The Wordsworth Dictionary of Drink

THE WORDSWORTH

Dictionary of Drink

AN A–Z OF ALCOHOLIC BEVERAGES

New Edition
Expanded, Updated, Illustrated

NED HALLEY

Wordsworth Reference

For customers interested in other titles from
Wordsworth Editions visit out website at
www.wordsworth-editions.com

For our latest list and a full mail order service contact
Bibliophile Books, 5 Thomas Road, London E14 7BN
Tel: +44 0207 515 9222   Fax: +44 0207 538 4115
e-mail: orders@bibliophilebooks.com

This edition published 2005 by Wordsworth Editions Limited
8B East Street, Ware, Hertfordshire SG12 9HJ

ISBN 1 84022 302 2

Text Ned Halley © Wordsworth Editions Limited 2005

2 4 6 8 10 9 7 5 3 1

Wordsworth® is a registered trademark of
Wordsworth Editions Limited

Typeset by Antony Gray
Printed in Great Britain by
Mackays of Chatham, Chatham, Kent

Introduction

Welcome to the new, updated, expanded and illustrated edition of this encyclopaedia of alcoholic beverages. As in its original, shorter, first edition, the book aims to be a straightforward reference guide to the words that describe every kind of intoxicating drink.

My prime intention is to identify as many types and brands of drinks as possible. Thousands of brewers, distillers and winemakers, as well as the names of their products, are listed. The idea is that the dictionary should be of real, practical help in locating beers and ciders, wines and spirits of every hue to their maker and place of origin.

Here, too, are the descriptive terms used on labels, along with the less-formal words used by producers and purveyors to promote their products in the market place. Origins, from village breweries to entire wine-producing regions, are located by nation, province and district. In many cases, there is mention of when a producer or product was established, perhaps a word about the founder or a brief explanation of a curious-sounding brand name.

This is not a 'critical' dictionary. There is little room here for effusive appreciations of (or withering animadversions against) the thousands of beverages mentioned. But where a beer, a wine or a spirit has an acknowledged reputation, this renown is duly noted. Inevitably, all the drinks known personally to the compiler are included. Those omitted – and they are legion – are either seriously obscure or (more likely) they have been innocently overlooked by the compiler.

As to using the dictionary, it has been written with maximum simplicity in mind. No 'technical' word is used which is not (I hope) explained under its own entry. Non-English descriptive terms are translated. Abbreviations are few and, it is hoped, of immediately obvious meaning.

Again for ease of reference, where the alcohol level is given for individual drinks, this is always stated in terms of alcohol by volume (for example beer at 3.6% alc, wine at 12.5% alc, spirits at 40% alc). There are several systems of measuring alcohol in beer, wine and spirits, and these are, of course, explained under their own entries. But it seems only fair to the general reader to use a scale that makes it simple to compare alcohol levels in all different types of drink.

A new feature of this edition is a series of short essays stranded through the text. These deal with generic topics – from beer and brewing to vermouth and vodka – and with a few of the world's most-famous drinks brands, particularly those which have a good story behind them.

A word about wine. Where practicable, the constituent grapes of individual wines are mentioned. Exceptions are the wines of the classic regions, where the great majority of producers use the grape varieties specified by local rules. For example, most of the famous estates of the Médoc region of Bordeaux in France make their wine with Cabernet Sauvignon, Merlot etc. The same goes for Burgundy and Champagne, where the wines are largely made from just three grape varieties.

So, to find the names of the grapes at the centre of any of the countless estates of the Médoc see the entry for Médoc. Here will be found details of the grape varieties in use under the prevailing Appellation Contrôlée rules. And so on for other well-known regions, from Asti and Barolo to Jerez and Rioja.

German wines occupy a good deal of space in this book. This is simply because the laws of that country call for labels detailing vineyards and villages, regional names, quality classifications, producer and grape variety. The numerous German-wine entries in this dictionary will, it is hoped, be of some real help in deciphering these peculiar designations.

Finally, a reiteration that this book does not attempt to be comprehensive. Even at ten times its size it could not list every branded drink. But it does try to explain, briefly, what most types of alcoholic drink consist of, where they come from, how their names are spelled and, here and there, a little bit more detail. I hope the book will prove a useful companion in that most companionable of diversions – intelligent drinking. ❦

A

Aalborg brand name for akvavits of De Danske Spritfabrikker (Danish Distilleries), Aalborg, Jutland, Denmark. **Aalborg Akeleje Snaps** (herb flavoured); **Aalborg Export** (with madeira); **Aalborg Fuselfri** (caraway flavoured, reduced strength); **Aalborg Jubiloeums** (dill flavoured); **Aalborg Porse Snaps** (sweet-gale flavoured); **Aalborg Taffel** (original 1846 brand, caraway flavoured).

Aan De Doorns Koöp Wynkelder South African wine co-operative in Worcester region of the Cape. Cabernet Sauvignon and Chenin Blanc wines.

Aargau northern Swiss vineyard district west of Zürich. Pinot Noir reds and lightweight whites.

Aarschotse Bruine brown ale from Biertoren brewery, Kampenhout, Belgium.

Aass brewery at Drammen, Oslo, Norway. Beer brands include **Aass Bayer Ø1; Aass Bokk; Aass Export; Aas Jule Ø1**. Name is locally pronounced *awss* and means 'summit'.

Aba brewery at Aba, Nigeria.

Abad, Tomás sherry *bodega* at Jerez de la Frontera, Spain. Owned by Emilio Lustau. Wines under **Tomás Abad** brand are Dry Amontillado; Dry Oloroso; Fino; Manzanilla; Medium Amontillado; Medium Oloroso; Palo Cortado; Sweet.

Abadia see Raimat.

Abanico very dry fino sherry brand produced by Bobadilla at Jerez de la Frontera, Spain. Also sold under 'Victoria' label.

Abazia di Nervesa winery in Montello e Colli Asolani DOC, Veneto, Italy.

Abbaia red wine of the Monti co-operative, Sardinia.

abbaye also called abbey and abdij bier, a style of European strong, bottle-conditioned beer made by Trappist monks, or by their imitators. Mainly Belgium and northern France.

Abbaye de Crespin St Landelin range of beers brewed by Enfants de Gayant, Douai, France.

Abbaye de Grâce Dieu monastery-producer of Trappistine herbal liqueur near Dijon, France.

Abbazia dell'Annunziata Barolo-producing vineyard in the commune of La Morra, Piedmont, Italy.

Abbazia di Rosazzo winery in Colli Orientali del Friuli DOC, north-east Italy.

Abbazia di Vallechiara Dolcetto-producing winery at Ovada, Piedmont, Italy, owned by actress Ornella Muti.

Abbazia Monte Oliveto Vernaccia-producing estate in the commune of San Gimignano, Tuscany, Italy.

abbey see abbaye.

Abbey Cocktail. Over ice shake 2 parts dry gin, 1 Lillet, 1 fresh orange juice, 1 dash Angostura bitters. Strain.

Abbey Ales brewery at Lansdown, Bath, England.

Abbey Bells Cocktail. Over ice shake 4 parts dry gin, 2 apricot brandy, 1 fresh orange juice, 1 dry vermouth, 1 dash grenadine. Strain.

Abbeydale brewery at Sheffield, Yorkshire, England.

Abbey Ridge vineyard in the Dundee Hills, Oregon, USA. Chardonnay and Pinot Noir wines.

abboccato medium-dry. Italian wine style, especially for Orvieto.

Abbot One of Belgium's strongest beers, at 10.6% alc. Produced by the Trappist Monastery of St Sixtus, Westvleteren.

Abbot Ale bitter ale (5.0% alc) of Greene King Brewery, Bury St Edmunds, Suffolk, England.

Abbot's Aged Bitters traditional-recipe bitters made in Baltimore, USA.

Abbot's Choice blended scotch whisky brand created by Perthshire farmer John McEwan.

Abbots Double Stout dry stout beer brewed by Carlton & United Breweries, Melbourne, Australia.

Abbotsford brewery at Abbotsford, Victoria, Australia. Owned by Carlton and United Breweries.

Abbuoto grape variety of central Italy.

abdij bier see abbaye.

Abeille de Fieuzal second wine of Château de Fieuzal, Graves, France.

Abel & Co winery at Kumeu, New Zealand.

Abel Brown's pub brewery (The Stag) at Stotfold, Bedfordshire, England.

Abelé, Henri champagne house est 1757 Reims, France. Known for NV Brut Sourire de Reims.

Abel Lepitre champagne house est 1944 Reims, France.

Abelsberg vineyard at Stuttgart in Württemberg region, Germany.

Aberdeen Amber beer brand of Weinkeller brewery, Chicago, Illinois, USA.

Aberdeen Angus Cabernet Sauvignon/Syrah wine from Goyenechea winery, Argentina.

Aberdeen Cows liqueur from Scotch whisky and cream by Old Boston company, USA.

Aberfeldy Highland malt whisky distillery est 1896, Perthshire, Scotland. Single malts: 13- and 15-year-old.

Aberfeldy vineyard in Clare Valley, South Australia. Notable for Shiraz and other varieties.

Aberlour-Glenlivet Speyside malt whisky distillery, Upper Spey, Scotland. Aberlour single malts: five- and 10-year-old.

Abfüller bottler, German. **Abfüllung** bottling.

Abiet, Château second wine of Château Cissac, Bordeaux, France.

Abir Lager produced at the Abir brewery in Israel.

Abisante aniseed spirit, USA.

Abita small brewery at Abita Springs, Louisiana, USA. Amber and Golden lagers.

ABM Cocktail. Over ice, shake 1 part Absolut vodka, 2 tomato juice, 1 dash Tabasco. Strain. Initials stand for Absolutely Bloody Marvellous.

abocado semi-dry wine style. Spanish.

Abolengo sherry-cask-matured brandy made by Sánchez Romate at Jerez de la Frontera, Spain.

Abouriou grape variety permitted in AC Côtes du Marmandais, but declining in use.

Abrau Black Sea sparkling-wine-producing centre, Russia.

Abricotine apricot liqueur produced by Garnier at Enghien-les-Bains, France.

Abruzzi Adriatic wine region of central Italy incorporating two DOCs, Montepulciano d'Abruzzo and Trebbiano d'Abruzzo.

absinth(e) see box.

Absinthe Cocktail. Over ice shake 1 part pastis, 1 water, 1 dash Angostura bitters, 1 dash sugar syrup. Strain.

Absinthe American cocktail. Over ice shake, until almost frozen, 1 part pastis, 1 water, 1 dash Angostura, 4 dashes sugar syrup. Strain and add lemon peel twist.

Absinthe Cooler Cocktail. Stir 4 parts whisky, 1 lemon juice, 2 dashes Angostura bitters in a tall glass with ice. Top up with ginger ale and 3 dashes of pastis.

Absinthe Drip Cocktail. Over a measure of pastis in a small glass, hold a sugar lump on a perforated drip spoon (or other strainer). Drip iced water on to the lump to dissolve the sugar into the drink.

Absinthe Frappé Cocktail. Over ice shake, until almost frozen, 2 parts pastis, 1 anisette syrup, 3 water. Strain.

Absinthe Friend Cocktail. Over ice shake 1 part pastis, 1 part dry gin, 1 dash Angostura bitters, 1 dash sugar syrup. Strain.

Absinto brand of 'absinthe', Portugal.

Absolut Vodka brand of Vin & Sprit AB, Sweden. Est 1879. Neutral and flavoured vodkas.

absolute alcohol also known as anhydrous alcohol. Spirit entirely free of water.

Absolute Peach Cocktail. Over ice stir 1 part Absolut vodka, 1 peach schnapps. Strain.

Absolut Nectar Cocktail. Into an ice-filled tall glass pour 2 parts Absolut vodka, 1 peach brandy, 1 fresh lime juice.

Abson aniseed liqueur, USA.

Abtei vineyards at Bernkastel-Kues in Mosel-Saar-Ruwer region and at Sponheim in Nahe region, Germany.

Absinthe

green goddess with a
cloudy history

Absinthe is the ancestor of today's anis and pastis. It was the creation of French doctor Pierre Ordinaire, a royalist refugee from France's Revolution, at Neuchâtel in Switzerland in 1792. His recipe for what he intended as a medical *digestif* included an infusion of wormwood (*Artemesia absinthium*) and 15 other herbs, notably anise, badiane, chamomile, coriander, parsley and veronica. These botanicals were steeped in 68% alcohol.

Dr Ordinaire, perhaps unsurprisingly, died within a year of devising the drink. He had no heirs, and the recipe came into the hands of his housekeeper, Madame Henriot. She established a retail shop, staffed by her daughters, to sell the product to a burgeoning clientele. It was a regular customer, Henri Dubied, who put absinthe into commercial production. He bought the formula from Mme Henriot in 1797, built a factory, and promoted the new elixir as a sovereign aid to digestion, a miraculous aphrodisiac – and a cure for drunkenness. Dubied's partner in this enterprise was his son-in-law, Henri-Louis Pernod.

Inheriting the business in 1805, Pernod expanded into a yet-larger factory over the border in France and began to label the drink with his own name. This distinguished it from the many imitators already crowding into the market. A particular boost to sales came in the 1840s when French troops fighting in Algeria were issued with a daily absinthe ration, allegedly to stave off malaria. The drink, whose powers of intoxication were readily appreciated, was christened with a number of soubriquets including *la déesse verte* (the green goddess). Soldiers returning to France on leave took their thirst for the new potion home with them, and established a firm domestic market.

Soon, absinthe was earning popularity as a recreational drink on the bohemian fringes of Paris café society. The painter Toulouse-Lautrec became a renowned consumer, the poet Verlaine a notorious addict. The drink was credited with hallucinogenic properties, and is believed to have fostered some of the delusions that drove the painter Vincent Van Gogh to cut off his ear.

Absinthe was outlawed in Switzerland in the wake of an infamous murder in 1905. A farmer, Jean Lanfray, shot to death his pregnant wife and two daughters after a drinking bout. The court resolved that the two glasses of absinthe Lanfray drank daily were to blame. The magistrates chose, for unknown reasons, to overlook the gallon of wine and pint of brandy the defendant also consumed each day. Lanfray was convicted of homicide in 'an absinthe-induced delirium' and sentenced to life imprisonment, but hanged himself in his cell shortly afterwards. In a 1907 referendum, the Swiss people voted to ban the manufacture and sale of absinthe, even for export.

France followed Switzerland's example in 1915 on grounds of the drink's alleged toxicity, and absinthe was subsequently proscribed elsewhere in Europe and in the United States – but never in Great Britain. A revived version of the product, Trenet Absinthe, is currently made in Le Havre, but all production is exported, as the ban on sales of the spirit in France remains in force.

Another popular recent brand is Hill's Absinth, at 70% alcohol by volume, produced by the Jindrichhuv Hradec distillery in Prague, Czech Republic.   ❦

Abteiberg vineyard at Mesenich in Mosel-Saar-Ruwer region, Germany.

Abtei Kloster Stuben vineyard at Bremm in Mosel-Saar-Ruwer region, Germany.

Abteilikoer herbal liqueur. Germany.

Abtei Ruppertsberg vineyard at Bingen in Nahe region, Germany.

Abtey *Grosslage* incorporating vineyards in the Rheinhessen region, Germany at, respectively, Appenheim, Gau-Algesheim, Nieder-Hilbersheim, Ober-Hilbersheim, Partenheim, Sankt Johann, Sprendlingen, Wolfsheim.

Abtsberg vineyards at Offenberg in Baden region, at Alzenau in Franken region, at Graach and at Mertesdorf in Mosel-Saar-Ruwer region, and at Impflingen in Rheinpfalz region, Germany.

Abtsfronhof vineyard at Bad Dürkheim in Rheinpfalz region, Germany.

Abtsleite vineyard at Würzburg in Franken region, Germany.

Abundante grape variety of southern Portugal.

ABV alcohol by volume. See alcohol.

Abymes white-wine *cru* (vineyard district) of Savoie, France. AC Vin de Savoie.

AC Appellation Contrôlée.

Acacia wine estate in the Carneros area of the Napa Valley, California, USA. Chardonnay and Pinot Noir wines.

Acadian Canadian distiller of 100 per cent rye whisky.

Acapulco Cocktail. Over ice shake 1 part white rum, 1 tequila, 1 freshly squeezed lime juice, 4 pineapple juice. Strain into ice-filled glasses.

Acapulco Gold Cocktail. Over ice shake 1 part golden (*anejo*) tequila, 1 golden rum, 1 coconut cream, 1 grapefruit juice, 2 pineapple juice. Strain into ice-filled glass.

Accademia Torregiorgi Italian winery in Neive, Piedmont, making Barbaresco, Barolo, Barbera and Dolcetto wines.

Accomasso, Lorenzo Italian vineyard-owner and winemaker in La Morra, Piedmont. Barolo and Dolcetto wines.

Accra Brewery producer of Club beer brand, Accra, Ghana.

Ace Lager product of Federation (of working men's clubs) Brewery of Newcastle upon Tyne, England.

acerbe acid-tasting (wine). French.

acerbo sour-tasting, unripe (wine). Italian.

acetaldehyde the major aldehyde in wines, particularly in sherry. Excess acetaldehyde is a fault in wine characterised by an oxidised smell.

acetic vinegary in smell or taste (wine).

acetic acid volatile acid giving wine keenness of flavour but, in excess, turning it vinegary.

acetification the 'pricking' of wines etc arising from exposure to air, allowing invasion by acetic organisms and conversion of alcohol to vinegar.

acetone distinctive smell in wine associated with ethyl acetate or amyl acetate (resembling nail varnish).

Achaia Clauss winery at Patras, Greece. Major producer of dry red and white table wines plus Mavrodaphne red liqueur wine, Muscat of Patras.

Achard, Jean-Pierre producer of Clairette-de-Die sparkling wines, Rhône Valley, France. Organic methods.

Achard, Michel producer of Chaume rich white wine, Coteaux du Layon, France.

Achkarren wine village of Kaiserstuhl, Baden region, Germany.

Achouffe, d' brewery at Houffalize in the Ardennes, France, known for fruit beers.

Achs wine producer in Neusiedlersee, Burgenland, Austria.

Achs-Tremmel wine producer in Neusiedlersee, Burgenland, Austria.

acid, acidity beneficial in wine's crispness of flavour and longevity. Lack of acidity is indicated by dull flavour. Wine with excess or immature acidity tastes tart and raw.

acin(ac)iform shaped like a bunch of grapes.

Ackermann-Laurance large sparkling-wine producer at Saumur in the Loire region, France.

Aconcagua valley forming the prime area of cultivation in Chile's central vineyard region.

Acquabona wine estate at Porto-ferraio on the island of Elba, Italy. Red and white Elba DOC wines.

acquette French aromatic liqueur sold as **Acquette d'Argent** (with silver trace added) or **Acquette d'Or** (gold trace).

Acqui Terme winemaking centre in Piedmont, Italy. See Brachetto d'Acqui and Dolcetto d'Acqui.

âcre harsh-tasting (wine). French.

Adabag medium red wine. Turkey.

Adakarasi white grape variety. Turkey.

Adam Cocktail. Over ice shake 2 parts Jamaica rum, 1 grenadine, 1 fresh lemon juice. Strain.

adamado sweet-tasting (wine). Portuguese.

Adam and Eve Cocktail. In ice stir 2 parts Plymouth gin, 3 orange curaçao, 1 yellow Chartreuse. Strain.

Adam-Garnotel grower-producer of champagne, Rily-la-Montaigne, France.

Adam's Apple Cocktail. In ice stir 2 parts calvados, 1 dry gin, 1 vermouth, 2 dashes yellow Chartreuse. Strain.

Adams, Samuel American revolutionary, signatory of Declaration of Independence and sometime brewer, whose name adorns the ales of the Boston Brewing Company, USA. Includes **Samuel Adams Boston Ale; Samuel Adams Boston Lager; Samuel Adams Cranberry Lambic**.

Adams, Tim maker of varietal wines under **Tim Adams** label in Clare Valley, South Australia.

Adams Vineyard producer of Chardonnay and Pinot Noir wines at Portland, Oregon, USA.

Adamstown Amber lager by Stoudt brewery, Pennsylvania, USA.

Addington Cocktail. Over ice stir 1 part dry vermouth, 1 sweet vermouth. Strain into tall, ice-filled glass. Top with soda water. Add orange twist.

Addlestones Draught Cider cask-conditioned dry cider produced by Matthew Clark, Shepton Mallet, Somerset, England.

adega winery, wine cellar or store. Portuguese.

Adega Cooperativa da Vidigueira winemaking co-operative in Alentejo region of Portugal. Notable young white wine Colheita do Ano.

Adega Cooperativa de Almeirim winemaking co-operative in Ribatejo region of Portugal. Quality wines including white Quinta das Varandas.

Adega Cooperativa de Arruda dos Vinhos winemaking co-operative in Oeste region of Portugal. Wines include red Arruda.

Adega Cooperativa de Borba wine-making co-operative in Alentejo region of Portugal. Notable red wines.

Adega Cooperativa de Labrugeira small winemaking co-operative in Oeste region of Portugal. Quality red wines.

Adega Cooperativa de Ponte da Barca producer of *aguardente* (grape spirit) Ponte da Barca, Portugal.

Adega Cooperativa de Redondo winemaking co-operative in Alentejo region of Portugal. Red wines.

Adega Cooperativa de Reguengos de Monsaraz winemaking co-operative in Alentejo region of Portugal.

Adega Cooperativa de Torres Vedras large winemaking co-operative in Oeste region of Portugal. Red and white wines.

Adega Cooperativa de Ponte de Lima winemaking co-operative in Portugal's vinho verde region. White wine brand is Loureiro.

Adega Mar de Frades producer of Albariño wines in Rías Baixas, north-west Spain.

Adega Regional de Colares sole winemaker in Colares region of Portugal.

Adegas do Torreão Vinhos madeira producer, Funchal, Madeira.

Adega Velha brandy distilled by Sociedade Agricola e Comercial da Quinta de Avelada, Penafiel, Portugal.

Adelaide Hills upland wine region north east of Adelaide, South Australia.

Adelaide Metropolitan Area wine region of Adelaide, South Australia. Now largely covered by urban development.

Adelaide Plains wine region north of Adelaide, South Australia. Includes famed Magill vineyard.

Adelaide Sparkling Ales traditionally made beers produced by Cooper & Sons of Adelaide, South Australia.

Adelberg *Grosslage* (collective vine-yard) incorporating vineyards in the Rheinhessen region of Germany at, respectively, Armsheim, Bermers-heim vdH, Bornheim, Ensheim, Erbes-Büdesheim, Flonheim, Lons-heim, Nack, Nieder-Wiesen, Sülz-heim, Wendelsheim, Wörrstadt.

Adelmann, Graf, Weingut great wine estate of the Württemberg region, Germany. Red and white wines under the 'Brüssele' label.

Adelpfad vineyard at Englestadt in Rheinhessen region, Germany.

Adelsberg vineyard at Bayerfeld-Steckweiler in Nahe region, Germany.

Adelscott Bière au Malt à Whisky pale, peated beer made with whisky malt by Adelshoffen brewery in Alsace, France.

Adelscott Noir near-black, peated-malt beer by Adelshoffen brewery in Alsace, France.

Adelsheim Vineyard Oregon, USA, producer of notable Pinot Noir wines and others.

Adelshoffen brewery at Strasbourg, Alsace, France. Owned by brewer Fischer/Pêcheur.

Adeneuer, JJ, Weingut red-wine producer at Bad Neuenahr-Ahrweiler in Ahr region, Germany.

Adgestone vineyard at Sandown, Isle of Wight, UK. Planted 1968 with Müller-Thurgau, Seyval Blanc and Reichensteiner vines. Dry white wines.

Adios Amigos Cocktail. Over ice shake 2 parts white rum, 1 cognac, 1 dry gin, 1 dry vermouth, 1 fresh lime juice. Strain.

Adler vineyard at Zell in Mosel-Saar-Ruwer region, Germany.

Adler Brauerei brewer at Schwanden, Switzerland.

Adler Fels Winery wine producer at Santa Rosa, California, USA.

Adler of Appleton small brewery at Appleton, Lake Winnebago, Wisconsin, USA.

Admiral second wine of Château Labégorce Zédé, Haut-Médoc, France.

Admiral Benbow rum brand of Halewood International, Huyton, Merseyside, England. Named after British Admiral John Benbow (1653-1702), naval Commander in Chief of the West Indies. Hero of a renowned action against a vastly larger French fleet off Jamaica, in which he was mortally wounded.

Admiral's Ale bitter brand of Southsea Brewery, Portsmouth, Hampshire, England.

Admirault, Claude & Thierry wine producer at St-Nicolas-de-Bour-gueil, Touraine, France.

Adnams renowned brewery and fine wine merchant, Sole Bay Brewery, Southwold, Suffolk, England. Mild, Bitter and Extra cask ales plus bottled beers including famed Broadside Pale Ale and Suffolk Strong Ale.

adomado sweet-tasting (wine). Portuguese.

Adom Atic red wine sold under Carmel co-operative label. Israel.

Adonis VSOP brandy by SODAP co-operative, Limassol, Cyprus.

Adonis Cocktail. In ice stir 2 parts dry sherry, 1 sweet vermouth, 1 dash orange bitters. Strain. Squeeze orange peel over glass.

Adriatic Wines producer of wines from Chenin Blanc, Grenache and other grapes, plus fortified wines, at Herne Hill, Western Australia.

adulterated alcoholic drink illicitly altered or augmented with an inferior substance; as, watered beer or sugared wine.

advocaat Dutch liqueur prepared from brandy, fresh egg yolks, sugar and vanilla to an alcohol content around 15%. Around 100 brands include Bols, Warnink and Zwarte Kip. UK consumes three-quarters of all exports. The name is abbreviated from the Dutch *advokaatenborrel*, an advocate's dram, taken to clear the throat while speaking in court.

Aecht Schlenkerla Rauchbier Märzen smoked beer by Schlenkerla Rauchbier brewery, Bamberg, Germany.

Aegean the major wine-growing islands of Greece are Lemnos, Lesbos and Samos.

Aegypter red grape variety of Austria. Synonymous with Schiava grossa.

aerate to charge a liquid, such as beer, with air (usually carbon dioxide) to cause effervesence. Also, to expose to air to release impurities, as in decanting wine.

aerobic in the presence of air; as, fino sherry is made in aerobic conditions.

Aerts 1900 strong traditional bottle-conditioned ale by Palm brewery, Brabant, Belgium.

Afames red wine brand from Troodos mountains, Cyprus.

Afdis see African Distillers.

Äffchen vineyard at Wöllstein in Rheinhessen region, Germany.

Affenberg vineyard at Worms in Rheinhessen region, Germany.

Affenthal literally 'monkey's valley' (but more likely a contraction of 'Ave Maria Tal'). A wine-growing area of the Ortenau in the Baden region, Germany. Red Spätburgunder wines are traditionally bottled in **Affenflaschen** – bottles embossed with a monkey emblem.

Affinity Cocktail. In ice stir 1 part scotch whisky, 1 dry vermouth, 1 sweet vermouth, 2 dashes Angostura bitters. Strain. Squeeze lemon peel over glass.

Affleck Vineyard small-scale producer of table and fortified wines near Lake George, New South Wales, Australia.

Affligem strong abbaye beer from De Smedt brewery, Belgium.

Afonso III wine brand of Lagoa co-operative, Algarve, Portugal.

African Distillers wine producer in Zimbabwe with vineyards at Bulawayo, Gweru and Mutare. Known as Afdis.

afrikoko type of coconut and chocolate liqueur produced in Sierra Leone and other west African locations.

After Dinner Cocktail. Over ice shake 1 part apricot brandy, 1 Cointreau, 1 fresh lime juice. Strain. Alternatively, over ice shake 1 part cherry brandy, 1 prunelle liqueur, 1 lemon juice. Strain.

After One Cocktail. In ice stir 1 part dry gin, 1 Campari, 1 sweet vermouth, 1 Galliano. Strain.

Aftershock Flavoured spirit brand, UK.

After Supper Cocktail. Over ice shake 1 part apricot brandy, 1 Cointreau, 1 lemon juice. Strain.

aftertaste the remaining flavour, in the mouth and throat, of a swallowed drink. Good-quality wines, spirits and beers are marked by the pleasantness of their aftertaste.

Agadir Cocktail. Pour 1 part Tia Maria and 1 orange juice into a tall, ice-filled glass and stir. Top with chilled sparkling wine.

Aganac, Château d' wine estate of AC Haut-Médoc, Bordeaux, France.

Agassac, Château d' wine estate of AC Haut-Médoc, Bordeaux, France. Classified *Grand Cru Bourgeois Exceptionnel*.

Agavana tequila brand of Pernod-Ricard, Mexico.

agave cactus plant and source of *pulque*, from which tequila is distilled. Species cultivated in Mexico for this purpose are **Agave Tequilana** and **Agave Tequilana Weber**.

Agavero tequila-based liqueur flavoured with damiana herb. Mexico.

Agawam grape variety, Ontario, Canada.

AGE Bodegas Unidas major winemaking concern at Fuenmayor, Spain. Largest exporter of Rioja wines, formerly owned by Guinness, now by Spanish Banesto group.

Age des Epices 13-year-old cognac known for dried-herb character. Leopold Gourmel, Cognac, France.

Age des Fleurs 10-year-old cognac known for floral character. Leopold Gourmel, Cognac, France.

Age du Fruit 8-year-old cognac. Leopold Gourmel, Cognac, France.

âge inconnu 'age unknown'; unofficial classification for old French brandies.

Agenais *vin de pays* zone south-east of Bordeaux, France. Bordeaux-style wines.

Agessimo wine brand of AGE Bodegas Unidas, Rioja, Spain.

agglomerated cork reconstituted cork used wholly or partially for stoppering sparkling wines and some table wines.

aggressive too immature to drink with pleasure; tannic (wine).

Agiorgitiko 'the vine of St George' red grape variety. Makes strong red wines of Nemea valley, Peloponnese, Greece.

Aglianico red grape variety of southern Italy, used especially in wines of Aglianico del Vulture, Cilento and Taurasi.

Aglianico del Taburno DOC zone for red and *rosato* wines, Campania, Italy.

Aglianico del Vulture DOC zone for rich red still and sparkling wines, Basilicata region, Italy. Still wines aged 2 years in cask and 3 in bottle are labelled Riserva. Vineyards lie largely on the slopes of the volcano of Monte Vulture.

Agliano red grape variety of Italy. Synonymous with Aleatico.

Agnus abbey ale by Du Bocq brewery, Purnode, Belgium.

agrafe metal clip securing cork on champagne bottle during the second fermentation. Lately replaced by crown cap.

Agramont wine brand of Bodegas Cenalsa, Navarra, Spain.

agraria farm producing wine. Italy.

Agrelo Vineyard brand name for wines of Nicholas Catena, Mendoza, Argentina.

agressif unripe-tasting (wine). French.

Agricola Castellana winemaking co-operative at La Seca in the Rueda region of Spain.

Agricola de Gandesa winemaking co-operative at Gandesa, Tarragona, Spain.

Agricola Monferrato noted producer of Barbera d'Asti wines at Nizza Monferrato, Piedmont, Italy.

Agricola Viña Los Vascos wine producer in the Maipo Valley, Chile.

Agritiusberg vineyard at Konz in Mosel-Saar-Ruwer region, Germany.

Agronavarra Cenal producer of Camponuevo red wine at Pamplona, Navarra, Spain.

Agua Bianca Italian bergamot-flavoured liqueur with added silverleaf. Name means 'white water'.

aguamiel honey water. The sap of the agave plant of Mexico fermented to make pulque.

aguardenta alternative spelling of aguardente. Portuguese.

aguardente 1 neutral grape spirit of 77% alcohol added in ratio of 1 to 4 to fermenting grape must to make port. Usually from Portuguese grapes. **2** Portuguese single-distilled brandy. Brands include Antiqua (Caves Alianca), Delaforce Fine Brandy, Espirito (JM Da Fonseca), 5 Estrelas (Kopke). Name means 'burning water'.

aguardente bagaceira colourless, fiery spirit distilled from grape-pressing residue. Producers include Carvalho, Ribeiro & Ferreira. Portugal.

aguardente de cana colourless and fiery Brazilian sugar-cane spirit, popularly known as cachaça. In effect, the national spirit drink of Brazil.

aguardiente 1 generic name for Spanish spirits distilled from grapes or other materials. **2** sugar-cane spirit of Bolivia, Chile, Colombia.

aguardiente de orujo colourless, fiery spirit distilled from grape-pressing residue. Spain.

aguja new-made wine with semi-sparkling character due to residual gas from fermentation. Spain.

Agulha brand of vinho verde wine sold in stone bottles. Portugal.

Ahéra, Domaine d' quality red wine from grapes including Cabernet Franc and Grenache, made by Keo. Cyprus.

Ahern Winery producer of noted Zinfandel wine, Los Angeles County, California, USA.

Ahlgren Vineyard winery in Santa Cruz County, California, USA.

Ahr tributary of the Rhine river giving its name to northernmost wine region of Germany. Mainly pale red wines from co-operatives.

Ahrenberg vineyard at Nack in Rheinhessen region, Germany.

Ahsis flavoured wine of the ancient world. Biblical.

Ahumat vine variety, SW France.

Ahuss Taffel caraway-flavoured aquavit. Sweden.

Aichinger wine producer in Kamptal, Niederösterreich, Austria.

Aigner wine producer in Kremstal, Niederösterreich, Austria.

Aidani sweet grape variety grown in Aegean islands, Greece.

Aigéchate heavy red wine. Armenia.

aigre in winetasting, sour flavour. French.

Aigrots, Les Premier Cru vineyard of Beaune, Côte de Beaune, France.

Aiguebelle herbal liqueur made at Valence, France.

Aile d'Argent white wine by Château Mouton-Rothschild, Bordeaux, France.

Ailenberg vineyards at Esslingen and at Stuttgart in Württemberg region, Germany.

Ain *vin de pays département* of eastern France. Some good white wines from around Seyssel.

aîné elder, as in senior partner in family firm such as famed *négoçiant-éleveur* Bouchard Aîné of Beaune in France.

Aïne Bessem Bouira easternmost wine region of Algeria in the province of Alger. Good light red and rosé wines.

Aïn Merane quality wine-growing area, formerly named Rabelais by French colonists, in the hills near Dahra, Algeria. Full-bodied red wines.

Ainslie and Heilbron Highland scotch whisky distiller, Clynelish, Scotland. Brands include blended

Ainslie's Royal Edinburgh and Clynelish.

Aiola Chianti Classico wine estate at Vagliagli, Tuscany, Italy.

Airén most-planted vine variety of Spain. White wines of La Mancha.

airlock trap for filling with water, used by winemakers to allow carbon dioxide to escape from fermenting vessel, but preventing invasion by oxygen or bacteria.

Aït Souala red wine of the Mekriés region, Morocco.

Aix-en-Provence winemaking centre of southern France. See Coteaux d'Aix-en-Provence.

Ajaccio AC wine zone of hills around capital city of Ajaccio, Corsica. Red and rosé wines mainly from Sciacarello grapes; whites from Malvoisie de Corse grape.

Ajudhia Distillers rum producer at Raja-Ka-Sahaspur, Distt Morada-bad, India.

AK Mild renowned ale brewed by McMullen & Sons, Hertford, England.

AK Bitter ale by Simpkiss Brewery, Brierley Hill, Staffordshire, England.

Akadama 'the symbol of the Rising Sun'. Japan's first (1907) locally grown sweet white wine, made by Suntory.

Akarangi small-scale wine producer. Havelock North, North Island, New Zealand.

Akeleje herb-flavoured akvavit. Denmark.

Akhaïa red wine of Peloponnese, Greece.

Aktiebolaget Vin & Spritcentralem Swedish state spirit monopoly producing 19 different *brannvins* (clear spirits from potatoes or grain) at the Stockholm distillery which may be the largest in central Europe. The monopoly, now restructured under conditions of membership of the European Union, is responsible for all Sweden's domestic spirit production – apart from the annual 10,000,000 litres said to be distilled illicitly.

akvavit 'water of life'. Potato- or grain-based spirit flavoured with herbs (caraway is most common) distilled in Denmark since the 1400s and now accounting for three-quarters of all spirit sales there. Also widely made in Norway and Sweden. The akvavit-drinking excesses of Denmark's King Christian IV inspired Shakespeare's portrayals of the Danish court in *Hamlet*. Also called aquavit. From Latin *aqua vitae*. These spirits are also commonly known as schnap(p)s.

Alabama Fizz Cocktail. Over ice shake 3 parts dry gin, 2 lemon juice, 1 powdered sugar. Strain into medium glass and top up with soda. Add mint sprig.

Alabama Slammer Cocktail. Over ice stir 1 part Southern Comfort, 1 amaretto, 1 teaspoon sloe gin, 1 dash lemon juice. Strain into a shot glass.

Alacanon white grape variety of Spain. Synonymous with Macabeo.

alaki said to be the first potable spirit, distilled from rice beer by ancient Chinese before 800 BC.

alambic prototype pot still attributed to Arab inventors of the ancient world.

alambic armagnacais type of continuous still for production of armagnac in Gascony, France.

alambic charentais pot still for production of cognac in Charentes, France.

alambique pot still in France and elsewhere.

alambrado wire net originally used to secure valuable Rioja bottles. Now decorative only. Spain.

Alameda winemaking county in the Central Coast area of California, USA.

Alamo Cocktail. In an ice-filled tall glass stir 2 parts tequila, 1 orange juice, 1 pineapple juice.

Alamos Ridge brand name for wines of Nicholas Catena, Mendoza, Argentina. Cabernet Sauvignon and Chardonnay wines.

Alaskan Brewing Co North America's northernmost brewery, formerly called Chinook. Famed for seasonal brews including Autumn Ale, Smoked Porter (Christmas) and **Alaskan Amber**.

Alaska Cocktail. Over ice shake 3 parts dry gin, 1 yellow Chartreuse. Strain.

Alavesa one of the three sub-zones of the Rioja region, Spain, along with Rioja Alta and Rioja Baja.

Alavesas, Bodegas wine producer at Alava, Rioja, Spain.

Albachtaler vineyard at Wasserliesch in Mosel-Saar-Ruwer region, Germany.

Alba Flora medium white wine of island of Majorca, Spain.

Albalonga German white grape variety widely planted in the Rheinhessen region.

Alban white wine of ancient Rome recorded by Pliny the Elder as beneficial for the stomach.

Albana white grape variety making dry, sweet and sparkling wines in Emilia-Romagna region, Italy.

Albana di Romagna DOCG for white wines from the Albana grape, Emilia-Romagna region, Italy.

Albanibräu strong beer of Haldengut Brauerei, Switzerland.

Albani brewer of brands including Giraf lager. Odense, Denmark.

Albano white grape variety of Italy. Synonymous with Trebbiano.

Albany Amber Beer lager brand originally of Newman brewery at Albany, New York, USA and now made by FX Matt at Utica, New York.

Albany Surprise New Zealand vine variety. Mostly for grape juice.

Albaranzeuli blanco and **nero** respectively, white and black grape varieties, Sardinia.

Albariño sweet white grape variety of Galicia, Spain. Synonymous with Alvarinho of Portugal.

albariza most-prized soil-type – chalk, sand and clay – for sherry vineyards of Andalucia, Spain.

Albarola white grape variety of northern Italy.

Albatros white grape variety of South Africa. Synonymous with Cinsaut blanc.

Albemarle Fizz Cocktail. Over ice shake 4 parts dry gin, 2 lemon juice, 1 powdered sugar. Strain into ice-fiiled glass, top with soda and add dash of raspberry syrup.

Alben white grape variety of Germany. Synonymous with Elbling.

Alberello vine-training system based on pruning plants low and bushy. Italy.

albero type of albariza soil found in the vineyards south of Jerez de la Frontera, Spain.

Alberta Distillery producer of 100 per cent rye whisky. Canada.

Albertine Cocktail. Over ice shake 1 part kirsch, 1 green Chartreuse, 1 Cointreau, 1 dash maraschino. Strain.

Albig white grape variety of Germany. Synonymous with Elbling.

Albillo white grape variety of Spain. Synonymous with Pardina.

Albillo Castellana white grape variety of Andalucia and Canary Isles, Spain.

Albino Rhino beer brand of Whistler Brewing, near Vancouver, Canada.

Albling alternative spelling of Elbling.

Albra Brauerei Heineken-owned brewery group, Alsace, France.

Albuquerque Brewing small brewery at Albuquerque, New Mexico, USA. Brands include Michael's Golden Ale.

Alcamo DOC dry white wine of Alcamo, Sicily, Italy.

Alcañol white grape variety of Spain. Synonymous with Macabeo.

Alcanón alternative spelling of Alcañol.

Alantara wine estate in Bucelas region, Portugal.

Alcayata red grape variety of Spain. Synonymous with Monastrell.

Alchermes liqueur from cinnamon, cloves, nutmeg and other spices. Italy.

Alcobaca winemaking region of western Portugal. Red and white wines.

alcohol class of several hundred distinct colourless flammable organic chemical substances. The alcohol in beverages is principally ethyl alcohol, produced from sugar by the action of enzymes present in yeast cells. From Arabic *al-kuhl*.

alcohol by volume is a measure based on the French Gay Lussac (*qv*) system of expressing the alcoholic content of drinks in proportional terms. Examples are, commonly, 3 to 8 per cent in beer; 8 to 14 per cent in table wines; 15 to 21 per cent in fortified wines; typically 40 per cent in spirits. Frequently abbreviated to ABV.

Alcola 'alcoholic cola' by Brothers Drinks Co, Shepton Mallet, Somerset, England.

alcool alcohol. French, Italian.

alcool svolto partially fermented sweet wine. Italy.

alcopops informal term for 'alcoholic soft drink' usually fruit-based and designed, reputedly, to appeal to younger drinkers.

Alcudia Cocktail. Over ice shake 2 parts dry gin, 1 Galliano, 1 banana liqueur, 1 grapefruit juice. Strain.

Aldabo rum-based liqueur of Cuba.

Aldanueva major winemaking centre of the Rioja Baja, Spain. Known as 'the town of three lies' because it is neither an *aldea* (small village), nor *nueva* (new), nor situated on the Ebro river.

Aldchlappie Hotel brewery at Kirkmichael, Perthshire & Kinross, Scotland.

Alde Gott four vineyards in the Baden region, Germany, at, respectively, Achern, Lauf, Sasbach, Sasbachwalden.

aldehyde organic chemical compound produced by oxidation of alcohol. Some aldehydes, such as esters (*qv*) are important in the development of bouquet in wine.

Aldeia Velha Minho valley *bagaceira* brand of Sandeman & Co, Lisbon, Portugal.

Alden grape variety, Canada.

Alderbrook Vineyards wine estate at Healdsburg, California, USA. Barrel-fermented white wines from Chardonnay and other varieties.

Aldermoor vineyard at Ringwood, Hampshire, England.

ale beer produced from an infusion of malt, with a distinct flavour imparted by the action of a top-fermenting yeast. Colour, flavour and strength of ales vary widely and include bitter ale, brown ale, India Pale Ale (IPA), light ale, mild, strong etc. In the Middle Ages, the term ale described a type of beer made without the use of hops – an additive first used in brewing in the tenth century AD or even earlier. Ale is still a name given to beers fast-brewed at high temperatures in the USA. English, from Old Norse *öl*.

Aleatica red grape variety of Chile. Sweet 'Moscatel' wines.

Aleatico red grape variety of Italy. Also a sweet red vino da tavola wine of Tuscany.

Aleatico di Gradoli DOC of Latium, Italy. Sweet red wines including fortified *liquoroso*.

Aleatico di Portoferraio sweet red wine from Aleatico grapes, Isle of Elba, Italy.

Aleatico di Puglia DOC of Apulia, Italy. Medium sweet *dolce naturale* and rich, fortified *liquoroso* red wines. Riserva wines have been aged three years.

alebench seat in or outside an alehouse.

aleberry lost beverage of warmed ale flavoured with sugar and spices and with bread added. English from *ale* and *bre* (broth).

ale-bush sign at an ale-house or tavern (originally from bunch, or bush, of ivy hung up as a tavern sign).

Ale Flip to make, bring 2 pints ale slowly to boil in a saucepan. Beat 2 egg whites and, separately, 4 yolks. Into a jug containing 4 tablespoons soft brown sugar and 1 teaspoon ground nutmeg gently pour the beaten eggs and mix thoroughly. Add the boiling ale gradually, stirring the while to ensure a consistent, creamy mixture. Serve piping hot in mugs as a sovereign prophylactic against imminent colds.

Ale Fresco bottle-conditioned summer ale (4.5% alc) by Tisbury Brewery, Wiltshire, England.

alegar vinegar made from sour ale; malt vinegar.

A Legendary Man – A Legendary Tequila spirit brand of Pernod-Ricard, Mexico, offering evidence that brevity is not always considered a virtue in the naming of drinks brands.

Aldeia Velha & Nova Portuguese wine brand of Pernod-Ricard.

ale-house public house for sale and consumption of ale.

Alejandro Fernández estate at Pesquera de Duero and also at Roa de Duero in the Ribera del Duero region, northern Spain, producing highly prized Tinto Pesquera wines including Janus Gran Reserva.

Alella shrinking DO winemaking district north of Barcelona, Spain, producing still and sparkling wines.

Alella Co-operative major producer of dry and sweet white wines, Alella, Spain.

Ale Mary strong (6% alc) winter ale by RCH brewery, Gloucestershire, England. Described by the producer as 'dark, rich and spicy with a warm, sweet aroma of cloves, coriander and ginger, touches of rum, raisins and sultanas.'

Alemannenbuch vineyard at Schallstadt in Baden region, Germany.

alembic early name for the pot still, from Arabic *alambic*.

Alenquer wine-producing region of western Portugal best known for Quinta de Porto Franco wines.

Alentejo winemaking province of southern Portugal now divided into five designated wine regions: Borba, Portalegre, Redondo, Reguerngos de Monsaraz and Vidigueira. Formerly noted for white wines but now for fine reds from new-built wineries.

ale-pole pole or stake used as a marker, or, later, to carry a sign, for an ale-house (thus, 'up the pole', meaning demented or drunk).

Alesme, Château d' wine estate of AC Margaux, Médoc, Bordeaux, France. Formerly named Château Marquis d'Alesme Becker. Classified *3ème Grand Cru Classé*.

Alexander Cocktail. Over ice shake 2 parts dry gin, 1 crème de cacao, 1 cream. Strain. Alternatively, over ice shake 1 part brandy, 1 crème de cacao, 1 cream. Strain.

Alexander Dunn scotch whisky brand of Alexander Dunn, Bracknell, Berkshire, England. Blended three-, five- and 12-year-old and 12-year-old Old Vatted Malt.

Alexander's Sister Cocktail. Over ice shake 2 parts dry gin, 1 crème de menthe, 1 cream. Strain.

Alexander's Sister-in-Law Cocktail. Over ice shake 1 part dry gin, 1 crème de menthe, 1 cream. Strain.

Alexander Valley AVA winegrowing region of Sonoma County, California, USA.

Alexander Valley Fruit & Trading Co small wine producer in Sonoma County, California, USA.

Alexander Valley Vineyards noted wine producer in Sonoma County, California, USA. Cabernet Sauvignon, Chardonnay and Johannisberg Riesling wines.

Alexandra's Sister's Cocktail. Over ice shake 1 part dry gin, 1 crème de menthe, 1 cream. Strain.

Alexandre, Serge cognac producer, Cognac, France.

Alexant, Domaine Jean spirit distiller, Beaune, Burgundy, France. Marc de Bourgogne, fine de Bourgogne.

aleyard long glass once widely used for serving and measuring ale. Now rare.

Aleyor red table wine, island of Majorca, Spain.

Alezio DOC for red and *rosato* wines east of Gallipoli in Apulia region, Italy. Negroamaro and Malvasia Rosso grapes.

Alfa Brouwerij small brewery at Limburg, Netherlands, producing all-malt beers, notably strong brand Super-Dort.

Alfaro winemaking centre of Rioja Baja zone, Spain.

Alfie Cocktail. Over ice shake 2 parts lemon vodka, 1 pineapple juice, 1 dash Cointreau. Strain.

Alfonso Cocktail. Over ice shake 2 parts Grand Marnier, 1 dry gin, 1 dry vermouth, 1 sweet vermouth, dash Angostura bitters. Strain.

Alfonso El Sabio brandy by Valdespino, Jerez de la Frontera, Spain.

Alfrocheiro (Preto) major red grape variety of Dão region, Portugal.

Algaco estate and winery at Villarejo de Salvanés south-east of Madrid, Spain. Known for Jeromín white wine and others.

Algarve demarcated wine region of southern Portugal.

Algeria principal winemaking nation of North Africa, planted by French *pied noir* colonists from 1830, but in decline as a producer since independence in 1962. Quality-wine-producing zones in Alger province: Aïne Bessem Bouira, Côtes de Zaccar, Haut Dabra and Médéa; in Oran province: Côteaux de Mascara, Côteaux de Tlemcen, Monts du Tessalah, Mostaganem, Mostaganem-Kenenda, Oued-Imbert.

Algonquin microbrewery at Formosa, Ontario, Canada.

Algonquin Cocktail. Over ice shake 2 parts rye whisky, 1 Noilly Prat, 1 pineapple juice. Strain.

Alhambra premium lager (4.6% alc) by Cervezas Alhambra, Spain. Also **Alhambra Star** (5.4% alc).

Aliança, Caves major wine producer of Bairrada region, Portugal. Quality red wines and still and sparkling whites. Also, brandies: Antiquissima, VS Antiqua, VSOP.

Alicante DO wines mainly from the Levante villages of Monóvar, Pinosa and Villena in the hills inland from the resort of Alicante, Spain. Red wines mainly from Monastrell grape plus rosé and white wines.

Alicante red-fleshed grape variety widely planted in Almansa, Spain. Synonymous with Garnacha Tintorera.

Alicante Bouschet prolific *teinturier* (dyer) grape variety giving red juice, primarily used to improve colour of inexpensive wines in southern France and California.

Alicante Branco grape variety crossing, Portugal.

Alicante Ganzin French grape variety from which *teinturier* (dyer) varieties have been hybridised.

Alice Mine Cocktail. Over ice shake 2 parts sweet vermouth. 2 kümmel, 1 scotch whisky. Strain.

Alice Springs brand name for red and white wines of Chateau Hornsby, Alice Springs in Australia's Northern Territory. Possibly the most improbable vineyard in the world, depending on irrigation and a climate-controlled subterranean winery.

Aligoté white grape best known in Burgundy, France, where it is the only variety apart from Chardonnay permitted under the region's AC rules. Bourgogne Aligoté is an appellation in its own right, and many of the best wines are made under the sole village appellation of Bourgogne Aligoté de Bouzeron. Good Aligoté wines are also grown in northern Burgundy in the Yonne at St Bris le Vineux and Chîtry. The vine is cultivated elsewhere, particularly in Bulgaria and Russia.

Alimony Ale strongly hop-flavoured beer made by Buffalo Bill's brewpub, Hayward, California, USA. Billed as 'the most bitter beer in America.'

alisier, eau-de-vie d' rowanberry spirit of Alsace, France.

Alize brand of pastis by Pernod-Ricard, France.

Alizé brand of liqueur from cognac and passion-fruit juice, France.

Aljarafe fortified white wine of Andalucia, Spain.

Alkemaer *jenever* brand, Belgium.

Alken-Maes major Belgian brewer owned by Kronenbourg of France. Products include Cristal Alken pilsner, Grimbergen abbey beers and Judas golden ale.

alkermes cochineal-red-coloured liqueur of France and Italy.

Alkoomi Wines vineyard at Frankland, Western Australia, noted for wines from Cabernet Sauvignon, Sémillon and other grape varieties.

Allandale Winery producer of quality wines including Cabernet Sauvignon, Chardonnay, Pinot Noir, Sémillon and Shiraz, each from individual vineyard named on label. Hunter Valley, New South Wales, Australia.

Allanmere small winery of the Hunter Valley, New South Wales, Australia.

Allasch birthplace of Russian kümmel (introduced by Tsar Peter the Great following a visit to Amsterdam in 1696) made by the von Blanckenhagen family at Allasch castle, near Riga, until confiscation in 1918.

Allegheny pub-brewery in Pittsburgh, Pennsylvania, USA, famed for Penn Dark brown lager.

Allegheny Cocktail. Over ice shake 1 part bourbon, 1 dry vermouth, 2 dashes crème de cassis, 2 dashes lemon juice. Strain and squeeze lemon peel over.

Allegrini wine estate in Veneto region, Italy, producing top-quality Valpolicella plus vino da tavola wines La Poja and Pelara.

Allegro Vineyards wine producer at Brogue, Pennsylvania, USA. Noted for Cabernet Sauvignon and Chardonnay wines.

Allemand French synonym for German Elbling white grape variety.

Allen, Herbert inventor in 1979 of the revolutionary Screwpull corkscrew. Mr Allen was at the time an engineer involved in the extraction of oil in Texas, USA.

Allen Cocktail. Over ice shake 2 parts dry gin, 1 maraschino, 1 dash lemon juice. Strain.

Allenberg vineyard at Raumbach/Glan in Nahe region, Germany.

Allendorf, Fritz long-established family wine concern at Winkel in the Rheingau region, Germany. High-quality wines from numerous vineyards, notably in Winkeler Jesuitengarten.

Allesvorlen Estate wine producer in the Cape, South Africa, long known for 'port' but lately also for fine table wines.

Allianico Italian red grape variety. Synonymous with Aleatico.

Allied Domecq British-based drinks company incorporating former Allied Breweries, Pedro Domecq and many other concerns. Brands include Ballantyne's scotch whisky, Beefeater gin, Canadian Club whisky, Courvoisier cognac, Harveys sherries, Kahlua liqueur, Laphroaig single malt whisky, Maker's Mark Bourbon whisky, Malibu rum liquor, GH Mumm and Perrier-Jouët champagnes, Sauza tequila, Stolichnaya vodka, Teacher's whisky.

allier variety of close-grained French oak used for wine barrels.

Allies Cocktail. Over ice shake 1 part dry gin, 1 dry vermouth, 2 dashes kümmel. Strain.

All Ireland Cocktail. Over ice stir 1 part Irish whiskey, 2 dashes green Chartreuse, 1 dash green crème de menthe. Strain and add a green olive.

All Nations brewpub at Madeley, Telford, Shropshire, England.

Alloa Brewery Company producer of famed Arrol's 80/- ale. Alloa, Central Scotland.

Allobrogie *vin de pays* zone north of Grenoble in eastern France. Mainly dry white wines.

Allram wine producer in Kamptal, Niederösterreich, Austria.

All Saints brewery at Stamford, Lincolnshire, England.

All Saints winery at Wahgunyah, Victoria, Australia. Owned by Brown Brothers. Table and fortified wines.

Allsopp believed to be the original brewing dynasty at Burton upon Trent, England, founded by Hugh de Allsopp in the 12th century. Allsopp brewery, pioneers of Burton pale ale, amalgamated with Ind Coope to form Allied Breweries.

Allt-á-Bhainne Speyside malt whisky distillery est 1975 by Chivas Brothers, Banffshire, Scotland. Name is Gaelic meaning 'burn of milk' and is pronounced (approximately) awlt-a-vane.

All tua salute 'cheers' in Italian.

almacenista stockholder. In Spain, a sherry dealer purchasing wine from producers for ageing and later sale to shippers. So-called almacenista sherries are fine wines that escape the oblivion of commercial blending and are bottled straight from their original casks.

Almaden Vineyards major wine producer in the Central Coast area of California, USA. Premium wines are marketed under the name Charles Lefranc, French co-founder of the vineyard in 1852.

Almansa town of SW Spain and name of local DO wine region. Robust red wines mainly from Monastrell grapes.

Almeirim wine district of Ribatejo, Portugal. See Adega Cooperativa de Almeirim.

Almond Cocktail. Over ice shake 6 parts warmed gin in which a few blanched almonds have steeped until mixture has cooled, 6 sweet white wine, 3 dry vermouth, 1 peach brandy, 1 kirsch. Strain.

almude a measure of, and small barrel for, port. Traditionally, the quantity a man could carry on his head, namely 25.44 litres. There are 21 almudes to a pipe (port barrel).

Aloha whisky-based coffee liqueur. Scotland.

Aloha Fizz Cocktail. In a tall wine glass stir 1 part dry white wine, 1 pineapple juice, 1 soda water. Add crushed ice and a teaspoon of caster sugar. Top with soda.

Aloxe-Corton village and AC commune of the Côte de Beaune, Burgundy, France. Aloxe-Corton AC 'village' wines are almost exclusively red.

Aloxe-Corton Premier Cru AC red wines from Aloxe-Corton *Premiers Crus* vineyards of Les Chaillots, Les Fournières, Les Guérets, Les Maréchaudes, Les Meix, Les Paulands, Les Valozières, Les Vercots, and neighbouring Ladoix-Serrigny *Premiers Crus* vineyards of Basses Mourettes, La Coutière, La Toppe au Vert, Les Grandes Lolières, Les Maréchaudes, Les Moutottes, Les Petites Lolières.

Alpes de Haute-Provence *vin de pays département* of southern France. Red and white wines.

Alpes-Maritimes *vin de pays département* of southern France. Red and rosé wines, few whites.

Alpestre liqueur from Alpine herbs by Maristri fathers, Carmagnola, Italy.

Alphart wine producer in Thermenregion, Niederösterreich, Austria.

Alphen Wines wine range of Gilbeys company, Stellenbosch, South Africa.

Alpina yellow liqueur flavoured with Alpine flowers. Bottles contain twig to which sugar adheres and crystallises. Italy.

Alpine beer brand of Moosehead brewery, Nova Scotia, Canada.

Alpine Village brewery producing esteemed Lager and Pilsner in Los Angeles, California, USA.

alquitara pot-still brandy. Spain.

Alrode brewery at Alrode, South Africa. Owned by South African Breweries Ltd.

Alsace Rhineland region of northeast France with famed vineyards lying in the plains and foothills beneath the Vosges mountains. The only French region to make its wines on a largely varietal basis, ie labelled according to the name of the constituent grape – mainly noble German varieties Gewürztraminer and Riesling but also Muscat, Pinot Blanc, Tokay Pinot Gris (formerly known as Tokay d'Alsace), Sylvaner and (for the few red wines of the region) Pinot Noir. Wines range from simple dry whites to great, rich late-harvested (*vendange tardive*) 'dessert' wines from single vineyards. Alsace's wines, vineyards and producers commonly have German names, and the bottles used are traditionally German-style *flûtes*. The wines are nevertheless quite distinct from those made in the German Rhineland to the immediate north.

Alsace AC all wines made in Alsace, France, carry either this designation or a more specific one such as Alsace Grand Cru AC or Crémant d'Alsace AC.

Alsace Grand Cru AC forty-eight vine-growing sites in Alsace, France, can make wine under this appellation provided they meet certain quality criteria, including the use only of the classic grape varieties Gewürztraminer, Muscat, Riesling, Tokay-Pinot Gris. The vineyards are Altenberg de Bergbieten, Altenberg de Bergheim, Altenberg de Wolxheim, Brand, Eichberg, Engelberg, Frankstein, Froehn, Furstentum, Geisberg, Gloeckelberg, Goldert, Hatschbourg, Hengst, Kanzlerberg, Kastelberg, Kessler, Kitterlé, Kirchberg de Barr, Kirchberg de Ribeauvillé, Mambourg, Mandelberg, Markrain, Moenchberg, Muenchberg, Ollwiller, Osterberg, Pfersigberg, Pfingstberg, Praelatenberg, Ranger, Rosacker, Saering, Schlossberg, Schoenenbourg, Sommerberg, Sonnenglanz, Spiegel, Sporen, Steinert, Steingruber, Steinklotz, Vorbourg, Wiebelsberg, Wineck-Schlossberg, Winzenberg, Zinnkoepflé, Zotzenberg.

Alsace Sélection des Grains Nobles AC the greatest wines of Alsace, France, made from late-harvested grapes which have achieved exceptionally high sugar levels due to *botrytis cinerea* or 'noble rot' while still on the vine. Only classic grape varieties Gewürztraminer, Muscat, Riesling, Tokay-Pinot Gris qualify. Wines are intensely rich and alcoholic, made for very long keeping (25 years or more) and very expensive.

Alsace Vendange Tardive AC late-harvested wines of Alsace, France.

Only classic grape varieties Gewürztraminer, Muscat, Riesling, Tokay-Pinot Gris qualify and grape sugar content must reach specified levels. In some years, the sugar levels can be achieved well within normal ripening time, and this has led to criticism of these wines' consistency of style.

Alsheim winemaking village in Krötenbrunnen collective vineyard (*Grosslage*) of Rheinhessen region, Germany.

Alsterweiler Kapellenberg vineyard at Maikammer in Rheinpfalz region, Germany.

Alt short form of Altbier commonly used in northern Germany and, more loosely, elsewhere.

Altarberg vineyard at Ellenz-Poltersdorf in Mosel-Saar-Ruwer region, Germany.

Altärchen vineyard at Trittenheim in Mosel-Saar-Ruwer region, Germany.

altar wine any wine used for the Eucharist. Most commonly purpose-made fortified wine.

Alta Vineyard Cellar winery at the Alta Vineyard in the Napa Valley, California, USA, immortalised in Robert Louis Stevenson's *The Silverado Squatters* in the words 'the smack of Californian earth shall linger on the palate of your grandson'.

Altbairisch Dunkel dark lager beer made by Ayinger brewery near Munich, Germany.

Altbayerische Weissbier wheat beer of Paulaner brewery, Munich, Germany.

Altberg vineyard at Au in Baden region, Germany.

Altbier 'old beer'. German for top-fermenting beers made in a range of traditional ways in many parts of Germany, but principally in Düsseldorf.

Altdörr vineyards at Dalheim and at Friesenheim in Rheinhessen region, Germany.

Alte Burg vineyards at Bad Mergentheim, at Emmendingen, and at Tenningen in Baden region, and at Zwingenberg in Hessische Bergstrasse region, Germany.

Alte Lay vineyard at Bad Neuenahr-Ahrweiler in Ahr region, Germany.

Altenbamberg winemaking village in the Burgweg collective vineyard (*Grosslage*) of the Nahe region, Germany.

Altenberg the name of 38 individual vineyards in Germany. Region by region, as follows: in Baden at Baden-Baden, Ballrechten-Dottingen, Boxberg, Bruchsal, Lauda-Königshofen (Lauda), Lauda-Königshofen (Oberlauda), Müllheim (Britzingen), Müllheim (Dattingen), Staufen im Breisgau, Sulzburg, Sulzburg (Laufen); in Franken at Abtswind, Ergersheim, Theilheim; in Mosel-Saar-Ruwer at Kanzem, Konz (Filzen), Konz (Hamm), Konz (Krettnach), Konz (Oberemmel), Trier, Wellen; in Nahe at Meddersheim, Niedern-hall, Weissbach; in Rheinhessen at Hillesheim; in Rheinpfalz at Bad Bergzabern, Weisenheim am Sand; in Württemberg at Brackenheim, stein, Obersulm, Stuttgart, Weinsberg, Weinstadt (Beutelsbach), Weinstadt (Schnait), Weinstadt (Strümpfelbach).

Altenburg vineyards at Waldlaubersheim in Nahe region, and at Wachenheim in Rheinpfalz region, Germany.

Altenmünster village brewery and export beer, Augsburg, Germany.

Alter Berg vineyards at Triefenstein in Franken region, at Römerberg (Heiligenstein) at Römerberg (Mechtersheim) in Rheinpfalz region, and at Aspach in Württemberg region, Germany.

Alte Reben old vines. A designation given to some wines made from such vines. Austria.

Alter Graben vineyard at Bamberg in Franken region, Germany.

Alte Römerstrasse vineyards at Mandel in Nahe region and at Freilaubersheim and at Volxheim in Rheinhessen region, Germany.

Altesino wine estate est in 15th century near Siena, Tuscany, Italy. Renowned Brunello di Montalcino red plus *vino da tavola* brands.

Altes Löhl vineyard at Landau in der Pfalz mit und Mörlheim, Rheinpfalz region, Germany.

Altesse white grape variety best known in Savoie region, France, for making rich and aromatic white wines.

Altforster Altbier-type beer made by Arcen brewery, Netherlands.

Alt Franken Export Dunkel dark beer by Tucher brewery, Nürnberg, Germany.

Althof vineyard at Ottersweier in Baden region, Germany.

Altia state-owned distiller, Finland.

Alt-Münchner Dunkel dark beer made by Paulaner brewery, Munich, Germany.

Alto wine estate in Stellenbosch, South Africa. Alto Rouge red wine from Cabernets Franc and Sauvignon, Merlot and Shiraz; also unblended Cabernet Sauvignon.

Alto Adige DOC quality wine zone within the Trentino-Alto Adige region of northeast Italy. Also known as Südtirol. Fine red varietal wines include Cabernet (both Franc and Sauvignon), Merlot and Pinot Nero. Whites include Chardonnay, Gewürztraminer, Pinot Bianco and Pinot Grigio. Some *rosato* wines. German grape names are also commonly used.

Alto Estate wine property in Stellenbosch, South Africa. Long-keeping Cabernet Sauvignon and Shiraz reds.

Altstadthof small brewery at Nürnberg, Germany, known for Hausbrauerei Altstadthof dark beer.

Altus AVA wine area of Arkansas, USA.

Altydgedacht Estate wine property at Durbanville, South Africa. Tintoretto red from Barbera and Shiraz grapes plus Chardonnay and other varietals.

Alvarelhão red grape variety of northern Portugal including Douro and Minho regions. Table wines.

Alvarinho white grape variety used for Portugal's white vinho verde wines. Uniquely in Portugal, Alvarinho can be vinified as an individual variety and the wine labelled as a varietal. Synonymous with Albarino grape of Spain.

Alvarinho de Monção Cepa Velha renowned vinho verde brand made entirely from Alvarinho grapes. Portugal.

Alvear longest-established producer of Montilla wines est 1729, Montilla, Andalucia, Spain.

Alzinger wine producer in Wachau, Niederösterreich, Austria.

amabile medium-sweet (wine). Italy.

Amadeus Almond Orange liqueur brand of Halewood International, Huyton, Merseyside, England.

Amador Foothill Winery wine property in Shenandoah Valley, California, USA. Zinfandel and other varietals.

Amaretto almond and apricot liqueur of Italy.

Amaretto Coffee add 1 part amaretto to a cup of hot, black coffee. Float whipped fresh cream over.

Amaretto Cream Cocktail. Over ice shake 1 part amaretto, 1 cream. Strain.

Amaretto di Saronno the original Amaretto, said first to have been made in 1525 by a young widow for Bernardino Luini, painter of the frescoes in Santa Maria delle Grazie in Saronno, Italy. She was keeper of the inn where Luini lodged, and model for his Madonna.

Amaretto Rose Cocktail. Into a tall, ice-filled glass pour 1 part amaretto and 1 teaspoon Rose's Lime Juice cordial. Top with soda water.

Amaretto Stinger Cocktail. Over ice stir 2 parts amaretto, 1 crème de menthe. Strain.

Amarit lager brand, Thailand.

amaro bitter (wine and spirits). Italy.

amarone strong (14% or more), dry, slightly bitter red wine style of DOC Valpolicella, Veneto, Italy. From the 2004 vintage, Amarone

della Valpolicella was elevated to DOCG status (see DOCG). Production method includes adding part-dried grapes during vinification to increase concentration and flavour. The first commercially marketed Amarone della Valpolicella was a 1950 vintage made by Bolla, released in 1953. See also Recioto della Valpolicella.

Amarula Cream liqueur from fruit of marula or 'elephant' tree and cream. Southern Liqueur Co, South Africa.

Amatitan tequila brand, Mexico.

Ambar brewery and lager brand, Spain.

Ambari lager (5% alc) by Impala Brewery, Goa, India.

Amber Lager beer produced by Abita Springs brewery, Louisiana, USA.

Amber Wheaten wheat beer produced under Pyramid label by Hart Brewing Inc at Kalma, Washington, USA.

Amberley lager brand of Heineken brewery, Netherlands.

Amberley Estate wine property at Margaret River, South Australia. Mainly white wines.

Amberley Estate Vineyard wine property at Amberley, New Zealand. Chardonnay and Pinot Noir wines.

Ambier brewery in Milwaukee, Wisconsin, USA, founded (1985) to re-create Vienna-style lager beer.

Ambonnay wine village of Montagne de Reims, Champagne, France.

Ambrato di Comiso rich dessert wine of Sicily, Italy.

Ameisenberg vineyards at St Goar and at St Goar (Werlau) in Mittelrhein region, Germany.

amelioration euphemistic description for the process of adding sugar to grape juice before fermentation in order to 'improve' wine.

Amer Campari bitter liqueur brand. Italy.

Americana Cocktail. Into a champagne glass put 1 sugar lump then add a dash of Angostura bitters and a measure of bourbon. Stir to dissolve sugar. Top with chilled sparkling wine and add an orange slice.

American Beauty Cocktail. Over ice shake 1 part dry vermouth, 1 brandy, 1 grenadine, 1 fresh orange juice, 1 dash crème de menthe. Strain and add a dash of port.

Americano Cocktail. Over ice, pour 1 part Campari, 2 sweet vermouth. Top with soda, stir and add lemon peel.

American Proof system of indicating alcohol levels in liquor, USA. Related to Gay Lussac (GL) system of measuring alcohol by volume by a factor of two. Thus pure spirit of 100%GL equates to 200% American proof.

American vines phylloxera-resistant vines, grown in the USA, used for grafting to European stock.

Amer Picon bitters flavoured with gentian and orange. French.

Amer Picon Highball Cocktail. Into tall glass containing one or two large ice cubes pour 1 part Amer Picon bitters, 1 or 2 dashes grenadine. Top with soda or ginger ale. Add lemon peel.

Amery Vineyards wine producer in McLaren Vale, South Australia. Table wines and liqueur Muscat.

Am Gaisberg vineyard at Herxheimweier in Rheinpfalz region, Germany.

Am heiligen Häuschen vineyard at Worms in Rheinhessen region, Germany.

Am hohen Stein vineyard at Rittersheim in Rheinpfalz region, Germany.

Amigne traditional Swiss grape variety for dry white wine.

Amiral, Château de l' second wine of Château Labégorce Zédé, Bordeaux, France.

Amity Vineyards producer of varietal wines, notably Chardonnay and Pinot Noir, at Amity, Oregon, USA.

Amizetta Vineyards wine producer in Napa County, California, USA. Known for Sauvignon wines.

Ammerlanden vineyard at Möckmühl in Württemberg region, Germany.

Amon, Chateau L' wine estate at Bendigo, Victoria, Australia. Named after owner Ian Leamon.

Amontillado 'in the style of Montilla'. Correctly, a *fino* sherry matured long enough to become darker in colour and nutty in flavour, but in current usage, just about any 'medium' (sweetened) sherry. Spain.

amoroso 'loving'. A sweet, velvety variation of *oloroso* (dark and fragrant) sherry. Spanish.

Amos small independent brewer in Lorraine, France.

Ampeau, Robert leading winemaker in Meursault, Burgundy, France. Vineyards in Meursault (les Perrières and les Charmes), Puligny-Montrachet (les Combettes), Pommard and Volnay Santenots.

ampelography the study of vines and their varietal characteristics.

amphora two-handled earthenware wine jar of ancient Greece and Rome. Full, an amphora equated to the value of a slave.

Ampuis winemaking village at centre of the Côte Rôtie vineyards of the Rhône Valley, France.

Ampurdán, Cavas del wine producer at Gerona, Catalonia, Spain. Cazador and Reserva Don Miguel reds.

Ampurdán-Costa Brava DO wine zone of Catalonia, Spain. Mostly rosé.

Amrut distiller and whisky brand, Bangalore, India. Of **Amrut Single Malt Whisky**, launched in Scotland in 2004, the distillery claimed: 'Indian single malt whisky has its own character – the product is made from 100 per cent Indian barley, grown in the foothills of the Himalayas.'

Amselberg vineyard at Genenbach in Baden region, Germany.

Amselfelder sweet Pinot Noir red wine of Kosovo, putative former province of Serbia.

Amstel brewery in Hamilton, Ontario, Canada. Produces Dutch Amstel beer brands plus local products including Grizzly beer.

Amstel Brouwerij major brewing company based in Amsterdam, Netherlands. Owned by Heineken.

Amstel Bier is a worldwide lager

Amtgarten vineyard at Mülheim in Mosel-Saar-Ruwer region, Germany.

Amtliche Prüfungsnummer (AP) certification number displayed on labels of all German quality wines, intended to affirm wine has passed analytical and tasting tests.

Amynteon wine appellation of northern Greece.

añada Spanish term for young ('one year') wine ready for the first stage of sherry production. Also any wine of one vintage only.

anaerobic 'in the absence of air'. The condition in which most wines are made in order to avoid oxidation.

ananas pineapple-flavoured liqueur. Usually prefixed with *crème de*. Mostly French.

Anatolia winemaking region of Turkey.

Anbaugebiet region of wine production, Germany. See Qualitätswein.

Ancient Age bourbon whiskey brand, USA.

Anchialos wine appellation of Gulf of Pegassitikos, Greece.

Anchor Beer brand name of Archipelago Brewery, Kuala Lumpur, Malaysia.

Anchor Brewing Company brewery est 1896 in San Francisco, California, USA. Famed for **Anchor Steam Beer**, Liberty Ale (6% alc), Old Foghorn Barley Wine and other brands.

An Cnoc Highland malt whisky of Knockdhu distillery est 1893, Knock, Banffshire, Scotland. Single malt: 12-year-old. Name dates from 1993.

Andalucia southernmost province of Spain and home of sherry production.

Andalusia WO wine district north of Kimberley, South Africa.

Andaluzas, Bodegas vineyard and winery, Colombia.

Andechs Brauerei monastery brewery on the Ammersee lake, Bavaria, Germany. Known not only for exceptionally malty beers but for liqueurs and fruit brandies.

Andeker beer brand by Pabst Brewery, Los Angeles, California, USA, said to be inspired by a recipe of Bavaria's Andechs brewery.

Anderson, O P akvavit producer, Sweden.

Anderson Valley AVA wine zone of Mendocino, California, USA.

Anderson Valley brewery at Boonville, Mendocino County, California, USA. Curiously named but highly regarded ales include Boont Amber and Poleeko Gold.

Anderson Valley Vineyards wine producer at Albuquerque, New Mexico, USA.

Anderson, S, Vineyard winery in Napa Valley, California, USA. Still and sparkling wines.

André, Pierre major wine producer and *négociant-éleveur* in Burgundy, France. Founded by Pierre André 1923 and based at Château de Corton-André, Aloxe-Corton.

Andreasberg vineyards at Ortenberg in Baden region and at Trier in Mosel-Saar-Ruwer region, Germany.

Andres Wines major wine producer in British Columbia and in Ontario, Canada. Known for 'Canadian Champagne', Baby Duck brand and quality table wines.

Andrew Garrett wine producer in McLaren Vale, South Australia. Noted for Chardonnay and Riesling. Owned by Suntory of Japan.

Andrew Wolf Wine Cellars wine producer at Cochrane, Alberta, Canada.

Andron-Blanquet, Château wine estate of AC St-Estèphe, Bordeaux, France. Classified *Cru Bourgeois*.

Añejas, Bodegas vineyard and winery, Colombia.

Aney, Château wine estate of Haut-Médoc, Bordeaux, France.

Angel Face Cocktail. Over ice shake 1 part dry gin, 1 apricot brandy, 1 apple brandy. Strain.

Angeles Brewery producer of British-style ales, notably **Angeles Amber Ale**, in suitably named Chatsworth, a suburb of Los Angeles, California, USA.

Angelica sweet liqueur of Basque country, Spain. Flavoured with angelica and plants of the Pyrenees.

Angelica traditional sweet wine of California, USA, made by fortifying new-pressed grape juice.

Angel's Kiss Cocktail. Into a shot glass pour one part each of the following, all chilled beforehand, and poured with a steady hand to prevent mixing: crème de cacao, sloe gin, brandy, single cream.

Angelus Bière de Froment, L' wheat beer by Annoeullin brewery, France.

Angélus, Château L' great wine estate of AC St-Emilion, Bordeaux, France. Classified *1er Grand Cru Classé* (1996).

Anghelu Ruju rich red dessert wine (vino da tavola) made by Sella & Mosca of Sardinia, Italy.

Angler Cocktail. Over ice shake 1 part dry gin, 2 dashes orange bitters, 1 dash Angostura bitters, 1 dash grenadine.

Anglo-German brewery at Barking, Essex, England.

Angludet, Château wine estate of AC Margaux, Bordeaux, France. Wine is labelled **Château d'Angludet**. Classified *Cru Bourgeois Supérieur Exceptionnel*.

CHATEAU D'ANGLUDET
MARGAUX

APPELLATION MARGAUX CONTROLÉE

1983

MIS EN BOUTEILLE AU CHATEAU
Produce of France   75 cl

Angos dry gin brand of Angostura company, Port of Spain, Trinidad.

Angostura aromatic bitters from a recipe devised as a restorative by German-born surgeon Johan Siegert (1796-1870) on duty in the town of Angostura, Venezuela, in 1824. Dr Siegert established a company to manufacture the bitters in 1867 but his heirs were forced to leave Venezuela during political upheavals and removed to Port of Spain, Trinidad, where the business is still based. Angostura town was renamed Cuidad Bolivar (after Venezuelan national Simon Bolivar) in 1846. The bitters are based in Trinidad rum flavoured with a secret recipe of herbs and spices.

Angove's large winery at Renmark, South Australia. Wide range of red and white varietals.

Anheuser, Weingut Okonomierat August E largest wine estate of Nahe region, Germany.

Anheuser, Weingut Paul wine producer of Nahe region, Germany. Noted *halbtrocken* Riesling wines.

Anheuser-Busch largest beer-producer in the USA, and probably in the world, based at St Louis, Missouri. The company has 13 brewing centres in the USA and produces more than ten billion litres of beer annually. Famous brands include **Anheuser Märzen**, Budweiser, Busch and Michelob.

Animator strong bock beer by Hacker-Pschorr brewery, Bavaria, Germany.

Añina district of *albariza* soil for sherry production, Andalucia, Spain.

Anis del Mono aniseed liqueur brand. Barcelona, Spain.

Anisetta Stellata aniseed liqueur brand. Aurum, Pescara, Italy.

anisette aniseed liqueur. First and still leading brand is that of Marie Brizard of Bordeaux, France.

Anjou AC wine zone of Loire Valley, France. Many good red wines from Saumur area, some whites, and, under **Anjou Rosé AC**, famous rosé wines.

Anjou Coteaux de La Loire AC small wine zone for white wines only, south of Angers in Loire Valley, France.

Anjou Gamay AC designation for red wines made from Gamay grapes grown in the Anjou AC, Loire Valley, France.

Anjou Mousseux AC designation for white and rosé sparkling wines made by the 'champagne method' from specified grape varieties grown in the Anjou AC, Loire Valley, France.

Anjou Pétillant AC designation for white and rosé semi-sparkling wines made in Anjou AC, Loire Valley, France.

Anjou-Saumur winemaking district of Loire Valley, France.

Annaberg vineyards at Schweich in Mosel-Saar-Ruwer region and at Kallstadt in Rheinpfalz region, Germany.

annata vintage/year of wine. Italy.

Annereaux, Château des wine estate of AC Lalande-de-Pomerol, Bordeaux, France.

Annoeullin, Brasserie d' small but famed brewery in the town of Annoeullin in northern France. Known for Pastor Ale *bière de garde*.

Ann Street brewery at St Helier, Jersey, Channel Islands, UK, producing **Ann's Treat** bitter.

Ansac cognac brand of Unicognac brandy co-operative, Jonzac, France. XXX, VSOP, Napoléon, XO.

Ansells brewery and beer brand based in Birmingham, England. Popular brands include **Ansells Mild** and **Ansells Traditional**.

Ansonica Costa dell'Argentario DOC for white wines from Ansonica B grapes, Grosseto province, Tuscany, Italy.

Anthemis green mint liqueur of Benedictine monastery, Montevergine, France.

anthocyans pigments in grape skins imparting much of the colour into wine.

Anthonic, Château wine estate of AC Moulis, Bordeaux, France. Classified *Cru Bourgeois Supérieur*.

anthracnose disease of vines prevalent in humid weather.

Antilliaanse Brouwerij brewery at Willemstad, Curaçao, West Indies.

Antinori Florentine winemaking dynasty (est 1385) with estates in Chianti Classico zone of Tuscany, Italy. Wines include Villa Antinori Riserva Chianti Classico and renowned Tignanello. Antinori's property at Castello della Sala in Orvieto, Umbria, produces one of the region's finest wines.

Antiquary, The blended scotch whisky brand of J & W Hardie, South Queensferry, Scotland.

Antique whisky brand originally of Seagram, Canada and USA.

Antofagasta Cocktail. Over ice shake 1 part scotch whisky, 1 dry vermouth, 1 curaçao, 2 dashes lemon juice. Strain.

Antoniusberg vineyard at Serrig in Mosel-Saar-Ruwer region, Germany.

Antoniusbrunnen vineyard at Saarburg in Mosel-Saar-Ruwer region, Germany.

Anvil Ale brand of Hydes Anvil Brewery, Manchester, England.

Aotea wine producer in Gisborne, New Zealand.

aperitif, apéritif a drink served as an appetiser. French, ultimately from Latin *aperire*, to open.

Apetlon village in Burgenland, Austria, at the centre of the many vineyards cultivated by winemaker Lenz Moser.

Aphrodite dry white wine of Keo company, Cyprus. Name alludes to myth of goddess Aphrodite's appearance from the sea at Cyprus.

Apitiv dry white port brand of House of Sandeman, Vila Nova de Gaia, Portugal. Until 1985, Apitiv was a fino sherry brand of Sandeman.

Apostelberg vineyard at Guldental in Nahe region, Germany.

Apostelgarten vineyard at Alzenau in Franken region, Germany.

Apotheke vineyard at Trittenheim in Mosel-Saar-Ruwer region, Germany.

Apparent Cocktail. Over ice shake 1 part dry gin, 1 Dubonnet, 1 dash anis. Strain.

Appellation Contrôlée (AC) familiar abbreviation of **Appellation d'Origine Contrôlée**, the designation of authenticity for quality wines in France. Since the founding of the Institut National des Appellations d'Origine in 1935, more than 400 ACs have been created in a continuing process. About 30 per cent of France's wine production qualifies to carry the label designation, meeting regulations and standards concerning location of vineyards and wineries, grape varieties and yields, methods of cultivation and vinification, alcohol content and, as determined by state-appointed committees, wine quality. The French system has been adopted with varying refinements by numerous wine-producing nations throughout the world.

Appetizer Cocktail. Over ice shake 1 part dry gin, 1 Dubonnet, 2 fresh orange juice. Strain.

Apple Cocktail. Over ice shake 2 parts sweet cider, 2 apple brandy, 1 dry gin, 1 brandy.

Apple Blow Fizz Cocktail. Over ice shake 1 generous measure apple brandy, 4 dashes lemon juice, 1 teaspoon powdered sugar, 1 egg white. Strain into medium glass and top with soda.

Apple Brandy correctly, a spirit distilled from fermented apple juice (cider). Sole licensed brand in UK labelled as such is J B Reynier's Herefordshire Apple Brandy.

Apple Day Cocktail. Over ice shake 1 part vodka, 1 apple brandy, 1 apple juice, 1 teaspoon lemon juice. Strain.

Apple Eau de Vie colourless apple spirit distilled by Somerset Cider Brandy Co, Kingsbury Episcopi, Somerset, England.

applejack cider spirit. USA.

Applejack Cocktail. Over ice shake 1 part apple brandy, 1 sweet vermouth, 1 dash Angostura bitters. Strain.

Applejack Rabbit Cocktail. Over ice shake 1 part apple brandy, 1 lemon juice, 1 orange juice, 1 maple syrup. Strain.

Applejack Special Cocktail. Over ice shake 2 parts white rum, 2 sweet vermouth, 1 apricot brandy, 1 lemon juice, 1 dash grenadine. Strain.

Apple Pie Cocktail. Over ice shake 1 part rum, 1 sweet vermouth, 2 dashes apple brandy, 2 dashes lemon juice, 1 dash grenadine. Strain.

apples in winetasting, a smell indicating the presence of malic acid, particularly in immature wine.

Appleton rum brand of J Wray Nephew, Jamaica.

Approved Viticultural Area (AVA) controlled appellation zone resembling AC of France, introduced in USA in 1980. To carry AVA designation on labels, wines must originate from within the defined area. More than 100 AVAs have been established in a continuing process, but criteria as defined under the French system are not yet in place.

âpre in winetasting, harsh-tasting, tannic. French.

Apremont dry white wine from the Jacquère grape in Savoie, France. AC Vin de Savoie.

Apricot Cocktail. Over ice shake 2 parts apricot brandy, 1 lemon juice, 1 orange juice, 1 dash dry gin. Strain.

apricot brandy correctly, a spirit distilled from fermented apricots. More usually, an apricot liqueur.

Apricot Cooler Cocktail. Over ice shake 1 part apricot brandy, 1 lime juice, 2 dashes grenadine. Strain into tall glass and top with soda.

apricot liqueur usually, the product of apricots macerated in grape brandy.

Aprilia DOC red and white wines from surroundings of town of Aprilia, Latium, Italy.

Apry apricot liqueur brand of Marie Brizard, Bordeaux, France.

Apulia Puglia, the wine region of Italy's 'heel'. Large production of simple wines, many for vermouth, but also a growing output of quality *vino da tavola* and wines from 24 DOC zones.

Aqua d'Oro liqueur decorated with powdered gold leaf. Italy.

aquavit see akvavit.

Aqueduct Cocktail. Over ice shake 2 parts vodka, 1 fresh lime juice, 2 dashes apricot brandy, 2 dashes curaçao. Strain.

Aquilea DOC wine zone of Friuli-Venezia Guilia, Italy. Good wines from Cabernet Franc, Pinot Grigio and Tocai Friuliano grape varieties, among others.

Arabier strong, top-fermenting summer-season beer by De Dolle Brouwers ('Crazy Brewers'), Diksmuide in Flanders, Belgium.

Aramon red grape once widely planted in southern France. Now only for ordinary wines.

Ararat brandy of Armenia.

Arban(n)e grape variety allowed for champagne production, but little used. France.

Arbin a *cru* (vineyard district) of Vin de Savoie, France.

Arbois white grape variety once much used for wines of the Orléanais, France, but now much less so.

Arbois wine AC of the Jura region, France. Red and rosé wines notably from Pinot Noir grapes, and white from Chardonnay and Savagnin.

Also **Arbois Mousseux AC** sparkling wines, **Arbois Vin de Paille AC** 'straw wine' from dried grapes, **Arbois Vin Jaune AC** long-aged wine. It was in the town of Arbois that the locally born Louis Pasteur conducted his researches into vinification.

Arbor Crest wine producer at Spokane, Washington, USA. High-quality wines from Cabernet Sauvignon and other varieties.

Arborea DOC of Sardinia, Italy. Red, *rosato* and white wines.

Arcen town brewery, Limburg, Netherlands, famous for top-fermenting beers including very strong (10% alc) **Arcener Grand Prestige**. Also **Arcener Stout** and **Arcener Tarwe** wheat beer.

Archambeau, Château d' wine estate of AC Graves, Bordeaux, France.

Archanes sweet red wine of Crete.

Arche, Château d' great wine estate of AC Sauternes, Bordeaux, France. Classified *2ème Cru Classé*.

Arche-Lafaurie, Château d' vineyard of AC Sauternes, Bordeaux, France, formerly part of Château d'Arche estate.

Archers peach schnapps brand, USA. Owned by Diageo.

Archers Ales brewery est 1979 at Swindon, Wiltshire, England. Ales include Best (4.0% alc), Golden (4.7% alc) and Village (3.6% alc) bitters and Blackjack Porter (4.6% alc).

Archers Aqua Flavoured alcoholic beverage blended from Archers schnapps, water and other ingredients, marketed in single-serve bottles by Diageo.

Arcins commune of the Haut-Médoc, Bordeaux, France.

Arcins, Château d' wine estate of AC Haut-Médoc, Bordeaux, France. Classified *Cru Bourgeois*.

Ardennes, Château d' wine estate of AC Graves, Bordeaux, France.

Ardbeg Island malt whisky distillery est 1794, Islay, Scotland. Single malts: 10-year-old, 18-year-old.

Ardmore East Highland malt whisky distillery est 1898, Kennethmont,

Aberdeenshire, Scotland. Single malt: 15-year-old.

are a hundredth of a hectare. Ownership of French vineyards, particularly in Burgundy, is commonly reckoned in *ares*.

arena sandy red soil of Andalucia, Spain in which sherry grapes are grown.

Arganda-Colemenar de Oreja winemaking area of Tierra de Madrid, Spain.

Argentina major wine-producing nation said to be world's fifth largest, but still a very minor exporter. Vineyards mainly in Mendoza region plus Rio Negro valley and Salta and San Juan regions.

Argile Grise apple variety traditionally valued for cidermaking. French.

argol tartar deposit occurring in wine casks.

Argueso, Manuel de sherry *bodega* est 1822, Jerez de la Frontera, Spain.

Argyll blended and single malt scotch whisky brand of Beinn Buidhe, Argyll, Scotland.

arika spirit distilled from kefir (fermented milk). Tartar.

Arinto white grape variety of Portugal, notably in Bucellas wines.

Arkansas minor wine-producing state of USA but with one major winery, Wiederkehr Cellars at Altus.

Arkell Best Bitter beer by Wellington County brewery, Ontario, Canada.

Arkell's brewery at Kingsdown, Swindon, Wiltshire, England. Ales include BBB and Bitter.

Arlay, Château d' wine estate of AC Côtes du Jura, France.

Arlesgarten vineyard at Gerolzhofen in Franken region, Germany.

Armada bottle-conditioned beer (4.0% alc) by Wood Brewery, Winstanstow, Shropshire, England. 'Brewed to celebrate the defeat of the Spanish fleet in 1588.'

Armada Cream *oloroso* sherry brand of House of Sandeman, Jerez, Spain. The name commemorates a pivotal moment in the history of the British sherry trade, as described in Sandeman's seminal history *200 Years of Port and Sherry*, concerning the occasion on which Sir Francis Drake 'singed the King of Spain's beard' in 1587: 'Drake's mission was to destroy the Armada being prepared at Cadiz for the invasion of England. This he did with his customary despatch, blasting his way into the port with a squadron of 24 naval vessels, boarding 32 enemy warships in various states of completion, stripping them of every valuable in sight, then burning all but those in which he carried home the mountainous booty. Incredibly, Drake remained three days in the great dockyard, finding time in the midst of this epic naval action to loot the huge quantity of sack that happened to be waiting on the quayside – 2,900 butts in all. The loss of this cargo is said to have been, on balance, of long-term benefit to the sherry trade, because its triumphal arrival in England popularised the wine there as never before.'

Armadillo 'British wine' brand of Matthew Clark, Bristol, England.

Armagnac

Armagnac the brandy of Gascony, France. Designated spirit must be distilled from wine of one of three defined regions: Bas Armagnac, Haut Armagnac and Ténarèze. Unblended Armagnac can be sold as the product of a dated vintage.

Armailhac, Château d' wine estate of AC Pauillac, Médoc, Bordeaux, France. Formerly named Château Mouton Baronne Philippe. Classified *5ème Grand Cru Classé*.

Armenia possibly the first wine-making nation, as grape pips carbon-dated to 7000 BC, the oldest ever found, have been discovered there. Limited production of wine continues.

Armigne medium-sweet white wine from Valais grape. Switzerland.

Arms Park Ale beer (4.0% alc) by SA Brain brewery, Cardiff, Wales. Commemorates former Welsh national Rugby Union stadium, Cardiff Arms Park, displaced 1999 by the Millennium Stadium in the city.

Arnaud-Jouan, Château d' wine estate of AC Premières Côtes de Bordeaux, France.

Arnauld, Château d' wine estate of AC Haut-Médoc, Bordeaux, France.

Arneis white grape variety and renowned varietal wines of Piedmont, Italy.

Arnould, Michel & Fils *récoltant-manipulant* champagne producer of Verzenay, France.

aroma in winetasting, a smell which indicates the presence of a particular grape variety.

aroma hops hop varieties used in brewing to enhance bouquet.

aromatic in winetasting, the type of smell associated with wines made from spicily scented grape varieties including the Gewürztraminer and Muscat and some others.

Arrack Punsch flavoured liqueur adaptation of Batavian arrak. Sweden.

arrak sugar (molasses fermented with rice yeast) spirit, originally of Batavia, Indonesia, but now imitated from the East Indies to the Mediterranean.

Arran Malt single malt whisky of Isle of Arran Distillers, Scotland. Production was interrupted in 1845 but resumed in 1995.

Arrasburg Schlossberg vineyard at Alf in Mosel-Saar-Ruwer region, Germany.

Arricaud, Château d' wine estate of AC Graves, Bordeaux, France.

arrière-gout in winetasting, after-taste. French.

arrope grape-sugar syrup used to colour and sweeten sherry. Spain.

Arrol's 80/- ale produced by Alloa Brewery Company, Scotland.

Arrosée, Château l' wine estate of AC St-Emilion, Bordeaux, France. Classified *Grand Cru Classé*.

Arrowfield wine producer of upper Hunter Valley, New South Wales, Australia.

Arroyo Seco AVA of Monterey County, California, USA.

Arruda Dos Vinhos wine region of western Portugal known for inexpensive table wines.

Arsac, Château d' wine estate of AC Haut-Médoc, Bordeaux, France. Classified *Cru Bourgeois Supérieur*.

Arsinoe white wine brand of Sodap winery, Cyprus.

Artigues-Arnaud, Château d' second wine of Château Grand-Puy-Ducasse, Bordeaux, France.

Artist's Special Cocktail. Over ice shake 2 parts whisky, 2 dry sherry, 1 lemon juice, 1 redcurrant syrup. Strain.

Artners wine producer in Carnuntum, Niederösterreich, Austria.

Artois Belgium's largest brewery, founded by the Artois family in 1366 and now based in Leuven. Known for Pilsener-style Stella Artois lager but also produces Loburg lager. Owned by Interbrew.

Arundel brewery at Arundel, West Sussex, England.

Arusha brewery at Arusha, Tanzania.

Arve-et-Lac wine district of Geneva canton, Switzerland.

Arve-et-Rhône wine district of Geneva canton, Switzerland.

Arvine medium-sweet white wine from Valais grape. Switzerland.

Arvois, Jean-Paul *récoltant-manipulant* champagne producer, Chavot-Courcourt, Champagne, France.

Arzley vineyard at Cochem in Mosel-Saar-Ruwer region, Germany.

Asahi brewing company of Japan. Dry Beer (5.0% alc) and **Asahi Black Beer**.

Asbach renowned brandy producer of Rudesheim, Germany. **Asbach Uralt** brandy. Sold by British owners Diageo to Bols of the Netherlands in 1999.

Asenovgrad wine area of Upper Maritsa Valley, Bulgaria. Known for quality red wines from Cabernet Sauvignon and Mavrud grapes.

Ashburnham vineyard at Battle, Sussex, England.

Ashes Cocktail. Over ice shake 2 parts dry gin, 1 lemon juice, 1 Marnique liqueur, 2 dashes yellow Chartreuse. Strain and add cocktail cherry to glass.

Ashill cider producer, Ilminster, Somerset, England.

Ashland Amber ale brand of Bay Front and Rogue breweries, Newport, Oregon, USA.

Ashley Wilkes Cocktail. Into a tumbler place three crushed mint sprigs, a teaspoon of sugar and a teaspoon of fresh lime juice. Add ice cubes. Pour in 2 parts bourbon, 1 peach brandy, and stir. Add a mint sprig.

Ashtarak sherry-style wine of Armenia.

Ashton co-operative wine producer, Robertson, South Africa.

Ash Vine brewery formerly of White Hart pub, Trudoxhill, Somerset, England. Brands including Hop & Glory, Longleat, Penguin Porter, Sweet FA.

Ask Mama Cocktail. Over ice shake 2 parts vodka, 1 Cointreau, 1 fresh lime juice. Strain.

Aspall cidermaker est 1728, Suffolk, England. Renowned 'cyder' products including bestselling vinegar.

aspect defining characteristic of vineyards. South and southwest facing slopes are most prized in colder latitudes (the classic regions of France, for example) for maximum sunlight hours.

Aspenberg vineyards at Bayerfeld-Steckweiler and at Oberndorf in the Nahe region, Germany.

aspersion frost-combatting technique employed by vine growers. Budding vines are sprayed as temperature approaches freezing point, forming a protective covering of ice.

Asprin(i)o semi-sparkling dry white wine of Basilicata and Campania regions, Italy.

assemblage assembling different *cuvées* (vats) of wine to form the desired blend, especially in Bordeaux, where wines from various grape varieties are vatted separately. French.

Assenovgrad town and winery (est 1948) of Rhodope Mountains, southern Bulgaria. Red wines from Cabernet Sauvignon, Mavrud and Merlot grapes.

Assmannshausen winemaking village of Steil collective vineyard (*Grosslage*) in Rheingau region, Germany.

Assyrtiko white grape variety for Retsina and fortified wines of Greece, now increasingly planted for dry whites of Aegean island of Santorini.

Asti Spumante DOCG sparkling wine, usually sweet, from Moscato grapes made at the town of Asti, Piedmont, Italy. Low in strength (typically 7% alc) and characterized by aromatic-grape flavour.

Astley vineyard at Stourport-in-Severn, Worcestershire, England.

Astoria Cocktail. Over ice stir 2 parts dry gin, 1 dry vermouth, 1 dash orange bitters. Strain and add cocktail olive.

Astra brand name of beers produced by Bavaria St Pauli brewery, Hamburg, Germany. Includes **Astra Exclusiv** beer, **Astra Pilsener** and **Astra Urtyp** lager.

astringency in winetasting, the mouth-drying character of a young wine due to high acidity or tannin.

aszú 'rotten'. Style of sweet wine made in Hungary from late-harvested, botrytis-affected grapes; as, Tokaji Aszú.

As We Get It vatted scotch malt whisky blend by Macallan-Glenlivet, Craigellachie, Scotland.

As You Like It 'finest sweet sherry' brand of Williams & Humbert, Jerez de la Frontera, Spain.

Atholl Brose traditional Scottish Highland drink of malt whisky with oatmeal, cream, honey and other even more mysterious ingredients.

Atlantic Amber beer brand of New England Brewing Company, Connecticut, USA.

Atlantic Cocktail. Over ice shake 1 part Sandeman Ruby port, 1 brandy. Strain into a small wine glass filled with crushed ice and add a black cherry.

Atlantic Tawny port brand of Taylor Fladgate & Yeatman, Vila Nova de Gaia, Portugal.

atmosphere measure of pressure in sparkling wine (as at 20°C). One atmosphere = 15lbs per square inch. At a typical 6 atmospheres, champagne is bottled under a pressure similar to that of a heavy vehicle tyre.

Atom Bomb Cocktail. Over ice stir 1 part pastis and 1 brandy. Strain.

Atta Boy Cocktail. Over ice shake 2 parts dry gin, 1 dry vermouth, 2 dashes grenadine. Strain.

attenuation extent of reduction of sugars by the action of yeasts during fermentation of beer.

Attica vineyard region near Athens, Greece. Retsina and other white wines plus light reds.

Attilafelsen *Grosslage* (collective vineyard) incorporating vineyards in the Baden region of Germany at, respectively, Breisach (Niederrimsingen), Breisach (Oberrimsingen), Freiburg (Munzingen), Freiburg (Opfingen), Freiburg (Tiengen), Freiburg (Waltershofen), Gottenheim, Merdingen.

Atty Cocktail. Over ice shake 3 parts dry gin, 1 dry vermouth, 1 pastis, 2 dashes Crème de Violette. Strain.

Aube winemaking *département* of Champagne region, France.

Aubun red grape variety of southern Rhône, France. Synonymous with Counoise.

Auchentoshan Lowland malt whisky distillery est 1800, Dalmuir, Dunbartonshire, Scotland. Single malt: 10-year-old.

Auchroisk Speyside malt whisky distillery, Banffshire, Scotland. Single malt: The Singleton of Auchroisk 10-year-old (or more).

audit ale special-occasion strong ale traditionally brewed in colleges of Oxford and Cambridge universities, originally for Audit Day feasts.

Auf dem Zimmerburg vineyard at Oberstreit in Nahe region, Germany.

Auf der Heide vineyard at Traben-Trarbach in Mosel-Saar-Ruwer region, Germany.

Auf der Wiltingerkupp vineyard at Konz in Mosel-Saar-Ruwer region, Germany.

Aufgesetzter pure grain spirit with blackcurrant flavouring, traditionally drunk as a 'chaser' to beer. Germany.

Auflangen *Grosslage* (collective vineyard) incorporating vineyards at Nierstein and at Nierstein (Schwabsburg) in Rheinhessen region, Germany.

Augenscheiner vineyard at Trier in Mosel-Saar-Ruwer region, Germany.

Augier oldest *maison* of Cognac, France, est 1643.

Augustiner brewery in Munich, Bavaria, Germany. Produces Munich's best-known pale beer, **Augustiner Hell**, and a famed Export beer, Edelstoff (marketed in USA as **Augustiner Munich Light**). Dark beers include Maximator Doppelbock, sold in USA as Munich Dark.

Augustinerberg vineyard at Breisach in Baden region, Germany.

August Schell brewery in New Ulm, Minnesota, USA.

Aulenberg vineyard at Uelversheim in Rheinhessen region, Germany.

Aulerde vineyard at Westhofen in Rheinhessen region, Germany.

Aultmore Speyside malt whisky distillery, Strathisla, Scotland. Single malt: 12-year-old.

Aume wine barrel of Alsace, France. Capacity 114 litres.

Aurian, Philippe armagnac producer, Condom en Armagnac, Gascony, France. Hors d'Age, Extra Vieux, XO etc.

Aurora white grape variety of France, but more widely planted in USA.

Aurum brandy-based orange and herb liqueur of Pescara, Italy.

ausbruch style of very rich Austrian wine made from botrytis-affected grapes.

ausgehängt 'hung out', Austrian. *Heurigen* (qv) hang bushes or vine cuttings from their premises to denote that they have the new-season's wines, from their own vineyards, on sale, and are thus *ausgehängt*.

auslese 'selected harvest'. German wine-quality designation within the *Prädikat* range. The third level (after *kabinett* and *spätlese*) of grape ripeness which must reach a minimum Oechsle (sugar density) level of between 83° and 105° according to the region of production. Because grapes need to be very ripe and usually affected by botrytis or 'noble rot' the resulting wines tend to be golden in colour and richly flavoured, with considerable ageing potential.

Ausone, Château great wine estate of AC St-Emilion, Bordeaux, France. Named after Gaul-born Latin poet Ausonius who reputedly lived close by in the fourth century. Classified *1er Grand Cru Classé (A)* and ranked, with Château Cheval Blanc, above all other St-Emilion properties.

Ausoniusstein vineyard at Lehmen in Mosel-Saar-Ruwer region, Germany.

austere in winetasting, a wine affected by high acidity or excessive tannins which may or may not diminish with ageing.

Australia winemaking was initiated by British settlers in the 1790s but began today's era of high-quality production only in the 1970s. Vineyards are concentrated in South Australia (Barossa Valley, Clare-Watervale, Coonawarra, Padthaway-Keppoch, Southern Vale districts); in New South Wales (Hunter Valley, Mudgee); in Victoria (Geelong, Goulburn Valley, Great Western, Milawa, Rutherglen, Yarra Valley). Western Australia has vineyards in Margaret River, Mount Barker and Swan Valley. Many varieties of European grapes are cultivated and sophisticated controlled fermentation and vinification technology are employed. The growth of the Australian wine industry is unprecedented. The 1999 harvest was the first to produce more than a million tonnes of grapes – at 1,177,610, the harvest was 20 per cent greater than the previous year's record figure of 975,674 tonnes. The vineyard area of Australia doubled in the 1990s and the value of wine exports (more than half going to the UK) rose from Aus $135 million in 1990 to more than Aus $1 billion in 2000. Australia overtook France as the principal exporter of wine into the UK in 2001, with sales worth more than Aus $2 billion in 2004.

Austria vineyards all lie in the east, both to the north and south of Vienna. Mostly grapey white wines from Grüner Veltliner, Riesling and other German varieties, made according to a classification system closely resembling that of Germany. Red wines from Blauer Portugieser and other varieties.

Authental vineyard at Guntersblum in Rheinhessen region, Germany.

Autreau Père & Fils *récoltant-manipulant* champagne producer, Champillon, Champagne, France.

autovinificator fermenting vat for port grapes which exploits natural carbon dioxide to maximise colour extract from grape skins. Portugal.

Auxerrois grape variety of Cahors, France. Synonymous with Malbec.

Auxerrois collective term for the vineyards of Auxerre and Chablis, Burgundy, France. Includes the winemaking villages of Chitry-le-Fort, Coulanges-la-Vineuse, Epineuil, Irancy, St-Bris-le-Vineux.

Auxerrois Blanc white grape variety of Alsace, France.

Auxil armagnac by Fatima Brothers, St-Georges-de-Marsan, France.

Avalanche schnapps brand, Canada.

Avalanche Ale beer brand of Breckenridge brewery, Colorado, USA.

Avalon vineyard at Shepton Mallet, Somerset, England. Organic methods.

Avalon Springtime seasonal ale of Moor Beer Co, Ashcott, Somerset, England. At appropriate times of year the name changes to Avalon Summertime, Autumn and Winter.

Aveleda vinho verde brand of Quinta da Aveleda, Penafiel, Minho region, Portugal. Also an important producer of *bagaceira* and brandies from vinho verde grapes.

Avelsbach winemaking village of Römerlay collective vineyard (*Grosslage*) in Mosel-Saar-Ruwer region, Germany.

Avenoise L' beer brand of Monceau St Waast brewery, Aulnoye-Aymeries, France.

Avensan wine-producing commune of Bordeaux, France.

Aventinus wheat beer brand of Schneider brewery, Kelheim, Bavaria, Germany. Named after Bavaria's foremost historian, Johannes Aventinus. **Aventinus Duppelbock** (8% alc).

Aviation Cocktail. Over ice shake 2 parts dry gin, 1 lemon juice, 2 dashes maraschino. Strain.

Aviator Cocktail. Over ice stir 1 part dry gin, 1 dry vermouth, 1 Dubonnet, 1 sweet vermouth. Strain.

Aviemore brewery at Dalfaber, Aviemore, Scotland.

Avize village location of prized Côtes des Blancs vineyards, Champagne, France.

Avonside Premium Blend 8-year-old scotch whisky by James Gordon, Elgin, Scotland.

Avontuur Estate wine producer at Helderberg, Stellenbosch, South Africa. Renowned Avon Rouge Cabernet-Merlot red plus numerous varietals: Chardonnay, Dolcetto, Pinotage etc.

awamori millet-based spirit of Japan.

A Winter's Tale 'rare old sherry' by Williams & Humbert, Jerez de la Frontera, Spain.

Aÿ village location of prized Montagne de Reims vineyards, Champagne. Also the home of Bollinger.

Ayala *Grande Marque* champagne house, est 1860 at Aÿ-Champagne, France.

Ayinger brewery, particularly of dark lagers, at Aying, near Munich, Germany.

Ayl winemaking village in Scharzberg collective vineyard (*Grosslage*) in Mosel-Saar-Ruwer region, Germany.

Aymaville red wine of Valle d'Aosta, Italy.

Ayze sparkling wine *cru* (vineyard district) of Savoie, France.

azienda agricola farm producing wine. Italian.

AVONTUUR ESTATE

1996

Cabernet Sauvignon / Merlot

WINE OF ORIGIN STELLENBOSCH

GROWN MADE & BOTTLED ON
AVONTUUR ESTATE, SOMERSET WEST
REPUBLIC OF SOUTH AFRICA

11,5% Vol.   e 75cl

B

Babic red wine of the Dalmatian peninsular, Croatia. From Babic grapes.

Babich wine producer of Dalmatian origin est 1916 in Henderson district, North Island, New Zealand. Famed for Irongate Chardonnay white.

Babycham sparkling perry drink devised by Francis Showering 1949 and produced at Shepton Mallet, Somerset, England – currently by Matthew Clark.

Baby Duck Canadian sparkling wine brand from Labrusca grapes.

Bacardi see box.

Bacardi Cocktail. Over ice shake 2 parts Bacardi rum, 1 grenadine, 1 fresh lime (or lemon) juice. Strain.

Bacardi Breezer branded 'premixed' fruit drink of Bacardi. Rum, fruit juices and sparkling water and 5.4% alc.

Bacardi Rigo branded rum-lime-soda drink of Bacardi.

Bacchus German grape-variety cross (Silvaner & Riesling with Müller Thurgau) widely planted in Rheinhessen region for Liebfraumilch.

Bacchus 'red ale' sold under St Louis label by Van Honsenbrouck brewery, Ingelmunster, Belgium.

Bacharach principal town and winemaking centre of Mittelrhein region, Germany.

back brewery vessel, English.

Back Alley microbrewery at Davis, California, USA.

Back Bay Cocktail. Over ice shake 2 parts rum, 1 brandy, 1 teaspoon peach brandy, 2 dashes fresh lime juice. Strain.

Backdykes brewery at Thornton, Fife, Scotland.

Backöfchen vineyard at Wallhausen in Nahe region, Germany.

Backofen vineyard at Kaub in Mittelrhein region, Germany.

Backsberg wine estate est 1936 by Sydney Back at Klapmuts, Paarl, South Africa. Notable red and white wines, plus sparkling and estate brandy. A brand of the Backsberg Estate is Freedom Road, for wines made by black workers on land leased from the estate under a 1996 agreement between owner Michael Back, his workforce, and the South African government, which provided extensive subsidies. Freedom Road wines include a red

Bacardi

the biggest spirit brand in the world

Bacardi was founded by Spanish-born brothers Facundo and José Bacardi y Maso at Santiago, Cuba, in 1862. Their rum was in a new style, clearer and milder than traditional coarse island rums, and it quickly earned a following throughout Cuba, then in the United States. In 1876 at the US Centennial Exhibition in Philadelphia, Pennsylvania (location in that year of Alexander Graham Bell's first public demonstration of the telephone) Bacardi confirmed its international status by winning a product medal – the first of many.

In 1898, Cuba obtained independence from Spain with military help from the US, and with considerable financial support from the Bacardi family. Bacardi sales in the US grew exponentially from this time. Prohibition (1919–1933) was an interruption but, as the company itself has said, 'During this challenging period, although no sales were permitted, enthusiastic and inventive consumers found ways to bring Bacardi into the market.' Nevertheless, the company determined to avoid over-dependence on the US market, and expanded into Mexico, establishing a distillery there in 1931. A further plant was built in Puerto Rico, the American protectorate, where rum could be distilled and imported into the US free of the swingeing one-dollar excise duty imposed on each bottle of spirits from outside the States.

Political unrest in Cuba was later to drive Bacardi from the island. The regime of Fidel Castro, established 1959, confiscated all Bacardi assets (then valued at $76 million) but missed the opportunity to seize the international trademarks. The company, with commendable foresight, had re-registered these in the Bahama Islands in 1958. Homeless, Bacardi had now, unwillingly, become the first multi-national drinks company.

A distillery was built in Spain to cater for the growing number of northern-Europeans holidaying there. By the 1990s, Bacardi rum was the biggest-selling spirit brand worldwide. In 1992 the company, still substantially controlled by descendants of the founding family, amalgamated with Martini-Rossi of Turin, Italy, to become one of the largest drinks corporations in the world. The company's official home is now the British Crown Colony of Bermuda. ❦

from Cabernet Sauvignon and a white from Sauvignon Blanc grapes. Of the agreement, Michael Back said, 'We have three options in this country, namely: evaporate, emigrate or participate. I believe that participation is the only viable alternative.'

backward in winetasting, a wine not as developed as might be expected for its age.

Baco Noir hybrid black grape variety of eastern USA.

Badascony mountainous winemaking region on north shore of Lake Balaton, Hungary. Good white wines.

Bad Dürkheim winemaking centre and spa town of Rheinpfalz region, Germany.

Baden German wine region. The most southern of all, its main vineyards are parallel with those of Alsace and are increasingly noted for drier white wines. There are seven *Bereichen* (subregions).

Baderbrau Bohemian-style Pilsner beer by Pavichevich Brewing Co, Elmhurst, Illinois, USA.

Badger brewery and beer range of Hall & Woodhouse brewers, est 1777, Blandford Forum, Dorset, England. Brands include **Badger Original (4.6% alc), Badger Best** (4.0% alc), **Badger Golden Champion** (4.60% alc), Badger Golden Glory (4.5%) and **Badger Tanglefoot** (5% alc).

Badia a Coltibuono wine producer in the Chianti Classico zone, Tuscany, Italy.

Badischer Winzerkeller major co-operative wine producer at Breisach, Baden region, Germany.

Bad Kreuznach winemaking centre and spa town of Nahe region, Germany.

Bad Münster Am Stein-Ebernberg winemaking centre and spa town of Burgweg collective vineyard (*Grosslage*), Nahe region, Germany.

Badstube *Grosslage* (collective vineyard) incorporating villages at Bernkastel-Kues and at Lieser in the Mosel-Saar-Ruwer region, Germany.

Baerenfang honey liqueur of Germany.

Baga major black grape variety of Portugal. Bairrada and Dão regions and others.

bagaceira colourless grape spirit of Portugal. Similar to the grappa of Italy and marc of France, it is prepared from the biproducts of the winemaking process. Production is mainly centred in the Douro and Minho valleys.

Bagborough Vineyard cider and wine producer, Pylle, Shepton Mallet, Somerset, England.

bag-in-box wine-packaging method of filling a vacuum bag which contracts as the wine is tapped off, in theory preventing oxidation. Bag is carried in a labelled box. Sizes range from 2 to 10 litres. Devised in Australia.

Bahans-Haut-Brion, Château second wine of Château Haut-Brion, Bordeaux, France.

Bahia coffee liqueur of Brazil.

Bahia Blanca white rum brand of Halewood International, Huyton, Merseyside, England.

baie d'alisier *eau de vie* distilled from rowanberries, Alsace, France.

baie de sureau *eau de vie* distilled from elderberries, Alsace, France.

Baiken vineyard at Eltville in Rheingau region, Germany.

Bailie Nicol Jarvie blended scotch whisky by Nicol Anderson, Leith, Scotland.

Bailey's Irish Cream liqueur compounded of Irish whiskey, fresh double Irish cream, neutral alcohol and flavourings including chocolate. Produced by R & A Bailey, Dublin, Eire. Bailey's was launched 1974. Now the World's leading cream liqueur brand selling more than 70 million bottles annually, and said to account for a third of Ireland's total liquid-milk production. Reportedly, one per cent of all the Republic's export earnings is accounted for by Bailey's. Owned by Diageo.

Baileys Vineyards wine-producer at Bundurra, Victoria, Australia, renowned for Liqueur Muscat.

Bailleux, Brasserie small restaurant-brewery at Gussignies, northern France, specialising in cooking with beer, and producing *bières de garde* including Cuvée des Jonquilles and Saison Saint Médard.

Bailly-Reverdy wine-producer of AC Sancerre in Clos du Chêne Marchand, Loire Valley, France.

Bairrada quality wine region of central Portugal producing mainly red but increasing quantities of sparkling wine.

baissage in viticulture, securing new vine shoots on to training wires as soon as spring frosts are over. French.

Baix de Houx hip-flavoured *eau de vie* of Alsace, France.

Baja California Mexico's northern-most, and prime, vineyard region.

Bajuvator bock beer by Tucher brewery, Nürnberg, Germany.

baked in winetasting, a 'hot' wine that indicates it has been made from grapes grown in excessive heat.

Balac, Château d' wine estate of AC Haut-Médoc, Bordeaux, France.

Balalaika Cocktail. Over ice shake 2 parts vodka, 1 Cointreau, 1 lemon juice. Strain.

balance in winetasting, the relationship between the vital characteristics of the wine – acidity, alcohol, fruit, tannin. In a good wine, these components must be in harmony.

Balardin, Domaine du second wine of Château Malescot-St-Exupéry, Bordeaux, France.

Balaton regional name for wines (mainly white) grown in vineyards close to Lake Balaton, Hungary.

Balatonfüred-Csopak white-wine region of Lake Balaton, Hungary.

Balbach important winemaking family and estate (Weingut Bürger-meister Anton Balbach Elben) of Rheinhessen region, Germany.

Balbaina vineyard district of *albariza* soil, Jerez de la Frontera, Spain.

Balblair North Highland malt whisky distillery, Dornoch Firth, Scotland. Est 1749. Single malt: 5-year-old.

Baleau, Château wine estate of AC St-Emilion, Bordeaux, France. Classified *Grand Cru Classé*.

Balestard-la-Tonnelle, Château de wine estate of AC St-Emilion, Bordeaux, France. Classified *Grand Cru Classé*.

Balfour sherry brand of Hijos de Agustin Blazquez, Jerez de la Frontera, Spain.

Balgownie winery in Bendigo, Victoria, Australia.

Ballantine Ale and **Ballantine IPA** beer brands of Pabst brewery, Milwaukee, Wisconsin, USA.

Ballantine's blended scotch whisky brand of George Ballantine (b 1807), Dumbarton Scotland. **Ballantine's Finest**, **Ballantine's Founder's Reserve, Ballantine's Gold Seal** (12-year-old) and older blends.

Ballarat wine region of Victoria, Australia.

Ballard Bitter ale brand of Redhook brewery, Seattle, Washington, USA.

Ballard's brewery at Nyewood, Hampshire, England.

Balling, Carl Joseph Napoleon Bohemian deviser of **Balling** measure of gravity (sugar density) in beer and in grape sugar.

Balluet, J producer of Fine Cognac VSOP and Cognac Très Vieille Réserve. Cognac, France.

Balm Cocktail. Over ice shake 6 parts sherry, 1 Cointreau, 1 orange juice, 1 dash orange bitters, 1 dash Pimento Dram Liqueur. Strain.

Balseiro Portuguese maturing vat mounted on stone legs. For port.

Balthazar champagne bottle size. At 12 litres, equates to 16 standard 75cl bottles.

Baltimore Brewing Company producer of noted lager beers. Baltimore, Maryland, USA.

Baltimore Egg Nog Cocktail. Over ice shake 10 parts milk, 2 madeira, 1 brandy, 1 rum, 1 teaspoon sugar, 1 egg. Strain and grate nutmeg over.

Balvenie, The Speyside malt whisky distillery, Dufftown, Scotland. Single malts: Founder's Reserve 10-year-old, Classic 18-year-old.

Bamberg town and centre – with nine breweries – of 'smoked beer' production, Franconia, Germany.

Bamberger Rauchbier, smoked beer from malted grain dried over beechwood fires produced by breweries including Heller and Spezial.

Bamboo Cocktail. Over ice stir 2 parts dry sherry, 1 dry vermouth, 1 sweet vermouth. Strain.

Banana Cocktail. Over ice shake 1 part rum, 1 banana liqueur, 1 fresh cream. Strain into an ice-filled tumbler and add a dash of grenadine.

Banana Colada Cocktail. In a kitchen blender, whizz 2 measures rum, 1 coconut liqueur, 4 pineapple juice and a banana (peeled and sliced) with a handful of ice. Serve in tall glasses with straws.

Banana Daiquiri Cocktail. In a kitchen blender, whizz 2 measures rum, 1 Cointreau, 1 fresh lime juice and a banana (peeled and sliced) with a handful of ice. Serve in stemmed glasses with straws.

Banana Rum Cocktail. Over ice shake 2 parts rum, 1 banana liqueur, 1 orange juice. Strain.

Banana Slip Cocktail. Into a shot glass, carefully pour 1 measure each of chilled banana liqueur and Baileys Irish Cream. The ingredients should not mix.

Banana Split Cocktail. Pour equal measures of marsala and crème de banane over ice in a small tumbler. Stir.

Banat wine region of Croatia. Laski Rizling whites.

Banda Azul 'Blue Riband'. Brand name for Rioja wine of Federico Paternina, Spain.

B & B Bénédictine and Brandy, a drier-tasting brand of Bénédictine liqueur.

B & B Cocktail. Over ice stir 1 part Bénédictine, 1 brandy. Strain.

Bandersnatch brewery in Phoenix, Arizona, USA. Known for Premium Bitter and Milk Stout.

ban de vendange traditional declaration of the start of the grape harvest, still widely observed in France and officially announced by *préfets* throughout the wine regions.

Bandol town and wine AC zone of Provence, France. Quality reds from Mourvèdre and other grapes, plus some whites and rosés.

B & T brewery at Shefford, Bedfordshire, England.

Banff East Highland malt whisky distillery, Banff, Scotland. Closed 1983.

Banfi major wine importer of USA and founders of Villa Banfi, Montalcino, Tuscany, Italy, in 1977. Now one of the largest quality-wine producers of Italy.

Banger Cocktail. Over ice stir 2 parts dry gin, 1 sweet vermouth, 2 dashes Angostura bitters. Strain.

Banjino Cocktail. Over ice shake 1 part dry gin, 1 orange juice, 1 dash Crème de Banane. Strain.

Banks & Taylor brewery at Shefford, Bedfordshire, England. Produces Shefford Bitter and felicitously named **Banks & Taylor Old Bat**.

Banks Lager malty lager brand by **Banks Brewery**, Bridgetown, Barbados, West Indies.

Banks's brewer at Wolverhampton, West Midlands, England. Renowned for **Banks's Mild** ale.

Bank Top brewery at Bolton, Greater Manchester, England.

Banner Bitter ale brand of Butterknowle Brewery, Newcastle-upon-Tyne, England.

Bannockburn Scottish ale (5.0% alc) by Bridge of Allen Brewery, Stirling, Scotland. 'Brewed to celebrate the battle at Bannockburn, where Robert the Bruce defeated the English army in 1314. At this famous victory Scotland at last gained its independence.'

Bannockburn wine producer in Geelong, Victoria, Australia. Red wine from Pinot Noir grapes.

Banshee Cocktail. Over ice shake 2 parts banana liqueur, 1 crème de cacao, 1 fresh cream. Strain.

Bantu tropical passion fruit liqueur. Germany.

Banyuls seaside town and wine AC of Pyrenees region, France. Red *vin doux naturel* wines from interrupted fermentation. **Banyuls Grand Cru** must be made with at least 75% Grenache grapes and be cask-aged for 3 years. **Banyuls Rancio** is a madeira-style wine cask-aged up to 20 years.

Bara, Paul *récoltant-manipulant* champagne producer, Bouzy, Champagne, France.

Baraccas Cocktail. Over ice shake 3 parts sweet vermouth, 1 Fernet Branca. Strain.

Barack Palinka colourless brandy made from fermented apricots. Hungary.

Barancourt champagne house, Bouzy, Champagne, France.

Barbadillo, Antonio longest-established sherry-producer (founded 1821) of Sanlúcar de Barrameda, Andalucia, Spain. Noted for *manzanilla* and other sherries.

Barbados Distillers major rum producers of Barbados, West Indies.

Barbados island rum style known for lightness and sweet, smoky flavour.

Barbaresco classic red wine of Piedmont, Italy. DOCG wines from Nebbiolo grapes only grown in zone around Barbaresco town and aged minimum 2 years. *Riserva* has 3 years' ageing and *riserva speciale* 4. Well-known co-operative Produttori del Barbaresco. Leading individual producers include Angelo Gaja.

Barbarossa black grape variety of Emilia Romagna region, Italy.

Barbe, Château de wine estate of AC Côtes de Bourg, Bordeaux, France.

Barbé, Château de wine estate of AC Blaye, Bordeaux, France.

Barbera black grape variety widely grown in Italy. Variety for DOCs in Piedmont and also grown as far south as Apulia. Wines are notable for freshness and acidity.

Barbera d'Alba DOC for red wines from Barbera grapes from Alba, Piedmont, Italy. *Superiore* wines must reach 13% alc and have 2 years' ageing.

Barbera d'Asti DOC for red wines from Barbera grapes from Asti and Alessandria, Piedmont, Italy. *Superiore* wines must reach 13% alc and have 3 years' ageing.

Barbera del Monferrato DOC for red wines from Barbera grapes of Monferrato hills, Piedmont, Italy. *Superiore* wines must reach 12.5% alc and have 2 years' ageing.

Barbie White Cocktail. Over ice shake 2 parts vodka, 1 Cointreau, 1 fresh cream.

Barclay Square Canadian whisky brand of Jas Barclay & Co, Canada.

barco rabelo prior to rail and road transport, this flat-bottomed, single-sail boat was the only means of carrying new-made port in pipes (casks) from the heights of Portugal's Douro Valley to Vila Nova de Gaia on the coast.

Barco Reale DOC wine of Carmignano, Tuscany, Italy.

Barde, Château la wine estate of AC Côtes de Bourg, Bordeaux, France.

Barde-Haut, Château wine estate of AC St-Emilion, Bordeaux, France.

Bardinet distiller and liqueur producer, Bordeaux, France. Operates major rum distillery at Dillon, Martinique, West Indies.

Bardingley vineyard at Staplehurst, Kent, England.

Bardolino lakeside village and DOC for light red wines of Lake Garda, Veneto, Italy.

Bardone red-wine brand of Fontanafredda company, Piedmont, Italy.

Bärental vineyard at Margetshöchheim in Franken region, Germany.

Baret, Château de wine estate of AC Pessac-Léognan, Bordeaux, France.

Barfly Cocktail. Over ice shake 1 part dry gin, 1 rum, 1 pineapple juice. Strain.

Barker, Château wine estate in Great Southern district, Western Australia.

Barkham Manor vineyard and winery at Uckfield, East Sussex, England. Noted white wines.

Barland pear variety traditionally valued for perry-making. English.

barley the principal cereal ingredient in beer worldwide and in Scottish malt whisky.

barley wine type of ale, usually strong (up to typical wine alcohol level of 12% or so) and dark, but having no other associations with wine.

Barnes Wines winery known for Heritage Estates brand, Ontario, Canada.

Barney Barnato Cocktail. Over ice stir 1 part brandy, 1 Caperitif, 1 dash Angostura bitters, 1 dash curaçao. Strain.

Barney Flats Oatmeal Stout specialty beer of Anderson Valley brewery, Boonville, California, USA.

Barnfield brewery at Slaithwaite, West Yorkshire, England.

Barngates brew pub (The Drunken Duck Inn) at Barngates, Ambleside, Cumbria, England.

Barn Owl Bitter beer brand (4.5% alc) of Cotleigh Brewery, Somerset, England.

Barnsley brewery at Elsecar, Barnsley, Yorkshire, England.

Barolo DOCG wine of Piedmont with claims to be Italy's greatest red. Made from Nebbiolo grapes only, grown around Barolo village south of Alba. Minimum ageing 3 years (2 in barrel), 4 for *riserva* wines and 5 for *riserva speciale*. Very dark, strong (min 13% alc) and long-lived.

see label opposite ➡

Baron Cocktail. Over ice stir 2 parts dry gin, 1 dry vermouth, 1 curaçao. Strain.

Baron vineyard at St Martin in Rheinpfalz region, Germany.

Baron Geymüller, Domaine wine producer in Kremstal, Niederösterreich, Austria.

Baronnet-de-Pichon, Château le second wine of Château Pichon Baron de Longueville, Bordeaux, France.

Baronnie, La major wine company in Pauillac, Bordeaux, France. Owns Châteaux Clerc-Milon, d'Armailhac and Mouton-Rothschild and produces leading Bordeaux branded wine Mouton Cadet and others.

Barossa Valley important wine region of South Australia, northeast of Adelaide. Extensive Riesling vineyards were first planted by original German settlers but French Shiraz and Grenache grapes are also widely grown.

Barossa Valley Estates wine producer of Adelaide Plains district, Barossa Valley, South Australia.

Barozzi Ernesto grappa producer, Lizzana di Rovereto, Trentino, Italy.

Barrabaque, Château wine estate of AC Canon-Fronsac, Bordeaux, France.

MONFORTE   BUSSIA

RED WINE
ESTATE BOTTLED
BAROLO
DENOMINAZIONE DI ORIGINE CONTROLLATA E GARANTITA

DAI VIGNETI DELLA
BUSSIA SOPRANA
PRODUCED AND BOTTLED IN ITALY BY:
PODERI ALDO CONTERNO
750 ML e   Piemonte MONFORTE Italia   Alcohol 13,5%vol.

Barracas Cocktail. Over ice stir 3 parts sweet vermouth, 1 Fernet Branca. Strain.

Barrail, Château wine estate of AC Cérons, Bordeaux, France.

barrel in brewing, a specific measure, e.g. in UK 36 gallons (165 litres) and in USA 31.5 US gallons (117 litres).

Barreyres, Château wine estate of AC Haut-Médoc, Bordeaux, France. Classified *Cru Bourgeois*.

barrica wine barrel of 225 litres. Spain.

barrique wine barrel of Bordeaux, France, containing 225 litres – or 24 dozen 75cl bottles.

barro dark mud-clay soil-type of vineyards at Jerez de la Frontera, Spain. Less valued for sherry-growing than *albariza*.

Barros Almeida major port company, Vila Nova de Gaia, Portugal. Vintages: 1955, 57, 58, 60, 63, 65, 66, 70, 74, 75, 77, 78, 79 80, 82, 83, 85, 87, 89, 91, 94, 97, 2000, 03.

Barsac village AC of Sauternes, Bordeaux, France, for classic dessert wines.

Bartender Cocktail. Over ice stir 1 part dry gin, 1 sherry, 1 Dubonnet, 1 dry vermouth, 1 dash Grand Marnier. Strain.

Barton & Guestier leading Bordeaux wine shipper est 1725 by Irish merchant Thomas Barton. Blanquefort, France.

Barton Manor vineyard at East Cowes, Isle of Wight, England. Vines include rare Gewürztraminer (under glass).

Basedow wine producer est 1896 Barossa Valley, South Australia. Renowned 'White Burgundy' from Semillon grapes and formidable Shiraz red.

Basilicata wine region of southern Italy known for DOC Aglianico del Vulture.

Baska-Dropper wormwood-infused brannvin, Sweden.

Bas-Médoc the northern area of the Médoc vineyard region, Bordeaux, France. Qualifying wines are designated AC Médoc, as distinct from AC Haut-Médoc in the southern part of the region.

Baso DO red wine brand of Compañia do Vinos de La Granja, Lerin, Navarra, Spain. Garnacha grapes

Bass leading British brewer based at Burton on Trent, Staffordshire. Known for Draught Bass bitter, Imperial Ale and Worthington's White Shield bottled strong ale. The company owns the three West Midland breweries of Mitchell & Butler and Tennent's in Scotland. Co-owner of Carlsberg-Tetley. Bought by Interbrew, 2000.

Bassermann-Jordan great wine estate (Weingut Geheimer Rat Dr von Bassermann-Jordan) of Rheinpfalz region, Germany. Founded 1250, with vineyards at Deidesheim, Forst, Ruppertsberg, Ungstein.

Bassgeige vineyard at Vogtsburg im Kaiserstuhl in Baden region, Germany.

Bass Wyatt Cocktail. For four glasses add to 4 beaten eggs 4 parts dry gin, 1 cherry brandy, 1 lemon juice, 4 dashes orange bitters, 1 teaspoon powdered sugar, 2 teaspoons vanilla essence. Shake over ice. Grate nutmeg over filled glasses.

Bastard ill-defined wine of 16th century England mentioned by Shakespeare as 'brown and white bastard'. Possibly from Bastardo grapes cultivated at the time in Madeira.

Bastardo heavy-cropping, sweet grape variety of Portugal.

Bastei vineyards at Castell in Franken region and at Traisen in Nahe region, Germany.

Bastor-Lamontagne, Château wine estate of AC Sauternes, Bordeaux, France. Classified *Cru Bourgeois*.

Batailley, Château wine estate of AC Pauillac, Médoc, Bordeaux, France. Classified *5ème Grand Cru Classé*.

Bâtard-Montrachet *Grand Cru* vineyard site at Puligny-Montrachet, Burgundy, France. Highly prized white wines.

Batavia ar(r)ak strongly flavoured rum from fermented molasses produced around Batavia on the island of Java, Indonesia.

Batemans brewery at Skegness, Lincolnshire, England. XB bitter and XXXB best bitter ales.

Batham's Best bitter ale by Daniel Batham, Delph Brewery, Brierley Hill, West Midlands, England.

Batterieberg vineyard at Enkirch in the Mosel-Saar-Ruwer region, Germany.

Battin small brewery at Esch, Luxembourg, producing beers under Gambrinus label.

Batzenberg six vineyards in Baden region, Germany, at, respectively: Ehrenkirchen (Kirchhofen), Ehrenkirchen (Norsingen), Ehrenkirchen (Scherzingen), Pfaffenweiler, Schallstadt, Schallstadt (Wolfenweiler).

Bauer wine producer in Donauland, Niederösterreich, Austria.

Bauer wine producer in Weinviertel, Niederösterreich, Austria.

Bäuerl wine producer in Wachau, Niederösterreich, Austria.

Baumard, Jean major wine producer in Loire Valley, France, with vineyards in Coteaux du Layon, Quarts de Chaume and Savennières.

Baumé French measuring scale for grape-must weight and thus potential alcohol in wine.

Bausch vineyard at Castell in Franken region, Germany.

Baux Bier lager brand of MDT International produced at Thomas Hardy brewery, Dorchester, England.

Bavaisienne, La sweet *bière de garde* of Theillier family brewery, Bavay, France.

Bavaria brewery at Liesbout, Brabant, Netherlands. Brands include **Bavaria** and Swinkels.

Bavaria St Pauli brewery in Hamburg, Germany. Produces beers under Astra label.

Bavenjager honey-flavoured liqueur, Germany.

Bavik-De Brabandere brewery at Bavikhove, Belgium. Produces Petrus red ale.

Baxter's Barley Bree blended scotch whisky by James Watson, Dundee, Scotland.

Bayerische Staatsbrauerei Weihenstephan German brewery said to be the oldest in the world (founded as a monastic brewery in 1040), and an important training centre associated with Munich University. Bavarian state-owned and produces beers including Kristal Export Weizenbier.

Bayern Gasthaus Brauerei brewery in Missoula, Montana, USA.

Bay Front brewery in Newport, Oregon, USA.

Baynards Brewhouse brew pub (The Thurlow Arms) at Baynards Rudgwick, West Sussex, England.

Bay of Plenty wine region of North Island, New Zealand.

Baziliques, Château Les wine estate of AC St-Emilion, Bordeaux, France.

Bazooka Cocktail. Over ice stir 3 parts Green Chartreuse, 1 brandy, 1 cherry brandy, 1 dry gin. Strain.

Beachcomber Cocktail. Over ice shake 3 parts rum, 1 Cointreau, 1 fresh lime juice, 2 dashes grenadine. Strain into cocktail glasses with rims encrusted in sugar.

Beacon Barley Wine beer brand of Front Street brewery, Santa Cruz, California, USA.

Beacon Bitter ale (3.8% alc) by Everards Brewery, Narborough, Leicestershire, England.

Beadle Cocktail. Over ice shake 1 part, 1 scotch whisky, 1 dry vermouth. Strain.

Beagle Cocktail. Over ice shake 2 parts brandy, 1 cranberry juice, 3 dahes kümmel, 1 dash lemon juice. Strain.

Beals Cocktail. Over ice stir 2 parts scotch whisky, 1 dry vermouth, 1 sweet vermouth. Strain.

Beam, Jim see Jim Beam.

Beamish Irish stout brewed by **Beamish & Crawford**, Cork, Ireland. Owned by Scottish Courage.

Bear Ale bottled beer (5.0% alc) by Traquair House Brewery, Peeblesshire, Scotland. Named after the heraldic-bear-adorned gates to the house which the Maxwell Stuart family, resident since 1107, have forsworn to open until a Stuart monarch reascends the Scottish throne.

Béarn wine AC of Pyrenees region, SW France. Red, white and rosé .

Beartown brewery at Congleton, Cheshire, England.

Beaucastel, Château de leading wine estate of AC Châteauneuf-du-Pape, Rhône Valley, France. Long-lived wines made by organic methods.

Beaufort & Fils, H *récoltant-manipulant* champagne producer, Bouzy, Champagne, France.

Beaujolais southern wine region of Burgundy, France, producing mostly red wine from Gamay grapes and a little white from Chardonnay. The southern part of the region (Bas Beaujolais) produces most of the wine for **Beaujolais AC** and, accounting for much of the average annual total of 90 million bottles, **Beaujolais Nouveau** (also called **Beaujolais Primeur**) for sale worldwide from the third Thursday of November (date was 15 November until 1985), just a few weeks after the harvest and made by an accelerated vinification process. In the northern part of the region (Haut Beaujolais) lie 38 communes whose wines qualify for the superior appellation **Beaujolais-Villages AC**, with a total annual production averaging 45 million bottles. Ten *crus* produce the most-valued wine of Beaujolais under their own AC labels: Brouilly, Chénas, Chiroubles, Côte de Brouilly, Fleurie, Juliénas, Morgon, Moulin-à-Vent, Régnié, St Amour. The name Beaujolais derives from Beaujeu, the region's first capital (before Villefranche). A Beaujolais vin de pays classification was created in 2005.

Beaulieu early revivalist vineyard est 1960 at Lymington, Hampshire, England.

Beaulieu-sur-Layon village of Coteaux de Layon, Loire Valley, France. Village wines may be described as such on labels.

Beaulieu Vineyard winery est 1900 in Napa Valley, California, USA, particularly known for Georges de Latour Private Reserve Cabernet.

Beau Mazerat, Château second wine of Château Grand-Mayne, Bordeaux, France.

Beaumes-de-Venise wine village of Côtes du Rhône, France. Red wines and an AC for famed *vin doux naturel* from Muscat grapes.

Beaumet-Chaurey champagne house, Epernay, France.

Beaumont, Château wine estate of AC Haut-Médoc, Bordeaux, France. Classified *Cru Grand Bourgeois*.

Beaumont, Château de wine estate of AC Côtes de Blaye, Bordeaux, France.

Beaune town at centre of Côte de Beaune wine region of Burgundy, France. Informally known as the wine capital of Burgundy, with famed Hospices de Beaune (funded from donated vineyards), wine museum and headquarters of many famous Burgundy growers and shippers.

Beaunois local name in Chablis, France, for Chardonnay grape.

Beauregard, Château de wine estate of AC Pomerol, Bordeaux, France.

Beaurenard, Domaine de wine estate at Châteauneuf-du-Pape, Rhône Valley, France.

Beau-Rivage brand of red AC Bordeaux wine of Borie-Manoux. France.

Beau-Rivage, Château wine estate of AC Premières Côtes de Bordeaux, France.

Beauroy *1er Cru* vineyard of Chablis, France.

Beauséjour, Château wine estate of AC St-Estèphe, Médoc, Bordeaux, France.

Beauséjour-Bécot, Château wine estate of AC St-Emilion, Bordeaux, France. Classified *1er Grand Cru Classé* (1996).

Beauséjour (Duffau-Lagarrosse), Château great wine estate of AC St-Emilion, Bordeaux, France. Classified *1er Grand Cru Classé*.

Beau-Site, Château wine estate of AC Premières Côtes de Bordeaux, France.

Beau-Site, Château wine estate of AC St-Estèphe, Médoc, Bordeaux, France. Classified *Cru Grand Bourgeois Exceptionnel*.

Beau-Site-Haut-Vignoble, Château wine estate of AC St-Estèphe, Médoc, Bordeaux, France. Classified *Cru Bourgeois*.

Beautiful Cocktail. Over ice shake 2 parts white rum, 2 dark rum, 2 lemon juice, 1 Cointreau, 1 grenadine. Strain.

Beautrait, Yves *récoltant-manipulant* champagne producer, Louvois, Champagne, France.

Beauty Spot Cocktail. Over ice shake 2 parts dry gin, 1 dry vermouth, 1 sweet vermouth, 1 teaspoon orange juice. Add a drop of grenadine to glass before straining and serving.

Beaux Arts Cocktail. Over ice shake 1 part dry gin, 1 dry vermouth, 1 sweet vermouth, 1 Amer Picon bitters, 1 Forbidden Fruit liqueur.

Beaver Bottle whisky brand of Hudson's Bay Company, Canada.

Bebidas das Americas leading brewing corporation of Brazil.

Bécade, Château La wine estate of AC Listrac, Médoc, Bordeaux, France. Classified *Cru Bourgeois*.

Bécasse, Château La wine estate of AC Pauillac, Médoc, Bordeaux, France.

Becherbrunnen vineyard at Mandel in Nahe region, Germany.

Becherovka yellow herbal liqueur by Karlovanska, Karlsbad, Czech Republic.

Beck brewery est 1874 at Bremen, Germany (and est at Philadelphia, USA, 1876), producing renowned **Beck's Bier**.

Beck wine producer in Neusiedler-see, Burgenland, Austria.

Becker brewery at St Ingbert, Saarland, Germany.

Beckett's brewery at Basingstoke, Hampshire, England.

Beecham's bar and brewery at St Helens, Merseyside, England.

Beefeater London dry gin by James Burrough distillers, London, England. Owned by Allied Domecq.

beer in the widest sense, a fermented beverage made from malted grain (usually, but not exclusively, barley) and flavoured with hops. The term encompasses ale, lager, malt liquor, porter and stout. Beer is at least as old as recorded history; the word derives ultimately from Latin *bibere* (to drink). See box.

beerenauslese 'selected berries'. German wine-quality designation within the *Prädikat* range. The fourth level (after *auslese*) of grape ripeness which must reach a minimum Oechsle (sugar density) level of between 110° and 128° according to the region of production. Grapes need to be very ripe and affected by botrytis or 'noble rot'. Made in best vintages only, the wines are golden in colour and richly flavoured, with considerable ageing potential.

beerenburg alternative spelling of Dutch *berenburg*.

Beer Engine brewery at Sweetham, Exeter, Devon, England.

beesengenever blackcurrant-flavoured 'London Dry' *genever* gin. Netherlands.

Bee's Knees Cocktail. Over ice shake 4 parts rum, 1 Cointreau, 1 teaspoon lemon juice, 1 teaspoon sugar. Strain.

beeswing the fine crust forming naturally in very old port.

Bégadan wine village in AC Médoc, Bordeaux, France.

Beichun red hybrid grape variety. China.

Beilberg vineyards at Grossinderfeld and at Werbach in Baden region, Germany.

Beiras wine province of eastern Portugal.

Bekáa Valley wine region of Lebanon, north of Beirut.

Belair, Château wine estate of AC Côtes de Blaye, Bordeaux, France.

Belair, Château wine estate of AC St-Emilion, Bordeaux France. Classified *1er Grand Cru Classé*.

Bel-Air, Château wine estate of AC Haut-Médoc, Bordeaux, France.

Bel-Air, Château wine estate of AC Pomerol, Bordeaux, France.

Bel-Air, Château wine estate of AC Puisseguin-St-Emilion, Bordeaux, France.

Bel-Air, Château wine estate of AC Ste-Croix-du-Mont, Bordeaux, France.

Bel-Air, Château de wine estate of AC Lalande-de-Pomerol, Bordeaux, France.

Bel-Air Lagrave, Château wine estate of AC Moulis, Médoc, Bordeaux, France.

Bel-Air-Marquis-d'Aligre, Château wine estate of AC Margaux, Médoc, Bordeaux, France. Classified *Cru Bourgeois Supérieur Exceptionnel*.

Beer

a simplified chemistry

The raw materials are malted barley, water, hops and yeast. In Germany, the rules (enshrined in the Reinheitsgebot Purity Law of 1516) permit no other ingredients, but in many countries other grains, sugar and flavourings may also be used.

Malted barley is prepared by steeping – soaking barley in water – then arresting the sprouting of the seeds by heat (kilning). Malting turns starch into simpler saccharides (sugars). Certain barley varieties are suitable for lagers (such as pilsner malt). Kilning methods give specific effects producing different malts. Examples are pale malt, crystal malt and chocolate malt – the latter very dark and used primarily in stout.

Brewers mill malt plus other grains then 'mash' it by soaking in hot water (typically 65° C), which uses the grain's enzymes to convert the remaining starch into simple sugar and the malt's proteins into amino acids. The resulting 'wort' may include added sugar before being boiled with hops to produce bitterness to balance the sweetness from the malt. Hops also provide antiseptic protection and, especially if whole hops are used (rather than pellets or extracts) a distinctive flavour.

Yeast is added to the cooled, oxygenated 'hopped wort'. The yeast grows on the amino acids, sugar and oxygen. The yeast's growth is gradually slowed by the lack of oxygen and available nutrient. Alcohol and carbon dioxide are produced. When fermentation is complete, the beer is usually chilled, racked and either fined for sale as real ale or filtered for keg, bottled or canned products.

Bel-Air-Marquis-de-Pomereu, Château second wine of Château Bel-Air-Marquis-d'Aligre, Bordeaux, France.

Belair-Montaiguillon, Château wine estate of AC St-Georges-St-Emilion, Bordeaux, France.

Belair-St Georges, Château wine estate of AC St-Georges-St-Emilion, Bordeaux, France.

Belcier, Château de wine estate of AC Côtes de Castillon, Bordeaux, France.

Belgrave, Château wine estate of AC Haut-Médoc, Bordeaux, France. Classified *5ème Grand Cru Classé*.

Belgravia dry gin brand of Hall & Bramley, Aintree, Liverpool, England.

Belhaven Brewery at Dunbar, Scotland, founded 1719. Brands include 90/- ale and Fowler's Wee Heavy.

Belic Pinot Balkan name for Pinot Blanc grape variety.

Belimnita Quadrata chalk soil base of Champagne region, France, imparting unique character to wine. Also suitable for excavation of underground cellars.

Bell Brewery reputed originator of porter (a dark beer similar to but lighter than stout) in Shoreditch, London, England in 1722.

Bellapais lightly sparkling white wine brand of Keo company, Cyprus.

Bellefont-Belcier, Château wine estate of AC St-Emilion, Bordeaux, France. Classified *Grand Cru*.

Bellegarde, Château second wine of Château Siran, Bordeaux, France.

Belle Gueule lager brand of Les Brasseurs GMT brewery, Montreal, Canada.

Belle-Rose, Château wine estate of AC Pauillac, Bordeaux, France.

Belle Terre vineyard of Alexander Valley, California, USA.

Belle Vue brewery and beer brand of Vandenstock company, Brussels, Belgium.

Bellevue-La-Foret, Château leading wine estate of AC Côtes du Fronton, SW France.

Bellet AC for red, rosé and white wines in commune of Nice, Provence, France. Château de Crémat is notable producer.

Bellevue, Cave Coopérative major wine producer of the Médoc, Bordeaux, France. Vinifier of numerous single-estate wines and a popular AC Médoc Pavillon de Bellevue.

Bellevue, Château wine estate of AC Côtes de Blaye, Bordeaux, France.

Bellevue, Château wine estate of AC Médoc, Bordeaux, France.

Bellevue, Château wine estate of AC Pomerol, Bordeaux, France.

Bellevue, Château wine estate of AC St-Emilion, Bordeaux, France.

Bellingham Wines wine producer of Franschoeck, South Africa. Est 1948 and noted for introducing French-style winemaking to South Africa.

Bellini Cocktail. Fill a good-sized wine glass with crushed ice and pour over a measure of peach juice and a dash of grenadine; fill with sparkling wine (ideally, Prosecco) and add a peach slice.

Bellinitini Cocktail. Over ice shake 2 parts vodka, 1 peach schnapps, 1 fresh peach juice. Strain into wine glasses and top with chilled sparkling wine.

Bellonne-St-Georges, Château second wine of Château Maquin St-Georges, Bordeaux, France.

Bell's blended scotch whisky by Arthur Bell & Sons, Perth, Scotland. Heir to the whisky of Thomas Sandeman, whisky merchant est 1825, who employed Arthur Bell 1845. Bell took control 1865, incorporated 1895 with his two sons as directors under the name Arthur Bell & Sons, and died 1900. Guinness took over 1985. Slogan is 'Afore Ye Go' and the brand is the second-largest seller in Britain.

Bell's Beer hoppy, top-fermenting ale by Kalamazoo Brewing Company (prop Larry Bell), Michigan, USA.

Belmont pub-brewery at Long Beach, California, USA.

Belmont Cocktail. Over ice shake 2 parts dry gin, 1 grenadine, 1 teaspoon fresh cream. Strain.

Belon, Château wine estate of AC Graves, Bordeaux, France.

Bel-Orme-Tronquoy-de-Lalande, Château wine estate of AC Haut-Médoc, Bordeaux, France. Classified *Cru Grand Bourgeois*.

Belvoir brewery at Old Darby, Leicestershire, England.

Belz vineyard at Wachenheim in Rheinpfalz region, Germany.

Ben Aigen blended scotch whisky by Strathnairn, Inverness, Scotland.

Ben Alder blended scotch whisky by Gordon & MacPhail, Elgin, Scotland.

Bench grafting nursery grafting of vine rootstocks.

Benchmark whiskey brand originally of Seagram, USA.

Ben Crossman's Prime Farmhouse Cider cider by Mayfield Farm, Hewish, Weston-super-Mare, Somerset, England.

Bendigo wine zone of Victoria, Australia.

Beneagles blended scotch whisky by Waverly Vintners, Perth, Scotland.

Benede-Orange wine Region of Origin, South Africa.

Bénédictine elixir originally discovered 1510 by Don Bernardo Vincelli of the monastery at Fécamp, Normandy, France. The liqueur is now produced in a reconstructed centre (in the form of a Gothic château) on the site, from a recipe said to date from 1863. The monastery was destroyed in the French Revolution. Bottles still bear the Benedictine dedication 'DOM' – *Deo Optimo Maximo*, To God, most good, most great.

Benediktinerberg vineyard at Trier in Mosel-Saar-Ruwer region, Germany.

Benediktinusberg vineyard at Zellingen in Franken region, Germany.

Bengel vineyard at Meersburg in Baden region, Germany.

Beni di Batasiolo wine producer at La Morra, Piedmont, Italy. Red wines from Barbera grapes.

Beni M'Tir wine appellation of Meknès Fez region, Morocco, known for Tarik red.

Benin brewery at Benin City, Bendel State, Nigeria.

Beni Sadden wine appellation of Meknès Fez region, Morocco.

Benmarl wine estate of Hudson River Valley, New York, USA.

Benmore blended scotch whisky by Benmore Distilleries, Glasgow, Scotland.

Benn vineyards at Westhofen in Rheinhessen region and at Obrigheim in Rheinpfalz region, Germany.

Bennett Cocktail. Over ice shake 3 parts dry gin, 1 fresh lime juice, 2 dashes Angostura bitters. Strain.

Bennett's cider producer, Edithmead, Burnham-on-Sea, Somerset, England.

Ben Nevis West Highland malt whisky distillery, Fort William, Scotland. Single malts: 19-year-old, 25-year-old.

Ben Riach Speyside malt whisky distillery, Elgin, Scotland. Owned by Pernod-Ricard.

Benrinnes Speyside malt whisky distillery, Upper Spey, Scotland. Single malt: 15-year-old.

Ben Roland blended 5-year-old scotch whisky by Ben Roland Scotch Whisky, Dartford, Kent, England.

Benromach Speyside's smallest working malt whisky distillery, Scotland, est 1898, mothballed 1983, reopened by Gordon & MacPhail 1998. Produced first **Benromach Speyside Single Malt** in 2004.

Ben Shalom liqueur from Jaffa oranges, Israel. Name means Son of Peace.

Bentley Cocktail. Over ice shake 1 part apple brandy, 1 Dubonnet. Strain.

Bentonite clay fining used in clarifying wine. Now more widely employed in 'vegetarian' wines to obviate use of animal fining products such as gelatin and isinglass.

Ben Wyvis North Highland malt whisky distillery, Invergordon, Scotland.

Beowulf brewery at Yardley, Birmingham, England. No connection with the epic Old English poem (written *c.* 1000 AD) is claimed.

Berberana, Bodegas wine producer at Cenicero, Spain. Carta de Plata (3 yr) and Carta de Oro (5 yr) Rioja.

bere type of barley sometimes used for brewing purposes in Scotland.

Bereich under German wine-law, a sub-region of a vineyard region or *Anbaugebiet*. Usually named after main local town or village, such as Bereich Piesport.

berenburg type of Dutch bitters based on brandewijn flavoured with herbs.

Berg the name of 24 individual vineyards in Germany. Region by region, as follows: in Ahr at Bad Neuenahr-Ahrweiler; in Baden at Neudenau, Neudenau (Herbolzheim); in Franken at Markt Eisenheim, Volkach; in Mittelrhein at Unkel; in Nahe at Bad Kreuznach, Roxheim; in Rheingau at Felsberg (Schwalm-Eder-Keis), Hocheim, Mainz; in Rheinpfalz at Neustadt an der Weinstrasse; in Württemberg at Asberg, Korb, Langenbrettach, Markgröningen, Stuttgart (Bad Cannstatt), Stuttgart (Feuerbach), Stuttgart (Münster), Stuttgart (Wangen), Stuttgart (Zuffenhausen), Winnenden, Winnenden (Hanweiler).

Bergamot Liqueur Mediterranean lemon liqueur.

Bergat, Château wine estate of AC St-Emilion, Bordeaux, France. Classified *Grand Cru Classé*.

Berg-Bildstock vineyard at Walluf in Rheingau region, Germany.

Bergborn vineyard at Langenlonsheim in Nahe region, Germany.

Bergel vineyards at Edenkoben and at Grünstadt in Rheinpfalz region, Germany.

Berger wine producer in Kremstal, Niederösterreich, Austria.

Bergerac AC wine region of SW France, adjacent to Bordeaux. Red, rosé and white (dry and sweet) wines from same grape varieties planted in Bordeaux.

Berghalde vineyards at Kressbronn/Bodensee and at Remshalden in Württemberg region, Germany.

Berghoff brand name for beers made by Huber brewery, Monroe, Wisconsin, USA, including **Berghoff Beer; Berghoff Bock; Berghoff Dark**.

Berg Kaisersteinfels vineyard at Rüdesheim in Rheingau region, Germany.

Bergkelder wine-producing co-operative and distributor of Stellenbosch, South Africa. Wine ranges include Fleur du Cap, Stellenryck Collection, Two Oceans and others.

Bergkirche vineyard at Nierstein in Rheinhessen region, Germany.

Bergkloster *Grosslage* (collective vineyard) incorporating vineyards in the Rheinhessen region of Germany at, respectively, Bermersheim, Eppelsheim, Esselborn, Flomborn, Gundersheim, Gund-heim, Hangen-Weisheim, Westhofen.

Bergle vineyards at Freiburg and at Offeburg in Baden region, Germany.

Bergpfad vineyard at Friesheim in Rheinhessen region, Germany.

Berg-Rondell vineyard at Dettelbach in Franken region, Germany.

Berg Roseneck vineyard at Rüdesheim in Rheingau region, Germany.

Bergschlösschen vineyard at Saarburg in Mosel-Saar-Ruwer region, Germany.

Berg Schlossberg vineyard at Rüdesheim in Rheingau region, Germany.

Bergsig Estate leading wine producer of Breede River, Worcester, South Africa. Cabernet Sauvignon and Pinotage red wines; Gewürztraminer, Sauvignon, Weisser Riesling and sparkling white wines, plus renowned 'Port'.

Bergstrasse-Kraichau, Badische *Bereich* (sub-region) of Baden wine region, Germany.

Bergwäldle vineyard at Wiesloch in Baden region, Germany.

Bergweiler-Prüm Erben wine estate of Mosel-Saar-Ruwer region, Germany.

Beringer Wine estate, founded 1873, at St Helena, California, USA. Formerly owned by Nestlé and sold to Australian brewer Foster's in 2000.

Berkane-Oujda wine region of Morocco.

Berkeley farm brewery (Bucketts Hill) at Berkeley, Gloucestershire, England.

Berlin Cocktail. Over ice shake 1 part dry gin, 1 madeira, 1 orange juice. Strain.

Berliner Kindl Brauerei brewery in Berlin, Germany, famed for Berliner Weisse wheat beers.

Berliner Weisse German top-fermenting wheat beer low in alcohol (typically 3%) and high in sparkle. Commonly drunk in Berlin with the addition of a flavouring syrup.

Berliquet, Château wine estate of AC St-Emilion, Bordeaux, France. Classified *Grand Cru Classé*.

Bermuda Bloom Cocktail. Over ice shake 2 parts dry gin, 2 lemon juice, 2 orange juice, 1 apricot brandy, 3 dashes Cointreau, 1 teaspoon sugar. Strain into tall ice-filled glasses.

Bermuda Pink Cocktail. Over ice shake 2 parts dry gin, 1 apricot brandy, 1 teaspoon grenadine. Strain.

Bern wine-producing canton, Switzerland.

Bernardine, Domaine de la Château-neuf-du-Pape wine by Max Chapoutier, Rhône Valley, France.

Bernkastel *Bereich* (sub-region) of Mosel-Saar-Ruwer region, Germany.

Bernkasteler Badstube *Einzellage* (vineyard) of Bernkastel *Bereich*, Germany. Famed Riesling wines notably produced by Deinhard of Koblenz.

Bernkasteler Doktor *Einzellage* (vineyard), the most renowned of Bernkastel *Bereich*, Germany. So named after the alleged therapeutic properties of its wines.

Bernkasteler Pils Pilsener beer made by Bürger brewery, Bernkastel, Germany.

Bernreither, Peter wine producer in Wien (Vienna), Austria.

Bernstein vineyard at Oberwesel in Mittelrhein region, Germany.

Beronia, Bodegas wine producer at Ollauri, Rioja, Spain.

Berri Estates large-scale co-operative wine producer, Riverland, South Australia. Premium wines sold under Renmano label.

Berro spirit brand of distillers HDL Comercial, Brazil.

Berrow brewery at Burnham on Sea, Somerset, England.

Berry Bros & Rudd Ltd Distiller of Cutty Sark whisky and noted wine merchant at 3 St James's Street, London, England. Founded, as a grocery, in late 17th century, this private company claims: 'No other family has been selling wine from one building for so long'.

Berry Good Ale seasonal (autumn) ale (4.5% alc) by Hydes Brewery, Manchester, England.

Berry's All Malt vatted malt scotch whisky by Berry Bros & Rudd, London, England.

Berry's Best blended scotch whisky by Berry Bros & Rudd, London, England.

Berry Wall Cocktail. Over ice shake 1 part dry gin, 1 sweet vermouth, 2 dashes curaçao. Strain and add lemon peel.

Bersano wine producer of Piedmont, Italy, known for Barbaresco and Barolo.

Bertani large-scale producer at Verona of Bardolino and Valpolicella red wines and Soave whites. Veneto region, Italy.

Berthiers, Les wine-producing village of AC Pouilly-Fumé, Loire region, France.

Bertin, Château de wine estate of AC Bordeaux, France.

Bertineau, Château wine estate of AC Lalande-de-Pomerol, Bordeaux, France.

Bertins, Château des wine estate of AC Médoc, Bordeaux, France.

Bertola sherry brand of Marcos Eguizábal, Jerez de la Frontera, Spain.

Bertolo, Lorenzo grappa producer, Turin, Italy.

Bertrams brand of Van der Hum liqueur. South Africa.

Bertrams VO five-year-old brandy of South Africa.

Bertrand, Gilbert *récoltant-manipulant* champagne producer, Chamery, Champagne, France.

Besserat de Bellefon champagne house est 1843, Reims, France.

Bestheim wine brand of Les Vignerons Réuinis de Bennwihr-Westhalten, Alsace, France.

Best's Wines producer at Great Western, Victoria, Australia. Renowned sparkling (**Best's Western**) and still wines.

Betschgräber vineyard at Bühl in Baden region, Germany.

Betsy Ross Cocktail. Over ice stir 1 part brandy, 1 port, 1 dash triple sec.

Bettelhaus vineyard at Bad Dürkheim in Rheinpfalz region, Germany.

Between-the-Sheets Cocktail. Over ice shake 1 part white rum, 1 brandy, 1 Cointreau, 1 dash lemon juice. Strain.

Beucher, Michel calvados producer at Sainte-Marie-du-Bois, Normandy, France. Organic methods.

Beukelaer, de producer of Elixir d'Anvers green liqueur – described as 'the Belgian national liqueur' – in Antwerp, Belgium.

Beulsberg vineyard at Oberwesel in Mittelrhein region, Germany.

Beutelstein vineyard at Oberndorf in Nahe region, Germany.

beyaz 'white' (wine). Turkish.

Beychevelle, Château great wine estate of AC St Julien, Médoc, Bordeaux, France. Classified *4ème Grand Cru Classé*.

Beyer, Léon major vineyard owner and wine producer at Eguisheim, Alsace, France.

Beyers Truter wine producer in Stellenbosch region, South Africa. Pinotage and other varietals.

Biac, Château du wine estate of AC Premières Côtes de Bordeaux, France.

Bianchello del Metauro DOC wine region for dry white from Bianchello grape, Marches region, Italy.

Bianchi wine-producer, Mendoza region, Argentina.

bianco white (wine). Italian.

Bianco Capena DOC white wine zone at Capena, Latium, Italy.

Bianco dei Colli Maceratesi DOC white wine zone at Maceratesi, Marches, Italy.

Bianco dei Roeri white wine of DOC Roero, Tuscany, Italy, made from Arneis grape.

Bianco della Lega white wine of Chianti Classico zone, Tuscany, Italy.

Bianco della Valdinievole DOC white wine zone at Montecatini Terme, Tuscany, Italy.

Bianco dell'Empolese DOC white wine zone, Tuscany, Italy.

Bianco di Custoza DOC white wine zone at Custoza, Veneto, Italy. Dry white wines rivalling local Soave for quality.

Bianco di Gravina DOC white wine zone, Apulia, Italy.

Bianco di Pitigliano DOC white wine zone at Pitigliano, Tuscany, Italy.

Bianco di Scandiano DOC sparkling white wine zone at Scandiano, Emilia-Romagna, Italy.

Bianco Pisano di San Torpè DOC white wine zone south of Pisa, Tuscany, Italy.

Bianco Val d'Arbia DOC white wine zone in Arbia Valley, Tuscany, Italy.

Bianco Vergine della Val di Chiana DOC white wine zone in Chiana Valley, Tuscany, Italy.

bibulexicographer compiler of drink dictionaries; harmless drudge.

Bical white grape variety, Bairrada region, Portugal.

Bichot, Albert wine-producer and *négociant-élèveur*, Beaune, Burgundy, France. Noted for wines from Clos Frantin estate, AC Vosne-Romanée.

Bich's Special Cocktail. Over ice shake 2 parts dry gin, 1 Lillet, 1 dash Angostura bitters. Strain and add orange peel.

Biddenden Vineyard wine producer at Biddenden, Ashford, Kent, England. Renowned white wine from Ortega grapes.

Biddy Early brewery at Inagh, County Clare, Ireland.

Biegler wine producer in Thermenregion, Niederösterreich, Austria.

Bienenberg vineyards at Achern, at Malterdingen and at Teningen in Baden region, and at Niederburg and at Oberwesel in the Mittelrhein region, Germany.

Bienengarten vineyards at Koblenz and at Senheim in Mosel-Saar-Ruwer region, Germany.

Bienenlay vineyard at Ediger-Eller in Mosel-Saar-Ruwer region, Germany.

Biengarten vineyards at Frankweiler and at Neustadt an der Weinstrasse in Rheinpfalz region, Germany.

Bienvenues-Bâtard-Montrachet *Grand Cru* vineyard at Puligny-Montrachet, Burgundy, France. Highly prized white wines. Name 'bastards welcome' derives, according to one parish myth, from the large number of local people owing their origins to the amorous activities of visiting aristocrats from 11th century onwards.

bierbrouwerij brewery. Netherlands.

Bière de Démon devilishly strong (12%) lager brewed by Enfants de Gayant, Lille, France.

bière de garde style of strong, bottle-conditioned beer, originally French, made for long keeping.

bière de Mars 'March beer'; style of beer made only in season. France.

Bière des Sans Culottes *bière de garde* of La Choulette brewery, Hordain, France.

Bière des Templiers abbey ale made by St Sylvestre brewery, Steenvoorde, France.

Bierschaum 'Beer foam'; Germany's answer to zabaglione – made with strong ale in place of Marsala.

Biferno DOC wine zone of Biferno Valley, Molise, Italy. Red, *rosato* and white wines.

Biffy Cocktail. Over ice shake 2 parts dry gin, 1 lemon juice, 1 Swedish Punsch. Strain.

big in winetasting, a flavour marked by richness and weight.

Bigaroux, Château wine estate of AC St-Emilion, Bordeaux, France.

Big Boy Cocktail. Over ice shake 2 parts brandy, 1 Cointreau, 1 lemon syrup. Strain.

Big Foot Ale barley wine brewed by Sierra Nevada Brewing Co, Chico, California, and once the USA's strongest beer at 11%.

Big Horn Bitter ale by Walnut Brewing, Colorado, USA.

Bigi wine producer in Umbria, Italy. Wines of Est! Est!! Est!!!, Orvieto and others.

Big Lamp brewery at Newburn, Newcastle upon Tyne, Tyne & Wear, England.

Big Rock Brewery Irish-immigrant-founded brewery at Calgary, Canada, noted for malty ales made in the Irish style.

Big Time pub-brewery in Seattle, Washington, USA. Ales include **Big Time ESB**, Here-Ryzen rye beer and Old Woolly barley wine.

Bijou Cocktail. Over ice stir 1 part dry gin, 1 sweet vermouth, 1 green Chartreuse, 1 dash orange bitters. Strain and add cherry and lemon peel.

Bikini rum brand of Halewood International, Huyton, Merseyside, England.

Bilbaínas, Bodegas wine producer in Rioja, Spain. Brands include Viña Pomal.

Bildberg vineyard at Freimersheim in Rheinpfalz region, Germany.

Bildstock vineyards at Worms in Rheinhessen region, and at Nierstein in Rheinpfalz region, Germany.

Billecart-Salmon *Grande Marque* champagne house at Mareuil-sur-Aÿ, France. Est 1818 and lately prominent.

Bill Gibb Cocktail. Over ice shake 4 parts fresh orange juice, 1 Mandarine liqueur, 1 dash Angostura bitters. Strain into ice-filled tall glass.

Biltong Dry Cocktail. Over ice shake 1 part dry gin, 1 Dubonnet, 2 Caperitif, 1 dash orange bitters. Strain.

Binding largest brewer in Germany, with beer brands including Export Privat and Steinhauser Bier.

bin storage space in wine cellar. In 18th century English architecture, a shelved opening of a size to accommodate a hogshead (25 dozen) of wine in bottles.

bin-end residual bottle(s) of wine from a bin or any large quantity.

bin-label descriptive label for wine bins used before introduction of individual bottle-labelling.

Bingen *Bereich* (sub-region) of Rheinhessen region, Germany.

Bingerberg vineyards at Flonheim, at Flonheim (Uffholen) and at Erbes-Büdesheim in Rheinhessen region, Germany.

biodynamic method a growing movement among wine producers wishing to reduce use of synthetic materials in vineyard and winery and to take maximum advantage of natural phenomena. First promoted in 1920s by Austrian philosopher-educationist Rudolph Steiner (1861–1925). In some ways similar to organic methods. Followers include Chapoutier in the Rhône Valley, France, and Robinvale in Australia.

Biondi-Santi wine producer at Montalcino, Tuscany, Italy. Renowned for Brunello di Montalcino red wine of Il Greppo vineyard, the longest-lived and most expensive wine of Italy.

Bios abbey ale producer of Ertvelde, Belgium. Brands include Pater Noster.

Bird of Paradise Cocktail. Over ice shake 3 parts tequila, 1 crème de cacao, 1 Galliano, 2 orange juice, 1 fresh cream. Strain.

Birdrock brewery at Tywyn, Gwynedd, Wales.

Birkenberg vineyards at Roxheim and at Sommerloch in Nahe region, Germany.

Biron, Château wine estate of AC Premières Côtes de Bordeaux, France.

birra beer, Italian.

Birra Perfetto oregano-flavoured pale ale by Pike Place brewery, Seattle, Washington, USA.

Bischofstein vineyard at Burgen in Mosel-Saar-Ruwer region, Germany.

Bischofsberg vineyards at Arnstein, Arnstein (Halsheim), Arnstein (Heugrumbach), Arnstein (Müdesheim), Arnstein (Reuchelheim) and Grossheubach in Franken region, and at Rüdesheim in Rheingau region, Germany.

Bischofsgarten

Bischofsgarten vineyards at Forst an Weinstrasse, at Friedelsheim and at Wachenheim in Rheinpfalz region, Germany.

Bischofshub vineyard at Oberdiebach in Mittelrhein region, Germany.

Bischofskreuz *Grosslage* (collective vineyard) incorporating vineyards in Rheinpfalz region of Germany at, respectively, Böchingen, Burrweiler, Flemingen, Gleisweiler, Knöringen, Landau in der Pfalz (Dammheim), Landau in der Pfalz (Nussdorf), Roschbach, Walsheim.

Bischöfliches Konvit great wine estate at Trier, Mosel-Saar-Ruwer region, Germany. Founded as an abbey vineyard 1653.

Bischöfliches Priesterseminar great wine estate at Trier, Mosel-Saar-Ruwer region, Germany.

Bischofstuhl vineyard at Cochem in Mosel-Saar-Ruwer region, Germany.

Bischofsweg vineyard at Neustadt an der Weinstrasse in Rheinpfalz region, Germany.

Bishop type of mulled-wine drink. Claret or port flavoured with orange, nutmeg and cloves.

Bishop Cocktail. Over ice stir 1 part white rum, 1 teaspoon claret, 1 dash lemon juice, 1 drop sugar syrup. Strain.

Bishops brewery at Borough Market, London, England.

Bishop's Bitter ale produced by Sherlock's Home brewery, Minnetonka, Minnesota, USA.

Bishops Finger strong (5.4% in bottle) ale brand of Shepherd Neame brewery, Kent, England.

see label opposite ➡

Bishops Waltham vineyard at Bishops Waltham, Hampshire, England.

Bison pub-brewery in Berkeley, California, USA.

Bisquit cognac producer, est 1819, Jarnac, France. XXX, Napoléon, Extra Vieille and others. Owned by Pernod-Ricard.

Bisquit No. 1 branded mixed drink of cognac, guarana and sparkling water by Bisquit.

Biston-Brillette, Château wine estate of AC Moulis, Médoc, Bordeaux, France. Classified *Cru Bourgeois*.

Bitburger Brauerei Theo Simon famed family-run Pilsner brewery at Bitburg in the Rheinpfalz region, Germany, producing **Bitburger Pils**.

bite in winetasting, a flavour indicating high acidity or the presence of tannin.

Biter Cocktail. Over ice shake 2 parts dry gin, 1 green Chartreuse, 1 lemon juice, 1 dash pastis, 1 drop sugar syrup. Strain.

bitter style of ale, originally English, characterised by a pronounced bitterness imparted by hops. Ordinary bitter typically has 4% alcohol; 'best' or 'special' bitter has up to 5%.

Bitterbier lager brand of Hövels Haus-Brauerei, Dortmund, Germany.

bittering hops in brewing, hop varieties selected for their ability to add bitterness and dryness to beers.

bitter top informal term for a pub shandy stronger on beer than it is on lemonade. A near-pint of bitter, topped with a little lemonade. UK.

Blaauwklippen wine estate in Stellenbosch region, South Africa. Noted Cabernet Sauvignon and Zinfandel red wines among others.

Black & White blended scotch whisky by James Buchanan, London, England.

Blackawton Brewery brewer in Totnes, Devon, England, producing **Blackawton Bitter**, Devon Best and Squires ales.

Black Bavarian dark lager by Sprecher Brewing Co, Milwaukee, Wisconsin, USA.

black beer style of dark lager beer original to Germany but now also produced elsewhere, particularly in Japan.

Black Beer from Hell black pilsner lager (4.4% alc) by Hell Brewery, Slovakia.

Black Bess Sweet Stout beer produced seasonally by Timothy Taylor brewery, Keighley, West Yorkshire.

Blackbirch red wine brand of Grove Mill, Marlborough, New Zealand.

Black Bottle blended scotch whisky by Gordon Graham, Aberdeen, Scotland.

Black Bull brewery at Fenny Bentley, Ashbourne, Derbyshire, England.

Black Butte Porter ale brand of Deschutes brewery, Bend, Oregon, USA.

Black Cuillin dark ale (4.5% alc) by Isle of Skye Brewery, Scotland.

blackcurrant in winetasting, aroma indicating presence of Cabernet Sauvignon grapes.

Black Death aquavit brand of state alcohol monopoly, Iceland. The Icelandic government has a policy of discouraging the consumption of spirits.

Black Death spirit brand of Richmond Distillers, Jersey, Channel Islands, UK.

Black Devil Cocktail. Over ice stir 2 parts rum, 1 dry vermouth. Strain.

Black Diamond ale brand of Butter-knowle Brewery, Newcastle-upon-Tyne, England.

Black Douglas Scottish ale (5.2% alc) by Broughton Ales, Biggar, Peeblesshire, Scotland. Named after Sir James Douglas, a comrade of Robert the Bruce (1274–1329). 'Black Douglas, a powerful knight and one of Scotland's heroes whose daring exploits often brought him to the Border country of Scotland, home of Broughton Ales, is famous for carrying the Bruce's heart into battle on the Crusades.'

Blackdown Bonfire 'celebration porter' of former Eldridge Pope brewery (now Thomas Hardy brewery), Dorset, England.

Blackened Voodoo dark lager by Dixie brewery, New Orleans, Louisiana, USA.

Black Forest Porter beer brand of Columbus Brewing Company, Ohio, USA.

Black Fox strong (7% alc) sparkling organic cider brand of Dunkertons, Pembridge, Herefordshire, England.

7% alc by vol
500ml ℮

Black Fox•
cider

from traditional cider apples
grown in unsprayed orchards

pressed, fermented and bottled by
DUNKERTONS
Pembridge, Herefordshire

Black Hamburg red grape variety synonymous with Schiava.

Black Hawk Cocktail. Over ice stir 1 part bourbon, 1 sloe gin. Strain and add a maraschino cherry.

Black Hawk Stout dry stout produced by North Coast brewery, Fort Bragg, California, USA.

Black Heart Jamaican dark rum brand, United Rum Merchants, England.

Black Jack brand name of Pernod-Ricard.

Black Mac dark lager brand of Mac's microbrewery, Stoke, New Zealand.

Black Magic Cocktail. Over ice shake 2 parts vodka, 1 Tia Maria, 1 dash lemon juice.

Black Maria Cocktail. With ice in a brandy glass, stir 1 part Tia Maria, 1 rum, 1 chilled black coffee, 1 teaspoon sugar.

Black Mountain Gold beer brewed by Crazy Ed's Black Mountain brewery, Phoenix, Arizona, USA.

Black Nikka whisky brand of Nikka Distilleries, Japan.

Blackout Cocktail. Over ice shake 2 parts dark rum, 1 Kahlúa, 2 dashes lemon juice.

Black Prince blended scotch whisky brand of Burn Stewart Distillers, Glasgow, Scotland. **Black Prince Select, Black Prince 12-Year-Old, Black Prince 17-Year-Old**.

Black Radish dark lager by Weeping Radish brewery, Roanoke Island, North Carolina, USA. Name derives from Bavarian tradition of eating salted (and thus 'weeping') black-skinned radishes with beer.

Black Ram Ale beer by Black Sheep Brewery, Masham, North Yorkshire, England.

Black Rock Porter beer by Triple Rock brewery, Berkeley, California, USA.

Black Rose Cocktail. In a tumbler, stir 1 teaspoon sugar and 1 part rum. Add ice and fill with iced black coffee.

black rot vine disease characterized by blackening of leaves and shrivelling of grapes.

Black Russian Cocktail. Over ice stir 2 parts vodka, 1 Kahlúa. Strain.

Black's Beach beer by Old Columbia brewery, California, USA.

Black Sea Gold Pomorie distiller and winery est 1954 (and privatised 1997) of eastern Bulgaria. Brandies and light wines from indigenous and imported grape varieties.

Black Sheep brewery est 1992 in former Lightfoot Brewery at Masham, North Yorkshire, England. **Black Sheep Ale** (4.4% alc), **Black Sheep Bitter** (3.8% alc), Black Ram Ale (4.2% alc), Harry Ramsden's Ale (4.4% alc), Riggwelter (5.7% alc), Yorkshire Square Ale (5.0% alc).

Black Spanish red grape variety for table wines, Madeira.

blackstrap local term for molasses in rum-distilling. Caribbean islands.

Black Taunton apple variety traditionally valued for cider-making. English.

Blackthorn cider originally by Taunton Cider, Norton Fitzwarren, Somerset, England, now part of Matthew Clark and made at Shepton Mallet, Somerset.

Blackthorn Cocktail. Over ice shake 1 part Irish whiskey, 1 dry vermouth, 2 dashes pastis, 2 dashes Angostura bitters. Strain.

Blackthorn Bush Cocktail. Over ice shake 1 part Irish whiskey, 1 dry vermouth, 2 dashes pastis, 2 dashes Angostura bitters.

Black Tower brand of Liebfraumilch wine, Rheinhessen region, Germany.

Black Tusk beer brand of Whistler Brewing, near Vancouver, Canada.

Black Velvet Canadian whisky brand of Gilbey Canada.

Black Velvet Cocktail. Gently pour equal parts chilled stout and chilled champagne into a tall glass.

Black Watch, The whisky brand of Pernod-Ricard.

Blackwell Stout dry stout by Elm City brewery, New Haven, Connecticut, USA.

Blackwych Stout ale by Wychwood brewery, Witney, Oxfordshire, England.

Bladnoch Lowland malt whisky distillery, Machars, Scotland. Single malt: 10-year-old.

Blagny

Blagny village and red-wine AC of Puligny-Montrachet, Burgundy, France. Also known as **Blagny-Côte-de-Beaune** AC.

Blagny 1er Cru AC for red wines of seven classified vineyards at Meursault and Puligny-Montrachet, Burgundy, France.

Blaignan, Château wine estate of AC Médoc, Bordeaux, France.

Blair Athol Highland malt whisky distillery, Pitlochrie, Perthshire, Scotland. Single malt: 12-year-old.

blanc white (wine). France.

blanc de blancs white wine from white grapes. In Champagne, wine made only from Chardonnay grapes. French.

Blanc de la Salle white wine of Valle d'Aosta, Italy.

Blanc de Marbonne dry white wine of Koopmanskloof winery, Stellenbosch, South Africa.

Blanc de Morgex white wine of Valle d'Aosta, Italy.

Blanc de Noirs white wine from black grapes, particularly in Champagne, France.

Blanc Fumé de Pouilly synonym for white wine of Pouilly Fumé. Loire Valley, France.

Blanche Cocktail. Over ice shake 1 part Cointreau, 1 white curaçao, 1 Anisette. Strain.

Blanche de Namur wheat beer by Brasserie du Bocq brewery, Purnode, Belgium.

Blancherie (Peyret), Château la wine estate of AC Graves, Bordeaux, France.

Blanch-ke wheat beer by Van Honsebrouck brewery, Belgium.

Blanchots *Grand Cru* vineyard, Chablis, France.

blanco white (wine). Spanish.

Blandford Fly bottled 'premium ale' (5.2% alc) by Hall & Woodhouse brewers, Blandford Forum, Dorset, England. Flavoured with ginger, the ale 'celebrates the infamous Blandford Fly, a resident biting insect of Dorset's River Stour. Local folklore has it that a constituent in ginger could help reduce the inflictions of the creature's bite.'

Blandy's brand of **Blandy Brothers**, Funchal, Madeira. Wines include Duke of Sussex Sercial (dry), Duke of Cambridge Verdelho (medium dry), Duke of Clarence Malmsey and 10-year-old Rich Malmsey (sweet).

Blanquet, Château second wine of Château Andron-Blanquet, Bordeaux, France.

Blanquette white grape variety of SW France. Synonymous with Mauzac.

Blanquette de Limoux sparkling wine AC of Limoux in SW France producing wine by the 'champagne method'.

Blarney Stone Cocktail. Over ice stir 1 part Irish whiskey, 2 dashes white curaçao, 2 dashes pastis, 1 dash maraschino.

Blatina red grape, and wine, of Herzegovina.

Blattenberg vineyard at Mehring in Mosel-Saar-Ruwer region, Germany.

Blatz beer brand of Heileman brewery, Wisconsin, USA.

Blaubeere liqueur from fermented bilberries of the Black Forest. Germany.

Blau(er)burgunder German synonym for Pinot Noir grape.

Blaufrankisch red grape variety of Austria.

Blauer Limberger red grape variety of Germany. Synonymous with Blaufrankisch.

Blauer Portugieser red grape variety, Austria, Germany and eastern Europe.

Blavod black-coloured vodka brand of Original Black Vodka Company, UK.

Blayais AC for white wines of Côte de Blaye, Bordeaux, France.

Blaye town of Blaye wine region, Bordeaux, France.

Blazquez, Hijos de Augustin Domecq-owned sherry *bodega*, Jerez de la Frontera, Spain. Sherries under brands Carta Blanca, Carta Roja etc.

Bleasdale wine producer est 1850 in Langhorne Creek, South Australia.

Bleidenberg vineyard at Alken in Mosel-Saar-Ruwer region, Germany.

blended whisky spirit made with a mixture of grain and malt whiskies.

Blenders Pride brand name of Pernod-Ricard.

blending in wine-making, the combining of new-made wines from differing grape varieties, vineyards or vintages to produce an improved, or annually consistent, style.

Blenton Cocktail. Over ice stir 2 parts dry gin, 1 dry vermouth, 1 dash Angostura bitters. Strain.

Blériot Cocktail. Over ice stir 4 parts dry gin, 2 dry vermouth, 1 cherry brandy, 1 peach bitters. Strain and add cherry.

Blinding Sunrise Cocktail. Over ice shake 1 part tequila, 1 vodka, 3 orange juice, 1 teaspoon triple sec. Strain into a tall, ice-filled glass and add a dash of grenadine and an orange slice. A fortified version of the popular Tequila Sunrise cocktail.

Blind Man's Brewery microbrewery est 2002 at Leighton, Somerset, England. Ales include Firkin Dog (3.8% alc) and Mine Beer (4.2% alc). The brewery is situated amidst Somerset's stone-quarrying district, but founder David Capps-Tunwell, who sold the business in 2003, admitted Mine Beer is so-called 'because it's mine'.

blind tasting assessing quality and type of anonymous wine. Necessary for objective evaluation.

Block and Tackle Cocktail. Over ice shake 2 parts brandy, 2 Cointreau, 1 apple brandy, 1 pastis. Strain.

Bloemendal Estate wine producer in Durbanville, South Africa. Still and sparkling wines, plus 'port'.

Blood and Sand Cocktail. Over ice shake 1 part scotch whisky, 1 cherry brandy, 1 sweet vermouth, 1 orange juice. Strain.

Bloodhound Cocktail. Into a blender put 2 parts chilled gin, 1 chilled dry vermouth, 1 chilled sweet vermouth, 2 or 3 chilled fresh strawberries. Whizz and serve.

Blood Transfusion Cocktail. Over ice shake 2 parts white rum, 1 fresh lime juice, 1 dash grenadine. Strain.

Bloody Butcher apple variety traditionally valued in cider-making. English.

Bloody Maria Cocktail. Over ice shake 1 part tequila, 2 tomato juice, 1 dash lemon juice, 1 dash Tabasco, 1 dash Worcestershire sauce.

Bloody Mary Cocktail. Over ice shake 2 parts vodka, 3 tomato juice, 1 lemon juice, 2 dashes Worcestershire sauce, pinch celery salt. Strain.

bloom surface accumulation of yeasts and other organisms on ripening skin of grapes. Also known as pruina.

Blossom Hill winery and popular table-wine brand, Paicine, California, USA.

Blücherhöhe vineyard at Edenkoben in Rheinpfalz region, Germany.

Blücherpfad vineyard at Ober-Flörsheim in Rheinhessen region, Germany.

Blüchertal vineyard at Kaub in Mittelrhein region, Germany.

Blue Anchor brewery at Helston, Cornwall, England.

Bluebird Cocktail. Over ice stir 2 parts dry gin, 1 dry vermouth, 1 teaspoon cherry brandy, 1 dash peach bitters. Strain and add a maraschino cherry.

Blue Bird Cocktail. Over ice shake 3 parts dry gin, 1 orange curaçao, 3 dashes Angostura bitters. Strain.

Blue Devil Cocktail. Over ice shake 2 parts dry gin, 1 fresh lime (or lemon) juice, 1 maraschino, 1 dash blue food colouring. Strain.

Blue Grass Cocktail. In a tall, ice-filled glass, mix 2 parts bourbon, 1 apricot brandy, 1 sprinkle of sugar. Top with soda water and stir.

Blue Hanger blended 'Scots Whisky' by Berry Bros & Rudd, London, England.

Blue Hawaii Cocktail. Over ice shake 1 part white rum, 1 blue curaçao, 1 coconut liqueur, 2 pineapple juice. Strain.

Blue Heron brand name of two unrelated ales produced respectively by BridgePort Brewery, Portland, Oregon, USA and Mendocino County Brewery, Hopland, California, USA.

Blue Imperial red grape variety, Australia. Synonymous with Cinsaut.

Blue Label pale ale (3.6% alc) by Harveys Brewery, Lewes, East Sussex, England.

Blue Label mild ale by Farsons brewery, Malta.

Blue Lagoon Cocktail. In an ice-filled tall glass, combine 2 parts vodka, 1 blue curaçao. Top with chilled clear grape juice and stir.

Blue Margarita Cocktail. Over ice shake 3 parts tequila, 1 blue curaçao, 2 fresh lime juice. Strain.

Blue Marlin Cocktail. Over ice shake 2 parts white rum, 1 blue curaçao, 2 fresh lime juice. Strain.

Blue Monday Cocktail. Over ice shake 3 parts vodka, 1 Cointreau, 1 dash blue food colouring. Strain.

Blue Moon brewery at Seamere Hingham, Norfolk, England.

Blue Moon Cocktail. Over ice stir 2 parts dry gin, 1 blue curaçao. Strain.

Blue Nun popular Liebfraumilch wine brand of H Sichel company, Alzey, Germany. Curiously, the famous blue-clad nun was originally depicted in a brown habit. The bottle remained brown until a 1997 relaunch of the wine by Ehrmann Group, UK, who opted for a blue bottle.

Blue Ridge pub-brewery at Charlottesville, North Carolina, USA.

blue ruin nickname for low-grade gin of early 18th-century England.

Blues Cocktail. Over ice shake 4 parts whisky, 1 curaçao, 1 teaspoon Syrup of Prunes.

Blue Train Cocktail. Over ice shake 2 parts dry gin, 1 Cointreau, 1 fresh lemon juice, 1 dash blue food colouring. Strain.

Blue Train Special Cocktail. Over ice shake 2 parts brandy, 1 pineapple syrup. Strain into wine glass and top up with chilled champagne. Stir carefully.

Blümchen vineyard at Nittel in Mosel-Saar-Ruwer region, Germany.

Blume vineyards at Rech in Ahr region, and at Stadecken-Elsheim in Rheinhessen region, Germany.

blush style of white wine from red grapes, in which some skin colour is imparted to produce a pink hue. Commonly from Zinfandel grapes in California, USA.

Boag, J brewery at Launceston, Tasmania, Australia. Produces **Boag's Lager**.

Boavista port brand of Forrester & Cia, Vila Nova de Gaia, Portugal.

Bobadilla major brandy and sherry producer, Jerez de la Frontera, Spain. 103 White Label, 103 Negro and Gran Capitan brandies; Victoria fino, Alcazar *amontillado* and Capitan *oloroso* sherries.

Bobal red grape variety of Mediterranean Spain. Red and *rosado* wines.

Bobby Burns Cocktail. Over ice shake 2 parts scotch whisky, 2 sweet vermouth, 1 Bénédictine. Strain.

Boberg Wine of Origin region for fortified wines, South Africa.

Bobtail, Brasserie de brewery at St Séverin, SW France, making naturally fermented beers using wild yeasts.

Boca DOC red-wine zone, Piedmont, Italy.

Boccalino's Brewpub restaurant-brewery in Edmonton, Alberta, Canada. Brands include **Bocca Ale** and **Bocca Blonde**.

Bocchino major grappa producer, Canelli, Piedmont, Italy.

bock beer a type of strong, usually dark, lager originally made in the 14th century at Einbeck in northern

Germany. Bock beers are now also made elsewhere in Europe, in Australia and the USA.

Bock Damm dark beer brand of Damm brewery, Barcelona, Spain.

Bockor brewery at Bellegem, Belgium. Bottle-fermenting *gueuze* beer and Vander Ghinste Ouden Tripel red ale.

Bocksbeeren blackcurrant liqueur of Eastern Europe.

Bocksberg vineyard at Feilbingert in Nahe region, Germany.

Bocksbeutel 'goat's bottle' – a squat, flask-like bottle traditional for wines of Franconia, Germany. Shape is said to imitate a goat's scrotum.

Bockshaut vineyards at Gau-Bickelheim and Wöllstein in Rheinhessen region, Germany.

Bockstein vineyards at Ockfen in Mosel-Saar-Ruwer region, and at Ingelheim and at Stadecken-Elsheim in Rheinhessen region, Germany.

Boddingtons brewery est 1778, Manchester, England. Draught and canned ales. **Boddingtons Pub Ale** and **Boddingtons Export** in cans incorporate a patented 'Draughtflow' system whereby a device releases air into the can when opened, replicating the aerating effects of pulling draught beer from the barrel. Formerly owned by Whitbread, the brand was sold to Interbrew in 2000 and the original brewery was closed in 2005.   *see label opposite* ➧

bodega 'wine cellar'. Spanish. Term also applies to a winemaking centre, wine shop, or producing company.

Bodegas Crillon producer of Crillon sparkling wines, Argentina.

Bodenheim riverside winemaking town of Rheinhessen region, Germany.

Bodensee *Bereich* (sub-region) of Baden region, Germany.

Bodental-Steinberg vineyard at Lorch in Rheingau region, Germany.

Bodicote brew pub (Plough Inn) at Bodicote, Banbury, Oxfordshire, England.

body in winetasting, the alcoholic weight and quantity of grape extract detectable in the mouth.

boerenjongens fruit-flavoured *brandewijn*, Netherlands. Name means 'farm boys'.

boerenmeisjes fruit-flavoured *brandewijn*, Netherlands. Name means 'farm girls'.

Bogdanusa white grape variety and wine of Brac and Hvar islands, Croatia.

Bohannon brewery at Nashville, Tennessee, USA, known for Market Street Pilsener and Market Street Oktoberfest beers.

Bohemia Pilsener beer brand by Cuauhtémoc brewery, Mexico.

Böhlig vineyard at Wachenheim in Rheinpfalz region, Germany.

bois in winetasting, woody, dried out. French.

Bois Communs designated area for production of wine for distilling into Cognac. Charente, France.

Bois Ordinaires designated area for production of wine for distilling into Cognac. Charente, France.

boisson cider with water added during or after production. French.

Boizel champagne producer, Epernay, France.

Bokkøl brand name of bock beer by Aass brewery, Norway.

Bokma distillery at Leeuwarden, Netherlands. *Genever* and other spirits. Owned by Heineken.

Bolandse leading co-operative wine producer of Paarl, South Africa.

Bolgheri DOC white and *rosato* wine zone at Bolgheri, Tuscany, Italy.

Bolla major producer of red Bardolino and Valpolicella wines, and Soave white. Verona, Italy. Est 1883 as Fratelli Bolla by innkeeper Abele Bolla at Soave and still under family management in spite of sales above 1.5 million cases annually.

Bollhayes cider by Vigo, Hemyock, Somerset, England.

Bollinger *Grande Marque* champagne house at Aÿ, France. Founded 1829. Brands include non-vintage **Bollinger Special Cuvée, Bollinger RD** ('recently disgorged'), **Bollinger RD Année Rare, Bollinger Vieilles Vignes** (from vines pre-dating phylloxera and thus ungrafted on to American rootstocks).   *see label opposite* ➡

Bollinger Club informal association of Oxford undergraduates, wistfully believed to have existed in the early 20th century but in fact an invention of Evelyn Waugh in his novel *Decline and Fall*.

Bolly-Stolly mythical cocktail composed of Bollinger champagne and Stolichnaya vodka. Attributed to BBC drama serial *Absolutely Fabulous*.

Bols liqueur and spirit producer founded by Lucas Bols in Amsterdam, Netherlands, 1575. Now at Nieuw Vennep.

Bolsberry blackcurrant-based liqueur by Bols, Netherlands.

Bolscherwhisk liqueur from cherry brandy and scotch whisky by Bols, Netherlands.

Bolskaya vodka brand of Hiram Walker & Sons, Canada.

bomba inexpensive colourless grain spirit of Aegean islands.

Bombadier Celebration Ale strong ale (5.5% alc) by Charles Wells brewery, Bedford, England.

Bombarral white-wine region of western Portugal.

Bombay Cocktail. Over ice shake 3 parts East Indian Punch, 1 lemon juice. Alternatively, over ice shake 2 parts brandy, 1 dry vermouth, 1 sweet vermouth, 2 dashes curaçao, 1 dash pastis. Strain.

Bombay Sapphire Gin brand of Greenhall Whitley, Warrington, Cheshire, England.

Bombay Punch chill all ingredients beforehand, and in a large punch bowl combine 1.5 litres brandy, 1.5 litres sherry, 20cl maraschino, 20cl orange curaçao, 6 litres sparkling wine, 3 sparkling mineral water. Stir and add slices of seasonal fruit.

Bombino Bianco white grape variety for bulk-wine production, southern Italy.

Bombona glass vessel for ageing wine, Spain.

Bombshell Cocktail. Over ice stir 2 parts dry marsala, 1 tequila, 1 dash Campari, 1 dash cherry brandy. Strain and add a maraschino cherry and lemon slice.

Bommerlunder aquavit distiller, Munich, Germany.

Bommes winemaking village in AC Sauternes, France.

Bonalgue, Château wine estate of AC Pomerol, Bordeaux, France.

Bonarda red grape variety of northern Italy. Synonymous with Croatina.

Bonarda Piemontese red grape variety of Piedmont, Italy.

Bon Courage Estate wine producer of Robertson, South Africa. Noted Late Harvest wines from Gewürztraminer, Riesling and other grapes, plus many sparkling and still wines.

bonde wine-cask bung, France.

Bondi Beach Blonde lager brand of Melbourne's brewery at Strongsville, Cleveland, Ohio, USA.

Bond 7 whisky brand of Gilbeys, Melbourne, Australia.

Bone Idyll red wine from Shiraz grapes by Idyll winery, Geelong, Victoria, Australia.

Bonheur, Le wine estate in Simonsig-Stellenbosch, South Africa.

Bonnaire-Boquemont *récoltant-manipulant* champagne producer, Cramant, Champagne, France.

Bonneau, Château wine estate of AC Haut-Médoc, Bordeaux, France.

Bonneau du Martray wine producer at Pernand-Vergelesses, Burgundy, France. Wines include Corton-Charlemagne.

Bonnes Mares *Grand Cru* vineyard of AC Chambolle-Musigny, Burgundy, France.

Bonnet, Alexandre *récoltant-manipulant* champagne producer, les Riceys, Champagne, France.

Bonnet, Château wine estate of AC Entre-Deux-Mers, Bordeaux, France.

Bonnet, Château wine estate of AC St-Emilion, Bordeaux, France.

Bonnezeaux village and AC within AC Coteaux du Layon, Loire Valley, France. High quality sweet wines from Chenin Blanc grapes.

Bonnie Scot Cocktail. Over ice shake 2 parts scotch whisky, 1 Drambuie, 1 lemon juice. Strain.

Bonny Doon vineyard and winery of innovative winemaker Randall Grahm, established in 1980s at Santa Cruz, California, USA, and producing famed wines such as Le Cigare Volant and Old Telegram from Rhône grapes. Bonny Doon also has plantings of Italian grape varieties of which great things are anticipated.

Bon Pasteur, Château Le wine estate of AC Pomerol, Bordeaux, France.

Bon Secour beer (7.0% alc) by Brasserie Caulier, France.

Bon Vivant Canadian whisky brand of Canadian Gibson Distilleries. Canada.

Boodles 'British Gin' brand originally of Seagram, Canada. Now owned by Pernod-Ricard.

Boomerang Cocktail. Over ice shake 1 part rye whisky, 1 dry vermouth, 1 Swedish Punsch, 1 dash lemon juice, 1 dash Angostura bitters. Strain.

Boomsma distillery for *genever* and other spirits, Leeuwarden, Netherlands.

Boon, Frank brewer of lambic beers at Lembeek, Belgium.

Boon Rawd Brewery German-built brewery, est 1934, in Thailand. Known for Singha Lager.

Booster Cocktail. Over ice shake 1 generous measure brandy, 1 egg white, 2 dashes curaçao. Strain and grate nutmeg over glass.

Booth's High & Dry London dry gin brand of Buchanan Booth distillers est 1740 London, England.

bootleg to smuggle liquor. The term is said to date from 1889, deriving in the USA from the habit of smugglers to hide bottles of illicit drink in the upper sections of their long boots. Thus the notorious **bootleggers** of America's Prohibition of 1920–34.

Bootlegger Navy rum brand of Hall & Bramley, Aintree, Liverpool, England.

booze to drink morbidly. From Middle English *bousen* (to drink deeply), the term was in use as early as 1589 when quoted in Edmund Spenser's *Faerie Queene*: 'a bousing can, Of which he supt so oft.'

Boplaas Estate wine producer of Klein Karoo, South Africa. Table wines and renowned 'Vintage Port'.

Bopser vineyard at Gerlingen in Württemberg region, Germany.

Bordeaux city and winemaking region of SW France. About 7,000 individual estates produce wines under their own labels, including many of the greatest wines of France. The region, lying within the Gironde *département*, encompasses the vineyard sub-region of the Médoc, lying north-west of the city, and, encircling the city in clockwise order, the sub-regions of Blaye, Bourg, Libournais (including Fronsac, Pomerol, St-Emilion), Entre-Deux-Mers, Graves (including Barsac, Cérons, Pessac-Léognan, Sauternes). Quality wines of the region are classified under more than 50 distinct ACs. In the last decade of the 20th century, sales of all Bordeaux wines grew from 450 million litres to 640 million litres, accounting for 12 per cent of total national wine production of 5,300 million litres. France accounts for 60 per cent of consumption, Belgium and the Netherlands for ten per cent, Germany for eight per cent, UK for six per cent, Japan four per cent, USA three per cent.

Bordeaux AC appellation for simple red, rosé and white wines of Bordeaux, France. Reds are light and dry; whites slightly sweet unless labelled *sec* (dry).

Bordeaux bottle the standard cylindrical, square-shouldered wine bottle owes its origins to the Bordeaux region of France. The shape was introduced in the latter part of the 18th century following the discovery that quality Bordeaux wine was better conserved in glass than in barrels. The cylinder shape allowed bottles to be stacked on their sides, unlike their bulbous precursors. First patent for moulded uniform bottles was held from 1821 by British manufacturer Rickettes, and mechanised mass production was launched in Cognac, France, in the factory of glass-maker Claude Boucher in 1894. For Bordeaux wines, full-bottle capacities ranged from 68-76 cl until the imposition of a standard size of 75 cl in 1930, though this was not universally adopted in the region until enforcement by the European Community directive of 1979. The Bordeaux bottle is now standard at this size worldwide. Once a standard weight of 725 grams, the bottles are now very much lighter. Four principal standard weights are Traditional at 550 grams, Semi-Heavy at 460 grams, Standard at 400 grams and Light at 380 grams. Heavier, costlier bottles are usually reserved for wines intended for long keeping. The bottles are manufactured with a punt in the base, around which sediment collects, facilitating decanting. Lighter bottles are used for wines made for immediate consumption.

Bordeaux Clairet AC for rosé wine, Bordeaux, France.

Bordeaux Mixture traditional name for copper sulphate mixture (with chalk and water) used for treating mildew on vines.

Bordeaux Supérieur AC for generic red wines of superior quality and 10.5% alc (compared to 10% for Bordeaux AC). White wines are 11.5% (compared to 10.5%).

Border brewery at Berwick on Tweed, Northumberland, England.

Border Gold organically produced beer (6% alc) by Broughton Ales, Peeblesshire, Scotland. 'Guaranteed free of genetically modified products.'

Bordéries designated area for production of wine for distilling into Cognac. Charente, France.

Boreale beer brand of Les Brasseurs du Nord brewery, St Jerome, Canada.

Borges & Irmão port-shipping company, Vila Nova de Gaia, Portugal. Single quinta ports and vintages: 1955, 58, 60, 63, 70, 79, 82, 83, 85, 88, 89, 94, 97, 2000.

Borgogno, Giacomo & Figli leading wine producer of DOCG Barolo, Piedmont, Italy.

Borie Manoux wine company of Bordeaux, France. Owns Châteaux Baret, Batailley, Beau-Site, Belair, Domaine de L'Eglise, Haut-Bages Montpelou, Trottevieille.

Borlido brandy by Caves Borlido, Bairrada region, Portugal.

Börnchen vineyard at Harxheim in Rheinhessen region, Germany.

Bornpfad vineyard at Guntersblum in Rheinhessen region, Germany.

Borovicka strongly juniper-flavoured style of gin. Slovakia.

Borve Cairm Porter ale produced by **Borve Brew House**, Ruthven, Grampian region, Scotland.

Bory, Château second wine of Château Angludet, Bordeaux, France.

Bosanquet Estate wine producer of Happy Valley, Southern Vales, South Australia.

Boschendal Estate major wine property of Paarl, South Africa. Numerous sparkling and still wines from French grape varieties. **Boschendal Brut** is a leading South African sparkling wine brand.

see label opposite ➡

Bosco Eliceo DOC zone for red and white wines, Emilia Romagna region, Italy.

Boskeun 'Easter bunny'; a honeyed beer by De Dolle Brouwers, Belgium.

Bosom Caresser Cocktail. Over ice shake 2 parts brandy, 1 curaçao, 1 egg yolk, 1 teaspoon grenadine. Strain.

Bosq, Château Le wine estate of AC Médoc, Bordeaux, France.

Bosq, Château Le wine estate of AC St-Estèphe, Médoc, Bordeaux, France.

Boston Beer Company producer of Samuel Adams range of ales. Boston, Massachusetts, USA.

botanicals flavouring ingredients in distilled spirits.

bothy in Scottish highlands, a hovel or refuge formerly used for the operation of illicit whisky distilling. Location was determined according to proximity of a fresh water supply.

Botobolar wine estate of Mudgee, New South Wales, Australia. Renowned wines by organic methods.

botrytis cinerea benificent mould precipitating 'noble rot' in grapes, causing them to shrivel, concentrating the juice and enabling production of fine sweet wines.

Bottchen vineyard at Wittlich in Mosel-Saar-Ruwer region, Germany.

botte wine barrel. Italy.

Botticino

Botticino town and DOC for red wine mainly from Barbera grapes, Lombardy, Italy.

bottiglia bottle. Italy.

bottle Roman writer Pliny reckoned that glass was the invention of the Phoenicians as early as 700 BC. The Romans themselves used glass extensively for windows as well as for tableware, and some of their glass bottles, still filled with wine, have been unearthed by archaeologists. But glass bottles remained an expensive item until large-scale manufacturing techniques were developed in the 19th century, making the product cheap enough for the bottling of beers and cider as well as wine and spirits. The first Bordeaux wines to be sold direct from the vineyard in glass began to appear in the 17th century, in blown bulbous bottles made by a new manufacturing method that was the forerunner of modern production. In 1696, England had 39 factories making glass bottles. The first vintage ports – made to be aged in new cylindrical bottles that could be stacked one on top of the other – appeared in the following century. Otherwise, glass bottles then served as decanters, to be refilled from casks – of wine or brandy – in the home or inn.

bottle age quality characteristic important in many wines especially champagne, great red wines and vintage port.

bottle-conditioning in brewing, an aroma- and flavour-enhancing process in which beer is allowed to undergo a secondary fermentation, and period of maturation, in bottle before going on sale.

bottlescrew the original device for drawing corks from wine bottles. The first implements of this kind appeared in the early 17th century and were adaptations of the helix or 'worm' used for extracting wadding and shot from the barrels of guns when they failed to discharge.

bottle sickness condition affecting newly bottled wine. Should disappear within a month or so.

bottle stink smell from air trapped between wine and cork, released when bottle is opened. Should disperse quickly.

Bottle Stopper apple variety traditionally valued for cider-making. English.

bottom-fermenting yeast in brewing, the kind of yeast mostly used in cool-fermenting process for making lager. Once the yeast has consumed the sugars in the wort, it settles on the bottom of the vessel. In ale-brewing, top-fermenting yeasts are more usual.

Boubée, La armagnac brandy of Jean Ladevèze La Boubée, Montréal-du-Gers, France.

Bouchard Aîné & Fils *négoçiant* and wine producer (from vineyards largely in Côte Chalonnaise) in Beaune, Burgundy, France.

Bouchard Père & Fils major wine producer and *négociant* in Beaune, Burgundy, France. Owner of renowned vineyards including Clos de la Mousse and Grèves Vignes de l'Enfant Jésus in Beaune.

Boucher, Claude glass maker of Cognac, France, credited with introducing mechanised mass production of glass bottles, 1894.

Bouchet synonym for Cabernet Franc grape. St-Emilion, France.

bouchonné in winetasting, corky. French.

Boudier, Gabriel leading liqueur producer, Dijon, France.

Bouilh, Château du wine estate of AC Bordeaux Supérieur, France.

Boukha fig brandy of Tunisia, usually enjoyed locally (by infidels) mixed with cola.

Boulder Creek Brewing Company brewery known for St Severin Kölsch beer. Boulder Creek, California, USA.

Boulder Porter ale brand of Rockies Brewing Co, Boulder, Colorado, USA.

Boulevard small brewery in Kansas City, Missouri, USA.

Boundary Waters Bock and **Boundary Waters Wild Rice Beer** ale brands made with a proportion of wild rice by James Page brewery, Minneapolis, Minnesota, USA.

bouquet in winetasting, smell or 'nose' of well-developed wine. French and English.

Bourbon whiskey of the USA. See box.

Bourbon Deluxe Bourbon whiskey brand of National Distillers, USA.

Bourboulenc white grape variety of Rhône Valley, France.

Bourdieu, Château wine estate of AC Premières Côtes de Blaye, Bordeaux, France.

Bourdieu, Château Le wine estate of AC Haut-Médoc, Bordeaux, France.

Bourdy, Jean leading winemaking concern at Arlay, Jura, France. AC Côtes de Jura and Château Chalon wines and *vin jaune*.

Bourgneuf-Vayron, Château wine estate of AC Pomerol, Bordeaux, France.

Bourgogne generic AC for wines of Burgundy, France. All red and rosé wines from Pinot Noir grapes; all whites from Chardonnay.

Bourgogne Aligoté AC for white wine of Burgundy, France, made from Aligoté grapes. The wine traditionally mixed with cassis liqueur to make Kir.

Bourgogne Aligoté de Bouzeron AC for white wine from Aligoté grapes grown around the village of Bouzeron, Burgundy, France.

Bourgogne des Flandres ale brand of Timmermans brewery, Brabant, Belgium.

Bourgogne Grand Ordinaire generic wine AC of Burgundy, France. Red

Bourgogne Hautes Côtes de Beaune

and rosé wines from Gamay or Pinot Noir grapes. White wines from Chardonnay, Melon de Bourgogne, Pinot Blanc.

Bourgogne Hautes Côtes de Beaune AC for wines of 20 villages lying on the back slopes of the Côte de Beaune, Burgundy, France. Red wines from Pinot Noir grapes. Whites mainly from Chardonnay.

Bourgogne Hautes Côtes de Nuits AC for wines of 14 villages lying on the back slopes of the Côte de Nuits, Burgundy, France. Red wines from Pinot Noir grapes. Whites mainly from Chardonnay.

Bourgogne Irancy new (1998) AC for red wines from Pinot Noir grapes of village of Irancy, Auxerrois, Burgundy, France.

Bourgogne Mousseux AC for ordinary sparkling wines of Burgundy, France.

Bourgogne Passe-Tout-Grains AC for red wines made from Gamay and Pinot Noir grapes in Burgundy, France.

Bourgueil AC for red wine from Cabernet Franc and Cabernet Sauvignon grapes in Bourgueil village and surrounding vineyards in Loire Valley, France. Longer-lived wine than other Loire reds.

Bourgueneuf, Château wine estate of AC Pomerol, Bordeaux, France.

Bournac, Château wine estate of AC Médoc, Bordeaux, France.

Boursault, Château de champagne producer at Boursault, Champagne, France.

bourrut new wine in latter stages of fermentation. France.

Bouscaut, Château wine estate of AC Pessac-Léognan, Bordeaux, France. Classified *Cru Classé*.

Bousquet, Château du wine estate of AC Côtes de Bourg, Bordeaux, France.

Bouteilley, Domaine de wine estate of AC Premières Côtes de Bordeaux, France.

boutique small winery with high-quality production. Usually California, USA.

Bouvet-Ladubay sparkling wine producer and *négociant*, Saumur, Loire Valley, France

Bouzeron AC village of Côte Chalonnaise, Burgundy, France, known for high-quality Bourgogne Aligoté white wine.

Bouzy village of Montagne de Reims, Champagne, France. Champagne and red **Bouzy Rouge** still wine.

Bovard, Louis leading wine producer of Cully, Switzerland. Wines from Chasselas grapes.

Bowen Estate wine producer at Penola, Coonawarra, South Australia. Cabernet Sauvignon and Shiraz wines of repute.

Bowmore Island malt whisky distillery, Islay, Scotland. Single malts: 12-year-old and others.

Boyar, Domaine leading wine-producing company of Bulgaria. Wineries at Iambol, Shumen and Sliven. Benefiting from the privatisation of formerly state-owned Bulgarian wine production, the company has been backed by the European Bank of Reconstruction and Development. Boyars were the former aristocracy of Russia.

Boyd-Cantenac, Château wine estate of AC Margaux, Médoc, Bordeaux, France. Classified *3ème Grand Cru Classé*.   *see label opposite* ➡

Boysenberry Wheat ale by Rogue brewery, Oregon, USA.

Brachetto red grape variety of Piedmont, Italy.

Brachetto d'Acqui DOCG of Acqui Terme, Piedmont, Italy. Sparkling wines from Brachetto grapes.

Brachetto d'Asti DOC of Asti, Piedmont, Italy. Sparkling wine from Brachetto grapes.

Braes of Glenlivet Speyside malt whisky distillery, Dufftown, Scotland. Built 1973 by Seagram.

Bragdy Dyffryn Clwyd brewery at Denbigh, Denbighshire, Wales.

Braidoire, Château second wine of Château Launay, Bordeaux, France.

Brain, SA brewery in Cardiff, Wales. Ales include renowned **Brains SA Bitter** (4.2% alc) and Dark Mild.

Brainstorm Cocktail. Over ice stir generous measure Irish whiskey, 2 dashes Bénédictine, 2 dashes dry vermouth. Strain and add orange peel.

Brakspear, W H brewery at Henley-on-Thames, Oxfordshire, England. Ales include renowned Bitter.

Bramaterra DOC of village of Bramaterra, Piedmont, Italy. Red wine mainly from Nebbiolo grapes.

Brame-les-Tours, Château wine estate of AC St-Estèphe, Médoc, Bordeaux, France.

Bourbon

American liquor with the flavour of France

America's own whiskey originated in Bourbon County, Kentucky. The district was so-named in grateful tribute to the royal family of France, whence had come material assistance in America's fight for independence against Great Britain.

Traditionally, the first commercial still in Bourbon County was established in 1789 (coinciding with the outbreak of the French Revolution and the inauguration of George Washington as the first President of the United States) by the Reverend Elijah Craig at Georgetown. Revd Craig made the spirit principally from maize (corn) with a little barley and rye and marketed it as 'Kentucky Bourbon Whiskey.'

Under the US regulations (Congress 1964) Bourbon must be made from 'a mash of not less than 51 per cent corn grain'. Most Bourbon is distilled from 60 to 70 per cent maize with malt and rye and matured in scorched white-oak barrels.

Straight Bourbon is the whiskey of a single distillery. Blended straight Bourbon is a blend of whiskeys from different distilleries. Blended Bourbon is a blend of true Bourbon with other whiskeys.

Kentucky Bourbon must be distilled and aged for at least a year in the State of Kentucky. About half the Bourbon made in the USA originates in Kentucky.

Bramtôt apple variety traditionally valued for cider-making. French.

Branaire-Ducru, Château great wine estate of AC St Julien, Médoc, Bordeaux, France. Classified *4ème Grand Cru Classé*.

Branas-Grand-Poujeaux, Château wine estate of AC Moulis, Médoc, Bordeaux, France.

branco white (wine). Portugal.

Brand *grand cru* vineyard, Turckheim, Alsace, France.

Brand Brouwerij brewery at Wijke, Limburg, Netherlands. Produces **Brand-Up** Pilsner and other beers.

brandewijn light grain spirit similar to *genever*. Netherlands.

brandy spirit from wine or other fruit preparations. First recorded in English 1657, a corruption by British troops returning from Lowlands of Dutch *brantjwyn*, 'burnt wine' – the name of a spirit in fact made from grain. See *brandewijn*.

Brandy Cocktail. Over ice stir 3 parts brandy, 1 curaçao. Strain.

Brandy Blazer Cocktail. Into a chunky glass put 1 sugar lump, 1 strip lemon peel, 1 strip orange peel, 1 generous measure brandy. With care, set alight, stir with long metal spoon and strain into a fresh glass.

Brandy Cask brewery at Pershore, Worcestershire, England.

Brandy Crusta Cocktail. Over ice stir 3 parts brandy, 1 curaçao, 4 dashes lemon juice, 3 dashes maraschino, 1 dash Angostura bitters. Strain into wine glass dipped first in lemon juice then in castor sugar to frost rim, and filled with crushed ice and decorated with a spiral of lemon peel.

Brandy de Jerez appellation for brandy distilled in Jerez de la Frontera, Spain. Wine for distilling comes principally from Airén and Palomino grapes grown in regions including Cordoba, Huelva, La Mancha and Valencia – but not from the sherry-producing vineyards of Jerez itself. Jerez brandies are aged in oak butts previously used for sherry, in criadera and solera systems, as for sherry. There are three official quality classifications: **Brandy de Jerez Solera** with minimum six months ageing in solera; **Brandy de Jerez Solera Reserva** with minimum 12 months ageing in solera; **Brandy de Jerez Solera Gran Reserva** with minimum 36 months ageing in solera.

Brandy Fix in a small glass combine 2 parts brandy, 1 cherry brandy, 1 lemon juice, 2 teaspoons sugar syrup. Add crushed ice and lemon slice. Stir and serve with a straw.

Brandy Fizz over ice shake 2 parts brandy, 1 lemon juice, 1 teaspoon powdered sugar. Strain into medium glass and top with soda water.

Brandy Gump Cocktail. Over ice shake 1 part brandy, 1 lemon juice, 2 dashes grenadine. Strain.

Brandy Punch add ingredients to the punch bowl in order: juice of 15 lemons and 4 oranges, 500g sugar, 25cl curaçao, 5cl grenadine, 2 litres brandy. Chill and add 1 litre (or more) sparkling mineral water immediately before serving.

Brandy Shrub a delicious mixed drink for home bottling. To 2 litres brandy add juice of 5, and fine peel of 2, lemons. Cover and leave for 48 hours. Add 1 litre dry sherry, 1 kilo soft brown sugar. Stir, strain through muslin, and bottle.

Brandy Vermouth Cocktail. Over ice stir 3 parts brandy, 1 sweet vermouth, 1 dash Angostura bitters. Strain.

Brane-Cantenac, Château great wine estate of AC Margaux, Médoc, Bordeaux, France. Classified *2ème Grand Cru Classé*.

Branik brewery in Prague, Czech Republic. Makes popular dark lager Tmavé.

brannvin the national spirit of Sweden. Originally (14th century) 'burnt wine' but now distilled from grain and made in many variations. Also produced elsewhere in Scandinavia and Iceland.

Branntwein brandy. German.

Branscombe Vale brewery at Branscombe Seaton, Devon, England.

brantjwyn brandy. Dutch.

Braquet red grape variety of Bellet, Provence, France. Synonymous with Brachetto.

brasserie brewery. French.

Brasserie à Vapeur brewery at Pipaix, southern Belgium, founded in 1785 and so named because it has been powered by steam since 1919. Beers include spice-seasoned Saison de Pipaix.

Brassin Robespierre heady *bière de garde* made by La Choulette brewery, Hordain, France.

Bratenhöfchen vineyard at Bernkastel-Kues in Mosel-Saar-Ruwer region, Germany.

Brauerei brewery. German.

Brauhaus brewery. German.

Braunchweiger Mumme tonic beer by Nettelback brewery, Brunswick (Braunschweig), Germany. The beer was first brewed in 1492 and for centuries was a favourite in England, as evinced by Samuel Pepys's reference to a 'mum-house' in his *Diaries* of the 1660s.

Brauneberg vineyards at Bekond, at Hetzeratz, at Klotten, at Oberfell and at Rivenich in Mosel-Saar-Ruwer region, Germany.

Braune Kupp vineyard at Wiltingen in Mosel-Saar-Ruwer region, Germany.

Bräunersberg vineyard at Ottersheim in Rheinpfalz region, Germany.

Braunfels vineyard at Wiltingen in Mosel-Saar-Ruwer region, Germany.

Braunstein wine producer in Neusiedlersee Hügelland, Burgenland, Austria.

Brautrock vineyard at Bullay in Mosel-Saar-Ruwer region, Germany.

Brazil wine-producing nation, mainly from vineyards in Rio Grande do Sol province, for local consumption. Spirit production includes Pisco and rum.

Brazil Cocktail. Over ice stir 1 part sherry, 1 dry vermouth, 1 dash pastis, 1 dash Angostura bitters. Strain.

Breakfast Cocktail. Over ice shake 2 parts dry gin, 1 grenadine, 1 egg white. Strain.

Breakfast Egg Nogg Cocktail. Over ice shake 10 parts milk, 3 brandy, 1 curaçao, 1 egg. Strain.

Breaky Bottom vineyard at Lewes, East Sussex, England. Noted Seyval Blanc white wine.

Breckenridge pub-brewery at Breckenridge, Colorado, USA. Brands include Avalanche Ale; End of Trail Ale and Wheat Beer.

Breda/Oranjeboom British-owned (Allied Breweries) brewery combine at Breda, Netherlands. Products include **Breda Royal Lager**. Also Drie Hoefijzers (Three Horseshoes); Oranjeboom and Skol lagers.

Brédif, Marc wine producer at Vouvray, Loire Valley, France.

Breede River Valley winemaking region, South Africa.

Breganze DOC for red and white wines, Veneto region, Italy.

Breidecker white grape variety crossing, New Zealand.

Breinsberg vineyard at Rüssingen in Rheinpfalz region, Germany.

Breisgau winemaking sub-region (*Bereich*) of Baden region, Germany.

Bremer Weisse wheat beer brand by Beck's brewery, Bremen, Germany.

Brentano'sche Gutsverwaltung major wine estate at Winkel in Rheingau region, Germany.

Brestnik Controliran (designated quality) wine region, Bulgaria.

Brethous, Château wine estate of AC Premières Côtes de Bordeaux, France.

Brettvale brew pub (The Kings Head) at Bildeston, Ipswich, Suffolk, England.

Breuil, Château du wine estate of AC Haut-Médoc, Bordeaux, France. Classified *Cru Bourgeois Supérieur*.

Brewer's Choice dark ale by Farsons brewery, Malta.

brewing see box.

Brewmaster export ale (3.8% alc) by Whitbread, London, England.

Brewpub on the Green golf-course-adjacent pub-brewery at Fremont, California. Beers include Hole-in-One Lager.

Breysach, Eugénie *eau de vie* brand of Distillerie Wolfberger, Colmar, Alsace, France.

Brewing

a brief history

Brewing is as old as civilisation. It probably dates from the first settlements in the Fertile Crescent made possible by the retreat of the glaciers from the eastern shores of the Mediterranean around 10,000 years ago. Neolithic people discovered that the cereals found growing in river deltas could be harvested and separated from their seeds. Hunter-gatherers had stumbled on a means by which they could replant grain for a subsequent crop, instead of stripping the land and moving on. Thus were the original farms founded, communities established, and cultures cradled.

Archaeological evidence suggests that as soon as man learned to make bread, he learned to make beer. Mixed with warm water, sprouting grains attracted airborne yeasts and spontaneously fermented. By a magic no doubt attributed to the gods, the brew became an alcoholic potion which transported the drinker beyond earthly cares.

This was something to celebrate. The first civilisation with a recorded language, the Sumerians, has left us the lines of one poet, writing 5,000 years ago: 'I feel full of wonder, drinking beer in a state of bliss with joy in my heart – and liver.'

Beer production was already one of man's most-eagerly pursued activities by the time of Ancient Egypt. Pharaohs took huge supplies with them into their tombs and, it is to be hoped, into the world beyond. There is much evidence of a widespread beer trade throughout the Middle East long before the rise of Greece and Rome.

Over the millennia, however, climate change pushed cereal farming and brewing farther north, making way for grape-growing and wine production in the south. This created the pattern of alcohol-production we know today. By the time of the Romans, northern Europe was dominated by brewing and southern Europe by viticulture. The sweet and watery products of barley and wheat did not suit the Roman legions. As they colonised the north, they planted the vineyards that still prosper today in Alsace and the Rhine, Bordeaux and Burgundy.

In Britain, Germany, Denmark and the Low Countries, now the major brewing nations, beer survived the distaste of the Romans. With the breakdown of the Roman Empire and the rise of the Saxons and Vikings, a new beer culture spread, based on a recent innovation, the addition of hops to the brew. This not only introduced bitterness to the flavour, but acted as a preservative in the beer. In 14th century Britain, two distinct brewing styles emerged – ale from Old Norse *öl*, made without hops, and beer from Old German *beor*, made with hops.

During the Middle Ages, brewing skills were honed in the monasteries of Europe, the only establishments in which beer was made in quantity, supplying the needs of the monks but making sufficient, too, for town dwellers and pilgrims. Households in the countryside, from great manor to humblest hovel, all did their own brewing. At a time when piped water was scarcely known and rivers were even more polluted than they are now, beer was the principal potation of entire populations. And large numbers of the people were, indeed, almost perpetually under the influence.

The conclusion of the Middle Ages in England is marked by the end of the Wars of the Roses on Bosworth Field in 1485. With the consequent accession of the Tudor monarchs comes a turning point in British history – and beer history. By breaking the stranglehold on 'commercial' brewing held for centuries by the monasteries, Henry VIII in the 1530s made room for the privately owned taverns and breweries that have come to dominate the beer business.

Large-scale brewing had to wait until the 18th century when natural scientists finally discovered how fermentation actually worked, and in what ways the process could be manipulated. With the industrial revolution that followed came the opportunity to build large brewhouses, and railways on which to send bulk quantities of beer over great distances.

The 19th century also brought cultured yeasts, lager and continued refinements in the production and preservation of cask-conditioned beers. The 20th century ushered in mass-production, bottle-conditioned beers, canned beers and worldwide distribution.

The 21st century will no doubt bring genetically engineered beer and organic beer, therapeutic beer and non-fattening beer – and perhaps some real surprises as well.

Bricco del Drago quality red wine brand by Cascine Drago, Alba, Piedmont, Italy.

Bricco Manzoni quality red wine brand by Podere Manzoni, Monforte d'Alba, Piedmont, Italy.

Bricco Roche label of Ceretto, producer of Barbaresco and Barolo wines, Piedmont, Italy.

Brick brewery at Waterloo, Canada, with brands including **Brick Bock** and **Brick Premium Lager**.

Bricout & Koch champagne house, Avize, France. Noted for Charles Koch Brut vintage.

Bridal Cocktail. Over ice shake 2 parts dry gin, 1 sweet vermouth, 1 dash maraschino, 1 dash orange bitters. Strain.

Bridal Veil Ale beer brand of Butterfield brewery, Fresno, California, USA.

Bridane, Château La wine estate of AC St Julien, Médoc, Bordeaux, France. Classified *Cru Bourgeois*.

Brideshead Bitter beer (4.0% alc) by York Brewery, York, England. 'Brewed within the city walls of York, and developed in conjunction with Castle Howard, setting for the evergreen television series [based on Evelyn Waugh's novel] *Brideshead Revisited*.'   *see label opposite* ➡

Bridge Bitter ale brand of Burton Bridge brewery, Burton upon Trent, England.

Bridge Farm cider producer, East Chinnock, Somerset, England.

Bridgehampton winery of Long Island, New York, USA.

Bridge of Allan brewery at Stirling, Scotland. Bannockburn ale, Stirling Brig beer.

BridgePort brewery at Portland, Oregon, USA. **BridgePort Ale**, Blue Heron ale, Old Knucklehead bottled barley wine.

Brigand strong (9% alc) from top-fermenting beer by Van Honsenbrouck brewery, Belgium.

bright in winetasting, having a clarity with no trace of imperfection.

Bright Brothers international wine-making company of Australian-born Peter Bright, originally of JM Fonseca in Setubal, Portugal. Bright Bros wines are made in several locations in Europe and Latin America.

Brights Wines wine producer est 1874 in Ontario, Canada. The oldest in Ontario and the largest in Canada.

Briljant Dortmund-style beer by De Kroom brewery, Brabant, Netherlands.

Brillat Savarin armagnac brand of drinks company Tradition Brillat Savarin, France.

Brillette, Château wine estate of AC Moulis, Médoc, Bordeaux, France. Classified *Cru Grand Bourgeois*.

Brindisi DOC zone of Apulia, Italy, for red and *rosato* wines. *Riserva* reds are aged two years.

Bristol Classic Rum range of long-aged 'golden' rums from a number of Caribbean distilleries aged and bottled (at cask strength of 46% alc) by Bristol Spirits Ltd of Wickwar, Gloucestershire, England. Included are Enmore Still 12-year-old, Port Morant Still 20-year-old, Rockley Still 12-year-old, Long Pond 13-year-old, Providence Esate 10-year-old, Versailles Still 16-year-old, Monymusk Still 23-year-old.

Bristol Cream popular sweet sherry brand of Harveys of Bristol, England.

Bristol Milk style of sweet sherry originally shipped by merchants in Bristol, England.

Britannia Ales brew pub (Britannia Inn) at Upper Gornall, West Midlands, England.

British Columbia wine-producing province, Canada.

British Festival Cocktail. Over ice shake 2 parts dry gin, 1 Drambuie, 1 fresh lime juice. Strain.

British Red ale by Tampa Bay Brewing Co using English (Fuggles and Kent Goldings) hops. Tampa, Florida, USA.

British Wine 'wine' or 'sherry' made in UK from imported grape must. Not related to English wine.

Brix German system of measuring original sugars in wine grapes. A development of the brewing system devised by Balling in 1843. Also used in USA.

Broad-Leaved Norman apple variety traditionally valued for cider-making. English.

Broadoak cider producer at Clutton, Bristol, England. Brands include Black Out, Mega Gold, Moonshine, Pheasant Plucker, Red Oak, Rustic Gold.

Broad Ripple Brewing Company brewery at Indianapolis, Indiana, USA.

Broadway Brewing Company brewery in Denver, Colorado, USA, known for Flying Dog beer brands, including Flying Dog Road Dog Scottish Ale (5.5% alc) originally labelled with the legend 'Good beer, no shit' but latterly moderated to 'Good beer, no Censorship.' Other brands include Flying Dog Old Scratch Lager (4.7% alc), Flying Dog Old Tire Biter (4.7% alc), Flying Dog Snake Dog Ale (5.3% alc), Flying Dog Doggie Style Ale (5.0% alc). The beers were initially made for the Flying Dog Brew Pub in the nearby resort of Aspen, but are now more widely distributed and exported.

Broadway Smile Cocktail. Into a small glass carefully pour 1 part crème de cassis, 1 Cointreau, 1 Swedish Punsch. The parts should not mix.

Broken Hill Lager brand of South Australia Brewing, Adelaide, South Australia.

Broken Spur Cocktail. Over ice shake 4 parts white port, 1 dry gin, 1 sweet vermouth, 1 teaspoon Anisette, 1 egg yolk. Strain.

Brünnchen

Brokenwood famed wine estate at Pokolbin, Hunter Valley, New South Wales, Australia.

Brolio estate of Ricasoli family and birthplace of Chianti Classico in Tuscany, Italy. The name is the wine and grappa brand of producer Casa Vinicola Barone Ricasoli.

Brombeergeist blackberry brandy of Switzerland.

Brondelle, Château wine estate of AC Graves, Bordeaux, France.

Brontë brandy-based liqueur with honey, orange and herb flavouring. Yorkshire, England.

Bronx Cocktail. Over ice shake 3 parts dry gin, 1 dry vermouth, 1 sweet vermouth, 1 orange juice. Strain.

Bronx Empress Cocktail. Over ice shake 1 part dry gin, 1 dry vermouth, 1 orange juice, 2 dashes pastis. Strain.

Bronx Terrace Cocktail. Over ice shake 2 parts dry gin, 1 dry vermouth, 1 fresh lime juice. Strain.

Brooklyn Cocktail. Over ice shake 2 parts rye whisky, 1 dry vermouth, 1 dash Amer Picon bitters, 1 dash maraschino. Strain.

Brooklyn Brewery producer of **Brooklyn Brown** ale and **Brooklyn Lager** in New York City, USA.

Brora North Highland malt whisky distillery, Sutherland, Scotland.

Brotwasser vineyard at Kernen in Württemberg region, Germany.

Broughton Ales brewery at Broughton, Peebleshire, Scotland. Black Douglas, **Broughton Special**, The Ghillie, Greenmantle Ale (Broughton is birthplace of John Buchan, author of the novel *Greenmantle*), Merlin's Ale, Old Jock, Scottish Ale.

Broughton Pastures fruit-wine producer at Tring, Hertfordshire, England. All wines, including blackcurrant, elderberry, elderflower, ginger, made by organic methods. Mead from organic honey imported from Tanzania and Zambia.

Brouilly largest of the 10 *crus* of Beaujolais wine region, France.

Brousteras, Château de wine estate of AC Médoc, Bordeaux, France.

Broustet, Château wine estate of AC Sauternes, Bordeaux, France. Classified 2ème *Cru Classé*.

brouwerij brewery. Belgium and Netherlands.

Brown, Château wine estate of AC Pessac-Léognan, Bordeaux, France.

brown ale traditional dark-coloured ale of north-east England made at about 4.5% to 5% alc. Also, in southern England, a sweeter, weaker (3.5% or less) type of dark ale. Flemish (Belgium) brown ale (*bruin bier*) is strong at 5% upwards and ranges from dry, high-acidity, spicy styles to very sweet indeed.

Brown Betty English traditional festive drink of brown ale flavoured with brown sugar and spices and garnished with baked apples. Brandy is sometimes added.

Brown Brothers major family wine producer est 1889 at Milawa, Victoria, Australia. Red and white wines and famed Liqueur Muscat.

Brown Forman leading wine and spirit corporation of USA. Brands include Fetzer wines and Finlandia vodka.

Brown's Apple apple variety widely used in cider production. English.

brown sherry English term for ordinary sweet, dark-coloured sherry.

Brown Snout apple variety traditionally valued for cider production. English.

Brown Street pub-brewery in Napa, California, USA. Range includes a Ginseng Beer.

Broyhan Alt *Altbier* by Lindener Gilde brewery, Hanover, Germany.

Brückchen vineyard at Nierstein in Rheinhessen region, Germany.

Brückes vineyard at Bad Kreuznach in Nahe region, Germany.

Brückstück vineyard at Winningen in Mosel-Saar-Ruwer region, Germany.

Bruderberg vineyard at Mertesdorf in Mosel-Saar-Ruwer region, Germany.

Brüderberg vineyard at Langsur in Mosel-Saar-Ruwer region, Germany.

Brudersberg vineyard at Nierstein in Rheinhessen region, Germany.

Bruderschaft vineyard at Klüsserath in Mosel-Saar-Ruwer region, Germany.

Brugnon, M *récoltant-manipulant* champagne producer, Ecueil, Champagne, France.

Brugs Tarwebier wheat beer by De Gouden Boom brewery, Flanders, Belgium.

Bruichladdich Island malt whisky distillery, Isla, Scotland. Single malts: 10-year-old, 15-year-old, 20-year-old, Stillman's Dram.

Bruisyard vineyard at Saxmundham, Suffolk, England.

Brûle-Sécaille, Château wine estate of AC Premières Côtes de Bourg, Bordeaux, France.

Bruna dark, all-malt beer by Moretti brewery, Udine, Italy.

Bründelsberg vineyard at Schwegenheim in Rheinpfalz region, Germany.

Bründlmayer wine producer in Kamptal, Niederösterreich, Austria.

Brunelle Cocktail. Over ice shake 1 part pastis, 3 lemon juice, 1 teaspoon sugar. Strain.

Brunello grape variety related to Sangiovese of Tuscany, Italy.

Brunello di Montalcino DOCG red wine from Brunello grapes grown in zone around Montalcino near

Siena, Tuscany, Italy. *Riserva* wines are aged five years in oak and are among the longest-lasting and costliest wines of Italy. Leading producer is Biondi Santi.

Brünnchen vineyard at Nochern in Mittelrhein region, Germany.

Brunnenhäuschen vineyard at Westhofen in Rheinhessen region, Germany.

Brunswiek Alt bottled *Altbier* by Feldschlosschen brewery, Braunschweig, Germany.

Brusco dei Barbi brand of red wine from Brunello grapes by Fattoria dei Barbi, Montalcino, Italy.

brut 'very dry' (champagne and sparkling wine). French, but now widely used on labels of sparkling wines in Italy, Spain, Australia, USA etc.

Bual sweet style of Madeira wine from Bual grapes.

Bubeneck vineyard at Ellerstadt in Rheinpfalz region, Germany.

Bubenstück vineyard at Bingen in Rheinhessen region, Germany.

Buçaco famed winery at the Palace Hotel do Buçaco, central Portugal.

Bucel(l)as designated wine growing area near Lisbon, Portugal. White wines mainly from Arinto grapes.

Buchanan's 12-year-old blended scotch whisky by James Buchanan, London, England.

Bücher brewery at Gundelfingen, Bavaria, Germany. Bücher Organic Pilsner (5.2% alc).

Buchmayer wine producer in Weinviertel, Niederösterreich, Austria.

buchu brandy popular style of brandy of South Africa, flavoured with buchu (*Barosma betulina*) herb.

Reputed to cure digestive upsets and snake bites.

Buckingham gin brand of Hiram Walker & Sons, Canada.

Bucks Fizz pour a measure of chilled fresh orange juice into a champágne glass and top with chilled champagne or other sparkling wine.

Budels brewery in Brabant, Belgium, producing German-style **Budels Alt** plus smoky Trappist beer, Capucijn.

Bud Ice beer brand (5.2% alc) of Anheuser Busch, USA.

Budweiser since the Middle Ages, the style of golden lager produced in and around the Bohemian city of Budweis. Today, the brand name of two famous beers. **Budweiser Budvar** is made at the 1895-founded Budvar brewery in Budweis (now in the Czech Republic) and **Budweiser** lager (5.2% alc) by Anheuser-Busch, founded 1875, in St Louis, Missouri, USA. American Budweiser is the world's biggest-selling beer, with sales of around 5 billion litres annually.

Bué winemaking village of AC Sancerre, Loire Valley, France.

Buffalo Bill innovative pub-brewery at Hayward, California, USA. Operated by Bill Owens, publisher of *American Brewer* magazine.

Buffalo Bitter ale brand of Firehouse Brewery, Rapid City, South Dakota, USA.

Buffalo Brewpub pub-brewery at Williamsville, New York, USA. Known for Oatmeal Stout made annually for St Patrick's Day; also Nickel City Dark ale.

Buff Bitter 'Elixir Stomachique' liqueur, Luxembourg.

Buffy's brewery at Tivetshall St Mary, Norwich, Norfolk, England.

Bugey wine region and appellation of south-eastern France known for sparkling wines made by the *méthode traditionnelle*.

Bühl vineyard at Merdingen in Baden region, Germany.

Bukettraube white grape variety of South Africa.

Buitenverwachting new (1980s) wine estate of Constantia, Cape Town, South Africa. Already-renowned wines from several French grape varieties.

Bulgaria the major quality wine-producing nation of eastern Europe. Indigenous and imported grape varieties are grown in 20 demarcated Controliran regions of origin. Top-quality wines are labelled Reserve.

Bulldog Cocktail. In an ice-filled tumbler stir 1 part dry gin, 2 fresh orange juice. Top with ginger ale.

Bulldog pale ale brand of Courage brewers, UK.

Bulleit bourbon brand of Diageo.

Bullion Bitter ale by Old Mill brewery, Snaith, East Yorkshire, England.

Bullmastiff brewery at Cardiff, South Glamorgan, Wales.

Bulloch Lade blended scotch whisky by Bulloch Lade, Glasgow, Scotland.

Bull's Blood popular branded wine of Eger, Hungary.

Bull's Head English-style, top-fermenting bitter-ale brand of The Pumphouse brewery, Sydney, Australia.

Bull Shot Cocktail. Over ice shake 2 parts vodka, 3 chilled beef consommé. Strain.

Bully! porter by Boulevard brewery, Kansas City, Missouri, USA.

Bulmer, HP major cider producer, Hereford, England. It produces 60 per cent of all cider made in the UK. Famed brands include **Bulmer's Number 7**, Strongbow, Woodpecker. See box.

Bunnahabhain Island malt whisky distillery, Isla, Scotland. Single malt: 12-year-old.

HP Bulmer

from 4,000 gallons to 56 million

The world's largest cider producer began as a small family concern in the village of Credenhill, Hereford, England. H P (Percy) Bulmer was the youngest son of the village's rector and is said to have first pressed apples, from the family's own orchard, in 1887. The Revd Charles Bulmer was an enthusiastic amateur cidermaker himself, but it was Percy's mother who encouraged him into the trade, wisely advising him that 'food and drink never go out of fashion'.

In 1888, aged 21, Percy rented a warehouse in Hereford and contracted to buy apples in large quantities from a number of local farmers. In that first year he made 4,000 gallons. He moved immediately to a larger building and took into partnership his brother Fred, in charge of sales. Fred, a teacher, had been given a choice between two interesting job offers. The one he turned down was that of tutor to the children of the King of Siam. The post was later filled by a deserving alternative candidate, Anna Leonowens, immortalised in the musical *The King & I*.

Bulmers won its first Royal Warrant in 1911 and expanded progressively through the 20th century with annual production peaking at 56 million gallons. It is said to supply 60 per cent of all the cider consumed in Britain, and exports to 60 nations worldwide. After a difficult start to the 21st century, Bulmer was sold to Scottish & Newcastle Breweries in 2003. The Chairman until 2000 had been Esmond Bulmer, Percy's great grandson.

Bunce's brewery at Netheravon, Salisbury, Wiltshire, England. Ales include **Bunce's Benchmark** and **Bunce's Vice** (a rendering of German *Weiss* or wheat beer).

Bundesverband der Deutschen Spirituosen Industrie federation of 60 leading German distillers producing majority of all domestic spirits.

Buorren ale brand of Friese brewery, Leeuwarden, Netherlands.

Bur champagne brand of Centre Vinicole de la Champagne co-operative, Chouilly, France.

Burdon, John William former sherry *bodega* and now brand of Luis Caballero, Puerto de Santa Maria, Spain.

Burg vineyards at Heidelberg in Baden region, and at Esslingen in Württemberg region, Germany.

Burg *Grosslage* (collective vineyard) incorporating vineyards in Franken region of Germany at, respectively, Elfershausen (Engenthal), Elfershausen (Machtilshausen), Elfershausen (Trimberg), Euerdorf (Wirmsthal), Hammelburg, Hammelburg (Feuerthal), Hammelburg (Saaleck), Hammelburg (Westheim), Ramstahl.

Burgas winery est 1963 (and privatised 1998) in Black Sea region of Bulgaria. Red and white wines from (mostly) French grape varieties.

Burgberg the name of 10 individual vineyards in Germany. Region by region, as follows: in Ahr at Mayschoss; in Mosel-Saar-Ruwer at Alken, Lösnich, Traben-Trarbach, Trier; in Nahe at Dorsheim; in Rheinhessen at Ingelheim; in Württemberg at Abstatt, Ilsfield, Steinheim.

Burg Bischofsteiner vineyard at Löf in Mosel-Saar-Ruwer region, Germany.

Burg Coreidelsteiner vineyard at Klotten in Mosel-Saar-Ruwer region, Germany.

Burg Ehrenberg vineyard at Bad Rappenau in Baden region, Germany.

Bürgel vineyard at Flörsheim-Dalsheim in Rheinhessen region, Germany.

Burgenland major wine region of Austria sub-divided into four defined areas: Mittelburgenland, Neudsiedlersee, Neudsiedlersee-Hügelland, Südburgenland.

Bürgergarten vineyard at Neustadt an der Weinstrasse in Rheinpfalz region, Germany.

Burgerspital zum Heilig Geist wine estate in Franken region, Germany, said to have been founded 1319.

Burgess Cellars winery in Napa Valley, California, USA.

Burggarten vineyards at Dernau in Ahr region, and at Bad Neuenahr-Ahrweiler and Bockenheim an der Weinstrasse in Rheinpfalz region, Germany.

Burggraf vineyards at Rauenberg in Baden region, and at Alf in Mosel-Saar-Ruwer region, Germany.

Burg Gutenfels vineyard at Kaub in Mittelrhein region, Germany.

Burghalde vineyards at Weinstadt (Beutelsbach) and Weinstadt (Schnait) in Württemberg region, Germany.

Burg Hammerstein *Grosslage* (collective vineyard) incorporating vineyards in Mittelrhein region of Germany at, respectively, Bad Hönningen, Dattenberg, Hammerstein, Leubsdorf, Leutesdorf, Linz, Ohlenberg, Rheinbrohl, Unkel.

Burg Hoheneck vineyards at Dietersheim, Ipsheim and Ipsheim (Kaubenheim) in Franken region, Germany.

Burg Katz vineyard at St Goarshausen in Mittelrhein region, Germany.

Burglay vineyards at Kröv and Minheim in Mosel-Saar-Ruwer region, Germany.

Burgley-Felsen vineyard at Zell in Mosel-Saar-Ruwer region, Germany.

Burg Lichteneck *Grosslage* (collective vineyard) incorporating vineyards in Baden region of Germany at, respectively, Emmendingen, Ettenheim, Ettenheim (Altdorf), Herbolzheim, Herbolzheim (Bleichheim), Herbolzheim (Broggingen), Herbolzheim (Tutschfelden), Herbolzheim (Wagenstadt), Kenzingen, Kenzingen (Bombach), Kenzingen (Hecklingen), Kenzingen (Nordweil), Malterdingen, Ringsheim, Teningen (Heimbach), Tenningen (Köndringen).

Burgmauer vineyard at Scheich in Mosel-Saar-Ruwer region, Germany.

Burg Maus vineyard at St Goarshausen in Mittelrhein region, Germany.

Burg Neuenfels *Grosslage* (collective vineyard) incorporating vineyards in Baden region of Germany at, respectively, Auggen, Bad Bellingen, Badenweiler, Badenweiler (Lipburg), Ballrechten-Dottingen, Müllheim, Müllheim (Britzingen), Müllheim (Dattingen), Müllheim (Feldberg), Müllheim (Hügelheim), Müllheim (Niederweiler), Müllheim (Vögisheim), Müllheim (Zunzingen), Neuenburg am Rhein, Schliengen, Schliengen (Liel), Schliengen (Mauchen), Schliengen (Niedereggnen), Schliengen (Obereggnen), Sulzburg, Sulzburg (Laufen).

Burg Ravensburger Dicker Franz vineyard at Sulzfeld in Baden region, Germany.

Burg Ravensburger Husarenkappe vineyard at Sulzfield in Baden region, Germany.

Burg Ravensburger Löchle vineyard at Sulzfield in Baden region, Germany.

Burg Rheinfels *Grosslage* (collective vineyard) incorporating vineyards at St Goar and St (Werlau) in Mittelrhein region, Germany.

Burg Rodenstein *Grosslage* (collective vineyard) incorporating vineyards at Bermershei, at Flörsheim-Dalsheim, at Flörsheim-Dalsheim

(Niederflörsheim), at Mörstadt and at Ober-Flörsheim in Rheinhessen region, Germany.

Burgstall vineyards at Hagnau, Immenstaad, Immenstaad (Kippenhausen) and Markdorf in Baden region, and at Ingelfingen and Niedernhall in Württemberg region, Germany.

Burgundy great wine region of France lying between Dijon in the north and Lyon to the south. Five quality-wine areas are dominant: Chablis, Côte d'Or (incorporating Côte de Nuits and Côte de Beaune), Côte Chalonnaise, Mâconnais, Beaujolais. All wines from these regions can be described as **burgundy**.

Burg Warsberg vineyard at Wincheringen in Mosel-Saar-Ruwer region, Germany.

Burgweg *Grosslage* (collective vineyard) incorporating vineyards in Franken region of Germany at, respectively, Iphofen, Iphofen (Possenheim), Markt Einersheim, Willanzheim.

Burgweg *Grosslage* (collective vineyard) incorporating vineyards in Nahe region of Germany at, respectively, Altenbamberg, Bad Münster am Stein Ebernburg, Bad Münster am Stein Ebernburg (Münster), Duchroth, Niederhausen an der Nahe, Norheim, Oberhausen an der Nahe, Schlossböckelheim, Traisen, Waldböckelheim.

Burgweg *Grosslage* (collective vineyard) incorporating vineyards in Rheingau region of Germany at, respectively, Geisenheim, Lorch, Lorch (Lorchhausen), Rüdesheim.

Burgweg vineyards at Bodenheim and Worms in Rheinhessen region, and at Grosskarlbach, Kindenheim, Lambsheim and Weisenheim am Sand in Rheinpfalz region, Germany.

Burg Wildeck vineyard at Abstatt in Württemberg region, Germany.

Burg Windeck Kastanienhalde vineyard at Bühl in Baden region, Germany.

Burgwingert vineyards at Bruchsal (Helmsheim) and at Bruchsal (Obergrombach) in Baden region, Germany.

Burg Zähringen *Grosslage* (collective vineyard) incorporating vineyards in Rheingau region of Germany at, respectively, Denzlingen, Emmendingen, Freiburg, Freiburg (Lehen), Glottertal, Gundelfingen Wiedtal, Heuweiler, Sexau, Waldkirch.

Buring, Leo winery in Barossa Valley, Australia. Noted Riesling wines.

Burkardus beer brand of Würzburger Hofbräu brewery, Germany.

Burlington Brewing brewery at Burlington near Toronto, Canada.

Bürklin Wolf leading wine producer based in Wachenheim, Rheinpfalz region, Germany.

Burly Irish Ale beer brand of Vermont Pub & Brewery, Burlington, Vermont, USA.

Burmester, JW port producer and shipper, Vila Nova de Gaia, Portugal. Old tawnies (up to 40 years) and vintages: 1958, 60, 63, 64, 70, 77, 80, 84, 85, 89, 91, 92, 94, 97, 2000, 03.

Burn Stewart three-year-old and 12-year-old blended scotch whiskies by Burn Stewart Distillers, Glasgow,

Scotland. The company is part-owned by Angostura of Trinidad.

Burntisland brewery at Burntisland, Fife, Scotland.

Burragorang Bock beer brand of Scharer's brewery, Picton, New South Wales, Australia.

Burrow Hill cider producer, Kingsbury Episcopi, Somerset, England. Brands include bottle-fermented, single-variety ciders from Kingston Black and Stoke Red apples respectively. Also producer of Somerset Royal Cider Brandy.

Burton Ale bitter-ale brand of Ind Coope brewery, Burton upon Trent, West Midlands, England.

Burton Bitter ale by Marston brewery, Burton upon Trent, England.

Burton Bridge brewery at Burton upon Trent, England. **Burton Porter** (4.5% alc), Empire strong pale ale (7.5% alc), Tickle Brain Abbey-style beer (8% alc).

Burton upon Trent West Midlands town at the centre of England's brewing industry. Beer was probably first produced at the abbey known to have existed at Burton before the Conquest of 1066, where the quality of the Trent river water supply was clearly appreciated. Major brewers in the town today are Bass, Ind Coope and Marston, and most recently, Coors.

Burtonwood brewery at Warrington, Cheshire, England.

Burts brewery at Sandown, Isle of Wight, England.

Busca-Maniban, Château du armagnac producer, Masencome, Gascony, France.

Busch beer brand of Anheuser-Busch brewery, St Louis, USA.

Busch brewery at Limburg, Germany producing Golden Busch Pils and other beers.

Bush Beer extra-strong barley-wine-style ale produced by Brasserie Dubuisson, Pipaix, Belgium. First made in 1933, when English beers were in vogue in Belgium, this is the country's strongest ale at 12% alc. Exports to the USA are labelled Scaldis to avoid confusion with the major American beer brand Busch.

bushel in brewing, a measure of grain, originally named from a vessel with a capacity of eight gallons of water – equvalent to 42lb of malts.

Bushmills whiskey brand of Irish Distillers. **Bushmills' Black Label** and **Bushmills' Three Star** are blends from the pot stills of Old Bushmills distillery and grain whiskey of the Coleraine distillery.

Bush Ranger Cocktail. Over ice stir 1 part white rum, 1 Caperitif, 2 dashes Angostura bitters. Strain.

Bushy's brewery of the Mount Murray Brewing Co, Braddan, Isle of Man, UK.

Busslay vineyard at Erden in Mosel-Saar-Ruwer region, Germany.

Butcombe brewery at Butcombe, Bristol, England, est 1978 by Simon Whitmore with his £24,000 redundancy payment from Courage brewers. Sold 2003 but still in independent hands.

Butler Cocktail. Over ice shake 1 part dry gin, 1 pineapple juice, 3 dashes apricot brandy. Strain.

Butler, Nephew port shippers late of Vila Nova de Gaia, Portugal. Vintages: 1955, 57, 58, 60, 63, 64, 65, 67, 70, 75.

Buton brand name of Trieste Distilleries, liqueur producers, Bologna, Italy.

butt sherry barrel of 500 litres and formerly a beer barrel.

Butterfield brewery at Fresno, California, USA, produces Bridal Veil Ale and Tower Dark.

Butterknowle brewery in Newcastle-upon-Tyne, England. Brands include Black Diamond bitter and Old Ebenezer barley wine.

Butts brewery at Great Shefford, Newbury, Berkshire, England.

Buxy village of AC Montagny, Côte Chalonnaise, Burgundy, France. Cave Coopérative de Buxy is a principal wine producer.

Buyer's Own Brand term used in champagne trade for wine bottled and labelled under name of importing merchant.

Buzbag red wine from Bogazkarasi grapes, Anatolia, Turkey.

Buzet AC zone of SW France. See also Côtes de Buzet. *see label opposite* ➡

Buzzetto di Quiliano white wine from Buzzetto grapes, Quiliano, Liguria, Italy.

BVD Cocktail. Over ice stir 1 part Bacardi rum, 1 dry gin, 1 dry vermouth. Strain.

By, Château de wine estate of AC Médoc, Bordeaux, France. Classified *Cru Bourgeois*.

Bybline sweet wine of ancient Greece.

Byculla Cocktail. Over ice shake 1 part ginger liqueur, 1 curaçao, 1 port, 1 sherry. Strain.

Byron Vineyard wine producer at Santa Maria in Santa County, California, USA. Est 1984 by Byron Brown, owned since 1990 by Robert Mondavi and dedicated to producing Burgundian-style varietal wines. Quality is renowned.

Byrrh

Byrrh apéritif wine-based drink made with tree bark of Peru plus quinine and herbs. Brand of Violet Frères, Thuir, France.

Byrrh Cocktail. Over ice stir 1 part Byrrh, 1 rye whisky, 1 dry vermouth. Strain.

Byrrh Cassis Cocktail. In ice-filled glass mix 2 parts Byrrh, 1 crème de cassis. Top with soda water.

Bytown Lager beer brand of Ottawa Valley brewery, Nepean, Ontario, Canada.

C

Caballero, Luis sherry *bodega* est 1830 Puerto de Santa Maria, Spain. Sherry brands: Benito, Burdon, Troubador.

Cabanes, Château second wine of Château Toumilon, Bordeaux, France.

Cabanne, Château La wine estate of AC Pomerol, Bordeaux, France.

Cabannieux, Château de wine estate of AC Graves, Bordeaux, France.

Cabardès new AC (1998) for red and rosé wines from area north of Carcassonne, Aude, France. Principally Cabernet Sauvignon and Merlot grapes.

Cabaret Cocktail. Over ice shake 1 part dry gin, 1 Caperitif, 1 dash pastis, 1 dash Angostura bitters. Strain and add cherry.

Cabernet d'Anjou AC of Loire Valley, France for rosé wines made from Cabernet Franc and Cabernet Sauvignon grapes.

Cabernet Franc red grape variety of France. Important blended with other varieties in Bordeaux, esp. St-Emilion. Sole variety in quality red wines of Loire Valley, esp Bourgueil, Chinon, Saumur. Widely planted in northern Italy.

Cabernet Sauvignon major red grape variety of Bordeaux, now adopted widely elsewhere in France and throughout the wine-growing world. Characterized by smell and flavour of blackcurrants, makes long-lived wines in northern climates, and many of the best red wines of Australia, Chile, eastern Europe, Italy, Portugal, South Africa, Spain and USA.

Cablegram Cocktail. Over ice shake 2 parts rye whisky, 1 lemon juice, 1 teaspoon powdered sugar. Strain. Top with ginger ale.

Cabreros wine region of Avila, Spain.

Cabrière Estate wine estate est 1694, Franschhoek, South Africa. Well-known Pierre Jourdan range of wines named after Huguenot founder of estate.

Cacao mit Nuss white liqueur from chocolate, flavoured with hazel nuts. Germany.

Cacao mit Nuss white liqueur from chocolate, flavoured with almonds. Switzerland.

cachaça colourless sugar-cane spirit of Brazil.

Cacc'e Mmitte di Lucera DOC red wine, Apulia, Italy.

Cacique rum brand of Diageo. Market leader in Venezuela.

Cactus Rose Cocktail. Over ice shake 2 parts tequila, 1 Drambuie, 2 dashes lemon juice. Strain.

Cadbury apple variety traditionally valued for cider-making. English.

Cadenhead's independent bottler of single malt scotch whiskies from numerous distilleries. Based in Campbeltown and with a famous shop in the Royal Mile, Edinburgh, Scotland.

Cadet-Bon, Château wine estate of AC St-Emilion, Bordeaux, France. Classified *Grand Cru Classé* (1996).

Cadet-Piola, Château wine estate of AC St-Emilion, Bordeaux, France. Classified *Grand Cru Classé*.

Cadet-Pontet, Château wine estate of AC St-Emilion, Bordeaux, France. Classified *Grand Cru*.

Cadillac AC of Bordeaux, France, for sweet white wines.

Cadiz Cocktail. Over ice shake 1 part dry sherry, 1 blackberry liqueur, 1 equal mix Cointreau and fresh cream. Strain.

Café Bénédictine coffee liqueur including Bénédictine. France.

Café de Paris Cocktail. Over ice shake generous measure dry gin, 3 dashes Anisette, 1 teaspoon fresh cream, 1 egg white. Strain.

Café Kirsch Cocktail. Over ice shake 1 part Kirsch, 2 cold coffee, 1 teaspoon sugar, 1 egg white. Strain.

Cahors AC wine region lying along the Lot river east of city of Cahors, SW France. Red wines from Auxerrois (Malbec) grapes blended with Merlot and Tannat varieties. Once famed for 'black wine' which included concentrated product of sun-dried grapes but is no longer produced. Noted wines include Château St Didier-Parnac, Château Haut Serre, Château de Gaudou.

Caillavet, Château de wine estate of AC Premières Côtes de Bordeaux, France.

Caillou, Château wine estate of AC Sauternes, Bordeaux, France. Classified *2ème Cru Classé*.

Caillou, Château Le wine estate of AC Pomerol, Bordeaux, France.

Caillou Blanc white wine brand of Château Talbot, Bordeaux, France.

Cains Formidable Ale beer by Robert Cain & Company, Merseyside, England.

Caipirinha Cocktail. Into a tumbler place chopped chunks of fresh lime and crush along with a teaspoon of sugar. Top with crushed ice and pour in cachaca.

Cairanne winemaking village of AC Côtes du Rhône Villages, France.

Cairm Porter ale by Borve brewery, Ruthven, Scotland. Name derives from Gaelic *car meal*, meaning liquorice.

cajuada coarse spirit distilled from mash of cashew nuts, West Africa.

Cakebread Cellars winery in Napa Valley, California, USA.

Calabria winemaking region of the 'toe' of southernmost Italy, incorporating eight separate DOC zones.

calamich boiled grape must added as a sweetening agent to Marsala wine. Sicily.

Calatayud DO wine zone of Zaragoza, Spain.

Caldaro DOC zone for red wine, Trentino/Alto Adige region, Italy. Calder's beer brand of Carlsberg-Tetley brewers, UK. Known for **Calder's Premium Cream Beer**.

Caledonian Brewing Company brewery in Edinburgh, Scotland, specialising in organic ales. Brands include Edinburgh Ale (5.1% alc), 80/- Export Ale (4.1% alc), Flying Scotsman Ale (5.1% alc) and Merman ale. **Caledonian Ale** is marketed in the USA as MacAndrew's.

Calem & Filho, AA Portuguese-owned port producer and shipper, Vila Nova de Gaia, Portugal. Vintages: 1955, 58, 60, 63, 66, 70, 75, 77, 80, 82, 83, 84, 85, 86, 87, 88, 89, 90, 91, 92, 94, 97, 99, 2000, 03.

Calera Wine Co winery est 1977 at Hollister, California, USA, known for Pinot Noir reds and more recently for white wines from Chardonnay and Viognier.

California the major winemaking state of USA. Vineyards first planted late 1700s by Spanish missionaries. European vines still predominate, notably Cabernet Sauvignon, Chardonnay, Pinot Noir, Sauvignon Blanc. Principal regions include Mendocino, Monterey, Napa Valley, Sonoma Valley.

Calisay sweetened brandy-based liqueur flavoured with tree barks, principally cinchona. Mollfulleda distillery, Barcelona, Spain.

Calistoga Inn pub-brewery of Napa Valley Brewing Company at Calistoga, California, USA.

Caliterra, Viña winery with highly rated production from various vineyard regions of Chile. Est 1989.

Callestock Cider Farm cider, country wine, mead and perry producer, Penhallow, Truro, Cornwall, England.

Calmont vineyards at Bremm and at Ediger-Eller in Mosel-Saar-Ruwer region, Germany.

Calm Sea Cocktail. Over ice shake 1 part Strega, 1 rum, 1 crème de cassis, 4 dashes lemon juice, 1 egg white. Strain.

Calon, Château wine estate of AC Montagne-St-Emilion, Bordeaux, France.

Calona Wines wine-producer in British Columbia, Canada.

Calon-Ségur, Château great wine estate of AC St-Estèphe, Médoc, Bordeaux, France. Classified *3ème Grand Cru Classé*. The label is decorated with the outline of a heart in commemoration of the Marquis Nicholas-Alexandre de Ségur, who owned not just this humble property, but Châteaux Lafite, Latour and Mouton, too. The Marquis, who died in 1755, once remarked: 'I make my wine at Lafite and Latour, but my heart is at Calon.'

Caloric Punsch liqueur from sweetened and flavoured Batavia arrak. Sweden.

Caluso Passito rich dessert wine from part-dried Erbaluce grapes of Caluso, Piedmont, Italy. **Caluso Passito Liquoroso** is a fortified (16% alc) version of renowned longevity.

Calvados the apple brandy of Normandy, France. First distilled from cider in 1553 by Gilles de Gouberville. Name, adopted in 19th century, derives from the *département* of Calvados, so-called after a vessel of the Spanish Armada, the *Calvador*, which foundered on a Normandy reef in 1588. Quality spirit is blended from casks of differing maturity, typically four to ten years and up to 25 years for finest.

Calvados Cocktail. Over ice shake 2 parts calvados, 2 orange juice, 1 Cointreau, 1 orange bitters.

Calvert gin brand originally of Seagram, UK.

Calvert whiskey brand originally of Seagram, USA.

Calvet major wine *négoçiant* est 1818 Bordeaux, France.

Calvi town and wine district of the island of Corsica, France.

Calvimont, Château de wine estate of AC Graves, Bordeaux, France.

Camarate red wine brand of J M da Fonseca, Alentejo, Portugal.

Camarsac, Château de wine estate of AC Entre-Deux-Mers, Bordeaux, France.

Cambon-la-Pelouse, Château wine estate of AC Haut-Médoc, Bordeaux, France. Classified *Cru Bourgeois Supérieur*.

Cambridge Brewing Company the first brewery in the USA to produce abbey beers, starting in 1989. Brands include aromatic Tripel Threat. Boston, Massachusetts.

Camel distillery at Udine, Italy. Fogolar brandies.

Camensac, Château de wine estate of AC Haut-Médoc, Bordeaux, France. Classified *5ème Grand Cru Classé*.

Cameron Brig single grain distillery of John Haig & Co, Markinch, Fife, Scotland. Single grain: 9-year-old.

Cameron's Kick Cocktail. Over ice shake 2 parts scotch whisky, 2 Irish whiskey, 1 lemon juice, 1 Orgeat Syrup. Strain.

Cameron Strongarm beer brand (4.0% alc) of Wolverhampton & Dudley brewery, Wolverhampton, England.

Camino Real coffee liqueur by Montini, Mexico.

Campania historic vineyard region, Italy.

Campari Italian herbal bitters flavoured with bitter-orange peel, Chinese rhubarb, quinine and other herbs and distinctively coloured with cochineal. The invention of Gaspare Campari, whose name, from Italian *campi* for fields, denotes his rural birthplace. He opened an eponymous café and liqueur shop in Milan and is said to have devised the famous red drink to mark the birth of his son Davide, not long before Gaspare's death in 1882. Davide introduced the popular single-serve, pre-mixed Campari-Soda in 1932. In 2002 the company introduced Campari Mixx, a ready-to-drink product including grapefruit flavouring.

Campbeltown Loch ten-year-old blended scotch whisky by J & A Mitchell, Campbeltown, Scotland.

Campden Cocktail. Over ice shake 2 parts dry gin, 1 Cointreau, 1 Lillet. Strain.

Campidano di Terralba DOC zone for red wine, Sardinia, Italy.

Campo de Borja DO wine region of Aragon, Spain.

Campo del Lago noted red *vino da tavola* from Merlot grapes by Villa dal Ferro, Veneto region, Italy.

Campo Fiorin rich red wine by Masi of Valpollicella, Veneto, Italy.

Campo Viejo major *bodega* of Rioja, Spain. Renowned crianza, reserva and gran reserva wines. Owned by Allied Domecq, UK.

CAMRA the Campaign for Real Ale. Consumer group founded in Britain in 1971 to combat the threat posed to cask-conditioned ales by conglomerate brewers intent on centralised production of 'keg' beers. The Campaign has helped to save many smaller breweries and ales from extinction, and continues actively to encourage production and consumption of natural beers.

Camus brandy producer of Cognac, France. Est 1863. Célébration, Napoléon, XO.

canada measure of port wine equal to 2.1 litres. Formerly the recommended daily port ration for one man. Portugal.

Canada well-established brewing and distilling nation and now emerging as a producer of quality wines. Vineyards are concentrated in British Columbia and Ontario.

Canada Cocktail. Over ice stir 1 part of Canadian rye whisky, 2 dashes Cointreau, 1 dash Angostura bitters. Strain.

Canadian Cherry Cocktail. Over ice shake 3 parts Canadian rye whisky, 1 cherry brandy, 1 equal mix lemon and orange juice. Strain.

Canadian Club whisky brand of Hiram Walker & Sons, Canada.

Canadian Cocktail. Over ice shake 3 parts curaçao, 1 rum, 1 lemon juice, 1 teaspoon powdered sugar. Strain.

Canadian Double Distilled whisky brand of Canadian Distillers, Canada.

Canadian Mist whisky brand of Canadian Mist Distillers, Collingwood, Ontario, Canada.

Canadian whisky whisky made in Canada, typically distilled from seven parts corn to one part rye.

Canadian Whisky Cocktail. Over ice shake 1 generous measure rye whisky, 2 dashes Angostura bitters, 2 teaspoons Gomme Syrup. Strain.

Canaiolo black grape variety diminishingly included in chianti. Italy.

Canandaigua Canadian drinks company with many brands world-wide, including Paul Masson wines of California, USA. In UK, brands include Babycham perry, Blackthorn, Gaymer and Taunton cider and British wines QC and Stone's. Now part of Constellation Wines.

Canard-Duchêne *Grand Marque* champagne house est 1868, Rilly-la-Montagne, France.

Canary Islands formerly known (16th-17th centuries) for **canary wine** and sack, now for simple reds and whites from volcanic vineyards. Spain.

Candia dei Colli Apuani DOC zone for white wine, Tuscany, Italy.

Candolini grappa producer, Friuli, Italy.

cane double-distilled neutral spirit from molasses, South Africa.

Cane End vineyard at Reading, Berkshire, England.

Canet, Château wine estate of AC Entre-Deux-Mers, Bordeaux, France.

Cannabia beer (5.0% alc) by Kronenbrauerei brewery, Gundelfingen, Bavaria, Germany. 'The first and original hemp beer' it is brewed with organic hemp and sold with Home Office approval in the UK.

cannellino style of sweet Frascati wine. Italy.

Cannonau di Sardegna DOC for red wines of Cannonau grape, Sardinia, Italy.

Canon (Horeau), **Château** wine estate of AC Canon-Fronsac, Bordeaux, France.

Canon (Moueix), **Château** wine estate of AC Canon-Fronsac, Bordeaux, France.

Canon, Château great wine estate of AC St-Emilion, Bordeaux, France. Classified 1er *Grand Cru Classé*.

Canon-de-Brem, Château wine estate of AC Canon-Fronsac, Bordeaux, France.

Canon-la-Gaffelière, Château wine estate of AC St-Emilion, Bordeaux, France. Classified *Grand Cru Classé*.

Canon-Moueix, Château wine estate of AC Canon-Fronsac, Bordeaux, France. Formerly Château Pichelèbre.

Cannon Royal brewery at Fruiterer's Arms, Uphampton, Worcestershire, England.

Canorgue, Château de la distinguished wine estate of AC Côtes du Luberon, Provence, France. Red wine from blend of Cabernet Sauvignon, Grenache, Merlot, Mourvèdre and Syrah grapes. Dry white from Bourboulenc, Clairette and Sauvignon.

Cantebeau, Château second wine of Château La Louvière, Bordeaux, France.

Cantegril, Château second wine of Château Doisy-Daëne, Bordeaux, France.

canteiros in Madeira, the storing of wine casks in warm, moist cellar conditions over long periods for ideal maturation. Portuguese.

Cantemerle, Château great wine estate of AC Haut-Médoc, Bordeaux, France. Classified *5ème Grand Cru Classé*.

Cantenac village of the commune of Margaux in Bordeaux, France, in which famed châteaux including Brane-Cantenac, d'Issan and Palmer are situated.

Cantenac-Brown, Château wine estate of AC Margaux, Médoc, Bordeaux, France. Classified *3ème Grand Cru Classé*.

Canterayne wine co-operative of AC Haut-Médoc, Bordeaux, France.

Canterbury ale brand of Pacific Western brewery, British Coumbia, Canada.

Canterbury southernmost wine region of New Zealand.

Cantillon, Brasserie small brewery at Anderlecht, Brussels, Belgium, producing lambic beers including Lambic Grand Cru and a raspberry-cherry fruit beer, Rosé de Gambrinus.

cantina 'cellar' in Italian. Commonly precedes wine brands of family producers.

cantina sociale wine co-operative, Italy.

cantina vinicola wine merchant or producer. Italy.

Can-y-Delyn whisky-based liqueur 'inspired by the mountains and valleys of Wales' by Hallgarten, London, England.

Caol Ila Island malt whisky distillery est 1846, Port Askaig, Islay, Scotland. Single malts: 12-, 15-, 17-, 18-year-old. Name is pronounced (approximately) carl-eela.

Capa Branca bagaceira by Sandeman, Oporto, Portugal.

Capa Negra brandy by Sandeman, Jerez de la Frontera, Spain.

Caparina Cocktail. Chop half a fresh lime into 4 pieces and place in a tumbler; add 2 teaspoons sugar; gently crush fruit with a spoon; add 1 part cachaca and crushed ice. Stir.

Capbern-Gasqueton, Château wine estate of AC St-Estèphe, Médoc, Bordeaux, France. Classified *Cru Grand Bourgeois Exceptionnel.*

Cap Bon vineyard region of coastal Tunisia known for Muscat wines.

Cap-de-Mourlin, Château wine estate of AC St-Emilion, Bordeaux, France. Classified *Grand Cru Classé.*

Cape Cocktail. Over ice shake 1 part dry gin, 1 Caperitif, 1 orange juice. Strain.

Cape Bay popular export wine range of Cap Bay Wines, West Somerset, South Africa.

Cape Cellars wine brand of KWV, South Africa.

Cape Cavendish brand of 'sherry' by KWV, South Africa.

Cape Mentelle vineyard in Margaret River, Western Australia.

Cape Riesling white grape variety, South Africa. Synonymous with Cruchen Blanc.

Caperdonich Speyside malt whisky distillery est 1897, Rothes, Morayshire, Scotland.

Caperitif wine and spirit based herbal-flavoured apéritif of South Africa.

Capetown Cocktail. Over ice stir 1 part rye whisky, 1 Caperitif, 3 dashes curaçao, 1 dash Angostura bitters.

Capezzana wine estate in Tuscany, Italy, known for Chianti and renowned Ghiaie della Furba.

Capital small brewery at Middleton, Wisconsin, USA. Known for Gartenbrau Weizen wheat beer and several lager brands.

capiteux in winetasting, high in alcohol. French.

Cap-Léon-Veyrin, Château wine estate of AC Listrac, Médoc, Bordeaux, France. Classified *Cru Bourgeois.*

Capri island and DOC wine region of Campania, Italy.

Capriano del Colle DOC wine region of Lombardy, Italy.

Capricornia tropical fruit liqueur, Australia.

Capsule Congé French duty stamp appearing on wines for inland sale.

Captain Morgan Jamaican dark spiced rum brand. Commemorates Welsh-born privateer Sir Henry Morgan (1635–88), appointed Lieutenant-Governor of Jamaica, 1674. Made in Puerto Rico, the former Seagram brand was sold to Diageo, 2002.

Captain Smith bottle-conditioned ale (5.2% alc) by Titantic Brewery, Stoke-on-Trent, England. Commemorates Edward J. Smith, Master of the SS *Titanic*, who went down with his ship following her collision with an iceberg off Newfoundland on 15 April 1912.

Capucijn abbey ale brand of Budels brewery, Netherlands.

Capucine Cafe Creme coffee liqueur brand of Halewood International, Huyton, Merseyside, England.

Cara Claudia Cocktail. Over ice shake 1 part tequila, 2 orange juice. Strain.

carafe wine vessel. In catering, 'carafe' wine is that sold identified only as house wine.

Caramany village AC of Côtes du Roussillon, France. Red wines.

caramayole traditional flask-shaped wine bottle of Chile.

Caramino heavy red-wine brand of Luigi Dessaliani at Faro in Piedmont, Italy.

Cara Sposa Cocktail. Over ice shake 1 part Tia Maria, 1 Cointreau, 1 fresh cream.

caratello barrel of up to 50 litres for vinifying and ageing wine. Italian.

Carbine Stout dry stout brand of Castlemaine brewery, Brisbane, Australia.

Carboj wine brand of Sciacca, Sicily, Italy.

carbonation in brewing, cider-making or winemaking, the appearance of a sparkle from carbon dioxide. Created either naturally during fermentation or by an injection process.

carbon dioxide (CO_2) a natural product of fermentation. In brewing and winemaking, it may be kept in contact with the fermenting matter to introduce a sparkle. It may also be introduced artificially.

Carbonnel armagnac brand of St Vivant, Condom, France.

Carbonell Montilla wine producer, Cordoba, Andalucia, Spain.

Carbonnieux, Château wine estate of AC Pessac-Léognan, Bordeaux, France. Classified *Cru Classé*.

carboy large glass or plastic vessel supported by a basketwork frame used for carrying wine.

Carcanieux, Château wine estate of AC Médoc, Bordeaux, France.

Carcavelos fortified white wine of central Portugal.

Cardaillan, Château du second wine of Château de Malle, Bordeaux, France.

Carden Park vineyard at Malpas, Cheshire, England.

Cardenal Cisneros brandy by Sánchez Romate, Jerez de la Frontera, Spain.

Cardenal Mendoza renowned brandy matured for 20 years in *oloroso* sherry casks by Sánchez Romate, Jerez de Frontera, Spain.

Cardeneu, Château wine estate of AC Fronsac, Bordeaux, France.

Cardhu Speyside malt whisky distillery est 1824, Upper Knockando, Scotland. Single malt: 12-year-old.

Cardinal-Villemaurine, Château wine estate of AC St-Emilion, Bordeaux, France. Classified *Grand Cru*.

Cardonne, Château La wine estate of AC Médoc, Bordeaux, France. Classified *Cru Grand Bourgeois*.

Carema DOC zone for red wine from Nebbiolo grapes, Piedmont, Italy.

Caribbean Twist cooler brand of Halewood International, Huyton, Merseyside, England.

Carib brewery at Champs Fleurs, Trinidad, West Indies.

Caribe Cocktail. Over ice shake 2 parts rum, 2 orange juice, 1 lemon juice, 2 teaspoons sugar.

Carib Lager domestic and export lager brand, Trinidad.

Carignan black grape variety widely planted in southern France. Synonymous with Cariñena.

Carignan Blanc white grape variety, southern France.

Carignane black grape variety, California, USA. Synonymous with Carignano.

Carignano black grape variety of Italy. Synonymous with Carignan.

Carignano del Sulcis DOC for red and *rosato* wines from Carignano grapes in Sulcis and isles of Sant' Antonio and San Pietro, Sardinia, Italy.

Cariñena village, DO and black grape variety of Aragón, Spain.

Carles, Château de wine estate of AC Fronsac, Bordeaux, France.

Carleton Tower Canadian whisky brand of Hiram Walker & Sons, Canada.

Carl G Platin Extra Fin brand of arrak-punsch liqueur. Göteborg, Sweden.

Carling O'Keefe major Canadian brewing company known for **Carling** (formerly **Carling Black Label**) lager brand. Along with its subsidiary, Ireland's Beamish & Crawford stout brewer, Carling was formerly owned by Foster's of Australia but was purchased by Adolph Coors 2001. In UK Carling is the leading lager brand (2004) and brewed at Coors' own purpose-built brewery at Burton on Trent.

Carlonet renowned red wine brand of Uitkyk Estate, Stellenbosch, South Africa.

Carlos I and **Carlos III** brandies by Pedro Domecq, Jerez de la Frontera, Spain.

Carlsberg international brewing company based in Copenhagen, Denmark, with brands licensed for production in many nations. World-renowned beers include **Carlsberg Lager Beer** (labelled **Carlsberg Hof** for some markets); **Carlsberg '68** (labelled Elephant for some markets); **Carlsberg Special Brew** (also known as **Carlsberg Special Strong Lager**). Domestic brands include seasonal **Carlsberg Påske Bryg 1847** (Easter) and **Gamle Carlsberg Special Dark** lager (Christmas). The company was founded in 1845 by Jacob Christian Jacobsen. It was at the brewery in 1883 that scientist Emil Hansen first isolated the single-cell yeast that made fully controlled fermentation possible. Bottom-fermenting yeast was thenceforth described as *Saccharomyces carlsbergensis*.

Carlsberg bitter-tasting herbal liqueur of Czech Republic and Germany.

Carlsberg vineyard at Veldenz in Mosel-Saar-Ruwer region, Germany.

Carlsberg-Tetley brewing company of Bass and Carlsberg, UK.

Carlsfelsen vineyard at Palzem in Mosel-Saar-Ruwer region, Germany.

Carlshamma brand of arrak-punsch liqueur. Sweden.

Carlsheim white wine brand of Uitkyk Estate, Stellenbosch, South Africa.

Carlton & United Breweries Australian brewer based in Melbourne, Victoria, with other production centres including the Tooth brewery at Sydney, New South Wales. Brands include notable Abbots Double Stout, **Carlton Draught**, and Victoria Bitter. Owned by Foster's Brewing of Australia.

Carmarthen brewery at Llandello, Carmarthenshire, Wales.

Carmel AVA of Monterey County, California, USA.

Carmel brand of kosher wines of Société Coopérative Vigneronne des Grandes Caves, Israel.

Carmeline green herb liqueur of Bordeaux, France. Now extinct.

Carmel Valley AVA of Monterey County, California, USA.

Carmenère historic black grape variety of Bordeaux, France. Now rare in Europe but increasingly widely planted in Latin America.

Carmes-Haut-Brion, Château Les wine estate of AC Pessac-Léognan, Bordeaux, France.

Carmignano DOC red wine from Sangiovese and some Cabernet Sauvignon grapes, Tuscany, Italy.

Carmine black grape variety crossing, California, USA.

Carnegie Porter renowned top-fermenting beer of Pripps brewery, Stockholm, Sweden.

Carnelian black grape variety crossing, California, USA.

Carneros wine zone and AVA, California, USA.

Carneros, Domaine winery est 1989 in Napa Valley, California, USA, by Champagne Taittinger and Kobrand Corp. 'Méthode Traditionelle' sparkling wines and still wines.

Carneros Creek winery of Napa County, California, USA.

Carolans 'Irish Cream Liqueur' brand of C&C International, Dublin, Eire.

Caroni rum producer, Jamaica.

Caronne-Ste-Gemme, Château wine estate of AC Haut-Médoc, Bordeaux, France. Classified *Cru Grand Bourgeois Exceptionnel*.

Carpenè Malvolti distiller est 1868 at Conegliano, Veneto, Italy. Brandy and grappa.

carrageen species of seaweed or 'Irish Moss' used in fining beer.

Carras, Château wine estate in Khalkidhiki, Greece.

Carrascal vineyard district of *albariza* soil, Jerez de la Frontera, Spain.

Carré, Lucien *récoltant-manipulant* champagne producer, Vertus-Marne, Champagne, France.

Carrelles, Château Les wine estate of AC Côtes de Blaye, Bordeaux, France.

Carrington Canadian whisky brand of Carrington Distillers, Canada.

Carrion apple variety traditionally valued for cider-making. English.

Carrol Cocktail. Over ice stir 2 parts brandy, 1 sweet vermouth. Strain and add pickled walnut (or cocktail onion).

Carr Taylor Vineyards

Carr Taylor Vineyards wine producer at Hastings, Sussex, England. Est 1974. Sparkling and still wines.

Carruades de Château Lafite second wine of Château Lafite-Rothschild, Bordeaux, France.

Carstairs whiskey brand originally of Seagram, USA.

Carta Blanca beer brand of Cuauhtémoc brewery, Mexico.

Cartaxo undesignated wine region of Ribatejo, Portugal.

Carteau-Côtes-Daugay, Château wine estate of AC St-Emilion, Bordeaux, France. Classified *Grand Cru*.

Carte et Le Châtelet, Château La wine estate of AC St-Emilion, Bordeaux, France. Classified *Grand Cru Classé*.

Cartier wine and liqueur producer at Niagara Falls, Ontario, Canada.

Cartillon, Château du wine estate of AC Haut-Médoc, Bordeaux, France.

Cartmel brewery at Cartmel, Cumbria, England.

Caruso Cocktail. Over ice shake 1 part dry gin, 1 dry vermouth, 1 crème de menthe. Strain.

Casa Alta Vino Nuevo red 'nouveau' wine of San Isidro co-operative, Jumilla, Spain.

Casabello Wines major winery of British Columbia, Canada.

Casablanca designated wine region of Morocco comprising appellations of Doukkla, Sahel and Zennata.

Casablanca coastal wine region of Chile, south of Valparaiso.

Casablanca, Viña wine producer of Lontué region, Chile. Quality varietal wines under **Casablanca White Label** brand, and Cabernet Sauvignon, Chardonnay and Sauvignon Blanc under **Casablanca Grey Label**.

Casablanca Cocktail. Over ice shake 2 parts vodka, 1 advocaat, 1 equal mix lemon and orange juice, 1 teaspoon Galliano. Strain into an ice-filled tumbler.

Casa Blanca Cocktail. Over ice shake 1 part rum, 2 dashes each of Cointreau, maraschino, fresh lime juice. Strain.

Casa da Calçada vinho verde producer, Amarante, Portugal.

Casa da Tapada vinho verde producer, Fiscal, Portugal.

Casa de Cabanelas vinho verde producer, Penafiel, Portugal.

Casa de Compostela vinho verde producer, Requião, Portugal.

Casa de Penela vinho verde producer, Adaúfe, Portugal.

Casa de Santa Leocádia vinho verde producer, Geraz do Lima, Portugal.

Casa di Vila Nova vinho verde producer, Santa Cruz do Douro, Portugal.

Casa do Douro port-wine grape-growers' association, Douro Valley, Portugal.

Casa do Landeiro vinho verde producer at Carreira, Portugal.

Casa dos Cunhas vinho verde producer at Quintado Belinho, Portugal.

Casa Girelli grappa producer, Italy.

Casa La Teja red and white wines by Campo Nuestro Padre Jesus Perdón co-operative, La Mancha, Spain.

Casalbaio wine producer at Rionero, Puglia, Italy. Brands include Allora, Colori, La Piazza.

Casal Garcia vinho verde by Aveleda, Penafiel, Portugal.

Casal do Monteiro noted red and white wines of Casa Agricola Herdeiros de Dom Luís de Margaride, Ribatejo, Portugal.

Casalinho vinho verde brand of Caves do Casalinho, Minho region, Portugal.

Casa Lo Alto wine estate of Utiel-Requena, Valencia, Spain.

Casal Thaulero co-operative producing Montepulciano red wines and Trebbiano whites, Abruzzi, Italy.

Cascade Brewery Australia's oldest, founded 1824, in Tasmania. Beers include **Cascade Draught; Cascade Export Stout; Cascade Premium Lager.**

cascina farmhouse. Italian. Describes an estate producing wine.

Casco Viejo tequila by La Arandina, Jalisco, Mexico.

Casillero del Diablo popular red wine brand of Concha y Toro, Maipo, Chile.

Casino Cocktail. Over ice stir 1 generous measure of gin, 2 dashes lemon juice, 2 dashes orange bitters, 2 dashes maraschino. Add cherry.

cask-conditioned in brewing, a beer which undergoes a secondary fermentation – becoming naturally carbonated – in the barrel.

Cassagne-Haut-Canon,   Château wine estate of AC Canon-Fronsac, Bordeaux, France.

Cassaigne, Château de armagnac producer, Condom, Gascony, France.

casse darkening or haziness in wine, commonly due to contamination. French.

Cassemichère, Château de la leading wine estate of AC Muscadet, Loire Valley, France.

Cassegrain winery in Hastings Valley, New South Wales, Australia.

Cassevert, Château second wine of Château Grand-Mayne, Bordeaux, France.

cassis blackcurrant. See crème de cassis, liqueur de cassis.

Cassis AC of the Côte d'Azur, Provence, France. Rosé and white wines. Vineyards are threatened by resort development.

Castaigne armagnac brand of St Vivant, Condom, France.

Castarède leading Armagnac house at Pont-de-Bordes, France. Armagnacs exclusively from Bas-Armagnac district: Domaine de Maniban VSOP, Nismes-Delclou and vintages back to 1900.

Castegens, Château wine estate of AC Côtes de Castillon, Bordeaux, France.

Castéja armagnac brand of Emile Castéja of Borie-Manoux wine firm, Bordeaux, France.

Castelain, Brasserie brewery at Bénifontaine near Wingles in northern France. Produces *bières de garde* under the Ch'Ti label.

Castel Daniels wine brand of Achaia Clauss, Patras, Greece.

Castel del Monte DOC for red, *rosato* and white wines, Apulia, Italy.

Castellane, De champagne house est 1890, Epernay, France.

Castellani leading wine producer in Tuscany, Italy. Campomaggio chianti, Villa Teseo 'Supertoscana' and other brands.

Castellberg vineyards at Ballrechten-Dottingen, at Ihringen and at Vogtsburg in Kaiserstuhl in Baden region, Germany.

Castell de Vilarnau *cava* brand of Sant Sadurni d'Anoia, Penedes, Spain.

Casteller DOC red wine of Trentino-Alto Adige, Italy.

Castelli Romani inexpensive red, *rosato* and white wines of Rome produced in the hill vineyards south-east of the city.

castello 'castle' in Italian. Broadly equivalent to, but less commonly used than, French château to signify a wine estate with a castle or country house.

Castello di Volpaia leading wine estate of DOCG Chianti Classico, Tuscany, Italy.

Castle Cary Cocktail. Over ice stir 1 part vodka, 1 sloe gin. Strain into a shot glass.

Castle Dip Cocktail. Over ice stir 1 part apple brandy, 1 white crème de menthe, 3 dashes pastis.

Castelot, Château Le wine estate of AC St-Emilion, Bordeaux, France. Classified *Grand Cru*.

Castel San Michele DOC for red wine made by San Michele all'Adige agricultural college, Trentino-Alto Adige, Italy.

Castéra, Château wine estate of AC Médoc, Bordeaux, France. Classified *Cru Bourgeois*.

Castillo rum brand, Mexico.

Castle Dip Cocktail. Over ice shake 1 part apple brandy, 1 white crème de menthe, 3 dashes pastis. Strain.

Castle Lager leading beer brand, South Africa.

Castlemaine-Perkins Brewery brewer in Brisbane, Queensland, Australia of **Castlemaine XXXX** and other brands including Carbine Stout. Castlemaine XXXX is brewed under licence in the UK by Allied-Domecq.

Castle Rock brewery in Nottingham, England.

Catalina Cocktail. Over ice shake 2 parts tequila, 1 peach brandy, 1 blue curaçao, 2 lemon juice, 2 fresh lime juice. Strain.

Catalunya generic Catalan Denominacio d'Origen (since 1999) wine-producing region of Spain. Incorporates nine distinct sub-regions.

Catamount brewery at White River Junction, Vermont, USA. Brands include **Catamount Amber; Catamount Gold; Catamount Porter**.

Catarratto white grape variety, Sicily, Italy. Marsala wine.

Catawba red grape variety indigenous to North Carolina, USA.

Catena, Nicholas leading wine producer of Mendoza region, Argentina.

Cathedral Cellars premium wine brand of KWV, South Africa.

Catherine's Ale beer by Traquair House Brewery, Scotland, named for Lady Catherine Maxwell Stuart in 1985 by her father, late laird of Traquair.

Cat's-Eye Cocktail. Over ice shake 4 parts dry gin, 3 dry vermouth, 1 Cointreau, 1 Kirsch, 1 lemon juice, 1 water. Strain.

cat's pee not-entirely jocular winetasting term describing the smell of white wine, particularly from Sauvignon grapes, with harsh acidity. Incredibly, the name **Cat's Pee on a Gooseberry Bush** was briefly adopted as a brand for Gisborne Sauvignon Blanc wine by Coopers Creek winery, New Zealand. The wine included Semillon.

Cattier *récoltant-manipulant* champagne producer, Chigny-les-Roses, Champagne, France.

Catto's blended scotch whisky brand of James Catto, est 1861 Aberdeen, Scotland. **Catto's Rare Old Scottish Highland Whisky** and **Catto's 12 Years Old**.

Catz Dutch bitters producer, Netherlands.

cava sparkling wine of Spain as defined by DO – made by 'champagne method' with production and best-quality centred on Penedés region.

Cavallino Rosso brandy by Martini & Rossi, Turin, Italy.

cave cellar. French.

cave coopérative wine growers' co-operative for members lacking their own production and marketing facilities. France.

Caveau *gueuze* beer by Timmermans brewery, Belgium.

Cavendish Cape 'sherry' brand, South Africa.

Cave Spring Cellars wine producer at Jordan, Ontario, Canada.

caviste 'cellarman'. French.

Cayla, Château wine estate of AC Premières Côtes de Bordeaux, France.

Caymana 'cream liqueur' brand of IDV, UK.

Caymus winery of Napa Valley, California, USA. Known for Cabernet Sauvignon and Pinot Noir reds and popular Liberty School wines.

Cayo Verde spirit-based lime liqueur, USA.

Cayrou, Château de wine estate of AC Cahors, SW France.

Cazebonne, Château wine estate of AC Graves, Bordeaux, France.

Cecubo red wine of Caccabum, Gaeta, Latium, Italy. Revival of the name (but not, thankfully, the syle of famed sweet **Cecubus** wine of ancient Rome.

cedarwood smell characterising the presence of Cabernet Sauvignons in fine red wines of Bordeaux, France.

Cederlunds Torr Caloric brand of arrak-punsch liqueur. Sweden.

Celebrated Pottsville Porter bottom-fermented beer by Yuengling brewery, founded 1829 and the oldest in the USA, at Pottsville, Pennsylvania.

Celebration Ale popular beer brand name of, among many others, Morrell's brewery, Oxford, England; Sierra Nevada Brewing Co, California, USA and Whitbread plc, owner of the Exchange Brewery, Sheffield, Yorkshire, England, which had a special extra-strong (11.5% alc) Celebration Ale made there in 1992 to mark Whitbread's 250th anniversary and then closed the brewery.

Celis Brewery producer of **Celis White** wheat beer and other ales at Austin, Texas, USA.

cellar for wine, ideally, a dark, mildly humid, tranquil and securely lockable underground space with a constant temperature of 10°C.

Cellatica DOC for light red wines, Cellatica, Lombardy, Italy.

Celtia lager brand, Tunisia.

Celtic Ale beer brand of Bert Grant brewery, Yakima, Washington, USA.

Celtic Premium Pils Lager brand of Federation Brewery, Scotland.

Cencibel regional name for Tempranillo grape, La Mancha, Spain.

Centenario brandy by Fernando A de Terry, Puerto da Santa Maria, Andalucia, Spain.

Centerbe mint liqueur allegedly compouned from a hundred herbs (thus the name). Abruzzi mountains, Italy. Synonymous with Mentuccia.

Centgericht vineyard at Heppenheim in Hessische Bergstrasse region, Germany.

Centgrafenberg vineyard at Bürgstadt in Franken region, Germany.

Cento Años tequila *reposado* brand of Tequila Sauza, Jalisco, Mexico.

Central Valley main production area for bulk wine, California, USA.

centrifuge in winemaking, a rotating device for separating liquid from grape must.

Centurion grape-variety crossing of Cabernet Sauvignon and Carignan. California, USA.

Centurion Best beer brand of Hadrian brewery, Northumberland, England.

Centurion's Ghost Ale 'Special Millennium Brew' by York Brewery, York, England. 'York is home to literally hundreds of ghosts, none stranger than the phantom Roman Legion doomed to patrol the city for all eternity. The ghostly soldiers, dead for 2,000 years, terrified a local man when they marched silently out through a wall in his cellar . . . The haunting taste of Centurion's Ghost Ale can now be sampled by us all.'

Century of Malts scotch whisky brand of Pernod-Ricard.

cépage grape variety. The variety or varieties selected for making a wine. French.

cépage améliorateur grape variety planted in a non-traditional region for blending with indigenous varieties to improve local wines. French.

Cephalonia wine-producing island of Ionian sea, Greece. Mavrodaphne, Muscat and Robola wines.

Cerasella cherry liqueur, Abruzzi mountains, Italy.

Cerasella di Fra Guiepro cherry and fruit liqueur, Pescara, Italy.

Cerasuolo light, cherry-red wine style of Italy.

Cerasuolo di Vittoria DOC for light, cherry-red wine of Vittoria, Sicily, Italy.

Cerdon VDQS wine district of Savoie, France. Still and sparkling wines.

Ceres Danish brewery producing **Ceres Pilsner** and many other brands.

Ceretto renowned family producer of Barbaresco and Barolo wines, Piedmont, Italy. Also renowned for spirits Grappa di Dolcetto and Grappa di Nebbiolo.

Cérons AC district of the southern Graves, Bordeaux, France. Sweet and dry white wines and some reds.

Cérons, Château de wine estate of AC Cérons, Bordeaux, France.

Certan-de-May, Château wine estate of AC Pomerol, Bordeaux, France.

Certan-Giraud, Château wine estate of AC Pomerol, Bordeaux, France.

Certan-Mazelle, Château wine estate of AC Pomerol, Bordeaux, France.

certosa red liqueur originally of Certosa di Pavia monastery, Lombardy, Italy. Also called **certosino**.

cerveceria brewery, Spanish.

Cerveteri town and DOC north of Rome, Italy. Red wines from Montepulciano and Sangiovese grapes; white wines from Malvasia and Trebbiano.

cerveza beer, Spanish. The word derives from Latin *servicia*, a primitive kind of ale derived from the fruit of the species of tree now known as a service (*Sorbus domestica*).

Cerveza Cristal leading beer brand of Cuba, by Cerveceria Bucanero brewery, Holguin, Cuba.

Cerveza Rosanna 'Red Chili Ale' of Pike Place brewery, Seattle, USA.

Cesanese red grape variety of Latium region, Italy. Wines include **Cesanese del Piglio, Cesanese di Affile, Cesanese di Olevano Romano.**

César red grape variety of Auxerrois region, Burgundy, France. Also known as Romain and so-called in the belief that Julius Caesar introduced it to the region.

Ceylon Brewery producer of lagers and popular Lion Stout at Nuwara Eliya, Sri Lanka.

CFH Cocktail. Over ice shake 2 parts dry gin, 1 apple brandy, 1 Swedish Punsch, 1 grenadine, 1 lemon juice. Strain.

Chablais wine region of the Vaud, Switzerland.

Chablis white wine of vineyards surrounding the town of Chablis, Burgundy, France. Ordinary wines designated AC Chablis or AC Petit Chablis. Fine wines are classed AC Chablis *Premier Cru* and labelled with vineyard of origin. Exceptional wines are labelled AC Chablis *Grand Cru* from seven nominated vineyards. 'Chablis' is also commonly and erroneously used as a generic term for dry white wines in the USA.

Chablis Grand Cru fine white wine from seven designated vineyards: Blanchots, Bougros, Les Clos, Grenouilles, La Moutonne, Preuses, Valmur, Vaudésir. Burgundy, France.

Chablisienne, La main co-operative of Chablis, France, producing high-quality wines for sale under labels of many *négociant* firms.

Chablis Premier Cru white wine from 30 vineyards grouped under 12 names: Beauroy, Côte de Léchet, Fourchaume, Les Fourneaux, Mélinots, Mont de Milieu, Montée de Tonnerre, Montmains, Vaillons, Vaucoupin, Vaudevey, Vosgros. Burgundy, France.

Chabot armagnac brand of Compagnie Viticole des Grands Armagnacs, Villeneuve de Marsan, France.

Chacoli light white wine of Guernica, Spain.

chai above-ground 'cellar' for maturing wines in cask. Bordeaux, France.

Chainette, Clos de La vineyard in Auxerre, Burgundy, France. Mostly white wine.

Chaintre, Château de wine estate of AC Saumur-Champigny, Loire Valley, France.

Chairman's Fine Scotch Whisky eight-year-old blended scotch whisky of Eldridge Pope, Dorchester, Dorset, England.

Chalice Wines American-backed winery of Republic of Georgia, mostly selling to Russia.

chalk important element of the *terroir* of Champagne, France. Its presence in the soil of the vineyards contributes to the unique character and flavour of champagne, and has enabled spectacular subterranean excavations for the champagne cellars or *crayères*.

Chalk Hill AVA of Sonoma County, California, USA.

Chalk Hill brewery at Thorpe Hamlet, Norwich, Norfolk, England.

Chalon, Château wine estate est 14th century at Arlay, Jura region, France. Brand of Jean Bourdy.

Chalone AVA of Monterey County, California, USA.

Chalone Group leading wine producer, USA.

Chambave wine village in Valle d'Aosta, Italy, known for **Chambave Rouge** red and sweet white Passito di Chambave.

Chambertin, Le *Grand Cru* vineyard of the Côtes de Nuits, Burgundy, France. One of the greatest of red burgundies, rich and long-lived, and said to have been the favourite of Napoleon Bonaparte.

Chambertin Clos de Bèze *Grand Cru* vineyard adjacent, and wines of similar stature, to Le Chambertin, Burgundy, France. Property of

Bèze Abbey from 7th to 18th century.

Chambert-Marbuzet, Château wine estate of AC St-Estèphe, Médoc, Bordeaux, France. Classified *Cru Bourgeois*.

Chambolle-Musigny AC and village of the Côtes de Nuits, Burgundy, France. Great red wine of outstanding fragrancy and elegance. Within the 420-acre AC lie two *Grand Cru* vineyards, Bonnes Mares and le Musigny, and 19 *Premiers Crus*: les Amoureuses, les Baudes, aux Beaux Bruns, les Borniques, les Charmes, les Châtelots, aux Combottes, les Combottes, les Cras, Derrière la Grange, les Fouselottes, les Fuées, les Groseilles, les Gruenchers, les Haut Doix, les Noirots, les Plantes, les Sentiers.

chambré 'as the room' – meaning at room temperature, or the ideal temperature at which to serve red wine. French. In fact, few red wines are at their best warmed to the level of a centrally heated room at a typical 21°C. Best temperature range is 15-18°C.

Champagne, La AC region of NE France producing the world's greatest sparkling wine – **le champagne**. The region comprises five principal vineyard districts:

Aube, Côtes des Blancs, Côte de Sézanne, Montagne de Reims, Vallée de la Marne, with two major producing centres at Epernay and Reims. Vineyards are variously classified for quality and divided among 14,000 owners. Permitted grape varieties are black Pinot Meunier (48% of total) and Pinot Noir (28%) and white Chardonnay (24%). In a method progressively developed since 17th century, blended wine (the *cuvée*) is bottled, treated with yeast and sugar to cause a second fermentation, producing the bubbles, and sealed with a cap. After maturing (minimum one year for non-vintage and three for vintage), bottles are turned and angled (*remuage*) so detritus of fermentation collects behind the cap. Neck is flash-frozen, the cap removed and detritus expelled (*dégorgement*) to leave wine clear. Bottle is topped up with champagne and sugar (*dosage*), in quantity varying according to whether champagne is to be *brut* (very dry), *demi sec* (sweet) or a more esoteric style. Most champagne is blended from the wines of two or more vintages but there are many single-vintage and de luxe wines made.

Champagne Cocktail. Into champagne glass place 1 sugar lump and soak with Angostura bitters or orange bitters. Add 1 teaspoon brandy (optional, especially if good champagne is involved). Top with chilled champagne.

Champagne bottle sizes the standard bottle, as for still wines, contains 75cl. Larger sizes are: magnum (2 bottles);

Jeroboam (4); Rehoboam (6); Methuselah (8); Salmanazar (12); Balthazar (16); Nebuchadnezzar (20).

Champagne Cobbler Cocktail. Into a wine glass pour 1 part brandy, 1 curaçao. Top with chilled champagne.

Champagne Cooler Cocktail. Into a wine glass containing ice cubes, pour 1 part brandy, 1 Cointreau. Top with chilled champagne and add a mint sprig.

Champagne Cup make this famous and expensive punch in a very large jug. Place 1 sliced orange and 1 sliced lemon in the jug and add 4 measures brandy, 3 maraschino, 2 Bénédictine. Leave to steep for half an hour. Add a handful of ice cubes then a bottle of chilled champagne and a litre of chilled sparkling water.

champagne method means of producing champagne. See champagne.

Champagne Moment cricketing award inseparably associated with BBC Radio Test Match Special commentator Brian Johnston (1912–94). The first award, of a Jeroboam of Veuve Clicquot champagne, was made by Johnston to England batsman David Gower during the third test match in the 1992 season against Pakistan. At 11.52 on 6 July, Gower struck a boundary through the covers to bring his aggregate score in test cricket past the England record of 8,114 held by Geoffrey Boycott. Champagne Moment awards of Veuve Clicquot continue to be made by Johnston's successors in the TMS team, as often to members of opposing teams as to English players.

Champagne Normandy Cocktail. In a champagne glass dissolve 1 teaspoon sugar in 1 measure of calvados and add a dash of Angostura bitters. Top with chilled champagne and add an orange slice.

Champagne Pick-Me-Up Cocktail. Over ice shake 1 part brandy, 1 equal mix lemon and orange juice, 2 dashes grenadine. Strain into a wine glass and top with chilled champagne.

Champagne Sidecar Cocktail. Over ice shake 2 parts brandy, 1 Cointreau, 1 lemon juice. Strain into champagne glass and top with chilled champagne.

champána informal name for sparkling wine (true champagne included) in Latin America. Spanish.

champanski popular and undefining name for the sparkling wines of Georgia and other former Soviet Union states.

champenisé wine made sparkling by the champagne method (*qv*).

Champet, Emile renowned producer of Côte Rôtie wines, northern Rhône valley, France.

Champflower ale brand (4.2% alc) of Cottage Brewing Co, Lovington, Somerset, England.

Champoreau coffee reinforced with brandy. France.

Champs-Elysées Cocktail. Over ice shake 3 parts cognac, 1 Chartreuse, 2 lemon juice, 1 teaspoon sugar, 1 dash Angostura bitters. Strain.

Chandon, Domaine sparkling and still wine producer, Napa Valley, California, USA. Brands include **Chandon Napa Valley Brut**. Est 1977 by Moët & Chandon of Champagne, France.

Chandon, Domaine sparkling wine producer of Yarra Valley, Victoria, Australia. 'Cuvée' branded wines of renowned quality. Est 1986 by Moët & Chandon of Champagne, France.

Chanson Père & Fils wine grower and *négociant* of Beaune, France. Known for wines of Beaune *Premiers Crus* vineyards and Pernand-Vergelesses and Savigny-lès-Beaune.

Chantalouette second wine of Château de Sales, Bordeaux, France.

Chante Alouette white Hermitage wine by Max Chapoutier, Rhône valley, France.

Chantegrive, Château de wine estate of AC Graves, Bordeaux, France.

Chanticleer Cocktail. Over ice shake 2 parts dry gin, 1 lemon juice, 1 raspberry syrup, 1 egg white. Strain.

Chantovent large-scale producer of table wines in the Midi, France.

Chantre *Weinbrand* by Eckes distillery, Neider-Olm, Germany.

Chanturgue vineyard *cru* of Côtes d'Auvergne, Loire Valley, France.

Chapala Cocktail. Over ice shake 2 parts tequila, 1 equal mix lemon and orange juice, dash triple sec, teaspoon grenadine. Strain.

chapeau 'cap'. French. In winemaking, the cap of grape skins and stalks that forms on the surface of fermenting must in the vat.

Chapel Hill brand of Balatonboglat Winery, Balaton, Hungary.

Chapel Hill leading wine producer of McLaren Vale, Adelaide, South Australia.

Chapelle-Chambertin *Grand Cru* vineyard of Côtes de Nuits, Burgundy, France. In the village of Gevrey-Chambertin.

Chapelle-Lescours, Château La wine estate of AC St-Emilion, Bordeaux, France. Classified *Grand Cru*.

Chapelle-Madeleine, Château La wine estate of AC St-Emilion, Bordeaux, France. Classified *Grand Cru Classé*.

Chapellet Vineyards wine producer in Napa Valley, California, USA.

Chapoutier, Max major wine grower and *negoçiant* of Tain l'Hermitage, Rhône Valley, France.

chaptalize in winemaking, to boost the alcohol level by adding sugar to the fermenting must. Widely practised in northern climates where natural grape sugar levels are lower. Process was devised by Jean-Antoine Chaptal, c. 1800.

Chapterhouse pub-brewery in Ithaca, New York, USA.

Charal wine producer, Ontario, Canada.

Charbaut, A & Fils champagne house est 1948, Epernay, France

Charbono red grape variety, California, USA. In decline.

Chardonnay classic white grape variety of Burgundy, where it is the sole constituent of all the region's great white wines, and of blanc de blanc champagne. Hardy and early-ripening, the variety thrives in northern vineyards but is now also planted worldwide. Chardonnays mature very successfully in oak casks, and are among the most sought-after of all white wines. The name of the grape may derive from

that of the village of Chardonnay in the Mâconnais region of southern Burgundy. White wine from the village (which was founded in 988 AD) is produced under the appellation name **Chardonnay de Chardonnay**.

Charles Cocktail. Over ice stir 1 part brandy, 1 sweet vermouth, 1 dash Angostura bitters. Strain.

Charleston Cocktail. Over ice shake 1 part dry gin, 1 kirsch, 1 curaçao, 1 dry vermouth, 1 sweet vermouth, 1 maraschino. Strain.

Charlie Chaplin Cocktail. Over ice shake 1 part sloe gin, 1 apricot brandy, 1 lemon juice. Strain.

Charmail, Château wine estate of AC Haut-Médoc, Bordeaux, France.

Charmat the 'tank method' of making cheap sparkling wine. Large vats of made wine are treated with sugar and yeast then sealed. Secondary fermentation causes carbonation and wine is filtered and bottled under pressure. Devised by French winemaker Eugène Charmat, 1910.

Charmes, Château des wine estate at St Davids, Niagara Peninsula, Ontario, Canada.

Charmes-Chambertin *Grand Cru* vineyard of Gevrey-Chambertin, Côtes de Nuits, Burgundy, France.

Charpignat obscure winemaking *cru* of Savoie, France.

Charron, Château wine estate of AC Premières Côtes de Blaye, Bordeaux, France.

Charros brand name of Pernod-Ricard.

Charta association of wine estates in Rheingau region, Germany. High-quality Riesling wines.

Chartreuse The famed liqueur has been produced at the Carthusian monastery of La Grande Chartreuse since 1764 to the same recipe, incorporating 130 different flavouring ingredients. Yellow Chartreuse is 40 per cent alc ('75° proof' on label), and the drier, spicier, Green is very much stronger at 55 per cent ('96° proof' on label). The monastery was established 1084 by St Bruno at Voiron, Grenoble, France.

Chartreuse, Château La second wine of Château St Amand, Bordeaux, France.

Chartreuse Daisy Cocktail. Over ice shake 2 parts brandy, 1 green Chartreuse, 4 dashes lemon juice. Strain into a wine glass and top with chilled sparkling water.

Chartron & Trebuchet wine producer and *négociant-éleveur* of Puligny-Montrachet, Burgundy, France.

Chassagne-Montrachet village and large (750-acre) AC of Côte de Beaune, Burgundy, France. Red and, more famously, white wines. Several *crus* are shared with neighbouring village and AC Puligny-Montrachet. White wine *Grand Cru* vineyards are Bâtard-Montrachet, Criots Bâtard-Montrachet, Le Montrachet; *Premiers Crus*: Abbaye de Morgeot, la Boudriotte, les Brussonnes, Chassagne/Cailleret, les Champs Gains, les Chenevottes, Clos Saint-Jean, Grandes Ruchottes, les Macherelles, la Maltroie, Morgeot, la Romanée, les Vergers.

Chassart *jenever* distillery, Chassart, Charleroi, Belgium.

Chasse-Spleen, Château wine estate of AC Moulis, Médoc, Bordeaux, France. Classified *Cru Grand Bourgeois Exceptionnel.* The name supposedly commemorates a visit to the estate by the splenetic Lord Byron in 1821. He liked the wine so much, so the story goes, that he declared 'it chases away my spleen.' Before the poet's visit, the wine had simply been sold as an anonymous *cuvée* of the huge Château Grand Poujeaux estate.

Chasselas white grape variety principally of Switzerland (locally named Dorin or Fendant). Some cultivation in England.

Chastelet, Château wine estate of AC Premières Côtes de Bordeaux, France.

Chatauqua vineyard region of New York State, USA.

château 'castle'. French. Used to designate a wine estate, particularly in Bordeaux and less commonly throughout France and beyond. Most wines thus labelled are from estates with a mansion or villa, or a mere farmhouse. In this dictionary, wine estates preceded with 'Château' are listed under their given names.

Chateau & Estates wine importer and distributor of USA, owned by Diageo.

château-bottled wine bottled by the producer rather than by a dealer or merchant. French.

Château-Chalon village and AC of Jura, France, producing sherry-like *vin jaune*.

Châteaugay wine-producing commune of Côtes d'Auvergne, France.

Châteaumeillant VDQS district for red and rosé wines of Loire Valley, France.

Châteauneuf-du-Pape village and AC for red (and some white) wines of southern Rhône Valley, France. Name alludes to the summer palace built (ruins stand in the village) by the Avignon popes of the 14th century, who also planted the vineyards. Red wines known for complexity and diversity (13 grape varieties are permitted) and strength (minimum 12.5% alc).

Château-Paulet brandy producer, Cognac, France. Labels include **Château Paulet Age Inconnu**.

Châtelet, Château Le wine estate of AC St-Emilion, Bordeaux, France.

Châtelleine wine co-operative at Vertheuil in AC Haut-Médoc, Bordeaux, France. Wines produced for single-estate members include Château Ferré Portal, Château Fondeminjean, Château Julian, Château Laride, Château Miqueau, Château Tamière.

Châtillon-en-Diois village and wine brand of AC Côtes du Rhône, France, made by Cave Coopérative de Die.

Chauché Gris white wine grape of California, USA, also known as 'Gray Riesling'.

chaufferette oil-burning heater used in vineyards to protect budding vines from frost damage. France.

Chauffeur Cocktail. Over ice stir 1 part dry gin, 1 vermouth, 1 whisky, 1 dash Angostura bitters. Strain. (Attrib. H.E. Bates in *The Darling Buds of May*, 1958.)

Chaume village and sweet-wine designation of AC Coteaux du Layon, Loire Valley, France.

Chaumes, Château Les wine estate of AC Premières Côtes de Blaye, Bordeaux, France.

Chaumet perry brand of Halewood International, Huyton, Merseyside, England.

Chaunac, de hybrid grape variety principally grown in Canada.

Chautagne wine *cru* of Savoie, France.

Chauvenet, F *négociant* of Nuits-St-Georges, Burgundy, France.

Chauvet, A champagne house, Tours-sur-Marne, France.

Chauvin, Château wine estate of AC St-Emilion, Bordeaux, France. Classified *Grand Cru Classé*.

Chave, Jean-Louis winemaking dynasty of AC Hermitage, Rhône Valley, France. The vineyards on the famed Hermitage slopes have passed from father to son since 1481.

cheese in cider-making, the build-up of layers of pomace (apple pulp) spaced with straw or cloth-and-board in the press.

Chelois hybrid white grape variety mainly of USA.

Chelsea Arts Cocktail. Over ice shake 1 part dry gin, 1 Cointreau, 1 teaspoon lemon juice. Strain.

Chénas AC and smallest of the 10 *crus* of Beaujolais wine region, France.

chêne oak. French. In winetasting, a wine with characteristic rich, vanilla flavours associated with new oak.

Cheng Nien Feng Kang Chiew rice-based 'wine' of state trading monopoly, Kwantung, People's Republic of China.

Chenin Blanc white grape variety indigenous to Touraine, France, producing classic rich wines of Coteaux du Layon, and many dry whites of the Loire. Also widely planted in the New World.

Chente brand name of Pernod-Ricard.

Chequers blended scotch whisky by John McEwan, Elgin, Scotland.

Chéreau-Carré wine producer of AC Muscadet, France.

Chéret-Pitres, Château wine estate of AC Graves, Bordeaux, France.

Cherie Cocktail. Over ice shake 2 parts white rum, 1 cherry brandy, 1 triple sec, 1 fresh lime juice. Strain into a cocktail glass and add a maraschino cherry.

Cheri-Suisse pink-coloured, cherry-and-chocolate flavoured liqueur, Switzerland.

Cheriton brewery at Cheriton, Alresford, Hampshire, England.

Cherry Blossom Cocktail. Over ice vigorously shake 5 parts cherry brandy, 4 brandy, 1 curaçao, 1 grenadine, 1 lemon juice. Strain.

Cherry Blossom Liqueur pink liqueur brand of Suntory, Japan.

cherry brandy cherry liqueur, usually composed of at least 20 per cent spirit distilled from fermented cherries along with fruit macerated in brandy.

Cherry Cobbler Cocktail. Into a tall, ice-filled glass pour 2 parts dry gin, 1 cherry brandy, 1 lemon juice, 1 teaspoon sugar. Stir and add a lemon slice and maraschino cherry.

Cherry Heering cherry brandy by Peter Heering, Denmark.

Cherry Marnier cherry brandy brand of Rocher, France.

Cherry Mixture Cocktail. Over ice shake 1 part dry vermouth, 1 sweet vermouth, 1 dash Angostura bitters, 1 dash maraschino. Strain and add cherry.

Cherry Norman apple variety traditionally valued for cider-making. English.

Cherry Pearmain apple variety traditionally valued for cider-making. English.

Cherry Rum Cocktail. Over ice shake 2 parts rum, 1 cherry brandy, 1 fresh cream. Strain.

Cherry's Irish Ale brewery at Waterford, Eire. Owned by Guinness.

cherry whisky spirit produced by compounding cherries with whisky.

Chesky cherry whisky brand of Fremy, France.

Chesters 'strong and ugly' beer by the Barngates Brewery at the Drunken Duck Inn, Ambleside, Cumbria, England.

Cheurlin champagne house, Mussy-sur-Seine, France.

Cheval Blanc, Château great wine estate of AC St-Emilion, Bordeaux, France. The name is linked, without substantiation, to the post house on the site at which King Henri IV (1553–1610), renowned for riding only white horses, is said to have changed mounts en route from Paris to his birthplace at Pau in the Basses Pyrénées. Classified *1er Grand Cru Classé* 'A' and ranked,

with Château Ausone, above all other St-Emilion properties.

Chevalier solera reserva brandy by Luis Caballero, Puerto de Santa Maria, Spain.

Chevalier, Domaine de great wine estate of AC Pessac-Léognan, Bordeaux, France. Classified *Cru Classé*.

Chevalier de Malle second wine of Château de Malle, Bordeaux, France.

Chevalier-de-Malle second wine of Château Cardaillan, Bordeaux, France.

Chevalier de Stérimberg white Hermitage wine by Paul Jaboulet, Rhône Valley, France.

Chevalier Lascombes wine brand of Alexis Lichine, AC Médoc, Bordeaux, France.

Chevalier-Montrachet *Grand Cru* vineyard at Puligny-Montrachet, Burgundy, France.

Chevaliers du Roi Soleil growers' co-operative and wine range of AC Haut-Médoc, Bordeaux, France.

Cheval Quancard wine company of Bordeaux, France. Châteaux and branded wines.

Chevergny VDQS zone for sparkling and still wines, Touraine, France.

cheville a champagne cork so long in place that it does not resume its swollen shape when drawn from the bottle. French.

Chevillon, Robert leading wine producer in AC Nuits-St-Georges, Burgundy, France.

Chia Fan rice-based 'wine' of state trading monopoly, Shanghai, People's Republic of China.

Chian island wine of ancient Greece.

Chianti red wine principally from Sangiovese grapes grown in DOCG zone of Tuscany, Italy. See box.

Chianti Classico DOCG production zone for quality Chianti wine lying between cities of Florence and Siena in Tuscany, Italy. **Chianti Classico Conzorio** of growers, est 1924 with 33 members, now with 600 and famed for its Gallo Nero (black cockerel) emblem, maintains its own quality standards in vineyard and winery.

Chianti Putto collective term for the *consorzio* of six Chianti-producing areas outside the Chianti Classico zone. The member-areas are Colli Aretini, Colli Fiorentini, Colline Pisane, Colli Senesi, Montalbano, Rufina.

Chiaretto pale red wine particularly

of, but not exclusive to, Bardolino DOC, Italy.

Chiarlo, Michele leading wine producer in Piedmont, Italy.

Chibuku brewery at Harare, Zimbabwe. Also, a name for home-made maize beers, East Africa.

Chicago Brewery producer of lager in Chicago, Illinois, USA.

Chicago Cocktail. Over ice shake 1 part brandy, 1 dash curaçao, 1 dash Angostura bitters. Strain into glass with castor-sugar-frosted rim and top with chilled champagne.

Chicago Vice wheat (*Weiss*) beer brand by Goose Island brewery, Chicago, Illinois, USA.

Chicane, Château wine estate of AC Graves, Bordeaux, France.

chicha corn beer of Peru, first brewed by the Incas.

Chicuva liqueur of brandy, aged sherry and herbs. Spain.

Chiddingstone vineyard est 1976 by Dudley Quirk at Edenbridge, Kent, England. Distinguished white wines from grape varieties including Pinot Noir and Seyval and a famed red wine from Triomphe d'Alsace grapes. Sadly, the vineyard, one of England's largest, was grubbed up in 2003.

Chianti

a jealously guarded formula

Chianti is named after a range of hills that runs south from Florence towards Siena in Tuscany. The raffia-clad wine that first put Italy on the world wine map in the early part of the 20th century has a romantic story behind its creation. Its begetter was a Florentine politician, Baron Bettino Ricasoli, who became the second prime minister of newly united Italy in 1861.

The story goes something like this. When just married, young Bettino took his new wife, Anna Bonacorssi, to a grand society ball in Florence. Known unaffectionately by his acquaintances as *il Barone de Ferro*, the Iron Baron, because of his unbending moral uprightness, the groom lived up to his name when he discovered that a handsome young guest at the ball was paying enthusiastic court to his beautiful bride.

By no means a comely figure himself, and jealous in the way that only an Italian knows how, Bettino took umbrage. He angrily summoned his carriage and conveyed *la bella signora* through the night to his gloomy family seat, Castello Brolio, far away in the Tuscan hinterland.

There, she was to languish for the rest of her days, watched over by her green-eyed protector – who beguiled the wilderness years of his political life in Brolio's extensive vineyards, devising what we now call chianti wine.

The Baron's artful blend of grape varieties (two black, Sangiovese and Canaiolo, plus two white, Malvasia and Trebbiano) remained the formula for chianti for more than a century and the wine certainly still owes its essential character to his experiments. The estate, dominated by the vast and formidable castle where wine has reputedly been in continuous production since 1141, is still a major producer within the Chianti Classico zone. And its wine is made today by the present Baron Bettino – great-great grandson of old jellybags himself.

Chief Mouse Cocktail. Into an ice-filled tumbler pour 1 part armagnac, 1 marc de Bourgogne. Top with dry ginger ale and stir.

Chiefs Brewing Company pub-brewery in Champaign, Illinois, USA.

Chieftain's Choice blended and malt scotch whisky brand of Peter J Russell, Broxburn, Scotland.

Chignin wine-producing *cru* of Savoie, France.

Chignin-Bergeron white-wine AC of Savoie, France.

Chihuahua beer brand of Cuauhtémoc brewery, Mexico.

Chile the most important wine-producing nation of South America. Vineyards created in 16th century by missionaries from Spain were later planted with French varieties from vine stocks pre-dating the Phylloxera outbreak of the mid-1800s. Protected by the Andes to the east and the Pacific Ocean to the west, the vines have remained unaffected by this otherwise worldwide disease. Principal vineyard regions are Aconagua, Cachapoal, Casablanca, Lontué, Maipo, Maule, Rapel.

Chilford Hundred vineyard at Linton, Cambridgeshire, England.

chili beer flavoured fruit (or, arguably, vegetable) beer made by a variety of brewers, notably in Mexico and the USA.

Chill Blane seasonal (winter) dark strong ale (5.0% alc) by Hydes Anvil brewery, Manchester, England.

Chilli Willy Cocktail. Over ice shake 2 parts vodka, 1 teaspoon chopped hot chilli. Strain, with care.

Chilsdown Vineyard vineyard at Chichester, Sussex, England.

Chiltern brewery at Terrick, Aylesbury, Buckinghamshire, England.

Chiltern Valley Wines vineyard and winery at Hambleden, Oxfordshire, England.

Chimay Belgium's principal Trappist brewery, at the Abbaye de Notre-Dame de Scourmont in the Ardennes. Brewing by the monks began in 1861 and Chimay was the world's first monastic brewery to offer 'Trappist Beer' for sale. Range of strong, fruity ales includes dry, hoppy **Chimay Capsule Blanche** (names follow colour of crown cork) vintage-dated, strongest (9% alc) **Chimay Capsule Bleu**; original **Chimay Capsule Rouge**.

China-China spiced liqueur, France.

Chinchon anis liqueur brand, Spain.

Chinese Cocktail. Over ice shake 2 parts rum, 1 grenadine, 3 dashes curaçao, 3 dashes maraschino, 1 dash Angostura bitters. Strain.

Ch'ing-tao vodka-making centre (est 20th century by Soviet emigrés), People's Republic of China.

Chinon town and AC of Loire Valley, France. Red wines from Cabernet Franc grape, said to have been a favourite of locally born writer François Rabelais (1494–1553). The wine is said to be best drunk young, but the best improve for many years.

Chip Dry white port brand of Taylor Fladgate & Yeatman, Vila Nova de Gaia, Portugal.

Chiquita Cocktail. Over ice shake 3 parts rum, 1 banana liqueur, 2 fresh cream, 2 dashes grenadine. Strain.

Chiroubles wine-producing *cru* of Beaujolais region, France.

Chisel Jersey apple variety traditionally valued for cider production. English.

Chiswick Bitter ale brand of Fuller's brewery, London, England.

Chitry wine-producing village of Auxerrois in Burgundy, France.

Chivas Regal leading brand of 12-year-old blended scotch whisky. See box.

chlorosis disease of vines planted in chalky soil.

chocolate in winetasting, a characteristic, vanilla-like smell or taste found in rich Bordeaux and Burgundy.

Chocolate Cocktail. Over ice shake 1 part yellow Chartreuse, 1 maraschino, 1 teaspoon powdered chocolate, 1 egg. Strain. Alternatively, over ice shake 3 parts port, 1 yellow Chartreuse, 1 teaspoon powdered chocolate, 1 egg yolk. Strain.

Chocolate Rum Cocktail. Over ice shake 2 parts white rum, 1 crème de cacao, 1 crème de menthe, 2 teaspoons fresh cream. Strain.

Choc Shock Cocktail. Over ice shake 3 parts port, 1 yellow Chartreuse, 1 teaspoon powdered chocolate, 1 egg. Strain into small wine glasses.

Chopin rye vodka brand of distillers Polmos Siedlce, Poland. Named after composer Frederic Chopin (1810–49).

Chorey, Château de wine estate of AC Chorey-lès-Beaune, Burgundy, France.

Chorey-lès-Beaune village and AC of Côte de Beaune, Burgundy, France.

Chorherrenhalde vineyard at Meersburg in Baden region, Germany.

Chorherren Klosterneuburg wine producer in Donauland, Niederösterreich, Austria.

chota peg 'a little drink' – customarily of whisky with soda or water – in colonial India. Hindustani.

Chouao style of crème de cacao (chocolate liqueur) of Caracas, Venezuela.

Chivas Regal

first among blended Scotch whiskies

James Chivas learned the food and drink trade on the shop floor – at the grocery in Aberdeen in the Scottish Highlands where he worked as a sales assistant. He had become the owner of the shop by 1843, when the business received a Royal Warrant as Purveyors to Her Majesty Queen Victoria, who was later to acquire the nearby estate of Balmoral Castle.

Chivas was a pioneer in the blending of single malt and grain Scotch whiskies, and produced his first blend, with the suitably regal name Royal Glendee, later in the 1840s. Joined by his brother John in 1857, Chivas began to extend sales into England, and further afield in the British Empire.

Chivas Brothers launched their famous Chivas Regal brand in the 1890s. It is blended from casks of malts and grains of differing ages, none less than 12 years old and more than 30 million bottles are now sold in more than 150 countries.

Chivas Brothers' Master Blender Colin Scott describes it thus: 'smooth, with a honeyed richness, round and full-bodied, slightly smoky with a long, lingering finish. The classic, premium Scotch whisky.'

Formerly owned by Canadian giant Seagram, which acquired the brand in 1949. Chivas Regal brand was sold to French multi-national Pernod-Ricard in 2001. 🍸

Christian Brothers major wine producer of Napa and San Joaquin valleys, California, USA.

Christian Merz Spezial small brewery at Bamberg, Germany, specialising in *Rauchbier*.

Christian Moerlein lager brand of Hudepohl-Schoenling brewery, Cincinnati, Ohio, USA.

Christmas beer seasonally brewed strong ale widely produced in Europe, the United States and elsewhere.

Christmas Cracker bottle-conditioned beer (6.0% alc) by Wood Brewery, Winstanstow, Shropshire, England.

Christmas Pudding seasonal bottle-conditioned-beer (6.8% alc) by Pilgrim Brewery, Reigate, Surrey, England.

Christoffel beer brand of Bierbrouwirij St Christoffel, Netherlands. Unrelated beer by Roermond microbrewery, Limburg, Netherlands, is also made under this label.

Christwein symbolic name for *Eiswein* from grapes picked on 24th or 25th of December. Germany.

Chrysanthemum Cocktail. Over ice shake 2 parts dry vermouth, 1 Bénédictine, 3 dashes anis. Strain and add orange peel.

Ch'Ti brand name of *bières de garde* produced by Castelain brewery at Bénifontaine, France, including **Ch'Ti Ambrée; Ch'Ti Blonde; Ch'Ti Brune.**

Church End brewery Shustoke, Warwickshire, England. Rugby Ale.

Churchill port brand of Churchill Graham port house, est 1982. Crusted Port, Vintage Character and vintage ports: 1982, 83, 84, 85, 86, 87, 89, 90, 91, 92, 94, 97, 2000, 03.

Churchill Cocktail. Over ice shake 3 parts scotch whisky, 1 Cointreau, 1 sweet vermouth, 1 fresh lime juice. Strain.

Church Parade Cocktail. Over ice shake 2 parts dry gin, 1 dry vermouth, 4 dashes orange juice, 1 dash orange bitters. Strain.

Church Road winery at Hawke's Bay, est 1897, and premium wine brand of Montana Wines, New Zealand.

Churchward cider by Yalberton Farm, Paignton, Devon, England.

Chusclan village of AC Côtes du Rhône Villages, France.

Chymos fruit-liqueur producer and brand. Sweden.

cider fermented liquor from the juice of pressed apples. In England, production is traditionally concentrated in Herefordshire and in Devon and Somerset. France and Germany, Australia and the United States are among the producing nations worldwide. The name cider derives from Hebrew *shekar* (strong drink). See box.

cider apples varieties for cider-production are grouped in four types: bittersharp (high acidity, high tannin), bittersweet (low acidity, high tannin), sharp (high acidity, low tannin), sweet (low acidity, low tannin). Scores of varieties (from among more than 350 known) are being replanted in the cider renaissance.

Cider Cup to make this punch, combine 2 measures each of brandy and Cointreau in a large jug. Add 1

Cider

apples into alcohol, an ancient art

Cider is a European device, probably first contrived by the Celts of what is now southern Germany. According to Roman historians, Celts worshipped an apple god and regarded the apple tree as sacred. During their great migrations from 500 BC they brought cidermaking skills to all the regions of Europe where production still continues – principally Brittany, Normandy and south-western England.

Cider apples tend to thrive better at the western extremities of land masses where rainfall is higher. Hereford and Somerset are thus the main growing areas in Britain. Likewise the north-western provinces of France. Climate changes meant these regions ceased to be suitable for vine-growing around 2,000 years ago, and cider made a palatable alternative, particularly in England during the long periods of embargo on wine due to wars with France.

Modern cidermaking plants take in thousands of tons of apples – there are 350 different suitable varieties – during the two-three month harvest. The fruit is first reduced to a pulp in a rotary mill before pressing. Very modern plants press the pulp much in the way grapes are crushed for wine, but traditionally, juice extraction for cider is by a process called 'cheese building'. A slatted square board provides the base. On to it is placed a frame about 4in (10cm) deep to form a shallow box. This is covered by a cloth much larger than the frame. The lined box is then filled with apple pulp. The cloth is folded over to cover the pulp. A second slatted board is placed over the top, and the whole process repeated 10 to 15 times to build up the 'cheese'.

The cheese then goes under a hydraulic press which can extract about 80 per cent of the weight of the apples as juice, leaving behind a solid residue known as the pomace. The juice is now ready for fermentation. In small-scale production, all will be fermented, in vats, immediately. In larger centres, some will be stored as concentrate for later fermentation, staged through the year to ensure consistency of supply.

The pomace is a valuable byproduct. Some will be processed for the extraction of pectin, a gelling agent used in food production such as jam-making, and finally as animal feed.

Fermenting vessels may be oak casks in small cider centres, but stainless steel vats are now the norm for commercial cidermaking. The juice will normally be treated with sulphur products to combat the effect of bacteria, and cultured yeasts are added for a controlled fermentation, lasting up to three weeks. When fermentation is complete, the cider is racked (pumped) off the yeast detritus into a maturing vat, kept carefully topped up to avoid oxidation. Maturing is a matter of weeks rather than months or years as for some wines.

Commercially produced cider is pasteurised and filtered before going on sale. It is clear, unlike unfiltered 'farmhouse' cider. Some draught and bottled brands have sugar added, plus a vigorously fermenting yeast, to produce a sparkle known in the trade as 'condition'.

Some sparkling bottled ciders are carbonated by injection with carbon dioxide. Others, particularly in Brittany and Normandy, are sparkling through the absorption of carbon dioxide given off by the natural activities of fermentation when trapped inside a closed tank or in a sealed bottle.

pint (0.5 litre) chilled dry cider, half pint (0.25 litre) chilled sparkling water, 1 tablespoon sugar, ice cubes, apple, orange and lemon slices. Serve in wine glasses.

cidre de Normandie the cider of Normandy, France. First made from cultivated apples on the orders of Charlemagne in eighth century.

Cienega, La AVA of San Benito County, California, USA.

Cien Años premium tequila brand of Jalisco, Mexico.

Cigales wine zone of NW Spain known for light (*clarete*) reds.

Cigare-Volant renowned red wine by Randall Grahm of Bonny Doon winery, California, USA. The grape varieties are based on those used for Châteauneuf-du-Pape in the Rhône Valley, France, where a local by-law forbids unauthorised landings by flying saucers (*cigares-volants* in French).

Ciliegiolo red grape variety of central Italy.

Cinderella Cocktail. Over ice shake 3 parts rum, 1 port, 1 lemon juice, 1 egg white, 1 teaspoon sugar syrup. Strain.

Cinq Cents beer brand of Chimay Trappist brewery first made in 1986 marking 500th anniversary of Chimay town, Belgium.

Cinqueterre white wine of five villages of coastal Liguria, Italy.

Cinsau(l)t red grape variety of southern France, much blended with other varieties, especially Carignan, Grenache and Syrah. Also grown in South Africa under the name Hermitage.

Cinzano vermouth manufacturer and wine producer based in Turin, Italy. Brands include **Cinzano Bianco** and **Cinzano Secco**. **Cinzano Brut** is a leading brand of Asti Spumante. Sold by former British owner Diageo to Campari in 1999.

Cirò DOC for red, *rosato* and white wines, Calabria, Italy. Notable rich (13.5% alc) reds from the *classico* zone closest to Cirò town.

Cissac winemaking commune of AC Haut-Médoc, Bordeaux, France.

Cissac, Château wine estate of AC Haut-Médoc, Bordeaux, France. Classified *Cru Grand Bourgeois Exceptionnel*.

Cisk beer brand of Malta

Citran, Château wine estate of AC Haut-Médoc, Bordeaux, France. Classified *Cru Grand Bourgeois Exceptionnel*.

citric acid a natural constituent of grape juice. It is commonly added to wine to improve acidity.

Citro lemon-based liqueur (21.9% alc) by Martini & Rossi, Italy.

Citronella Cocktail. Over ice shake 1 part lemon vodka, 1 cranberry juice, 2 dashes lime juice. Strain.

Citronen-eis Likor yellow liqueur from distilled lemon-peel and lemon juice. Germany.

citroengenever lemon-flavoured 'London Dry' *genever* gin. Netherlands.

City of Cambridge brewery in Cambridge, England.

CIVC Comité Interprofessionel du Vin de Champagne. Association of producers of Champagne, France, responsible for promoting champagne and a renowned litigant in cases where the product's name is taken in vain.

Civrac, Château de wine estate of AC Côtes de Bourg, Bordeaux, France.

Claerkampster herbal liqueur with monastic origins by Boomsma distillery, Netherlands.

Claeryn brand of *jonge* (young) *genever* by Bols, Netherlands.

Clair, Domaine Bruno wine producer based in Marsannay-la-Côte, Burgundy, France.

Clair, Domaine Michel wine producer in Santenay, Burgundy, France.

Clairefort, Château de second wine of Château Prieuré Lichine, Bordeaux, France.

Claire Riesling white grape variety of Australia. Synonymous with Cruchen Blanc.

clairet light red wine of Bordeaux, France. Source of English term 'claret'.

Clairette white grape variety of southern France.

Clairette de Bellegard AC for dry white wines from Clairette grapes, Costières du Gard, France.

Clairette de Die sparkling wine AC of Drôme, Rhône Valley, France. **Clairette de Die Brut** is dry and from Clairette grapes only. **Clairette de Die Tradition** is sweet, from a blend of Clairette and Muscat grapes and made by a unique protracted-single-fermentation method.

Clairette du Languedoc white wine from Clairette grapes, l'Hérault region, France.

Clairette Rousse white grape variety of southern France. Synonymous with Bourboulenc.

Clan Ardroch blended scotch whisky by Hall & Bramley, Liverpool, England.

Clan Campbell blended scotch whisky of Campbell Distillers, Brentford, Middlesex, England. Also **Clan Campbell Highlander** 12-year-old, **Clan Campbell Legendary** 21-year-old.

Clan MacGregor blended scotch whisky by J G Thompson, Glasgow, Scotland.

Clan Murdock blended scotch whisky by Murdoch McLennan, Edinburgh, Scotland.

Clanrana whisky-based herb liqueur, Scotland.

Clan Roy blended scotch whisky by Morrison Bowmore, Glasgow, Scotland.

Clansman blended scotch whisky by Glen Catrine, Catrine, Ayrshire, Scotland.

Clape, Auguste leading wine producer of AC Cornas, Rhône Valley, France.

Clape, La wine district of AC Coteaux du Languedoc, SW France.

Clapham Omnibus Cocktail. Over ice shake 2 parts Absolut vodka, 2 Campari, 1 sweet vermouth. Strain.

clara white, Spanish. Describes some uncoloured spirits, particularly tequila of Mexico.

Clare, Château La wine estate of AC Médoc, Bordeaux, France. Classified *Cru Bourgeois*.

Claremont Wines leading wine producer of British Columbia, Canada.

claret the red wine of Bordeaux. English via French from Latin *vinum claratum* (clear wine).

clarete light red wine. Spanish.

Clare-Watervale northernmost wine-producing district of South Australia.

Claridge Cocktail. Over ice shake 2 parts dry gin, 2 dry vermouth, 1 apricot brandy, 1 Cointreau. Strain.

Claridge Wines sparkling and still wine producer, Wellington, South Africa.

Clarin first-distillation rum, Haiti, West Indies.

Clark, HB brewery at Wakefield, West Yorkshire, England.

Clark, William brewery at South Cliff, Scarborough, North Yorkshire, England.

Clarke, Château wine estate of AC Listrac, Médoc, Bordeaux, France. Classified *Cru Bourgeois*.

Clarksburg AVA of Yolo County, Central Valley, California, USA.

Clarysse brewery in Oudenaarde, Belgium. Known for Felix brown ale.

Class Axe Classic ale brand of Manzano Mountain brewery, Tijeras, New Mexico, USA. Named in connection with Class Axe pop group.

Classic Cocktail. Over ice shake 3 parts brandy, 1 curaçao, 1 maraschino, 1 lemon juice. Strain into glass with caster-sugar-frosted rim. Add lemon peel.

Classico term appended to the regional names of numerous wines of Italy, denoting proximity to the region's centre, and a superior quality. Examples are Chianti Classico and Soave Classico.

clavelin wine bottle for *vin jaune* of the Jura, France. The capacity, 62 cl, is traditionally the proportion remaining of each litre of new wine once it has had the customary six years' ageing in cask.

Clawford Cider cider by Clawford Vineyard, Clawton, Devon, England.

Claymore, The blended scotch whisky by Whyte & Mackay, Glasgow, Scotland.

clean in winetasting, a fresh smell with no discernible faults.

Clear Lake AVA of Lake County, California, USA.

Clément-Pichon, Château wine estate of AC Haut-Médoc, Bordeaux, France.

Clerck brewery in Picardy, northern France, known for Pot Flamand *bière de garde*.

Clerc-Milon, Château wine estate of AC Pauillac, Médoc, Bordeaux, France. Classified *5ème Grand Cru Classé*.

Clerget, Raoul wine producer and *négoçiant* est 1270 in St-Aubin, Burgundy, France.

Clessé wine village of Mâconnais region, Burgundy, France.

Cleveland Brewing Company producer of Erin Brew ale, Pittsburgh, Pennsylvania, USA.

Clevner regional name for Pinot Blanc (and sometimes Pinot Noir) grape. Alsace, France.

climat an individually identified, but officially unclassified, vineyard. Mainly Burgundy region of France. Synonymous with *lieu dit* (mainly Alsace and Rhône).

Climens, Château great wine estate of AC Barsac, Bordeaux, France. Classified *1er Cru Classé*.

Clinet, Château wine estate of AC Pomerol, Bordeaux, France.

Clinton American red grape variety cultivated since 18th century in Veneto region, Italy.

CLOC Cumin Liquidum Optimum Castelli – 'The Best Caraway in the Castle' – colourless caraway liqueur. Denmark.

Clocher, Clos du wine estate of AC Pomerol, Bordeaux, France.

clone in viticulture, a derived vine with a specific variation from the original plant. Botanists have isolated clones of all major vine varieties to produce stocks suitable for particular plantings.

Cloquet, Château wine estate of AC Pomerol, Bordeaux, France.

clos an enclosed vineyard (French). Many wine properties in France and elsewhere are prefixed with this name, and these are listed under their main titles (eg **Clos de Vougeot** under **Vougeot**).

Clos, Les largest of the *Grand Cru* vineyards of Chablis, France.

Clos de l'Amiral second wine of Château Beychevelle, Bordeaux, France.

Clos-des-Jacobins, Château wine estate of AC St-Emilion, Bordeaux, France. Classified *Grand Cru Classé*.

Clos du Bois wine producer in Sonoma Valley, California, USA.

Noted for Cabernet Sauvignon, Chardonnay, Pinot Noir etc.

Closerie-Grand-Poujeaux, Château La wine estate of AC Moulis, Médoc, Bordeaux, France. Classified *Cru Bourgeois*.

Clos la Madeleine wine estate of AC St Emilion, Bordeaux, France. Classified *Grand Cru* (1996).

Clot, François liqueur producer of Grenoble, France. Organic liqueurs including Cérise (cherry) and Vinoix (walnut).

Clotte, Château de wine estate of AC Côtes de Castillon, Bordeaux, France.

Clotte, Château La wine estate of AC St-Emilion, Bordeaux, France. Classified *Grand Cru Classé*.

Cloudy Bay wine estate est 1985, Marlborough district, South Island, New Zealand. Renowned Chardonnay and Sauvignon white wines and latterly Pinot Noir red.

Clover Club Cocktail. Over ice shake 2 parts dry gin, 1 grenadine, 1 fresh lime juice, 1 egg white. Strain.

Clover Leaf Cocktail. Over ice shake 2 parts dry gin, 1 grenadine, 1 fresh lime juice, 1 egg white. Strain. Add sprig of mint.

cloying in winetasting, a sweet wine unredeemed by balancing acidity.

Club blended scotch whisky by Justerini & Brooks, London, England.

Club Cocktail. Over ice shake 2 parts dry gin, 1 sweet vermouth, 1 dash yellow Chartreuse. Strain.

Club-Weisse wheat beer by Spaten brewery, Munich, Germany.

Cluny blended scotch whisky by John E MacPherson, Edinburgh, Scotland. Also 12-year-old and 21-year-old.

Clusière, Château La wine estate of AC St-Emilion, Bordeaux, France. Classified *Grand Cru Classé*.

Cluss brewery in Heilbronn, Bavaria, Germany, making **Cluss Bock Dunkel** dark beer.

Clynelish North Highland malt whisky distillery est 1967, Brora, Sutherland, Scotland. Single malts: 12-year-old, 14-year-old.

Cnudde small brown-ale brewery, Oudenaarde, Belgium.

Coan historic white wine of ancient Greece. From the island of Cos.

coarse in winetasting, rough and unknit in the mouth.

Coastal Region a designated wine region of South Africa, encompassing Wines of Origin districts of Constantia, Durbanville, Paarl, Stellenbosch, Swartland, Tulbagh.

Coates former cider producer of Somerset, England, after Redvers Coates, whose large-scale farmhouse-style production plant at Nailsea, Bristol, was bought by Showerings (*qv*) of Shepton Mallet in 1956. The Coates brand was latterly merged with Gaymers and absorbed by Matthew Clark Brands.

Coates & Co distillers of Plymouth Gin in the Blackfriars Distillery, Plymouth, England. Distillery, in a former Dominican monastery, opened 1793.

Cobaneshof Schneider wine producer in Kamptal, Niederösterreich, Austria.

Cobenzl wine producer in Wien (Vienna), Austria.

Cobbler American-style cocktail consisting of spirit poured over crushed ice into which powered sugar has been mixed. Traditionally decorated with slices of seasonal fruit.

Cobra Indian lager brand (5.0% alc) of Cobra Beer Co, originally of Bangalore, India. Now brewed internationally under licence.

Cockburn's Highland Malt vatted malt scotch whisky by Cockburn & Co, Edinburgh, Scotland.

Cockburn

Cockburn port brand of **Cockburn Smithes**, Vila Nova de Gaia, Portugal. Popular Special Reserve brand, old tawnies, Dry Tang white port and vintages: 1955, 60, 63, 67, 70, 75, 83, 85, 87, 91, 92, 94, 97, 2000, 03.

Cocker Hoop beer brand of Jennings Brothers brewery, Cockermouth, Cumbria, England.

Cock o' the North fruit-flavoured, malt-whisky-based liqueur brand by Drumguish distillery, Scotland.

Cocks et Féret oft-quoted reference guide to the wine estates of Bordeaux, France.

Cockspur leading Bajan rum brand by West India Rum Refinery, Black Rock, Barbados. Blended and bottled by Hanschell Inniss, est 1884 by Danish-born chandler and liquor-store operator Valdemar Hanschell.

cocktail a concocted drink. The custom began in the newly independent United States of the late 1700s. The first 'definition' of the word cocktail is possibly that given in the 1801-08 edition of New York's *Columbian Repository*: 'a stimulating liquor composed of spirits of any kind, sugar, water and bitters.' As to the word itself, the likeliest source is a drink in which the spoon used to stir the mixture is left in the glass. At American horseracing courses two centuries ago, it was common for punters to watch the races while holding a glass of spirit mixed with water or fruit juice. The spoon (or other implement) was retained to give the mix an occasional stir. The story goes that the projecting spoon reminded equestrian enthusiasts of the upright, docked tails of mixed-bred hunters and draught horses, as distinct from thoroughbred racehorses. 'Cocktailed' is still a common description in the US for a non-thoroughbred animal. There are countless other suggested origins, including claims that the cocktail was an invention of American barkeeper Betsy Flanagan. Allusions to poultry feathers seem wide of the mark. Likelier is some connection with a wine-based drink from Bordeaux long known as the *coquetel*. One improbable, but perennially popular, explanation centres on a truce amidst the Mexican-American hostilities of the early 1800s. King Axolotl VIII proposed a toast to the US general, but only a single cup was brought. The king, concerned that the general might be insulted to share, hesitated to take the cup first. Seeing his predicament, the cup-bearer – a beautiful girl – drained the vessel herself, and saved the day. Impressed, the general asked his host for the girl's name. The king, who had no idea, sensibly replied that she was his daughter, Coctel. The rest, were any of this true, would be history.

Cocomacoque Cocktail. Over ice shake 1 part white rum, 1 orange juice, 1 pineapple juice. Strain into an ice-filled wine glass and top with red wine.

coconut liqueur style of white-rum based liqueur in which coconut flesh has been macerated. West Indies.

Coconut Tequila Cocktail. Over ice shake 1 part tequila, 2 dashes coconut liqueur, 2 dashes lemon juice, dash maraschino.

Coconut Whisqueur scotch whisky-based coconut liqueur.

Cocuy spirit distilled from fermented sisal roots, Venezuela.

Codorníu *cava* sparkling wine producer, Barcelona, Spain. Raventó family, winemakers since 1551, devised cava-making 1872 and Codorníu is now the largest producer. Brands include Gran Codorníu Brut, Non Plus Ultra.

Coebergh *genever* distiller, Netherlands.

Coeur d'Alene brewery of TW Fisher pub at Coeur d'Alene, Idaho, USA.

Coffee Cocktail. Over ice shake 2 parts port, 1 brandy, 1 dash curaçao, 1 teaspoon sugar, 1 egg yolk. Strain and grate nutmeg over. Cocktail is so-called because it looks like coffee, not because it tastes of it.

Coffee House rum-based sweet liqueur made with coffee extracts. Virgin Islands, West Indies.

Coffey Still type of continuous still devised by Aeneas Coffey, 1830.

cognac brandy from grapes grown in a defined zone of the River Charente basin, western France, with production centred on the towns of Cognac and Jarnac.

Cognac Combo Cocktail. Over ice shake 2 parts cognac, 1 port, 1 pastis, 4 dashes lemon juice. Strain.

Cointreau colourless liqueur from double-distilled Caribbean bitter-orange peels and sweet Mediterranean oranges compounded with spirit. Created 1849 by Edouard and Adolphe Cointreau at Angers, France, where production still continues.

Colares designated coastal wine region and long-lived red wine from Ramisco grapes grown in vineyards of sand. West of Lisbon, Portugal.

Colchester Brewery Company extinct brewery once famed in Essex, England, for Oyster Feast Stout.

Cold Cock porter brand of Big Rock brewery, Calgary, Canada.

Cold Deck Cocktail. Over ice shake 2 parts brandy, 1 sweet vermouth, 1 white crème de menthe.

Cold Duck to make this punch mix the juice of 1 lemon and 6 teaspoons of sugar in a punch bowl. Add 2 bottles chilled moselle, 1 bottled chilled sparkling wine and plenty of ice. Slice 1 lemon and float slices on top. Serve in wine glasses.

cold fermentation in winemaking, the use of vats equipped with immersion coils through which cold water is pumped to control temperature of fermenting must. Common for white wines in hot areas of Australia, SW France etc.

Cold Spring brewery at Cold Spring, Minnesota, USA.

Coldstream Hills vineyard in Yarra Valley, Australia, est by lawyer-writer James Halliday. Renowned wines from Pinot Noir, Chardonnay, Cabernet Sauvignon and Merlot, grapes. Now owned by Southcorp.

Coleraine Cabernet Sauvignon/Merlot red wine by Te Mata Estate, Hawke's Bay, New Zealand.

Coleburn Speyside malt whisky distillery est 1897, Longmorn, Morayshire, Scotland. Now closed.

Cole Ranch AVA of Mendocino County, California, USA.

Cole's brewery in Salt Lake City, Utah, USA.

colheita 'vintage' in Portuguese. Colheita ports, as made by Portuguese rather than British shippers, are tawny wines of individual vintages, aged in wood for a minimum of seven years before bottling. The wines are commonly kept in cask for 20 or even 30 years before bottling, with occasional mild filtering to preserve freshness. The wine should not be expected to develop in bottle in the manner of vintage port bottled on its lees and 'ruby' in colour.

Colio wine producer at Harrow, Essex County, Ontario, Canada.

collage fining (clarifying wine). French.

Colleen Cocktail. Over ice shake 3 parts Irish whiskey, 2 Irish Mist, 1 Cointreau, 1 teaspoon lemon juice.

Colle Picchioni red wine of Castelli Romani, Latium, Italy. Cesanese, Merlot, Montepulciano and Sangiovese grapes.

Collery champagne house, Aÿ, France.

colli hills in Italian. Common in wine-region descriptions.

Colli Albani DOC for sparkling and still white wines from Malvasia and Trebbiano grapes, Lake Albano, Latium, Italy.

Colli Altotiberini DOC for red and *rosato* wines from Merlot and Sangiovese grapes, and white wines from Trebbiano and others, Tiber Valley, Umbria, Italy.

Colli Aretini zone of Chianti Putto, Tuscany, Italy.

Colli Berici DOC for red, *rosato* and white wines, Vicenza, Veneto, Italy. Well-known red wines from Cabernet Franc and Cabernet Sauvignon grapes.

Colli Bolognesi DOC close to Bologna, Emilia-Romagna, Italy. Red wines from Barbera and Cabernet Sauvignon grapes; white wines from Sauvignon and others.

Colli del Trasimeno DOC for red wines from Ciliegiolo, Gamay and Sangiovese grapes and white wines from Grechetto, Malvasia, Trebbiano and Verdicchio. Lake Trasimeno, Umbria, Italy.

Colli di Bolzano DOC for red wine from Schiava grapes, Bolzano, Trentino-Alto Adige, Italy.

Colli di Parma DOC for red wines from Barbera, Bonarda Piemontese and Croatina grapes and white wines from Malvasia and Sauvignon. Emilia-Romagna, Italy.

Colli Euganei DOC for sparkling and still red and white wines, Po Valley, Veneto, Italy. Includes sweet wines from Muscatel grapes.

Colli Fiorentini zone of Chianti Putto, Tuscany, Italy.

Colli Goriziano DOC for red, *rosato* and white wines from numerous grape varieties, Friuli-Venezia Giulia, Italy.

Colli Lanuvini DOC for dry white wines from Malvasia and Trebbiano grapes, Lake Nemi, Latium, Italy.

Colli Morenici Mantoveani del Garde DOC for red and *rosato* wines from Merlot, Rondinella and Rossanella grapes and white wines from Garganega and Trebbiano. Mantua, Lombardy, Italy.

Colline Tortonesi DOC for red wines from Barbera grapes and white wines from Cortese. Tortona, Piedmont, Italy.

Collins lemon gin brand formerly of Seagram, Canada.

Collio alternative name of DOC Colli Goriziano.

Colli Orientali del Friuli DOC of westernmost Friuli-Venezia Giulia, Italy.

Collioure AC for regional red wines of Roussillon, France.

Collioure Blanc new (from 2002 vintage) AC for regional white wines of Roussillon, France.

Colli Perugini DOC for red and *rosato* wines from Barbera, Merlot, Montepulciano and Sangiovese grapes and white wines from Grechetto, Malvasia, Trebiano and Verdicchio. Perugia, Umbria, Italy.

Colli Piacentini series of DOCs for sparkling and still wines from individual grape varieties in Emilia-Romagna, Italy. Varieties are Barbera, Bonarda, Malvasia, Pinot Grigio, Pinot Nero, Ortrugo, Sauvignon.

Colli Piacentini Val Nure DOC for white win from Malvasia, Ortrugo and Trebbiano grapes. Emilia-Romagna, Italy.

Colli Pisani zone of Chianti Putto, Tuscany, Italy.

Colli Senesi zone of Chianti Putto, Tuscany, Italy.

Colombard white grape variety of SW France for brandy production and some table wines. Also widely planted in California, USA and, as **Colombar**, in South Africa.

Colombier-Monpélou, Château wine estate of AC Pauillac, Médoc, Bordeaux, France. Classified *Cru Grand Bourgeois*.

Colonel Collins Cocktail. In a tall-ice-filled tumbler mix 2 parts bourbon, 1 lemon juice, 1 teaspoon sugar. Top with chilled sparkling water and add a lemon slice.

Colonial Cocktail. Over ice shake 2 parts dry gin, 1 grapefruit juice, 3 dashes maraschino. Strain.

Colony House Canadian whisky brand of Palliser Distillers, Canada.

Colori wine brand of Casalbaio, Apulia, Italy. Primitivo and Sangiovese.

colori

1997 PUGLIA
INDICAZIONE
GEOGRAFICA TIPICA
SANGIOVESE

Colorino red grape variety permitted for use in DOCG Chianti. Tuscany, Italy.

Coltassala prestige *vino da tavola* from Sangiovese grapes by Chianti-producer Castello di Volpaia, Tuscany, Italy.

Columbia Brewing brewery at Creston, British Columbia, Canada.

Columbia Cocktail. Over ice shake 2 parts rum, 1 raspberry syrup, 1 lemon juice. Strain.

Columbia River former name of BridgePort brewery, Oregon, USA.

Columbia Winery wine producer est 1962 Bellevue, Washington, USA.

Columbus ale brand of 't IJ brewery, Amsterdam, Netherlands.

Columbus Brewing Company small brewery at Columbus, Ohio, USA. Brands include **Columbus Gold**; **Columbus Nutbrown Ale**; **Columbus Pale Ale**; Blackforest Porter.

Combo Cocktail. Over ice shake 2 parts dry vermouth, 4 dashes brandy, 2 dashes curaçao, 1 dash Angostura bitters, pinch of sugar. Strain.

Comet Cocktail. Over ice stir 4 parts dry gin, 1 Strega, 1 Van der Hum. Strain and add lemon peel.

Comet Year wine producers are prone to the belief that great vintages coincide with the appearance of Halley's Comet, identified by Sir Edmund Halley (1656–1742). Of the most recent comet years 1835, 1910 and 1986, only the last has been above average – but not exceptional – in Europe. The famed 1811 vintage in which Château Lafite made its legendary *vin de la comète*, coincided with another comet altogether.

Comfortable Blend Cocktail. Over ice shake 2 parts bourbon, 1 Southern Comfort, 1 equal mix lemon and peach juice, 4 dashes dry vermouth, 1 teaspoon sugar. Strain into an ice-filled tumbler.

Commandaria classic sweet wine of Cyprus named by twelfth century crusaders. Still made, from semi-dried grapes.

Commanderie, Château de la wine estate of AC Lalande-de-Pomerol, Bordeaux, France.

Commanderie du Bontemps association of wine producers in AC Médoc, Bordeaux, France. The members produce a respected joint-venture wine typical of the region, under the label Cuvée de la Commanderie du Bontemps.

Commanderie, Château La wine estate of AC Pomerol, Bordeaux, France.

Commanderie, Château La wine estate of AC St-Estèphe, Médoc, Bordeaux, France. Classified *Cru Bourgeois*.

Commando brandy by Castle Wine & Green, South Africa.

Commemorativa Christmas beer brand by Cuauhtémoc brewery, Mexico.

Commodore Cocktail. Over ice shake 4 parts rye whisky, 1 fresh lime (or lemon) juice, 2 dashes orange bitters, 1 teaspoon sugar syrup. Strain.

Commonwealth brewery at Nassau, New Providence, Bahama Islands.

Commonwealth pub-brewery in Boston, Massachusetts, USA.

Communard mixed drink of red wine and crème de cassis. Dijon, France.

Commuter Cocktail. Over ice shake 3 parts bourbon, 1 sweet vermouth, 1 grenadine.

complet in winetasting, perfectly balanced between fruit and acidity. French.

Completer white grape variety of Switzerland.

Comte Georges de Vogüé wine estate of AC Chambolle-Musigny, Burgundy, France. Renowned red Bonnes Mares and Chambolle-Musigny les Amoureuses. Domaine les Musigny.

Comtes de Champagne vintage-champagne brand of Taittinger, Reims, France.

Comtes Lafon, Domaine des wine estate of AC Meursault and part owner of Le Montrachet vineyard. Burgundy, France.

coñac informal name, imitative of cognac of France, for brandy of Spain. Proscribed with Spain's joining EEC (now EU) 1985, but not extinct.

Conca de Barbera DO wine region of Catalonia, Spain. Sparkling and still white wines from Macabeo and Parellada grapes. Few reds.

Concannon wine estate of Livermore Valley, California, USA.

Concertina Band Club brewery at Mexborough, South Yorkshire, England.

Concha y Toro major wine producer of Maipo Valley, Chile. Casillero del Diablo and Don Melchor red wines, Chardonnay and Sauvignon whites, etc.

concia the process of treating base wine with boiled must, wine or wine alcohol to complete Marsala wine. Italian.

Conciliation Ale brand of Butterknowle Brewery, Newcastle-upon-Tyne, England.

Concord red grape variety widely planted in New York State, USA.

Concorde 'British wine' brand of Matthew Clark, Bristol, England.

Condado de Tea vineyard region of Galicia, NW Spain.

Conde de Osborne fine pot-still brandy, aged 20 years, by Osborne, Jerez de la Frontera, Spain. Unusual bottle design by Salvador Dali.

Conde Duque brandy by Gonzalez Byass, Jerez de la Frontera, Spain.

condition in brewing, the natural

carbonation in beer brought about during maturation.

Condrieu AC white wine from Viognier grapes, northern Rhône Valley, France.

Confrérie des Chevaliers du Tastevin association est 1934 of wine producers of Burgundy, France. Dedicated to promoting the region's wines, its members meet (and not infrequently dine) in the château of the Clos de Vougeot vineyard. Wines selected by the Confrérie's tasting committees may bear the distinctive Tastevinage label.

congeners in wine and spirits, complex chemical components contributing much to the flavours.

Congress Springs winery known for Chardonnay and Pinot Blanc whites, Santa Cruz, California, USA.

Conhaque Dreher the biggest-selling domestic spirit brand of Brazil. In spite of the name's allusion to cognac, the spirit is distilled from sugar cane and flavoured emphatically with distilled ginger. Originally launched as a 'brandy' in 1955 by Dreher family of German origin, the maker was bought by Heublein in 1973; they added the ginger flavouring 1982 and moved production to Sorocaba, São Paulo.

Conn Creek vineyard and winery in Napa Valley, California, USA. Cabernet Sauvignon and Zinfandel red wines and Chardonnay white.

Connemara Irish whiskey brand of Cooley Distillery, Riverstown, Dundalk, County Louth, Republic of Ireland. Also Connemara Cask Strength (59.7% alc) Pure Pot Still Peated Single Malt whiskey.

Conner's brewery in Don Valley, Ontario, Canada.

Connétable Talbot second wine of Château Talbot, Bordeaux, France.

Connoisseurs Choice brand of Gordon & MacPhail, Elgin, Scotland, independent bottlers of single malt whiskies from most of the nation's distilleries.

cono regional term for oak wine vats, Valencia, Spain.

Cono Sur new (1993) wine producer at Santa Elisa Estate, Chimbarongo in the Rapel Valley, Chile. Cabernet Sauvignon and Pinot Noir red wines and Chardonnay, Gewürztraminer and Riesling whites. The name sounds facetious (a phonetic rendering of 'connoisseur') but in fact alludes to Latin American topography.

con retrogusto in winetasting, 'with aftertaste'. Italian.

Conseillante, Château La great wine estate of AC Pomerol, Bordeaux, France.

Consejo Regulador local governing body for wine production in each of Spain's DO regions.

Consolidated brewery at Ijebu-Ode, Ogun State, Nigeria.

consorzio local association of wine producers working to their own standards (above and beyond the requirements of state regulations) in vineyard and winery. Italy.

Constantia designated Wine of Origin region, Cape Town, South Africa. The remains of the original Constantia vineyard, est 1685, now accommodate the Groot (Great) Constantia and Klein (Small) Constantia estates. Famed liqueur Muscat of Constantia, extinguished by Phylloxera in 19th century, has been revived by Klein Constantia as Vin de Constance.

Constantino popular brandy of Portugal, by port shipper Ferreira of Vila Nova de Gaia.

Constellation Wines US-based multinational drinks corporation and world's largest wine company, following acquisition of Australian giant BRL Hardy in 2003. Constellation also owns US wine brands Arbor Mist, Blackstone, Paul Masson and others plus New Zealand's Nobilo and Stowell's of Chelsea in UK. Owner of Matthew Clark, UK, which manufactures brands including Babycham perry, Blackthorn and Gaymers ciders, Stone's ginger wine. Constellation also owns Italy's largest brewing company, Peroni.

Conterno, Aldo and **Giacomo** two distinguished, and separate, wine producers of DOCG Barolo, Piedmont, Italy.

Continental Cocktail. Over ice shake 3 parts white rum, 1 crème de menthe, 1 fresh lime juice, 1 teaspoon caster sugar.

Continental Chocolate liqueur brand of Halewood International, Huyton, Merseyside, England.

Continental's Charter Oak bourbon whiskey brand, USA.

Contratto, Guiseppe producer of sparkling and still wines, Alba, Piedmont, Italy.

Controguerra DOC of Abruzzi region, Italy. Red wines from Montepulciano with Merlot, Cabernet Sauvignon and other grape varieties. Still and sparkling white wines from Trebbiano Toscano, Passerina etc.

Controliran designated quality-wine zone of Bulgaria. There are 27 such zones, and wines thus labelled are claimed to be Bulgaria's best.

Convalmore Speyside malt whisky distillery est 1893, Dufftown, Scotland. Now closed.

Cooks major wine producer est 1969 Te Kauwhata, Waikato, New Zealand. Cabernet Sauvignon, Chardonnay, Gewürztraminer, Sauvignon.

cooler style of diluted wine-based fruit drink. USA.

Cooley Irish whiskey distillery, Riverstown, Dundalk, County Louth, Republic of Ireland. Brands include Connemara, Inishowen, Kilbeggan, Locke's, Tyrconnell.

cool ship in brewing, an open cooling vessel into which the wort is run after boiling. No longer widely used outside the Low Countries, where open-vessel cooling is still employed in 'lambic' breweries.

Coombes cider and perry producer at Japonica Farm, Mark Causeway, Highbridge, Somerset, England.

Coonawarra wine region of South Australia.

cooper barrel-maker.

Coopers Brewery producer of **Coopers Extra Stout; Coopers Original Pale Ale; Coopers Sparkling Ale** and other beers at Adelaide, South Australia.

Cooper's Creek winery at Huapai, New Zealand. Noted white wines.

Cooper Smith's pub-brewery in Fort Collins, Colorado, USA.

Cooperstown Cocktail. Over ice shake 1 part dry gin, 1 dry vermouth, 1 sweet vermouth. Strain and add mint sprig.

Coors major US brewing company est 1873 at Golden, Colorado and operator of the world's largest brewery at Golden, Denver. Brands include **Coors; Coors Extra Gold; Coors Light** and seasonal **Coors Winterfest**. Coors introduced the original aluminium drinks can in 1959. Purchased Carling 2001. The British brewery for Carling, at Burton upon Trent, is the UK's largest.

Cooymans *genever* and liqueur producer, Netherlands.

Copenhagen Cocktail. Over ice stir 3 parts dry gin, 1 aquavit, 3 dashes dry vermouth. Strain.

Copertino DOC for red and *rosato* wines from Negroamaro grapes, Apulia, Italy. Noted *riserva* two-year-old wines with lasting qualities.

Copet-Bégaud, Château wine estate of AC Canon-Fronsac, Bordeaux, France.

Copperhead cider brand of Matthew Clark, Shepton Mallet, Somerset, England.

Copperhead wheat beer brand of Lion Brewery, Adelaide, South Australia.

Corbans large wine-producing group est 1902 Henderson, New Zealand.

Corbett Canyon winery known for Coastal Classics brand, San Luis Obispo, California, USA.

Corbières major AC (since 1985) of the Midi, France, for red wines from Carignan, Cinsaut, Grenache, Mourvèdre and Syrah grapes. Few white wines.

Corbin, Château wine estate of AC St-Emilion, Bordeaux, France. Classified *Grand Cru Classé*.

Corbin-Michotte, Château wine estate of AC St-Emilion, Bordeaux, France. Classified *Grand Cru Classé*.

Corby's Reserve American blended whiskey brand, USA.

Cordat, Clos second wine of Château Monbrison, Bordeaux, France.

cordial liqueur of fruit macerated in spirit, USA.

Cordial Médoc sweet red liqueur based on Médoc wine. Bordeaux, France.

Cordier, Gérard distinguished producer of AC Reuilly wine, Loire Valley, France.

Cordier major wine-estate owner of Bordeaux, France. Châteaux include Cantemerle, Clos des Jacobins, Gruaud Larose, Lafaurie Peyraguey, Meyney, Talbot. Also a shipper of branded wines.

Cordier Estates major white-wine producer, Ste Genevieve Vineyards, Texas, USA. Associated with Cordier of Bordeaux.

Cordless Screwdriver Cocktail. Prepare a slice of orange by dipping it in sugar. Pour a measure of iced vodka into a shot glass. Drink the vodka in one shot and take a suck of the orange.

cordon vine-training system based on horizontal wire support for vine trunks.

Cordon Argent, Cordon Rubis and Cordon Supreme are all brands of Pernod-Ricard.

Cordon Rouge *brut* non-vintage champagne brand of GH Mumm, Champagne, France. **Cordon Vert** is the *demi-sec* (sweet) counterpart.

Cordova Cocktail. Over ice shake 2 parts dry gin, 1 sweet vermouth, 1 dash anis, 1 teaspoon fresh cream. Strain.

Corent *cru* for rosé wines, Côtes d'Auvergne, Loire Valley, France.

corenwijn unflavoured, all-grain spirit of renowned quality. Netherlands. Name means 'corn wine'.

Corenwyn renowned brand of wood-aged *corenwijn* by Bols, Netherlands.

Cori DOC for red wines from Cesanese, Montepulciano and Nero Buono grapes and white wines from Malvasia and Trebbiano, Cori, Latium, Italy.

Coria wine producer of DOC Cerasuolo di Vittoria, Sicily, Italy.

Corio whisky brand of United Distillers, Melbourne, Australia.

cork since the 18th century, the principal closure for wine bottles. Cut from bark of cork oak trees cultivated largely in Portugal and Spain. Diminishing quality and quantity of supply has resulted in progressively wider use of plastic substitutes and screwcaps.

corkage charge made by hoteliers and restaurateurs per bottle for opening and serving wines brought into their premises by customers.

corked in winetasting, a 'dead' smell usually caused by oxidation – due to an invasion of air via a faulty cork. Wine in this condition is emphatically undrinkable, but this does not deter *soi disant* experts from applying the term to just about any fault or unfamiliar characteristic in wine they dislike.

corkscrew device for drawing the cork from a bottle. The term dates, according to the Oxford dictionaries, from 1720 – fully a century after the first corkscrews came into use. Previously, these implements were known as bottlescrews – a term now no longer in use and not, mysteriously, even mentioned in the Oxford dictionaries.

Corkscrew Cocktail. Over ice stir 3 parts rum, 1 peach brandy, 1 dry vermouth. Strain.

corky in winetasting, a mushroomy smell of desiccated cork, which may also invade the flavour. Caused by infected or infested cork.

Cormeil-Figeac, Château wine estate of AC St-Emilion, Bordeaux, France. Classified *Grand Cru*.

Cornas AC for rich, long-lived red wines from Syrah grapes, northern Rhône Valley, France.

Cornell Cocktail. Over ice shake 2 parts dry gin, 4 dashes maraschino, 2 dashes lemon juice, 1 egg white. Strain.

Cornish Brewery Company famed for Domesday II, a barley wine first made in 1986 and said to be the strongest beer ever brewed, at 1143·7 original gravity (15.86% alc). Redruth, Cornwall, England.

Cornish Coaster ale (3.6% alc) by Sharp's Brewery, Rock, Cornwall, England.

Cornish Knocker bottle-conditioned ale (4.5% alc) by Skinners Brewing Co, Truro, Cornwall, England. 'Cornish Knockers are the local tin mine fairies who, through their knocking, used to lead miners to the best seams in return for the crusts of Cornish pasties.'

Cornucopia strong (6.5% alc) bottled ale by King & Barnes brewers, formerly of Horsham, Sussex, England. Now made by Hall & Woodhouse, Blandford Forum, Dorset.

Corona beer brand of Cerveceria Modelo brewery, Mexico. Leading bottled product is **Corona Extra** (4.6% alc). Owned by Constellation Wines.

Coronation Cocktail. Over ice shake 1 part sherry, 1 dry vermouth, 2 dashes orange bitters, 1 dash maraschino. Strain. Alternatively, over ice shake 1 generous measure brandy, 3 dashes curaçao, 1 dash peppermint, 1 dash peach bitters. Strain.

Corowa wine region of New South Wales, Australia, along border with Victoria State. Known for 'port' and 'sherry' wines.

corps in winetasting, body. French.

Corpse Reviver Cocktail. Over ice shake 2 parts brandy, 1 apple brandy, 1 sweet vermouth. Strain. Alternatively, over ice shake 1 part dry gin, 1 Cointreau, 1 Lillet, 1 lemon juice, 1 dash anis. Strain.

corsé in winetasting, a young, heavy wine. France.

Corsendonk Belgian abbey beers named after former priory of Corsendonk near Turnhout, including **Corsendonk Agnus** and **Corsendonk Pater Noster**.

Corsica wine-producing island covered by AC Vin de Corse, France. Other ACs and *vin de pays* designation Ile de Beauté cover the island's diverse red, rosé and white wines, plus *vin doux naturel*.

Corsican Breeze Cocktail. In a tall glass combine 1 part Mandarine Napoléon, 3 chilled bitter lemon, 3 chilled orange juice. Add ice and a mint sprig.

Cortaillod wine village of Neuchâtel, Switzerland.

Cortese white grape variety principally of Piedmont, Italy. Sparkling and still white wines of DOC **Cortese dell'Alto Montferrato** and DOC **Cortese di Gavi.**

Corton AC and large (200 acres) *Grand Cru* vineyard grouping within or partially within AC of village of Aloxe-Corton, Côte de Beaune, Burgundy, France. Highly prized red wines sold as Corton or appended with the name of the individual *climat* (site) within the vineyard: Les Bressandes, Le Charlemagne (white wines), Les Chaumes, Les Chaumes de la Voirosse, Le Clos du Roi, Les Combes, Le Corton, Les Frêtres, Les Grèves, Les Languettes, Les Maréchaudes, Les Meix, Les Meix Lallemand, en Pauland, Les Perrières, Les Pougets, Les Renardes, Le Rognet et Corton, Les Vergennes, La Vigne au Saint.

Corton-Charlemagne AC and *Grand Cru* within Corton *Grand Cru* for white (Chardonnay) wines, Côte de Beaune, Burgundy, France. Renowned and costly long-lived wines. Vineyard is traditionally believed planted on orders of Holy Roman Emperor Charlemagne (742–814).

Corton-Grancey, Château AC Corton of Louis Latour, Burgundy, France.

Corvina red grape variety of Veneto, Italy. Main constituent of Valpolicella.

Corvo wine brand of Duca di Salaparuta, Sicily, Italy.

Cos d'Estournel, Château great wine estate of AC St-Estèphe, Médoc, Bordeaux, France. Classified *2ème Grand Cru Classé.*

cosecha vintage. Spanish.

Cos Labory, Château wine estate of AC St-Estèphe, Médoc, Bordeaux, France. Classified *5ème Grand Cru Classé.*

Cosmo Cocktail. Over ice shake 2 parts vodka, 1 Cointreau, 2 cranberry juice, 1 fresh lime juice. Strain and squeeze lemon peel over.

Cosmos Cocktail. Over ice shake 3 parts vodka, 1 fresh lime juice. Strain into shot glasses.

Cossack Cocktail. Over ice shake 1 part vodka, 1 cognac, 1 fresh lime juice, sprinkling of sugar. Strain.

Cossart Gordon leading wine shipper of Island of Madeira, Portugal. Est 1745, now a brand of Madeira Wine Co.

Coste, Château de la second wine of Château Paveil de Luze, Bordeaux, France.

Coste, Edmund & Fils wine producer in Graves, Bordeaux, France. Château Chicane and Domaine de Gaillat and branded wines.

Costières de Nîmes AC zone between Montpelier and Nîmes in the Midi, France. Red wines of improving reputation from Carignan, Cinsaut, Grenache, Mourvèdre and Syrah grapes. Some rosé and white. Formerly known as AC Costières du Gard.

Cot name in SW France, especially in AC Cahors, for Malbec (or Auxerrois) grape.

côte coast or 'hillside' in French. In naming wine-producing districts of France, the term has commonly been adopted to emphasise that vines are grown on sites with the best exposure to (or shelter from) the sun – in other words, the hillsides. In reality, many wines labelled Côtes are from vineyards on level ground.

Côte, La lakeshore wine region of Vaud, Switzerland.

coteaux in wine descriptions, similar to côtes. Strictly speaking, applies to vineyards on individual hill sites rather than lying along continuous ranges of hills.

Côte-Baleau, Château wine estate of AC St-Emilion, Bordeaux, France. Classified *Grand Cru*.

Coteaux Champenois AC for red and white still wines of Champagne, France.

Coteaux d'Aix-en-Provence AC for red, rosé and white wines of Provence, France. Red and rosé wines from Cabernet Sauvignon, Cinsaut, Grenache and Syrah grapes; white wines from Clairette, Grenache Blanc, Sauvignon, Ugni Blanc.

Coteaux d'Aix-en-Provence Les Baux AC for red, rosé and white wines within Coteaux d'Aix-en-Provence AC. Vineyards have been planted in excavated bauxite rock.

Coteaux d'Ancenis VDQS wines, mostly red from Cabernet and Gamay grapes, Loire Valley, France.

Coteaux de Cap Corse vineyard district of AC Vin de Corse, Island of Corsica, France. Mainly white wines and *vin doux naturel*.

Coteaux de Carthage wine brand of UCCVT, Tunisia.

Coteaux de La Méjanelle vineyard district of AC Coteaux de Languedoc, the Midi, France. Red wines from Carignan, Cinsaut and Grenache grapes.

Coteaux de L'Aubance AC for sweet white wines from Chenin Blanc grapes, Loire Valley, France.

Coteaux de Pierrevert VDQS for red, rosé and white wines, Alpes-de-Haute-Provence, France.

Coteaux de Saumur sweet white wine from Chenin Blanc grapes, Saumur, Loire Valley, France.

Coteaux de Tlemcen wine district of Oran, Morocco.

Coteaux du Giennois VDQS of Loire Valley, France. Red wines from Gamay and Pinot Noir grapes; white wines from Chenin Blanc and Sauvignon.

Coteaux du Languedoc sprawling AC (since 1985) of the Midi, France, including many emerging wine districts: Cabrières, La Clape,

Coteaux de la Méjanelle, Coteaux de St-Christol, Coteaux de Vérargues, Montpeyroux, Picpoul de Pinet, Pic St-Loup, Quatourze, St-Dézery, St-Georges d'Orques, St-Saturnin. Mainly red wines.

Coteaux du Layon AC for sweet white wines from Chenin Blanc grapes, Loire Valley, France. Coteaux du Layon Villages is designation for wines from villages of Beaulieu sur Layon, Faye d'Anjou, Rablay sur Layon, Rochefort sur Loire, Saint Aubin de Luigné, Saint Lambert de Lattay.

Coteaux du Loir wine district of northern Loire Valley, France.

Coteaux du Lyonnais AC for red, rosé and white wines from near Lyon in southernmost Burgundy.

Coteaux du Mascara wine district of Oran, Algeria.

Coteaux du Quercy *vin de pays* zone of Tarn & Garonne, SW France.

Coteaux d'Utique red wine of Bizerte-Mateur-Tebourda region, Tunisia.

Coteaux du Tricastin AC for red wines from Carignan, Cinsaut, Grenache, Mourvèdre and Syrah, southern Rhône Valley, France. Few rosé and white wines.

Coteaux du Vendômois VDQS for red (Pinot d'Aunis grape and others), rosé and white (mainly Chenin Blanc) wines, Vendôme, Loire Valley, France.

Coteaux Varois VDQS for red and rosé wines from Cabernet Sauvignon, Carignan, Cinsaut, Grenache, Mourvèdre and Syrah grapes. Brignoles in Var *département*, Provence, France.

Côte Blonde and **Côte Brune** the principal hillside vineyards of AC Côte Rôtie of the northern Rhône Valley, France. The names are dated to a medieval lord of Ampuis who divided the adjacent slopes between his two daughters – one a blonde, the other a brunette. The wines are commonly labelled Côte Rôtie Brune et Blonde.

Côte Chalonnaise vineyard district of Burgundy, France, lying south of the Côte d'Or. Four ACs: Givry, Mercurey, Montagny, Rully.

Côte de Beaune the southern district of the Côte d'Or of Burgundy, France.

Côte de Beaune AC for red and white wines from slopes immediately surrounding the town of Beaune, Burgundy, France.

Côte de Beaune-Villages AC for red and white wines from 16 designated villages of the Côte de Beaune, Burgundy, France. Wines from more than one of the villages can be blended. The villages are Auxey-Duresses, Blagny, Chassagne-Montrachet, Cheilly-les-Maranges, Dezizes-les-Maranges, Chorey-lès-Beaune, Ladoix-Serrigny, Meursault, Monthélie, Pernand-Vergelesses, Puligny-Montrachet, St-Aubin, St-Romain, Sampigny-les-Maranges, Santenay, Savigny-lès-Beaune.

Côte de Brouilly *cru* of Beaujolais region, France.

Côte de Léchet *premier cru* vineyard of Chablis, France.

Côte de Nuits the northern district of the Côte d'Or, Burgundy, France.

Côte de Nuits-Villages AC for red (and a very few white) wines from six designated villages of the Côte de Nuits, Burgundy, France. Villages are: Brochon, Comblanchien, Corgoloin, Couchey, Fixin, Prissey.

Côte des Blancs major vineyard district of AC Champagne, France. Chardonnay grapes.

Côte de Sézanne vineyard district of Champagne, France. Mainly Chardonnay grapes.

Côte d'Or the 'golden hillside' of Burgundy, France, is a *département* name given to the gentle hills extending 30 miles south-southwest from Dijon and incorporating the designated vineyard districts of Côte de Nuits and Côte de Beaune.

Côte Rôtie the 'roasted hillside' – AC for red wine from Syrah (and sometimes Viognier) grapes grown on the slopes surrounding the village of Ampuis, northern Rhône Valley, France. Wine is traditionally matured in old oak casks but some growers now use new wood.

Côtes d'Agly traditional, but fading, *vin doux naturel* of the Midi, France.

Côtes d'Auvergne VDQS of upper Loire Valley, France. Red wines from Gamay grapes are compared with Beaujolais. Five communes within the region can append their names to the Côtes designation on labels of their wines: Boudes, Chanturgue, Châteaugay, Corent, Médargues.

Côtes de Bergerac AC for superior-quality regional wines of Bergerac, SW France. Red and white wines.

Côtes de Blaye AC for white wines of Blaye, Bordeaux, France.

Côtes de Bordeaux overall term for the satellite ACs of Bordeaux, France: Côtes de Blaye, Côtes de Bourg, Côtes de Castillon, Côtes de Francs, Premières Côtes de Bordeaux.

Côtes de Bordeaux St-Macaire AC for sweet white wine, Bordeaux, France.

Côtes de Bourg AC for red wines from Bourg, the district facing Médoc across the Gironde river, Bordeaux, France.

Côtes de Brulhois VDQS of the Lot et Garonne, SW France. Principally red wines.

Côtes de Buzet former AC name of Buzet, SW France.

Côtes de Canon-Fronsac AC for vineyards of upper slopes within commune of Fronsac, Bordeaux, France.

Côtes de Castillon AC adjacent to St-Emilion, Bordeaux, France.

Côtes de Duras AC for red, rosé and white wines lying immediately south of AC Entre-Deux-Mers of Bordeaux, France. Bordeaux grape varieties.

Côtes de Forez new (1999) AC of Southern Loire, France, for wines from Gamay grapes.

Côtes de Francs AC of Bordeaux, France.

Côtes de Frontonnais AC north of Toulouse, SW France, for red wines from Negrette grapes (and many others in lesser quantities) and some rosé.

Côtes de La Malpère VDQS for red and rosé wines of Carcassonne, the Midi, France.

Côtes de Montravel AC for dry and medium white wines, Bergerac, SW France.

Côtes de Provence extensive AC of Provence, southern France. Mostly rosé wine from co-operative producers.

Côtes de Saint-Mont VDQS for red, rosé and white wines of Cave Coopérative de Saint-Mont, SW France.

Côtes de Toul VDQS of Toul, NE France, for distinctive *vin gris* from Gamay grapes plus red and white wines.

Côtes de Zaccar wine-producing district of Alger, Algeria.

Côtes d'Olt, Les dominant co-operative wine producer of AC Cahors, SW France.

Côtes du Forez VDQS for red and rosé wines of upper Loire Valley, France.

Côtes du Jura AC of Jura region, France. Red and rosé wines from Pinot Noir, Poulsard and Trousseau grapes; white wines from Chardonnay and Savagnin. AC covers sparkling wines as well as *vin de paille* and *vin jaune*.

Côtes du Lubéron AC for red, rosé and white wines, Vaucluse, Rhône Valley, France.

Côtes du Marmandais VDQS of Marmande, SW France. Red wines from regional grapes plus Bordeaux varieties. Few whites.

Côtes du Rhône AC of Rhône Valley (mainly southern regions), France. Mostly red wines (and some rosé) from Carignan, Grenache, Mourvèdre and Syrah grapes (among others) plus white wines from Marsanne, Roussanne and others. Quality varies wildly.

Côtes du Rhône Villages AC for the wines of 16 villages lying within AC Côtes du Rhône, France. Wines may be blends from more than one village's production. Wine from a single village may be labelled with its name: Beaumes-de-Venise, Cairanne, Chusclan, Laudun, Rasteau, Roaix, Rochegude, Rousset-les-Vignes, Sablet, St Gervais, St Maurice-sur-Eygues, St Pantaléon-les-Vignes, Séguret, Valréas, Vinsobres, Visan. Village wines are made to stricter standards and higher alcohol levels than basic Côtes du Rhône AC.

Côtes du Roussillon AC of the Midi, France, for red and rosé wines largely from Carignan grapes with some Cinsaut, Grenache and Mourvèdre. White wines from Maccabéo grapes.

Côtes du Roussillon Villages AC for higher-quality wines from within AC Côtes du Roussillon, France.

Côtes du Roussillon les Aspres AC (from 2003 vintage) for regional wines within Roussillon, France.

Côtes du Ventoux AC of southern Rhône Valley, France, for red, rosé and white wines.

Côtes du Vivarais VDQS for red, rosé and white wines, Ardèche, Rhône Valley, France.

Côtes Roannaises VDQS for red and rosé wines from Gamay grapes, upper Loire Valley, France.

Côte St-Jacques vineyard at Joigny, Burgundy, France. Red, white and long-established *vin gris*.

Côte Vermeille *vin de pays* of Banyuls and Collioure, the Midi, France.

Cotleigh brewery at Wiveliscombe, Somerset, England. Barn Owl Bitter (4.5%), Harrier SPA (3.6%), Old Buzzard (4.8%), Tawny Bitter (3.8%).

Cotnari traditional sweet wine of Moldavia, Romania.

Cottage Brewing microbrewery at West Lydford, Somerset, England.

cotto boiled-down grape concentrate used in colouring wine (particularly marsala of Sicily). Italy.

Coucheroy, Château second wine of Château La Louvière, Bordeaux, France.

Coudert, Château wine estate of AC St-Emilion, Bordeaux, France. Classified *Grand Cru*.

Coudert-Pelletan, Château wine estate of AC St-Emilion, Bordeaux, France. Classified *Grand Cru*.

Coudoulet de Beaucastel wine brand of Château de Beaucastel, Châteauneuf-du-Pape, France.

Coufran, Château wine estate of AC Haut-Médoc, Bordeaux, France. Classified *Cru Grand Bourgeois*.

Couhins, Château wine estate of AC Pessac-Léognan, Bordeaux, France. Classified *Cru Classé*.

Couhins-Lurton, Château wine estate of AC Pessac-Léognan, Bordeaux, France. Classified *Cru Classé*.

Coulac, Château wine estate of AC Ste-Croix-du-Mont, Bordeaux, France.

Coulanges-la-Vineuse village of northern Burgundy, France, known for red wine from Pinot Noir grapes. Classified AC Bourgogne Rouge.

coulant in winetasting, quaffable. French.

coulure vine disorder. Untypical spring weather causes vine to develop foliage at the expense of grape buds, which wither. Reduction in harvest can be dramatic.

Couly Dutheuil wine producer and *négociant* of AC Chinon, Loire Valley, France.

Country Club Cooler Cocktail. Into ice-filled tumbler pour 1 generous measure dry vermouth, 1 teaspoon grenadine. Stir and top with soda water.

Country Gentleman's, The blended scotch whisky of the Country Gentleman's Association, Baldock, Hertfordshire, England.

Countryman cider of Felldown Head, Milton Abbot, Tavistock, Devon, England.

Country Manor perry brand of Matthew Clark, Shepton Mallet, Somerset, England.

County ale brand of Ruddles brewery, Rutland, England.

County Ale beer brand of Wellington County brewery, Ontario, Canada.

County Fair bourbon whiskey brand, USA.

County Fair Raspberry Ale fruit beer by Stratcona Brewing Co, Edmonton, Alberta, Canada.

coupage in winemaking, blending made wines, usually to disguise faults. A wine thus made is known as a **coupé**.

Courage Former major British brewing company owned by Scottish & Newcastle Breweries since 1995. Brands still in production include **Courage Best Bitter; Courage Director's Bitter**; bottled Bulldog pale ale; Imperial Russian Stout.

Courbon, Château de wine estate of AC Graves, Bordeaux, France.

Courbu Blanc white grape variety mostly of Jurançon, SW France.

Couronne, Château La wine estate of AC Pauillac, Médoc, Bordeaux, France. Classified *Cru Bourgeois Supérieur Exceptionnel*.

Cour Pavillon, La wine brand of Gilbey de Loudenne, Bordeaux, France.

court in winetasting, short, lacking finish. French.

Courteillac, Château de wine estate of AC Entre-Deux-Mers, Bordeaux, France.

courtier broker of wines, usually representing small-scale producers in dealings with *négoçiants*.

Courvoisier leading brandy producer of Cognac, France, owned by Diageo. The firm's association with the Emperor Napoleon (his 'N' symbol and hat appear on the labels)

dates from 1815, the year of his defeat at Waterloo. After the battle, Napoleon attempted to escape to America, and Emmanuel Courvoisier gallantly provided the Emperor with several barrels of spirit to take with him into exile. But the ship was intercepted by the Royal Navy, which handed Napoleon over to the allies, and confiscated the cognac. Courvoisier's current range includes a three-star, a VSOP and a Napoleon among others.

Cousiño Macul leading wine producer est 1862 Santiago, Chile. Renowned Cabernet Sauvignon reds Antiguas Reservas and Don Luis, plus white wines from Chardonnay and Semillon grapes.

Couspaude, Château La wine estate of AC St-Emilion, Bordeaux, France. Classified *Grand Cru Classé* (1996).

Coustolle, Château wine estate of AC Canon-Fronsac, Bordeaux, France.

Coutelin-Merville, Château wine estate of AC St-Estèphe, Médoc, Bordeaux, France. Classified *Cru Grand Bourgeois*.

Coutet, Château wine estate of AC Barsac, Bordeaux, France. Classified *1er Cru Classé*.

Coutet, Château wine estate of AC Graves, Bordeaux, France.

Coutet, Château wine estate of AC St-Emilion, Bordeaux, France. Classified *Grand Cru*.

Coutras satellite vineyard region of Bordeaux, France. Bordeaux AC wines.

Couvent, Château Le wine estate of AC St-Emilion, Bordeaux, France. Classified *Grand Cru*.

Couvent Les Jacobins, Château wine estate of AC St-Emilion, Bordeaux, France. Classified *Grand Cru Classé*.

Covifruit wine producer of Vin d'Orléanais district, Loire Valley, France. Also renowned for delectable Eau de Vie de Poire William, including magnum bottle complete with whole pear.

Cowarne Red apple variety traditionally valued for cider-making. English.

Cowboy Cocktail. Over ice shake 2 parts rye whisky, 1 fresh cream. Strain into crushed-ice-filled glass.

Coxley Vineyard wine producer, Wells, Somerset, England.

Cox's sweet cider (3.5% alc) by Thatcher's Cider, Sandford, Somerset, England. Made from Cox's apples.

Coyote spirit brand of Pernod-Ricard.

Coyote Spring Brewing Company pub-brewery in Phoenix, Arizona, USA, known for Cologne-style beer branded Koyote Kölsch.

Crabbie's blended scotch whisky by John Crabbie, Leith, Scotland.

Crabitey, Château wine estate of AC Graves, Bordeaux, France.

Cracker Ale beer brand of Barngates Brewery at the Drunken Duck Inn, Ambleside, Cumbria, England.

Crackshot beer (5.5% alc) 'brewed to a 17th century recipe found in a recipe book in Ripley Castle' by Daleside Brewery, Harrogate, Yorkshire, England.

cradle in serving wine, a basket to hold the bottle for gentle pouring that will not disturb sediment. Mechanical cradles are elaborate contraptions operated by a rotating handle.

Cragganmore Speyside malt whisky distillery est 1869, Ballindalloch, Banffshire, Scotland. Single malt: 12-year-old.

Craigellachie Speyside malt whisky distillery est 1891, Banffshire, Scotland. Single malts: 14-year-old, 15-year-old.

Craigmoor wine estate est 1858 in Mudgee, New South Wales, Australia.

Cramant vine-growing village of Côte des Blancs, Champagne, France. Highly prized Chardonnay grapes.

Cramer, Christian wine producer in Südsteiermark, Austria.

Cranmore vineyard at Cranmore, Isle of Wight, England.

Crawford's 3 Star blended scotch whisky of Whyte & Mackay and A & A Crawford, Glasgow, Scotland.

crayères underground wine-storage cellars of Champagne, France. First excavated in the chalk subsoil by the Romans.

Crazy Ed's Black Mountain brewery at Cave Creek, Phoenix, Arizona, USA, producing beers including Black Mountain Gold and sweet, hoppy Frog Light.

Cream Puff Cocktail. Over ice shake 2 parts white rum, 1 fresh cream, 1 teaspoon caster sugar. Strain into a wine glass and top with chilled sparkling water.

cream sherry style of dark sherry blended from *oloroso* and sweet Pedro Ximénez wine. Jerez de la Frontera, Spain.

Creamy Orange Cocktail. Over ice shake 2 parts cream sherry, 2 orange juice, 1 brandy, 1 fresh cream. Strain.

Creemore Springs brewery at the ski resort of Creemore, Ontario, Canada, known for unpasteurized **Creemore Springs Premium Lager.**

crémant 'champagne method' sparkling wines of Alsace, Burgundy, Limoux and the Loire Valley, France, as made under ACs est since 1975. The term *crémant* for champagne made to a lower atmospheric pressure than usual, to produce a 'creaming' mousse rather than a fully sparkling one, has been abolished.

Crémat, Château de noted producer of red, rosé and white wines of AC Bellet, Nice, France.

crème in liqueur-making, a style flavoured entirely or predominantly with a single ingredient. Examples are **crème de cassis, crème de menthe**. French, but a term applying to liqueurs made worldwide.

crème d'amandes sweet almond liqueur.

crème d'ananas pineapple liqueur, commonly rum-based. Brands/producers include Lamb & Watt, Liverpool, England, and Hulstkamp, Netherlands.

crème de banane yellow liqueur from macerating ripe bananas in spirit.

crème de cacao chocolate liqueur made by macerating or percolating cacao beans then distilling and sweetening.

crème de café liqueur usually of spirit extracts of coffee, coloured and sweetened.

Crème de Cassis de Dijon blackcurrant liqueur indigenous to Dijon, Burgundy, France.

Crème de Cumin former brand of kümmel by Wolfschmidt of Riga, Latvia. Extinguished by Second World War.

crème de fraises des bois liqueur from cultivated 'wild' strawberries.

crème de framboise liqueur from raspberries.

crème de Genièvre liqueur from macerated juniper berries.

Crème de Kobai plum liqueur brand of Suntory, Japan.

crème de mandarine liqueur from tangerine peel. Denmark, France, Netherlands.

crème de menthe mint-flavoured green or white liqueur.

Crème de Menthe Frappé Cocktail. Fill a small brandy glass with crushed ice and pour a measure of green crème de menthe over. Serve with two short straws.

crème de mokka liqueur usually of spirit extracts of mocha coffee, coloured and sweetened.

crème de mûres sauvages liqueur from wild blackberries. Southern France.

crème de myrtilles liqueur from bilberries. Southern France.

crème de noisettes liqueur from nuts, usually hazel. Southern France.

crème de noix liqueur from walnuts. Speciality of walnut-growing area of Perigord, SW France.

crème de noyau liqueur from apricot and peach kernels. France.

Crème de Nuits blackcurrant liqueur by Carton, Nuits-St-Georges, France.

crème de pêches liqueur from peaches. France and Netherlands.

crème de poire liqueur from pears. France and Netherlands.

crème de prunelle liqueur from plums. France and Netherlands.

crème de roses liqueur from extract of rose petals. France.

crème de vanille rich liqueur from vanilla beans. France.

crème de violettes liqueur from citrus extracts coloured and lightly flavoured violet.

Crème Yvette leading brand of crème de violettes, produced by Jacquin, Philadelphia, USA.

Creole Cocktail. Over ice stir 1 part rye whisky, 1 sweet vermouth, 2 dashes Bénédictine, 2 dashes Amer Picon bitters. Strain.

crépitant softly sparkling wine in style of AC Crépy, France.

Crépy AC for softly sparkling white wine, Haute Savoie, France.

Cresta Run Cocktail. Over ice stir 4 parts kirsch, 3 dry vermouth, 1 crème de noyau. Strain and add orange peel.

Crete island of Aegean with traditional red wines designated as Archanes, Daphnes, Peza, Sitia. Greece.

creux in winetasting, hollow-tasting, thin. French.

criadera 'nursery' in Spanish. The first series of casks in a sherry *solera*, into which the new wine is run. Andalucia, Spain.

crianza 'nursing' in Spanish. The period in which Rioja wine is 'brought up' for at least a year in cask and subsequently in the bottle before going on sale. Rioja *con crianza* is released for sale no earlier than the third year after its vintage.

Crimson Cocktail. Over ice shake 2 parts dry gin, 1 lemon juice, 3 dashes grenadine. Strain into a small wine glass and gently pour 2 parts port on top.

Crinian Canal Water blended scotch whisky of Cockburn & Co, Leith, Scotland.

Criolla red grape of Argentina. Widely planted in Mendoza region.

Cripple Cock 'strong farmyard scrumpy' cider (7.5% alc) by Thatcher's Cider, Sandford, Somerset, England. 'Have your crutches handy this be a toe curler.'

crisp in winetasting, a white wine with notable acidity.

Cristal de luxe vintage *cuvée* of Champagne Louis Roederer, Reims, France. Bottled in clear glass, as per original specification of the Romanov Court of St Petersburg in 19th century. Claimed by some aficionados to be the best of all champagnes, and unquestionably one of the most expensive.

Cristal Alken lager brand of Brouwerij Alken, Belgium.

Cristall grain vodka by Cristall Distillery (Stolichnaya), Moscow, Russia.

Croatino red grape variety of Lombardy and Piedmont, Italy.

Crochet, Lucien noted wine producer of AC Sancerre, Loire Valley, France.

Crock, Château Le wine estate of AC St-Estèphe, Médoc, Bordeaux, France. Classified *Cru Grand Bourgeois Exceptionnel*.

Crocodile Cocktail. Over ice shake 2 parts vodka, 1 Cointreau, 1 melon liqueur, 2 lemon juice. Strain.

Croft port producer and shipper, est 1678 Vila Nova de Gaia, Portugal. Acquired by Taylor-Fonseca, 2001. Popular Finest Distinction Reserve, old tawnies and vintages: 1955, 60, 63, 66, 67, 70, 75, 77, 78, 82, 83, 85, 87, 91, 94, 97, 2000, 03.

Croft Jerez sherry operation est 1970 by International Distillers & Vintners of London in Jerez de la Frontera, Spain and acquired by Gonzalez Byass of Jerez, 2001. Popular brands include the suitably named, first-ever 'pale cream' sherry **Croft Original**, plus 'medium' **Croft Particular** and others.

Croix, Château La wine estate of AC Fronsac, Bordeaux, France.

Croix, Château La wine estate of AC Pomerol, Bordeaux, France.

Croix, Château La second wine of Château Ducru-Beaucaillou, Bordeaux, France.

Croix-Blanche, Château La second wine of Château des Tours, Bordeaux, France.

Croix-de-Gay, Château La wine estate of AC Pomerol, Bordeaux, France.

Croix de Mazerat, Château La second wine of Château Beauséjour-Duffau-Lagarosse, Bordeaux, France.

Croix de Millorit, Château La wine estate of AC Côtes de Bourg, Bordeaux, France.

Croix de Pez, Château La wine estate of AC St-Estèphe, Médoc, Bordeaux, France.

Croix du Casse, Château La wine estate of AC Pomerol, Bordeaux, France.

Croix-Landon, Château La wine estate of AC Médoc, Bordeaux, France.

Croix-St-André, Château La- wine estate of AC Lalande-de-Pomerol, Bordeaux, France.

Croix-St-Georges, Château La wine estate of AC Pomerol, Bordeaux, France.

Croix-Toulifaut, Château La wine estate of AC Pomerol, Bordeaux, France.

Croizet-Bages, Château wine estate of AC Pauillac, Médoc, Bordeaux, France. Classified *5ème Grand Cru Classé*.

Crombe brewery in Zottegem, Belgium, specialising in brown ale.

Cropton brewery at Cropton, Pickering, North Yorkshire, England.

Croque-Michotte, Château wine estate of AC St-Emilion, Bordeaux, France. Classified *Grand Cru* (1996).

Cros, Château de wine estate of AC Loupiac, Bordeaux, France.

Crossman, Ben see Ben Crossman's.

Cross River brewery at Uyo, Akwa Ibom State, Nigeria.

Crouch Vale Brewery producer at Chelmsford, Essex, England, of ales including Essex Porter and Willie Warmer.

Crow Cocktail. Over ice shake 1 part rye whisky, 2 lemon juice, 1 dash grenadine. Strain.

Crown City pub-brewery in Pasadena, California, USA.

Crown of Crowns Liebfraumilch brand by Langenbach, Worms, Germany.

Crown Royal Canadian whisky brand of Seagram, Canada, sold to Diageo 2001.

Crozes-Hermitage AC for red wines from Syrah grapes and white wines from Marsanne and Roussanne grapes, Tain l'Hermitage, northern Rhône Valley, France.

cru 'growth' in French. The term for a vineyard or grouping of vineyards with designated status. Mainly Bordeaux and Burgundy.

Cru Bourgeois category of wine estates in the Médoc and Sauternes regions of Bordeaux, France. Ranked below *cru classé* wines. Properties are members of Syndicat des Crus Bourgeois.

Cru Bourgeois Supérieur higher category of *Cru Bourgeois*. Wines must be aged in oak barrels.

Cruchen Blanc near-extinct white grape variety, France.

Crucial Brew strong lager by Red Stripe brewery, Jamaica.

Cruet *cru* of Vin de Savoie, France.

Cru Grand Bourgeois alternative to *Cru Bourgeois Supérieur*.

Cru Grand Bourgeois Exceptionnel designation of top properties among those ranked *Cru Grand Bourgeois* in the Médoc region of Bordeaux, France.

Cruse et Fils Frères major shipper of Bordeaux wines. France.

Crusius, Weingut Hans wine estate at Traisen in Nahe region, Germany.

Cru St-Marc second wine of Château La Tour-Blanche, Bordeaux, France.

crusted port informal term for 'vintage character' port intended for ageing in bottle so that it forms a sediment or 'crust'.

Cruzcampo popular bottled and draught beer brand of Spain, est 1904.

Cruzeau, Château du wine estate of AC Pessac, Léognan, Bordeaux, France.

Cruzeta tall T-shaped support carrying wires for vines in Minho region, Portugal. For *vinho verde* wines.

Crystal beer brand of Budweiser Bürgerbräu, Budweis, Czech Republic.

Crystal gin brand of Hiram Walker & Sons, Canada.

Crystal Bronx Cocktail. Over ice shake 1 part dry vermouth, 1 sweet vermouth, 1 orange juice. Strain into ice-filled glass and top with soda water.

Csopák village of Lake Balaton, Hungary, known for white wines.

CSR Leading cider-producing company of France. Sold by Pernod-Ricard to Cidreries de Calvados La Fermiere, 2002.

Cuarante y Tres orange-based 'licvor mirabilis' claimed to be from a Roman recipe of 2000 years old and incorporating 43 different herbs. Diego Zamora & Compania, Cartagena, Spain.

Cuauhtemoc brewery in Moctezuma, Mexico. Cerveza Superior lager (6.0% alc).

Cuba Libre Cooler Cocktail. Over ice shake 2 parts Bacardi rum, 1 fresh lime juice. Strain into ice-filled glass and top with Coca-Cola.

Cuban Cocktail. Over ice shake 2 parts brandy, 1 apricot brandy, 1

fresh lime (or lemon) juice. Strain.

Cubzac vineyard region of Bordeaux, France. Bordeaux AC wines.

Cuckmere Haven brewery of The Golden Galleon, Exceat Bridge, Seaford, East Sussex, England.

Cuello rum brand, Belize.

Cuesta sherry brand of Diageo.

Cugat, Château de wine estate of AC Entre-Deux-Mers, Bordeaux, France.

cul de bouteille wine-bottle punt. French.

Culemborg popular Cape wine brand of Douglas Green Bellingham, Johannesburg, South Africa.

Culotta wine producer at Oakville, Ontario, Canada.

Culross Cocktail. Over ice shake 1 part rum, 1 apricot brandy, 1 Lillet, 1 lemon juice. Strain.

cultivar named grape variety on wine label. South Africa.

culture biologique organic cultivation in vineyard. French.

Cumberland Ale beer brand of Jennings Brothers brewery, Cumbria, England.

Cumbrae Castle blended scotch whisky by Macduff International, Glasgow, Scotland.

Cumières wine village of Montagne de Reims, Champagne, France. Champagne and still red wines.

Cummy Norman apple variety traditionally valued for cider-making. English.

Cupid Cocktail. Over ice shake 1 generous measure sherry, 1 teaspoon sugar, 1 fresh egg, 1 drop Tabasco. Strain.

curaçao liqueur from orange peel steeped in spirit and distilled. Originally from island of Curaçao, West Indies. Widely produced, particularly in France and Netherlands. Colours: blue, brown, green, orange, white.

Curaçao Cocktail. Over ice shake 1 part curaçao, 1 orange juice, 1 teaspoon brandy, 1 teaspoon dry gin, 1 dash orange bitters. Strain.

Curate's Choice ale (4.8% alc) by Exe Valley brewery, Silverton, Devon, England.

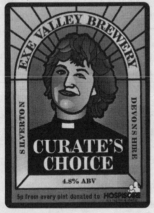

Curé-Bon-la-Madeleine, Château wine estate of AC St-Emilion, Bordeaux, France. Classified *Grand Cru Classé*.

Curebourse, Domaine de second wine of Château Durfort-Vivens, Bordeaux, France.

Curious & Ancient twenty-year-old tawny port brand of Delaforce, Vila Nova de Gaia, Portugal.

Cusenier major distiller and liqueur producer, originally of Jura, France. Now centred in Marseilles and Paris.

Cussac wine-producing commune of Médoc region, Bordeaux, France.

Custodian blended scotch whisky by Douglas Denham, London, England.

Cutty Sark blended scotch whisky of Berry Bros & Rudd, London, England. Also 12-year-old and 18-year-old. The name is that of the famed tea clipper now preserved at Greenwich, London, but cutty sark is originally a Scots term for a short shirt, as in Robert Burns's *Tam o' Shanter*:

'Her cutty sark, o' Paisley harn
That while a lassie she had worn
In longitude tho' sorely scanty
It was her best, and she was
vauntie.'

cuvaison in winemaking, the stage in which the grape skins steep in the pressed juice. French.

Cuvaison winery in Napa Valley, California, USA. Cabernet Sauvignon red wines and Carneros Chardonnay white.

cuve close tank-method of producing sparkling wines. See Charmat.

cuvée the wine contained in a *cuve* (vat). French. The term has been incorporated into the brand names of many wines. Those listed appear under their more-distinguishing names (eg **Cuvée Galius** under **Galius**).

Cuvée de l'Ermitage strong all-malt beer by Union brewery, Jumet, Belgium.

Cuvée de Noël dark *bière de garde* by Brasserie Bailleux, Gussignies, France.

Cuvée des Jonquilles *bière de garde* by Brasserie Bailleux, Gussignies, France.

Cuvée du Patron popular name for 'own-label' or 'house' wines, supposedly chosen by the patron of the establishment. French.

Cuvée Napa popular sparkling wine of Napa Valley, California, USA. Established by champagne house GH Mumm.

cuverie the vats that make up the winemaking capacity of a cellar. French.

CVNE Compania Vinicola del Norte de España. Major *bodega* in Haro, Rioja, Spain. Imperial and Viña Real reserva red wines, Monopole white.

Cynar Liqueur brand of Italy.

Cyprus Mediterranean island known for 'sherry' (a term disallowed by the European Union, 1996), table wines and Commandaria dessert wine.

Cyriakusberg vineyard at Sulzfeld in Franken region, Germany.

Cytrynowka lemon vodka brand, Poland.

Czarina Cocktail. Over ice stir 4 parts vodka, 1 dry vermouth, 1 apricot brandy, 1 dash Angostura bitters. Strain.

Czech Republic vineyards of Bohemia and Moravia produce red and white table wines. Pinot Blanc and Pinot Gris white wines are improving in reputation.

1993
CZECH

PINOT BLANC
Dry White Wine

Hustopece – Hodonin region

11.0% vol   Produce of the Czech Republic   75 d e

D

DAB Dortmunder Actien Brauerei, Dortmund, Germany.

Dabinett apple variety commonly cultivated for cider-making. English.

Dabug vineyard at Randersacker in Franken region, Germany.

DAC Districtus Austria Controllatus, wine-quality designation system of Austria, introduced 2003.

Dachgewann vineyard at Zornheim in Rheinhessen region, Germany.

Dachs vineyard at Oberschwarzach in Franken region, Germany.

Dachsberg vineyards at Brackenheim in Württemberg region and Oestrich-Winkel and Wiesbaden in Rheingau region, Germany.

Dachsbuckel vineyard at Heidelberg in Baden region, Germany.

Dachsteiger five vineyards in Württemberg region, Germany at, respectively: Ohringen, Pfedelbach (Harsberg), Pfedelbach (Heuholz), Pfedelbach (Oberohrn), Pfedelbach (Untersteinbach).

Daguin, André armagnac producer, Auch, Gascony, France.

Dailuaine Speyside malt whisky distillery est 1852, Carron, Aberlour, Upper Spey, Scotland. Single malt: 16-year-old. Name is Gaelic for 'green vale' and is pronounced dal-yoo-an.

Daiquiri Cocktail. Over ice shake 3 parts rum, 1 fresh lime juice, 1 teaspoon sugar. Strain. See box.

Daiquiri Habit Sam Roughton told this story: A fastidious Canadian doctor was in the habit of enjoying a daiquiri in the same bar across the road from his surgery at the stroke of one o'clock every weekday lunchtime. He liked the drink flavoured with a little nutmeg. On one occasion, he noticed it tasted quite different from usual. 'What the hell have you done to my daiquiri?' he demanded. The barman replied that he had run out of nutmeg and had substituted another flavouring. 'It's a hickory daiquiri, doc.'

Dalem, Château wine estate of AC Fronsac, Bordeaux, France.

Daleside brewery at Harrogate, Yorkshire, England. Crackshot (5.5% alc), Duff Beer (5.0% alc), Greengrass (4.5% alc), Monkey Wrench (5.3% alc), Morocco (5.5% alc), Old Legover (4.1% alc).

Dallas Brewing Company brewery at Dallas, Texas, USA.

Dallas Dhu North Highland malt whisky distillery, Forres, Scotland. Est 1889, closed 1983. Whisky from 1969 and 1974 bottlings exists, but is becoming rare.

Dalmatia wine-producing region now synonymous with Croatia.

Dalmato-Friulana dei Marchesi Ricci grappa producer, Friuli, Italy.

Dalmeny blended scotch whisky of J Townend, Hull, England.

Daiquiri

commemorating a courageous cavalry charge

The story of this famous cocktail recalls the exploits of a brave American President. Theodore Roosevelt, aged 40 and assistant secretary in the US War Department, resigned his post in 1898 to lead a regiment of volunteer cavalry in that year's invasion of Cuba. Their mission was to support Cuban revolutionaries in their struggle for independence from Spain.

The regiment, popularly known as 'Rough Riders' because they were mostly cowboys, college athletes and New York policemen, landed on the beach at Daiquiri on the island's south coast on 3 July. Under withering fire, they swept the Spanish forces from their trenches and opened the way for the capture of strategically vital Santiago. The city surrendered on 15 July.

Victory was toasted with a cocktail that had been devised in 1896 by a resident American, Jennings Cox. An engineer at the Daiquiri copper mines, he had named the mix of Bacardi rum and lime juice after his place of work, but it was the Daiquiri's association with the landing place of the Rough Riders that brought the drink its great fame.

Spain handed Cuba to the United States 'in trust for its local inhabitants' in 1899 and the island continued under American influence until the revolution of 1959. Theodore Roosevelt was President of the US from 1901 to 1909.

Dalmore

Dalmore North Highland malt whisky distillery est 1839, Alness, Ross-shire, Scotland. Single malt: 12-year-old.

Dalwhinnie North Highland malt whisky distillery est 1897, Drumochter, Inverness-shire, Scotland. Single malts: 8-year-old and 15-year-old.

Dalwhinnie wine estate at Moonambel, Victoria, Australia. Distinguished Cabernet Sauvignon and Chardonnay wines.

Damaso Mediola brand of Pernod-Ricard.

Damblat armagnac producer, Castelnau d'Auzan, Gascony, France.

Dame Blanche, La white wine Château du Taillan, Bordeaux, France.

dame-jeanne wicker-clad glass container for up to 50 litres of wine. French. The dame-jeanne of Bordeaux holds 2.5 litres.

Dames Hospitalières one of the *cuvées* of wine sold annually in the charitable auction of the Hospices de Beaune, Burgundy, France.

Dà Mhìle 'the world's very first organic Scotch whisky' bottled by Springbank distillery, Campbeltown, Scotland from 1999. A 'Millennium Malt' from organic barley grown in England and Scotland – by a Welshman, John Savage-Onstwedder.

Damm brewery in Barcelona, Spain. Est 1876 by Alsace-born August K Damm.

Damn-the-Weather Cocktail. Over ice shake 2 parts dry gin, 1 sweet vermouth, 1 orange juice, 3 dashes curaçao. Strain.

Damoiseau rum distiller on Grande-Terre, Guadeloupe. Brands include Rhum Blanc at between 43 and 55% alc, Rhum Vieux and Rhum Vintage at 45% alc. One single vintage rum is dated 1953.

D'Amour Cocktail. Over ice shake 1 egg white, 2 parts dry gin, 1 Anisette, 1 fresh lime juice. Strain.

Dampfbier brand of steam beer by Maisel Brothers, Bayreuth, Germany.

damson beer fruit beer made with damsons.

Dandy Cocktail. Over ice shake 1 part Dubonnet, 1 rye whisky, 1 dash Angostura bitters, 3 dashes Cointreau. Strain.

D'Angelo Vineyards wine producer at Amherstberg, Ontario, Canada.

Daniels, Jack see Jack Daniels.

Daniel Visser *genever* distiller, Netherlands.

Danziger Goldwasser sweet herbal liqueur with added gold flakes first produced by Der Lachs of Danzig (Gdansk), Poland in 1598. Now made in Germany. Also, **Danziger Silberwasser**.

Dão designated wine zone of central Portugal. Red wines age for minimum three years in wood and further years in bottle. *Reserva* wines are kept longer. White wines are also made.

Daphnes sweet red wine of island of Crete, Greece.

Darb Cocktail. Over ice shake 1 part apricot brandy, 1 dry gin, 1 dry vermouth, 3 dashes lemon juice. Strain.

Daredevil Strong Ale strong (7.1% alc) ale brand of Everards brewery, Leicester, England.

Dark & Stormy Cocktail. In an ice-filled tumbler combine 1 part Gosling's Black Seal rum, 2 ginger beer. The favourite cocktail, it is said, of Bermuda – home to Gosling's famous distillery.

Dark de Triomphe beer brand of the Paris Real Ale Brewery, France.

Dark Horse bock beer by Virginia Brewing Co, Virginia, USA.

Dark Horse brewery at Hertford, Hertfordshire, England.

Dark Island brand of dark beer (4.6% alc) by Orkney Brewery, Sandwick, Orkney, Scotland.

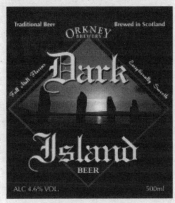

dark lager traditional malty, dark-coloured beer style of Germany said to have preceded lighter-coloured modern lagers but still popular. Locally known as *Dunkel*.

Dark Peak brewery at Caulden Lowe, Stoke-on-Trent, England.

Dark Ruby bottle-conditioned beer (6.0% alc) by Sarah Hughes Brewery, Dudley, West Midlands, England.

Dark Star ale brand originally brewed by former Pitfield brewery, London, England.

Dark Star brewery of Skinners Ales, Brighton, East Sussex, England.

Darktribe brewery at Scunthorpe, Lincolnshire, England.

Darroze, Francis armagnac house specialising in brandies from individual producers of Bas-Armagnac region. Based at Roquefort, Gascony, France.

Darwin brewery at Crook, County Durham, England.

Das Kleine Brauhaus 'The Little Brewhouse'. Inn-brewery of Prince Luitpold of Bavaria, Munich, Germany.

Dassault, Château wine estate of AC St-Emilion, Bordeaux, France. Classified *Grand Cru Classé*.

Daubhaus vineyards at Appenheim and Oppenheim in Rheinhessen region and at Bad Neuenahr-Ahrweiler in Ahr region, Germany.

Daubhaus *Grosslage* incorporating vineyards in Rheingau region, Germany at, respectively: Flörsheim, Flörsheim (Wicker), Hochheim, Hochheim (Massenheim), Mainz.

Daudet Naudin wine producer at Savigny-lès-Beaune, Burgundy, France.

Dauphin-Château-Guiraud, Le second wine of Château Guiraud, Bordeaux, France.

Dauphin-de-Lalague, Le second wine of Château Guiraud, Bordeaux, France.

Dauphine, Château de la wine estate of AC Fronsac, Bordeaux, France.

Dauphiné-Rondillon, Château wine estate of AC Loupiac, Bordeaux, France.

Dautenpflänzer vineyard at Münster-Sarmsheim in Nahe region, Germany.

Dauzac, Château wine estate of AC Margaux, Médoc, Bordeaux, France. Classified *5ème Grand Cru Classé*.

Davenport Arms brewery at Worfield, Bridgnorth, Shropshire, England.

Davis Cocktail. Over ice shake 2 parts dry vermouth, 1 rum, 1 fresh lime (or lemon) juice, 2 dashes Grenadine. Strain.

Davis Brandy Cocktail. Over ice shake 2 parts brandy, 1 dry vermouth, 4 dashes grenadine, 1 dash Angostura bitters. Strain.

Dawn Cocktail. Over ice shake 1 part champagne, 1 fresh lime juice, 1 fino sherry. Strain.

Dead Horse India Pale Ale brand of McNeill's Brewery, Brattleboro, Vermont, USA.

Dealul Mare wine region of SE Romania known for red wines.

Deanston Highland malt whisky distillery est 1965, Doune, Perthshire, Scotland. Single malt: 12-year-old.

Deauville Cocktail. Over ice shake 1 part apple brandy, 1 brandy, 1 Cointreau, 1 lemon juice. Strain.

De Bortoli wine company of New South Wales, Australia. Famed for sweet Botrytis Semillon, but also a major generic producer.

De Boutville apple variety traditionally valued for cider-making. English.

Debrö Hárslevelü noted medium white wine of Debrö in Métraalya region, Hungary.

Débutante Cocktail. Over ice shake 1 egg white, 2 parts dry gin, 2 lemon juice, 1 crème de noyau, 1 lime juice. Strain.

Decano solera brandy by Luis Caballero, Puerto de Santa Maria, Spain.

decant to pour wine from its original bottle into another container. To aerate the wine or remove it from its sediment. A **decanter** is a carafe for the purpose.

Dechantsberg vineyard at Treis-Karden in Mosel-Saar-Ruwer region, Germany.

De Dolle Brouwers brewery at Esen, Belgium. Name means 'the mad brewers'.

De Drie Fonteinen café-brewery in Beersel, Belgium.

Deeping Ales brewery at Market Deeping, Lincolnshire, England.

Deep Sea Cocktail. Over ice shake 1 part dry vermouth, 1 dry gin, 1 dash pastis, 1 dash orange bitters. Strain and add an olive to glass.

Deep Shaft Stout bottle-conditioned beer (6.2% alc) by Freeminer Brewery, Forest of Dean, Gloucestershire, England.

Deerstalker twelve-year-old Highland single malt scotch whisky brand of Bass Export, Glasgow, Scotland.

De Gans small brewery in Zeeland province, Netherlands.

dégorgement in champagne production, the removal of sediment from the wine. The neck of the bottle, in which the sediment has accumulated through the action of *remuage*, is frozen and the ice-plug of sediment removed with the crown cap, prior to topping up with *liqueur d'expédition* and final closing with a champagne cork. French.

De Goulden Boom brewery at Bruges, Belgium.

dégustation winetasting. French.

De Hop Bloem brewery at Middelburg, Zeeland province, Netherlands.

Deidesheim major wine centre of Rheinpfalz region, Germany. Important producers include Bassermann-Jordan, Deinhard, Fitz-Ritter, Von Bühl. *Grosslagen*: Hofstück, Mariengarten, Schnepfenflug; vineyards include: Grainhübel, Hergottsacker, Hohenmorgen, Kalkofen, Kieselberg, Maushöhle, Nonnengarten, Paradiesgarten.

Deinhard wine producer and merchant est 1794, Koblenz, Germany. Vineyards in Bernkastel (including part of Doctor), Graach and Wehlen in Mosel-Saar-Ruwer region; Geisenheim, Oestrich, Rüdesheim and Winkel in Rheingau region; Deidesheim, Forst and Ruppertsberg in Rheinpfalz region. Brands include Lila *sekt* sparkling wine.

Deiss, Marcel wine producer in Bergheim Alsace, France. Renowned Riesling of Grand Cru Schoenenberg.

De Keersmaecker brewery at Kobbegem, Belgium.

De Kluis brewery at Hoegaarden, Belgium. Brands include Hoegaarden wheat beer. Name means 'cloister' commemorating monastery where brewing began at Hoegaarden.

De Koninck brewery and beer brand, est 1833, at Antwerp, Belgium.

De Koning major malt distillery for *genever* industry, Schiedam, Netherlands. Owned by Bols.

De Kroon brewery at Neerijse, Belgium.

De Kuyper major distillery company est 1695 in Rotterdam, Netherlands. Cherry brandy and many famous liqueurs.

Delabarre, Pierre *récoltant manipulant* champagne producer, Vandières, Champagne, France.

Delaire Vineyards wine producer at Helshoogte Pass, Stellenbosch, South Africa.

Delaforce port producer, Vila Nova de Gaia, Portugal. Owned by Croft, with which it was taken over in 2001 by Taylors, but with own wines such as His Eminence's Choice tawny and vintages: 1955, 58, 60, 63, 66, 70, 74, 75, 77, 78, 80, 82, 83, 84, 85, 87, 91, 92, 94, 97, 2000, 03.

Delamain distinguished cognac house est 1762 Jarnac, France. Brandies are all of Grande Champagne district, bought at minimum of 15 years old, kept for ten or more further and all styled 'Pale & Dry'. Brands include Très Vieux 50-year-old.

Delas wine producer and *négoçiant* of Rhône Valley, France.

Delatite wine estate of Victoria, Australia. Riesling and other wines of growing repute.

De Leeuw brewery at Valkenburg, Netherlands.

Delegat's wine producer of Henderson, New Zealand. 'Auslese' white wine, Cabernet Sauvignon and Oyster Bay brand of Chardonnay and Sauvignon.

Delicator bock beer brand of Hofbräuhaus brewery, Munich, Germany.

Delirium Tremens ale brand of Du Bocq brewery, Naumur, Purnode, Belgium. The name cheerfully evokes the notorious psychosis of acute alcoholism symptomised by hallucination and uncontrollable trembling.

Della Morte producer of DM brands of grappa, Valpolicella, Italy.

Dellchen vineyards at Mandel and Norheim in Nahe region, Germany.

Delmonico Cocktail. Over ice stir 3 parts dry gin, 1 brandy, 1 dry vermouth, 1 sweet vermouth, 1 dash Angostura bitters.

Delorme, André wine producer and *négoçiant* of Côte Chalonnaise, Burgundy, France. Vineyards at Rully and for sparkling Crémant de Bourgogne.

Delpech Fougerat cognac producer, Barbezieux, France.

Delta Cocktail. Over ice shake 3 parts scotch whisky, 1 Southern Comfort, 2 dashes fresh lime juice, 1 teaspoon sugar. Strain into a tall, ice-filled glass and add orange slice.

Demerara style of dark rum distilled from bi-products of demerara sugar. Guyana. Formerly the rum issued on board the ships of the British Navy. Demerara rums are commonly labelled 'Navy Rum' or similar. Production is in the control of Demerara Distillers, with distilleries in Guyana and on St Kitts.

Demestica ubiquitous red and white wine brand of Achaia-Clauss, Greece.

demi-john wicker-clad glass container for between, approximately, five and 50 litres of wine.

demi-sec 'half-dry' (wine) but often meaning sweet. French.

Demockaat coffee-flavoured advocaat brand of Bols, Netherlands.

Demolition ale brand of Goose Island Brewery, Chicago, USA.

Dempsey Cocktail. Over ice shake 1 part apple brandy, 1 dry gin, 1 dash pastis, 1 dash grenadine. Strain.

Dempsey's ale brand of Huber brewery, Wisconsin, USA.

Denargo lager brand of Tabernash brewery, Denver, Colorado, USA.

Denbies largest vineyard and wine producer of England, of 250 acres at Ranmore Common, Surrey.

De Neve brewery at Schepdaal, Belgium.

Denis-Mounie cognac producer est 1838 Jarnac, France. Owned by Hine.

Denois Père & Fils *récoltant manipulant* champagne producer, Cumières, Champagne, France.

Denominación de Origen (DO) Spain's system of regulating wine production, similar to France's *appellation contrôlée*. Introduced (first region was Rioja) in 1926.

Denominación de Origen Calificada (DOCa) a new superior-quality designation for Spanish wines. So far (2005) only applying to Rioja and Priorat.

Denominação de Origem Controlada (DOC) designation for Portugal's top-rated wine regions.

Denominazione di Origine Controllata (DOC) Italy's system of regulating quality-wine production, introduced

1963 but not fully comparable with France's *appellation contrôlée*. Wines labelled DOC must be from appropriate grape varieties grown in designated vineyard regions, and made by accepted methods. Rules were revised 1992, providing for demotion of underperforming DOCs and promotion to DOCG (*qv*) status of outstanding ones. There are about 280 DOCs, including DOCGs and inter-regional denominations, but this number may ultimately be reduced to under 200.

Denominazione di Origine Controllata e Garantita (DOCG) the upper echelon of Italy's quality-wine ranking system. Any DOC can qualify for elevation by reaching the prescribed standards (including maximum grape yields per acre and tasting scrutiny) consistently over five years. In 2004 the DOCGs were: Albana di Romagna, Amarone della Valpolicella, Asti and Moscato d'Asti, Barbaresco, Barolo, Brachetto d'Acqui, Brunello di Montalcino, Carmignano, Chianti, Chianti Classico, Franciacorta, Gattinara, Ghemme, Sagrantino de Montefalco, Sassicaia, Taurasi, Torgiano, Vermentino di Gallura, Vernaccia di San Gimignano, Vino Nobile di Montepulciano.

Dent brewery at Cowgill, Dent, Cumbria, England.

Dentergems Witbier wheat beer brand of Riva group's Liefman brewery, Dentergem, Belgium.

deoch-an-doris a stirrup-cup and, broadly, 'one for the road'. Gaelic, from *deoch*, drink, and *dorus*, door. Scotland.

DePaz rum distiller on Martinique, West Indies. Rhum Blanc, Rhum Paille and Rhum Vieux, plus occasional single vintages. Marketed mainly in France, by Bardinet.

Depth-Bomb Cocktail. Over ice shake 1 part brandy, 1 calvados, 4 dashes grenadine, 1 dash lemon juice. Strain.

Depth-Charge Cocktail. Over ice shake 1 part dry gin, 1 Lillet, 2 dashes pastis. Strain.

Derby Cocktail. Over ice shake 1 part dry gin, 2 dashes peach bitters, 2 sprigs fresh mint. Strain.

Derby Fizz Cocktail. Over ice shake 2 parts rye whisky, 1 lemon juice, 4 dashes curaçao, 1 egg, 1 teaspoon sugar. Strain into a tall, ice-filled glass and top with soda water.

Derby Special three-, five- and 12-year-old blended scotch whiskies by Kinross Whisky Co, Haywards Heath, West Sussex, England.

De Ridder brewery at Maastricht, Belgium. Owned by Heineken.

De Rigueur Cocktail. Over ice shake 2 parts rye whisky, 1 grapefruit juice, 1 clear honey. Strain.

Deschutes Brewery pub-brewery at Bend, Oregon, USA. Brands include Black Butte Porter, Cascade Golden Ale, Mirror Pond Pale Ale.

Desert Healer Cocktail. Over ice shake 4 parts dry gin, 4 fresh orange juice, 1 cherry brandy. Strain.

De Smedt brewery at Affligem, Belgium.

Desmirail, Château wine estate of AC Margaux, Médoc, Bordeaux, France. Ceased production 1957, resumed 1983. Classified *3ème Grand Cru Classé*.

Desmoulins, A champagne house, Epernay, France.

De Sousa Cellars wine producer at Beamsville, Ontario, Canada.

Despagnet, Château wine estate of AC St-Emilion, Bordeaux, France.

Desperados Mexican-style 'Tequila Beer' (5.9% alc) by Fischer brewery, France.

dessert wine sweet wine such as France's Barsac and Sauternes of Bordeaux, Coteaux du Layon of the Loire and *vendanges tardives* of Alsace, or late-harvested Rieslings of the Mosel and Rhine. Tokaji of Hungary, *Recioto* white wines of the Veneto, Italy and sweet table wines from Muscat grapes in Australia are also classed as dessert wines. Gastronomically, such wines are ill-suited to accompany sweet puddings; they are at their best as apéritifs, or with savouries, fresh fruit or blue cheeses. In France, *foie gras* is widely promoted as the natural companion.

de Torens *jenever* and liqueur brand of Geens Benelux, Aarschot, Belgium.

De Troch brewery at Wambeek, Belgium.

Déthune, Paul *récoltant manipulant* champagne producer, Ambonnay, Champagne, France.

Deuchars India pale ale brand (4.4% alc) of Caledonian brewery, Edinburgh, Scotland.

Deugniet ale brand of Du Bocq brewery, Naumur, Belgium. Name means 'rascal'.

Deuslay vineyard at Mesenich in Mosel-Saar-Ruwer region, Germany.

Deutelsberg *Grosslage* (collective vineyard) incorporating vineyards at Eltville (Erbach) and Eltville (Hattenheim) in Rheingau region, Germany.

Deutsches Erzeugnis 'made in Germany'. German.

Deutschherrenberg vineyards at Ober-Flörsheim in Rheinhessen region and at Trier, Trier (Olewig) and Zeltingen-Rachtig in Mosel-Saar-Ruwer region, Germany.

Deutschherrenköpfchen vineyard at Trier in Mosel-Saar-Ruwer region, Germany.

Deutz & Gelderman *Grande Marque* champagne house est 1838 Aÿ, Champagne, France.

Deutz sparkling wine brand of Montana Wines, Marlborough, New Zealand. Established by Champagne Deutz.

De Valcourt brand of Pernod-Ricard.

Deveaux, A champagne brand of Union Auboise co-operative, Champagne, France.

Devenish brewery at Redruth, Cornwall, England.

Devilliers, Raymond *récoltant manipulant* champagne producer, Villedommange, Champagne, France.

Devil Mountain brewery at Benicia, California, USA.

Devil's Cocktail. Over ice shake 1 part port, 1 dry vermouth, 2 dashes lemon juice. Strain.

Devil's Lair wine producer in Margaret River, Western Australia.

Devil's Lake Red Lager beer brand of Great Dane brewery, Madison, Wisconsin, USA.

Devil's Tail Cocktail. Over ice shake 3 parts rum, 2 vodka, 1 fresh lime juice, 4 dashes apricot brandy, 2 dashes grenadine. Strain.

Devil's Thumb Stout beer by Walnut Brewing, Colorado, USA.

Devizes Bitter ale by Wadworth brewery, Devizes, Wiltshire, England.

Devon Ales brewery at Sauchie, Alloa, Scotland.

Devon Glory ale (4.7% alc) by Exe Valley Brewery, Silverton, Devon, England.

Devonia Cocktail. Over ice shake, gently, 2 parts sparkling cider, 1 dry gin, 1 dash orange bitters. Strain.

Devonshire Pride Cocktail. Over ice shake 2 parts apple brandy, 1 Swedish Punsch, 1 dash lemon juice. Strain.

Dewar's White Label blended scotch whisky by John Dewar, Perth, Scotland.

De Wetshof wine estate of Robertson region, South Africa.

Deyrem-Valentin, Château wine estate of AC Margaux, Médoc, Bordeaux, France. Classified *Cru Bourgeois*.

Dezberg vineyards at Eberstadt and Weinsberg in Württemberg region, Germany.

Dézelay designated vineyard of Lavaux, Switzerland.

Dhron wine village in Michelsberg *Grosslage*, Mosel-Saar-Ruwer region, Germany. Hofberger and Roterd vineyards.

Diablo Cocktail. Over ice shake 3 parts white port, 2 dry vermouth, 4 dashes lemon juice. Strain.

Diabola Cocktail. Over ice shake 2 parts Dubonnet, 1 dry gin, 2 dashes Orgeat Syrup. Strain.

Diageo corporate name of conglomerated UK companies Grand Metropolitan and Guinness, following £24 billion merger in 1997. Believed to be the world's largest drinks company with annual sales approaching £12bn in 2002.

Diamond Fizz Cocktail. Over ice shake 2 parts dry gin, 1 lemon juice, 1 teaspoon sugar. Strain into a tall, ice-filled glass, top with chilled sparkling wine and stir.

Diana Cocktail. Fill a small wine glass with crushed ice and add 3 parts white crème de menthe, 1 brandy.

Diana disappearing grape variety of Germany.

Diät Pils 'diet' beer brand, originally developed for diabetic drinkers, of Holsten brewery, Hamburg, Germany. Low in carbohydrate but high (5.8%) in alcohol.

Dickens dry gin brand of William Lundie & Co, Glasgow, Scotland.

Dickkopp vineyard at Ellerstadt in Rheinpfalz region, Germany.

Diebels brewery at Issum, Germany. Renowned for altbier.

Dieblesberg vineyards at Löwenstein, Obersulm (Affaltrach) and Obersulm (Willsbach) in Württemberg region, Germany.

Diekirch brewery of Grand Duchy of Luxembourg.

Dienheim wine village in Rheinhessen region, Germany. Neighbour of Oppenheim.

Diet Pils informal name for Diät Pils brand of Holsten brewery, Germany.

Dietrich Jooss wine producer at Iberville, Quebec, Canada.

Diez Hermanos port shipper late of Vila Nova de Gaia, Portugal. Vintages: 1960, 63, 70, 77, 80, 82.

Digby, Sir Kenelm the acknowledged inventor of the mass-produced glass bottle. Digby (1603–65) devised the technique for blowing bottles from the base, which left a punt in the bottom after the blowpipe was withdrawn. The bottle could thus stand upright – something predecessors, blown from the mouth and consequently round-bottomed, could not do.

digestif 'digestive' after-dinner drink of wine or spirit. French.

digestion in liqueur-making, the maceration of ingredients in a heated solvent.

Diki-Diki Cocktail. Over ice shake 4 parts apple brandy, 1 grapefruit juice, 1 Swedish Punsch. Strain.

Diktiner German liqueur style, said to resemble Bénédictine of France.

Dillon rum distiller of Martinique, West Indies, est 1690. Brands include Rhum Blanc, Rhum Paille and Negrita plus long-matured Rhum Très Vieux 15-year-old and single vintage. Mostly sold in France, by Bardinet.

Dillon, Château wine estate of AC Haut-Médoc, Bordeaux, France. Classified *Cru Bourgeois*.

Dilworth pub-brewery at Charlotte, North Carolina, USA.

Dimiat white grape variety of Bulgaria.

Dimple de luxe blended scotch whisky brand of John Haig, Markinch, Scotland. In North America, branded Pinch.

Dinah Cocktail. Over ice shake, gently, 1 part rye whisky, 1 part lemon juice, 1 teaspoon sugar, 1 lightly crushed sprig fresh mint. Strain and add mint sprig (not crushed) to glass.

Diner's blended and vatted malt scotch whiskies by Douglas Denham, London, England. Five-, eight-, 12- and 21-year-old blends; 15-year-old vatted malt.

Dingac traditional heavy red wine from part-dried Plavac Mali grapes, Peljesac, Croatia.

Dinkelacker brewery in Stuttgart, Germany. Brands include CD-Pils, Cluss Bock Dunkel, Sanwald Hefe Weiss.

Dinstigut Loiben wine producer in Wachau, Niederösterreich, Austria.

Dionysus ancient Greek god of wine (among other things). Immaculately conceived offspring of Theban princess Semele and Zeus. Bacchus to the Romans. In Dyonisian rites, celebrants worshipped the grape as the god's flesh, the wine as his blood.

Dioralyte rehydration preparation recommended by habitual over-indulgers for overcoming the ill-effects of alcoholic dehydration. Rorer Pharmaceuticals, UK.

Diplomat Cocktail. Over ice shake 2 parts dry vermouth, 1 sweet vermouth, 1 dash maraschino. Strain and add maraschino cherry and lemon slice to glass.

Directors Bitter ale brand of Courage brewery, Bristol, England.

Dirkzwager major distiller of *genever* and other spirits, Netherlands.

Di Saronno leading brand of amaretto liqueur, Italy.

distillation the process of separating alcohol from fermented material by the application of heat.

Distillers Company major Scotch whisky distillery owner, est 1877, acquired in controversial circumstances in 1986 by Guinness. Operator of 50 malt and grain distilleries.

D'Istinto wine brand of BRL Hardy Europe by Casa Vinicola Calatrasi, Sicily, Italy.

Disznoko ancient wine domain classified 'first growth' in 1700 at Tokaji, Hungary. Name means 'pig of a rock' after boar-like crag over-looking the valley estate. National-ised 1946 and sold to French combine AXA in 1992. Producer of Tokaji wines.

Disnoko Dry Furmint white wine brand from Furmint grapes by Domain Disznoko, Tokaji, Hungary.

Disnoko Oremus white wine brand from Oremus grapes by Domain Disznoko, Tokaji, Hungary.

distilling see box

Ditchling vineyard at Ditchling, East Sussex, England.

Divino Estate wine producer at Oliver, British Columbia, Canada.

Distilling

a long history of a mystic art

In the fourth century BC Aristotle wrote about a system he had observed for extracting drinking water from sea water. It involved heating the sea water and collecting the condensed vapour (steam) from it. In effect, this is the art of distilling. You start with what is now called a 'wash' – wine (for brandy), malted grain and water (for gin, whisky and vodka), sugar molasses and water (for rum) – and end up with a purified form of it.

The science of distilling goes back a very long way. Some archaeologists claim to have found remains of distilling-type equipment during excavations of Mesopotamian settlements dating back to 3,500 BC.

It is much later that the Persian philosopher-physician Avicenna (980–1036) records methods of distillation that can be related to modern practices. Avicenna, who did much to interpret Aristotle's work for the Islamic world, uses the Arabic word *alambic* which is the 'alembic' still of today, producing *al- kuhl*, a black-powder distillate used as eye make-up, and the source of the English word 'alcohol'.

It is an irony that the technology and language associated with the strongest liquors should derive from a culture that is forbidden alcohol, but it is certainly from the Arabs (who distilled to create oils and perfumes) that the West learned this art. French, German, Irish, Italian and Spanish pioneers of the 12th and 13th centuries have all laid claims to making the first distilled spirits, each describing their discovery in alchemic terms as a sort of fifth element mystically called 'water of life' – *aquae vitae* in Latin, *eau de vie* in French, *usquebaugh* in Gaelic, and so on. Both wine and grain (in effect, beer) were in use as base materials by this time.

The first identifiable alembic was what is now called a 'pot' still. The closed copper kettle or pot is positioned over a heat source which raises the contents – wine or wash – to 173°F, the temperature at which the most volatile element in the base, the ethyl alcohol, vaporises (water doesn't vaporise until its boiling point at 212°F) and can thus be separated from the rest of the base. The vapour rises into the neck of the kettle and is carried through a water-cooled condenser which turns it back into liquid.

Spirits are redistilled at least once, perhaps twice and very occasionally three times to increase the purity. But a certain number of impurities – substances other than ethyl alcohol – will nevertheless persist in the spirit, notably higher or 'fatty' alcohols, aldehydes, acids and esters.

The pot still's inability to eliminate these substances, and other disadvantages such as the slowness of the process and relatively small quantities of spirit that could be produced, kept scientists occupied for centuries trying to find a means of improving the process. This came to fruition in 1801 with the discovery by French academic Edouard Adam of an integrated means of redistilling or 'rectifying' to produce purer spirits with higher alcohol.

The first apparatus to perform this function effectively was a 'continuous' still designed in 1826 by a Scotsman, Robert Stein, who was related to the family of William Haig, the renowned Perthshire whisky distillers. Stein's prototype was subsequently improved on by Aeneas Coffey, and patented as the first commercially viable continuous still in 1830. This type of still, known as the 'patent' or Coffey, has been the principal apparatus for most spirit production ever since.

The typical modern continuous still consists of two tall columns both divided into sections by horizontal, perforated copper plates. The interiors of the columns are heated by steam. Rather than heating the wine or wash in a pot, this system feeds the base liquid into a copper tube coiled between the plates from the top to the bottom of the first, 'rectifier' column. Steam rising through the plates heats the liquid. Now the heated wash is carried up the pipe to the top of the second column (called the analyser) where it disperses and falls through the series of perforated plates.

Superheated steam rising from the bottom of the analyser causes vaporisation of the hot wash, separating the alcohol vapour from the rest. The alcohol vapour is returned to the bottom of the rectifier by a pipe exiting the top of the analyser, while the 'spent wash' is tapped off at the bottom of the analyser. Now the hot alcohol vapour rises in the rectifier, but is cooled by the cold new wash running through the chamber in its pipe. The effect is to condense (reliquefy) the heavier volatiles in the vapour, which run back to the bottom of the column and are tapped off. The best spirit condenses at a higher point in the column, where it is drawn off. The most volatile elements rise all the way to the top of the column and are drawn off separately. These lightest elements, known as the 'heads' are, along with the heaviest, drawn off at the bottom of the column and known as the 'tails', can be redistilled.

Continuous stills are cheap to operate and produce much purer alcohol in far greater quantities than pot stills. White spirits and grain whiskies along with most brandies are virtually all now made with continuous stills. But pot stills remain in use for relatively small-scale production of malt whiskies, Irish whiskeys, some dark rums and cognac.

Dixie beer brand and brewery of New Orleans, Louisiana, USA. Producer of **Dixie Amber Light** beer.

Dixie Cocktail. Over ice shake 2 parts dry gin, 1 dry vermouth, 1 pastis. Strain.

Dizy champagne-producing village, Montagne-de-Reims, Champagne, France.

DNA 'alcoholic spring water' drink brand. Australia.

D'n Schele Os strong (7.5% alc) Tripel beer brand of Maasland Brewery, Oss North Brabant, Netherlands. Name translates to 'The Dizzy Bull'.

DO see Denominación de Origen.

Dobbel Palm ale brand of Palm brewery, Steenhuffel, Belgium.

DOC see Denominazione di Origine Controllata, Denominación de Origen Calificada and Denominaçoes de Origem Controlada.

DOCG see Denominazione di Origine Controllata e Garantita.

Dock Street brewery in Philadelphia, Pennsylvania, USA.

Doctor great vineyard of Riesling vines at Bernkastel-Kues in Mosel-Saar-Ruwer region, Germany. Also rendered as Doktor.

Doctor Cocktail. Over ice shake 2 parts Swedish Punsch, 1 part fresh lemon or lime juice. Strain.

Doctor's Special blended scotch whisky by Hiram Walker, Dumbarton, Scotland.

Doctor's Thirsty's ale by Wychwood brewery, Witney, Oxfordshire, England.

Dodge Special Cocktail. Over ice shake 1 part Cointreau, 1 dry gin, 1 dash grape juice. Strain.

Dogbolter lager by Matilda Bay brewery, Western Australia.

Dogs Bollocks strong (6.5% alc) ale by Wychwood brewery, Witney, Oxfordshire, England.

Dog's Hair bottle-conditioned beer (4% alc) by Wickwar Brewing, Gloucestershire, England. 'The beer for the morning after – the world famed, palatable, effervescing, invigorating, cooling and effective remedy for all known alements.'

Dog's Nose a 'sly-grog' drink reputedly devised in the wardrooms of Royal Navy warships. It is a glass of beer with a generous measure of gin added to it.

Doisy-Daëne, Château wine estate of AC Barsac, Bordeaux, France. Classified 2ème Cru Classé.

Doisy-Dubroca, Château wine estate of AC Barsac, Bordeaux, France. Classified *2ème Cru Classé*.

Doisy-Védrines, Château wine estate of AC Barsac, Bordeaux, France. Classified *2ème Cru Classé*.

Doktor vineyards at Dexheim in Rheinhessen region and at Venningen in Rheinpfalz region, Germany. See also Doctor.

Doktorberg vineyard at Waldrach in Mosel-Saar-Ruwer region, Germany.

Doktorgarten vineyard at Ihringen in Baden region, Germany.

dolce sweet (wine). Italian.

Dolcetto red grape variety of Piedmont, Italy. Known for making vigorously fruity red wines for drinking young, under seven separate DOCs. Wines for keeping longer are labelled *superiore* and have an extra year's ageing before release for sale.

Dolcetto d'Acqui DOC for red wine from Dolcetto grapes, Acqui Terme, Piedmont, Italy.

Dolcetto d'Alba DOC for red wine from Dolcetto grapes, Alba, Piedmont, Italy.

Dolcetto d'Asti DOC for red wine from Dolcetto grapes, Monferrato hills of Asti province, Piedmont, Italy.

Dolcetto delle Langhe Monregalesi DOC for red wine from Dolcetto grapes, Langhe hills, Piedmont, Italy.

Dolcetto di Diano d'Alba DOC for red wine from Dolcetto grapes, Diano, Piedmont, Italy.

Dolcetto di Dogliano DOC for red wine from Dolcetto grapes, Dogliano, Piedmont, Italy.

Dolcetto di Ovada DOC for red wine from Dolcetto grapes, Ovada, Piedmont, Italy.

Dôle red wine from Gamay and Pinot Noir grapes, Valais, Switzerland.

Dolfi leading producer of *eau de vie*, Alsace, France.

Dolle wine producer in Kamptal, Niederösterreich, Austria.

Dolly Hoskins Cocktail. Over ice shake 3 parts dry gin, 2 peach brandy, 1 fresh cream, 4 dashes grenadine.

Dolly O'Dare Cocktail. Over ice stir 2 parts dry gin, 2 dry vermouth, 1 apricot brandy. Strain.

Dolores Cocktail. Over ice stir 1 part Spanish brandy, 1 cherry brandy, 1 crème de cacao.

Dom *Kölschbier* brand. Cologne, Germany.

domaine estate or property (French). The term prefixes the names of many wine estates in France and elsewhere and these are listed under their main titles (eg **Domaine de Chevalier** under **Chevalier**).

Domaine bottled a wine bottled at the point of production rather than on the premises of a merchant or *négociant*.

Domberg vineyard at Sobernheim in Nahe region, Germany.

Domblick *Grosslage* (collective vineyard) incorporating vineyards in Rheinhessen region, Germany at, respectively: Hohen-Sülzen, Mölsheim, Monsheim, Monsheim (Kriegsheim), Offstein, Wachenheim.

Domdechaney vineyard at Hochheim in Rheingau region, Germany.

Domecq, Pedro great sherry house est 1830 by Irish-born Patrick Murphy, and later acquired by French-born Pedro Domecq at Jerez de la Frontera, Spain. La Ina Fino, Double Century, Rio Viejo sherries. Fundador and other brandies. As Allied-Domecq, part of a major European drinks combine with interests worldwide.

Domesday II barley wine brand brewed by Cornish Brewery Company, Redruth, Cornwall, England. At time of production (1986), its 15.86% alcohol made it the strongest beer ever brewed.

Domherr vineyards at Iphofen in Franken region and at Piesport in Mosel-Saar-Ruwer region, Germany.

Domherr *Grosslage* (collective vineyard) incorporating vineyards in Rheinhessen region, Germany at, respectively: Essenheim, Gabsheim, Klein Winternheim, Ober-Olm, Saulheim, Schornsheim, Stadecken-Elsheim (Elsheim), Stadecken-Elsheim (Stadecken), Udenheim.

Domherrenberg vineyards at Trier (Kürenz), Trier (Ruwer) and Zell in Mosel-Saar-Ruwer region, Germany.

Dominie, The blended scotch whisky by Cockburn & Co, Edinburgh, Scotland.

Dominikanerberg vineyards at Kasel and Morscheid in Mosel-Saar-Ruwer region, Germany.

Dominion Bitter brand of Maxim brewery, Greymouth, New Zealand.

Dominique, Château La wine estate of AC St-Emilion, Bordeaux, France. Classified *Grand Cru Classé*.

Dominus red wine from Bordeaux grape varieties of Napanook vineyard, Napa Valley, California, USA. Franco-American-made by Christian Moueix of Bordeaux with US partners.

Domlay vineyard at Bad Neuenahr-Ahrweiler in Ahr region, Germany.

Dommels brewery at Brabant, Netherlands.

Dom Pérignon

Dom Pérignon 'prestige' vintage and vintage rosé champagne by Moët & Chandon, Epernay, France. Named after Dom Pérignon (1638-1715), cellarmaster of Hautvillers abbey, Epernay, who is credited with making important improvements to champagne-making methods.

Domprobst vineyard at Graach in Mosel-Saar-Ruwer region, Germany.

Doms, Château wine estate of AC Graves, Bordeaux, France.

Don, the world-renowned symbol of the House of Sandeman, port and sherry shippers est London, England, 1790. The character, wearing a cape of the type worn by Portuguese students and wide-brimmed hat of a Spanish *caballero*, was painted by artist George Massiot-Brown and submitted by his employers, Lochend Printing Co of London, as a poster visual to Sandeman in 1928. It was purchased outright for 50 guineas. The Don is registered as a trademark in 120 nations and has appeared on more than a billion bottles of wine.

Donabaum wine producer in Wachau, Niederösterreich, Austria.

Donatien Bahaud wine producer and *négociant* of Loire Valley, France.

Don Cortez brand for Spanish table wine of Matthew Clark, Bristol, England.

Don Fino dry sherry by House of Sandeman, Jerez de la Frontera, Spain.

Don Giovanni *vino da tavola* red wine of Sicily by Casa Vinicola Calatrasi.

Donjon aux Amandes strongly nut-flavoured almond liqueur. French.

Don Julio premium tequila brand of Tequila Tres Magueyes, Atotonilco El Alto, Jalisco, Mexico.

Don Leonico brand of Pernod-Ricard.

Donnaz red wine from Nebbiolo grapes grown in DOC Valle d'Aosta, Piedmont, Italy.

Dönnhoff, Weingut Hermann wine estate of Nahe region, Germany. Noted Riesling wines from Kreuznach etc.

Donnici DOC red wine from Gaglioppo and Greco Nero grapes. Cosenza, Calabria, Italy.

Dooley's 'Vodka Toffee' liqueur of United Brands, UK.

Doom Bar Bitter ale by Sharp's Brewery, Rock, Cornwall, England.

Doorly's rum distiller of Barbados, West Indies.

Doosberg vineyard at Oestrich-Winkel in Rheingau region, Germany.

Dopff & Irion wine producer est 1945 Riquewihr, Alsace, France. Single vineyard wines from les Amandiers, les Maquisards, les Murailles, les Sorcières.

Dopff au Moulin wine producer est 1500s Riquewihr, Alsace, France. Original and currently leading producer of Crémant d'Alsace sparkling wines as well as top-rated still wines.

Doppel 'double' in German. In brewing, a common prefix for names of extra-strong beers. Also appears on spirit labels, eg Doppel Wacholder.

Doppelbock strong (7.5% alc) type of dark beer of southern Germany.

Doppelkorn neutral spirit from corn mash, sometimes flavoured. Germany.

Doppo Cedro lemon-flavoured liqueur, Italy.

Dor cognac house est 1858 Jarnac, France, by Amadée-Edouard Dor. Rare dated cognacs including 'The Oldest 1805'.

Doradillo white grape variety originally of Spain now of Australia for fortified wines.

Dorin white wine from Fendant (also called Dorin) grape, Vaud, Switzerland.

Dormenacker vineyard at Heidelberg in Baden region, Germany.

Dornfelder red grape variety of Germany.

Dornkaat leading *Korn* producer, Norden, Germany.

Dornpfad vineyard at Gabsheim in Rheinhessen region, Germany.

Dorothy Goodbody ale brand of Wye Valley Brewery, Herefordshire, England. Dorothy Goodbody Wholesome Stout and Golden Ale.

Dorsheim wine village of *Grosslage* Schlosskapelle, Nahe region, Germany.

Dortmund city and major brewing centre of Westphalia, Germany.

Dortmunder light-coloured, dry style of beer traditionally made in Dortmund, Germany. Description permitted only to Dortmund-made German beers, but also adopted by brewers in other countries.

Dortmunder Actien Brauerei (DAB) major brewing group in Dortmund, Germany, est 1868. Brands include Export, Maibock, Original Premium.

Dortmunder Hansa brewer in Dortmund, Germany. Brands include Hansa Export, Hansa Pils.

Dortmunder Kronen brewery at Dortmund, Germany. Brands include Classic, Export, Pilskrone, Steinbock.

Dortmunder Ritter brewery at Dortmund, Germany. Brands include Export, Pils.

Dortmunder Thier brewery at Dortmund, Germany. Brands include Export, Pils.

Dortmunder Union Brauerei (DUB) brewery at Dortmund, Germany. Brands include Brinckhoff's No. 1, Export, Siegel Pils.

dosage in champagne-making, the sugar content of the *liqueur d'expédition* that tops up the bottle after *dégorgement*. The sweetness of the dosage governs that of the wine. In brewing, dosage is adding sugar or yeast to promote secondary fermentation.

Dos Equis beer brand (4.8% alc) of Moctezuma brewery, Orizaba, Mexico.

Double Diamond pale ale brand of Ind Coope brewery, Burton upon Trent, England.

Double Dragon beer brand of Felinfoel brewery Llanelli, Wales.

Double Maxim brown ale brand of Vaux brewery, Sunderland, England.

Douglas Cocktail. Over ice stir 2 parts scotch whisky, 1 dry gin, 1 grenadine, 3 dashes Angostura bitters. Strain.

Douglas export ale brand of McEwan's brewery, Scotland.

Douglas Wine of Origin district of Orange River, South Africa.

Douglas of Drumlanrig 12-year-old malt whisky brand launched 1995 by Drumlanrig Castle (prop Duke of Buccleuch), Dumfriesshire, Scotland.

Douro river of Portugal and valley of vineyards for cultivation of port grapes. Also renowned red table wines.

Douves, Domaine des second wine of Château Beauregard, Bordeaux, France.

Douzico Macedonian ouzo. Greece.

Downside House Cocktail. Over ice shake 1 part vodka, 1 green crème de menthe, 1 fresh lime juice. Strain.

Dow's port brand of Symington-owned Silva & Cosens, est 1798 Vila Nova de Gaia, Portugal. Boardroom 15-year-old tawny, ten-year-old tawny, crusted port and vintages: 1950, 55, 60, 63, 66, 70, 72, 75, 77, 80, 83, 85, 91, 94, 97, 2000, 03.

Drachenbrunnen vineyard at Waldböckelheim in Nahe region, Germany.

Drachenfels vineyards at Bad Honnef and Königswinter in Mittelrhein region, Germany.

Dragasani wine region of Romania.

Drake, Sir Francis the Elizabethan swashbuckler is credited with popularising sherry in Britain. In 1587, he made a daring raid on the Armada being prepared at Cadiz and not only destroyed the Spanish fleet, but seized 2,900 barrels of sherry from the quayside, loaded them into captured galleons, and sailed home in triumph. The booty was sold for high prices in London, and the fashion for 'sack' was launched.

dram a shot of spirit, usually whisky. Contracted from drachm, a sixteenth of an ounce avoirdupois. From the ancient Greek measure of weight and silver coin drachma, still in use as the standard unit of Greek currency until 2001.

Drambuie scotch whisky liqueur by Drambuie Liqueur Co, Kirkliston, Edinburgh, Scotland. Said to be a recipe of Prince Charles Edward Stuart (1720–88), bonnie Young Pretender to the throne of Scotland. After the massacre of his highlanders at Culloden in 1746, the prince found refuge with a loyalist, Captain John Mackinnon of Strathaird, on Skye. It was Mackinnon who spirited the prince out of Scotland back to exile in France, and the story goes that the grateful escapee gave the recipe in thanks. The Mackinnons were slow to exploit the formula on a commercial basis, waiting until 1906 before putting the drink on general sale. Members of the family are still at the helm of the company today and the recipe remains their closely guarded secret.

Drappier, André champagne house, Bar-sur-Aube, France.

Drathen, Ewald Theodor wine producer, Mosel-Saar-Ruwer region, Germany.

dray delivery vehicle operated by a brewery. Originally a four-wheeled wagon drawn by dray horses and driven by dray men.

DRC popular abbreviation of Domaine de la Romanée Conti. See Romanée Conti.

Dream Cocktail. Over ice stir 2 parts brandy, 1 curaçao, 1 dash pastis. Strain.

Dreher beer brand of Italy.

Dressler beer brand of Holsten brewery, Germany.

Dr Fischer great wine estate of Mosel-Saar-Ruwer region, Germany. Centred at Wawerner Herrenberg with further vineyards in Ockfen and Saarberg.

Dr Loosen great wine estate at St Johannishof, Mosel-Saar-Ruwer region, Germany. Famed Riesling wines from Bernkastel, Erden, Graach, Urzig, Wehlen.

see label opposite ➡

Dr McGillicuddy spirit and liqueur brand allegedly named after American Aloysius Percival McGillicuddy,

1808–1891 whose last will and testament decalred 'I bequeath my home, livestock, and half interest in the Shady Eye Saloon to my fifth wife, Hermione, age 22. To my son, I leave my watch, dueling pistols and favorite pipe. To the world, I present the recipe for Dr McGillicuddy's Mentholmint Schnapps, whose refreshing taste made me a bit of a legend in these parts. It's good chasing beer, even better on-the-rocks.'

Drioli leading brand of maraschino liqueur. Venice, Italy.

Drosselborn vineyard at Appenheim in Rheinhessen region, Germany.

Drostdy 'sherry' brand, South Africa.

Drouhin, Joseph major wine producer and *négoçiant* of Beaune, Burgundy, France.

Druivenlambic grape-flavoured ale brand of Cantillon brewery, Belgium.

drunk as a lord phrase believed to have derived from the habits of the nobly-born 'three bottle men' notorious for drinking excessive quantities of wine in eighteenth-century England – a time when regular drunkenness was an indulgence to which few outside the aristocracy could afford to aspire. Twenty-first-century peers are models of sobriety.

Drunken Parliament the members of the Scottish assembly at Parliament House in Edinburgh in 1661 were said to have been the most inebriated in the nation's proud history. Gilbert Burnet, the historian and cleric who enrolled as a probationer in the Church of Scotland in the same year, described the assembly as 'almost perpetually drunk.' The Scottish assembly was dissolved in 1707 under the terms of the Act of Union with England and Wales, but reconvened in 1999.

Drupeggio white grape variety of Orvieto, Umbria, Italy.

dry in tasting, a flavour without sweetness, signifying that all sugar has been fermented out.

Dry Blackthorn cider brand of Taunton Cider, Somerset, England.

Dry Creek Valley AVA of Sonoma County, California, USA.

Dry Creek Vineyard winery in Sonoma County, California, USA. Renowned Chardonnay and Fumé Blanc white wines.

Dry Don *amontillado* sherry brand of The House of Sandeman, Jerez de la Frontera, Soain.

Dry Fly *amontillado* sherry brand of Findlater Mackie Todd, London, England.

dry-hopping in brewing, adding hops at late stages in process to enhance aromas and flavours.

Dry Martini Cocktail see Martini.

Dry Sack *amontillado* sherry by Williams & Humbert, Jerez de la Frontera, Spain. Created 1906 and possibly named after generic term 'sack' for SW European wine popularised by Shakespeare.

Du Barry Cocktail. Over ice shake 2 parts dry gin, 1 dry vermouth, 2 dashes pastis, 1 dash Angostura bitters. Strain.

Dubliner 'Irish cream liqueur' brand of IDV, UK.

Duboeuf, Georges leading producer and *négociant* of Beaujolais, France.

Dubonnet wine-based, vermouth-style aperitif. Flavourings include quinine. Sweet red and drier Blonde (white) styles. France.

Dubonnet Cocktail. Over ice stir 1 part Dubonnet, 1 part dry gin. Strain.

Dubonnet Fizz Cocktail. Over ice shake 2 parts Dubonnet, 1 cherry brandy, 1 orange juice, 4 dashes lemon juice. Strain into tall, ice-filled glasses and top with soda water.

Dubory, Château second wine of Château Launay, Bordeaux, France.

Dubuisson brewery at Pipaix, Belgium, renowned for Bush Beer barley wine.

Dubuque Star Private Reserve beer by Zele brewery, Dubuque, Iowa, USA.

Duc d'Ejas armagnac brand of Duc d'Ejas growers' co-operative in

Panjas region of Bas Armagnac, Gascony, France.

Duc de Magenta wine estate of Louis Jadot at Chassagne-Montrachet, Burgundy, France.

Duché de Longueville leading apple grower and cider producer of Normandy, France, renowned for sparkling ciders from gros oeillet apples.

Duchess Cocktail. Over ice stir 1 part dry vermouth, 1 pastis, 1 sweet vermouth. Strain.

Duchesse de Bourgogne, La red ale brand of Verhaeghe brewery, Belgium.

Duckhorn Vineyards wine producer in Napa Valley, California, USA. Long-lived red wines from Cabernet Sauvignon and Merlot grapes.

Duck's Bill apple variety traditionally valued for cider-making. English.

Duck's Fizz Cocktail. Half-fill a champagne glass with chilled Canard-Duchêne champagne. Top with chilled freshly squeezed orange juice.

Duckstein pale ale brand of Feldschlossen brewery, Braunschweig, Germany.

Ducru-Beaucaillou, Château great wine estate of AC St Julien, Médoc, Bordeaux, France. Classified *2ème Grand Cru Classé*.

Duff Beer dark beer (5.0% alc) by Daleside Brewery, Harrogate, Yorkshire, England. 'Duff' is from Gaelic for dark or black.

Duffield pub-brewery (Thorold Arms) at Harmston, Lincolnshire, England.

Duff Gordon sherry company est 1768 by Sir James Duff and Sir William Gordon, Puerto de Santa Maria, Spain.

Dufftown Speyside malt whisky distillery est 1887, Dufftown, Banffshire, Scotland. Single malts: 10-year-old, 15-year-old.

Duhart-Milon-Rothschild, Château wine estate of AC Pauillac, Médoc, Bordeaux, France. Classified *4ème Grand Cru Classé*.

Dujac, Domaine wine producer in Morey St-Denis, Burgundy, France. Vineyards in Bonnes Mares, Chambolle-Musigny, Echézeaux.

Dujardin brandy distiller, Urdingen, Germany.

Duke of Marlborough Cocktail. Over ice shake 1 part dry sherry, 1 sweet vermouth, 2 dashes orange bitters. Strain and decorate glass with orange-peel twist.

Dulce Apagado extra-sweet sherry used in blending 'cream' sherry. Spain.

Dulce de Alimbar sweetening sherry of pale colour used for mixing with fino sherry to produce 'pale cream'. Spain.

Dulce Pasa sweetening wine for sherry-blending. Spain.

Dullgärten

Dullgärten vineyard at Igel in Mosel-Saar-Ruwer region, Germany.

dumb in winetasting, flavour and smell of an immature wine with potential but as yet undeveloped.

Dunbar's blended whisky brand of Kirin Breweries and Pernod-Ricard. Japan.

Duncan brewery at Auburndale, Florida, USA.

dunder detritus from cane sugar distillations added to molasses before fermentation in rum production. Caribbean region.

Dunkel bock beer brand of Einbecker brewery, Germany.

Dunkel generic term for dark-coloured beers, Germany.

Dunkel Export lager brand of Spaten brewery, Germany.

Dunkeld Atholl Brose branded scotch whisky liqueur by Gordon & MacPhail, Elgin, Scotland.

Dunkertons cider and perry producer est by Ivor and Susie Dunkerton 1982 at Hays Head, Luntley, Pembridge, Herefordshire, England. Organic production of brands including Black Fox sparkling cider (7% alc) and Dunkertons Perry (7.5% alc).

Dunlop Cocktail. Over ice stir 2 parts rum, 1 dry sherry, 1 dash Angostura bitters. Strain.

Dunnewood wine brand of Canandaigua Wine Co, California, USA.

Dupeyron armagnac producer, Condom, Gascony, France.

Dupeyron, Château second wine of Château Cannet, Bordeaux, France.

Duplessis-Fabre, Château wine estate of AC Moulis, Médoc, Bordeaux, France. Classified *Cru Bourgeois*.

Duplessis Hauchecorne, Château wine estate of AC Moulis, Médoc, Bordeaux, France. Classified *Cru Grand Bourgeois*.

Dupont brewery at Tourpes-Leuze, Belgium. Beers from organically grown grains include Saison Dupont (5.5% alc), Moinette (7.5% alc).

Duque de Bragança distinguished 20-year-old tawny port by Ferreira, Vila Nova de Gaia, Portugal.

Duquesne-Trois-Rivières rum distiller of Martinique, West Indies.

Duras red grape variety of SW France.

Durbach wine village of Baden region, Germany. *Grosslage* Fürsteneck.

Durban, Domaine leading producer of Muscat wine, AC Beaumes-de-Venise, Rhône Valley, France.

Durfort-Vivens, Château wine estate of AC Margaux, Médoc, Bordeaux, France. Classified *2ème Grand Cru Classé*.

Durham brewery at Bowburn, County Durham, England.

Dürrenberg vineyard at Schallstadt in Baden region, Germany.

Durup, Jean wine producer of Chablis, France. Château de

7.5% alc by vol
500ml ℮

organic
PERRY
from traditional perry pears
grown in unsprayed orchards

pressed, fermented and bottled by
DUNKERTONS
PEMBRIDGE, HEREFORDSHIRE

Maligny and *premier cru* vineyards.

Dutch Courage soubriquet for the gin of the Low Countries, consumed by British servicemen to emboldening effect. Early 17th century.

Dutchess white grape variety of New York State, USA.

Dutch gin the neutral and flavoured gins of the Netherlands. Distilled with fuller flavour and at lower strength than London gin. Also known as Genever, Hollands, Schiedam.

Dutellier, Château second wine of Château Ramage-la-Bâtisse, Bordeaux, France.

Dutruch-Grand-Poujeaux, Château wine estate of AC Moulis, Médoc, Bordeaux, France. Classified *Cru Grand Bourgeois Exceptionnel*.

Duval Leroy champagne house est 1859 Vertus, Marne, Champagne, France.

Duvel strong (8.5% alc) ale brand of Moortgat brewery, Belgium. Name means 'devil'.

Duyck brewery at Jenlain, France, known for *bière de garde*. Brands in-clude Jenlain and Printemps.

Dyffryn Clwyd brewery at Denbigh, Clwyd, Wales.

Dylan's ale brand (4.8% alc) of SA Brain brewery, Cardiff, Wales. Named after renowned Welsh poet and notorious drinker Dylan Thomas (1914-53).

Dymock Red apple variety traditionally valued for cider-making. English.

Dynasty branded white wine of Tianjin region, People's Republic of China.

E

Eagan's Irish Ale beer by Tap and Growler brewery, Chicago, USA.

Eaglehawk Estate large-scale winery in Clare Valley, South Australia.

Eagle Hawk Hill brewery in Canberra, Australia.

Eagle Rare bourbon whiskey brand originally of Seagram, USA.

Eagle's Dream Cocktail. Over ice shake 1 egg white, 3 parts dry gin, 1 Crème Yvette, 1 teaspoon sugar. Strain.

Earl Soham brewery at Earl Soham, Suffolk, England.

Earl Street brewery at Rugby, Warwickshire, England.

Early Times bourbon whiskey brand, Kentucky, USA.

Earthquake Cocktail. Over ice stir 1 part bourbon, 1 dry gin, 1 pastis. Strain.

Earthquake Pale Ale beer by San Andreas brewery, Hollister, California, USA. The brewery is situated on the San Andreas Fault and appears to be under unsuperstitious ownership.

earthy in winetasting, a flavour or smell evoking the character of the vineyard's soil – as the 'gravelly' style of a Graves (Bordeaux) wine, or some Pinot Noir reds. Usually a positive rather than a critical note. More loosely, an unsubtle but not unlikable wine.

Eastern Brewing major brewer at Hammonton, New Jersey, USA, producing 'own brand' beers for retailers.

East India Cocktail. Over ice shake 6 parts brandy, 1 orange curaçao, 1 pineapple juice, 1 dash Angostura bitters. Strain.

East Indian Cocktail. Over ice shake 1 part dry sherry, 1 dry vermouth, dash orange bitters. Strain.

Easingwold brewery at Easingwold, York, North Yorkshire, England.

East Street Cream bottle-conditioned beer (5.0% alc) by RCH Brewery, Weston-Super-Mare, Somerset, England.

East Wind Cocktail. Over ice stir 2 parts vodka, 1 dry vermouth, 1 sweet vermouth, 2 dashes rum. Strain.

eau de clairette a sweetened *eau de vie* flavoured with herbs, lemon and rose leaves, said to be the first liqueur made in France. Thirteenth century.

Eau de ma Tante orange-flavoured liqueur, Netherlands.

eau de vie 'water of life' – spirit distilled from the fermented juice of fruit. Mainly France (especially Alsace) but also Germany, Switzerland and elsewhere. Many different fruits are employed.

Ebenrain vineyard at Wertheim in Baden region, Germany.

Eberfürst vineyards at Eberstadt and Neustadt am Kocher in Württemberg region, Germany.

Eberhardt and Ober former (1880-1952) brewery in Pittsburgh, Pennsylvania, USA, now home to Pennsylvania Brewing Co.

Ebersberg vineyards at Bodenheim, Nierstein and Nierstein (Schwabsburg) in Rheinhessen region, Germany.

Eblana Irish-whiskey-based liqueur by Cooley Distillery, Riverstown, Dundalk, County Louth, Republic of Ireland.

Eburneo white wine from Chardonnay and Trebbiano grapes, Podere di Cignano, Tuscany, Italy.

Eccentric Ale beer brand, with unusual flavourings including caraway, sassafras and snuff, of Kalamazoo brewery, Michigan, USA.

Eccleshall brewery at Eccleshall, Staffordshire, England.

Echézeaux *Grand Cru* vineyard of Vosne-Romanée, Burgundy, France.

Echo, Clos de L' leading wine property of AC Chinon, Loire Valley, France. Owned by Couly Dutheuil.

echt(er) 'genuine' in German. Asserted on German beverages.

echte 'genuine' in Dutch. Asserted on *genever* and other Dutch beverages.

Echter imported rum brand, Germany.

Echt Stonsdorfer herb-flavoured liqueur of Germany.

Eck vineyards at Altenahr and Altenahr (Reimerzhoven) in Ahr region, Germany.

Eckartsberg vineyard at Breisach in Baden region, Germany.

Eckberg vineyards at Baden-Baden and Bötzingen in Baden region, Germany.

Eckes liqueur distiller, Nieder-Olm. Germany.

Eckweg vineyard at Heppenheim in Hessische Bergstrasse region, Germany.

Eclipse Cocktail. Over ice shake 1 part dry gin, 1 sloe gin. Strain gently into glass containing a measure of grenadine. Squeeze orange peel over.

Ecusson cider brand of Cidreries du Calvados La Fermière, Messac, Brittany, France. Styles include, Brut, Doux, Traditionnel, Biologique etc.

Eddie Brown Cocktail. Over ice shake 1 part dry gin, 1 Lillet, 2 dashes apricot brandy. Strain.

edel 'noble' in German. Attached, without material significance, to names of many drinks, eg Edelkirsch, Edelkorn.

Edelberg vineyards at Enkirch in Mosel-Saar-Ruwer region, Lauschied and Meddersheim in Nahe region and Tauberbischofsheim in Baden region, Germany.

Edelfäule 'noble rot' from fungus *botrytis cinerea* affecting grapes and enabling production of concentrated sweet wine. German.

Edelfrau vineyard at Triefenstein in Franken region, Germany.

Edelkaur renowned sweet white wine from Steen and Riesling grapes, Nederburg Estate, Paarl, South Africa.

Edelmann vineyards at Mainz in Rheinhessen region and Oestrich-Winkel in Rheingau region, Germany.

Edelmann, Johann wine producer in Carnuntum, Niederösterreich, Austria.

Edelstoff Helles beer of Augustiner brewery, Munich, Bavaria, Germany.

Edelweiss Fior d'Alpi (Alpine Flowers) herb liqueur brand, Italy.

Edelzwicker inexpensive wine of Alsace, France. Originally, a blend of the region's *edel* ('noble') grape varieties (Gewürztraminer, Muscat, Tokay-Pinot Gris, Riesling) but now from other varieties as well.

Eden Ale beer (4.4% alc) by Sharp's Brewery, Rock, Cornwall, England.

Eden Valley district of Barossa Valley vineyard region, South Australia.

Eder wine producer in Kamptal, Niederösterreich, Austria.

Edinburgh Strong Ale beer brand of Caledonian Brewing Co, Edinburgh, Scotland.

Edle Weingärten vineyard at Dittelseim-Hessloch in Rheinessen region, Germany.

Edmund Fitzgerald Porter beer brand of Great Lakes brewery, Cleveland, Ohio, USA.

Edna Valley AVA of San Luis Obispo, California, USA.

Edradour Highland malt whisky distillery est 1825, Pitlochry, Perthshire, Scotland. Single malt: 10-year-old. Said to be Scotland's smallest distillery with a single-malt output of only 2,000 cases per annum.

Eersterivier Kelder co-operative wine producer of Stellenbosch, South Africa. Notable Chardonnay and Sauvignon white wines and 'port'.

egészégedre 'good health to you'. Hungarian toast.

Eggenberg brewery near Salzburg, Austria. Beers include Nessie 'Whisky Malz Bier'.

Eggleton Styre apple variety traditionally valued for cider-making. English.

Eglise, Domaine de l' wine estate of AC Pomerol, Bordeaux, France.

Eglise, Clos L' wine estate of AC Pomerol, Bordeaux, France.

Eglise-Clinet, Château L' wine estate of AC Pomerol, Bordeaux, France.

égrappage in winemaking, the stripping of grapes from their stalks. Usually by mechanical screw method in an **égrappoir**. French.

Egri Bikaver traditional red wine from Kadarka grapes of Eger, Hungary. Marketed abroad as Bull's Blood.

Eguisheim important winemaking town of Alsace, France.

Egypt probably the birthplace of brewing, more than 5,000 years ago. Egypt continues to produce beer, and wine from vineyards south of Alexandria.

Eherieder Berg vineyard at Kitzingen in Franken region, Germany.

Ehn, Ludwig wine producer in Kamptal, Niederösterreich, Austria.

Ehrenberg vineyards at Geringen in Württemberg region and Waldrach in Mosel-Saar-Ruwer region, Germany.

Ehrenfelser white grape variety from Riesling and Silvaner. Germany.

EH10 blended scotch whisky brand of UK supermarket Sainsbury's, by Macdonald & Muir, Edinburgh, Scotland. 'EH10' is the Edinburgh postal code.

Eibel, Alois wine producer in Süd-Oststeiermark, Austria.

Eichberg *Grand Cru* vineyard of Eguisheim, Alsace, France.

Eichberg vineyards at Denzlingen, Glottertal, Heuweiler and Vogtsburg im Kaiserstuhl in Baden region, Germany.

Eichelberg vineyards at Fürfeld and Neu-Bamberg in Rheinhessen region, Mühlacker in Württemberg region and Olbronn-Dürrn and Sinsheim in Baden region, Germany.

Eichert vineyard at Sasbach in Baden region, Germany.

Eichinger-Allram wine producer in Kamptal, Niederösterreich, Austria.

Eichwäldle vineyard at Sasbach in Baden region, Germany.

Eierlikors egg liqueur, Germany.

1845 bottle-conditioned Celebration Strong Ale (6.3% alc) by Fuller's brewery, London, est 1845.

1877 Solera Reserva brandy by Williams & Humbert (est 1877), Jerez de la Frontera, Spain.

1860 Imperial vodka brand of Hall & Bramley, Liverpool, England.

1812 vodka brand distributed by Alfred Shappard, Guernsey, Channel Islands, UK.

83 Canadian whisky brand originally of Seagram, Canada. Commemorates 1883 distillery purchase by Joseph Seagram, founder of eponymous former drinks empire.

Eikendal Vineyards wine producer of Stellenbosch, South Africa.

Eilfingerberg vineyard at Maulbronn in Württemberg region, Germany.

Eilfingerberg Klosterstück vineyard at Maulbronn in Württemberg region, Germany.

Einbeck city and brewing centre of Lower Saxony, Germany.

Einbecker brewery at Einbeck, Germany. Renowned for bock beers.

Ein Gedi Samson region wine brand of Israel Distillers, Richon le Zion, Israel.

Einsiedel vineyard at Klingenberg am Main in Franken region, Germany.

Einzellage individual vineyard in Germany. Many of the best Mosel and Rhine wines are identified by their village and *Einzellage* names, with the grapes deriving exclusively from the vineyard concerned. There are more than 2,500 vineyards entitled to be identified on labels, with their name appended to that of the appropriate village or town, eg Hattenheimer-Pfaffenberg, for wine of Pfaffenberg *Einzellage* at the village of Hattenheim in Rheingau region.

Eira Velha quinta (estate) port shipped by Cockburn, Vila Nova de Gaia, Portugal. Vintages: 1972, 78, 80, 82, 85, 87.

Eisbock brand of lager brewed by a process including water extraction by freezing. Reichelbräu brewery, Kulmbach, Germany.

Eisenstadt town and winemaking centre, Burgenland, Austria.

Eiserne Hand vineyard at Guntersblum in Rheinhessen region, Germany.

Eiskorn flavoured *Korn* spirit, Germany.

Eis-Liköre classification of liqueurs made to be drunk with ice. Germany.

Eiswein 'ice wine'. German. Describes a wine from grapes harvested from frozen vines during the winter months. Consequent loss of water produces high concentration of sugars and acids in the fruit and can make intensely sweet, long-lived wines of great quality and value.

Eitelsbach wine village of Mosel-Saar-Ruwer region, Germany. Known for Karthäuserhofberg vineyards. *Grosslage*: Römerlay.

EKU Erste Kulmbacher Actien-brauerei. Major brewery at Kulmbach, Germany, known for bock beer brands including Kulminator.

Elba island DOC for red and white wines, Tuscany, Italy.

El Bierzo DO wine region of Léon, Spain.

Elbling white grape variety, principally of Luxembourg.

Elbschloss brewery in Hamburg, Germany, known for Ratsherrn beer brands.

Elders IXL brewing company, Australia.

El Dorado AVA of Sierra Foothills, California, USA.

El Dorado rum brand of Demerara Distillers, Guyana. Dark, golden, white and aged (5, 12 and 15 years) rums.

Eldridge Pope & Co brewer, wine shipper and merchant, est 1833 Dorchester, Dorset, England. Beer brands include Blackdown Bonfire porter (6.0%), Hardy Country Bitter (4.2%), Liberation Commemorative Bitter (4.8%), Royal Oak (5.0%), Thomas Hardy's Ale. Brewery was sold in 1997 and the company now confines itself to operating pubs.

Electric Dave brewery at Bisbee, Arizona, USA, owned by former electrician Dave Harvan. Brands include two lagers, **Electric Dark** and **Electric Light**.

Electric Jam Cocktail. In a tall, ice-filled glass stir 2 parts Absolut vodka, 1 blue curaçao, 1 lemon juice, 1 orange juice.

Elegance white wine brand of Barkham Manor vineyard, East Sussex, England.

elegant in winetasting, a perfectly legitimate term for a wine noticeably well-balanced between fruitiness and crisp acidity.

Elegante pale sherry brand of Gonzalez Byass, Jerez de la Frontera, Spain.

Elephant Beer strong (7.2% alc) lager brand of Carlsberg brewery, Copenhagen, Denmark.

éleveur in winemaking, 'bringerup'. French. A producer who buys grapes or made wine from various sources to 'bring up' in casks or vats until ready for blending and/or bottling. Function usually combined with that of a *négoçiant*, thus the common label-description of producers (esp in Burgundy) as *négoçiants-éleveurs*. The process of bringing up wine in this way is **élèvage**.

Elfenhof wine producer in Neusiedlersee Hügelland, Burgenland, Austria.

Elfenley vineyard at Boppard in Mittelrhein region, Germany.

Elgood & Sons brewery at Wisbech, Cambridgeshire, England.

Eliot Ness beer brand of Great Lakes brewery, Cleveland, Ohio, USA. Named after Cleveland-born crimefighter.

Elisabethenberg vineyards at Hilzingen and Singen (Hohentwiel) in Baden region, Germany.

Elisenberg vineyards at Mülheim and Veldenz in Mosel-Saar-Ruwer region, Germany.

Elixir Amorique green herb liqueur of Brittany, France.

Elixir d'Anvers green, bitter-sweet herb liqueur by FX de Beukelaer of Antwerp, Belgium. Said to be the 'national liqueur of Belgium'.

Elixir de Mondorf liqueur of Luxembourg.

Elizabethan Ale strong (8.1%) ale by Harveys Brewery, Lewes, East Sussex, England. Named in tribute to HM Queen Elizabethan II, crowned 1953.

Elk Cocktail. Over ice shake 1 part dry gin, 1 prunelle liqueur, 2 dashes dry vermouth. Strain.

Elkersberg vineyard at Alsenz in Nahe region, Germany.

Ellergrub vineyard at Enkirch in Mosel-Saar-Ruwer region, Germany.

Elm City Connecticut Ale beer brand of New Haven Brewing, New Haven, Connecticut, USA.

Elmham Park vineyard at East Dereham, Norfolk, England.

El Presidente Cocktail. Over ice shake 2 parts rum, 1 curaçao, 1 fresh lime juice. Strain.

els Dutch herbal bitters by Hennekens distillery, Beek, Netherlands.

Elsnegg, Engelbert wine producer in Südsteiermark, Austria.

Elster vineyard at Forst an der Weinstrasse in Rheinpfalz region, Germany.

Eltville wine village of Rheingau region, Germany. Vineyards include Langenstück, Sandgrub, Sonnenberg. *Grosslage*: Steinmächer.

El Vino Connoisseur's Blend 7 Years Old blended scotch whisky of El Vino, London, England.

Elysium dessert wine from black Muscat grapes by Andrew Quady, California, USA.

Elzhofberg vineyard at Ediger-Eller in Mosel-Saar-Ruwer region, Germany.

Embassy Cocktail. Over ice shake 2 parts bourbon, 2 Drambuie, 1 sweet vermouth, 1 teaspoon orange juice. Strain.

Emerald Isle Cocktail. Over ice stir 2 parts dry gin, 1 teaspoon green crème de menthe, 1 dash Angostura bitters. Strain.

Emerald Riesling grape variety cross of Muscadelle and Riesling. California, USA.

Emery pub-brewery at Emeryville, San Francisco, California, USA. Brands include **Emery Pale Ale** and Powell Street Porter.

Emilia-Romagna wine-producing region of central Italy. Source of Lambrusco, but also of reputable wines from Sangiovese and other grape varieties.

Emilio Lustau sherry *bodega* est 1896 Jerez de la Frontera, Spain. Noted *fino*, *amontillado* and *oloroso* sherries and famed almacenista sherries.

Emmanuel Delicata wine producer of island of Malta. Export brands include Anchor rosé, Paradise Bay red and Golden Bay white.

Empire bottle-conditioned strong pale ale (7.5% alc) by Bridge Brewery, Burton upon Trent, England.

Empire Cocktail. Over ice stir 2 parts dry gin, 1 apple brandy, 1 apricot brandy. Strain.

empyreumatick Johnsonian term for the unlikeable characteristics of ardent spirit, as in his description of Scotch whisky, given on the only occasion upon which Dr Johnson (1709–84) drank it: 'I thought it preferable to any English malt brandy. It was strong, but not pungent, and was free from the empyreumatick taste or smell.'

Emva fortified wine producer, Cyprus. **Emva Cream** is from sun-dried grapes made into wines which mature in outdoor *soleras*.

encépagement the composition and ratio of grape varieties in a French wine.

Enclouse des Vignes, L' cognac house at Floirac, France.

En de L'EI, L' white grape variety of SW France. Regional name meaning 'far from the eye'.

Enclos, Château L' wine estate of AC Pomerol, Bordeaux, France.

Enclos de Moncabon second wine of Château Croizet-Bages, Bordeaux, France.

Enfants de Gayant brewery at Douai, France, known for Abbaye de Crespin Saint Landelin beers.

Enfer d'Arvier DOC for red wines, Valle d'Aosta, Italy.

Engelgrube vineyard at Neumagen-Dhron in Mosel-Saar-Ruwer region, Germany.

Engelmannsberg vineyard at Eltville in Rheingau region, Germany.

Engelsberg vineyards at Endingen in Baden region, Herxheim bei Landau in der Pfalz in Rheinpfalz region and Nackenheim and Offstein in Rhein-hessen region, Germany.

Engelsfelsen vineyard at Bühlertal in Baden region, Germany.

Engelstein vineyards at Boppard and Spay in Mittelrhein region, Germany.

Engelströpfchen vineyard at Edige-Eller in Mosel-Saar-Ruwer region, Germany.

Enggass vineyard at Thörnich in Mosel-Saar-Ruwer region, Germany.

England in renaissance as a wine-producing country since 1970s. Germanic white wines are giving way to drier styles. Red wines are still rare and good red wines rarer still.

English Challenger hop variety widely used in brewing. Imparts a distict citric character.

English Harbour rum brand of Antigua Distillery, Antigua, West Indies. Golden and white rums.

English Wine a description that may apply only to table wine made from grapes grown in England and Wales. Quite distinct from 'British wines' which are UK-manufactured products from imported grape concentrates.

English Rose Cocktail. Over ice stir 2 parts dry gin, 1 apricot brandy, 1 dry vermouth, 4 dashes grenadine, 1 dash lemon juice. Strain.

Engweg vineyards at Niedernhall and Weissbach in Württemberg region, Germany.

Enkirch wine village of Mosel-Saar-Ruwer region, Germany.

Enmore still named after the sugar estate established around 1840 in British Guiana (now Guyana), the still was made in Britain in 1880 and shipped to the former colony for rum production. Now operated by Guyana Distillers it is said to be the oldest working patent still (one copper pot still and one column) in the world.

enoteca wine 'library' or shop, Italy.

Enotria 'land of cultivated vines' in Greek. The name given to southern

Italy by Athenians who colonised it from *c.*800BC to plant vineyards, and later to beget Rome.

en primeur wine offered for sale at purportedly advantageous prices in advance of bottling. Usually that of Bordeaux, France.

Enselberg vineyards at Sasbach and Vogtsburg im Kaiserstuhl in Baden region, Germany.

Entre-Deux-Mers 'Between-Two-Seas' – AC for white wines from Sémillon and/or Sauvignon grapes of the region lying between the tidal rivers Dordogne and Garonne, Bordeaux, France.

Enville farm-brewery at Enville, Stourbridge, West Midlands, England. Bottle-conditioned **Enville Ale** (4.5% alc) 'is properly a 'bee-keeper's ale', one of the highly specialised beers brewed on the farm from an original family recipe dating back to the 1850s.' The farm grows its own barley and employs honey from its own hives in brewing its ales.

envasado 'bottling', Spanish.

Enzian colourless gentian-flavoured spirit of Bavaria, Germany.

enzyme in brewing and winemaking yeast-cell secretion precipitating fermentation by converting natural sugar into alcohol.

Epernay city and one of the two major centres (with Reims) of production of AC Champagne, France.

epi de Facon, L' wheat beer brand of St Arnould brewery, Lille, France.

Epineuil village and AC for red wines from Pinot Noir grapes, Auxerrois, Burgundy, France.

épluchage in champagne production, process of picking over grapes to exclude unhealthy fruit before pressing. France.

Erbach wine village of Rheingau region, Germany. Vineyards include Marcobrunn, Siegelsberg, Schlossberg. *Grosslage* (shared with Hattenheim): Deutelsberg.

Erbaluce di Caluso DOC for white wines from Erbaluce grapes of Caluso, Piedmont, Italy.

erdbeergeist *eau de vie* distilled from strawberries, Switzerland.

Erden wine village of Mosel-Saar-Ruwer region, Germany. Vineyards include Herrenberg, Prälat, Treppchen. *Grosslage*: Schwarzlay.

Erdinger Weissbräu major brewer of wheat beer at Erding, Bavaria, Germany.

Ergolzthaler fruit-brandy distiller, Ormalingen, Switzerland.

Erin lager brand produced by FX Matt Brewing Co, Utica, New York, USA.

Erkenbrecht vineyards at Geisenheim and Neustadt an der Weinstrasse in Rheinpfalz region, Germany.

Erlanger lager brand of Stroh brewery, Detroit, Michigan, USA.

Erntebringer *Grosslage* (collective vineyard) incorporating vineyards at Geisenheim, Geisenheim (Johannisberg), Oestrich-Winkel (Mittelheim) and Oestrich-Winkel (Winkel) in Rheingau region, Germany.

Errazuriz brand name of wine-producer Viña Errazuriz-Panquehue est 1879 Aconcagua Valley, Chile.

erzeugerabfüllung 'estate-bottled'. German. A wine bottled at the source of production rather than by a merchant.

Erzgrube vineyard at Bad Münster am Stein-Ebernburg in Nahe region, Germany.

Erzherzog Weine, Johann wine co-operative in Südsteiermark, Austria.

ESB Extra Special Bitter. Brand-style for strong ales by brewers, notably Fuller's in London and Mitchell's in Lancaster, England. In USA, brewers adopting the style include Oasis and Wynkoop in Colorado and Redhook and Big Time in Seattle.

Escadre, Château L' wine estate of AC Premières Côtes de Blaye, Bordeaux, France.

Escoubes, Domaine d' armagnac producer, Labastide d'Armagnac, France. Vintages from 1904.

Eselsberg vineyards at Flein in Württemberg region and Kitzingen and Kolizheim in Franken region, Germany.

Eselsbuckel vineyard at Niederotterbach in Rheinpfalz region, Germany.

Eselshaut vineyard at Neustadt an der Weinstrasse in Rheinpfalz region, Germany.

Eselspfad vineyard at Appenheim in Rheinhessen region, Germany.

Eselstreiber vineyard at Eckelsheim in Rheinhessen region, Germany.

Eschenauer, Louis wine *négoçiant*, Bordeaux, France.

Esk Valley Estate wine producer of Hawke's Bay, New Zealand.

espalier vine-training method. French.

Esper vineyard at Kerzenheim in Rheinpfalz region, Germany.

Espèrance Mon Repos rum distiller est 1895, Guadeloupe.

Espinglet, Château de l' wine estate of AC Premières Côtes de Bordeaux, France.

espumoso 'sparkling wine'. Spanish.

Essencia orange Muscat dessert wine by Andrew Quady, California, USA.

Essencia ultra-sweet wine of Tokaji, Hungary. Locally spelt **Eszencia**. Botrytis-affected and of low alcohol (6.0%).

Essex Porter beer brand of Crouch Vale brewery, Chelmsford, Essex, England.

Estaing VDQS of Lot Valley, SW France. Red and white wines in fast-diminishing quantities.

Estang, Château L' wine estate of AC Castillon, Bordeaux, France.

Esterhazy aristocratic family wine company of Burgenland, Austria. Renowned sweet wines.

estery in winetasting, a smell of varnishy-vapoury smell, indicating a faulty wine.

Est! Est!! Est!!! DOC for white wine from Malvasia and Trebbiano grapes of Montefiascone, Latium, Italy. Origin: Processing to Rome for coronation of Holy Roman Emperor in 1111, princely German Bishop Fugger sent his servant Martin ahead along the route to scout for inns with good wine, marking the door with Est! where appropriate. At Montefiascone, the magnificence of the wine was attested to by Martin's threefold endorsement and the bishop proceeded no further. Modern scholars endorse neither the story nor the wine.

Estrella beer brand of Damm brewery, Spain.

Estruelle, Château L' wine estate of AC Médoc, Bordeaux, France.

estufa in madeira winemaking, the vat in which wine is gently heated for three to six months to produce characteristics similar to those prevailing aboard ships on long voyages to the Tropics from the 16th century. The heating process is called the **estufagem**. Portuguese.

Etchart brand of wine producer Bodegas Arnaldo Etchart est 1850 Cafayate, Argentina. Noted wines from Cabernet Sauvignon, Chardonnay and Torrontes grapes.

Ethel Cocktail. Over ice shake 1 part apricot brandy, 1 curaçao, 1 white crème de menthe. Strain.

eticetta bottle label, Italian, as in spirits described as Eticetta Bianca or Eticetta Nera (Black Label, White Label).

Etienne Sauzet wine estate of Puligny-Montrachet, Burgundy, France. *Premier cru* vineyards including les Combettes.

étiquette bottle label. French.

Etko-Haggipavlu wine producing co-operative, island of Cyprus. Brands include Emva.

Etna brewery at Etna, California, USA.

Etna DOC for red, *rosato* (both from Nerello Mascalese grapes) and white wines (Carricante and Catarratto) of Etna volcano vineyards, Sicily, Italy.

Etoile, L' village and AC for white wine and *vin jaune* from Chardonnay, Poulsard and Savagnin grapes, Jura region, France.

Etoile, Château L' wine estate of AC Graves, Bordeaux, France.

Eton Blazer Cocktail. Over ice shake 3 parts dry gin, 1 kirsch, 1 lemon juice, 1 teaspoon sugar. Strain.

Ettaler Klosterlikor herbal liqueur of Ettel monastery, Bavaria, Germany.

eucalyptus in winetasting, a concentrated, spicily alcoholic smell associated with intense red (esp Cabernet Sauvignon) wines from particularly ripe vintages.

Euchariusberg vineyards at Konz, Konz (Krettnach), Konz (Niedermennig) and Konz (Obermennig) in Mosel-Saar-Ruwer region, Germany.

Eulengrund vineyard at Zeil am Main in Franken region, Germany.

Euler brewery at Wetzlar, Germany. Brands include **Euler Hell**, **Euler Pilsener**.

Evangile, Château L' wine estate of AC Pomerol, Bordeaux, France.

Evans & Tate leading wine producer in Margaret River and Swan Valley, Western Australia. Famed Chardonnay and Semillon white wines among others.

Eve O Cocktail. Over ice shake 2 parts apple brandy, 2 dry gin, 1 fresh orange juice, 1 dash Angostura bitters. Strain.

Everards brewery in Leicester, England. Beacon Bitter (3.8% alc) Original Premium Cask Ale (5.2% alc), Tiger Best Bitter (4.2% alc).

Evesham pub-brewery (The Green Dragon) at Evesham, Worcestershire, England.

Eve's Apple Cocktail. Over ice shake 1 part apple brandy, 1 Swedish Punsch, 1 grapefruit juice. Strain. Evesham

Ewig Leben collective vineyard (*Grosslage*) at Randersacker in Franken region, Germany.

Exchange Brewery former brewery in Sheffield, South Yorkshire, England. Closed c 1993.

Excise see box.

Executive Suite Cocktail. Into a champagne glass pour 2 parts brandy, 1 Grand Marnier, 1 dash orange bitters. Top with chilled sparkling wine.

Exe Valley brewery at Silverton, Exeter, Devon, England. Curate's Choice (4.8% alc), Devon Glory (4.7% alc), Exe Valley Bitter (3.7% alc).

Exmoor Ales brewery at Wiveliscombe, Somerset, England.

Expedition Superior Light rum brand of Hall & Bramley. Blended from rums of Barbados and Guyana.

Exshaw cognac house est 1805 Cognac, France. Owned by Otard.

extract in winetasting, elements in colour, weight and flavour due to the presence of non-sugar soluble solids in the wine.

Extra Zytnia fruit-flavoured rye vodka brand of Polmos Siedlce, Poland.

Eye of the Hawk strong-ale brand of Mendocino Brewing Co, Hopland, California, USA.

Eye-Opener Cocktail. Over ice shake 1 egg yolk, 1 part rum, 2 dashes crème de noyaux, 2 dashes curaçao, 2 dashes pastis, 1 teaspoon sugar. Strain.

Eylenbosch brewery at Schepdaal, Payottenland, Belgium.

Eyrie Vineyards wine producer of Oregon, USA. Noted Chardonnay and Pinot Noir wines.

Ezerjo white grape variety of Hungary.

Excise

taxing drink for the good of the people

Like many bad things, the Romans started it. The *vectigal rerum venalium* was the first excise duty, originally levied in the first century BC, on goods sold in open markets in Rome. It was introduced by Augustus at one per cent (*centesima*) of value, halved by Tiberius and finally abolished, in AD 38, by Caligula. It was, in common with all such taxes, imposed to fund the gross excesses of government.

Excise did not stage a comeback for sixteen centuries. No monarch even of the Middle Ages seems to have dared try it. But when the Puritan-dominated Parliament in Britain seized fiscal power from King Charles I during the English Civil War, it was quick to consider the tax.

The government of the day was, as ever since, reticent about its intentions. This is a statement of 1641: 'The Houses of Parliament, receiving information that divers public rumours and aspersions are by malignant persons cast upon this house, that they intend to assess every man's pewter and lay Excise upon that and other commodities, the said House, for their vindication do declare these rumours are false and scandalous.'

The first Excise Ordinance was duly introduced two years later for 'the speedy raising and levying of monies for the maintenance of the forces raising by Parliament' and, of course, 'only for the duration of the war.'

The method of collection was inspired by the indirect taxation levied in Holland, where to finance a burgeoning navy, the state collected percentages of the value of spirits, cider and beer. In Britain, the tax was extended to beer, meat, clothes, leather and salt. Further money-spinning schemes were added. Fees were demanded for issuing licences to sell game, medicines, imported wines, and snuff. Pawnbrokers, pedlars, auctioneers and other riff-raff were also required to buy a licence if they wished to continue their trades.

To enforce it all, Excise Commissioners were appointed. The original eight nominees worked on a commission of $3d.$ in every £1 collected – or $1^{1}/_{4}$ per cent. The commissioners and their officers had almost unlimited powers when it came to collections – including the right of entry and search into the homes of citizens. Overnight, this ended one the most basic privileges of British life, the inviolability of private homes.

The excise, the first such tax ever to be levied on ordinary working people, was spectacularly unpopular, and evaded on an epic scale. Excise officers were resisted, attacked and occasionally murdered. The army was regularly called out to assist with enforcement. For all that, collecting was profitable work, with generous salaries offered, and ample scope for corruption.

When Cromwell's Commonwealth came to its inevitable end in 1660 and the Crown was restored, it was widely anticipated that the new levies would be revoked. But King Charles II was not a man to overlook a source of ready income. Within his first year in power, the excise had been increased not only on alcoholic drinks, but extended to tea, coffee and chocolate. The proceeds, which went to the Crown, amounted to about £250,000 a year – uncountable millions at today's values.

Alongside customs duties, levied on imports since the Middle Ages, the revenue from excise funded the majority of public expenditure in Britain until the 20th century. The idea of taxing income – 'direct' tax – did not occur to politicians until the blackest days of the Napoleonic Wars, when Parliament again felt the need to introduce a temporary levy, in addition, of course, to hugely increased excise duties not just on alcohol but on such luxuries as bricks, glass, soap, salt and candles.

Rates of excise duty on drink have increased inexorably in most nations over the centuries. British excise on spirits moved from a few pence per gallon in 1660 to 11s. 8^1/$_2$d. in 1820. In the year 2000, it stood at £36.

In the European Union, Britain, Finland, Ireland and Sweden are the four members (out of 25) levying more than £1 on a bottle of wine. France takes a tiny duty, but Austria, Germany, Greece, Italy, Portugal and Spain are among the member states levying none at all. Every EU member imposes an excise on spirits.

European governments now openly declare it their duty to protect the physical and moral welfare of their citizens by imposing punitive excise duties on alcohol. By obliging us to pay ten times the actual value for a bottle of whisky in the United Kingdom, we are being done a service.

F

Faber white grape variety, Germany.
Faberrebe Niersteiner Spiegelberg wine by Niersteiner Winzergenossenschaft, Rheinhessen region, Germany.

Fabs UK drinks trade acronym for flavoured alcoholic beverages – more familiarly known as alcopops.
Fabuloso brandy by Vinicola Hidalgo y Cia, Sanlúcar de Barrameida, Spain. From the sherry region, 36% alc.
Fachern vineyard at Niederfell in Mosel-Saar-Ruwer region, Germany.
Factory House meeting place of British 'factors' (shippers) of the port trade, Oporto, Portugal. Present building dates from 1790.

Facundo premium rum brand of Bacardi. Name commemorates company founder Facundo Bacardi y Maso, born Sitges, Spain, 1813.
Fagnouse, Château La wine estate of AC St-Emilion, Bordeaux, France.
Fahrberg vineyards at Kopbern-Gondorf, Lehmen and Löf in Mosel-Saar-Ruwer region, Germany.
Fair and Warmer Cocktail. Over ice shake 2 parts rum, 1 sweet vermouth, 2 dashes curaçao. Strain.
Fairbanks Cocktail. Over ice shake 1 part apricot brandy, 1 dry gin, 1 dry vermouth, 1 dash grenadine, 1 dash lemon juice. Strain.
Fairbanks Senior Cocktail. Over ice shake 2 parts dry gin, 1 dry vermouth, 2 dashes crème de noyaux, 2 dashes orange bitters. Strain.
Fair Maid of Devon apple variety traditionally valued for cider-making. English.
Fair Valley wine producer in Paarl, South Africa, established 1998 with partial government funding and co-operation from neighbouring Fairview Estate (*qv*) as an employment and housing scheme for black workers. Chenin Blanc and Pinotage wines.
Fairview Estate leading vineyard of Paarl, South Africa. Renowned Chardonnay, Sauvignon and Semillon white wines, Cabernet Sauvignon red. Charles Back branded wines are named after the estate's winemaker.

Fairy Belle Cocktail. Over ice shake 1 egg white, 3 parts dry gin, 1 apricot brandy, 1 teaspoon grenadine. Strain.

Faiveley, Joseph major estate and *négoçiant* based in Nuits-St-Georges, Burgundy, France.

Falandy-Liandry cognac house, Cognac, France.

Falcon & Firkin pub-brewery at Hackney, London, England.

Falerio dei Colli Ascolani DOC for white wines from Trebbiano grapes, Ascoli Piceno, Marches, Italy.

Falernum historic wine of ancient Rome, still made in Latium and Mondragone. Red from Aglianico and Barbera grapes, white from Falanghina. Italy.

Falfas, Château wine estate of AC Côtes de Bourg, Bordeaux, France.

Falken major brewery at Falkenberg, Sweden.

Falkenberg vineyards at Alsenz in Nahe region, Dienheim in Rheinhessen region, Donnersdorf in Franken region and Piesport in Mosel-Saar-Ruwer region, Germany.

Falklay vineyards at Burg and Reil in Mosel-Saar-Ruwer region, Germany.

Fallen Angel Cocktail. Over ice shake 2 parts dry gin, 1 lemon juice, 2 dashes crème de menthe, 1 dash Angostura bitters. Strain.

Faller, Théo wine producer at Kayserberg, Alsace, France.

Famous Gate Pinot Noir red wine by Domaine Carneros, California, USA.

Famous Grouse, The blended scotch whisky by Matthew Gloag, Perth, Scotland.

Fandango Cocktail. Over ice stir 2 parts dry sherry, 1 rum, 1 dash orange bitters. Strain.

Fanfare bottle-conditioned seasonal (Spring) bitter ale (4.5% alc) by Tisbury Brewery, Wiltshire, England.

Fanny Hill Cocktail. Over ice stir 1 part Campari, 1 Cointreau, 1 brandy. Strain into champagne glasses and top with chilled sparkling wine.

Fantasia Cocktail. Over ice stir 2 parts brandy, 1 dry vermouth, 3 dashes crème de menthe, 3 dashes maraschino. Strain.

Fara village and hearty red wine from Bonarda and Nebbiolo grapes, Piedmont, Italy.

Fare Thee Well Cocktail. Over ice shake 3 parts dry gin, 1 dry vermouth, 4 dashes sweet vermouth, 1 dash lemon juice.

Fargues, Château de wine estate of AC Sauternes, Bordeaux, France. Classified *Cru Bourgeois*.

Farmer Cocktail. Over ice stir 2 parts dry gin, 1 dry vermouth, 1 sweet vermouth, 2 dashes orange bitters.

Farmer's Glory ale by Wadworth brewery, Devizes, Wiltshire, England.

farmyard in winetasting, a ripe, sweet whiff of manure in the smell of (usually) red wine. Not a fault, and found in many mature fine wines.

faro style of sweet lambic beer. Belgium.

Faro DOC for red wine from Nerello Macalese grapes, Messina, Sicily, Italy.

Faros red wine from Plavac grapes, island of Hvar, Croatia.

Farsons brewery at Mriehel, Malta. Brands include Cisk lager and Lacto milk stout.

Fascinator Cocktail. Over ice shake 2 parts dry gin, 1 dry vermouth, 2 dashes pastis, 1 sprig fresh mint. Strain.

Fass 'barrel' in German.

Fässerlay vineyard at Boppard in Mittelrhein region, Germany.

Fässla brewery at Bamberg, Germany.

Fastini perry brand of Halewood International, Huyton, Merseyside, England.

fat in winetasting, a glyceriney texture, often characterising oak-aged Chardonnay wines.

Fat Bastard Vin de Pays d'Oc brand of Gabriel Meffre, Gigondas, France. Chardonnay grapes aged in oak for a 'fat' flavour. Made in Languedoc by UK importer Guy Anderson and French winemaker Thierry Boudinaud. Anderson claims the name for the wine eluded them until 'we thought, sod it – if they can have Bâtard-Montrachet in Burgundy then why can't the Languedoc have a Fat Bastard Chardonnay. It's as simple as that.'

Fat God's brewery at The Queen's Head, Iron Cross, Evesham, Worcestershire, England.

Fat Tire Amber Ale beer brand of New Belgium Brewing Co at Fort Collins, Colorado, USA.

Fattor Angelo grappa brand of Friuli, Italy.

fattoria farm, Italian. Precedes name of numerous wine estates, especially in Tuscany.

Faubernet, Château wine estate of AC Bordeaux Supérieur, France.

Faugères AC zone of Coteaux du Languedoc, Midi, France. Red wines from Carignan, Cinsaut, Grenache, Mourvèdre and Syrah grapes.

Faurie-de-Souchard, Château wine estate of AC St-Emilion, Bordeaux, France. Classified *Grand Cru Classé*.

Faustino Martinéz leading wine producer of Rioja, Spain. **Faustino I** *gran reserva*, **156 Faustino V** *reserva* and white wine. A quirk of the Faustino wines is that the labels are adorned with portraits of distinguished composers. *Reserva* wines bear the benevolent image of Christoph Willibald Gluck (1714–87).

Favonio wine brand of Attilio Simonini, Apulia, Italy.

Favorita white wine of Roeri and Langhe, Piedmont, Italy.

Favourite Cocktail. Over ice shake 1 part apricot brandy, 1 dry gin, 1 dry vermouth, 1 dash lemon juice. Strain.

Faxe brewery known for **Faxe Fad** beer. Denmark.

Fayau, Château wine estate of AC Premières Côtes de Bordeaux, France.

Faye d'Anjou designated wine village of AC Coteaux du Layon Villages, Loire Valley, France.

Faygate Dragon bottled ale (4.7% alc) by King & Barnes brewers, formerly of Horsham, Sussex, England. Now made by Hall & Woodhouse, Blandford Forum, Dorset. The name, say the makers, commemorates 'the last reported sight of a living dragon in the 16th century.'

Fazi-Battaglia Titulus major wine producer of DOC Verdicchio, Marches, Italy.

FBR Cocktail. Over ice shake 3 parts brandy, 2 rum, 1 teaspoon lemon juice, 1 egg white, 1 teaspoon sugar. Strain into wine glasses half-filled with crushed ice. Initials stand for Frozen Brandy and Rum.

Feast & Firkin pub-brewery in Leeds, Yorkshire, England.

Featherstone brewery at Enderby, Leicester, England.

Federal Hill brewery at Forest, Virginia, USA.

Federation brewery at Gateshead, Newcastle upon Tyne, England.

Feher Burgundi white grape variety, Hungary. Synonymous with Pinot Blanc.

Feiler-Artinger wine producer in Neusiedlersee Hügelland, Burgenland, Austria.

feints rejected portions of the distilling process, typically the first and last quantities from the cycle.

Feist, H & CJ port shipper, Vila Nova de Gaia, Portugal. Vintages: 1957, 60, 63, 66, 70. 74, 75, 77, 78, 79, 80, 82, 83, 85, 87, 89, 91, 94, 97, 2000, 03.

Feldon brewery at The Coach & Horses, Shipston-on-Stour, Warwickshire, England.

Feldschlöschen brewery at Rheinfelden, Switzerland.

Feldschlosschen brewery at Braunschweig, Germany. Maker of Duckstein beer.

Felinfoel brewery at Llanelli, Dyfed, Wales. Produces Double Dragon ale.

Felix brown ale brand of Clarysse brewery, Oudenaarde, Belgium.

Fellows, Morton & Clayton brewery at Nottingham, England.

Felluga, Livio wine producer of DOC Collio, Friuli-Venezia Giulia, Italy.

Fels vineyards at Freilaubersheim in Rheinhessen region, Konz in Mosel-Saar-Ruwer region and St Katherinen in Nahe region, Germany.

Fels, Le wine village of VDQS Entraygues, SW France.

Felsen vineyard at Eppelsheim in Rheinhessen region, Germany.

Felsenberg vineyards at Durchroth, Eckenroth, Oberhausen an der Nahe and Schlossböckelheim in Nahe region, Germany.

Felseneck vineyards at Bad Münster am Stein-Ebernburg, Gutenberg and Wallhausen in Nahe region, Germany.

Felsengarten vineyards at Besigheim, Bietigheim-Bissingen, Gemmrigheim, Hessigheim, Löchgau and Walheim in Württemberg region and Uberlingen in Baden region, Germany.

Felsenköpfchen vineyard at Bretzenheim in Nahe region, Germany.

Felsenkopf vineyard at Trittenheim in Mosel-Saar-Ruwer region, Germany.

Felsensteyer vineyard and Niederhausen an der Nahe in Nahe region, Germany.

Felsentreppchen vineyard at Wittlich in Mosel-Saar-Ruwer region, Germany.

Felsina-Berardenga wine estate of DOC Chianti Classico, Tuscany, Italy.

Femsa abbreviated name for Fomento Economico, leading brewing company of Mexico.

Fendant white grape variety, Valais, Switzerland. Synonymous with Chasselas.

Fenland brewery at Chatteris, Cambridgeshire, England.

Fentimans revived ginger beer producer and brand of Yorkshire, England. Traditionally brewed to 0.5% alc and classified as a 'soft' drink.

Fer red grape variety of Argentina. Synonymous with Malbec.

Ferbos, Château de wine estate of AC Cérons, Bordeaux, France.

Ferintosh traditionally, the first named brand of scotch whisky, as described by John Knox (1513–1572), Protestant reformer and founder of the Church of Scotland: 'the sociable practice of Highlandmen in all ages to seal satisfy and wash down every compact or bargain in good old Ferintosh'.

fermentation the process in which sugar, through the action of yeast, is converted into alcohol and carbon dioxide.

fermentazione naturale 'natural fermentation'. A sparkling wine description implying the carbon dioxide creating the bubbles is naturally occurring. Italian.

Fermoselle wine region of Zamora, Spain.

Fernandes rum distiller of Trinidad. Vat 19 gold and white rums and other brands. Owned by Angostura.

Fernão Pires white grape variety of Portugal.

Fernet Branca Italian bitter-tasting liqueur with both aperitif and digestive properties. Allegedly, a remedy for hangovers. Produced as **Fernet** by Martini & Rossi in Turin and by Fratelli Branca in Milan. Leading brand is produced in France, by Distilleries Fernet-Branca, St Louis, Haut-Rhin.

Ferran, Château wine estate of AC Pessac-Léognan, Bordeaux, France.

Ferrand, Pierre cognac producer est 1702, Segonzac, France. Brandy entirely from Ferrand's own vineyards in Grande Champagne district. Brands include Réserve Ancestrale 50-year-old.

Ferrand, Château wine estate of AC Pomerol, Bordeaux, France.

Ferrand, Château de wine estate of AC St-Emilion, Bordeaux, France. Classified *Grand Cru*.

Ferrande, Château wine estate of AC Graves, Bordeaux, France.

Ferrari renowned producer of non-DOC sparkling wines from Chardonnay and Pinot Noir grapes, Trento, Trentino-Alto Adige, Italy. **Ferrari Brut, Ferrari Riserva Giulio Ferrari** and other wines.

Ferraud, Pierre wine estate of AC Beaujolais, France.

Ferreira, AA port producer and shipper, est 1751 Vila Nova de Gaia, Portugal. Dóna Antonia Personal Reserve is named after founder's grand-daughter-in-law who survived the notorious drowning incident in the Douro river of 1862 in which Baron James Forrester perished, and who in widowhood made Ferreira a leading port house. Also, ten- and 20-year-old tawnies and vintages: 1955, 58, 60, 63, 66, 70, 75, 77, 78, 80, 82, 83, 85, 87, 90, 91, 94, 97, 2000, 03.

Ferret & Firkin pub-brewery in Chelsea, London, England.

Ferrière, Château wine estate of AC Margaux, Médoc, Bordeaux, France. Classified *3ème Grand Cru Classé*.

Fer Servadou red grape variety of SW France.

Festbier style of beer specially brewed for consumption at festivals. Germany.

Fesles, Château de leading wine estate of AC Bonnezeaux, Loire Valley, France.

Feteasca white grape variety of Romania. Synonymous with Fetiaska of Bulgaria and Léanyka of Hungary.

Fetiaska white grape variety of Bulgaria. Synonymous with the Feteasca of Romani and Léanyka of Hungary.

Fettercairn East Highland malt whisky distillery, Laurencekirk, Scotland. Single malt: 10-year-old.

Fettgarten vineyard at Zell in Mosel-Saar-Ruwer region, Germany.

Fetzer leading wine producer in California, USA. Organically produced varietals from Chardonnay, Pinot Noir and Viognier grapes including Bonterra labels.

Feuer vineyard at Neustadt an der Weinstrasse in Rheinhessen region, Germany.

Feuerbach vineyard at Castell in Franken region, Germany.

Feuerberg vineyards at Bad Münster am Stein-Ebernburg, Duchroth and Feilbingert in Nahe region; Ediger-Eller and Ernst in Mosel-Saar-Ruwer region; Flomborn in Rheinhessen region; Vogtsburg im Kaiserstuhl in Baden region, Germany.

Feuerberg *Grosslage* (collective vineyard) incorporating vineyards in Rheinpfalz region, Germany at, respectively: Bad Dürkheim, Bobenberg am Berg, Ellerstadt, Gönnheim, Kallstadt, Weisenheim am Berg.

Feuerheerd port producer, Vila Nova de Gaia, Portugal. Est 1815 and owned by Barros Almeida. Old tawnies and vintages: 1957, 58, 60, 63, 66, 70, 74, 77, 78, 80, 83, 85, 87, 89, 91, 94, 97, 2000, 03.

Feuerley vineyard at Boppard in Mittelrhein region, Germany.

Feuermännchen vineyard at Neu-leiningen in Rheinpfalz region, Germany.

Feuerstein vineyard at Röttingen in Franken region, Germany.

Feuersteinrossel vineyard at Oberndorf in Nahe region, Germany.

feuillette unit of quantity, of 132 litres, traditionally used in Chablis wine trade. Based on barrel size no longer in use.

Feunig high-strength wine, Germany.

Fèvre, William leading wine producer of AC Chablis, particularly of AC Chablis Grand Cru. Oak-aged wines.

Feytit-Clinet, Château wine estate of AC Pomerol, Bordeaux, France.

Fiano di Avellino DOC white wine from Fiano grapes, Campania, Italy.

fiasco 'flask' in Italian. Style of wicker-clad wine bottle formerly associated with Chianti.

Fiddlers Ales brewery at The Fox & Crown, Old Basford, Nottinghamshire, England.

Fiddler & Firkin pub-brewery in Croydon, Surrey, England.

Fiddler's Elbow ale (5.2% alc) by Wychwood brewery, Witney, Oxfordshire, England.

Fiddletown AVA of Sierra Foothills, Amador County, California, USA.

Fiefs de la Grange, Les second wine of Château Lagrange, AC St Julien, Bordeaux, France.

Fiefs Vendéens VDQS for red and rosé wines from Cabernets Franc and Sauvignon, Gamay and Pineau d'Aunis grapes and whites from Chardonnay, Chenin Blanc, Gros Plant and Sauvignon. Vendés, Loire Valley, France.

Fielder & Firkin pub-brewery at Sutton, Surrey, England.

Fieuzal, Château de wine estate of AC Pessac-Léognan, Bordeaux, France. Classified *Cru Classé*.

Fifth Avenue Cocktail. Into a small wine glass gently pour 1 part apricot brandy, 1 crème de cacao, 1 sweetened cream. Avoid mixing ingredients.

Fifty-Fifty Cocktail. Over ice stir 1 part dry gin, 1 dry vermouth. Strain into a cocktail glass and add a cocktail olive. The original 'Martini'.

Figari wine district of AC Vin de Corse, Corsica, France.

Figaro red-wine brand of Villeveyrac co-operative, SW France.

Figeac, Château great wine estate of AC St-Emilion, Bordeaux, France. Classified *1er Grand Cru Classé*.

Filhot, Château wine estate of AC Sauternes, Bordeaux, France. Classified *2ème Cru Classé*.

fillette 'little girl' in French. Half-sized wine bottle.

Filliers *jenever* and liqueur producer, Bachte-Maria-Leerne, Belgium.

Fillioux, Jean cognac producer est 1880 Segonzac, France.

Filo brew pub (First In, Last Out) at Hastings, East Sussex, England.

Finch & Firkin pub-brewery in Liverpool, Merseyside, England.

Findlater's Finest blended scotch whisky by Findlater, London, England.

Findling vineyard at Nierstein in Rheinhessen region, Germany.

Findling white grape variety (related to Müller-Thurgau), Mosel-Saar-Ruwer region, Germany.

Fine and Dandy Cocktail. Over ice shake 2 parts dry gin, 1 Cointreau, 1 lemon juice, 1 dash Angostura bitters. Strain.

Fine Goule, La cognac producer, Archaic, France.

Fine Old FOB Canadian whisky brand of Hudson's Bay Company, Canada.

Fine Old Special blended scotch whisky by Joseph Holt, Manchester, England.

Finesko & Firkin pub-brewery in Norwich, Norfolk, England.

Fines Roches, Château des wine estate of AC Châteauneuf-du-Pape, Rhône Valley, France.

fine wine a term without statutory significance in any language, but as a sincere and objective description in winetasting, praise indeed.

Finger Lakes wine region of New York State, USA.

fining in brewing and winemaking, the process of, or substance used in, clarification. Bentonite, egg white, gelatine, isinglass and oxblood are among the materials employed.

finish in winetasting, the last sensation in the mouth. Good wines with correct acidity have a 'clean' finish; bad wines leave a watery impression.

Finlandia wheat vodka brand, Finland. Also **Finlandia Arctic Cranberry** vodka and **Finlandia Arctic Pineapple** vodka.

fino driest and palest style of sherry of Jerez de la Frontera, Spain. Typically 15–17% alc. See box.

Finotini Cocktail. Over ice stir 3 parts dry gin, 1 fino sherry. Strain and squeze lemon peel over.

Fiorano red and white wine brand of Principe de Venosa estate, Rome, Italy.

Fior d'Alpi yellow liqueur flavoured with Alpine flowers. Bottles contain twig to which sugar adheres and crystallises. Italy.

Fioupe Cocktail. Over ice stir 1 part brandy, 1 sweet vermouth, 1 teaspoon Bénédictine. Strain, add cocktail cherry to glass and squeeze lemon peel over.

Firebox premium bitter ale (6.0% alc) of RCH Brewery, Weston-Super-Mare, Somerset, England.

Firecracker strong ale (5.8% alc) by Harveys Brewery, in Lewes, East Sussex, England. 'A tribute to the emergency services.'

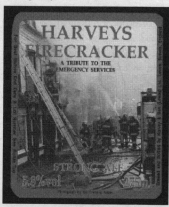

Fino sherry

the flowering of a competitor's idea

Fino is very pale, very dry sherry. It is made in Jerez de la Frontera in Spain's Andalucia, and is a variation on the original pale, dry sherry, the manzanilla of Sanlucar de Barrameda. The sherry is from Palomino grapes fermented to 11.5% alcohol and then fortified with grape spirit to a level of 15%. This mild fortification is not strong enough to inhibit the yeast growth vital to sherry's character, but is sufficient to protect the wine from infections during the maturing process.

This style of sherry is relatively modern, owing its origins to the introduction of the *solera* in the late 1920s. It's a succession of maturing casks through which quantities of wines can gradually be progressed to produce commercial quantities in a consistent style. Early users of this 'fractional blending' system discovered that in the casks of the *solera* a yeasty scum formed on the surface of the new wine. This mantle was found to have a miraculous effect, protecting the wine from air and light, keeping it very pale and fresh, and also inoculating it with delightfully pungent flavours. The frothy cap came to be perceived as a 'blooming' and Jerezanos now call it the *flor*, or flower. Much care is taken to keep the *flor* alive by continually refreshing the *solera* with younger wine to maintain the vital supply of nutrients.

The original process was first developed in the 19th century, long before the commercial use of soleras, in the seaside town Sanlucar de Barrameda, home of manzanilla, where the humid maritime air is particularly conducive to the growth of *flor*. The new style of pale dry sherry quickly earned popularity and Sanlucar began to gain dominance over Jerez in the sherry market. In the 1840s, *bodegas* in Jerez began to imitate the techniques of their counterparts in Sanlucar, and marketed their own pale, dry sherry as 'fino'. Manzanilla sales managed to stay ahead of those for fino for the next century or so, but in the 1950s major Jerez *bodegas* such as Gonzalez Byass and Pedro Domecq began to market their respective brands (Tio Pepe and La Ina) on an international scale, and manzanilla fell into the shadows.

While fino dominates the dry sherry market abroad (especially in Britain, the principal export market), manzanilla has lately regained supremacy at home. Sanlucar now claims to sell 56 per cent of all the sherry consumed in Spain.

Firehouse

Firehouse brewery in Rapid City, South Dakota, USA.

Fireman's Lift Cocktail. Over ice shake 2 parts rum, 1 fresh lime juice, sprinkling of sugar. Strain and add a cocktail cherry.

Firestone Vineyard renowned wine estate est 1973 by Brooks Firestone (grandson of tyre manufacturer), Santa Ynez Valley, California, USA.

firkin a small cask, especially for ale. Originally equivalent to a quarter of a barrel. English, from Dutch *vierde* (fourth).

Firkin pub-brewery chain, UK.

Firkin Dog ale brand of Blind Man's Brewery, Leighton, Somerset, England.

firm in winteasting, a well-knit flavour well-balanced between fruit and acidity. Opposite of flabby.

firn 'maderised', German. Describes a white wine that has darkened to brown over many years' ageing.

First vineyards at Eussenheim in Franken region and Wertheim in Baden region, Germany.

First Estate port brand of Taylor Fladgate & Yeatman, Vila Nova de Gaia, Portugal.

First Lord 12-year-old blended and vatted malt scotch whiskies by Edwin Cheshire, Stansted, Essex, England.

First River wine estate in Stellenbosch, South Africa.

Fischer vineyard at Frickenhausen in Franken region, Germany.

Fischer, Albert wine producer in Neusiedlersee Hügelland, Burgenland, Austria.

Fischer, Christian wine producer in Thermenregion, Niederösterreich, Austria.

Fischer Gasthaus restaurant-brewery in Vienna, Austria.

Fischerstube brewery in Basel, Switzerland. Beers are sold under Ueli ('jester') brand.

Fischer-Pêcheur major brewery group centred in Alsace, France.

Fischerpfad vineyard at Alsheim in Rheinhessen region, Germany.

Fitou important AC of Midi, France (first AC est in the region, 1946). Red wines from Carignan, Grenache, Laadoner, Mourvèdre and Syrah grapes.

Five-Fifteen Cocktail. Over ice shake 1 part curaçao, 1 dry vermouth, 1 sweetened cream. Strain.

Five Roses popular *rosato* wine by Leone de Castris, Apulia, Italy.

5757 Gin Margarita Cocktail. Over ice shake 3 parts dry gin, 2 lemon juice, 1 Cointreau, half teaspoon sugar. Strain.

Five Thirty Canadian whisky brand of Canadian Schenley Distilleries, Canada.

Fixin northern village and AC of Côte d'Or, Burgundy, France. *Premiers crus*: les Arvelets, aux Chensots, Clos du Chapitre, les Hervelets, les Meix Bas, la Perrière.

Fizz & Chip mixed drink of Taylor's Chip Dry white port with tonic water and ice.

flabby in winetasting, a watery flavour; lacking in acidity.

flacon pot-shaped 46-cl wine bottle of Lyons, France.

Flagey-Echézeaux wine village of Burgundy, France. Location of *grands crus* Echézeaux and Grands Echézeaux.

Flagship brewery at Chatham, Kent, England.

Flame Lily wine brand of Philips Central Cellars, Harare, Zimbabwe.

Flame Thrower ale brand of Fox & Hounds pub-brewery, Barley, Hertfordshire, England.

Flaming Ferrari Cocktail. Over ice stir 1 part rum, 1 Grand Marnier, 1 green crème de menthe. Strain.

Flamingo & Firkin pub-brewery in Derby, Derbyshire, England.

Flamingo Cocktail. Over ice shake 3 parts dry gin, 1 apricot brandy, 1 fresh lime juice. Strain into ice-filled tumblers and add dashes of grenadine.

Flannary's brewery at Capelbangor, Aberystwyth, Ceredigion, Wales.

flat in winetasting, a flavour marred by lack of acidity.

Flatterberg vineyards at Forchtenberg and Forchtenberg (Emsbach) in Württemberg region, Germany.

Fleur, Château La wine estate of AC St-Emilion, Bordeaux, France. Classified *Grand Cru*.

Fleur-Cailleau, Château La wine estate of AC Canon-Fronsac, Bordeaux, France.

Fleur Calon, Château La wine estate of AC Montagne-St-Emilion, Bordeaux, France.

Fleur-Canon, Château La wine estate of AC Canon-Fronsac, Bordeaux, France.

Fleur-Cardinale, Château wine estate of AC St-Emilion, Bordeaux, France.

Fleur du Cap popular wine brand of Bergkelder, Stellenbosch, South Africa.

Fleurie village, AC and most prestigious *cru* of Beaujolais region, France. The 825 hectares of the AC are divided up into 13 named vineyards: Les Côtes, Le Bon Cru, La Roilette, Les Moriers, Les Roches, Les Garants, Poncié, Montegnas, La Chapelle des Bois, Grille Midi, Champagne, La Joie du Palais and La Madone. Best known from labels is La Madone, named after the Chapelle de la Madone, a prominent landmark overlooking the village. The chapel's bronze statue of La Madone was blown down and destroyed during a storm in 1999, and the vineyards subsequently suffered a run of poor vintages.

Fleurie, Château de Beaujolais cru wine brand of Heritiers Loron, Fleurie, France.

Fleur-Milon, Château La wine estate of AC Pauillac, Médoc, Bordeaux, France. Classified *Cru Grand Bourgeois*.

Fleur-Pétrus, Château La great wine estate of AC Pomerol, Bordeaux, France.

Fleur-Pourret, Château La wine estate of AC St-Emilion, Bordeaux, France. Classified *Grand Cru*.

Fleuron Blanc de Château Loubens second wine of Château Loubens, Bordeaux, France.

Flichman wine estate of Mendoza, Argentina. Finca Flichman varietal brands.

Flinters aperitif brand of Halewood International, Huyton, Merseyside, England.

flinty in winetasting, a defined stoney flavour and smell. Characteristic of dry white wines, particularly Pouilly Blanc Fumé of Loire Valley, France.

floc de Gascogne regional apéritif of Armagnac region, SW France. From armagnac brandy and grape juice.

flor in sherry-making, the cap of saccharomyces yeast products forming on the surface of *fino* and *manzanilla* sherries as they mature in butts. *Flor* protects the wine from air, reducing the effects of oxidation and keeping the sherry pale and fresh as it ages. Conditions in the sherry-making centres of Jerez de la Frontera and Sanlucar de Barrameda are particularly conducive to the formation of *flor*. Name means 'flower' from the appearance of the yeasty 'bloom'.

Flora white grape-variety cross (Gewürztraminer and Semillon) of Australia and California, USA.

Floradora Cocktail. Over ice shake 2 parts dry gin, 1 fresh lime juice, 1 teaspoon grenadine, 1 teaspoon sugar. Strain into a tall, ice-filled glass and top with chilled dry ginger ale.

floraison flowering of vines, French.

Flor de Caña rum brand of Compañia Licorera, Nicaragua.

Florida Cocktail. Over ice shake 1 part dry gin, 5 orange juice, 1 teaspoon Cointreau, 1 teaspoon kirsch, 2 dashes lemon juice. Strain.

Florida Rum Cocktail. Over ice shake 2 parts rum, 1 grapefruit juice, 3 dashes dry vermouth, 3 sweet vermouth. Strain.

Florimond, Château de wine estate of AC Premières Côtes de Blaye, Bordeaux, France.

Florio marsala and brandy producer, Sicily, Italy. Brandies under Florio and Ingham labels.

Flounder & Firkin pub-brewery in London N7, England.

flower power bucolic English nickname for a mixed drink from elderflower cordial and gin or vodka.

flowery in winetasting, a smell reminiscent of flower blooms.

Fluffy Navel Cocktail. Over ice shake 1 part peach schnapps, 1 orange juice. Strain.

flute tall narrow-bowled wine glass for champagne.

flûte slim green wine bottle of Alsace, France.

Flying Dog pale ale brand of Broadway Brewing, Denver, Colorado, USA. Originally made exclusively for Flying Dog Brewpub of Aspen, Colorado, but now exported in bottle.   *see label opposite* ➤

Flying Horse lager by United Breweries, Bangalore, India.

Flying Dutchman Cocktail. Over ice stir 1 part Dutch gin, 1 teaspoon Cointreau, 1 dash orange bitters. Strain.

Flying Scotsman Cocktail. Over ice shake 3 parts scotch whisky, 1 sweet vermouth, 1 teaspoon sugar, 2 dashes Angostura bitters. Strain.

Fog Horn Cocktail. In an ice-filled tumbler mix 2 parts dry gin, 1 fresh lime juice. Top with chilled dry ginger ale and add a lime slice.

Fog Lifter Cocktail. Over ice shake 3 parts rum, 1 brandy, 1 dry gin, 1 orange juice. Strain into ice-filled tumbler and add a teaspoon of madeira to each.

Fogolar brandy brand of Distillerie Camel, Udine, Italy.

Fohrenberg vineyards at Ihringen, Meersburg and Stetten in Baden region, Germany.

Foianeghe red wine from Bordeaux grape varieties by Fedrigotti, Trentino-Alto Adige region, Italy.

Folle Blanche white grape variety of Charente and Gascony, France. Diminishingly used in armagnac and cognac production.

Fombrauge, Château wine estate of AC St-Emilion, Bordeaux, France. Classified *Grand Cru*.

Fomento Economico leading brewing company of Mexico. Name is usually shortened to Femsa.

Fonbadet, Château wine estate of AC Pauillac, Médoc, Bordeaux, France. Classified *Cru Bourgeois Supérieur*.

Fonchereau, Château wine estate of AC Entre-Deux-Mers, Bordeaux, France.

Fondarzac, Château wine estate of AC Entre-Deux-Mers, Bordeaux, France.

Fondillón traditional long-aged sweet wine of Alicante, Spain.

Fongrave, Château wine estate of AC Entre-Deux-Mers, Bordeaux, France.

Fonplégade, Château wine estate of AC St-Emilion, Bordeaux, France. Classified *Grand Cru Classé*.

Fonrazade, Château wine estate of AC St-Emilion, Bordeaux, France. Classified *Grand Cru*.

Fonréaud, Château wine estate of AC Listrac, Médoc, Bordeaux, France. Classified *Cru Bourgeois*.

Fonroque, Château wine estate of AC St-Emilion, Bordeaux, France. Classified *Grand Cru Classé*.

Fonscolombe, Château major wine estate of AC Coteaux d'Aix-en-Provence, France.

Fonseca, JM da major wine-producing company est 1834, Azeitao, Portugal. Red wines include Camarate, Pasmados, Periquita. Sparkling wine: Lancers.

Fonseca Guimaraens port producer and shipper est 1822 Vila Nova de Gaia, Portugal. Merged with Taylor Fladgate 1948, ports were labelled simply Fonseca until 1988. Bin 27 vintage character, old tawnies and vintages: 1958, 60, 61, 62, 63, 64, 65, 66, 67, 68, 70, 72, 74, 75, 76 77, 78, 80, 83, 84, 85, 86, 87, 88, 91, 92, 94, 97, 2000, 03.

Fonsèche, Château second wine of Château Lamothe-Cissac, Bordeaux, France.

Fontana Candida leading producer of Frascati, Latium, Italy.

Fontanafredda major wine producer and distiller est 1878 (by son of King Victor Emanuel II), Serralunga, Piedmont, Italy. Grappa, Asti Spumante sparkling wines and Barolo red wines.

Fontanelle, La second wine of Château Cantenac-Brown, Bordeaux, France.

Fontenay, Château wine estate of AC Côtes de Castillon, Bordeaux, France.

Fontenil, Château wine estate of AC Fronsac, Bordeaux, France.

Fontesteau, Château wine estate of AC Haut-Médoc, Bordeaux, France. Classified *Cru Grand Bourgeois*.

Fonthill vineyard at Salisbury, Wiltshire, England.

Footage & Firkin pub-brewery in Grosvenor Street, Manchester, England.

Forest Brown Ale beer brand (2.7% alc) of Whitbread, London, England.

Foretnik Winzerhof wine producer in Traisental, Niederösterreich, Austria.

Forgeron, Michel cognac house est 1977, Segonzac, France.

Formentini wine producer of DOC Collio, Friuli-Venezia Giulia, Italy.

Forrester port house named after Baron James Forrester, originally est as William Offley 1737. Known as Offley Forrester until purchase by Martini & Rossi, 1987. Baron Forrester ten-year-old tawny, Offley Boavista brands and vintages: 1955, 60, 62, 63, 66, 67, 70, 72, 75, 77, 80, 82, 83, 85, 87, 89.

Forrester & Firkin pub-brewery in Stafford, Staffordshire, England.

Forschungs brewery at Perlach in Munich, Germany.

Forst great wine village of Rheinpfalz region, Germany. *Grosslagen:* Mariengarten and Schnepfenflug. Producers include Bassermann Jordan, Bürklin Wolf, Deinhard.

Försterlay vineyard at Lösnich in Mosel-Saar-Ruwer region, Germany.

Forst vineyards at Bad Kreuznach in Nahe region and Edesheim in Rheinpfalz region, Germany.

Forstberg vineyards at Bad Neuenahr-Ahrweiler in Nahe region, Leutesdorf in Mittelrhein and Oberstenfeld and Oberstenfeld (Gronau) in Württemberg region, Germany.

Forstgrube vineyards at Illingen and Vaihingen in Württemberg region, Germany.

Forstreiter, Meinhard wine producer in Kremstal, Niederösterreich, Austria.

Forstweg vineyard at Walsheim in Rheinpfalz region, Germany.

Forta white grape variety, Germany.

Fort Collins Pride ale by Old Colorado brewery, Fort Collins, USA.

Fort-de-Vauban, Château wine estate of AC Haut-Médoc, Bordeaux, France.

Fort Garry Distillery formerly of Seagram, Canada.

Fortia, Château leading wine estate of AC Châteauneuf-du-Pape, Rhône Valley, France.

fortified wine wine to which grape spirit has been added during or after fermentation. Madeira, port and sherry are examples.

Fortilizio Il Colombaio Chianti Classico by Fattoria il Colombaio, Quercegrossa, Tuscany, Italy.

Magnificent label portrays Ottoman emperor Suleiman the Great.

Fortnum & Mason's Choice Old blended scotch whisky of Fortnum & Mason, Piccadilly, London, England. Also, 8- and 12-year-old blends and Linkwood 21-year-old malt.

Forts de Latour, Les second wine of Château Latour, Bordeaux, France.

Fort Spokane brewery at Spokane, Washington, USA.

Fortuna, La vineyard and wine brand of Lontue Valley, Chile. Noted wines from Malbec, Merlot and other grape varieties.

Fortunator lager brand of Ayinger brewery, Germany.

Fortyniner bottle conditioned strong ale (4.9% alc) by Ringwood Brewery, Hampshire, England.

forward in winetasting, a wine more mature than might be expected from its age.

Foster's major brewing company based in Melbourne, Australia. Best known for worldwide brand **Foster's Lager**.

foudre large wine barrel. French.

foulage in winemaking, the action of bursting grapes to allow yeasts on the skins into contact with the flesh. French.

Fountain Brewery principal production centre of Scottish & Newcastle Breweries in Edinburgh, Scotland, until 2004, when it was sold and the site redeveloped for housing.

Fourcas-Dupré, Château wine estate of AC Listrac, Médoc, Bordeaux, France. Classified *Cru Grand Bourgeois Exceptionnel*.

Fourcas-Hosten, Château wine estate of AC Listrac, Médoc, Bordeaux, France. Classified *Cru Grand Bourgeois Exceptionnel*.

Fourchaume *premier cru* vineyard of Chablis, Burgundy, France.

Fourcroy distillery company est 1862 Laken, Brussels, Belgium. Vodka, Mandarine Napoléon and other spirits.

Four Flush Cocktail. Over ice shake 2 parts Bacardi rum, 1 dry vermouth, 1 Swedish Punsch, 1 dash grenadine.

Fourneaux, Les *premier cru* vineyard of Chablis, Burgundy, France.

Fourney, Château wine estate of AC St-Emilion, Médoc, Bordeaux, France. Classified *Grand Cru*.

Fournier brand name for liqueurs of Berger company, France.

Four Rivers brewery at Newcastle upon Tyne, Tyne & Wear, England.

Four Roses bourbon whiskey brand of Seagram, USA, sold to Kirin Brewery Co of Japan, 2001.

Four Seasons whisky brand of United Distillers, Melbourne, Australia.

Four Score Cocktail. Over ice stir 3 parts brandy, 2 Lillet, 1 yellow Chartreuse. Strain.

Foursquare rum brand of RL Seale & Co, St Philip, Barbados.

Fourtet, Clos wine estate of AC St-Emilion, Bordeaux, France. Classified *Grand Cru Classé*.

Fourth Degree Cocktail. Over ice shake 2 parts dry vermouth, 2 dry gin, 2 sweet vermouth, 1 pastis. Strain.

Fowl & Firkin pub-brewery in Coventry, West Midlands, England.

Fowler's Wee Heavy beer brand of Belhaven brewery, Dunbar, Scotland.

Fox & Firkin pub-brewery in Lewisham, London, England.

Fox & Newt brewery in Leeds, Yorkshire, England.

Foxfield brewery at the Prince of Wales, Foxfield, Broughton in Furnace, Cumbria, England.

Fox River Cocktail. Place 1 ice cube into a small wineglass and add 3 parts rye whisky, 1 crème de cacao, 4 dashes peach bitters.

Fox Trot Cocktail. Over ice shake 4 parts Bacardi rum, 1 fresh lime juice, 2 dashes orange curaçao. Strain.

Foxwhelp apple variety traditionally valued for cider-making.

foxy in winetasting, earthy flavour and smell characterising wines from wild vine species particularly grown in USA.

fraise *eau de vie* distilled from strawberries. France (mainly Alsace) and Switzerland.

fraises de bois *eau de vie* distilled from wild strawberries. France (mainly Alsace) and Switzerland.

framboise *eau de vie* distilled from raspberries. France (mainly Alsace) and Switzerland.

Framboise Cocktail. Over ice shake 2 parts rum, 1 crème de framboise, 1 fresh cream. Strain.

frambozen raspberry beer. Belgian.

France the foremost quality-wine-producing nation of the world, from major regions of Alsace, Bordeaux, Burgundy, Champagne, Loire and Rhône plus many minor regions. Quality wine standards are assured under AC system (est 1936) with lesser quality wines graded VDQS or vin de pays. France is also the leading producer of grape spirits, notably armagnac and cognac. Normandy is one of the world's major cider-producing regions and Alsace a world-famous brewing centre.

France, Château de wine estate of AC Pessac-Léognan, Bordeaux, France.

France, Château La wine estate of AC Entre-Deux-Mers, Bordeaux, France.

France, Château La wine estate of AC Médoc, Bordeaux, France. Classified *Cru Bourgeois*.

Franc-Grâce-Dieu, Château wine estate of AC St-Emilion, Bordeaux, France. Classified *GrandCru*.

Franciacorta DOCG for red wines from Barbera, Cabernet Franc, Merlot and Nebbiolo grapes and white wines from Pinot Bianco grapes grown in area of Cortefranca, Lombardy, Italy. Also, *rosato* and white *spumante* wines from Pinot Grigio and Pinot Nero grapes.

Franc-Maillet, Château wine estate of AC Pomerol, Bordeaux, France.

Franc-Mayne, Château wine estate of AC St-Emilion, Bordeaux, France. Classified *Grand Cru Classé*.

Franco-Fiorino wine producer, Piedmont, Italy.

Francoli grappa distiller of Gattinara, Piedmont, Italy.

Franconia Franken wine region, Germany.

Frangelica hazelnut liqueur (24% alc) by Barbero (est 1891), Canale, Italy. 'According to legend Frangelica lived three centuries ago in a hilly area bound by the right bank of the river Po. He lived as a hermit and through his love of nature and knowledge of its secrets created unique recipes for liqueurs. The most precious one of all was a liqueur made from wild hazelnuts with infusions of berries and flowers to enrich the flavour.'

Frangelico hazelnut-flavoured liqueur brand of C&C International, Dublin, Eire.

Franken wine region of northern Bavaria, Germany. Three *Bereichen*: Maindreieck, Mainviereck, Steigerwald.

Frankenberg vineyards at Lauda-Königshofen (Lauda) and Lauda-Königshofen (Marbach) in Baden region, Germany.

Frankenhell vineyard at Damscheid in Mittelrhein region, Germany.

Frankenjack Cocktail. Over ice shake 2 parts dry vermouth, 2 dry gin, 1 apricot brandy, 1 Cointreau. Strain.

Frankenland *Bereich* of Baden region, Germany.

Frankenmuth brewery at Frankenmuth, Michigan, USA, well known for German-style beers.

Franken Riesling white grape variety of California, USA. Synonymous with Silvaner.

Frankenstein vineyard at Freimersheim in Rheinhessen region, Germany.

Frankenthal vineyard at Rüdesheim in Rheingau region, Germany.

Frankfort gin brand formerly of Seagram, USA.

Frankland River vineyard region, Western Australia.

Frank Sullivan Cocktail. Over ice shake 1 part brandy, 1 Cointreau, 1 lemon juice, 1 Lillet. Strain.

Franquet-Grand-Poujeaux, Château wine estate of AC Moulis, Médoc, Bordeaux, France. Classified *Cru Bourgeois*.

Fransdruif white grape variety of South Africa synonymous with Palomino of Jerez, Spain. Used in production of Cape 'sherry'.

Franzensberger vineyards at Offenburg and Offenburg (Fessenbach) in Baden region, Germany.

Franziskaner vineyard at Breisach in Baden region, Germany.

Franziskaner Hefe-Weissbier wheat beer by Spaten brewery, Munich, Germany.

Franziskus Heller Bock beer by Spaten brewery, Munich, Germany.

Fraoch Heather Ale beer (5.0% alc) by Heather Ale brewery, Strathaven, Scotland.

Frapin major cognac house, Segonzac, France.

Frascati DOC white wine from Malvasia and Trebbiano grapes of Frascati and Monteporzi Catone in Castelli Romani, Italy. The 'café wine' of Rome.

Fraser McDonald blended scotch whisky of Fraser McDonald, London, England.

Fraser's Supreme blended scotch whisky of Strathnairn, Inverness, Scotland.

frasqueiras single-variety Madeira wines of nominated vintages, aged at least 20 years in wood before bottling. Portuguese.

Fratelli Vallunga wine producer in Emilia-Romagna region, Italy.

Frauenberg vineyards at Bremm and Neef in Mosel-Saar-Ruwer region, Flöhrsheim-Dalsheim in Rhein-hessen region and Schliengen in Baden region, Germany.

Frauenfeld brewery at Frauenfeld, Switzerland.

Frauengarten vineyard at Winters-heim in Rheinhessen region, Germany.

Frauenländchen vineyard at Kleinkarlbach in Rheinpfalz region, Germany.

Frecciarossa leading wine producer of Oltrepò Pavese, Lombardy, Italy.

Freedom pilsner lager brand of **Freedom Brewing** Co of Fulham, London, England.

Freedom Fighter Cocktail. Over ice shake 3 parts sloe gin, 1 Crème Yvette, 1 lemon juice, 1 egg white. Strain.

Freedom Road wine brand of South Africa. See Backsberg Estate.

Freemark Abbey winery of Napa Valley, California, USA.

Freeminer brewery at Cinderford in Forest of Dean, Gloucestershire, England. Deep Shaft Stout (6.2% alc), **Freeminer Best Bitter** (4% alc), Hurricane (4% alc), Shakemantle (5.0% alc), Speculation Strong Ale (4.7% alc), Trafalgar (6.0% alc), Waterloo (4% alc). Bottled Ales include Golden Mile Celebration, originally brewed 2004 to mark the 50th anniversary of the first mile run in under four minutes, by Roger Bannister, at Oxford, England, on 6 May 1954.

Free State brewery at Lawrence, Missouri, USA.

Freezomint leading green crème de menthe brand by Cusenier, France.

Freie Weingärtner wine producer in Wachau, Niederösterreich, Austria.

Fritsch, Karl wine producer in Donauland, Niederösterreich, Austria.

Freisa d'Alba red wines from Freisa grapes, of varying fizziness and sweetness, Alba, Piedmont, Italy.

Freisa d'Asti DOC for red wines from Freisa grapes, of varying fizziness and sweetness, Asti, Piedmont, Italy.

Freisa di Chieri DOC for red wines from Freisa grapes, of varying fizziness and sweetness, Chieri, Piedmont, Italy.

Freisamer white grape variety prin-cipally of Baden region, Germany. Cross of Pinot Gris and Silvaner.

Freixenet major cava producer est 1889 San Sadurni de Noya, Cata-lonia, Spain. Cordon Negro brand. Name is pronounced 'frezhnay'.

French Connection

French Connection Cocktail. Over ice stir 2 parts brandy, 1 amaretto. Strain.

French Rose Cocktail. Over ice stir 2 parts dry gin, 1 cherry brandy, 1 dry vermouth. Strain.

French 75 Cocktail. Over ice shake 2 parts Plymouth gin, 1 fresh lime juice. Strain into small wine glasses and top with chilled sparkling wine.

Fréquin Audièvre apple variety traditionally valued for cider-making. English.

Frescobaldi leading wine producer of DOCG Chianti Rufina, Tuscany, Italy. Renowned wines incude Castello di Nipozzano, Montesodi and wines of DOC Pomino.

fresh in winetasting, flavour and smell of young wine with good acidity.

Fresian & Firkin pub-brewery in Clapham, London, England.

Freudental vineyard at Ortenberg in Baden region, Germany.

Freundstück vineyard at Forst an der Weinstrasse in Rheinpfalz region, Germany.

Freycinet leading wine producer of Tasmania, Australia.

Friar & Firkin pub-brewery in London NW1, England.

Friary Vintners producer of West Country range of flavoured liqueurs at Witham Friary, Somerset, England. Styles include Black Cherry, Blackcurrant Rum, Friar's Choice, Whisky & Mead, and vodka-based West Country Velvet liqueurs.

Friedrich Wilhelm Gymnasium great wine estate est 1563 at Trier in Mosel-Saar-Ruwer region, Germany. World-renowned Riesling wines.

Friese brewery in Friesland, Netherlands.

Friuli-Venezia Giulia wine region of NE Italy. DOCs include Aquilea, Collio Goriziano, Colli Orientali del Friuli, Grave del Friuli, Isonzo, Latisana.

frizzante lightly sparkling wine, Italy. Less effervescent than *spumante*.

frizzantino faintly sparkling wine, Italy.

Frog & Parrot brew pub in Sheffield, Yorkshire, England.

Frog Island brewery at Westbridge, Northampton, England.

Froher Weingarten vineyard at Niederheimbach in Mittelrhein region, Germany.

Fröhlich vineyard at Bechenheim in Rheinhessen region, Germany.

Frohnwingert vineyard at Oberhausen in Rheinpfalz region, Germany.

Frohwingert vineyards at St Goar and St Goar (Werlau) in Mittelrhein region, Germany.

Fromes Hill brewery at Wheatsheaf Inn, Fromes Hill, Ledbury, Herefordshire, England.

Fronhof vineyard at Bad Dürkheim in Rheinpfalz region, Germany.

Fronsac village and AC of Libourne, Bordeaux, France.

Fronsac, Château de wine estate of AC Fronsac, Bordeaux, France.

Frontignan AC of SW France. Sweet, liquorous white wines from Muscat grapes.

Frontignan informal name for original cylindrical Bordeaux wine bottle of 19th century. Grand Frontignan bottle held 74–76 cl, Medium Frontignan 72–74 cl, Petit Frontignan 68–70cl. Bordeaux bottle was officially decreed at 75 cl in 1930, but the region did not universally adopt this size until 1979 with the introduction of a European Community standard.

Frontignan New World synonym for white grape variety Muscat Blanc à Petits Grains.

Frosty Jack cider brand of Aston Manor cider producer, UK.

Froth Blower Cocktail. Over ice shake 1 egg white, 4 parts dry gin, 1 grenadine. Strain.

Froupe Cocktail. Over ice stir 2 parts brandy, 2 sweet vermouth, 1 Bénédictine. Strain.

Frozen Apple Cocktail. Over ice shake 3 parts apple brandy, 1 fresh lime juice, 1 egg white, 1 teaspoon sugar. Strain.

Fruchtaromalikors fruit liqueur made without additives. Germany.

Früh Echt Kölsch beer brand of **PJ Früh's Gölner Hofbräu**, Cologne, Germany.

Frühlingsplätzchen vineyard at Monzingen in Nahe region, Germany.

Frühmess vineyard at Gleiszellen-Gleishorbach in Rheinpfalz region, Germany.

Frühmesse vineyard at Alsheim in Rheinhessen region, Germany.

Frühmessler vineyard at Sinzheim in Baden region, Germany.

Fruit Bat Cocktail. Over ice stir 1 part cider brandy, 1 dry vermouth, 1 dry sherry. Strain.

fruit beer style of beer in which fruit is added to grain base for fermentation. Mainly Belgium.

Fruit Défendu, Le ('Forbidden Fruit') strong (7.2% alc) beer of Hoegaarden brewery, Belgium.

Fruitini Cocktail. Over ice shake 1 part vodka, 1 cranberry juice, 1 teaspoon sugar. Strain. Make this cocktail with any one of a wide variety of summer-fruit juices, preferably freshly pressed from blackberries, loganberries, raspberries, strawberries.

fruity in winetasting, a smell suggesting ripe grapes.

Fruska Gora vineyard area of Vojvodina, Serbia. Known for Laski Rizling.

Frydenlunds brewery in Oslo, Norway.

Fryns *jenever* producer, Hasselt, Belgium.

Fuchs vineyard at Saarburg in Mosel-Saar-Ruwer region, Germany.

Fuchsberg vineyard at Geisenheim in Rheingau region, Germany.

Fuchsen vineyard at Laubenheim in Nahe region, Germany.

Fuchshöhle vineyard at Kobern-Gondorf in Mosel-Saar-Ruwer region, Germany.

Fuchsloch vineyards at Gau-Odernheim in Rheinhessen region, at Hochdorf-Assenheim and Rödersheim-Gronau in Rheinpfalz region and at Wincheringen in Mosel-Saar-Ruwer region, Germany.

Fuchsmantel vineyards at Bad Dürkheim and Wachenheim in Rheinpfalz region, Germany.

Fuder large wine cask (approx 1000 litres) of Mosel-Saar-Ruwer region, Germany.

Fuggles

Fuggles hop variety widely used in British brewing, principally for bittering. Named after grower Richard Fuggle, who first propagated it in 1875.

Fuggles Imperial strong (5.5% alc) 'single varietal hop beer' brewed with Fuggles hops by Castle Dene brewery, County Durham, England. Owned by Whitbread.

Fuhrmann, Tobias wine producer in Neusiedlersee, Burgenland, Austria.

Fuie-St-Bonnet, Château La- second wine of Château La Tour St Bonnet, Bordeaux, France.

full-bodied in winetasting, flavour of wine high in alcohol and extract.

Fuller's brewer of Chiswick, London, England. Famed beers include Chiswick Bitter, ESB, London Pride.

Full House Cocktail. Over ice shake 2 parts Bacardi rum, 1 dry vermouth, 1 Swedish Punsch. Strain.

Full Monty Cocktail. Over ice shake 1 part vodka, 1 Galliano, sprinkle of freshly grated ginseng root. Strain.

Fumé Blanc white grape variety of Australia and USA. Synonymous with Sauvignon Blanc.

Funchal capital and winemaking centre of madeira trade, island of Madeira, Portugal.

Fundador solera reserva brandy by Pedro Domecq, Jerez de la Frontera, Spain.

Funkenberg vineyard at Müden in Mosel-Saar-Ruwer region, Germany.

Furmint white grape variety of Hungary. Major constituent of Tokay sweet wine and dry wines of other regions.

Fürst Bismarck popular brand of *Korn* by von Bismarck family distillery, Friederichsruh, Germany.

Fürstenberg brewery at Donauschingen, Germany.

Fürstenberg vineyards at Dettelbach, Volkach (Eschendorf) and Volkach (Köhler) in Franken region and at Oberdiebach and Oberdiebach (Rheindiebach) in Mittelrhein region, Germany.

Fürsteneck *Grosslage* (collective vineyard) incorporating vineyards in Baden region, Germany at, respectively: Appenweier, Berghaupten, Durbach, Gengenbach, Gengenbach (Bermersbach), Gengenbach (Reichenbach), Hohberg (Diersburg), Hohberg (Hofweiler), Hohberg (Niederschopfheim), Lautenbach, Oberkirch, Oberkirch (Bottenau), Oberkirch (Haslach), Oberkirch (Nussbach), Oberkirch (Odsbach), Oberkirch (Ringelbach), Oberkirch (Stadelhofen), Oberkirch (Tiergarten), Offenburg (Fessenbach), Offenburg (Rammersweier), Offenburg (Zell-Weierbach),

Offenburg (Zunsweier), Ohlsbach, Ortenberg, Renchen (Erlach), Renchen (Ulm).

Fürstenlager vineyard at Auerbach in Hessische Bergstrasse region, Germany.

Fürstliche Brauerei Thurn und Taxis brewery at Schierling, Bavaria, Germany. Known for rye beer, Schierlinger Roggenbier.

Fursty Ferret ale brand (4.4% alc) of Hall & Woodhouse, Dorset, England.

Fussigny, A De cognac house, Jarnac, France.

fût small wine barrel, France.

fûts de chêne oak barrels. The phrase *élevé en fûts de chêne* on a wine label indicates the wine has been 'brought up (matured) in oak barrels'. French.

Fyfe brewery at Kirkcaldy, Fife, Scotland.

G

'G' dry white wine of Château Guiraud, AC Sauternes, Bordeaux, France.

Gabiano DOC for red wines from Barbera grapes, Gabiano, Monferrato Casalese hills, Piedmont, Italy.

Gabriel Boudier leading producer of fruit liqueurs, Dijon, France.

Gachot-Monot leading wine producer of Nuits-St-Georges, Burgundy, France.

Gaby, Château du wine estate of AC Canon-Fronsac, Bordeaux, France.

Gaffel brand of *Kölsch* beer by **Gaffel-Becker** brewery, Cologne, Germany.

Gaffelière, Château La wine estate of AC St-Emilion, Bordeaux, France. Classified *1er Grand Cru Classé*.

Gager, Josef wine producer in Mittelburgenland, Austria.

Gaglioppo red grape variety of Italy, notably used in Cirò of Calabria, and elsewhere.

Gagnard, Château wine estate of AC Fronsac, Bordeaux, France.

Gai, Château sparkling and still wine producer, Ontario, Canada.

Gaillac vineyard area of SW France including **AC Gaillac** for red, rosé and white wine, **AC Gaillac Doux** for sweet wines, **AC Gaillac Mousseux** for rosé and white sparkling wines, **AC Gaillac Premières Côtes** for superior-quality whites, **AC Gaillac Sec Perlé** for whites with residual natural carbon dioxide.

Gaillard, Château wine estate of AC St-Emilion, Bordeaux, France. Classified *Grand Cru*.

Gaillat, Domaine de wine estate of AC Graves, Bordeaux, France.

Gairloch blended scotch whisky of McMullen & Sons, Hertford, England.

Gaisböhl vineyard at Ruppertsberg in Rheinpfalz region, Germany.

Gaispfad vineyard at Traben-Trarbach in Mosel-Saar-Ruwer region, Germany.

Gaja, Angelo greatest wine producer of DOCG Barbaresco, Piedmont, Italy. Also Barolo and other wines.

Galactica Cocktail. Over ice shake 1 part vodka, 1 blue curaçao, 1 fresh ime juice, 1 teaspoon crème de cassis. Strain.

Galaxy whiskey brand formerly of Seagram, USA.

Gale's ale brand of **George Gale & Co**, Horndean, Portsmouth, Hampshire, England. Ales include HSB (Horndean Special Bitter), Prize Old Ale.

Gale's eight-year-old blended scotch whisky of George Gale, Horndean, Hampshire, England.

Galestro white wine from Trebbiano and other grapes of Chianti zone, Tuscany, Italy.

galet flat circular stones of the vineyards of Châteauneuf du Pape, southern Rhône Valley, France. The stones' ability to absorb sun's heat and radiate it to the vines is said to give the wine its characteristic ripeness.

Galgenberg vineyards at Bad Kreuznach in Nahe region, Badenheim and Hackenheim in Rheinhessen region and Kandel in Rheinpfalz region, Germany.

Galicia wine-producing region of NW Spain. DOs Rias Bajas, Ribiero, Valdeorras.

Galissonière, Château de la leading wine producer in AC Muscadet, Loire Valley, France.

Galius, Cuvée wine brand of Union des Producteurs de St-Emilion, Bordeaux, France.

Gallagher & Burton whisky brand originally of Seagram, USA.

Gallais-Bellevue, Château second wine of Château Potensac, Bordeaux, France.

Gallimard Père & Fils *récoltant manipulant* champagne producer, les Riceys, Champagne, France.

Gallo, E&J winemaking company of Modesto, California, USA. Operates the world's largest winemaking centre in San Joaquin valley. Mainly 'jug' wines but also an important range of quality varietals from Sonoma vineyards. Total production exceeds 50 million bottles annually. Founded by Ernest and Julio Gallo.

Gallo Nero 'Black Cockerel' emblem of Chianti Classico consortium, Tuscany, Italy.

Gallwey coffee liqueur brand of Irish Distillers, Eire.

Gamay red grape variety principally of AC Beaujolais, Burgundy, France, where it is the sole constituent of all red wines of the region's appellations. Also grown in other Burgundy ACs, plus Anjou, Ardèche, Haut Poitou etc.

Gamay Beaujolais red grape variety of California, USA. Unrelated to Gamay.

gam bay 'cheers' in Chinese

Gambellara DOC white wine of Veneto region, Italy. Similar to Soave.

Gambrinus brewery est 1869 at Plzen (Pilsen), Czech Republic. Along with Pilsner Urquell, whose brewery site it shares, the only true pilsner beer, in the sense that it is made in Pilsen. Gambrinus is a strong (4.9% alc) lager.

Game Bird tawny port by Robertson Brothers, Vila Nova de Gaia, Portugal.

Gamefair ten-year-old vatted malt scotch whisky of Hynard Hughes, Leicester, England.

Gammel Jysk Porter beer brand of Ceres brewery, Aarhus, Jutland, Denmark.

Gammel Porter beer brand of Carlsberg brewery, Copenhagen, Denmark. Sometimes labelled **Gammel Imperial Stout**.

Gamot, Clos de wine estate of AC Cahors, SW France.

Gamza red grape variety of Bulgaria. Synonymous with Kadarka of Hungary.

Gancia leading producer of *spumante* wines est 1850 Asti, Piedmont, Italy. Also a major vermouth producer.

Gäns vineyard at Kobern-Gondorf in Mosel-Saar-Ruwer region, Germany.

Gänsberg vineyard at Baden-Baden in Baden region, Germany.

garagiste originally French for the owner or operator of a motor garage and, metaphorically, any small provinicial *petit bourgeois* entrepreneur. But from the 1990s the term has come to embrace makers of high-price cult Bordeaux wines from tiny vineyard plots outside the usual appellations and vinified in tiny wineries with the common soubriquet of garages.

Garcia, Tomas wine *bodega* est 1921, Montilla-Moriles, Spain.

Garde *Kölschbier* brewed in Cologne, Germany.

Garde, Château La wine estate of AC Pessac-Léognan, Bordeaux, France.

Gardera, Château Le wine estate of AC Premières Côtes de Bordeaux, France.

Gardet, Georges champagne producer, Rilly-la-Montagne, France.

Gardour, Château second wine of Château Moncets, Bordeaux, France.

Garganega white grape variety of Veneto region, Italy. Main constituent of Soave and other regional whites.

Gärkammer vineyard at Bad Neuenahr-Ahrweiler in Ahr region, Germany.

Garnacha one of the principal red grape varieties of Spain, grown in Navarra, Rioja, Vega Sicilia and elsewhere. Is commonly blended with Tempranillo. Synonymous with Grenache.

Garnacha Blanco white grape variety of Spain. Strong white wines of high colour, especially in Rioja region. Synonymous with Grenache Blanc.

Garrafeira quality designation for Portuguese wine. Red wines from qualifying vintage aged at least two years before bottling and one after. White wines from qualifying vintage aged at least six months before and after bottling. Alcohol of 0.5% higher than standard. Term is used by producers to denote their prestige wines.

Gärtchen vineyard at Piesport in Mosel-Saar-Ruwer region, Germany.

Gartenbrau wheat beer brand of Capital brewery, Madison, Wisconsin, USA.

Gartenlay vineyard at Leutesdorf in Mittelrhein region, Germany.

Garvey sherry *bodega* est 1780 by Irish-born William Garvey, Jerez de la Frontera, Spain. Company's fino sherry San Patricio commemorates Ireland's patron saint.

Gasper Cocktail. Over ice shake 1 part dry gin, 1 pastis. Strain.

Gässel vineyard at Neustadt an der Weinstrasse in Rheinpfalz region, Germany.

Gastenklinge vineyard at Weinstadt in Württemberg region, Germany.

Gatão popular *vinho verde* brand of Borges & Irmão, Minho, Portugal. Name means 'Cat'.

Gattinara DOCG red wine from Nebbiolo grapes, Vercelli hills, Piedmont, Italy.

Gaudou, Domaine de wine producer in AC Cahors, SW France.

Gauguin Cocktail. Over ice shake 2 parts rum, 1 equal mix lemon and fresh lime juice, 1 teaspoon passionfruit syrup. Strain and add a maraschino cherry.

Gauloise strong ale by Du Bocq brewery, Purnode, Belgium. Named after the Gauls, pre-Christian inhabitants of Belgium.

Gautier cognac house, Aigre, France. Owned by Berger.

Gavi DOC for white wine from Cortese grapes, Piedmont, Italy. Also known as DOC Cortese di Gavi.

Gavi di Gavi white wine of DOC Cortese di Gavi from La Scolca estate, Piedmont, Italy.

Gay, Château Le wine estate of AC Pomerol, Bordeaux, France.

Gay, Château Le wine estate of AC Entre-Deux-Mers, Bordeaux, France.

Gay Lussac French system of measuring alcoholic content of drinks. The most widely used of the three principal systems (British Proof and US Proof are the others) in brewing and cider industries as well as wines and spirits, it is based simply on the percentage of alcohol by volume in the drink. Thus a spirit of 40GL is 40 per cent alcohol. Devised by French chemist Joseph Louis Gay-Lussac (1778–1850).

Gazebo Cocktail. Over ice stir 3 parts dry gin, 1 Cointreau, 1 blue curaçao, 1 dash Angostura bitters. Strain.

Gazette Cocktail. Over ice shake 1 part brandy, 1 sweet vermouth, 3 dashes lemon juice, 3 dashes sugar syrup. Strain.

Gazin, Château wine estate of AC Graves, Bordeaux, France.

Gazin, Château wine estate of AC Pomerol, Bordeaux, France.

Gazin, Château du wine estate of AC Canon-Fronsac, Bordeaux, France.

Geary's brewery in Portland, Maine, USA. Geary Pale Ale.

Gedeonseck *Grosslage* (collective vineyard) incorporating vineyards at Boppard, Brey, Rhens and Spay in Mittelrhein region, Germany.

Geebung Polo Club pub-brewery in Melbourne, Australia.

Geelong wine district of Victoria, Australia.

Geens *genever* producer, Schiedam, Netherlands.

Geens Benelux *jenever* and liqueur producer, Aarschot, Belgium.

Geezer bottle-conditioned beer (4% alc) by Wood Brewery, Winstantow, Shropshire, England.

Gehringer Brothers wine producer at Oliver, British Columbia, Canada.

Geffard, Henri cognac producer, Segonzac, France.

Gehrn vineyard at Eltville in Rheingau region, Germany.

Geiersberg vineyards at Armsheim and Dittelsheim-Hessloch in Rheinhessen region, Germany.

Geierslay vineyard at Wintrich in Mosel-Saar-Ruwer region, Germany.

Geiershöhll vineyard at Klein-Winternheim in Rheinhessen region, Germany.

Geisberg vineyards at Ockfen, Rivenich, Schoden and Zell in Mosel-Saar-Ruwer region, Germany.

Geisenheim renowned wine village of Rheingau region, Germany. *Grosslagen*: Burgweg, Erntebringer. Vineyards include Klaus, Rothenberg, Schlossgarten.

Geisenheim Institut für Kellerwirtschaft der Forschungsanalt German wine industry's principal research establishment and winemaking college.

Geissberg vineyards at Heidesheim in Rheinhessen region and Wiesenbronn in Franken region, Germany.

Geissenkopf vineyards at Niedermoschel and Obermoschel in Nahe region, Germany.

Geisskopf vineyard at Kirchheim an der Weinstrasse in Rheinpfalz region, Germany.

Geisterberg vineyards at Erbes-Büdesheim, Flonheim and Flonheim (Uffenholden) in Rheinhessen region, Germany.

Geisweiler & Fils wine producer and *négoçiant-éleveur* of Nuits-St-Georges, Burgundy, France.

Gekkeikan *sake* and wine brand, Japan.

Gélas armagnac house est 1865 Vic-Fezensac, Gascony, France.

Gellewza red grape variety indigenous to island of Malta.

Gemaco cognac house and brand of Berger company, Aigre, France.

Gemischter Satz Austrian wine from a mix of grape varieties harvested together.

General Sutter leading *kirsch* brand by H Nebiker distillery, Sissbach, Switzerland. Named after Swiss-born Johann Sutter, US General and distillery-founder in California of 18th century.

generic loosely, the term for a wine defined only by its region of origin.

generoso wine style. In Italy, heavy table wine high in alcohol. In Spain, richer style of sherry or other fortified wine.

Genesee brewery at Rochester, New York, USA. Brands include Michael Shea's Irish Amber and 12-Horse Ale.

Gene Tunney Cocktail. Over ice shake 2 parts dry gin, 1 dry vermouth, 1 dash lemon juice, 1 dash orange juice. Strain.

geneva alternative spelling of *genever*.

Geneva canton and wine-producing region of Switzerland. Includes Arve-et-Lac, Arve-et-Rhône and Mandement vineyard zones.

Geneva Double Curtain vine-training system. Shoots are trained to form two high 'curtains' of foliage and bunches for improved sun exposure. Widely used in northerly vineyards.

genever the original gin, first distilled *c.*1550 by medical professor Fransicus de la Boe (also called Sylvius) at the university of Leyden, Netherlands. His intention in compounding juniper-berry juice with spirit was to produce a remedy for digestive ailments. First distilled commercially 1575 by Bols of Schiedam, Netherlands. 'London dry' gin is a derivative style of the sweeter, fuller-flavoured original *genever*.

genévrier *eau de vie* distilled from juniper berries. Alsace, France.

Genghiz Khan vodka brand, Mongolia.

Genoa Cocktail. Over ice stir 2 parts grappa, 2 dry gin, 1 Sambuca, 1 dry vermouth. Strain.

gentian herbaceous plant used in flavouring aperitif and liqueur drinks. In some places, preceded hops as a flavouring agent in brewing.

gentiane bitter colourless *digestif* liqueur from spirit flavoured with roots of yellow gentian plant. France and Switzerland.

Gentil Aromatique regional soubriquet for Riesling grape variety, Alsace, France.

Genus brand of Simonsvlei Winery, Paarl, South Africa. Renowned wines with labels known for illustrations of South African animal species.

Geoff Merrill winemaker of Reynella, Southern Vales, South Australia. Well-known Mount Hurtle wines and others.

George Dickel Tennessee sour mash whiskey of George A Dickel Cascade Distillery, Tullahoma, Coffee County, Tennessee, USA.

George Gale & Co brewery est 1730s, Horndean, Hampshire, England.

Georgia wine-producing Black Sea 'independent state' formerly of Soviet Union with extensive vineyards in Rion Valley and elsewhere. Large production of 'champanski' plus red wines including Mukuzani and whites including Napereuli and Tsinandal.

geraniums

geraniums in winetasting, a smell denoting a fault, usually due to infection during fermentation.

Gereons *Kölschbier* brand. Cologne, Germany.

Germain & Fils, H champagne house, Rilly-la-Montagne, France.

Germain, Jean leading producer of white wines of Meursault and Puligny-Montrachet, Burgundy, France.

Germany major brewing and wine-producing nation. Breweries cover the entire country from Hamburg in the north to Munich in the south with each region remaining loyal to the styles of beer brewed long before the unification of Germany in the 19th century and its reunification late in the 20th. Wine production is confined to the southwest of the country in the valleys of the Rhine river and its tributaries. Thirteen quality-wine regions have been defined under Germany's labyrinthine wine laws: Ahr, Baden, Franken, Hessische Bergstrasse, Mittelrhein, Mosel-Saar-Ruwer, Nahe, Rheingau, Rheinhessen, Rheinpfalz (usually called Pfalz), Saale-Unstrut, Sachsen, Württemberg. Wines are graded from simplest *Deutscher Tafelwein* and *Landwein* to basic-quality *Qualitätswein bestimmter Anbaugebiete* to top-quality *Qualitätswein mit Prädikat*. Greatest wines from driest to sweetest are from Riesling grapes but white wines from Riesling blends and other varieties are common; there are also red and sparkling (*Sekt*) wines. Traditionally wines are labelled according to their vineyard, village and region of origin. In one of many continuing attempts to simplify labelling of German wines, new quality classifications for wines 'Classic' and 'Selection' were added in 2001.

Gertrudenberg vineyard at Dattenburg in Mittelrhein region, Germany.

Gerümpel vineyards at Friedelsheim and Wachenheim in Rheinpfalz region, Germany.

Gesellmann, Engelbert wine producer in Mittelburgenland, Austria.

Gestühl vineyards at Sasbach (Jechtingen) and Sasbach (Leiselheim) in Baden region, Germany.

Getaufer watered wine. German.

Get Frères producers of Pippermint Get crème de menthe, created 1796 by Jean Get at Revel, Toulouse, France. Owned by Bénédictine.

Getreide spirit made from mixed grains, usually rye and wheat. Germany.

Gevrey-Chambertin wine village and AC of Côtes de Nuits, Burgundy, France. Vineyards include *Grands Crus* Chambertin, Chambertin Clos de Bèze, Chapelle-Chambertin, Charmes-Chambertin, Griotte-Chambertin, Latricières-Chambertin, Mazis-Chambertin, Mazoyères-Chambertin, Ruchottes-Chambertin. *Premiers Crus*: Bel-Air, Cazetiers, les Champeaux, Champonets, Cherbaudes, au Closeau, Clos du Chapitre, Clos du Fonteny, Clos Prieur, le Clos St-Jacques, Combe aux Moines, aux Combettes, les Corbeaux, Craipillot, Ergots, Estournelles, les Gemeaux, les Goulots, Issarts, Lavaux, la Perrière, Petite Chapelle, Pissenot, les

Véroilles. Important producers include Bassot, Boillot, Drouhin, Faiveley, Jadot, Labouré-Roi, Leroy, Rousseau, Trapet.

Gewürzgärtchen vineyard at Horrweiler in Rheinhessen region, Germany.

Gewürzgarten vineyard at Hackenheim in Rheinhessen region, Germany.

Gewürztraminer white (or, more specifically, copper-gold-coloured) grape variety originally of Tramin, a village of Alto Adige region, Italy. Name means 'spicy Traminer'. Principally grown in Alsace, France, but also in Austria and Germany and Australasia and the Americas. Highly distinctive aromatic wines with lychee bouquet and spicy-pungent flavour.

Geyer brewery at Frankenmuth, Michigan, USA.

Geyerhof wine producer in Kremstal, Niederösterreich, Austria.

Geyersberg vineyards at Bechtheim, Gau-Weinheim and Sakt Johann in Rheinhessen region, Germany.

Ghemme DOCG red wine principally from Nebbiolo grapes, Novara Vercelli hills, Piedmont, Italy. Aged three years in wood and one in bottle before sale.

Ghiaie della Furba prestige non-DOC red wine of Conte Contini Bonacossi's Tenuta Capezzana estate, Carmignano, Tuscany, Italy. Cabernet Franc, Cabernet Sauvignon and Merlot grapes.

Ghillie, The Scottish ale (4.5% alc) by Broughton Ales, Peeblesshire, Scotland. 'Originally the Clan Chief's bearer who stood behind him in battle, the Ghillie today is a much respected, pithy character who guides sportsmen of the world on the rivers of Scotland.'

Ghirgentina white grape variety of island of Malta.

Giacobazzi major producer of Lambrusco wines, Emilia-Romagna, Italy.

Giaconda wine estate of Beechworth, Victoria, Australia. Highly valued Chardonnay and Pinot Noir wines.

Gibeau, Château wine estate of AC Puisseguin-St-Emilion, Bordeaux, France.

Gibbs Mew brewer at Salisbury, Wiltshire, England.

Gibson Cocktail. Over ice stir 2 parts dry gin, 1 teaspoon dry vermouth. Strain, squeeze lemon peel over and add cocktail onion to glass.

Giebelhöll vineyard at Weinähr in Mittelrhein region, Germany.

Giesen wine producer at Christchurch, Canterbury, New Zealand. Noted Riesling wines.

Gigondas AC and wine village of southern Rhône, France. Red wines from Cinsaut, Grenache, Mourvèdre and Syrah grapes.

Gilbey, WA international wine and spirit company based in UK. Owned by IDV.

Gilbeys Gin worldwide gin brand of WA Gilbey, UK.

Gilden *Kölschbier* brand. Cologne, Germany.

Gildenbier brown ale by Haacht brewery, Belgium.

Gilette, Château wine estate of AC Sauternes, Bordeaux, France.

Gillespie's Malt Stout Scottish beer brand curtailed by rationing in 1915. Revived 1995.

Gillon's blended scotch whisky of John Gillon, Glasgow, Scotland.

Gilroy Cocktail. Over ice shake 2 parts cherry brandy, 2 dry gin, 1 dry vermouth, 1 lemon juice, 1 dash orange bitters. Strain.

Gilt Edge whisky brand of Gilbeys, Melbourne, Australia.

Gimlet Cocktail. Over ice pour 1 part dry gin, 1 lime juice cordial.

Gimmeldingen wine village of Rheinpfalz region, Germany. *Grosslage*: Meerspinne.

Gimmonet & Fils, Pierre *récoltant-manipulant* champagne producer, Cramant, Champagne, France.

gin colourless rectified spirit based on maize or molasses and flavoured principally with juniper. England, mainly London, dominates production. See box.

Gin and Cape Cocktail. Over ice stir 1 part Caperitif, 1 dry gin. Strain.

Gin and It Cocktail. Over ice stir 1 part dry gin, 1 sweet vermouth. Strain.

Gin Cocktail. Over ice shake 1 part dry gin, 2 dashes orange bitters. Strain.

Gin Daisy Cocktail. Over ice shake 1 part dry gin, 1 lemon juice, 1 teaspoon grenadine, sprinkling of sugar. Strain into ice-filled tall glass and add slices of lemon and orange.

Ginder Ale beer brand of Lamot brewery, Mechelen, Belgium.

Gin Fix Cocktail. In a tumbler mix 1 part lemon juice, 1 teaspoon sugar syrup. Add ice and pour 1 part dry gin over. Add lemon slice.

Gin Fizz Cocktail. Over ice shake 2 parts dry gin, 1 lemon juice, 1 teaspoon sugar. Strain and top with soda water.

Gin

the long road to London Dry

The spirit of England originated in Holland. In the 16th century, *genever* was the preferred *aqua vitae* of the Low Countries, while ardent British thirsts were being slaked with primitive brandy and rum. The sweet, yellow liquor taking its name from French *genièvre* for juniper, the principal flavouring, was discovered by British troops fighting alongside the Dutch against Spanish occupying forces in the 1570s. London merchants were soon importing the spirit for home-coming soldiers who had acquired a taste for this source of 'Dutch courage'. The name was soon corrupted to ginever, then abbreviated to gin.

Distillers were making 'London gin' – then indistinguishable from the Netherlands original – by the beginning of the 17th century. The spirit was soon being produced, too, in seaports including Bristol, Portsmouth and Plymouth. It gradually established its place in the market until 1688 when its fortunes received an unexpected upturn. In that year, Britain's new king, William of Orange, Dutch consort of Queen Mary, resolved to boost domestic farm values by banning imports of all foreign spirits. He agreed with the nation's farmers that grain prices would rise with the increase in demand for home-produced spirits.

British distilling went into overdrive. Gin production grew from half a million gallons a year to five million gallons by the 1720s. Records show that by 1733, London alone was making more than 10 million gallons. Prices had fallen as consumption rose. Public drunkenness was commonplace and large sections of the populace were clearly addicted.

Parliament was dismayed. Something had to be done. A Gin Act was passed in 1736. Gin shops, of which London had several thousand, were to pay £50 for a licence. The government knew perfectly well that this sum, more than the entire annual earnings of a labourer, would be beyond the means of all but a very few traders. As would the tax of £1 to be levied on every gallon of gin sold.

The Act backfired dramatically. The gin business went underground. By 1743 when the legislation was repealed, consumption in London had redoubled to an estimated 20 million gallons, most of it illicit. Public health and order were breaking down. Not until 1751 did Parliament regain control, with a further Gin Act levying a collectable duty on sales, and introducing badly needed quality controls.

Now gin became respectable. The filthy grog shops of old were displaced by ornately fitted-out taverns soon known as Gin Palaces – forerunners of today's mirror-and-glass-bedecked city pubs. Around the middle of the 19th century gin itself began to change. Equipped with a new kind of still, the Coffey, producers were able to make a lighter, drier style of spirit. It caught on as an excellent spirit for mixing with cordials and a new, bitter-tasting, quinine-based therapeutic potation imported from British India – tonic water.

By the 20th century dry gin was being exported worldwide, carried to every corner by the continuing taste for cocktails and the firm loyalty of the officers of the Royal Navy (divided about equally between London and Plymouth gins). The original gin, *genever*, is still in the sweet and aromatic style of old (though now very much refined), and continues to enjoy steady sales at home in Holland. ❧

Gin Rickey Cocktail. Into an ice-filled tall glass pour 2 parts dry gin, 1 fresh lime juice. Top with chilled sparkling wine and add maraschino cherry.

Ginseng Ju leading ginseng liqueur brand, by Jinro, Seoul, Korea.

Ginsin Cocktail. Over ice shake 1 part dry gin, 1 grapefruit juice, 1 orange juice, 1 dash grenadine. Strain and add a strawberry to the glass.

Gin Sling Cocktail. Into long tumbler with ice cube stir 1 part dry gin, 1 teaspoon sugar syrup. Top with soda water. To serve hot, top with boiling water and add a pinch of nutmeg to glass.

Ginza Fizz Cocktail. Over ice shake 3 parts dry sherry, 1 port, 1 lemon juice, 1 egg white, 1 teaspoon sugar. Strain into tumblers and top with soda water.

Ginzing gin-based spirit brand of Tanqueray Gordon & Co (United Distillers), UK. Ingredients include Korean ginseng, Brazilian guarana, oriental and American herbs, schinzandra, taurine, muira puama, wolfberry.

Gipfel *Grosslage* (collective vineyard) incorporating vineyards in Mosel-Saar-Ruwer region, Germany at, respectively: Fellerich, Nittel, Nittel (Köllig), Nittel (Rehlingen), Oberbillig, Onsdorf, Palzem, Palzem (Helfant und Esingen), Palzem (Kreuzweiler), Palzem (Wehr), Temmels, Wasserliesch, Weelen, Wincheringen.

Gippsland vineyard district of Victoria, Australia.

Gips vineyards at Fellbach and Stuttgart in Württemberg region, Germany.

Girard cognac house est 1884, now brand of Berger company of France.

Girardin brewery in Payottenland, Belgium. Lambic beers.

Girasol in sparkling wine production, a mechanical substitute for manual *remuage* (turning and gradual up-ending of bottles to manoeuvre sediment into neck). Used particularly in Spain (name is Spanish for 'sunflower') but also in Champagne, France, sometimes under the name **Giropalette**, and elsewhere.

Giraud *vigneron* family of Grande Champagne district of Cognac region since 1650 and lately cognac producers. Châteauneuf sur Charente, France.

Giro di Cagliari DOC sweet red wine from Giro grapes, Cagliari, Sardinia, Italy.

Gironde *département*, named after estuarial Gironde river, within which all of the defined vineyard region of Bordeaux lies. France.

Gisborne town and important vineyard district of Poverty Bay, New Zealand. Renowned white wines from Chardonnay and Sauvignon grapes.

Giscours, Château wine estate of AC Margaux, Médoc, Bordeaux, France. Classified *3ème Grand Cru Classé*.

Gisperg wine producer in Thermenregion, Niederösterreich, Austria.

Gisselbrecht, Louis wine producer, Dambach-la-Ville, Alsace, France.

Gisselbrecht, Willy & Fils wine producer, Dambach-la-Ville, Alsace, France.

Gitton wine producer of AC Sancerre, Loire Valley, France.

Givry village and AC of Côte Chalonnaise, Burgundy, France.

Glad Eye Cocktail. Over ice shake 2 parts pastis, 1 peppermint cordial. Strain.

Gladiator bitter ale brand of Hadrian brewery, Newcastle upon Tyne, England.

Gladstone bitter ale (4.8% alc) by McMullen brewery, Hertford, England.

Glana, Château du wine estate of AC St Julien, Bordeaux, France. Classified *Cru Grand Bourgeois Exceptionnel*.

Glaschu brewery in Glasgow, Scotland.

Glass Slipper Cocktail. Over ice stir 3 parts dry gin, 1 blue curaçao. Strain.

Glastonbury Ales microbrewery est 2002 at Somerton, Somerset, England. Chalice Gold bitter (4.2% alc), Hedge Monkey bitter (4.6% alc), Lady of the Lake bitter (4.2% alc), Mystery Tor bitter (3.7% alc).

Glatzen vineyard at Dettelbach in Franken region, Germany.

Glatzer, Walter wine producer in Carnuntum, Niederösterreich, Austria.

Glayva Scotch whisky liqueur by Invergordon Distillers, Edinburgh, Scotland.

Glen Albyn North Highland malt whisky distillery, Inverness, Scotland. Est 1846, closed 1983.

Glenallachie Speyside malt whisky distillery est 1968, Ruthie, Aberlour, Banffshire, Scotland. Single malt: 12-year-old.

Glen Baren five- and eight-year-old vatted malt whiskies of Kinross Whisky Co, Haywards Heath, West Sussex, England.

Glenburgie North Highland malt whisky distillery est 1829, Alves, Morayshire, Scotland. Gordon & MacPhail bottlings of single malts (eg 1970).

Glen Burn whisky brand of Merchant International, UK.

Glencadam East Highland malt whisky distillery est 1825, Brechin, Angus, Scotland. Single malt: 21-year-old.

Glen Cairn malt whisky brand of Tesco supermarkets, UK.

Glen Calder blended scotch whisky of Gordon & MacPhail, Elgin, Scotland.

Glen Carlou wine producer of Paarl, South Africa. Well-known Cabernet

Sauvignon, Chardonnay, Pinot Noir wines.

Glen Carren vatted malt scotch whisky of Kinross Whisky Co, Haywards Heath, West Sussex, England.

Glen Coe vatted malt scotch whisky by R N McDonald, London, England.

Glencraig Speyside single malt whisky by Glenburgie distillery, Forres, Scotland. Now extinct.

Glendarroch twelve-year-old blended scotch whisky by William Gillies, Glasgow, Scotland.

Glen Deveron East Highland malt whisky distillery est 1962, Banff, Scotland. Single malt: 12-year-old.

Glen Dochart single malt scotch whisky brand of Winerite Ltd, Leeds, England. Source is undisclosed.

Glendower vatted malt scotch (not, as name suggests, Welsh) whisky by Burn Stewart, Glasgow, Scotland.

Glendronach East Highland malt whisky distillery est 1826, Forgue, Aberdeenshire, Scotland. Single malt: 12-year-old, 18-year-old.

Glendullan Speyside malt whisky distillery est 1897, Dufftown, Banffshire, Scotland. Single malts: 12-year-old.

Glen Elgin Speyside malt whisky distillery est 1898, Longmorn, Morayshire, Scotland. Single malt: 12-year-old.

Glen Elgin vineyard of Hunter Valley district, Australia.

Glen Ellen major winery est 1980 in Sonoma Valley, California, USA. Well-known Cabernet Sauvignon, Chardonnay and Merlot wines.

Glenesk East Highland malt whisky distillery, Montrose, Scotland. Est 1897, closed 1985.

Glenfairn twelve-year-old blended scotch whisky made for Co-operative Wholesale Society, Manchester, England, by Invergordon Distillers, Scotland.

Glenfarclas Speyside malt whisky distillery est 1836, Ballindalloch, Banffshire, Scotland. Est 1836 and family-owned since 1865 by J&G Grant. Single malts: eight-, 10-, 12-, 15-, 21- and 25-year-old; cask-strength (60%) '105'.

Glenfiddich Speyside malt whisky distillery, Dufftown, Banffshire,

Scotland. The world's biggest-selling malt whisky, first made 1887 by William Grant and still managed by his descendants. Single malts: **Glenfiddich Special Reserve**; 18 Years Old, 21 Years Old, 30 Years Old and other export brands.

Glen Flagler vatted malt scotch whisky by Inver House, Airdrie, Lanarkshire, Scotland.

Glen Fruin whisky (blended and single malt) brand of William Lundie & Co, Glasgow, Scotland.

Glen Garioch East Highland malt whisky distillery est 1785, Old Meldrum, Aberdeenshire, Scotland. Single malts: eight-, 10-, 12- and 21-year-old. Garioch is pronounced GEERee.

Glen Garry blended scotch whisky by Inver House Distillers, Airdrie, Lanarkshire, Scotland.

Glen Ghoil blended scotch whisky by Hall & Bramley, Liverpool, England.

Glenglassaugh East Highland malt whisky distillery est 1875, Portsoy, Banffshire, Scotland.

Glen Gordon fifteen-year-old Speyside malt whisky by Glen Gordon Whisky Co, Elgin, Scotland.

Glen Goyne South Highland malt whisky distillery est 1833, Old Killearn, Stirlingshire, Scotland. Single malts: 10-, 12- and 17-year-old.

Glen Grant Speyside malt whisky distillery est 1840, Rothes, Morayshire, Scotland. Single malts: five-, 10-, 12-, 15-, 18-, 21- and 25-year-old; numerous vintage bottlings back to 1936. Bought by Pernod-Ricard, 2001.

Glen Gyle eight-year-old vatted malt whisky by Fraser Macdonald, London, England.

Glen Keith Speyside malt whisky distillery est 1957, Keith, Banffshire, Scotland. Single malt: 22-year-old. Owned by Pernod-Ricard.

Glenkinchie Lowland malt whisky distillery est 1837, Pencaitland, East Lothian, Scotland. Single malt: 10-year-old.

Glenlivet, The Speyside malt whisky distillery, Minmore, Ballindalloch, Banffshire, Scotland. Est 1824 by former illicit distiller George Smith, the high quality of the product had spawned 18 more 'Glenlivet' distilleries by 1880, when a court ruling was obtained protecting the name – thus *The* Glenlivet. Single malts: 12-, 15- and 21-year-old. See box.

Glenlivet Distillers scotch whisky company owned by Pernod-Ricard.

Glenlochy West Highland malt whisky distillery est 1898, Fort William, Inverness-shire, Scotland. Now closed.

Glenlossie North Highland malt whisky distillery est 1876, Elgin, Morayshire, Scotland. Single malt: 10-year-old.

Glen Lyon blended scotch whisky by Glen Lyon Blending, Glasgow, Scotland.

Glen Mhor Highland malt whisky distillery est 1892, Inverness, Scotland. Single malt: eight-year-old.

Glenmorangie North Highland malt whisky distillery est 1843, Tain, Ross-shire, Scotland. All the output of the distillery, which is pronounced glen-MOR-n'jee, is sold as single malts. Ten- and 18-year-old; 10-year-old cask strength (57.6%); vintage bottlings of 1963, 1971, 1972.

Glen Moray Speyside malt whisky distillery est 1897, Elgin, Morayshire, Scotland. Single malts: 12-, 15- and 17-year old; vintage bottlings of 1962, 1964, 1966, 1967, 1973.

Glen Nevis twelve-year-old blended scotch whisky by Gibson International, London, England.

Glen Niven blended scotch whisky by Douglas MacNiven, Leith, Scotland.

Glenora Wine Cellars wine producer in Finger Lakes region, New York, USA.

Glen Ord North Highland malt whisky distillery est 1838, Muir of Ord, Ross-shire, Scotland. Single malt: 12-year-old.

Glenrothes Speyside malt whisky distillery est 1878, Rothes, Morayshire, Scotland. Single malts: 8- and 16-year-old, and 12-year-old bottled by Berry Bros & Rudd, London.

Glen Scotia Campbeltown malt whisky distillery est 1832, Argyllshire, Scotland. Single malts: eight- and 12-year-old.

Glen Shee blended scotch whisky by Findlater Mackie Todd, London, England. Three- and five-year-old.

Glenside blended scotch whisky of Thresher, Welwyn Garden City, England.

Glen Spey Speyside malt whisky distillery est 1877, Rothes, Morayshire, Scotland. Single malt: eight-year-old.

Glen Stuart five-year-old blended scotch whisky by W Brown & Sons, Glasgow, Scotland. Also, five-, eight- and 12-year-old vatted malts.

Glentauchers Speyside malt whisky distillery est 1898, Mulben, Banffshire, Scotland.

Glentromie twelve- and 17-year-old vatted malt scotch whiskies by Speyside Distillery Co, Glasgow, Scotland.

Glenturret, The Highland malt whisky distillery, Crieff, Perthshire. Est 1775 and possibly the oldest malt whisky distillery in Scotland. Single malts: eight-, 12-, 15-, 21- and 25-year-old; vintage bottlings.

Glentworth brewery at Skellow, Doncaster, England.

Glenugie Highland malt whisky distillery est 1831, Peterhead, Aberdeenshire, Scotland. Closed 1982.

Glen Urquhart blended scotch whisky by Gordon & MacPhail, Elgin, Scotland.

Glenury-Royal East Highland malt whisky distillery est 1825, Stonehaven, Kincardineshire, Scotland. Closed 1985.

Glider Cocktail. Over ice shake 1 egg white, 3 parts dry gin, 1 fresh lime juice, 2 dashes grenadine, 1 dash pastis. Strain.

The Glenlivet

top single

The Glenlivet is the best-selling of all 12-year-old single malt Scotch whiskies. The name is that of a remote glen (valley) of the River Livet in the Scottish Highlands. In the 1700s the glen was a major centre for distilling, most of it illicit in defiance of the heavy taxes imposed by Parliament in London on whisky sales. Whisky distilling was outlawed in 1784 but production, from at least 200 different stills, continued undiminished in the glen. The excise men gave priority to raiding the more-accessible stills farther south.

The ban was finally lifted in 1823, and one major Glenlivet farmer-distiller, George Smith, was among the first to apply for an official licence under the new Excise Act. He distanced himself from his bootlegging neighbours and gradually came to dominate whisky production in the glen.

By now Glenlivet whisky, legal or otherwise, had acquired a considerable reputation. King George IV, visiting Edinburgh in 1822, insisted on trying Glenlivet in spite of its illegitimacy, and declared it so good he would drink no other. The fame of the malt was assured. In 1858, George Smith, now with his son John Gordon in partnership, built a new, larger distillery at Minmore. The Glenlivet single malt first appeared under its own label in 1932. Descendants of George Smith continued to run the business as a family concern until 1978, when the company was bought by Seagram, who sold it to Pernod-Ricard in 2001.

The Glenlivet is still made at Minmore, and is described as having 'a perfectly balanced nose with an array of floral notes, a soft smooth fruity sweetness on the palate and a finish which is subtle, smooth and gently warming.'

The name Livet is Gaelic and means 'smooth, flowing one.' ☙

Gloag, Matthew producer, at Perth, Scotland, of Famous Grouse blended whisky.

Gloag's gin brand of Highland Distilleries Co, UK.

Glockenberg vineyard at Gau-Bischofsheim in Rheinhessen region, Germany.

Glockenzehnt vineyard at Neustadt and der Weinstarsse in Rheinpfalz region, Germany.

Glöck vineyard at Nierstein in Rheinhessen region, Germany.

Gloom Chaser Cocktail. Over ice shake 1 part curaçao, 1 Grand Marnier, 1 grenadine, 1 lemon juice. Strain.

Gloom Lifter Cocktail. Over ice shake 4 parts rye whisky, 2 lemon juice, 1 egg white, 1 teaspoon sugar. Strain.

Gloria, Château wine estate of AC St Julien, Médoc, Bordeaux, France. Classified *Cru Bourgeois*.

glühwein mulled wine with sugar and spices. German recipe.

Gmeineder brewery at Deisenhofen, Bavaria, Germany. Wheat beers.

Gnats Piss white table wine from Sauvignon and Semillon grapes, Entre Deux Mers region, Bordeaux, France. Launched 1997 for export. Future uncertain, but one tasting note reported: 'The wine in no way resembles its nomenclature ... rather fetching pale-gold colour, delightful floral nose with orange-blossom highlights; fresh gooseberry-grassy fruit and finishing clean.'

Goacher's Bockingford brewery at Tovil Green, Maidstone, Kent, England.

Goats do Roam wine brand of Charles Back, Fairview Estate, Paarl, South Africa. The grape varieties used are similar to those for France's Côtes du Rhône. Back maintains the similarity in the name is coincidental to the fact that he named the wine in commemoration of a difficult day when the farm's goats got loose in the vineyard.

Goddard's brewery at Ryde, Isle of Wight, England.

Godeslberg vineyard at Aschaffenburg in Franken region, Germany.

Godet cognac house est 1838 La Rochelle, France. Now cognac and 'cream liqueur' brand of IDV, UK.

Godfather Cocktail. Over ice stir 2 parts scotch whisky, 1 amaretto. Strain.

Godmé, Bertrand *récoltant-manipulant* champagne producer, Verzenay, Champagne, France.

Godmother Cocktail. Over ice stir 2 parts vodka, 1 amaretto. Strain.

Godo Shusei whisky distiller, Japan.

Goélane, Château de wine estate of AC Entre-Deux Mers, Bordeaux, France. Classified *Cru Bourgeois*.

Goetheberg vineyard at Obernhof in Mittelrhein region, Germany.

Goff's brewery at Winchcombe, Gloucestershire, England.

Goldapfel vineyard at Worms in Rheinhessen region, Germany.

Goldatzel vineyard at Geisenheim in Rheingau region, Germany.

Goldbächel vineyard at Wachenheim in Rheinpfalz region, Germany.

Goldbäumchen *Grosslage* (collective vineyard) incorporating vineyards in Mosel-Saar-Ruwer region, Germany at, respectively: Briedern, Bruttig-

Fankel, Cochem, Cochem (Sehl), Ellenz-Poltersdorf, Ernst, Klotten, Moselkern, Müden, Pommern, Senheim, Treis-Karden.

Goldberg the name of 32 individual vineyards in Germany. Region by region, as follows: in Baden at Bad Schönborn, Sinsheim; in Mosel-Saar-Ruwer at Pommern, Wawern; in Rheingau at Oestrich-Winkel; in Rheinhessen at Alsheim, Eich, Mettenheim, Esselborn, Flörsheim-Dalsheim, Flomborn, Gau-Algesheim, Gensingen, Horrweiler, Jugenheim, Monzernheim, Nieder-Olm, Osthofen, Udenheim, Endenheim, Vendersheim, Worms; in Rheinpfalz at Bissersheim, Erpolzheim, Freinsheim, Weisenheim am Sand, Grünstadt; in Württemberg at Bretzfeld, Fellbach, Ohringen, Pfedelbach, Pfedelbach (Windischenbach).

Gold Blend blended scotch whisky by Kinross Whisky Co, Haywards Heath, West Sussex, England.

Goldblume vineyard at Löf in Mosel-Saar-Ruwer region, Germany.

Gold Crest Canadian whisky brand of Hiram Walker & Sons, Canada.

Goldemund vineyards at Damscheid and Oberwesel in Mittelrhein region, Germany.

Golden Ball apple variety traditionally valued for cider-making. English.

Golden Cadillac Cocktail. Over ice shake 1 part Cointreau, 1 Galliano, 1 cream. Strain.

Golden Cap blended scotch whisky by Palmer Brewery, Bridport, Dorset, England.

Golden Cock gin brand of Norway.

Golden Dawn Cocktail. Over ice shake 1 part apple brandy, 1 apricot brandy, 1 dry gin, 1 orange juice. Pour gently into glass containing 1 dash grenadine.

Golden Dream Cocktail. Over ice shake 2 parts Galliano, 1 Cointreau, 1 cream, 1 orange juice. Strain.

Goldene Luft vineyard at Nierstein in Rheinhessen region, Germany.

Goldener Oktober liebfraumilch brand of St Ursula Weinkellerei, Bingen, Germany.

Goldenes Horn vineyard at Siefersheim in Rheinhessen region, Germany.

Golden Gate Cocktail. Shake 3 parts frozen orange juice, 1 dry gin. Serve.

Golden Hill brewery at Wiveliscombe, Somerset, England.

Golden Pacific small brewery in Emeryville, California, USA.

Golden Pale organically produced pale ale by Caledonian Brewery, Edinburgh, Scotland.

Golden Piper blended scotch whisky by Lombard Scotch Whisky, Ramsay, Isle of Man, UK.

Golden Pride 'super strength ale' (8.5–9.2% alc) by Fuller's brewery, London, England.

Golden Promise organically produced ale by Caledonian Brewery, Edinburgh, Scotland.

Golden Slipper Cocktail. Over ice shake 1 egg yolk, 1 part Eau de Vie de Danzig, 1 yellow Chartreuse. Strain.

Golden Special Canadian whisky brand of Palliser Distilleries, Canada.

Golden Thread ale (5.0% alc) by Salopian Brewery, Shropshire, England.

Golden Velvet Canadian Whisky brand of Gilbey Canada.

Gold Fassl Spezial lager by Ottakringer brewery, Vienna, Austria.

Goldfinch brewery at Dorcester, Dorset, England.

Goldfüsschen vineyard at Königswinter in Rheinhessen region, Germany.

Goldgrube vineyards at Bockenheim an der Weinstrasse in Rheinpfalz region, Köngernheim in Rheinhessen region, Rüdesheim and Staudernheim in Nahe region, Traben-Trarbach in Mosel-Saar-Ruwer region, Germany.

Goldgrübchen vineyard at Mesenich in Mosel-Saar-Ruwer region, Germany.

Goldie barley wine by Eldridge Pope brewery, Dorchester, England.

Golding classic hop variety used in brewing. Imparts spice aromas and flavours.

Goldkaul vineyard at Dernau in Ahr region, Germany.

Goldkupp vineyard at Mehring in Mosel-Saar-Ruwer region, Germany.

Gold Label blended scotch whisky by Red Lion Blending, London, England.

Gold Label Canadian whisky brand of Jas Barclay & Co, Canada.

Gold Label 'Very strong' (10.9% alc) barley wine by Whitbread, London,

England. 'Two and a half times stronger than ordinary beers and matured for six times as long, Gold Label is no small beer.'

Goldlay vineyards at Niederfell, Oberfell, Pünderich and Reil in Mosel-Saar-Ruwer region, Germany.

Goldloch vineyards and Dorsheim in Nahe region and and Gauersheim in Rheinpfalz region, Germany.

Gold 1000 whisky brand of Suntory, Japan.

Goldroggen rye beer of Schlägl monastery brewery, Austria.

Goldschläger popular brand of cinnamon schnapps 'with real gold' by IDV, Genestrerio, Switzerland.

Gold Seal Vineyards major winery of New York State, USA.

Gold Stripe Canadian whisky brand of Thomas Adams Distillers, Canada.

Goldstückchen vineyard at Armsheim in Rheinhessen region, Germany.

Goldtröpfchen vineyards at Neumagen-Dhron, Piesport and Piesport (Niederemmel) in Mosel-Saar-Ruwer region, Germany.

Goldwater leading wine producer at Waiheke Island, New Zealand. Noted Cabernet Sauvignon and Merlot reds.

Goldwingert vineyard at Urzig in Mosel-Saar-Ruwer region, Germany.

Golf Cocktail. Over ice stir 2 parts dry gin, 1 dry vermouth, 1 dash Angostura bitters. Strain.

Gollenberg vineyards at Bellheim and Knittelsheim in Rheinpfalz region, Germany.

Goller brewery at Zeil, Bamberg, Germany.

Gombaude-Guillot, Château wine estate of AC Pomerol, Bordeaux, France.

Gomme sweet syrup used in cocktail making. French.

Gonnet, Michel *récoltant-manipulant* champagne producer, Avize, Champagne, France.

Gontier, Château wine estate of AC Premières Côtes de Blaye, Bordeaux, France.

Gonzalez Byass sherry *bodega* est 1835 Jerez de la Frontera, Spain, by Antonio Gonzalez y Rodriguez and English-born Robert Blake Byass. Famed sherries include Elegante and Tio Pepe *finos* and Matusalem rich *oloroso*.

Good Night Ladies Cocktail. Over ice shake 3 parts dry gin, 1 apricot brandy, 1 grenadine, 1 lemon juice. Strain.

gooseberries in winetasting, a redolence associated with Sauvignon Blanc grapes.

Goose Eye brewery at Keighley, West Yorkshire, England.

Goose Island pub-brewery in Chicago, Illinois, USA.

Gorby Cocktail. Over ice shake 1 part vodka, 1 apple juice, 1 dash grenadine. Strain.

Gordon & MacPhail famed 'Family Grocers, Tea, Wine & Spirit Merchants' est 1895, Elgin, Morayshire, Scotland, which has now become the best-known independent bottler of scotch single malt whiskies (from most of the distilleries) usually under the Connoisseurs Choice label, as well as vatted malts. Also produces blended malt and grain whiskies.

Gordon Biersch pub-brewery in Palo Alto, California, USA.

Gordon Highland Scotch Ale beer by McEwan's brewery, Edinburgh, Scotland.

Gordon's leading dry gin brand of Tanqueray, Gordon & Co, London, England. Other products include Lemon, Old Tom, Orange and Lemon gins.

Gorgeous Cocktail. Over ice shake 2 parts vodka, 1 cranberry juice, 1 equal mix lemon and orange juice. Strain into ice-filled tumbler.

Gorilka vodka brand of Russia.

gorzalka medieval precursor of vodka, Poland.

Gosling's rum distiller of Bermuda. Known principally for Black Seal rum. Also Gosling's Barbados Rum.

Gosset champagne house est 1584 (it is the oldest still trading) Aÿ, Champagne, France.

Gottesacker vineyards at Altdorf in Rheinpfalz region, Müllheim in Baden region and Walluf in Rheingau region, Germany.

Gottesfuss vineyard at Wiltingen in Mosel-Saar-Ruwer region, Germany.

Gottesgarten vineyard at Selzen in Rheinhessen region, Germany.

Gotteshilfe *Grosslage* (collective vineyard) incorporating vineyards at Bechtheim and Osthofen in Rheinhessen region, Germany.

Gottesthal collective vineyard (*Grosslage*) at Oestrich-Winkel in Rheingau region, Germany.

Götzenberg vineyards at Steinheim and Stuttgart in Württemberg region, Germany.

Götzenborn vineyard at Wolfsheim in Rheinhessen region, Germany.

Götzenfels vineyards at Bad Münster am Stein-Ebernburg in Nahe region, Germany.

Götzhalde vineyard at Neckarzimmern in Baden region, Germany.

Goudenband beer by Liefman brewery, Oudenaarde, Belgium.

Gouden Carolus dark ale brand of Het Anker brewery, Mechelen, Belgium.

Goudoulin armagnac brand of Veuve Goudoulin, Gondrin, Gascony, France.

Goulburn Valley wine region of Victoria, Australia.

Gould Campbell port shipper est 1797 Vila Nova de Gaia, Portugal. Ports now made by Symington-owned Smith Woodhouse. Vintages: 1950, 55, 60, 70, 75, 77, 80, 83, 85, 91, 94, 97, 2000, 03.

Goulet, Georges champagne house est 1834 Reims, France.

Goumin, Château second wine of Château Bonnet, Bordeaux, France.

Gourgazaud, Château de wine estate of AC Minervois, Midi, France.

Gourmel, Leopold cognac house, Cognac, France.

Goût Americain in champagne production, a sweeter style tailored to US market. Champagne, France.

goût de terroir in winetasting, a flavour suggestive of the soil of the vineyard, especially where this is more dominant than that of the constituent grape variety. French.

governo traditional winemaking feature of Chianti-production, Tuscany, Italy. Concentrated unfermented grape juice is added in proportion of 10–20 to one to fermented wine to stimulate second fermentation, boosting colour and strength, and giving wine characteristic 'prickliness'. Now rare in Chianti.

Graach wine village of Mosel-Saar-Ruwer region, Germany. *Grosslage*: Münzlay. Site of renowned Kesselstatt estate.

graan all-grain *genever*. Netherlands.

Graben vineyard at Bernkastel-Kues in Mosel-Saar-Ruwer region, Germany.

Gra-Car liqueur of monastery of Certosa di Pavia, Lombardy, Italy.

Grâce-Dieu, Château La wine estate of AC St-Emilion, Bordeaux, France. Classified *Grand Cru*.

Grâce-Dieu-Les-Menuts, Château La wine estate of AC St-Emilion, Bordeaux, France. Classified *Grand Cru*.

Gracia Hermanos leading wine *bodega* of Montilla-Moriles, Andalucia, Spain. Brands include Fino Corredera, Kiki, Maria del Valle.

Graciano red grape variety of Rioja region, Spain.

Gradeal Special

Gradeal Special Cocktail. Over ice shake 2 parts rum, 1 apricot brandy, 1 dry gin. Strain.

Graf Beyssel-Herrenberg vineyard at Bullay in Mosel-Saar-Ruwer region, Germany.

Grafenberg the name of 11 individual vineyards in Germany. Region by region, as follows: in Mosel-Saar-Ruwer at Neumagen-Dhron, Piesport; in Nahe at Sponheim; in Württemberg at Brackenheim, Eppingen, Leingarten (Grossgartach), Leingarten (Schluchtern), Nordheim, Schwaigern, Schwaigern (Niederhofen), Schorndorf.

Gräfenberg vineyards at Freckenfeld in Rheinpfalz region, Kiedrich in Rheingau region and Nordheim in Württemberg region, Germany.

Grafensprung vineyard at Gernsbach in Baden region, Germany.

Gräfenstein vineyard at Rottenberg in Franken region, Germany.

Grafenstuck *Grosslage* (collective vineyard) incorporating vineyards at Bockenheim an der Weinstrasse, Kindenheim, Obrigheim and Obrigheim (Mühlheim) in Rheinpfalz region, Germany.

Gräflich Stubenberg'sches Schlossweingut wine producer in Kamptal, Niederösterreich, Austria.

Grafschaft *Grosslage* (collective vineyard) incorporating vineyards at Alf, Beuren, Bremm, Bullay, Ediger-Eller, Neef, Nehren, St Aldegrund and Zell in Mosel-Saar-Ruwer region, Germany.

Grafschafter Sonnenberg vineyard at Veldenz in Mosel-Saar-Ruwer region, Germany.

grafting necessary precaution of growing new vine plants on phylloxera-resistant rootstocks – still the only method found of combatting the most serious of all vine pests, and not invariably successful.

Graf von Neipperg wine estate at Schwaigern, Württemberg region, Germany. Est 13th century and still a family property. Distinguished red wines.

Graham, W & J port producer and shipper est 1820 Vila Nova de Gaia, Portugal. Symington-owned. Old tawnies, Six Grapes ruby, Extra Dry White and vintages: 1955, 60, 63, 66, 70, 75, 77, 80, 83, 85, 91, 92, 94, 97, 2000, 03.

Graffiti Alt speciality beer of Stanislaus Brewing Co, Modesto, California, USA.

Graham Beck wine estate of Madeba valley, Robertson, South Africa.

Grain vineyard at Neustadt an der Weinstrasse in Rheinpfalz region, Germany.

Grain Belt Beer brand of Pete's Brewing Co, Palo Alto, California, USA.

Grainhübel vineyard at Deidesheim in Rheinpfalz region, Germany.

Grain Store brewery at Oakham, Rutland, England. Operated by Davis's Brewing Co.

Gran Capitan solera gran reserva brandy by Bobadilla, Jerez de la Frontera, Spain.

Gran Coronas red wine brand of Miguel Torres, Vilafranca del Penedes, Spain.

Grand-Abord, Château wine estate of AC Graves, Bordeaux, France.

Grand Bahama Cocktail. Over ice shake 2 parts rum, 1 brandy, 1 Cointreau, 2 fresh lime juice. Strain.

Grand-Barrail-Lamarzelle-Figeac, Château wine estate of AC St-Emilion, Bordeaux, France. Classified *Grand Cru* (1996).

Grand-Corbin, Château wine estate of AC St-Emilion, Bordeaux, France. Classified *Grand Cru* (1996).

Grand-Corbin-Despagne, Château wine estate of AC St-Emilion, Bordeaux, France. Classified *Grand Cru* (1996).

grand cru 'great growth' – a quality classification, defined by statute in French law, applying to vineyards and properties of regions including Alsace, Bordeaux and Burgundy. In Bordeaux regions of Médoc, Graves, St Emilion, Sauternes and Barsac, hundreds of individual properties carry official *grand cru* designations of various ranks from simple *Grands Crus* of St Emilion to *1er, 2ème, 3ème, 4ème* and *5ème Grands Crus* of the Médoc. In Alsace and Burgundy, *Grand Cru* applies to vineyards, which are commonly composed of numerous individual holdings in separate ownership. The wines of these vineyards, made either by the *vignerons* or sold to *négoçiant-éleveurs*, are generally the greatest of their respective regions, and invariably (regardless of quality) the most expensive.

Grand Cru Estate winery of Adelaide Hills, South Australia.

Grand Cru Vineyards winery of Sonoma Valley, California, USA.

Grand Cumberland passion-fruit liqueur brand, Australia.

Grand-Duroc-Milon, Château wine estate of AC Pauillac, Médoc, Bordeaux, France. Classified *Cru Bourgeois*.

Grande Brasserie Moderne de Terken brewery co-operative at Roubaix, France.

Grande Champagne AC zone of Charente region, France. Highest-ranked of vineyards for cognac production.

Grande Chouffe beer brand of Brasserie d'Achouffe, Achouffe, Belgium.

Grande Marque 'great brand name' claimed by a number of champagne producers. Use of the term pre-dated the formation in 1964 of the Syndicat de Grandes Marques de Champagne by 28 houses, later displaced by the Club des Grandes Marques, with 24 members, which broke up after failing to agree on a variety of proposed new qualifications for membership, in 1997. The producers are now represented by the Union des Maisons de Champagne. The term *grande marque* lingers, but has never been a guarantee of top quality. Many great producers are not, nor ever have been, *grandes marques*.

Grand-Enclos, Château wine estate of AC Cérons, Bordeaux, France

Grande Rue, La *Grand Cru* of Vosne-Romanée, Burgundy, France.

Grandes-Murailles, Château wine estate of AC St-Emilion, Bordeaux, France. Classified *Grand Cru Classé* (1996).

Grandis, Château wine estate of AC Haut-Médoc, Bordeaux, France. Classified *Cru Bourgeois*.

Grand-Jour, Château wine estate of AC Côtes de Bourg, Bordeaux, France.

Grand Listrac wine of Cave Coopérative of Listrac, Bordeaux, France.

Grand MacNish standard and 12-year-old blended scotch whiskies by MacDuff International, Glasgow, Scotland.

Grand Marnier cognac-based liqueur produced at Neauphle le Château, France. The liqueur is named after Marnier Lapostolle, who created the recipe in 1827. Lapostolle was a man of enormous wealth, but of diminutive stature. The story goes that he offered a sample of his new preparation to the hotelier César Ritz, asking him both for an opinion and to suggest a suitable name for it. Ritz pronounced the drink delicious, and with the ingratiation instinctive in hotel managers, recommended *Grand* Marnier.

Grand-Mayne, Château wine estate of AC St-Emilion, Bordeaux, France. Classified *Grand Cru Classé*.

Grand-Monteil, Château wine brand of Société du Grand Monteil des Pontons et de Lafite, AC Bordeaux Supérieur, France.

Grand-Moueys, Château wine estate of AC Premières Côtes de Bordeaux, France.

Grand-Moulin, Château wine estate of AC Haut-Médoc, Bordeaux, France. Classified *Cru Bourgeois*.

Grand-Moulinet, Château wine estate of AC Pomerol, Bordeaux, France.

Grand Panax sparkling wine with ginseng herb. Brand of Holmbru, California, USA.

Grand Passion Cocktail. Over ice shake 2 parts dry gin, 1 passionfruit juice, 1 dash Angostura bitters. Strain.

Grand-Pontet, Château wine estate of AC St-Emilion, Bordeaux, France. Classified *Grand Cru Classé*.

Grand Pré wine producer at Kings County, Nova Scotia, Canada.

Grand-Puch, Château de wine estate of AC Entre-Deux-Mers, Bordeaux, France.

Grand-Puy-Ducasse, Château wine estate of AC Pauillac, Médoc, Bordeaux, France. Classified *5ème Grand Cru Classé*.

Grand-Puy-Lacoste, Château wine estate of AC Pauillac, Médoc, Bordeaux, France. Classified *5ème Grand Cru Classé*. *see label opposite* ➤

Grand-Renouil, Château wine estate of AC Canon-Fronsac, Bordeaux, France.

Grand Ridge brewery at Mirbo North, Victoria, Australia.

Grand Roussillon AC for *vin doux natural* of Roussillon region, France.

Grand Royal Clover Club Cocktail. Over ice shake 1 egg, 2 parts dry gin, 1 grenadine, 1 lemon juice. Strain.

Grands-Echézeaux *Grand Cru* vineyard of Vosne-Romanée, Burgundy, France.

Grand Slam Cocktail. Over ice shake 2 parts Swedish Punsch, 1 dry vermouth, 1 sweet vermouth. Strain.

Gran Duque d'Alba brandy by Williams & Humbert, Jerez de la Frontera, Spain.

Grand-Village-Capbern, Le second wine Château Capbern-Gasqueton, Bordeaux, France.

grand vin the 'great wine' of a French vineyard – as opposed to lesser ones. Has no legally defined significance.

Grange Hermitage arguably the greatest red wine of Australia. From The Grange estate est 1844 by Penfold family at Magill, South Australia and made entirely from Shiraz grapes (local name for the Syrah of Hermitage in the Rhône Valley, France). First made 1951.

Grangeneuve, Domaine de wine estate of AC Graves, Bordeaux, France.

Granite pub-brewery at Halifax, Nova Scotia, Canada.

Gran Reserva in Spain, notably Rioja, a designation for wine from exceptional vintage aged at least two years in oak cask and three in bottle before going on sale.

Grans Muralles wine brand of Bodegas Miguel Torres, Penedes, Spain.

Grant, William see William Grant's.

Grant Burge large-scale winery of Barossa Valley, South Australia.

Grant's pub-brewery at Yakima, Washington, USA. Beers include **Grant's Scottish Ale**.

Granville Island brewery in Vancouver, Canada.

Grão Vasco Dão red wine by Sogrape, Portugal.

grape sole source of wine, almost always from vine species *vitis vinifera*. Other species including *vitis labrusca*, mostly grown in North America, are also used, particularly for grafting on to *vitis vinifera* vines because of their relative resistance to the vine-louse phylloxera.

Grapefruit Cocktail. Over ice shake 2 parts dry gin, 1 grapefruit juice. Strain.

Grape to glass
how wine is made

Wine is made by cultivating grapes, picking them at an ideal ripeness, crushing them to extract the juice then fermenting it until all the natural sugar turns into alcohol. It's then just a matter of maturing, clarifying and bottling the finished product.

Of course there are variations. Red, white and rosé wines are made by different processes. So are sparkling and fortified wines, which are made by methods described elsewhere in this book.

The red wine process

1. Black-skinned grapes are fed into an auger, a screw-threaded contraption that strips the bunches of their stems and crushes the fruit.

2. The crushed fruit or 'must' is fed into a fermenting vat. The juice is clear in all grapes, so the colour – and the health-giving antioxidant compounds such as tannins – come from fermenting the fruit with its skins.

3. A cultured yeast is usually added, and fermentation takes up to two weeks, turning the natural sugars in the fruit into alcohol and typically producing a dry wine usually of 11 to 14 per alcohol by volume.

4. The 'free-run' wine is piped to storage tanks and the skins and pips left behind are pressed to extract the remaining wine.

5. The final product is made by blending together the vats of free-run and pressed wine. Cheaper wines are clarified and bottled about six months after the harvest, while others may be matured in oak casks for varying periods before going on sale.

The white wine process

1. Grapes, usually white-skinned, are fed into a stemmer-crusher that strips off the stems and crushes the fruit.

2. The fruit is fed into a press, which extracts the juice.

3. The juice only, without the skins, now called 'must' is piped into a fermenting vat. A cultured yeast is usually added. If the wine is to be dry, fermentation will continue until the natural sugars become alcohol, up to two weeks and making wine typically of 11 to 14 per cent alcohol. If the wine is to be 'medium' or sweet, the fermenting process may be stopped by killing the yeast with spirit or sulphur or other means, leaving a controlled residue of sugar.

4. The wine is piped into storage tanks to await blending, clarifying and bottling. White wines can be bottled just a few weeks after the vintage.

Rosé wine

The process is the same as for red wines except that when the free-run juice has taken on the desired colour, it is piped off the skins into a separate vat to complete fermentation. Some cheap rosé is made simply by blending red and white wine.

Grapevine brewery near Lebec, California, USA.

Grape Vine Cocktail. Over ice shake 2 parts dry gin, 1 grape juice, 1 lemon juice, 1 dash grenadine. Strain.

grapey in winetasting, a smell redolent of the constituent grape in its natural (unfermented) state.

grappa spirit distilled from by-products of winemaking process, Italy. Made throughout the winemaking regions and said to number more than 2,000 different brands, including Andrea de Ponte, Branca, Bocchino, Brolio, Camel, Gravina, Julia, Langa Antica, Libarna, Nardini, Segnana.

Grappa-Strega Cocktail. Over ice shake 1 part grappa, 1 Strega, 1 equal mix lemon and orange juice. Strain.

Grapput red grape variety of SW France. Wines of the Lot Valley and Côte du Marmandais.

Grasa white grape variety of Cotnari, Romania.

Grasevina regional name in Balkn region for Laski Rizling grape variety.

Grasshopper Cocktail. Over ice shake 1 part crème de cacao, 1 crème de menthe, 1 Cream. Strain.

grassy in winetasting, a fresh lushness of fruit in the flavour. Often associated with Sauvignon Blanc grape.

Grate-Cap, Château wine estate of AC Pomerol, Bordeaux, France.

Gratien, Alfred champagne brand of Gratien & Meyer, Epernay, France.

Gratien, Meyer, Seydoux champagne and Loire Valley sparkling wine (Crémant de Loire) producer, Epernay and Saumur, France.

Graubünden red wine from Pinot Noir grapes, Switzerland.

Graukatz vineyards at Gaugrehweiler, Kalkhofen, Münsterappel, Niederhausen an der Appel, Oberhausen an der Appel and Winterborn in Nahe region and Tiefenthal in Rheinhessen region, Germany.

Grava, Château du wine estate of AC Premières Côtes de Bordeaux, France.

Grave, Domaine La wine estate of AC Graves, Bordeaux, France.

Grave, Château de la wine estate of AC Côtes de Bourg, Bordeaux, France.

Gravelines, Château wine estate of AC Premières Côtes de Bordeaux, France.

Grave-Martillac, La second wine Château La Tour Martillac, Bordeaux, France.

Gravensteiner *eau de vie* distilled from apples. Switzerland.

Graves wine region and AC for red and white wines, Bordeaux, France. Name derives from gravelly soil of region and red wines are said to have a characteristic style. Encompasses important AC of Pessac-Léognan and communes including

Cadaujac, Martillac, Talence etc. Château Haut Brion of Pessac was classified *1er grand cru classé* with 60 Médoc wines in 1855, but Graves wines were otherwise unclassified until 1953 (reclassified 1959). ACs of Barsac, Cerons and Sauternes, for sweet white wines, lie within Graves AC but are not designated part of it.

Graves de Vayres district of Entre-Deux-Mers, Bordeaux, France. Red and white wines.

Gravet, Château wine estate of AC St-Emilion, Bordeaux, France. Classified *Grand Cru*.

Grave-Trigant-de-Boisset, Château La wine estate of AC Pomerol, Bordeaux, France.

Graveyard Hermitage memorable red wine from Shiraz grapes by Brokenwood, Hunter Valley, Australia.

Gravière, Château La wine estate of AC Lalande-de-Pomerol, Médoc, Bordeaux, France.

Gravières de Marsac second wine of Château Marsac-Séguineau, Bordeaux, France.

Graville-Lacoste, Château wine estate of AC Graves, Bordeaux, France.

Gravina DOC for white and sparkling wines from Bianco d'Alessano, Greco di Tufo and other grape varietes, Bari, Apulia, Italy.

graybeard stoneware jug traditionally for spirits. USA.

Gray Monk wine producer at Okanagan Centre, British Columbia, Canada.

Gray Riesling white grape variety of California. Synonymous with Trousseau Gris.

Gray Whale Ale beer by Pacific Coast brewery, Oakland, California, USA.

Gray's farmhouse cider, Halstow, Tedburn St Mary, Devon, England.

Great Eastern golden ale (4.3% alc) by Woodforde's brewery, Woodbastwick, Norfolk, England.

Great Lakes popular name for breweries in northern United States and Canada, including **Great Lakes** pub-brewery at Cleveland, Ohio, USA and **Great Lakes** brewery at Brampton, Ontario, Canada.

Great Secret Cocktail. Over ice shake 2 parts dry gin, 1 Lillet, 1 dash Angostura bitters. Strain.

Great Southern wine region of Western Australia.

Great Wall vodka by China National Cereals, Oils and Foodstuffs Import and Export Corporation, Ch'ing-tao, People's Republic of China. Export only (mainly USA).

Great Western ale brand of Cottage Brewing Co, Lovington, Somerset, England.

Great Western wine region of Victoria, Australia.

Great Western winery est 1860, Hammondsport, New York, USA. Producers of **Great Western Champagne**.

Grechetto white grape variety of Umbria, Italy.

Greco white grape variety of southern Italy.

Greco di Bianco DOC for strong (17% alc) sweet white wine from Greco grapes, town of Bianco, Calabria, Italy.

Greco di Todo dry white *vino da tavola* from Grechetto grapes, Todi, Umbria, Italy.

Greco di Tufo DOC for dry white wine from Greco grapes, Tufo, Campania, Italy.

Greece wine-producing nation of antiquity, now with an antiquated wine industry. Production is localised throughout mainland and islands, with retsina still the dominant national style.

Greek Cocktail. Over ice shake 3 parts Greek brandy, 1 lemon juice, 1 teaspoon ouzo. Strain into icefilled tumblers and top with chilled dry ginger ale.

green in winetasting, a flavour with dominant acidity which may suggest grapes were insufficiently ripe.

Greenall Whitley brewery in Warrington, Lancashire, England.

Greenbriar Cocktail. Over ice shake 2 parts dry sherry, 1 dry vermouth, 1 dash peach bitters, 1 sprig fresh mint. Strain.

Green Dragon brew pub at Bungay, Suffolk, England.

Green Dragon Cocktail. Over ice shake 4 parts dry gin, 2 green crème de menthe, 1 kümmel, 1 lemon juice, 4 dashes peach bitters. Strain.

Greene King brewery at Bury St Edmunds, Suffolk, England. Famed products include Abbot Ale, St Edmund Ale, Strong Suffolk and bottled Beer to Dine For. Scions of the Greene brewing dynasty include novelist Graham (1904–1994).

Green Grape regional name for Sémillon grape variety, South Africa.

Greengrass ale brand of Daleside Brewery, Harrogate, Yorkshire, England.

Green Island cane spirit brand, Mauritius.

Greenjack brewer at Oulton Road brewery, Oulton Broad, Suffolk, England.

Green Label bottled ale by Wadworth brewery, Devizes, Wiltshire, England.

Green Lady Cocktail. Over ice shake 2 parts dry gin, 1 green Chartreuse, teaspoon fresh lime juice. Strain.

Greenmantle beer brand (3.9% alc) of Broughton brewery, Peeblesshire, Scotland. John Buchan (1875–1940), author of the novel *Greenmantle*, was born at Broughton village.

Green Room Cocktail. Over ice shake 2 parts dry vermouth, 1 brandy, 2 dashes curaçao. Strain.

Greenshields pub-brewery in Raleigh, North Carolina, USA.

Green Tea tea-flavoured liqueur by Suntory, Japan.

Green Valley Cyder cider by Marsh Barton Farm, Clyst St George, Devon, England.

Green Valley Solano AVA of Solano County, California, USA.

Green Valley Sonoma AVA of Sonoma County, California, USA.

Greifenberg vineyard at Sulzheim in Rheinhessen region, Germany.

Greifenklau inn-brewery in Bamberg, Franconia, Germany.

Greiner vineyard at Korb in Württemberg region, Germany.

Grenache red grape variety of southern France. Important in the *cépages* of Côtes du Rhône, Châteauneuf-du-Pape and other ACs of the Rhône Valley, and in many red wines of the Midi, Corsica and Sardinia. Also widely planted in Australia, California, South Africa. Originally Spanish. See Garnacha.

Grenache Blanc white grape variety of southern France. Synonymous with Garnacha Blanco.

Grenadier Cocktail. Over ice shake 2 parts brandy, 1 ginger brandy, 1 teaspoon sugar. Strain.

Grenon, Jean-Marie cognac producer, Dompierre sur Charente, France.

Grenouilles *Grand Cru* vineyard of Chablis, France. Name means 'Frogs' – so-called due to proximity of vineyard to spawning territory of river Serein.

Grenzquell pilsener beer by Bavaria St Pauli brewery, Hamburg, Germany.

Gressier-Grand-Poujeaux, Château wine estate of AC Moulis, Médoc, Bordeaux, France. Classified *Cru Grand Bourgeois Exceptionnel*.

Greth vineyard at Treis-Karden in Mosel-Saar-Ruwer region, Germany.

Grey Goose French-distilled vodka brand of Sydney Frank Co, New York, USA. The spirit is made in the Cognac region using corn, wheat, rye and barley and 'filtered through champagne limestone'.

Greyhound brew pub at Streatham, London, England.

Grey Riesling white grape variety of New Zealand. Synonymous with Trousseau Gris.

Greysac, Château wine estate of AC Médoc, Bordeaux, France. Classified *Cru Grand Bourgeois*.

Grgich Hills wine producer at Rutherford, Sonoma Valley, California, USA. Named after founder Dave Grgich and an associate called Hills.

Gribble Inn brew pub at Oving, Chichester, West Sussex, England.

Grierson's No. 1 twelve-year-old vatted malt scotch whisky by Grierson's, London, England.

Grignolino d'Asti DOC for red wines from Grignolino grapes, Asti, Piedmont, Italy.

Grignolino del Monferrato Casalese DOC for red wines from Grignolino grapes, Casale Monferrato, Piedmont, Italy.

Grillet, Château wine property at Condrieu, Rhône Valley, France. The estate comprises all of the AC Château Grillet, the smallest defined appellation of France. Extravagantly priced white wine from Viognier grapes.

Grillo white grape variety of Sicily, Italy. Marsala wines.

Grimond, Château wine estate of AC Premières Côtes de Bordeaux, France.

Grim Reaper bottle-conditioned beer by Freeminer Brewery, Forest of Dean, Gloucestershire, England. 'A hoppy, well-balanced bitter ideal for quenching the thirst after another grim day in the field.'

Gringet white grape variety of Savoie, France. Sparkling Ayze wines. Synonymous with Savagnin.

Grinzing wine village of Vienna region, Austria.

Griotte-Chambertin *Grand Cru* of Gevrey-Chambertin, Burgundy, France.

grip in winetasting, a wine with emphatic flavour and assertion, the antithesis of flabbiness. Immortalised in John Jorrocks's description of his beloved port: 'wine with a good grip o' the gob.' RS Surtees, *Handley Cross* (1843).

Gris de Boulaouane rosé wine of Casablanca region, Morocco.

grist in brewing, the milled grain.

Gritty McDuff's pub-brewery at Portland, Maine, USA.

Grivière, Château wine estate of AC Médoc, Bordeaux, France. Classified *Cru Bourgeois*.

Grivot, Jean wine producer of Côte de Nuits, Burgundy, France.

Grk white grape variety and strong wine of island of Korcula, Croatia.

Grodzisk town and 'smoked beer' style. Poland.

grog watered rum, as issued in place of undiluted spirit to Royal Navy crews on orders of Admiral Edward Vernon, 1740. Vernon's nickname 'Old Grog' – from his distinctive grogram cloak – was adopted as a pejorative soubriquet for the ration, which continued to be issued on board naval vessels until 1969.

Grolet, Château wine estate of AC Premières Côtes de Blaye, Bordeaux, France.

Grolleau red grape variety of Loire Valley, France. Anjou red and rosé.

Grolsch Dutch pilsener beer brand well known for its wire-and-pottery bottle closure.

Groot Constantia Estate great wine estate est 1685 by Simon van der Stel, first Governor of the Cape, Capetown, South Africa. Original estate was divided up then sold to the state in 1885 after vineyards for legendary Constantia sweet wine were destroyed by Phylloxera. Revived and in hands of government-appointed trustees, now produces famed table wines including Cabernet Sauvignon, Chardonnay, Gouverneurs Reserve red, Weisser Riesling etc.   *see label opposite* ➤

Gropello red grape variety and *vino da tavola*, Lake Garda, Lombardy, Italy.

gros gin a concocted winter-warming drink peculiar to the province of Quebec, Canada. Principal ingredients are gin or any other spirit and sweetened red wine. Also known as *p'tit caribou*.

Gros-Moulin, Château wine estate of AC Côtes de Bourg, Bordeaux, France.

Gros Plant regional name in western Loire Valley for Folle Blanche white grape variety, and the resulting dry and acidic white wine. Nantes, France.

Gross, Alois wine producer in Südsteiermark, Austria.

Grossenberg vineyard Gernsbach in Baden region, Germany.

Grosser Hengelberg vineyard at Neumagen-Dhron in Mosel-Saar-Ruwer region, Germany.

Grosser Herrgott vineyard at Wintrich in Mosel-Saar-Ruwer region, Germany.

Grosslage collective vineyard, Germany. Group name for a number of individual vineyards or *Einzellagen* whose wines may be marketed under that name. On labels, the *Grosslage* name is added to that of the village with which it is identified, eg Piesporter Michelsberg.

Grosslay vineyard at Müden in Mosel-Saar-Ruwer region, Germany.

Grossmulde vineyard at Waiblingen in Württemberg region, Germany.

Grove Mill wine producer at Blenheim, Marlborough, New Zealand. Well-known Chardonnay and other wines.

Growler's pub-brewery in Toronto, Canada.

Gruaud-Larose, Château great wine estate of AC St Julien, Médoc, Bordeaux, France. Classified *2ème Grand Cru Classé*.

Gruet & Fils Champagne brand of Coteaux de Bethon co-operative, Champagne, France.

Grumello DOC for red wines classified as Valtellina Superiore, Lombardy, Italy.

Grüner Veltliner white grape variety and wine of Austria and, to a lesser extent, elsewhere in central Europe.

Grupo Modelo leading brewing company of Mexico.

Gsellmann & Gsellmann wine producer in Neusiedlersee, Burgenland, Austria.

Guadet-Franc-Grâce-Dieu, Château former name of Château Franc-Grâce-Dieu, Bordeaux, France.

Guadet-St-Julien, Château wine estate of AC St-Emilion, Bordeaux, France. Classified *Grand Cru Classé*.

Guard's Cocktail. Over ice shake 2 parts dry gin, 1 sweet vermouth, 2 dashes curaçao. Strain.

Guedes Portuguese wine family known for creation of Mateus Rosé in 1950s, now incorporated into Sogrape company.

Guenoc Valley AVA of Lake County, California, USA.

Guernsey Brewery (1920) Ltd brewer at St Peter Port, Guernsey, Channel Islands, UK. Beers include Milk Stout, Pony Ale, Stein Lager.

Guerrieri-Rizzardi leading wine producer in Veneto region, Italy. Bardolino, Soave and Valpolicella by organic methods.

AZIENDA AGRICOLA
GUERRIERI-RIZZARDI

Valpolicella
Denominazione di Origine Controllata
V. Q. P. R. D.
Classico Superiore

Imbottigliato all'origine dal viticoltore
nella sede in Bardolino, Italia

0.750 lt   12 % Vol
NON PASTORIZZATO

Guerrouane designated wine region of Meknès Fez, Morocco. Red and rosé wines.

Guerry, Château wine estate of AC Côtes de Bourg, Bordeaux, France.

gueuze style of sparkling beer produced by blending mature lambic beer with a part-fermented lambic to promote secondary fermentation – and thus carbonation – in bottle. Name may derive from Old Norse *geysa* (to gush). Belgium.

Gueyrot, Château wine estate of AC St-Emilion, Bordeaux, France.

Guibeau, Château wine estate of AC Puisseguin-St-Emilion, Bordeaux, France.

Guibon, Château wine estate of AC Entre-Deux-Mers, Bordeaux, France.

Guiborat *récoltant-manipulant* champagne producer, Cramant, Champagne, France.

Guigal renowned wine producer of Rhône Valley, France. New-style red wines of Côte Rôtie vineyards of La Landonne, La Mouline, La Turque fetch enormous prices.

Guillon-Painturaud cognac grower and producer est 1615, Biard, Grande Champagne district of Cognac, France.

Guimaraens port shipper, Vila Nova de Gaia, Portugal. See Fonseca Guimaraens.

Guinness & Son, Arthur brewery founded 1759 by Arthur Guinness at St James's Gate, Dublin, Ireland. Produces ubiquitous dry stout **Draught Guinness** (which also appears in cans) and bottled **Guinness Original Stout** (4.3% alc). **Guinness Foreign Extra Stout** is 7.5% alc. There are other Guinness breweries (though the most famed, at Park Royal, London, closed in 2004) and licensed operations throughout the world. See box.

Guinness

the stout that built a dynasty

Arthur Guinness (1725–1803) bought his first brewery, at Leixlip on the upper reaches of Ireland's river Liffey, with £100 left to him in a clergyman's will. The generous benefactor was the rector of Celbridge, County Kildare, who had employed Arthur's father, Richard Guinness, as a factor. Richard had brewed beer for the rectory, and no doubt his young son had assisted.

Arthur proved a talented brewer, known to strive for the highest quality. His Irish ales gained him a solid reputation with the tavern-keepers of Kildare. Earnings from the small enterprise at Leixlip funded his purchase of a larger, but disused, brewery owned by a Mr Rainsford at St James's Gate, Dublin, in 1759. Thus began the history of the most famous beer in the world.

To start with, Guinness produced Irish ale rather than stout. Porter production dates from the 1770s and the word Stout does not appear to have figured on product descriptions until the launch of the Extra Stout Porter brand in 1820.

Arthur Guinness built not just a large business, but a considerable dynasty. He and his wife Olivia had 18 children. It was Arthur's grandson, Benjamin Lee Guinness (1798–1868), who developed the brewery into a major exporting concern. From 1825 when Benjamin took control, he established agencies for Guinness throughout the United Kingdom and its colonies worldwide as well as in the United States.

Benjamin became the owner of Guinness in 1855 on his father's death. Already Lord Mayor of Dublin (the city's first), he was the richest man in Ireland. The brewery was in continual expansion, and export business enormous. Guinness now began the philanthropic works for which it has long been celebrated. Benjamin spent £160,000 (a fabulous sum equal to £50 million at today's values) restoring St Patrick's Cathedral in Dublin from 1860–65.

Benjamin also launched his family into British politics. He represented Dublin as a Conservative MP, and in 1867 was created a baronet. His son, Sir Arthur Edward Guinness, succeeded to the title and was in turn elected for Dublin before becoming the first Guinness peer as Baron Ardilaun in 1880. Disdaining trade, the new peer sold his shares to his brother Edward Cecil Guinness (1847–1927) in 1881 – the year the brewery reached an annual ouput of a million barrels.

In 1886, Edward Cecil floated the company as Arthur Guinness, Son & Co Ltd on the London Stock Exchange. At a value of £6 million, it was the largest share issue the City had ever seen. Edward Cecil, created a baronet in 1885, retained a majority of the shares, and thus ranked as one of the world's wealthiest individuals. In 1889, he gave £250,000 for the establishment of the Guinness Trust to build housing for the benefit of the working poor in London and Dublin. He was raised to the peerage as the first Baron Iveagh in 1891, and subsequently to First Earl Iveagh.

Guinness is now sold in more than 100 countries around the world. It was brewed in London, at the Park Royal site, until its closure in 2004, but continues to be brewed at company-owned sites in Africa and the Far East. It is produced under licence in a further 30 different locations. The Guinness family continued to participate in the management of the publicly owned company until as recently as 1992. Guinness is now incorporated into the world's largest drinks company, Diageo.

Guionne, Château wine estate of AC Côtes de Bourg, Bordeaux, France.

Guiraud, Château great wine estate of AC Sauternes, Bordeaux, France. Classified *1er Cru Classé*.

Guiteronde, Château wine estate of AC Sauternes, Bordeaux, France.

Güldenkern vineyard at Aspach in Württemberg region, Germany.

Guldenmorgen vineyard at Zornheim in Rheinhessen region, Germany.

Güldenmorgen *Grosslage* (collective vineyard) incorporating vineyards at Dienheim, Oppenheim and Uelversheim in Rheinhessen region, Germany.

Guldenzoll vineyard at Heppenheim in Hessische Bergstrasse region, Germany.

Gulpen brewery at Limburg, Netherlands, renowned for X-pert pilsener beer.

Gumpoldskirchner red and white wine of Gumpoldskirchen district, Niederosterreich, Austria.

Gumpoldskirchner Königssekt sparkling (*sekt*) wine brand of Inführ, Austria.

gunflint in winetasting, a smell characterising Chablis.

Guntersblum wine town of Rheinhessen region, Germany. *Grosslagen*: Krötenbrunnen, Vogelsgärtchen.

Günterslay vineyards at Piesport and Minheim in Mosel-Saar-Ruwer region, Germany.

Guntrum, Louis wine producer in Rheinhessen region, Germany.

Gurgue, Château La wine estate of AC Margaux, Médoc, Bordeaux, France. Classified *Cru Bourgeois Supérieur*.

gusano worm, Spanish. The Mexican spirit mezcal is commonly bottled with the remains of a worm in it. See box.

Gut Alsenhof vineyard at Lauf in Baden region, Germany.

Gutedel white grape variety of Germany, also planted in England. Synonymous with Chasselas.

Gutenberg vineyards at Oestrich-Winkel (Mittelheim) and Oestrich-Winkel (Winkel) in Rheingau region, Germany.

Gusano

the worm in the bottle

Mexico's mezcal distillers include the *gusano* – the desiccated corpse of a worm – in bottles of their fiery spirit as a badge of authenticity. How did this curious practice arise? One unlikely source of the tradition is said to concern the legend of an American temperance preacher on tour in Mexico. In a packed church, he sought to demonstrate the evils of drink with an experiment. Taking a glass of water and another of mezcal spirit, he dropped a live worm into each. Holding the two glasses aloft for all the congregation to see, the preacher was able plainly to show the effect. The one in the water wriggled vigorously, the one in the spirit was quite dead. 'And what do you make of that?' the preacher demanded of his admiring audience. A lengthy silence was finally broken by the voice of a small boy from the back: 'If you've got worms, drink mezcal.'   ❦

Gutenborner

Gutenborner white grape variety of Germany, also planted in England.

Gutenhölle vineyard at Hüffelsheim in Nahe region, Germany.

Gutental vineyard at Bad Kreuznach in Nahe region, Germany.

Gützenberg vineyard at Königheim in Baden region, Germany.

Gutes Domtal *Grosslage* (collective vineyard) incorporating vineyards in Rheinhessen region, Germany at, respectively: Dalheim, Dexheim, Friesenheim, Hahnheim, Köngerheim, Mommenheim, Nackenheim, Nieder-Olm, Nierstein, Selzen, Sörgenloch, Undenheim, Weinolsheim, Zornheim.

Gutleuthaus vineyard at Oppenheim in Rheinhessen region, Germany.

Guttenberg *Grosslage* (collective vineyard) incorporating vineyards in Rheinpfalz region, Germany at, respectively: Bad Bergzabern, Dierbach, Börrenbach, Freckenfeld, Kandel, Kapsweyer, Minfeld, Niederotterbach, Oberotterbach, Schweigen-Rechtenbach, Scheighofen, Steinfeld, Vollmersweiler.

Guyana Distilleries principal rum distiller of Guyana (formerly British Guiana) est 1952. The company is an amalgamation of five smaller distilleries from the former Dutch colony of Demerara, the old stills, both pot and continuous types, remain in use, including those of Enmore, Uitvlugt and Port Morant.

Guy de Bersac cognac brand of Tradition Brillat-Savarin, Segonzac, France.

Guyon, Antonin wine producer at Aloxe-Corton, Burgundy, France. Notable wines of Corton etc.

Guyot vine-pruning and training method of France.

Gwalia distillery of Welsh Whisky Co at Penderyn, Brecon, Wales. First four-year-old single malt Penderyn Welsh whisky went on sale in 2004.

gypsum calcium sulphate. As *yeso* it is added to grape must in sherry-making to improve acidity.

H

Habitant Cocktail. Over ice shake 2 parts rye whisky, 1 teaspoon dry vermouth, 1 teaspoon maple syrup, 1 dash Angostura bitters. Strain.

H & H Cocktail. Over ice shake 2 parts dry gin, 1 Lillet, 2 dashes curaçao. Strain.

Haacht brewery at Boortmeerbeek, Belgium.

Haag, Fritz leading wine producer at Brauneberg, Mosel-Saar-Ruwer region, Germany.

Haag, Willi wine producer at Brauneberg, Mosel-Saar-Ruwer region, Germany.

Haake-Beck brewery in Bremen, Germany. Beers include Bremer Weisse, Edel Hell and Pils.

Haarberg-Katzensteg vineyard at Wöllstein in Rheinhessen region, Germany.

habillage dressings of French wine and spirit bottles: capsule and labels.

Habitant Cocktail. Over ice shake 4 parts rye whisky, 1 dry vermouth, 1 maple syrup, 1 dash Angostura bitters.

Hächnchen vineyard at Bornheim in Rheinhessen region, Germany.

Hacker-Pschorr brewery in Munich, Germany.

Häder vineyards at Kernen (Rommelshausen) and Kernen (Stetten) in Württemberg region, Germany.

Hadrian brewery in Newcastle upon Tyne, England. Beers include Centurion and Gladiator.

Haecht Tarwebier wheat beer by Haacht brewery, Belgium.

hagel en donder Friesian *brandewijn* flavoured with anis, Netherlands. Name means 'hail and thunder'.

Hägenich vineyard at Wiesloch in Baden region, Germany.

Hahn brewery at Camperdown, Sydney, Australia.

Hahn vineyards at Bacharach in Mittelrehein region and Rehborn in Nahe region, Germany.

Hahnen vineyard at Weisenheim am Sand in Rheinpfalz region, Germany.

Hahnenberg vineyards at Zaberfeld (Leonbrunn) and Zaberfeld (Ochsenburg) in Württemberg region, Germany.

Hahnenkamm vineyard at Bubenheim in Rheinpfalz region, Germany.

Hahnenschrittchen vineyard at Burg in Mosel-Saar-Ruwer region, Germany.

Hahnhölle vineyard at Niedermoschel in Nahe region, Germany.

Haig blended scotch whisky by John Haig & Co, Clackmannan, Scotland. Also, **Haig Gold Label**.

Hainault wine producer in Perth Hills, Western Australia.

Hainhölzer *Korn* brand of August Schmidt distillery, Hainholz, Germany.

Hainle Vineyards wine producer at Peachland, British Columbia, Canada.

hair of the dog an alcoholic drink taken as a hangover remedy, on the principle that in the source of an ailment lies the cure. The traditional belief that an infusion of hair from a dog that has inflicted a bite will forestall consequent infection is a variation on the homoeopathic maxim *simila similibus curantor* (treating like with like). Behavioural researchers warn that drinking more to alleviate the symptoms of drinking too much is at best ill-advised, and quite likely a step along the road to perdition.

Hair Raiser Cocktail. Over ice shake 2 parts vodka, 1 Dubonnet, 1 lemon juice. Strain.

Hakam Cocktail. Over ice shake 1 part dry gin, 1 sweet vermouth, 2 dashes curaçao, 1 dash orange bitters. Strain.

Hakutsuru *sake* brand of Hakutsuru Brewing Co, est 1743, Kobe, Japan. Name means 'white crane'.

Halbfuder wine cask of Mosel, Germany. About 500 litres.

halbsüss semi-sweet wine style with 12–45 g/l residual sugar. Austria.

Halbstück standard 600-litre wine cask of Germany.

halbtrocken 'medium dry' wine, Germany.

Halde vineyards at Emmendingen in Baden region, at Weisenheim am Sand in Rheinpfalz region and at Illingen, Mühlacker (Mühlhausen), Mühlacker (Lomersheim), Vaihingen and Vaihingen (Rosswag) in Württemberg region, Germany.

Haldengut brewery at Winterthur, Switzerland.

Halenberg vineyard at Monzingen in Nahe region, Germany.

Hale & Hearty brewery at Farnham, Surrey, England.

Hale's brewery with premises at Colville and Kirkland, Washington, USA.

Half om Half liqueur from equal parts curaçao and Dutch bitters. Netherlands.

Hall & Woodhouse brewer est 1777 now at Badger Brewery, Blandford Forum, Dorset, England. Cask beers include Badger Best (4% alc), Badger Original (4.6% alc), Tanglefoot (5.1%).

Haller's County Fair bourbon whiskey brand, Kentucky, USA.

Hallgarten wine and liqueur producer of Geisenheim, Germany and London, England.

Hallgarten wine village with well-known co-operative (Arthur Hallgarten GmbH) of Rheingau region, Germany. *Grosslage*: Mehrhölzchen.

Haltnau vineyard at Meersburg in Baden region, Germany.

Hambledon pioneering revivalist English vineyard est 1951 by Sir Guy Salisbury-Jones in Hampshire, England.

Hambleton Ales brewery at Holme-on-Swale, Thirsk, North Yorkshire, England.

Hambusch vineyard at Bacjarach in Mittelrhein region, Germany.

Hamilton Russell Vineyards wine estate in Walker Bay, South Africa. Noted Chardonnay and Pinot Noir brands.

Hamilton's Ewell Vineyards wine producer in Eden Valley, South Australia.

Hamm vineyards Koblenz (Lay), Koblenz (Moselsweiss) and Winningen in Mosel-Saar-Ruwer region and Waldböckelheim in Nahe region, Germany.

Hämmchen vineyard at Brey in Mittelrhein region, Germany.

Hammerstein vineyard at Trier in Mosel-Saar-Ruwer region, Germany.

Hampshire Brewery brewery at Romsey, Hampshire, England.

Hampshire Special Ale beer brand of Geary Brewing Co, Portland, Maine, USA.

Hanby Ales brewery at Wem, Shropshire, England.

Handsome Maid apple variety traditionally valued for cider-making. English.

Handsome Norman apple variety traditionally valued for cider-making. English.

Hanepoot regional name for Muscat d'Alexandrie grape variety, South Africa.

Hanging Rock wine estate within site of Hanging Rock, Macedon, Victoria, Australia. Well-known red and white wines including, inevitably, a range under the Picnic Wines label.

Hangdowns apple variety traditionally valued for cider-making. English.

Hankey Bannister standard and 12-year-old blended scotch whiskies by Hankey Bannister, est 1757 London, England. Now a brand of Inver House Distillers, Airdrie, Lanarkshire, Scotland.

Hanky Panky Cocktail. Over ice shake 1 part dry gin, 1 sweet vermouth, 2 dashes Fernet Branca. Strain and squeeze orange peel over.

Hanns Christof wine brand of Deinhard & Co commemorating Hanns Christof Deinhard, 17th century ancestor of the famous German firm's founder.

Hansenberg vineyard at Geisenheim in Rheingau region, Germany.

Hansje in de Kelder liqueur by Van Zuylekom, Amersterdam, Netherlands. Name 'Hans in the Cellar' is equivalent to 'jack in the box'.

Hanteillan, Château wine estate of AC Haut-Médoc, Bordeaux, France. Classified *Cru Grand Bourgeois*.

Hanwood brand of McWilliam's Wines, Chullora, New South Wales, Australia. Cabernet Sauvignon, Chardonnay and Shiraz wines.

Happenhalde vineyard at Weinstadt in Württemberg region, Germany.

Happy Return Cocktail. Over ice shake 4 parts dry gin, 2 Cointreau, 1 cherry brandy, 4 dashes lemon juice. Strain and add a maraschino cherry to glass.

Hapsburg absinthe brand of Bulgaria. Super De-Luxe Extra at 85% alc is claimed to be the strongest absinthe in the world.

hard in winetasting, the flavour of an immature wine dominated by tannin.

Hardcore Flavoured spirit-based drink brand, UK.

Hardt vineyard at Weikersheim in Württemberg region, Germany.

Hardtberg vineyards at Dernau and Rech in Ahr region, Germany.

Hardy, Antoine cognac house est 1863 Cognac, France. Brands include Noces d'Or 50-year-old brandy.

Hardy Country Bitter beer brand (4.2% alc) of Thomas Hardy (formerly Eldridge Pope) brewery, Dorset, England. Commemorates Dorset author Thomas Hardy (1840-1928) and quotes him on the label: 'Too much liquor is bad, and leads us to that horned man in the smoky house; but after all, many people haven't the gift of enjoying a wet, and since we be highly favoured with a power that way, we should make the most o't.'

Hardy's brand of leading wine company Thomas Hardy, est 1853, McLaren Vale, South Australia, now BRL Hardy. Hardy wines include Chateau Reynella, Houghton, Leasingham, Nottage Hill, Siegersdorf, Stanley and premium Eileen Hardy range. The company has further winemaking operations in Europe. BRL Hardy was merged with multinational drinks company Constellation in 2003 to form the world's largest wine producer.

Hardys & Hansons brewery at Kimberley, Nottinghamshire, England. Beers include Guinea Gold, Starbright IPA.

Harfenspiel vineyard at Bergtheim in Franken region, Germany.

Harlem Cocktail. Over ice shake 2 parts dry gin, 1 pineapple juice, 2 dashes maraschino. Strain.

Haro winemakng centre of Rioja Alta region, Spain.

Harp Lager beer brand of Diageo (Guinness) formerly brewed at Park Royal, London, England.

Harrier SPA Special Pale Ale brand (3.6% alc) of Cotleigh Brewery, Somerset, England.

Harrovian Cocktail. Over ice shake 1 part dry gin, 2 dashes orange juice, 1 dash lemon juice, 1 dash Angostura bitters. Strain.

Harry Lauder Cocktail. Over ice shake 1 part scotch whisky, 1 sweet vermouth, 2 dashes grenadine. Strain.

Harry Ramsden's Ale brand of Black Sheep Brewery, Masham, North Yorkshire, England. 'A rich full bodied ale specially brewed to complement fish & chips.' Harry Ramsden's is a renowned British chain of fish and chip restaurants.

Harry's Cocktail. Over ice shake 2 parts dry gin, 1 sweet vermouth, 1 dash pastis, 2 sprigs fresh mint. Strain and add cocktail olive to glass.

Harvey's Pick-Me-Up Cocktail. Over ice shake 2 parts brandy, 1 lemon juice, 1 teaspoon grenadine. Strain into wine glass and top with champagne.

Hárslevelü white grape variety of Tokay, Hungary.

Harsovo designated (Controliran) red-wine region of Bulgaria.

Harstell vineyard at Grossostheim in Franken region, Germany.

Hart brewery at Little Ecclestone, Lancashire, England.

Hart Brewing Co producer at Kalama, Washington, USA, of Pyramid wheat beer.

Hartley brewery at Ulverston, Cumbria, England.

Hart's blended scotch whisky by Donald Hart, Glasgow, Scotland.

Hartwall brewing company with sites in Karelia and Lapland, Finland. Brands include Joulo and Juhlaolut lagers. Owned by Scottish & Newcastle, UK.

Harvard Cocktail. Over ice shake 1 part brandy, 1 sweet vermouth, 2 dashes Angostura bitters, 1 dash sugar syrup. Strain.

Harvard Cooler Cocktail. Over ice shake 4 parts apple brandy, 1 lemon or lime juice, 1 teaspoon sugar. Strain into tumbler glass and top with soda water.

Harvest Tradition perry brand of Halewood International, Huyton, Merseyside, England.

Harvey & Son brewery est 1790 in Lewes, East Sussex, England. Bill Brewer Sussex Old ale ('not more than 1%' alc), Blue Label pale ale (3.8% alc), Christmas Ale (8.1%), Exhibition Brown old ale (3.5%

alc), Family Ale (2% alc), Firecracker Strong Ale (5.8%), India Pale Ale (3.2% alc), John Hop Sussex Bitter ('not more than 1% alc), Nut Brown Ale (3% alc), Porter (4.8% alc), South Down Harvest Ale (5.0% alc), Tom Paine Ale (5.5% alc), Sussex Stout.

Harveys wine merchants est 1796, Bristol, England as John Harvey & Son. Famed Bristol shop closed 2001 and John Harvey is now a wine-wholesaling brand of Allied Domecq. Harveys is also a major sherry shipper, with its own bodegas at Jerez in Spain since 1970,

renowned for **Harveys Bristol Cream** and other brands. Captain Thomas Harvey, father of the man who gave his name to the merchant company, was a seafarer with a fearsome reputation for holding his drink. Ashore in Bristol he once drank a companion, literally, under the table. Harvey summoned his servant. 'Kindly removed Mr Prothero,' he commanded, 'and bring me another bottle of port.'

Harvey's Special blended scotch whisky by John & Robert Harvey, Glasgow, Scotland.

Harveys Wallhanger Cocktail. Over ice shake 1 part Harveys Bristol Cream sherry, 1 rum, 2 pineapple juice, sprinkle of black pepper. Strain.

Harvey Wallbanger Cocktail. Over ice shake 1 part vodka, 2 orange juice. Strain into ice-filled tall glass and add 2 teaspoons Galliano to top.

Harviestoun brewery at Dollar, Scotland.

Harwood Canadian Canadian whisky by Duncan Harwood distillers, Vancouver, Canada.

Harztberg vineyards at Grossbottwar, Grossbottwar (Hof und Lembach), Grossbottwar (Winzerhausen), Oberstenfeld and Oberstenfeld (Gronau) in Württemberg region, Germany.

Häs'chen vineyard at Neumagen-Dhron in Mosel-Saar-Ruwer region, Germany.

Hasekamp *genever* distillery, Schiedam, Netherlands.

Haselstaude vineyards at Kippenheim, Laher and Mahlberg in Baden region, Germany.

Haselstein vineyards at Winnenden and Winnenden (Breuningsweiler) in Württemberg region, Germany.

Hasen vineyard at Eschbach in Rheinpfalz region, Germany.

Hasenberg vineyards at Bad Ems and Dausenau in Mittelrhein region, Endingen in Baden region and Perl in Mosel-Saar-Ruwer region, Germany.

Hasenbiss vineyard at Osthofen in Rheinhessen region, Germany.

Hasenlauf vineyard at Bermersheim in Rheinhessen region, Germany.

Hasenläufer vineyard at Burgen in Mosel-Saar-Ruwer region, Germany.

Hasennestle vineyard at Adelshofen in Franken region, Germany.

Hasensprung vineyards at Bechtheim, Dorn-Dürkheim and Jugenheim in Rheinhessen region, Ediger-Eller in Mosel-Saar-Ruwer region, Oestrich-Winkel in Rheingau region, Wallhausen in Nahe region and Walzbachtal in Baden region, Germany.

Hasenzeile vineyard at Weisenheim am Sand in Rheinpfalz region, Germany.

Haskovo winery est 1947, Rhodopes region, southern Bulgaria. Red wines from Cabernet Sauvignon, Merlot, Pamid and Tamianka grapes.

Hassel vineyard at Eltville in Rheingau region, Germany.

Hassmannsberg vineyard at Bockenheim an der Weinstrasse in Rheinpfalz region, Germany.

Hasty Cocktail. Over ice shake 2 parts dry gin, 1 dry vermouth, 4 dashes grenadine, 1 dash pastis. Strain.

Hatté, Bernard *récoltant-manipulant* champagne producer, Verzenay, Champagne, France.

Hattenheim famed wine village of Rheingau region, Germany. *Grosslage*: Deutelsberg. Vineyards (*Einzellagen*) include Engelmannsberg, Hassel, Nussbrunnen, Pfaffenberg, Wisselbrunnen.

Haubenberg vineyard at Saulheim in Rheinhessen region, Germany.

Hausbrauerei inn or restaurant incorporating its own brewery. Germany. Equivalent to brewpub in USA or pub-brewery in UK.

Haus Marienberg wine producer in Neusiedlersee Hügelland, Burgenland, Austria.

Haut-Badette, Château wine estate of AC St-Emilion, Bordeaux, France.

Haut-Bages-Averous second wine of Château Lynch-Bages, Bordeaux, France.

Haut-Bages-Libéral, Château wine estate of AC Pauillac, Médoc, Bordeaux, France. Classified *5ème Grand Cru Classé*.

Haut-Bages-Monpelou, Château wine estate of AC Pauillac, Médoc, Bordeaux, France. Classified *Cru Bourgeois*.

Haut-Bailly, Château wine estate of AC Graves, Bordeaux, France. Classified *Cru Classé*.

Haut Baron armagnac brand of growers' co-operative of Cazaubon, Gascony, France.

Haut-Batailley, Château wine estate of AC Pauillac, Médoc, Bordeaux, France. Classified *5ème Grand Cru Classé*.

Haut-Benauge AC for white wines within Entre-Deux-Mers AC, Bordeaux, France.

Haut-Bergey, Château wine estate of AC Pessac-Léognan, Bordeaux, France.

Haut-Bommes, Château wine estate of AC Sauternes, Bordeaux, France. Classified *Cru Bourgeois*.

Haut-Breton-Larigaudière, Château wine estate of AC Margaux, Médoc, Bordeaux, France.

Haut-Brignon, Château wine estate of AC Premières Côtes de Bordeaux, France.

Haut-Brion, Château great wine estate of AC Pessac-Léognan, Bordeaux, France. Classified *1er Grand Cru Classé*.

Haut-Canteloup, Château wine estate of AC Médoc, Bordeaux, France. Classified *Cru Bourgeois*.

Haut-Castenet, Château second wine of Château Launay, Bordeaux, France.

Haut-Chaigneau, Château wine estate of AC Lalande-de-Pomerol, Bordeaux, France.

Haut-Corbin, Château wine estate of AC St-Emilion, Bordeaux, France. Classified *Grand Cru Classé*.

Haut-Courgeaux, Château second wine of Château Launay, Bordeaux, France.

Haute Provence wine producer in Franschhoek, South Africa.

Hauterive, Château wine estate of AC Médoc, Bordeaux, France. Classified *Cru Bourgeois*.

Haut-Gueyrot, Château wine estate of AC St-Emilion, Bordeaux, France.

Haut-Justices, Château Les wine estate of AC Sauternes, Bordeaux, France.

Haut-Lavallade, Château wine estate of AC St-Emilion, Bordeaux, France.

Haut-Lignan, Château wine estate of AC Médoc, Bordeaux, France.

Haut-Logat, Château wine estate of AC Haut-Médoc, Bordeaux, France. Classified *Cru Bourgeois*.

Haut-Macau, Château wine estate of AC Côtes de Bourg, Bordeaux, France.

Haut-Madrac, Château wine estate of AC Haut-Médoc, Bordeaux, France.

Haut-Maillat, Château wine estate of AC Pomerol, Bordeaux, France.

Haut-Marbuzet, Château wine estate of AC St-Estèphe, Bordeaux, France. Classified *Cru Grand Bourgeois Exceptionnel*.

Haut-Mazeris, Château wine estate of AC Canon-Fronsac, Bordeaux, France.

Haut-Médoc extensive AC of southern Médoc, Bordeaux, France, within which commune ACs of Listrac, Margaux, Moulis, Pauillac, St Estèphe and St Julien all lie.

Haut Montravel medium-sweet white wine of Dordogne region, SW France.

Haut-Peyraguey, Château wine estate of AC Sauternes, Bordeaux, France. Classified *1er Cru Classé*.

Haut-Peyraguey, Clos wine estate of AC Sauternes, Bordeaux, France. Classified *1er Cru Classé*.

Haut Poitou AC north of Poitiers, Loire Valley, France. Quality wines labelled by grape variety (among first thus described in France) including Cabernet and Gamay reds, Chardonnay and Sauvignon whites.

Haut-Pontet, Château wine estate of AC St-Emilion, Bordeaux, France. Classified *Grand Cru*.

Haut-Prieuré wine brand of Château Prieuré-Lichine, Bordeaux, France.

Haut-Quercus wine brand of Union des Producteurs de St-Emilion, Bordeaux, France.

Haut-Sarpe, Château wine estate of AC St-Emilion, Bordeaux, France. Classified *Grand Cru Classé*.

Hauts-Conseillants, Château Les wine estate of AC Lalande-de-Pomerol, Bordeaux, France.

Hauts-de-Pontets second wine of Château Pontet-Canet, Bordeaux, France.

Haut-Ségottes, Château wine estate of AC St-Emilion, Bordeaux, France. Classified *Grand Cru*.

Haut-Tayac, Château wine estate of AC Margaux, Médoc, Bordeaux, France. Classified *Cru Bourgeois*.

Haut-Tuquet, Château wine estate of AC Côtes de Castillon, Bordeaux, France.

Haut-Tuileries, Château Les wine estate of AC Lalande-de-Pomerol, Bordeaux, France.

Hautvillers abbey near Epernay, France, widely and erroneously described as birthplace of champagne. Dom Pérignon, cellarman at Hautvillers, did establish important wine-blending principles there in 17th century. Site of abbey and ruins are now owned by Moët & Chandon.

Haux, Château de wine estate of AC Premières Côtes de Bordeaux, France.

Havana Club rum brand of Cuba Rum Corporation, Havana. Rums include Silver Dry, 3 and 5 year old and 7-year-old Anejo Reserva. The business is a venture between the

Cuban state and French worldwide drinks company Pernod-Ricard, reviving a brand that had been all-but extinguished by the Cuban revolution of 1959. In 1997, the Bacardi company bought the Havana Club trademark from its pre-Revolution owner, the Arechabala family. But the validity of the mark remained in question, since the family had allowed it to lapse in its most important location, the USA, in 1973 by failing to re-register it. But American law does not recognise trademarks nationalised by the Cuban government (which registered Havana Club for itself in 1966). Meanwhile, Bacardi has been selling its own brand of Havana Club in the United States.

Havana Cocktail. Over ice shake 2 parts apricot brandy, 1 dry gin, 1 Swedish Punsch, 1 dash lemon juice. Strain.

Havana Ron Cocktail. Over ice shake 1 part rum, 1 pineapple juice, 1 dash lemon juice. Strain.

Hawaiian Cocktail. Over ice shake 2 parts dry gin, 1 curaçao, 1 orange juice. Strain.

Hawkes Bay major wine region of North Island, New Zealand.

Haye, Château La wine estate of AC St-Estèphe, Médoc, Bordeaux, France. Classified *Cru Bourgeois Supérieur*.

HB see Hofbräuhaus.

Head Cracker 'Very stRong pale Norfolk ale' (7% alc) by Woodforde's brewery, Woodbastwick, Norfolk, England.   *see label opposite* ➤

heads in distilling, the first spirit of the distillation.

Healdsburg winemaking centre of Sonoma County, California, USA.

Heaumes, Château Les wine estate of AC Côtes de Bourg, Bordeaux, France.

Heather Ale brewery at Strathaven, Lanarkshire, Scotland.

Heather Cream liqueur brand of Inver House Distillers, Lanarkshire, Scotland.

Heatherdale blended scotch whisky made for Co-operative Wholesale Society, Manchester, England, by Invergordon Distillers, Scotland.

Heavenly Cocktail. Over ice stir 3 parts brandy, 1 cherry brandy, 1 plum brandy.

heavy in winetasting, a wine high in alcohol and extract.

hecho 'made' in Spanish; as, *hecho en Mexico* on a label indicates native-produced tequila. Past participle of *hacer* (to make).

Heck's renowned farmhouse cider and perry producer, Street, Somerset, England.

hectolitre a hundred litres. Common measure of wine quantities, France.

Hedge Monkey bitter ale (4.6% alc) by Glastonbury Ales, Somerton,

England. Name, according to brewer Greig Nicholls, is Somerset patois for 'the kind of traveller who descends on Glastonbury in the summer, sleeps in fields or people's gardens and finally departs, leaving the place looking like a toxic dump.'

Heemskerk wine producer at Pipers Brook, Tasmania, Australia. Est 1975 and named after flagship of Abel Tasman, discoverer of Tasmania, 1642.

Heerkretz vineyards at Neu-Bamberg and Siefersheim in Rheinhessen region, Germany.

Hefeabstich wine aged on its lees until bottling. Austria.

Hefeweizen style of sediment-bearing wheat beer. Originally German but now also made in France, the Low Countries and USA.

Heger leading estate for red wines from Spätburgunder grapes, Ihringen, Baden, Germany.

Heggies wine estate owned by Hill Smith in Adelaide Hills, South Australia. Noted Riesling wines.

Heide vineyard at Weyher in der Pfalz in Rheinpfalz region, Germany.

Heidegarten vineyard at Edenkoben in Rheinpfalz region, Germany.

Heidsieck, Charles *Grande Marque* champagne house est 1851 by Charles-Camille Heidsieck, a descendant of the founder of original Heidsieck house (est 1785) and who achieved notoriety as 'Champagne Charlie' in USA.

Heidsieck & Co Monopole *Grande Marque* champagne house derived from original house est by Florens-Louis Heidsieck 1785. Reims, France.

Heil vineyards at Frettenheim and Wallertheim in Rheinhessen region, Germany.

Heileman brewing company based at La Crosse, Wisconsin, USA.

Heilgarten vineyard at Manubach in Mittelrhein region, Germany.

Heilgraben vineyard at Dieblich in Mosel-Saar-Ruwer region, Germany.

Heiligborn vineyard at Albisheim in Rheinpfalz region, Germany.

Heiligenbaum vineyard at Nierstein in Rehinhessen region, Germany.

Heiligenberg vineyards at Eltville in Rheingau region, Heidelberg, Krautheim and Krautheim (Klepsau) in Baden region, Illingen and Sachsenheim in Württemberg region, Maikammer in Rheinpfalz region and Weiler bei Monzingen in Nahe region, Germany.

Heiligenborn vineyards at Albisheim in Rheinpfalz region and Serrig in Mosel-Saar-Ruwer region, Germany.

Heiligenhäuschen vineyards at Jugenheim in Rheinpfalz region, Morscheid, Riveris and Waldrach in Mosel-Saar-Ruwer region and Stetten in Rheinpfalz region, Germany.

Heiligenhaus vineyard at Saulheim in Rheinhessen region, Germany.

Heiligenkirche vineyard at Bockenheim an der Weinstrasse in Rheinpfalz region, Germany.

Heiligenpfad vineyard at Wendelsheim in Rheinhessen region, Germany.

Heiligenstein vineyards at Baden-Baden and Mühlhausen in Baden region, Germany.

Heiligenstock collective vineyard (*Grosslage*) at Kiedrich in Rheingau region, Germany.

Heiligenthal collective vineyard (*Grosslage*) at Grossostheim in Franken region, Germany.

Heiliger Blutberg vineyard at Alzey in Rheinhessen region, Germany.

Heiliger Dreikönigwein *Eiswein* from grapes picked on January 6th, traditionally the day the Three Kings (*Dreikönigen*) visited the infant Jesus. Germany.

Heilige Tanne vineyard at Brensbach in Hessische Bergstrasse region, Germany.

Heilighäuschen vineyard at Ingelheim in Rheinhessen region, Germany.

Heiligkreuz vineyard at Bechtheim in Rheinhessen region, Germany.

Heilig Kreuz vineyards at Edenkoben in Rheinpfalz region and Künzelsau in Württemberg region, Germany.

Heimberg vineyard at Schlossböckelheim in Nahe region, Germany.

Heineken brewery est 1873, lager brand and international exporter based in Amsterdam, Netherlands. **Heineken Lager Beer** is produced and marketed worldwide. The brand was immortalised in an advertising campaign on the theme that 'Heineken refreshes the parts other beers cannot reach.' See box over.

Heinrich, Gernot wine producer in Neusiedlersee, Burgenland, Austria.

Heinrich, Johann wine producer in Mittelburgenland, Austria.

Heisser Stein vineyard at Buchbrunn in Franken region, Germany.

Heisterberg vineyard at Königswinter in Mittelrhein region, Germany.

Heitersbrünnchen vineyard at Bodenheim in Rheinhessen region, Germany.

Heitz Wine Cellars wine producer in Napa Valley, California, USA. Noted wines include Bella Oaks and Martha's Vineyard Cabernet Sauvignon.

Helbon lost sweet white wine of the ancient world, made at Damascus, Syria.

Held vineyards at Bissersheim in Rheinpfalz region and Kenn, Köwerich, Langsur and Pölich in Mosel-Saar-Ruwer region, Germany.

Helenboch brewery at Helen, Georgia, USA.

Helenenkloster vineyard at Mülheim in Mosel-Saar-Ruwer region, Germany.

Helen Twelvetrees Cocktail. In an ice-filled tall glass stir 1 part Southern Comfort, 2 dashes blackberry concentrate. Top with chilled dry ginger ale.

Heineken

a valued inheritance

The worldwide success of Heineken lager has been the achievement of one remarkable man. Alfred (Freddy) Henry Heineken was the grandson of Gerard Adriaan Heineken, who bought an existing Amsterdam brewery, said to have been founded with the name 'Haystack' in 1592, and gave it his family's name, in 1864. Gerard pioneered the pilsner-type lager that remains the brewery's style today. The brand prospered, penetrating export markets including the United States – where it was the first foreign beer to be allowed an import licence at the end of Prohibition in 1933. By this time, Freddy's father, Henry Pierre, was at the helm, but he sold the family's share in the business in 1942.

Freddy, born in 1923, was already working for the Heineken company, and wrote his father a remarkably percipient letter concerning the sale of the stock he had hoped to inherit: 'I have my mind set on restoring the majority of Heineken shares into the hands of the family . . . It is not my plan to become very rich . . . but it is a matter of pride that any children I might have can inherit a stake in Heineken, like I did from my father and you inherited from your father.'

True to his word, Freddy succeeded in buying back a controlling interest in the company in 1954 in a stock market coup using private loans. Within ten years he was financial director and also took charge of marketing and advertising, later culminating in the hugely successful campaign centred on the slogan 'Heineken refreshes the parts other beers cannot reach,' originally voiced for television by Danish entertainer Victor Borge.

Among other promotional schemes attempted by Freddy was the 'World Bottle' in the 1970s. Proposed for Heineken bottled beers worldwide, it was square and intended for re-use as a building brick in developing countries. Sadly for this enterprising piece of environmental friendliness, the idea failed to win support.

In 1979 Freddy was appointed chairman of Heineken and within ten years it was the third largest brewing company in the world. Freddy was said to have been a dollar billionaire and was certainly the richest man in the Netherlands – a distinction for which he paid a high price when he was kidnapped by a gang from his company Amsterdam headquarters and held for 21 days. A ransom said to be equivalent to £9 million was paid for his release. Two men were later convicted for the crime, but only a fraction of the ransom money was recovered.

Freddy subsequently became a relative recluse, though much featured in the media for his reportedly tyrannical and eccentric management style. He died in 2002, leaving his shareholding to his only child, a daughter named Charlene. ❦

Hell brewery and lager brand (4.9% alc) at Banská Stiavnica, Slovakia. Brewery est 1473 in what was then an important gold-mining centre, is said to be one of the oldest in Central Europe and claims the name Hell 'may derive from the miner's traditional greeting.'

hell pale. German beer style.

Hell Cocktail. Over ice shake 1 part cognac, 1 crème de menthe. Strain into glass and add a pinch of cayenne pepper.

Hellenpfad vineyard in Braunweiler in Nahe region, Germany.

Heller brewery in Bamberg, Franconia, Germany.

Helles pale beer. German.

hempje licht op traditional 'ship's liqueur' once dispensed by Dutch naval surgeons. Netherlands. Name means 'lift up your shirt'.

Hemsberg vineyards at Bensheim, Bensheim (Zell) and Bensheim (Gronau) in Hessische Bergstrasse region, Germany.

Hendelberg vineyards at Eltville and Oestrich-Winkel in Rheingau region, Germany.

Hengl-Haselbrunner wine producer in Wien (Vienna), Austria.

Hengstberg vineyard at Desloch in Nahe region, Germany.

Henkenberg vineyard at Vogtsburg im Kaiserstuhl in Baden region, Germany.

Henkes major distiller of *genever* and other spirits, Schiedam, Netherlands.

Henkes liqueur brand of Canadian Schenley Distilleries, Canada.

Hennekens Dutch bitters producer, Beek, Netherlands.

Hennessy largest cognac house, est 1765 by Richard Hennessy (French soldier of Irish-immigrant ancestry), Cognac, France. Brands include Privilege VSOP, XO (a style devised by Hennessy) and Paradis, blended from cognacs up to 100 years old.

Henninger beer brand of Henninger Brau brewery est 1869, Frankfurt, Germany. Beers include Kaiser Pilsner and Premier Pilsner.

Henriot *Grande Marque* champagne house est 1808, Reims, France.

Henriques & Henriques family wine producer est 1850 island of Madeira, Portugal.

Henry McKenna bourbon whiskey brand formerly of Seagram, USA.

Henry of Pelham wine producer at St Catharines, Ontario, Canada. Named after Henry Smith, whose father served on the Loyalist side against the rebels in the American Revolutionary war in 1776 and fled to Canada.

Henry's farmhouse cider and 'scrumpy' producer est 1912 at Tanpits cider farm, Bathpool, Taunton, Somerset, England.

Henry's Original IPA pale ale by Wadworth brewery, Devizes, Wiltshire, England. Commemorates Henry Wadworth, who founded the brewery in 1875 and remained in charge until he died in a riding accident in 1929.

Henschke great wine estate est 1868 Keyneton, Adelaide Hills, South Australia. Classic wines include Cyril Henschke Cabernet Sauvignon, Hill of Grace Shiraz, Mount Edelstone Shiraz and Johann's Garden.

Hen's Tooth strong ale (6.5% alc) by Morland Brewery, Abingdon, England.

Henstridge brewery at Henstridge, Somerset, England.

Heppenstein vineyard at Ockfen in Mosel-Saar-Ruwer region, Germany.

Herbstthal vineyard at Karlstadt in Franken region, Germany.

Herforder brewery at Herford, Rhineland, Germany.

Herist, Johann wine producer in Südburgenland, Austria.

Heritage Selection brand of Pernod-Ricard.

Hermannsberg vineyard at Niederhausen an der Nahe in Nahe region, Germany.

Hermann's Dark ale by Vancouver Island brewery, Canada.

Hermannshöhle vineyard at Niederhausen an der Nahe in Nahe region, Germany.

Hermitage AC greatest red wine of northern Rhône Valley, France. From Syrah grapes grown on slopes above Tain l'Hermitage and made for long ageing. Some white wine from Marsanne and Rousanne grapes. Leading producer is J L Chave and others include Max Chapoutier, Jean-Louis Grippat, Paul Jaboulet Ainé.

Hermitage regional name for Cinsaut grape variety in South Africa.

Hermitage regional name for Syrah grape variety in Australia.

Hermitage La Chapelle brand of AC Hermitage by Paul Jaboulet Ainé, Tain l'Hermitage, France.

Hernder Estates wine producer at St Catharines, Ontario, Canada.

Heroldrebe red grape variety principally of Württemberg region, Germany.

Heroldsberg vineyard at Hammelburg in Franken region, Germany.

Herrenberg the name of 41 individual vineyards in Germany. Region by region, as follows: in Ahr at Rech; in Baden at Boxberg, Heidelberg, Kenzingen, Lauda-Königshofen, Leimen; in Franken at Oberschwarzach, Oberschwarzach (Düttingsfeld), Oberschwarzach (Mutzenroth), Ochsenfurt; in Mosel-Saar-Ruwer at Alf, Briedern, Cochen, Enkirch, Erden, Kasel, Kesten, Konz (Falkenstein), Konz (Filzen), Konz (Niedermennig), Kröv (Kövenig), Longuich, Schweich, Mertesdorf, Mertesdorf (Maximin Grünhaus), Ockfen, Schoden, Serrig, Trier, Valwig; in Nahe at Boos, Staudernheim, Rehborn; in Rheingau at Flörsheim, Hochheim; in Rheinhessen at Dienheim, Oppenheim; in Rheinpfalz at Bad Dürkheim, Kleinkarlbach, Nussdorf, Minfeld.

Herrenberg *Grosslagen* (collective vineyards) incorporating vineyards of Dörscheid and Kaub in Mittelrhein region and Castell in Franken region, Germany.

Herrenberger vineyards at Ayl and Wawern in Mosel-Saar-Ruwer region, Germany.

Herrenbuck vineyard at Eichsteffen in Baden region, Germany.

Herrenbuckel vineyard at Flemlingen in Rheinpfalz region, Germany.

Herrengarten vineyards at Dienheim and Oppenheim in Rheinhessen region, Germany.

Herrenhauser brewery in Hanover, Germany. Pilsner beers.

Herrenletten vineyard at Neustadt an der Weinstrasse in Rheinpfalz region, Germany.

Herrenmorgen vineyard at Bad Dürkheim in Rheinpfalz region, Germany.

Herrenpfad vineyards at Heuchelheim-Klingen and Göcklingen in Rheinpfalz region, Germany.

Herrenstück vineyard at Vogtsburg im Kaiserstuhl in Baden region, Germany.

Herrentisch vineyard at Lahr in Baden region, Germany.

Herrenwingert vineyard at Steinfeld in Rheinpfalz region, Germany.

Herrenzehntel vineyard at Weiler bei Monzingen in Nahe region, Germany.

Herrgards caraway- and whisky-flavoured *aquavit* matured in sherry casks for additional flavour. Sweden.

Herrgottsacker vineyards at Deidesheim, Dirmstein and Kleinkarlbach in Rheinpfalz region, Germany.

Herrgottsblick vineyard at Zellertal in Rheinpfalz region, Germany.

Herrgottshaus vineyard at Klein-Winternheim in Rheinhessen region, Germany.

Herrgottspfad vineyard at Gau-Odernheim in Rheinhessen region, Germany.

Herrgottsrock vineyard at Pellingen in Mosel-Saar-Ruwer region, Germany.

Herrgottsweg vineyard at Albertshofen in Franken region, Germany.

Herrlesberg vineyard at Neckarwestheim in Württemberg region, Germany.

Herrlich *Grosslage* (collective vineyard) incorporating vineyards in Rheinpfalz region, Germany at, respectively: Eschbach, Göcklingen, Herxheim bei Landau, Herxheimweyher, Ilbesheim, Impflingen, Insheim, Landau in der Pfalz (Mörzheim), Landau in der Pfalz (Wollmersheim), Leinsweiler, Rohrbach.

Herrnberg vineyards at Gross-Unstadt in Hessische Bergstrasse region, Flörsheim, Hochheim, Wiesbaden (Frauenstein) and Wiesbaden (Scheirstein) in Rheingau region and Gau-Bischofsheim in Rheinhessen region, Germany.

Herrnwingert vineyard at Bensheim in Hessische Bergstrasse region, Germany.

Herrschaftsberg vineyard at Ippesheim in Franken region, Germany.

Herrschaftsgarten vineyard at Hergenfeld in Nahe region, Germany.

Herte Kamp *jenever* by Bruggeman distillery, Ghent, Belgium.

Herttua lager brand of Olvi brewery, Finland.

Herzchen vineyard at Briedel in Mosel-Saar-Ruwer region, Germany.

Herzfeld vineyard at Bad Dürkheim in Rheinpfalz region, Germany.

Herzlay vineyard at Bausendorf in Mosel-Saar-Ruwer region, Germany.

Herzog vineyard at Neustadt an der Weinstrasse in Rheinpfalz region, Germany.

Herzogenberg vineyards at Felbach, Stuttgart (Bad Cannstatt) and Stuttgart (Untertürkheim) in Württemberg region, Germany.

Herzogsberg vineyards at Binau and Mosbach in Baden region, Germany.

Hesitation Cocktail. Over ice shake 3 parts Swedish Punsch, 1 rye whisky, 1 dash lemon juice. Strain.

Hesket Newmarket brewery at Hesket Newmarket, Cumbria, England.

Hessem vineyard at St Goarshausen in Mittelrhein region, Germany.

Hessiche Bergstrasse wine region of Germany lying between Darmstadt and Heidelberg. Two *Bereichen*: Starkenberg, Umstadt.

Hessweg vineyard at Odernheim am Glan in Nahe region, Germany.

Het Anker brewery at Mechelen, Belgium.

Heuchelberg *Grosslage* (collective vineyard) incorporating vineyards in Württemberg region, Germany at, respectively: Brackenheim, Brackenheim (Botenheim), Brackenheim (Dürrenzimmern), Brackenheim (Haberschlacht), Brackenheim (Hausen), Brackenheim (Meimsheim), Brackenheim (Neipperg), Brackenheim (Stockheim), Cleebronn, Eppingen, Güglingen, Güglingen (Eibensbach), Güglingen (Frauenzimmern), Heilbronn, Leingarten (Grossgartach), Leingarten (Schluchtern), Massenbachausen, Nordheim, Nordheim (Nordhausen), Pfaffenhofen, Pfaffenhofen (Weiler), Schwaigern, Schwaigern (Niederhofen), Schwaigern (Stetten), Zaberfeld, Zaberfeld (Leonbronn), Zaberfeld (Michelbach), Zaberfeld (Ochsenburg).

Heuriger new-made local wine as served by inns (**Heurigen**) of wine villages surrounding Vienna, Austria. The wine can be sold only between 11 November after the harvest until the end of the following year.

Hexelberg vineyard at Eimsheim in Rheinhessen region, Germany.

Hex vom Dasenstein vineyard at Kappelrodeck in Baden region, Germany.

Hibiscus Cocktail. Over ice shake 4 parts rum, 1 fresh lime juice, 1 dash grenadine. Strain.

Hickinbotham wine producers At Elgee Park, Melbourne and Mount Anakie, Geelong, Australia.

Hidalgo La Gitana leading producer of manzanilla and other sherries, est 1792, Sanlucar de Barrameda, Spain. The company has remained in family ownership throughout its history and is now in the control of the seventh successive generation. Brands include La Gitana manzanilla, Pastrana single-vineyard manzanilla and a number of sherries branded Napoleon in commemoration of the time when, during the occupation of the Peninsular War, the company supplied the French military.

Hiedler, Ludwig wine producer in Kamptal, Niederösterreich, Austria.

highball mixed drink of spirit and soda water or ginger ale served with ice and, optionally, with lemon peel or slice.

High Commissioner blended scotch whisky by Glen Catrine, Catrine, Ayrshire, Scotland.

High Flyer Cocktail. Over ice shake 3 parts dry gin, 1 Strega, 3 dashes Van der Hum. Strain.

High Force brewery at Barnard Castle, County Durham, England.

Highgate and Walsall brewery at Walsall, Staffordshire, England.

Highland Blend fifteen-year-old blended scotch whisky of Avery's of Bristol, England.

Highland Clan blended scotch whisky of Pernod-Ricard.

Highland Cooler Cocktail. In tall glass with ice stir 4 parts Scotch whisky, 1 lemon juice, 2 dashes Angostura bitters, 1 teaspoon sugar. Top with ginger ale.

Highland Fusilier vatted malt scotch whisky brand of Gordon & MacPhail, Elgin, Scotland. Five-, eight-, 15-, 21- and 25-year-old whiskies.

Highland Gathering blended scotch whisky brand of Lombard Scotch Whisky, Isle of Man, UK. Eight-, 12-, 15-, 18-, 21- and 25-year-old blends.

Highland Park Island malt whisky distillery est 1798, Kirkwall, Orkney, Scotland. Single malts: 12-year-old; 1967 vintage bottling.

Highland Pearl twelve-year-old blended scotch whisky by Hall & Bramley, Liverpool, England.

Highland Queen blended scotch whisky brand of Macdonald & Muir, Leith, Scotland. **Highland Queen Grand Reserve** (15-year-old),

Highland Queen Supreme (21-year-old).

Highland Stag blended scotch whisky by R N MacDonald, London, England.

Highland Woodcock blended scotch whisky of J T Davies & Sons, Croydon, Surrey, England.

High Level brown ale by Federation Brewery, Newcastle upon Tyne, England.

Highwood brewery at Barnetby, North Lincolnshire, England.

Hildegardisberg vineyard at Bermersheim vdH in Rheinhessen region, Germany.

Hildegardisbrünnchen vineyard at Bingen in Nahe region, Germany.

Hilden brewery at Lisburn, County Antrim, Northern Ireland.

Hillcrest wine producer in Umpqua Valley, Oregon, USA.

Hillebrand Estates wine producer at Niagara-on-the-lake, Ontario, Canada.

Hill's absinthe producer, Czech Republic.

Hillside Cellars wine producer at Penticton, British Columbia, Canada.

Hill Smith Estate wine producer in Adelaide Hills, South Australia. Part of Yalumba company.

Himbeergeist *eau de vie* distilled from raspberries, Germany and Switzerland.

Himmelacker vineyard at Alzey in Rheinessen region, Germany.

Himmelberg vineyards at Angelbachtal in Baden and Leinach (Oberleinach) and Leinach (Unterleinach) in Franken region, Germany.

Himmelchen vineyard at Bad Neuenahr-Ahrweiler in Ahr region, Germany.

Himmelgarten vineyard at Bad Kreuznach in Nahe region, Germany.

Himmelreich vineyards at Bretzfeld (Dimbach), Bretzfeld (Schwabbach), Bretzfeld (Siebeneich), Bretzfeld (Waldbach), Gundelsheim, Langenbrettach, Winnenden (Baach) and Winnenden (Hertmannsweiler) in Württemberg region, Graach, St Aldegund and Zeltingen-Rachtig in Mosel-Saar-Ruwer region, Herxheim am Berg in Rheinpfalz region, Sand am Main in Franken region, and Ubstadt-Weiher (Stettfeld) and Ubstadt-Weiher (Zeutern) in Baden region, Germany.

Himmelsbühl vineyard at Sand am Main in Franken region, Germany.

Himmelthal vineyard at Guntersblum in Rheinhessen region, Germany.

Hine distinguished cognac house est 1817 by Thomas Hine (1775–1822) of Dorset, England who was stranded on a visit to the region by the tumult of the French Revolution, in Jarnac, France, around 1790. Brands include Signature, Rare & Delicate, Antique and vintage 'landed' cognacs aged and bottled in England by the Bristol Brandy Company. The stag trademark of the company is a hind, chosen for its homonymity with the family name. Hine was sold by Hennessy to the Angostura company in 2003. *see label opposite* ➤

Hinkelstein vineyard at Bad Kreuznach in Nahe region, Germany.

Hintere Klinge vineyard at Weinstadt in Württemberg region, Germany.

Hinterer Berg vineyard at Fellbach in Württemberg region, Germany.

Hinterhalde vineyard at Ammerbuch in Württemberg region, Germany.

Hinterkirch vineyard at Rüdesheim in Rheingau region, Germany.

Hipperich vineyard at Guldental in Nahe region, Germany.

Hipping vineyard at Nierstein in Rheinhessen region, Germany.

hippocras early English spiced-wine drink. Named may derive from Greek physician Hippocrates' custom of making flavoured wines.

Hippocrene, the blushful Keats's immortal metaphor for the red wine of Provence in *Ode to a Nightingale* (1819). From Pegasus' fountain – *hippos* (horse) and *krene* (spring) – on Mt Helicon in ancient Greece, where the Muses sought inspiration.

Hiram Walker major Canadian distiller, est 1858.

Hirondelle lost international wine brand, of protean provenance, of former UK wine merchants Hedges & Butler.

Hirsch brewery at Ottobeuren in Baden-Württemberg region, Germany.

Hirsch, Josef wine producer in Kamptal, Niederösterreich, Austria.

Hirschberg vineyard at Werbach in Baden region, Germany.

Hirschlay vineyard at Longuich in Mosel-Saar-Ruwer region, Germany.

Hirschmugl, Franz wine producer in Südsteiermark, Austria.

Hintengarten vineyard at Oberillig in Mosel-Saar-Ruwer region, Germany.

Hiram Walker major Canadian distilling company, est 1858.

Hirtenhain vineyard at Bad Kreuznach in Nahe region, Germany.

Hirtzberger, Franz wine producer in Wachau, Niederösterreich, Austria.

His Eminence's Choice tawny port by Delaforce, Vila Nova de Gaia, Portugal.

His Majesty's Choice twenty-year old tawny port by Smith Woodhouse, Vila Nova de Gaia, Portugal.

Hitzlay vineyard at Kasel in Mosel-Saar-Ruwer region, Germany.

Hobgoblin ale (5.5% alc) by Wychwood brewery, Witney, Oxfordshire, England.

Hobson's brewery at Cleobury Mortimer, Kidderminster, Worcestershire, England.

Hoch vineyard at Bodenheim in Rheinhessen region, Germany.

Hochar, Gaston founder in 1930 of Château Musar, Bekaa Valley, Lebanon, now run by his son, Serge.

Hochbenn vineyard at Bad Dürkheim in Rheinpfalz region, Germany.

Hochberg vineyards at Erlenbach am Main and Klingenberg am Main in Franken region, Sasbach in Baden region and Worms (Herrnsheim) and Worms (Pfeddersheim) in Rheinhessen region, Germany.

Hochgericht vineyards at Altdorf and Obrigheim in Rheinpfalz region, Germany.

Hochheim wine village of Rheingau region, Germany. *Grosslage*: Daubhaus.

Hochlay vineyard at Cochem in Mosel-Saar-Ruwer region, Germany.

Hochmess *Grosslage* (collective vineyard) incorporating vineyards at Bad Dürkheim and Ungstein in Rheinpfalz region, Germany.

Höchstes Kreuz vineyard at Feilingbert in Nahe region, Germany.

Hochwart vineyard at Reichenau in Baden region, Germany.

hock English term for wine of the Rhine Valley, Germany. Contraction of 'hockamore' 17th-century rendering of Hochheimer, the wine of the village of Hochheim in Rheingau region, Germany.

Hock mild ale by Fuller's brewery, London, England.

Hockberg liqueur brand of Halewood International, Huyton, Merseyside, England.

Hockenmühle vineyard at Ockenheim in Rheinhessen region, Germany.

Hoegaarden 'white beer' (5.0% alc and from wheat as well as barley) brand of De Kluis brewery,

Hoegaarden, Brabant, Belgium. Beer was first brewed at Hoegaarden in 1445 but production lapsed until revival in 1966. Owned by Interbrew.

Hoe Langer Hoe Liever traditional 'ship's liqueur' once dispensed by Dutch naval surgeons. Netherlands. Name means 'the more the better'.

Hoeppeslei vineyard at Serrig in Mosel-Saar-Ruwer region, Germany.

Hofberg vineyards at Bernkastel-Kues and Konz in Mosel-Saar-Ruwer region and Möckmühl, Neudenau and Widdern in Württemberg region, Germany.

Hofberger vineyards at Neumagen-Dhron and Piesport in Mosel-Saar-Ruwer region, Germany.

Hofbräuhaus brewery and beer hall in Munich, Bavaria, Germany. Est 1589 as the brewery of the Bavarian royal household and now in state ownership. **Hofbräu** ('Court brew') beer brands labelled HB include Delicator, Edel Weizen, Export, Maibock.

Hofgarten vineyard at Bad Kreuznach in Nahe region, Germany.

Hofgut vineyard at Bretzenheim in Nahe region, Germany.

Höfinger, Egmont wine producer in Kamptal, Niederösterreich, Austria.

Höfkellerei Stiftung Fürst Liechtenstein wine producer in Weinviertel, Niederösterreich, Austria.

Hofmark brewery at Cham, Bavaria, Germany.

Hofmeister vineyard at Hochheim in Rheingau region, Germany.

Hofrat *Grosslage* incorporating vineyards at Albertshofen, Buchbrunn, Kitzingen, Kitzingen (Eherider Mühle), Mainstockheim, Markbreit, Marksteft, Segnitz and Sulzfeld in Franken region, Germany.

Hofstatter leading wine producer of Alto Adige region of northern Italy.

Hofsteige vineyards at Metzingen and Metzingen (Neuhausen) in Württemberg region, Germany.

Hofstück vineyard at Mainstockheim in Franken region, Germany.

Hofstück *Grosslage* incorporating vineyards at Deidesheim, Ellerstadt, Friedelsheim, Gönnheim, Hochdorf-Assenheim, Mechenheim, Niederkirchen, Rödersheim-Gronau and Ruppertsberg in Rheinpfalz region, Germany.

Hog & Stump brewery at Kingston upon Thames, Surrey, England.

Hogarth dry gin brand of Halewood International, Huyton, Merseyside, England.

Hogs Back brewery at Tongham, Farnham, Surrey, England.

hogshead beer barrel of 243 litres (54 imperial gallons). For wine, size is more variable around 250 litres.

Hogshead pale ale by Uley Brewery, Uley, Gloucestershire, England.

Hogshead small brewery at Sacramento, California, USA.

Hog's Head Dark ale by Plains Brewery, Christchurch, New Zealand.

Hohberg vineyards at Hassmersheim in Baden region and Lörzweiler and Weinolsheim in Rheinhessen region, Germany.

Höhe vineyard at Landau in der Pfalz in Rheinpfalz region, Germany.

Hoheberg vineyard at Ruppertsberg in Rheinpfalz region, Germany.

Höhe Domkirche important ecclesiastical wine estate of Mosel-Saar-Ruwer region, Germany.

Hohenberg vineyards at Pfaffenhofen, Pfaffenhofen (Weiler), Zaberfeld and Zaberfeld (Michelbach) in Württemberg region, Germany.

Hohenberg *Grosslage* incorporating vineyards in Baden region, Germany at, respectively: Eisingen, Kämpfelbach (Bilfingen), Kämpfelbach (Ersingen), Karlsruhe (Durlach), Karlsruhe (Grötzingen), Karlsruhe (Hohenwettersbach), Keltern (Dietlingen), Keltern (Ellmendingen), Olbronn-Dürrn, Pfinstal (Berghausen), Pfinztal (Söllingen), Pfinstal (Wöschbach), Walzbachtal (Jöhlingen), Wingarten.

Hohenbühl vineyard at Seinsheim in Franken region, Germany.

Hohenlandsberg vineyards at Weigenheim and Weigenheim (Reusch) in Franken region, Germany.

Hohenmorgen vineyard at Deidesheim in Rheinpfalz region, Germany.

Hohenneuffen *Grosslage* incorporating vineyards at Beuren, Frickenhausen, Frickenhausen (Linsenhofen), Kohlberg, Metzingen, Metzingen (Neuhausen), Neuffen, Neuffen (Kappishäusern) and Weilheim in Württemberg region, Germany.

Hohenrain vineyards at Eltville in Rheingau region and Knöringen in Rheinhessen region, Germany.

Hoher Berg vineyards at Ingelfingen, Ingelfingen (Criesbach), Künzelsau and Niedernhall in Württemberg region, Germany.

Hoher Hergott vineyard at Külsheim in Baden region, Germany.

Höhlchen vineyards at Dienheim in Rheinhessen region and Bad Münster am Stain-Ebernburg and Spabrücken in Nahe region, Germany.

Hohnart vineyard at Castell in Franken region, Germany.

Hokkaido Cocktail. Over ice stir 3 parts dry gin, 2 sake, 1 Cointreau. Strain.

holandas first-distillation grape spirit, originally so named because it was destined for Netherlands. Spain.

Holden's brewery at Woodsetton, Dudley, West Midlands, England. Ales include Black Country Bitter.

Hole in One Cocktail. Over ice shake 2 parts scotch whisky, 1 dry vermouth, 2 dashes lemon juice, dash orange bitters.

Höll brewery at Traunstein, Bavaria, Germany. Wheat beers.

Höll vineyards at Ediger-Eller in Mosel-Saar-Ruwer region and Markt Eisenheim in Franken region, Germany.

Holland House Cocktail. Over ice shake four parts dry gin, 2 dry vermouth, 1 lemon juice, 4 dashes maraschino, 1 slice pineapple. Strain.

Hollandia 11 important malt distillery supplying *genever* industry, Schiedam, Netherlands. Owned by Gist-Brocades.

Hollands alternative name for *genever*. Netherlands.

Höllberg vineyards at Bensheim in Hessische Bergstrasse region, Buggingen and Müllheim in Baden region and Siefersheim in Rheinhessen region, Germany.

Hölle the name of 18 individual vineyards in Germany. Region by region, as follows: in Mittelrhein at Hammerstein; in Mosel-Saar-Ruwer at Alf, Wiltingen; in Nahe at Alsenz, Eckenroth, Guldental, Rümmelsheim; in Rheingau at Geisenheim, Hochheim, Wiesbaden; in Rheinhessen at Alzey, Nierstein, Pfaffen-Schwabenheim, Sprendlingen, Wöllstein, Wonsheim; in Rheinpfalz at Geisweiler.

Höllenberg vineyards at Heidesheim in Rheinhessen region, Nussbaum in Nahe region and Rüdesheim (Assmannshausen) and Rüdesheim (Aulhausen) in Rheingau region, Germany.

Höllenbrand vineyards at Bad Kreuznach (Bosenheim) and Bad Kreuznach (Planig) in Nahe region and Gundersheim in Rheinhessen region, Germany.

Höllenpfad vineyards at Burgsponheim, Roxheim and Wallhausen in Nahe region, Germany.

Höllenpfad *Grosslage* incorporating vineyards at Battenberg, Grünstadt, Grünstadt (Asselheim), Grünstadt

(Sausenheim), Kleinkarlbach, Mertesheim and Neuleiningen in Rheinpfalz region, Germany.

Höllenweg vineyard at Ingelheim in Rheinhessen region, Germany.

Höllhagen vineyard at Ehrenkirchen in Baden region, Germany.

hollow in winetasting, a lack of 'middle' flavour.

Hollywood Boulevard Cocktail. Over ice shake 1 part vodka, 2 orange juice. Strain into an ice-filled wine glass, top with chilled dry white wine and add a mint sprig.

Holsten brewery and major beer exporter in Hamburg, Germany. Brands include **Holsten-Edel** and famed strong (5.8% alc), low-carbohydrate **Holsten Diät Pils**.

Holt brewery of Joseph Holt, Cheetham, Greater Manchester, England.

Holzenberg vineyards at Winnenden and Winnenden (Breuningsweiler) in Württemberg region, Germany.

Holzer wine producer in Donauland, Niederösterreich, Austria.

Homberg vineyards at Albig and Bechtolsheim in Rheinhessen region and Wiesbaden in Rheingau region, Germany.

Homburg vineyard at Gössenheim in Franken region, Germany.

Home Brewery brewery est 1880 at Daybrook, Nottingham, England. Closed 1996 following takeover by Scottish & Newcastle breweries. **Home Beers** brands now produced in Mansfield, Yorkshire.

Homestead whisky brand of Thomas Adams Distillers, Canada.

Homestead

Homestead Cocktail. Over ice shake 2 parts dry gin, 1 sweet vermouth, 1 slice orange. Strain.

hommelbier style of strongly hoppy beer. Belgium.

Honey Dew golden ale (4.3% alc) by Fuller's brewery, Chiswick, London. Honey is added 'for an aromatic smoothness'.

honeyed in winetasting, a smell indicating a mature botrytis-affected sweet wine.

Honey Mead Ale seasonal beer by Ridley's brewery, Chelmsford, Essex, England.

Honeymoon Cocktail. Over ice shake 2 parts apple brandy, 2 Bénédictine, 1 lemon juice, 3 dashes curaçao. Strain.

Honigberg the name of 12 individual vineyards in Germany. Region by region, as follows: in Mosel-Saar-Ruwer at Maring-Noviand; in Nahe at Bad Kreuznach, Dorsheim, Guldental; in Rheingau at Eltville; in Rheinhessen at Biebelsheim, Bingen, Bubenheim, Ludwigshöhe, Nieder-Hilbersheim, Sprendlingen, Sulzheim.

Honigberg *Grosslage* incorporating vineyards at Geisenheim, Oestrich-Winkel (Mittelheim) and Oestrich-Winkel (Winkel) in Rheingau region and Dettelbach, Dettelbach (Bibergau), Dettelbach (Brück) and Dettelbach (Schnepfenbach) in Franken region, Germany.

Honigsack vineyards at Grünstadt and Herxheim am Berg in Rheinpfalz region, Germany.

Honigsäckel collective vineyard (*Grosslage*) at Bad Dürkheim in Rheinpfalz region, Germany.

Honkajoki *sahti* (rye beer) brand, northern Finland.

Honker's Ale beer by Goose Island Brewery, Chicago, USA.

Honolulu Brewing Co producer in Hawaii, USA, of Ko'olau Lager and other beers.

Honolulu Cocktail. Over ice shake 1 part Bénédictine, 1 dry gin, 1 maraschino. Strain. Alternatively, over ice shake 1 part dry gin, 1 dash Angostura bitters, 1 dash lemon juice, 1 dash orange juice, 1 dash pineapple juice. Strain.

hooch colloquial American English for illicitly manufactured or obtained alcohol. Shortened from Alaskan Indian hoochinoo tribe known for making their own distilled liquor.

Hood River Brewing Co producer at Hood River, Oregon, USA, of Full Sail Ale brands.

Hook Norton brewery at Banbury, Oxfordshire, England. Brands include Jack Pot, Jubilee, Old Hookey.

Hooper, Richard port shipper late of Vila Nova de Gaia, Portugal. Vintages: 1980, 82, 83, 84, 85, 87.

Hooper's Ginger Brew 'beer strong in alcohol' (4.7%) by Bass Breweries, UK.

Hooper's Hooch 'alcoholic lemon' drink (4.7% alc) by Bass Breweries, UK. An early alcopop brand, extinguished 2002.

Hoopla Cocktail. Over ice shake 1 part brandy, 1 Cointreau, 1 lemon juice, 1 Lillet. Strain.

Hoots Mon Cocktail. Over ice stir 2 parts Scotch whisky, 1 Lillet, 1 sweet vermouth. Strain.

hop vine (*humulus lupulus*) cultivated for its flowers for use (most commonly in a processed form) in brewing to add bitterness, flavour and aroma to beer. Tannin present in hops acts as a natural preservative. Major varieties include Brewer's Gold, Cascade, Fuggles, Goldings, Hallertau, Progress, Saaz.

Hop & Glory bitter ale (5.0% alc) by Ash Vine Brewery, Frome, Somerset, England.

Hop Back brewery at Downton, Salisbury, Wiltshire, England. Ale brands include Crop Circle, GFB, Summer Lightning, Thunder Storm. A hop back is a kind of filter used to extract hop remains from the brew.

Hop Cane Toad Cocktail. Over ice shake 1 part rum, 1 apricot brandy, 2 dashes fresh lime juice. Strain.

Hop Leaf brewery at Reading, Berkshire, England.

Höpler wine producer in Neusiedlersee, Burgenland, Austria.

Hoppe distillery for *genever* and other spirits, Schiedam, Netherlands.

Hopping Mad bottle-conditioned beer (4.7% alc) byWood Brwery, Winstanstow, Shropshire, England.

Hopps Brau brewery in La Salle, Montreal, Canada.

Hops pub-brewery in Clearwater, Florida, USA. Maker of Hammerhead Red Ale.

Hopscotch Cocktail. Over ice shake 2 parts scotch whisky, 1 sweet vermouth, sprinkling of sugar, 1 dash orange bitters. Strain.

Hop Toad Cocktail. Over ice shake 3 parts apricot brandy, 1 lemon juice. Strain.

Hörecker vineyard at Kanzem in Mosel-Saar-Ruwer region, Germany.

Horiot Père & Fils *récoltant-manipulant* champagne producer, les Riceys, Champagne, France.

Horitschon Winzergenossenschaft wine co-operative in Mittelburgenland, Austria.

Horn vineyards at Ingelheim and Wachenheim in Rheinhessen region and Kallstadt in Rheinpfalz region, Germany.

Hornberg vineyard at Framersheim in Rheinhessen region, Germany.

Hörnchen vineyard at Laubenheimand Wallhausen in Nahe region, Germany.

Horndean Special Bitter (HSB) ale brand of George Gale brewery, Portsmouth, England.

Hornfelsen vineyard at Grenzach-Whylen in Baden region, Germany.

Hornitos tequila *reposado* by Tequila Sauza, Jalisco, Mexico.

Hörnle vineyards at Korb and Waiblingen in Württemberg region, Germany.

Hornsby, Château wine producer at Alice Springs, Australia.

Hornsby's cider brand of Ernest & Julio Gallo, Sonoma, California, USA.

Horse Ale beer by Lamot brewery, Mechelen, Belgium.

Horseshoe Bay brewery in Vancouver, Canada.

Horsepower beer brand (4.5% alc) of Titanic Brewery, Stoke-on-Trent, England.

Hortevie, Château wine estate of AC St Julien, Médoc, Bordeaux, France. Classified *Cru Bourgeois*.

Hosbag red wine from Gamay grapes, Trayka, Turkey.

Hoskins & Oldfield brewery at Frog Island, Leicester, England.

Hospices de Beaune the name on the label of some of the best (and some of the less good) wines of Burgundy, France. See box.

Hospices de Nuits charity est 1692 in Nuits St Georges, Burgundy, France. Endowed similarly to Hospices de Beaune. Auction is held two Sundays before Easter.

hospital brandy informal description used by distillers in Australia.

Implies neither medicinal powers nor risk, merely alluding to endowment of Australia's first hospitals (notably Sydney Hospital) by wealthy distillers.

Hoster pub-brewery in Columbus, Ohio, USA.

Hotcha Cocktail. Over ice stir 2 parts rum, 1 dry sherry. Strain.

Houbanon, Château wine estate of AC Médoc, Bordeaux, France. Classified *Cru Bourgeois*.

Houghton leading wine estate of Swan Valley, Western Australia. Numerous famed wines including the best-selling **Houghtons 'White Burgundy'**. Owned by Hardy's.

Houissant, Château wine estate of AC St-Estèphe, Médoc, Bordeaux, France. Classified *Cru Bourgeois Supérieur*.

Hourtin-Ducasse, Château wine estate of AC Haut-Médoc, Bordeaux, France. Classified *Cru Bourgeois*.

House of Lords eight- and 12-year-old blended scotch whiskies by William Whiteley, Pitlochry, Perthshire, Scotland.

House of Peers scotch whisky brand of Douglas Laing, Glasgow, Scotland. Blends: **House of Peers De Luxe, House of Peers XO Extra Old, House of Peers 12 Years Old**. Vatted malt: **House of Peers 22 Years Old**.

Hövel, Weingut von historic wine producer at Obermosel in Mosel-Saar-Ruwer region, Germany. Owner of Oberemmeler Hütte and part-owner of Scharzhofberg vineyards.

HSB see Horndean Special Bitter.

Hsiang Hsueh rice-based 'wine' of state trading monopoly, Shanghai, People's Republic of China.

Hospices de Beaune

a gift of wine

In the age of taxpayer-funded health and social security, it is tempting to believe that in earlier times, the poor were doomed to die of disease or starvation. But not so. In the centuries before the age of grim acquisitiveness brought about by the agricultural and industrial revolutions in Europe, the God-fearing rich were wont to will large parts of their fortunes to their parishes – in the sincere belief that this would buy them a place in Heaven.

In Burgundy, one of the most spectacular of charitable gifts made in the late Middle Ages is still very much in evidence. It is the Hôtel-Dieu in Beaune, endowed by Nicolas Rolin in 1443. He was a squire of Autun appointed Chancellor of Burgundy by the royal Valois Duke, Philip the Good, at a time when the duchy was richer and more powerful than the rest of France put together.

In control of the exchequer of one of Europe's wealthiest economies, Rolin naturally accumulated a great deal of money, and decided to invest some of it in a hospital and religious foundation for the poor. Thus the world-renowned Hospices de Beaune, now a museum and tourist mecca, but still intact under its precipitous roofs, luminously tiled in the local fashion and surmounted by a host of dormer windows with gables decorated in what is clearly the Flemish style.

As a hospital, the institution has been the recipient of many donations over the ensuing centuries, including a total of 131 acres of prime Burgundy vineyards. Each year, the wine from these plots (all, bar one, within the Côtes de Beaune) is auctioned, and the proceeds – as much as £2.5 million – invested in a state-of-the-art health centre in Beaune. Held in the spectacular council chamber, hung with priceless tapestries, the auction is held on the Sunday of Les Trois Glorieuses, the third in November.

High prices are paid by the throng of local *negoçiants-éleveurs* and invited guests from farther afield. In light of the good cause, it is understandable that bids are much higher than market forces would always dictate. The wines, still barely more than grape juice from a harvest only a few weeks past, are very difficult to evaluate anyway. But the auction is nevertheless regarded as a useful barometer for the prices the vintage will fetch when the wines are bottled and ready for sale in the following year, or later.

Nicolas Rolin's kindness to the poor of Beaune has had a welcome spin-off for the wealthy *vignerons* of the region. Because the auction is dedicated to raising funds for a famous charity, the event attracts worldwide attention, and does much to maintain the good name of Burgundy – not just for the 34 wines under the Hospices de Beaune label, but for all the wines, good and bad alike, of the entire region.

Hua Tiao rice-based 'wine' of state trading monopoly, Shanghai, People's Republic of China.

Huatusco Huammer Cocktail. Over ice shake 1 part tequila, 1 rum, 1 Cointreau, 1 lemon juice, 1 teaspoon sugar. Strain into a tall glass with ice, and top with Coca-Cola.

Hubacker vineyard at Flörsheim-Dalsheim in Rheinhessen region, Germany.

Hubberg vineyard at Weinheim in Baden region, Germany.

Huber brewery in Monroe, Wisconsin, USA. Beers made under Berghoff label.

Hubertusberg vineyards at Nittel, Onsdorf and Waldrach in Mosel-Saar-Ruwer region, Germany.

Hubertusborn vineyard at Koblenz in Mosel-Saar-Ruwer region, Germany.

Hubertuslay vineyards at Bausendorf and Kinheim in Mosel-Saar-Ruwer region, Germany.

Hübsch pub-brewery in Davis, California, USA.

Hudepohl-Schoenling brewery in Cincinnati, Ohio, USA. Beers include Christian Moerlein and Little Kings Cream Ale.

Hudson & Cooper lost 'British wine' brand of former Vine Products Co, England.

Hudson's Bay Company Distillery formerly of Seagram, Winnipeg, Canada.

Hudson Valley wine-producing region of New York State, USA.

Huelva DO wine region of SW Spain. Mostly ordinary wines for distilling.

Huet, Gaston wine producer of AC Vouvray, Loire Valley, France. Still and sparkling wines by biodynamic methods. Founder Gaston Huet (1910-2002) was mayor of the town of Vouvray and the leader of a successful campaign in the 1970s to dissuade SNCF, the French railways, from excavating a cutting for the high-speed TGV Atlantique through some of the appellation's prime vineyards. Instead, the rail was laid through a tunnel, constructed at an additional cost of several million francs. Even then, Huet and his campaigners insisted, successfully, that the track must be laid on shock-absorbing foundations – added at further enormous expense – to prevent the vibration from passing trains disturbing the vines.

Hugel leading wine producer of Alsace, France. Est Riquewihr 1639 and still family run. Originated *Vendange Tardive* (late-harvest) wines of the region.

Hughes, Sarah brewery at Beacon Hotel, Sedgley, West Midlands. Known for Original Dark Ruby Mild ale.

Huguenac brandy by Huguenot Wine Farmers, South Africa.

Hühnerberg vineyard at Traben-Trarbach in Mosel-Saar-Ruwer region, Germany.

Huia Vineyards wine producer est 1996 at Blenheim, Marlborough, New Zealand. Distinguished wines from Chardonnay, Gewürztraminer and Sauvignon Blanc, plus sparkling brand. *see label opposite* ➡

Hula-Hula Cocktail. Over ice shake 2 parts dry gin, 1 fresh orange juice, 1 dash Cointreau. Strain.

Hull Brewery Co brewery at Hull, East Yorkshire, England.

Humboldt pub-brewery at Arcata, Humboldt Bay, California, USA.

Hummelberg vineyard at Ostringen in Baden region, Germany.

Hundert vineyard at Oberwesel in Mittelrhein region, Germany.

Hundertgulden vineyard at Appenheim in Rheinhessen region, Germany.

Hundred Per Cent Cocktail. Over ice shake 4 parts Swedish Punsch, 1 lemon juice, 1 orange juice, 2 dashes grenadine. Strain.

100 Pipers blended scotch whisky brand of Seagram, Montreal, Canada, acquired by Diageo, 2001.

Hundsberg vineyards at Obersulm (Eichelberg) and Obersulm (Weiler) in Württemberg region, Germany.

Hundskopf vineyard at Albis in Rheinhessen region, Germany.

PRODUCE OF NEW ZEALAND

Huia

MARLBOROUGH
Sauvignon Blanc
19'98

PRODUCED AND BOTTLED BY
HUIA VINEYARDS LIMITED
BOYCES ROAD, RD 3, BLENHEIM
MARLBOROUGH

13.5% Vol.   750ml℮

Hungary the major quality-wine producer of eastern Europe. Wines include famed dessert Tokaj, table wines from vineyards surrounding Lake Balaton and from the Great Plain, and 'Bulls Blood' of Eger. New vineyards planted with French grape varieties have been established since 1990.

Hungerberg vineyard at Winterbach in Württemberg region, Germany.

Hungerbiene vineyard at Gundheim in Rheinhessen region, Germany.

Hungerford Hill major wine producer of Australia with vineyards and wineries in Hunter Valley, Coonawarra and Riverland.

Hung Mei grape-based tonic 'port' of People's Republic of China.

Hungriger Wolf vineyard at Bad Kreuznach in Nahe region, Germany.

Hunnenstein vineyard at Alken in Mosel-Saar-Ruwer region, Germany.

Hunolsteiner vineyard at Merxheim in Nahe region, Germany.

Hunter River Riesling regional name for Sémillon white grape variety, Australia.

Hunter's wine producer at Blenheim, Marlborough, New Zealand. Famed Chardonnay and Sauvignon white wines.

Hunter Valley major and long-established (1820s) wine-producing region of New South Wales, Australia. White wines from Chardonnay and Sémillon (locally called Hunter River Riesling) grapes and red wines most famously from Shiraz. The Upper Hunter Valley is a distinct and separate region exploited only since 1960s.

Huntingdon Estate leading wine producer in Mudgee, New South Wales, Australia. Red wines from Cabernet Sauvignon and Shiraz grapes and whites from Chardonnay and Sémillon.

Huntly blended scotch whisky by Huntly Blending, Hurlford, Ayrshire, Scotland.

Huntsman ale brand of Thomas Hardy (Eldridge Pope) brewery, Dorchester, England.

Huntsman Cocktail. Over ice shake 2 parts vodka, 1 rum, 1 fresh lime juice, sprinkling of sugar. Strain.

Hürlimann brewery in Zürich, Switzerland. Produces Samichlaus, the world's strongest lager.

Hurricane 'Amercian style pale ale' (4% alc) by Freeminer Brewery, Forest of Dean, Gloucestershire, England. 'Crammed with floral Cascade hops from the hopfields of Rattlesnake Hills, Washington.'

Hurricane Cocktail. Over ice shake 2 parts rum, 2 fresh lime juice, 1 passionfruit syrup. Strain.

Hüssberg vineyard at Suggenheim in Franken region, Germany.

Hütt vineyard at Grünstadt in Rheinpfalz region, Germany.

Hüttberg vineyard at Mainz in Rheinhessen region, Germany.

Hütte vineyard at Konz in Mosel-Saar-Ruwer region, Germany.

Hüttenberg vineyard at Roxheim in Nahe region, Germany.

Huttenheim brewery in Benicia, California, USA.

Hutter Weingut Silberbichlerhof wine producer in Wachau, Niederösterreich, Austria.

Hütte-Terrassen vineyard at Bornheim in Rheinhessen region, Germany.

Huxelrebe white grape variety of Germany and, lately, England.

Hwato grape-based medicinal tonic drink of People's Republic of China.

HWB popular white-wine brand of Houghton Winery, Western Australia. Stands for 'Houghton White Burgundy'.

Hydes Anvil brewery in Manchester, England. Anvil Bitter (3.8% alc), Anvil Light (3.5% alc), Anvil Mild (3.5% alc), Anvil Smooth ((4% alc).

see label opposite ➡

Hymettus white wine of Attica, Greece.

I

IBF Pick-Me-Up Cocktail. In a wineglass with an ice cube mix 1 part brandy, 3 dashes curaçao, 3 dashes Fernet Branca. Top with champagne.

Iby, Anton & Johanna wine producers in Mittelburgenland, Austria.

Ice Dragon cider brand of Matthew Clark, Bristol, England.

Ice Maiden Cocktail. To a tall glass add a scoop of ice cream (vanilla or other); add 2 parts marsala and top with chilled lemonade. Add a lemon slice and drink through a straw.

Iceni brewery at Ickburgh, Mundford, Norfolk, England.

Ice wine sweet white wine made from grapes picked frozen from the vine. World's leading producer is, unsurprisingly, Canada. Equivalent to Germany's *Eiswein*.

Ichbien Cocktail. Over ice shake 1 egg yolk, 1 sherry-glassful milk, 3 parts brandy, 1 orange curaçao. Strain and sprinkle ground nutmeg over.

Ichnusa beer brand of Italy.

Idaho wine-producing state of USA.

Ideal Cocktail. Over ice shake 2 parts dry gin, 1 dry vermouth, 1 grapefruit juice, 2 dashes maraschino. Strain and add blanched almond to glass.

Idig vineyard at Neustadt an der Weinstrasse in Rheinpfalz region, Germany.

Idyll wine producer in Geelong, Victoria, Australia.

Ightham vineyard at Ightham, Sevenoaks, Kent, England.

Igler, Waltraud wine producer in Mittelburgenland, Austria.

IGT see Indicazione Geografica Tipica.

Ijalba, Viña *bodega* est 1991, Rioja, Spain. Ecologically cultivated wines under the name Solferino.

Île de Margaux, Domaine de L' island wine estate of Bordeaux, France.

Illats wine village of AC Cérons, Bordeaux, France.

Im Felseneck vineyard at Bockenau in Nahe region, Germany.

Im Füchschen inn-brewery in Düsseldorf, Germany. Name means 'the fox'.

Im Heubusch vineyard at Morschheim in Rheinpfalz region, Germany.

imbottigliata bottled. Italian.

imbottigliata all'origine bottled at source. Italian.

Immengarten vineyard at Maikammer in the Rheinpfalz region, Germany.

Immortal Memory eight-year-old blended scotch whisky by Gordon & MacPhail, Elgin, Scotland. Name echoes January 25 toast to poet Robert Burns (1759–96).

Im Neuberg vineyard at Bockenau in Nahe region, Germany.

Imperial Speyside malt whisky distillery est 1897, Carron, Morayshire, Scotland. Single malt: 12-year-old.

Imperial Cocktail. Over ice stir 1 part dry gin, 1 dry vermouth, 1 dash Angostura bitters, 1 dash maraschino. Strain and add cocktail olive to glass.

Imperial Blue brand of Pernod-Ricard.

impériale large-format bottle size for wines of Bordeaux, France. Six litres.

Imperial Gold Medal blended scotch whisky by Cockburn & Co, Edinburgh, Scotland.

imperial stout dark, strong style of beer brewed in UK from 18th century, mainly for export. Now also made in northern Europe, North America and Japan.

Imperial Russian Stout classic brand of Courage brewers, England.

Im Röttgen vineyards at Koblenz and Winningen in Mosel-Saar-Ruwer region, Germany.

Im Sonnenschein vineyard at Siebeldingen in Rheinpfalz region, Germany.

Im Stein vineyard at Karlstadt in Franken region, Germany.

Ina, La renowned *fino* sherry brand. Pedro Domecq, Jerez de la Frontera, Spain.

Inca Cocktail. Over ice shake 1 part dry gin, 1 dry vermouth, 1 dry sherry, 1 sweet vermouth, 1 dash orange bitters, 1 dash Orgeat Syrup. Strain.

Inchgower Speyside malt whisky distillery est 1871, Buckie, Banffshire, Scotland. Single malts: 12-year-old, 14-year-old.

Inchmurrin South Highland single malt whisky by Loch Lomond distillery, Alexandira, Dumbartonshire, Scotland.

Inch's Cider cider producer originally of Winkleigh, Devon, England. Under ownership of Bulmer, reduced to Stonehouse and White Lightning brands.

Income Tax Cocktail. Over ice shake 4 parts dry gin, 2 dry vermouth, 2 sweet vermouth, 1 orange juice, 1 dash Angostura bitters. Strain.

Ind Coope major brewery of Allied Breweries company, Burton upon Trent, West Midlands, England.

In den Felsen vineyard at Schlossböckelheim in Nahe region, Germany.

In den Layfelsen vineyard at Hammerstein in Mittelrhein region, Germany.

In den siebzehn Moreg vineyard at Bad Kreuznach in Nahe region, Germany.

India brewing, distilling and winemaking continue amidst periodic regional prohibitions. Wine has been produced since the Indus civilisations contemporaneous with Pharaonic Egypt and vineyard planting was greatly increased in the Macedonian colonies established by Alexander the Great. During the British Empire, vineyards were planted in Kashmir and elsewhere.

Indianapolis Brewing Co brewery in Indianapolis, Indiana, USA.

Indians Bones Dark Strong Ale beer brand of Wessex Craft Brewers (Summerskills), England.

India Pale Ale beer style created by 19th century brewers in UK for export to India. Beers had high gravities and were extravagantly hopped in order to ferment, in a good state of preservation, during long duration needed for shipment. Usually abbreviated to IPA.

Indicaçãos de Proveniência Regulamentada wine-quality designation of Portugal. Wine made to set standards in a defined region. IPR for short.

Indicazione Geografica Tipica recent (1992) designation for wine of basic quality, Italy. IGT wines may carry name of geographical location followed by constituent grape variety. There are 115 IGTs accounting for around 20 per cent of national wine production. Broadly equivalent to *vin de pays* of France.

Indigo Hills premium wine brand of Ernest & Julio Gallo, California, USA.

Infernal Brew 'devilishly drinkable silky brown' bottle-conditioned beer (4.8% alc) by Wickwar Brewing, Gloucestershire, England.

Inferno DOC for red wines classified as Valtellina Superiore, Lombardy, Italy.

infusion in brewing, the steeping of grain mash in water.

Ingelheim important wine town of Rheinhessen region, Germany. *Grosslage*: Kaiserpfalz.

Ingham brandy of Ingham Whitaker, Marsala, Sicily, Italy. Owned by Marsala producer Florio.

Inglenook wine estate est 1881 Napa Valley, California, USA.

Inishowen Irish whiskey brand of Cooley Distillery, Riverstown, Dundalk, County Louth, Republic of Ireland.

Inkelhöll vineyard at Lettweiler in Nahe region, Germany.

Ink Street Cocktail. Over ice shake 1 part rye whisky, 1 lemon juice, 1 orange juice. Strain.

Innere Leiste vineyard at Würzburg in Franken region, Germany.

Inniskillin leading wine producer est 1975 at Niagara-on-the-lake, Ontario, Canada.

In Seine beer brand of the Paris Real Ale Brewery, France.

Insel Heylesen Werth vineyard at Bacharach in Mittelrhein region, Germany.

Institut National des Appellations d'Origine the governing body of France's wine industry est 1935 to formulate the manifold standards and practices of the nation's 400 *Appellations Contrôlées*. Usually abbreviated to INAO.

Instituto Nacional de Denominaciones de Origen national wine-regulating body of Spain. Est 1972 to oversee Consejo Reguladores, local enforcement agencies for Denominaciones de Origen (DOs).

Instituto do Vinho do Porto Portugal's official body supervising port production. The institute's seal is a guarantee of authenticity.

Interbrew international brewing company listed in Brussels, Belgium. More than 200 brands in 120 countries include Bass, Boddingtons, Hoegaarden, Stella Artois, Tennent's, Whitbread.

Invalid Stout beer by Carlton & United Breweries, Melbourne, Australia.

invecchiato aged. Italian.

Inveralmond brewery at Perth, Scotland. Lia Fail (4.7% alc), Ossian's Ale (4.1% alc).

Invergordon, The ten-year-old single grain scotch whisky of The Invergordon Distillery, Cromarty Firth, Scotland.

Inver House (Green Plaid) blended scotch whisky by Inver House Distillers, Airdrie, Lanarkshire, Scotland. Also, 12- and 17-year-old blends.

Inverleven Lowland malt whisky distillery est 1938, Dumbarton, Scotland. Single malt: Lomond 30-year-old.

Inycon wine brand of Settesoli, Sicily, Italy. Aglianico, Chardonnay, Merlot, Syrah and other varietal wines. Inycon was the Ancient Greek name of the Sicilian village of Menfi, now home to the winery.

Inzolia white grape variety of Sicily, Italy. Marsala and table wines.

see label opposite ➡

Iolanthe Cocktail. Over ice shake 2 parts brandy, 2 Lillet, 1 Grand Marnier, 1 orange juice, 2 dashes orange bitters. Strain.

IPA see India Pale Ale.

Irancy AC for red wine from Pinot Noir and, sometimes, César grapes grown around village of Irancy in northern Burgundy, France.

Irish Ale Breweries producers at Dundalk and Kilkenny of beers including Macardle's, Smithwick's, Twyford's.

Irish Ayes Cocktail. Over ice shake 4 parts Irish whiskey, 1 green Chartreuse, 1 dash Green Mint. Strain and add green olive to glass.

Irish Cocktail. Over ice shake 1 part Irish whiskey, 2 dashes curaçao, 2 dashes pastis, 1 dash Angostura bitters, 1 dash maraschino. Strain and add green olive to glass. Squeeze orange peel over.

Irish Coffee a mixed drink of hot coffee into which Irish whiskey is added, and then warmed double cream floated on top. Sugar is optional. Choose a stemmed or handled glass.

Irish Cooler Cocktail. Into a tall, ice-filled glass pour a measure of Irish whiskey. Top with soda water and add a twist of lemon peel.

Irish Mint Cocktail. Over ice stir 1 part Baileys Irish Cream, 1 white crème de menthe. Strain into a shot glass.

Irish Mist liqueur brand of C&C International, Dublin, Eire.

Irkutsk brewery of Lake Baikal, Irkutsk, Siberia, Russia. **Irkutsk** lager (4.4% alc), Vladimir lager (5.5% alc).

Irle brewery at Siegen, Sauerland, Germany. Pilsener beers.

Ironbrew ale by Sail and Anchor brewery, Fremantle, Western Australia.

iron casse in winemaking, a precipitate due to reaction of iron in the wine with oxygen in the air, and causing cloudiness.

Iron City Beer brand of Pittsburgh Brewing, Pennsylvania, USA.

Iron Duke strong (6.5% alc) ale by Wellington County brewery, Guelph, Ontario, Canada.

Iron Horse wine property in Sonoma County, California, USA.

Irouléguy village and AC for red and rosé wines from Cabernet Franc, Cabernet Sauvignon and Tannat grapes, Pyrenees region, SW France.

Irroy obscure *Grande Marque* champagne house, Reims, France.

Isabel leading wine estate at Marlborough, New Zealand. Chardonnay, Pinot Noir, Riesling and Sauvignon Blanc.

Isabella hybrid red grape variety of eastern Europe and Black Sea vineyards.

Ischia wine-producing island designated part of Campania region, Italy. Red wines from Guarnaccia and Pere Palummo grapes, whites from Biancolella and Forastera.

isinglass in brewing and winemaking, a gelatinous material used in fining. Derived from fish bladders.

Iskra sparkling wine of Bulgaria.

Islander blended scotch whisky by Arthur Bell, Perth, Scotland.

Islay Scottish island renowned for malt whisky. See box.

Islay Legend blended scotch whisky by Morrison Bowmore, Islay, Scotland.

Islay Mist vatted malt scotch whisky by MacDuff International, Glasgow, Scotland. Also, 17-year-old.

Isle of Jura Island malt whisky distillery est 1810, Isle of Jura, Scotland. Single malt: ten-year-old.

Isle of Skye blended scotch whisky brand of Ian MacLeod, Broxburn, Scotland. Also, eight-, 12- and 18-year-old blends.

Isle of Skye brewery at Uig, Skye, Scotland.

Isonzo DOC for red and white wines from Gorizia in Friuli-Venezia Giulia region, Italy. Ten different grape varieties permitted.

Israel the vineyards of biblical tradition have not survived but new plantings by Rothschilds in the last century began today's revival. Wines are produced from vineyards including the coastal plains and regions of Mount Carmel and the Sea of Galilee.

Issan, Château d' wine estate of AC Margaux, Médoc, Bordeaux, France. Classified *3ème Grand Cru Classé*.

Islay

burning to make whisky

The southernmost island of Scotland's Inner Hebrides, Islay (pronounced Eye-la) is just 25 miles from end to end. The ancient seat of the 'Lord of the Isles,' adopted around 1370 by local laird John Macdonald, Islay has been a stonghold of the Campbells since they evicted the Macdonalds in 1616. The Campbells' ancient domain, Islay House, still stands at the head of the great sea-loch of Indaal.

Islay is renowned for its peat which, at the beginning of the 20th century, locals said would last 1,500 years as a source of fuel. This optimism is certain to prove unfounded, but there is still sufficient from the original 60 square miles of the bog to supply the island's famous distilleries for the foreseeable future. The peat provides the heat source for drying their barley – imparting the famed peaty flavours that so distinguish Islay malts.

These weighty whiskies, also characterised by a pungent sea-weedy style credited to the distilleries' proximity to the sea, are said to be the most readily identifiable of all Scottish malts. Today's distilleries are Bowmore, named after the island's chief town, Port Ellen (the main fishing port), Ardbeg, Bruichladdich, Bunnahabhain, Caol Ila, Lagavulin and Laphroaig.

Istria wine-producing Adriatic peninsula of Croatia. Red wines from Bordeaux grape varieties, whites from Malvasia.

Italiano Cocktail. In an ice-filled glass mix 1 part amaretto, 1 brandy. Top with chilled pineapple juice and stir.

Italian Riesling white grape variety unrelated to noble Riesling of Germany. Synonymous with Rizling and Welschriesling.

Italian Swiss Colony major commercial wine producer of California, USA.

Italy all the 19 administrative regions of Italy are wine-producing, and the country is said to have a million vine-yards. Officially, Italy produces and exports more wine than any other nation. Wine-quality laws, revised in 1992, designate basic wine *vino da tavola* (table wine) on which labels carry only producer's own or brand name. Next grade up, IGT (*Indicazione Geografica Tipica*) wines display location and grape-variety. Next, DOC (*Denominazione di Origine Controllata*) wines must be from prescribed grape varieties grown within the defined vineyard or area, and conforming to certain standards in vineyard and winery. Top-ranked wines are DOCG (*Denominazione di Origine Controllata e Garantita*), those of particular regions including Barolo, Chianti etc or, under 1992 rule-revisions, outstanding individual properties. Red, *rosato*, sparkling and white wines are all made in every style and at every level of quality. Grape-based spirits, brandy and grappa, plus fortified wines and vermouths, are all produced on a major scale nationwide. Italy is growing in importance as a brewing nation, now ranked seventh in size in Europe with annual production over 12 million hectolitres. The industry has 15 major brewing companies employing 22,500 people.

Itchen Valley brewery at Bideford, Devon, England.

Izmir Aegean-coast wine-producing region of Turkey. Red and white wines from French grape varieties.

J

Jabberwock Cocktail. Over ice stir 1 part Caperitif, 1 dry gin, 1 dry sherry, 2 dashes orange bitters. Strain and squeeze lemon peel over.

Jaboulet Ainé, Paul wine grower and *négoçiant* of Rhône Valley, France. Renowned Hermitage wines and others.

Jaboulet Vercherre *négoçiant-éleveur*, Beaune, Burgundy, France.

Jack Daniel's Tennessee sour mash whiskey of Jack Daniel distillery, Lynchburg, Tennessee, USA. Est 1866 by Jasper Newton Daniel (1848-1911), the 'Oldest Registered Distillery in the United States'.

Jack in the Box Cocktail. Over ice shake 1 part apple brandy, 1 pineapple juice, 1 dash Angostura bitters. Strain.

Jack Kearns Cocktail. Over ice shake 3 parts dry gin, 1 rum, 1 dash lemon juice, 1 dash sugar syrup. Strain.

Jack-Op beer by Vandenstock brewery, Brussels, Belgium.

Jack Pine Cocktail. Over ice shake 2 parts dry gin, 1 dry vermouth, 1 orange juice, 1 slice pineapple. Strain.

Jack Rose Cocktail. Over ice shake 2 parts apple brandy, 1 grenadine, 1 lemon juice. Strain.

Jacobi spirit producer, Stuttgart, Germany. Brands include **Jacobi 1880** brandy.

Jacobins *gueuze* beer by Bockor brewery, Bellegem, Belgium.

Jacobite, The blended scotch whisky brand of Nurdin & Peacock, London, England.

Jacobite Ale beer by Traquair House Brewery, Peebles, Scotland. Introduced 1995 'to commemorate the rising of Bonnie Prince Charlie in 1745.'

Jacob's Creek popular red and white wine brand of Orlando, Australia.

Jacquart champagne brand of Coopérative des Regionales des Vins de Champagne, Reims, France.

Jacquart, André *récoltant-manipulant* champagne producer, le Mesnil-sur-Oger, Champagne, France.

Jacqueline Cocktail. Over ice shake 2 parts dark rum, 1 triple sec, 1 fresh lime juice, pinch of sugar. Strain.

Jacquère white grape variety of Savoie region, France. Main constituent of AC Vin de Savoie white wines.

Jacques-Blanc, Château wine estate of AC St-Emilion, Bordeaux, France.

Jacquesson & Fils champagne house est 1798 Dizy, France. Legendary Blanc de Blancs.

Jacquet synonym for Black Spanish grape, Spain. Also **Jacquez**.

Jade organic lager brand (4.6%) of Brasserie Castelain, Bénifontaine, France.

Jade Cocktail. Over ice shake 3 parts rum, 1 Cointreau, 1 crème de menthe, 1 fresh lime juice, teaspoon sugar. Strain.

Jadot, Louis leading grower and *négoçiant-éleveur* of Beaune, Burgundy, France. Beaune *Premier Cru* vineyards of Boucherottes, Les Bressandes, Clos des Ursules, Theurons etc. and *Grands Crus* Corton, Corton-Charlemagne, Corton-Pougets.

Jahrang 'vintage year' in German.

Jäger wine producer in Wachau, Niederösterreich, Austria.

Jagermeister leading brand of *Klosterlikor* herbal liqueur, Germany.

jaggery sweet palm sap of palmyra tree, extracted for fermenting into toddy spirit. India.

Jaime I brandy of Bodegas Miguel Torres, Penedes, Spain. Launched 1998, a *Reserva de la Familia*, blended from soleras 15 to 30 years old.

Jamaica Cocktail. Over ice shake 1 part Jamaican rum, 1 Tia Maria, 1 fresh lime juice, 1 dash Angostura bitters. Strain.

Jamaica Sunset Cocktail. Over ice shake 3 parts dry gin, 1 dark rum, 1 red wine, 1 orange juice. Strain.

Jamek wine producer in Wachau, Niederösterreich, Austria.

Jameson's Irish whiskey brand. See John Jameson.

James Foxe Canadian whisky brand formerly of Seagram, Canada.

James Gordon's blended scotch whisky by James Gordon, Elgin, Scotland.

James Martin's VVO eight-year-old blended scotch whisky by Macdonald Martin Distilleries, Leith, Edinburgh, Scotland. Also, 12-, 17- and 20-year-old blends. Martin's VVO was the brand aboard the SS *Politician* wrecked off Eriskay, Outer Hebrides, on February 4, 1941 – the inspiration for Sir Compton Mackenzie's novel *Whisky Galore* (1947).

Jamora Cocktail. Over ice shake 2 parts vodka, 1 orange juice, 1 apple juice, 1 teaspoon raspberry liqueur. Strain into wine glasses and top with chilled sparkling wine. Add a fresh raspberry per glass.

Janet's Jungle Juice cider brand of West Croft Farm, Brent Knoll, Somerset, England.

Janneau largest producer of armagnac brandy, based in Condom, Gascony, France. Est by Pierre-Etienne Janneau 1851. Tradition, VSOP, Napoléon, XO (12–20 year-old), Réserve (20–25 year-old), Cinquentenaire (30–35 year-old), Domaine de Mouchac (single estate).

J&B Jet blended scotch whisky by Justerini & Brooks, London, England.

J&B Rare eight-year-old blended scotch whisky by Justerini & Brooks, London, England. Also, **J&B Reserve 15 Years Old**.

Japan minor wine-producing country with vineyards mainly on Hokkaido, Honshu and Kyushu islands, but a major distiller of brandy, whisky and other spirits as well as rice beers/wines. Suntory operates the world's largest whisky distillery at Hakushu.

Japanese Cocktail. Over ice shake 1 part brandy, 4 dashes fresh lime juice, 3 dashes orgeat syrup, 1 dash Angostura bitters. Strain.

Jarana tequila by La Union en Totolan, Jalisco, Mexico.

Jarzebiak rowanberry-infused golden vodka, Poland.

Jasmin, Robert outstanding producer of Côte Rôtie wines, Rhône Valley, France.

Jasnières AC for white wines from Chenin Blanc grapes, Loire Valley in Loire region, France.

Jasper Hill wine estate of Bendigo, Victoria, Australia.

Jaubertes, Château wine estate of AC Graves, Bordeaux, France.

Jaubertie, Château wine estate of AC Bergerac, SW France. Known for fine red and white wines and, even more so, for being the creation of millionaire English stationer Nicholas Ryman.   *see label opposite* ➡

Jauga, Château second wine of Château Rabaud-Promis, Bordeaux, France.

Java Cooler Cocktail. In a tall, ice-filled glass combine 2 parts dry gin, 1 teaspoon fresh lime juice, 1 dash Angostura bitters. Top with chilled tonic water.

JCB strong ale (4.6% alc) of Wadworth Brewery, Devizes, Wiltshire, England, commemorating former chairman John Cairns Bartholomew. The company obtained the consent of UK earth-moving-equipment manufacturer JCB for use of the name. The beer is commonly known as 'Digger'.

Jeandeman, Château wine estate of AC Fronsac, Bordeaux, France.

Jean-Fauré, Château wine estate of AC St-Emilion, Bordeaux, France. Classified *Grand Cru*.

Jean-Gervais, Château wine estate of AC Graves, Bordeaux, France.

Jeanlain famed *bière de garde* of Brasserie Duyck, Jenlain, France.

Jeanne d'Arc brewery at Ronchin, Lille, France.

Jean Perico *cava* brand of Gonzalez Byass, Spain.

Jean-Voisin, Château wine estate of AC St-Emilion, Bordeaux, France. Classified *Grand Cru*.

Jeeper *récoltant-manipulant* champagne producer, Damery, Champagne, France.

Jekel Vineyard wine producer in Monterey, California, USA.

jenever alternative spelling of *genever*. Netherlands and Belgium.

Jennings Brothers brewery at Cockermouth, Cumbria, England. Brands include Cocker Hoop, Sneck Lifter.

Jentz Cocktail. Over ice shake 2 parts marsala, 1 dry gin, 1 dash each of Bénédictine, dry vermouth, fresh pink grapefruit juice. Strain.

Jerez capital of sherry country of Andalucia, Spain, and the Spanish word for the wine. As a Moorish settlement the town was known as Seris, which changed to Xeres and thus Jerez from 1264 under Christian occupation. Full name Jerez de la Frontera dates from 1380, as a mark of the town's strategic position at the frontier between the Muslim and Christian worlds.

Jericho Cocktail. Over ice shake 2 parts vodka, 1 blue curaçao, 1 lemon juice, 1 orange juice. Strain.

jeroboam wine bottle format. In Bordeaux, 4.5 litres, equivalent to six standard bottles. In Champagne, three litres, equivalent to four standard bottles. Named after Jeroboam I, first king of divided Israel in the 10th century BC.

Jersey Chisel apple variety traditionally valued for cider-making. English.

Jersey Lightning Cocktail. Over ice shake 2 parts brandy, 1 apple brandy, 1 sweet vermouth, 1 dash Angostura bitters. Strain.

Jerusalem vineyard at Ljutomer, Slovenia. White wines from 'Rizling' grapes.

Jesuitenberg vineyards at Elsenfeld in Franken region and Wawern in Mosel-Saar-Ruwer region, Germany.

Jesuitengarten vineyards at Bad Neuenahr-Ahrweiler in Ahr region, Neustadt an der Weinstrasse in Rheinpfalz region, Oestrich-Winkel in Rheingau region and Pellingen and Waldrach in Mosel-Saar-Ruwer region, Germany.

Jesuitenhofgarten vineyard at Dirmstein in Rheinpfalz region, Germany.

Jesuitenschloss vineyards at Frieburg and Merzhausen in Baden region, Germany.

Jesuitenwingert vineyard at Trier in Mosel-Saar-Ruwer region, Germany.

Jever town and brewery in Friesland, Germany, famed for **Jever Pilsener** beer.

Jewel Cocktail. Over ice shake 1 part dry gin, 1 sweet vermouth, 1 green Chartreuse, 2 dashes orange bitters. Strain and add maraschino cherry to glass.

Jeyplack Cocktail. Over ice shake 2 parts dry gin, 1 sweet vermouth, 1 dash pastis. Strain and squeeze lemon peel over.

Jezek lager brand of Jihlava brewery, Czech Republic. Jezek translates as 'hedgehog'.

Jimador, el tequila *reposado* by Tequila, Herradura, Jalisco, Mexico.

Jim Barry wine estate in Clare Valley, South Australia. Noted wines from Chardonnay and Riesling grapes and premium Armagh from Shiraz.

Jim Beam Kentucky straight bourbon whiskey of James B Beam distillery, Clermont, Kentucky, USA. 'The World's Finest Bourbon.'

Jimmy Blanc Cocktail. Over ice shake 2 parts dry gin, 1 Lillet, 3 dashes Dubonnet. Shake and squeeze orange peel over.

Jingle Knocker bottle-conditioned amber seasonal (Christmas) ale (5.5% alc) by Skinners Brewing, Truro, Cornwall, England.

Jinro Soju leading white spirit brand of South Korea.

João Pires dry Muscat wine brand of J.M. da Fonseca of Setubal, Portugal.

Jöbstl, Johannes wine producer in Weststeiermark, Austria.

Jo'burg Cocktail. Over ice stir 1 part rum, 1 Caperitif, 4 dashes orange bitters. Strain and squeeze lemon peel over.

Jockey Club Cocktail. Over ice shake 1 part dry gin, 4 dashes lemon juice, 2 dashes crème de noyaux, 1 dash Angostura bitters, 1 dash orange bitters.

Jock Scot three-, five-, eight- and 12-year-old blended scotch whiskies by Findlater Mackie Todd, London, England.

Johannesberg vineyards at Sobernheim and Waldböckelheim in Nahe region, Germany.

Johannisberg regional name for Silvaner white grape variety, Switzerland.

Johannisberg vineyards at Aspisheim, Gau-Algesheim, Mainz and Zotzenheim in Rheinhessen region, Dreis, Franzenheim and Mertesdorf in Mosel-Saar-Ruwer region, Elsenfeld and Thüngersheim in Franken region and Rümmelsheim mit Orsteil Burg Layen and Wallhausen in Nahe region, Germany.

Johannisberg wine village of Rheingau region, Germany. *Grosslage*: Erntebringer. Site of renowned Schloss Johannisberg estate and other *Einzellagen* of Hasenberg, Hölle, Mittelhölle, Schwarzenstein, Vogelsang etc. Confusingly, the village name Johannisberg can be used for wines of the *Bereich* of Rheingau as a whole.

Johannisberger white wine of Valais region, Switzerland.

Johannisberg Riesling regional name for Rhine Riesling white grape variety, California, USA.

Johannisbrünnchen vineyard at Bernkastel-Kues in Mosel-Saar-Ruwer region, Germany.

Johanniskirchel vineyard at Neustadt an der Weinstrasse in Rheinpfalz region, Germany.

Johannisweg vineyard at Wallhausen in Nahe region, Germany.

Johannitergarten vineyard at Neustadt an der Weinstrasse in Rheinpfalz region, Germany.

John Barr blended scotch whisky by John Walker, Kilmarnock, Scotland.

John Begg blended scotch whisky by John Begg, Glasgow, Scotland.

John Collins Cocktail. Over ice shake 2 parts Dutch gin, 1 lemon juice, 1 teaspoon sugar. Strain into tall glass with ice and top with soda water.

John Hampden's Ale brand of Chiltern Brewery, Buckinghamshire, England.

John Hop Sussex Bitter low-alcohol ('not more than 1%') beer by Harveys Brewery, Lewes, East Sussex, England.

John Jameson whiskey brand of Irish Distillers, Midleton, Eire.

Johnnie Mack Cocktail. Over ice shake 2 parts sloe gin, 1 orange curaçao, 3 dashes pastis. Strain.

Johnnie Walker Red Label blended scotch whisky by John Walker & Sons, Kilmarnock, Scotland. The biggest-selling scotch whisky brand in the world. John Walker began as a grocer, est 1820, in Kilmarnock, where he blended his own Walker's Kilmarnock Whisky. A statue to John Walker, sculpted by Sandy Stoddart and unveiled in 1998, stands in Kilmarnock's town centre. Red Label was introduced, with **Johnnie Walker Black Label**, 1909. Green Label, a blended malt, was launched in 2004.

John Player Special blended scotch malt whisky brand of Douglas Laing, Glasgow, Scotland.

John Wood Cocktail. Over ice shake 4 parts sweet vermouth, 2 Irish whiskey, 2 lemon juice, 1 kümmel, 1 dash Angostura bitters. Strain.

Jollyboat brewery at Alresford, Hampshire, England.

Joly, Madame A wine producer, Coulée de Serrant, AC Savennières, Loire Valley, France.

Joncarde, Château wine estate of AC Côtes de Bourg, Bordeaux, France.

Jones brewery est 1907 at Smithton, Pennsylvania, USA. Beers include Stoney's, after soubriquet 'Stoney' of Jones the founder.

jonge 'young' in Dutch. Style of lighter, less malty *genever*.

Jongieux *cru* of Vin de Savoie, France.

Jordan wine producer at Healdsburg, Sonoma, California, USA. Cabernet Sauvignon red wines in Bordeaux style, and others.

J.O.S. Cocktail. Over ice shake 1 part dry gin, 1 dry vermouth, 1 sweet vermouth, 1 dash brandy, 1 dash lemon juice, 1 dash orange bitters. Strain and squeeze lemon peel over.

Jose Cuervo leading tequila producer of Mexico. Est 1795.

Josefsberg vineyards at Wertheim (Bronnbach) and Wertheim (Reicholzheim) in Baden region, Germany.

Josephsberg vineyard at Durbach in Baden region, Germany.

Josephshöfer vineyard at Graach in Mosel-Saar-Ruwer region, Germany.

Jost Vineyards wine producer at Malagash, Nova Scotia, Canada.

Joulo Christmas beer by Hartwall brewery, Finland.

Jouluolut Christmas beer by Sinebrychoff brewery, Finland.

Jourdan, Château wine estate of AC Premières Côtes de Bordeaux, France.

Journalist Cocktail. Over ice shake 2 parts dry gin, 1 dry vermouth, 1 sweet vermouth, 2 dashes curaçao, 2 dashes lemon juice, 1 dash Angostura bitters. Strain.

joven young wine or spirit, Spanish. As Tequila Joven of Mexico and in Spain, Rioja Joven, new-season red wine made by carbonic maceration, the same method used in France for Beaujolais.

Jubilator lager brand by Schutzenberger brewery, Alsace, France.

Jubilee lager by United Breweries, Bangalore, India.

Judas ale by Alken-Maes brewery, Belgium.

Judenkirch vineyard at Wiesbaden in Rheingau region, Germany.

Judge's brewery at Rugby, Warwickshire, England.

Judgette Cocktail. Over ice shake 1 part dry gin, 1 dry vermouth, 1 peach brandy, 1 dash lime cordial. Strain.

Juffer vineyard at Brauenberg in Mosel-Saar-Ruwer region, Germany.

Juffermauer vineyard at Treis-Karden in Mosel-Saar-Ruwer region, Germany.

Juffer Sonnenuhr vineyard at Brauenberg in Mosel-Saar-Ruwer region, Germany.

jug wine regional term for ordinary wines, USA.

Juge, Château du wine estate of AC Cadillac, Bordeaux, France.

Juge, Château du wine estate of AC Premières Côtes de Bordeaux, France.

Juhfark white grape variety of Somló, Hungary.

Juhlaolut Christmas beer by Hartwall brewery, Finland.

Jule Ø1 Christmas beer by Aass brewery, Denmark.

julep bourbon-based drink with sugar and water and usually flavoured with mint. The name derives from Arabic *julab*, meaning rose-water. American.

Jules Robin brand of Pernod-Ricard.

Julia grappa by Stock distillery, Trieste, Italy.

Juliénas Beaujolais *cru*, from village said to be named after Julius Caesar, France.

Julius sparkling beer by Hoegaarden brewery, Belgium.

Julius-Echter-Berg vineyard at Iphofen in Franken region, Germany.

Julius Kayser major wine producer, Germany.

Juliusspital wine estate of Wurzburg, Franken region, Germany.

Jumilla DO for red wines from Monastrell grapes, Valencia, Spain.

Junayme, Château wine estate of AC Canon-Fronsac, Bordeaux, France.

Jungbrunnen vineyard at Dorsheim in Nahe region, Germany.

Jungfer vineyards and Eltville and Oestrich-Winkel in Rheingau region and Lauffen in Württemberg region, Germany.

Jungfernberg vineyard at Waldrach in Mosel-Saar-Ruwer region, Germany.

Jungfernstieg vineyard at Meersburg in Baden region, Germany.

Juniper Green organic London dry gin by Thames Distillers, London, England. 'The world's first organic gin ... produced from pure organic grain and botanical herbs sourced from around the world.'

Junkanoo Cocktail. Over ice shake 2 parts rum, 1 peach brandy, 1 curaçao, 2 dashes fresh lime juice, 1 dash orange bitters. Strain.

Junker vineyards at Bad Kreuznach and Laubenheim in Nahe region, Germany.

Jupiler brewery and pilsener beer brand, Jupille, Liège, Belgium.

Jupiterberg vineyard at Brackenheim in Württemberg region, Germany.

Jupiter Cocktail. Over ice shake 4 parts dry gin, 2 dry vermouth, 1 Parfait Amour liqueur, 1 orange juice. Strain.

juponne champagne cork. French.

Jura wine region of eastern France comprising four ACs: Arbois, Château-Chalon, Côtes du Jura, L'Etoile. Red, rosé and white wines (including sparkling) plus *vin de paille* and *vin jaune*.

Jurançon AC for white wines from (largely) Courbu and Manseng grapes, Pau, SW France. **Jurançon Moelleux** is sweet wine from late-harvested grapes, and was famously described by novelist Colette (1873–1954) as a 'great seducer'.

Jurançon grape variety of SW France with three strains: Blanc, Noir, Rouge.

Jurat, Château Le wine estate of AC St-Emilion, Bordeaux, France. Classified *Grand Cru*.

Juris, Stiegelmar wine producer in Neusiedlersee, Burgenland, Austria.

Jurtschitsch Sonnhof wine producer in Kamptal, Niederösterreich, Austria.

Justa, Château wine estate of AC Premières Côtes de Bordeaux, France.

Juvé y Camps leading producer of cava wines (and some still wines), San Sadurní d'Anoia, Barcelona, Spain.

Juwards brewery at Wellington, Somerset, England.

K

K cider brand of Matthew Clark, Bristol, England.

Kaapzicht Estate wine producer of Stellenbosch, South Africa.

Kabinett first of the levels of *Prädikat* wines, Germany. Name derives from 'Cabinet', an estate's private collection of fine wines, and applies to wines made from grapes of sufficient ripeness to obviate the addition of sugar. Required *oechsle* level varies by region and grape variety.

kachasu illicit spirit distilled from maize beer, East Africa.

Kachelberg vineyards at Ensheim and Wörrstadt in Rheinhessen region, Germany.

Kadarka indigenous red grape variety of Hungary. Synonymous with Gamza of Bulgaria.

Kaefferkopf renowned vineyard of Ammerschwir, Alsace, France.

Kafels vineyard at Norheim in Nahe region, Germany.

Kaffelstein vineyard at Kreuzwertheim in Franken region, Germany.

Kahlberg vineyard at Hirschberg in Baden region, Germany.

Kahlenberg vineyards at Bad Kreuznach and Feibingert in Nahe region and Ottersheim in Rheinpfalz region, Germany.

Kahllay vineyard at Niederfell in Mosel-Saar-Ruwer region, Germany.

Kahlúa Mexican coffee liqueur produced under licence by Peter Heering, Dalby, Denmark.

Kahlúa Cocktail. In an ice-filled tumbler stir 1 part Kahlúa, 1 dash crème de noyaux, 1 teaspoon fresh cream

Kailberg vineyard at Lauda-Königshofen in Baden region, Germany.

Kaiser wine producer in Neusiedlersee Hügelland, Burgenland, Austria.

Kaiserberg the name of 12 individual vineyards in Germany. Region by region, all follows: in Nahe region at Duchroth; in Baden region at Ettenheim, Ettenheim (Altdorf), Herbolzheim, Herbolzheim (Bleichheim), Herbolzheim (Broggingen), Herbolzheim (Tutschfelden) and Ringsheim; in Rheinpfalz region at Göcklingen and Landau in der Pfalz; in Württemberg region at Güglingen and Güglingen (Fraenzimmern).

Kaiserdom brewery in Bamberg, Germany.

Kaisergarten vineyard at Gau-Weinheim in Rheinhessen region, Germany.

Kaiser Karl vineyards at Kitzingen (Eherider Mühle) and Kitzingen (Repperndorf) in Franken region, Germany.

Kaiserpfalz *Grosslage* incorporating vineyards at Bubenheim, Engelstadt, Heidesheim, Ingelheim, Ingelheim (Gross-Winternheim), Jugenheim, Schwabenheim and Wackernheim in Rheinhessen region, Germany.

Kaiserstuhl vineyard at Neustadt an der Weinstrasse in Rheinpfalz region, Germany.

Kaiser Stuhl wine brand of Penfolds, Barossa Valley, South Australia.

Kaiserstuhl-Tuniberg *Bereich* of Baden region, Germany. *Grosslagen*: Attilafelsen, Vulkanfelsen.

Kaiser Wilhelm vineyard at Winterhausen in Franken region, Germany.

Kakao coffee liqueur, Germany.

Kakubin whisky brand of Suntory, Japan.

Kalamazoo Brewing Co producer at Kalamazoo, Michigan, USA, of Great Lakes Amber Ale, Third Coast Old Ale and other beers.

Kalashnikov Russian vodka brand first exported 2004 as 'military strength made in the traditional way from grain harvested in Russia and water drawn from the tributaries of the River Niva in St Petersburg'.

Kalb vineyard at Iphofen in Franken region, Germany.

Kalbenstein vineyard at Karlstadt in Franken region, Germany.

Kalbspflicht vineyard at Eltville in Rheingau region, Germany.

Kalkberg vineyard at Neustadt an der Weinstrasse in Rheinpfalz region, Germany.

Kalkgasse vineyard at Bernsheim in Hessische Bergstrasse region, Germany.

Kalkgrube vineyard at Frankenweiler in Rheinpfalz region, Germany.

Kalkofen vineyards at Bad Dürkheim and Deidesheim in Rheinpfalz region, Germany.

Kallenberg vineyard at Bubenheim in Rheinhessen region, Germany.

Kallmet wine brand of Albania.

Kallmuth vineyard at Triefenstein in Franken region, Germany.

Kallstadt wine village of Rheinpfalz region, Germany. *Grosslagen*: Kobnert, Saumagen.

Kalte Ernte 'cold duck'. Mixed drink of sparkling and still wine with added lemon and sugar. Germany.

Kaltenberg brewery at Kaltenberg castle, Bavaria, Germany. Brands include Pils and König Ludwig Dunkel, named after King Ludwig of Bavaria, an ancestor of the brewery's present owner, Prince Luitpold.

Kamikaze Cocktail. Over ice shake 1 part Cointreau, 1 vodka, 1 Rose's Lime Juice cordial. Strain.

Kammer liqueur distillery, Kammer, Germany.

Kammer vineyard at Brauenberg in Mosel-Saar-Ruwer region, Germany.

kampai 'cheers' in Japanese.

Kamptal-Klassik wine producer in Kamptal, Niederösterreich, Austria.

K & B Cornucopia Ale strong ale (6.5% alc) by King & Barnes brewery, Horsham, West Sussex, England.

Kandeel liqueur from cognac flavoured with cinnamon, cloves and vanilla. Van Zuylekom distillery, Amsterdam, Netherlands.

Kangaroo Cocktail. Over ice stir 2 parts vodka, 1 dry vermouth. Strain and squeeze lemon peel over.

Kanonkop leading wine estate of Stellenbosch, South Africa. Renowned Paul Sauer red wine from Bordeaux grapes plus Cabernet and Sauvignon and Pinotage reds. Kadette is 'second' label.

Kanterbräu brewer and beer brand (4.7% alc) of Strasbourg, Alsace, France.

kanyak domestic brandy of Turkey. The name (and the spirit) pretends, remotely, to a similarity with cognac.

Kanzel vineyard at Obernbreit in Franken region, Germany.

Kanzem wine village of Mosel-Saar-Ruwer region. *Grosslage*: Scharzberg. Vineyards: Altenberg, Schlossberg, Sonnenberg.

Kanzler white grape-variety crossing of Müller-Thurgau and Silvaner. Rheinhessen region, Germany.

Kao Liang Chiew grape-based tonic of People's Republic of China.

Kapellberg vineyard at Laumersheim in Rheinpfalz region, Germany.

Kapellchen vineyard at Minheim in Mosel-Saar-Ruwer region, Germany.

Kapelle vineyards at Bodenheim and Gau-Bickelheim in Rheinhessen region and Hainfeld in Rheinpfalz region, Germany.

Kapellenberg the name of 28 individual vineyards in Germany. Region by region, as follows: in Ahr at Bad Neuenahr-Ahrweiler; in Baden at Bad Bellingen (Bamlach), Bad Bellingen (Rheinweiler), Durbach, Freiburg, Klettgau (Erzingen), Klettgau (Rechberg), Ostringen; in Franken at Eibelstadt, Frickenhausen, Volkach; in Mosel-Saar-Ruwer at Alf, Briedern, Bruttig-Fankel (Bruttig), Bruttig-Fankel (Fankel), Nittel, Palzem, Treis-Karden; in Nahe at Münster-Sarmsheim, Odernheim am Glan; in Rheingau at Lorch; in Rheinhessen at Alzey, Alzey (Weinheim), Bingen, Fürfeld, Ober-Olm; in Rheinpfalz at Neustadt an der Weinstrasse; in Württemberg at Rottenburg.

Kapellenberg *Grosslage* incorporating vineyards at Ebelsbach, Knetzgau, Sand am Main, Zeil am Main (Schmachtenberg) and Zeil am Main (Ziegelanger) in Franken region, Germany.

Kapellengarten vineyard at Dackenheim in Rheinpfalz region, Germany.

Kapellenpfad vineyard at Bad Kreuznach in Nahe region, Germany.

Kapellenstück vineyard at Worms in Rheinhessen region, Germany.

Käppele vineyard at Weinstadt in Württemberg region, Germany.

Kapplay vineyard at Ediger-Eller in Mosel-Saar-Ruwer region, Germany.

Kaptenlojtnant liqueur brand from blend of Bénédictine and grape spirit. Sweden.

Kapuzinerbuck vineyard at Wittnau in Baden region, Germany.

Kardinalsberg vineyard at Bernkastel-Kues in Mosel-Saar-Ruwer region, Germany.

Karg brewery at Murnau, Bavaria, Germany. Wheat beer.

Karl K. Kitchen Cocktail. Over ice shake 3 parts scotch whisky, 1 grape juice, 4 dashes grenadine. Strain.

Karloff vodka brand, Australia.

Karlovacko brewery and beer brand. Karlovac, Croatia.

Karlsberg vineyards at Konz in Mosel-Saar-Ruwer region and Weikersheim in Württemberg region, Germany.

Karlskopf vineyard at Bad Neuenahr-Aherweiler in Ahr region, Germany.

Karpi cranberry liqueur by Lignell & Piispanen, Finland.

Karthäuser vineyards at Laubenheim in Nahe region and Volkach in Franken region, Germany.

Karthäuserhofberg vineyard at Trier in Mosel-Saar-Ruwer region, Germany.

Karthäuser Klosterberg vineyard at Konz in Mosel-Saar-Ruwer region, Germany.

Käsberg vineyards at Hessigheim and Mundelsheim in Württemberg region, Germany.

Kasel wine village of Mosel-Saar-Ruwer region, Germany. *Grosslage*: Römerlay. Vineyards: Dominikanerberg, Kehrnagel, Nies'chen etc. Producers include von Kesselstatt.

Käsleberg vineyard at Vogtsburg im Kaiserstuhl in Baden region, Germany.

Kasselberg vineyard at Durbach in Baden region, Germany.

Kastanienbusch vineyard at Birkweiler in Rheinpfalz region, Germany.

Kastaniengarten vineyard at Edenkoben in Rheinpfalz region, Germany.

Kasteelbier strong beer by Van Honsebrouck brewery, Ingelmunster, Belgium.

Kastell vineyards at Boos and Waldböckelheim in Nahe region, Germany.

Katergrube vineyard at Weinsheim in Nahe region, Germany.

Katnook Estate wine producer of Coonawarra, South Australia. Noted white wines including *botrytis* Riesling.

Kattus, Maria wine producer in Wien (Vienna), Austria.

Katy strong medium-dry cider (7.4% alc) by Thatcher's Cider, Sandford, Somerset, England. Made from Katy variety of apple.

Kätzchen vineyard at Osann-Monzel in Mosel-Saar-Ruwer region, Germany.

Katzenbeisser vineyard at Lauffen in Württemberg region, Germany.

Katzenberg vineyard at Weingarten in Baden region, Germany.

Katzenhölle vineyard at Bad Kreuznach in Nahe region, Germany.

Katzenkopf vineyards at Alf in Mosel-Saar-Ruwer region and Sommerach in Franken region, Germany.

Katzenöhrle vineyard at Brackenheim in Württemberg region, Germany.

Katzenstein vineyard at Kindenheim in Rheinpfalz region, Germany.

Kaulenberg vineyard at Auen in Nahe region, Germany.

Kauzenberg in den Mauem vineyard at Bad Kreuznach in Nahe region, Germany.

Kauzenberg-Oranienberg vineyard at Bad Kreuznach in Nahe region, Germany.

Kauzenberg-Rosenhügel vineyard at Bad Kreuznach in Nahe region, Germany.

Kayberg vineyards at Erlenbach-Binswangen (Binswangen), Erlenbach-Binswangen (Erlensbach) and Oedheim in Württemberg region, Germany.

KCB Cocktail. Over ice shake 3 parts dry gin, 1 kirsch, 1 dash apricot brandy, 1 dash lemon juice. Strain.

Keelings Advocaat liqueur by J Townend, Kingston upon Hull, England.

Kehr vineyard at Weinolsheim in Rheinhessen region, Germany.

Kehrberg vineyard at Kobern-Gondorf in Mosel-Saar-Ruwer region, Germany.

Kehrenberg vineyard at Altenbamberg in Nahe region, Germany.

Kehrnagel vineyard at Kasel in Mosel-Saar-Ruwer region, Germany.

Kekfrankos red grape variety of Hungary. Synonymous with Blaufrankisch.

Keknyelü white grape variety of Hungary, particularly for Badascony wines.

Kelham Island brewery in Sheffield, Yorkshire, England.

Keller cellar in German – beer and wine.

Kellerei winery in German.

Kellerberg vineyard at Weinsheim in Nahe region, Germany.

Kellerbier style of ale in which filtering is obviated by allowing the brew to settle in a tank before being tapped off. Traditional in Bavaria, Germany.

Kellermeister cellarmaster or winemaker in German.

Kellermilch perry brand of Halewood International, Huyton, Merseyside, England.

Kellersberg vineyard at Gau-Bischofsheim in Rheinhessen region, Germany.

Kelmer's pub-brewery at Santa Rosa, California, USA.

Keltek brewery at Redruth, Cornwall, England.

Kelter vineyard at Himmelstadt in Franken region, Germany.

Kelterberg vineyards at Arspach, Kirchberg and Marbach/Nektar in Württemberg region, Germany.

Kemelrain vineyards at Wertheim (Höhefeld) and Wertheim (Reichholzheim) in Baden region, Germany.

Kempinski Cocktail. Over ice shake 1 part rum, 1 Cointreau, 2 grapefruit juice. Strain and add a maraschino cherry. Recipe of Bristol Kempinski hotel, Berlin, Germany.

Kemper brewery at Poulsbo, Washington, USA.

Kemptown brewery at Kemptown, Brighton, East Sussex, England.

Kendermann, Hermann wine producer, Bingen, Germany. Black Tower Liebfraumilch and others.

Kent Old beer by Tooth Brewery (est 1835 by Kent-born John Tooth), Sydney, Australia.

Kent Town brewery in Adelaide, Australia, producing **Kent Town Real Ale**.

Kentucky Cocktail. Over ice shake 2 parts bourbon, 1 pineapple juice. Strain.

Kentucky Colonel Cocktail. Over ice stir 3 parts bourbon, 1 Bénédictine. Strain.

Kenya Cane cane spirit by International Distillers, Nairobi, Kenya.

Kenya Gold cane-spirit-based coffee liqueur by International Distillers, Nairobi, Kenya.

Keo wine producer, island of Cyprus. Aphrodite white wine, Othello red and fortified wines.

Keppoch-Padthaway wine region of South Australia.

Kerner white grape variety of Germany newly (1969) created by crossing Trollinger and Riesling. Also planted in England and South Africa.

Kernobsbranntwein apple or pear spirit of Germany.

Kerry Cooler Cocktail. Over ice shake 2 parts Irish whiskey, 1 dry sherry, 1 lemon juice, 4 dashes Amaretto. Strain into an ice-filled tumbler and top with soda water.

Kerschbaum, Paul wine producer in Mittelburgenland, Austria.

Kertz vineyard at Niederhausen an der Nahe in Nahe region, Germany.

Kesselstadt, Weingut Reichsgraf von major wine estate of Mosel-Saar-Ruwer region, Germany. Renowned Riesling wines from vineyards including Josephshöf at Graach.

Kessler brewery at Last Chance Gulch, Helena, Montana, USA.

Kessler whiskey brand formerly of Seagram, USA.

Kestellberg vineyards at Gernsbach and Weisenbach in Baden region, Germany.

Kesten wine village of Mosel-Saar-Ruwer region, Germany. *Grosslage*: Kurfürstlay.

Keulebuckel vineyards at Keltern (Dietlingen) and Keltern (Ellmendingen) in Baden region, Germany.

Keyneston wine district of Barossa Valley region, South Australia.

KGB Cocktail. Over ice shake 3 parts dry gin, 1 kümmel, 3 dashes apricot brandy, 3 dashes lemon juice. Strain.

Khalokhorio wine village of island of Cyprus, known for Commandaria wine.

Khan Krum Controliran wine region of Bulgaria. Chardonnay and Gewürztraminer wines.

Kickelskopf vineyard at Traisen in Nahe region, Germany.

Kicker Cocktail. Over ice shake 2 parts rum, 1 part apple brandy, 2 dashes sweet vermouth. Strain.

kick in the guts nickname for poor-quality English gin of early 18th century. Much gin was then adulterated with turpentine and sulphuric acid. Its toxicity may have been responsible for several thousand deaths between 1700 and 1750.

Kiedrich wine town of Rheingau region, Germany. *Grosslage*: Heiligenstock.

Kientzler, André wine producer, Ribeauvillé, Alsace, France.

Kierlinger, Martin wine producer in Wien (Vienna), Austria.

Kieselberg vineyards at Biebelsheim in Rheinhessen region, Bobenheim am Berg, Deidesheim, Erpolzheim and Kleinkarlbach in Rheinpfalz region and Oberhausen an der Nahe in Nahe region, Germany.

Kilbeggan Irish whiskey brand of Cooley Distillery, Riverstown, Dundalk, County Louth, Republic of Ireland.

Kiliansberg vineyard at Grosslangheim in Franken region, Germany.

Kilkenny Irish beer Irish ale by Smithwick's brewery, Kilkenny, Ireland.

Killawarra wine producer of Penfolds group, Barossa Valley, South Australia.

kill-devil the original generic name for Caribbean rum. The spirit was made by owners of sugar cane plantations first planted in the islands from the 1630s for sale to taverns and ships. By 1651, when the new name 'rumbullion' is said to have been first recorded, kill-devil production had already reached a reported 200,000 gallons a year.

Killerby Leschenault wine producer of Margaret River, Western Australia.

Killer Whale Stout beer by Pacific Coast brewery, Oakland, California, USA.

kill grief nickname for gin, 18th-century England.

Kilzberg vineyards at Geisenheim and Geisenheim (Johannisberg) in Rheingau region, Germany.

Kimberley Best Mild ale brand of Hardys & Hansons brewery, Nottingham, England. Also **Kimberley Best Bitter** and **Kimberley Classic**.

Kina Cocktail. Over ice shake 2 parts dry gin, 1 Lillet, 1 sweet vermouth. Strain.

Kinclaith Lowland malt whisky from a distillery at Moffat St, Glasgow, Scotland, demolished 1982.

Kindl brewery in Berlin, Germany, famed for wheat beers.

King & Barnes brewery in Horsham, West Sussex, England. Beers include Mild Ale, Old Ale, Sussex Bitter.

Brewery closed 2000 but brands and 65 pubs were taken over by Hall & Woodhouse of Dorset.

King Arthur gin brand originally of Seagram, Canada.

King Cole Cocktail. Over ice stir 1 part rye whisky, 2 dashes sugar syrup, 1 dash Fernet Branca. Add orange and pineapple slices to glass.

Kingfisher lager by United Breweries, Bangalore, India. Also brewed by Shepherd Neame, Faversham, England.

King George IV blended scotch whisky of United Distillers, Edinburgh, Scotland.

King Henry VIII five- and 12-year-old blended scotch whiskies by Highland Blending Co, London, England.

King James VI blended scotch whisky of Forth Wines, Milnathort, Kinross, Scotland.

King of Scots twelve-, 17- and 25-year-old blended scotch whiskies by Douglas Laing, Glasgow, Scotland. Also, **King of Scots Rare Extra Old**.

King Robert II blended scotch whisky of Ian MacLeod, Broxburn, Scotland. Also, 12-year-old.

King's Legend blended scotch whisky of Ainslie & Heilbron, Glasgow, Scotland.

Kingston Black apple variety traditionally valued for cider-making. Synonymous with Black Taunton. English.

Kingston Black cider-brandy/unfermented apple juice brand (20% alc) by Somerset Cider Brandy Co, England. Production method is similar to Pineau des Charentes.

Kingston Cocktail. Over ice shake 2 parts rum, 1 kümmel, 1 orange juice, 1 dash Pimento Dram liqueur.

Kingston Estate leading wine producer in Murray Valley, Australia.

Kinheim wine village of Mosel-Saar-Ruwer region, Germany. *Grosslage*: Schwarzlay.

Kinnleitenberg vineyard at Königsberg in Bayern in Franken region, Germany.

Kinzigtäler vineyards at Berghaupten, Gengenbach, Gengenbach (Bermersbach), Gengenbach (Reichenbach), Hohberg (Diersburg), Hohberg (Hofweiler), Hohberg (Niederschopfheim), Offenburg and Ohlsbach in Baden region, Germany.

Kir mixed apéritif drink named for French partisan and mayor of Dijon, Burgundy, Félix Kir. To a glass of chilled dry white wine (correctly, Bourgogne Aligoté) add 1 teaspoon crème de cassis.

Kirchberg the name of 48 individual vineyards in Germany. Region by region, as follows: in Baden at

Badenweiler, Efringen-Kirchen, Efringen-Kirchen (Huttingen), Efringen-Kirchen (Istein), Ehrenkirchen, Ettenheim (Münchweier), Ettenheim (Wallburg), Gottenheim, Kippenheim, Königsheim, Kraichtal, Lauda-Königshofen (Beckstein), Lauda-Königshofen (Königshofen), Vogtsburg im Kaiserstuhl (Schelingen), Vogtsburg im Kaiserstuhl (Oberrotweil); in Franken at Castell, Uettingen, Würzburg; in Hessische Bergstrasse at Bensheim; in Mosel-Saar-Ruwer at Burgen, Konz, Löf, Moselkern, Veldenz; in Nahe at Waldböckelheim; in Rheinhessen at Bingen, Eckelsheim, Freilaubersheim, Gabsheim, Hackenheim, Osthofen, Udenheim; in Rheinpfalz at Alberweiler, Barbelroth, Edenkoben, Gleiszellen-Gleishorbach, Gross-und Kleinfischlingen, Neustadt an der Weinstrasse, St Martin; in Württemberg at Bönnigheim, Bönnigheim (Hohenstein), Esslingen, Freudental, Kirchheim, Sachsenheim (Hohenhaslach), Sachsenheim (Kleinsachsenheim), Stuttgart (Obertürkheim), Vaihingen.

Kirchberg *Grosslage* incorporating vineyards in Franken region, Germany at, respectively: Dettelbach (Neues am Berg), Dettelbach (Neusetz), Fahr, Frankenwinheim, Kolitzheim (Lindach), Kolitzheim (Stammheim), Kolitzheim (Zeilitzheim), Markt Eisenheim (Obereisenheim), Markt Eisenheim (Untereisenheim), Neusetz, Nordheim, Schwarzach, Sommerach, Volkach, Volkach (Astehim), Volkach (Escherndorf), Volkach (Fahr), Volkach (Gaibach), Volkach (Hallburg), Volkach (Köhler), Volkach (Krautheim), Volkach (Obervolkach), Volkach (Rimach), Volkach (Vogelsburg), Waigolshausen (hergolshausen), Waigolshausen (Theinheim), Wipfeld.

Kirchenpfad vineyard at Rüdesheim in Rheingau region, Germany.

Kirchenstück the name of 13 individual vineyards in Germany. Region by region, as follows: in Rheingau at Hochheim; in Rheinhessen at Alzey, Bornheim, Ingelheim, Mainz; in Rheinpfalz at Bad Dürkheim, Ellerstadt, Forst an der Weinstrasse, Herxheim am Berg, Hainfeld, Kallstadt, Landau in der Pfalz, Maikammer.

Kirchenweinberg *Grosslage* incorporating vineyards at Flein, Heilbronn, Ilsfeld, Lauffen, Neckarswestheim, Talheim and Untergruppenbach in Württemberg region, Germany.

Kirchgärtchen vineyard at Welgesheim in Rheinhessen region, Germany.

Kirchhalde vineyard at Uhldingen-Mühlhof in Baden region, Germany.

Kirchöh vineyard at Dierbach in Rheinpfalz region, Germany.

Kirchlay vineyards at Ernst, Kröv and Osann-Monzel in Mosel-Saar-Ruwer region, Germany.

Kirchmayr wine producer in Kamptal, Niederösterreich, Austria.

Kirchplatte vineyard at Nierstein in Rheinhessen region, Germany.

Kirchspiel vineyard at Westhofen in Rheinhessen region, Germany.

Kirchstück vineyard at Hohen-Sülzen in Rheinhessen region, Germany.

Kirchtürmchen at Bad Neuenahr-Ahrweiler in Ahr region, Germany.

Kirchweinberg vineyards at Hassmersheim and Neckarsimmern in Baden region, Germany.

Kirchweingarten vineyard at Bullay in Mosel-Saar-Ruwer region, Germany.

Kirin largest brewery of Japan. Brands include **Kirin Lager Beer**.

kirmi red (wine). Turkey.

Kirnbauer, Walter wine producer in Mittelburgenland, Austria.

Kir Royale add sparkling wine to 1 teaspoon crème de cassis.

kirsch *eau de vie* distilled from cherries. France and Switzerland.

Kirschwasser *eau de vie* distilled from cherries. Germany.

Kirschgarten vineyards at Erpolzheim and Laumersheim in Rheinpfalz region, Germany.

Kirschheck vineyards at Norheim and Wallhausen in Nahe region, Germany.

Kirschwingert vineyard at Neu-Bamberg in Rheinhessen region, Germany.

Kirwan, Château wine estate of AC Margaux, Médoc, Bordeaux, France. Classified *3ème Grand Cru Classé*.

Kiss Kiss Cocktail. Over ice stir 1 part dry gin, 1 cherry brandy, 1 sweet vermouth. Strain.

Kitchen brewery at Aspley, Huddersfield, West Yorkshire, England.

Kitterlé *grand cru* vineyard, Guebwiller, Alsace, France.

Kittling Ridge Estate wine producer at Grimsby, Ontario, Canada.

Kiwi Lager beer brand by Maxim brewery, New Zealand.

Klamm vineyard at Niederhausen an der Nahe in Nahe region, Germany.

Klarers clear spirit, Germany.

Klaus vineyards at Geisenheim, Geisenheim (Johannisberg) and Oestrich-Winkel in Rheingau region, Germany.

Klausenberg vineyards at Worms in Rheinhessen region, Germany.

Kläuserweg vineyards at Geisenheim and Geisenheim (Johannisberg) in Rheingau region, Germany.

Klein Constantia Estate wine property within Constantia vineyard, Capetown, planted 1685 by Simon van der Stel, first Governor of the Cape, South Africa. Famed Cabernet Sauvignon, Chardonnay, Sauvignon etc plus Vin de Constance sweet wine, a revival of 18th–19th century Constantia, formerly the world's premier dessert wine.

Kleindal wine brand of Vinimark company, Stellenbosch, South Africa.

Klein Karoo vineyard region, South Africa.

Klepberg vineyards at Eisingen, Kämpfelbach (Bilfingen), Kämpfelbach (Ersingen) and Keltern in Baden region, Germany.

Kletterberg vineyards at Angelbachtal in Baden region and Neu-Bamberg in Rheinhessen region, Germany.

Klevner regional name for Pinot Noir grape variety, Switzerland.

Klingle vineyard at Remshalden in Württemberg region, Germany.

Klipdrift brandy by Castle Wine & Green, South Africa.

Klipfel, Domaine wine producer est 1824, Barr, Alsace, France. Renowned Clos Zisser Gewürztraminer and other wines.

Klisch Dark Lager Beer brand of Lakefront brewery, Milwaukee, Wisconsin, USA.

Kloppberg vineyard at Dittelsheim-Hessloch in Rheinhessen region, Germany.

Kloppenberg vineyard at Mommenheim in Rheinhessen region, Germany.

Klosterberg herbal liqueur by Eckes distillery, Germany.

Klosterberg the name of 23 individual vineyards in Germany. Region by region, as follows: in Baden at Bruchsal; in Mittelrhein at Oberheimbach in Mosel-Saar-Ruwer at Bengel, Bernkastel-Kues, Lehmen, Maring-Noviand, Perl, Platten, Saarburg, Schleich, Traben-Trarbach, Wiltingen, Zell; in Nahe at Norheim; in Rheingau at Kiedrich, Oestrich-Winkel, Rüdesheim; in Rheinhessen at Bechtolsheim, Mainz, Nieder-Olm, Osthofen; in Württemberg at Sachsenheim, Vaihingen, Weikersheim.

Klosterberg *Grosslage* incorporating vineyards in Ahr region, Germany at, respectively: Ahrbrück, Altenahr, Altenahr (Kreuzberg), Altenahr (Reimerzhoven), Bad Neuenahr-Ahrweiler (Ahrweiler), Bad Neuenahr-Ahrweiler (Bachem), Bad Neuenahr-Ahrweiler (Ehlingen), Bad Neuenahr-Ahrweiler (Heimersheim), Bad Neuenahr-Ahrweiler (Heppingen), Bad Neuenahr-Ahrweiler (Lohrsdorf), Bad Neuenahr-Ahrweiler (Marienthal), Bad Neuenahr-Ahrweiler (Neuenahr), Bad Neuenahr-Ahrweiler (Walporzheim), Dernau, Matschoss, Rech.

Klosterbergfelsen vineyard at Baden-Baden in Baden region, Germany.

Klosterbrauerei Furth monastery-brewery at Landshut, Bavaria, Germany.

Klosterbruder vineyard at Ingelheim in Rheinhessen region, Germany.

Kloster Disibodenberg vineyard at Odernheim am Glan in Nahe region, Germany.

Kloster Eberbach monastic site of state wine domain and wine academy of Germany. Hattenheim, Rheingau region.

Kloster Fürstental vineyard at Bacharach in Mittelrhein region, Germany.

Klostergarten the name of 24 individual vineyards in Germany. Region by region, as follows: in Ahr at Bad Neuenahr-Ahrweiler; in Franken at Grossheubach; in Mosel-Saar-Ruwer at Brauneberg, Cochem, Leiwen; in Nahe at Bingen, St Katharinen, Sponheim, Weiler; in Rheinhessen at Bermersheim vdH, Flonheim, Hackenheim,

Nierstein, Sankt Johann, Schwaben-heim, Sprendlingen, Zotzenheim; in Rheinpfalz at Edenkoben, Gönn-heim, Grünstadt, Landau in der Pfalz, Niederkirchen.

Klostergut Fremersberger Feigen-wäldchen vineyard at Sinzheim in Baden region, Germany.

Klostergut Schelzberg vineyard at Sasbachwalden in Baden region, Germany.

Klosterhofgut vineyard at Bern-kastel-Kues in Mosel-Saar-Ruwer region, Germany.

Klosterkammer vineyard at St Alde-gund in Mosel-Saar-Ruwer region, Germany.

Klosterlay vineyard at Rüdesheim in Rheingau region, Germany.

Kloster Liebfrauenberg *Grosslage* in-corporating vineyards in Rheinpfalz region, Germany at, respectively: Babelroth, Bad Bergzabern, Billig-heim-Ingenheim, Gleiszellen-Gleis-horbach, Göcklingen, Hergersweiler, Heuchelheim-Klingen, Kapellen-Drusweiler, Klingenmünster, Nie-derhorbach, Oberhausen, Pleis-weiler-Oberhofen, Rohrbach, Stein-eiler, Winden.

Klosterlikors herbal liqueur of Germany.

Klosterneuburg winemaking research centre and vineyard (Chorrenstift) of Donauland, Austria.

Klosterpfad vineyards at Dorsheim in Nahe region and Rhodt unter Rietburg in Rheinpfalz region, Germany.

Klosterschaffnerei vineyard at Bockenheim an der Weinstrasse in Rheinpfalz region, Germany.

Kloster Schwarz-Bier dark (but not black) beer by Kulmacher Mönchs-hof brewery, Kulmbach, Germany.

Klosterstück vineyards at Einsel-thum and Zellertal in Rheinpfalz region, Germany.

Klosterweg vineyards at Hupperath and Wittlich in Mosel-Saar-Ruwer region, Bingen and Ockenheim in Rheinhessen region and Gerols-heim in Rheinpfalz region, Germany.

Klotzberg vineyard at Bühlertal in Baden region, Germany.

Klüsserath wine village of Mosel-Saar-Ruwer region, Germany. *Grosslage*: St Michael. Producers include Friedrich Wilhelm Gym-nasium.

KMW Klosterneuberger Mostwaage. Austria's scale for measuring sugar levels in grape must.

Knickerbocker Cocktail. Over ice shake 2 parts dry gin, 1 dry ver-mouth, 1 dash sweet vermouth. Strain and squeeze lemon peel over.

Knickerbocker Special Cocktail. Over ice shake 1 part rum, 1 tea-spoon each lemon juice, orange juice, raspberry syrup, 2 dashes curaçao. Strain.

Knights Valley AVA of Sonoma County, California, USA.

Knipperlé lost white grape variety of Alsace, France.

Knockando Speyside malt whisky distillery est 1898, Morayshire, Scotland. Named after the *cnoc-an-dhu* ('black hillock') on which the distillery stands. Single malts bottled by Justerini & Brooks, London, as single vintages.

Knockdhu East Highland malt whisky distillery, Knock, Banff-shire, Scotland. Single malt: 12-year-old.

Knockeen brand of Irish Poteen by Knockeen Hills distillery, Water-ford, Ireland.

Knockendoch dark beer (5.0% alc) by Sulwath Brewery, Southerness, Scotland.

Knockout Cocktail. Over ice shake 1 part dry gin, 1 dry vermouth, 1 pastis, 1 teaspoon white crème de menthe. Strain.

Knoll, Emerich wine producer in Wachau, Niederösterreich, Austria.

Knopf vineyards at Friesenheim and Hahnheim in Rheinhessen region, Germany.

Knudsen Erath wine producer in Willamette Valley, Oregon, USA.

Knysna brewery in Cape Province, South Africa.

Kobánya brewery in Budapest, Hungary. Lager beers.

Kobersberg vineyard at Rimpar in Franken region, Germany.

Kobnert *Grosslage* incorporating vineyards at Bad Dürkheim (Lei-stadt), Bad Dürkheim (Ungstein), Dackenheim, Erpolzheim, Freins-heim, Herxheim am Berg, Kallstadt, Ungstein and Weisenheim am Berg in Rheinpflaz region, Germany.

Kochberg vineyard at Durbach in Baden region, Germany.

Kocherberg *Grosslage* incorporating vineyards in Württemberg region, Germany at, respectively: Dörzbach, Forchtenberg, Forchtenberg (Erns-bach), Hardthausen, Ingelfingen, Ingelfingen (Criesbach), Künzelsau, Künzelsau (Belsenberg), Möckmühl, Möckmühl (Signlingen), Neudenau, Niedernhall, Schöntal, Weissbach, Widdern.

Kocher-Jagst-Tauber *Bereich* of Württemberg region, Germany.

Koelenhof co-operative wine producer of Stellenbosch, South Africa.

Koff beer brand of Sinebrychoff brewery, Finland.

Köhler vineyards at Dingolshausen, Dingolshausen (Bischwind), Gerolz-heim and Sulzheim in Franken region, Germany.

Köhler-Köpfchen vineyard at Bad Münster am Stein-Ebernburg in Nahe region, Germany.

kokkineli rosé wine, Greece.

Kölbl, Ernst Johannes wine producer in Weinviertel, Niederösterreich, Austria.

Kolkmann, Horst & Gerhard wine producer in Donauland, Niederösterreich, Austria.

Kollwentz, Andi wine producer in Neusiedlersee Hügelland, Burgenland, Austria.

Kolomyka vodka brand formerly of Seagram, Canada.

Kölsch pale-coloured beer style of Cologne, Germany. Name is protected under an official convention of 1985.

König brewery in Duisburg, Germany. Beers include **König Alt, König Pilsener**.

König vineyards at Sternenfels and Sternenfels (Diefenbach) in Württemberg region, Germany.

König, HC noted distiller of Steinhäger spirit, Steinhägen, Westphalia, Germany.

Königin vineyard at Tauberrettersheim in Franken region, Germany.

Königin Viktoriaberg vineyard at Hocheim in Rheingau region, Germany.

König Johann Berg vineyards at Kastel Staadt and Serrig in Mosel-Saar-Ruwer region, Germany.

Königsbach wine village of Rheinpfalz region, Germany. *Grosslage*: Meerspinne. Vineyards: Idig, Jesuitengarten, Oelberg, Reiterpfad.

Königsbacher brewery in Koblenz, Germany.

Königsbecher vineyard at Ostringen in Baden region, Germany.

Königsberg vineyards at Klüsserath and Traben-Trarbach in Mosel-Saar-Ruwer region and Steinheim in Württemberg region, Germany.

Königsberg *Grosslage* incorporating vineyards at Albersweiler, Albersweiler (St Johann), Birkweiler, Frankweiler, Landau in der Pfalz mit Queichheim und Mörlheim, Landau in der Pfalz (Arzheim), Landau in der Pfalz (Godramstein, Ranschbach and Siebeldingen in Rheinpfalz region, Germany.

Königslay-Terrassen vineyard at Zell in Mosel-Saar-Ruwer region, Germany.

Königsschild vineyard at Langenlonsheim in Nahe region, Germany.

Königsschloss vineyard at Münster-Sarmsheim in Nahe region, Germany.

Königstuhl vineyards at Gundersheim and Lörzweiler in Rheinhessen region, Germany.

Königsweg vineyards at Zellertal (Niefernheim) and Zellertal (Zell) in Rheinpfalz region, Germany.

Königsweingarten vineyard at Bodman in Baden region, Germany.

Königswingert vineyard at Wachenheim in Rheinpfalz region, Germany.

König Wenzel vineyard at Rhens in Mittelrhein region, Germany.

König-Wilhelms-Berg vineyard at Flörsheim in Rheingau region, Germany.

konjac brandy of Albania. The resemblance to cognac extends to no degree beyond the phonetic.

Konzelmann wine producer of Niagara Peninsular, Ontario, Canada.

Kopf *Grosslage* incorporating vineyards in Württemberg region, Germany at, respectively: Korb, Korb (Kleinheppach), Remshalden, Schorndorf, Waiblingen, Waiblingen (Beinstein), Waiblingen (Neustadt), Winstadt, Winnenden,

Winnenden (Breuningsweiler), Winnenden (Bürg), Winnenden (Hanweiler), Winterbach.

Kopfensteiner, Manfred wine producer in Südburgenland, Austria.

Kopke, CN oldest port producer, est 1638 by German Cristiano Kopke, Vila Nova de Gaia, Portugal. Renowned Colheita tawnies and vintages: 1955, 58, 60, 63, 65, 66, 70, 74, 75, 77, 78, 79, 80, 82, 83, 85, 87, 89, 91, 92, 94, 97, 2000, 03.

Koppelstein vineyards at Braubach and Lahnstein in Mittelrhein region, Germany.

Korbel & Bros, F sparkling wine producer since 1881, Sonoma, California, USA.

korenwijn all-malt *genever* distilled without juniper. Netherlands.

Korn grain spirit (*Schnapps*) of Germany. Usually from rye (*Roggen*), sometimes wheat (*Weizen*) or both (*Getreide*). Also labelled **Kornbrantt** or **Kornbranntwein**.

Kornell, Hanns sparkling wine producer, Napa Valley, California, USA.

Korn-genever juniper-flavoured Korn, Germany.

Körper-Faulhammer, Walter wine producer in Südburgenland, Austria.

Koshu white grape variety of Japan.

Koskenkorva vodka brand, Finland.

Kosmet region of former Yugoslavia, now Serbia-Macedonia, known for Amselfelder wine from Pinot Noir grapes and Cabernet Sauvignon wines.

Kosovo alternative name of Kosmet.

Köstritzer Schwarzbier 'black beer' by **Köstritzer Schwarzbierbrauerei**, Bad Köstritz, Thüringen, Germany.

k(o)umiss liquor from fermented mare's milk. Traditional beverage of the Tartars. Also the spirit distilled therefrom. Tatar *kumiz*.

Kourtaki retsina brand of D Kourtakis, Marcopoulo Attica, Athens, Greece.

Kovosh vodka brand of Merchant International, UK.

Koyote Kölsch beer by Coyote Spring Brewing Co, Phoenix, Arizona, USA.

Kracher, Alois wine producer in Neusiedlersee, Burgenland, Austria.

Krähenberg vineyard at Massenbachhausen in Württemberg region, Germany.

Krähenschnabel vineyard at Erlenbach (bei Marktheidenfeld) mit Orsteil Triefenthal in Franken region, Germany.

Krajina vineyard region of Serbia.

Kralevo Controliran wine region of Bulgaria. Riesling wines.

Kranzberg vineyards at Dalheim amd Nierstein in Rheinhessen region, Germany.

Krapfenberg vineyard at Vollmer-weiler in Rheinpfalz region, Germany.

Kraski Teran red wine from Teran grapes grown in coastal limestone-subsoil ('krass') vineyards of Istria, Slovenia.

Kräusening in brewing, the process of adding wort to promote secondary fermentation and thus carbonation. German. Beer thus made may be described as **Kräusenbier**.

Kräuterberg vineyards at Bad Neuenahr-Ahrweiler in Ahr region and Oberdiebach in Mittelrhein region, Germany.

Kräuterhaus vineyard at Traben-Trarbach in Mosel-Saar-Ruwer region, Germany.

Krauterlikors herbal liqueur of Germany.

Kreidkeller vineyard at Kallstadt in Rheinpfalz region, Germany.

Krepkaya strong (56%) vodka brand, Russia.

Kretchma Cocktail. Over ice shake 2 parts vodka, 2 crème de cacao, 1 lemon juice, 1 dash grenadine. Strain.

kretzer German regional name for *rosato* wines of Alto Adige, Italy.

Kreuz vineyards at Dienheim, Ockenheim and Oppenheim in Rheinhessen region, Friedelsheim and Kirchheim and der Weinstrasse in Rheinpfalz region and Hammelburg in Franken region, Germany.

Kreuzberg the name of 16 individual vineyards in Germany. Region by region, as follows: in Baden at Achern, Kappelrodeck, Offenburg, Renchen, Tauberbischofsheim; in Franken at Nordheim, Volkach; in Mittelrhein at Koblenz; in Mosel-Saar-Ruwer at Traben-Trarbach; in Rheinhessen at Bodesheim, Dolgesheim, Worms; in Rheinpfalz at Einselthum, Zellertal (Niefernheim), Zellertal (Zell).

Kreuzblick vineyard at Worms in Rheinhessen region, Germany.

Kreuzhalde vineyards at Ihringen and Ihringen (Wasenweiler) in Baden region, Germany.

Kreuzkapelle vineyard at Guntersblum in Rheinhessen region, Germany.

Kreuzlay vineyard at Zell in Mosel-Saar-Ruwer region, Germany.

Kreuznach *Bereich* of Nahe region, Germany. *Grosslagen*: Kronenberg, Pfaffgarten, Schlosskapelle, Sonnenborn.

Kreuzpfad vineyard at Kolitzheim in Franken region, Germany.

Kreuzweg vineyards at Framersheim in Rheinhessen region and Leimen in Baden region, Germany.

Kreuzwingert vineyard at Piesport in Mosel-Saar-Ruwer region, Germany.

Kreydenweiss, Marc wine producer, Barr, Alsace, France.

Kriegsberg vineyard at Stuttgart in Württemberg region, Germany.

kriek lambic-based cherry beer. Belgium.

Krim Brut sparkling wine brand, Russia.

Kristall Weizen style of filtered (as opposed to sedimented) wheat beer. Germany.

Kroatenpfad vineyard at Neustadt an der Weinstrasse in Rheinpfalz region, Germany.

Kroatzbeere bramble-flavoured liqueur by Thienelt distillery, Düsseldorf, Germany.

Kroiss, Walter wine producer in Neusiedlersee, Burgenland, Austria.

Krolewska grain vodka brand of Polmos Zielona Gora distillers, Poland.

Krombacher brewery in Kreutzal-Krombach, Germany. Pilsener beers.

Kronberg vineyard at Sand am Main in Franken region, Germany.

Krondorf wine producer in Barossa Valley, South Australia.

Krone vineyards at Laubenheim in Nahe region, Lorch in Rheingau region, Prichsenstadt in Franken region and Waldrach in Mosel-Saar-Ruwer region, Germany.

Kroneberg vineyard at Bullay in Mosel-Saar-Ruwer region, Germany.

Kronen brewery in Dortmund, Germany.

Kronenberg vineyards at Alf in Mosel-Saar-Ruwer region and Kallstadt in Rheinpfalz region, Germany.

Kronenberg *Grosslage* incorporating vineyards at Bad Kreuznach, Bad Kreuznach (Bosenheim), Bad Kreuznach (Ippesheim), Bad Kreuznach (Planig), Bad Kreuznach (Winzenheim), Bretzenheim and Hargesheim in Nahe region, Germany.

Kronenbourg largest brewery of France, based at Strasbourg in Alsace. Est 1664, the date is identified with the company's premium lager. Bought by UK brewers Scottish & Newcastle, 2000.

Kronenbrauerei brewery at Gundelfingen, Bavaria, Germany. Organic beers including Oko-Krone Pilsner (5.0% alc).

Kronenbühl vineyards at Friesenheim, Friesenheim (Heiligenzell), Friesenheim (Oberschopfheim), Friesenheim (Oberweier), Lahr, Lahr (Hugsweier) and Lahr (Mietersheim).

Kronsberg vineyard at Iphofen in Franken region, Germany.

Krötenbrunnen *Grosslage* incorporating vineyards in Rheinhessen region, Germany at, respectively: Alsheim, Dienheim, Dolgesheim, Eich, Elmsheim, Gimbsheim, Guntersblum, Hillesheim, Ludwigshöhem Mettenheim, Oppenheim, Uelversheim, Wintersheim.

Krötenpfuhl vineyard at Bad Kreuznach in Nahe region, Germany.

Kröv wine village of Mosel-Saar-Ruwer region, Germany. *Grosslage*: Nacktarsch.

Krug *Grande Marque* champagne house est 1843 Reims, France. Grande Cuvée, Clos du Mesnil Blanc de Blancs and other famous and famously costly wines.

Krug, Charles wine producer in Napa Valley, California, USA.

kruidenbier style of beer flavoured with herbs or spices (instead of hops). Belgium.

Krupnik vodka-based, honey-flavoured liqueur. Poland and Russia.

Krutzler, Reinhold & Erich wine producer in Südburgenland, Austria.

Krusovice brewery and lager brand, Czech Republic.

Kubanskaya vodka brand of Russia.

Kübler 57 absinthe (57% alc) distilled at Val-de-Travers, Neuchatel, Switzerland.

Kuch Behar Cocktail. In an ice-filled tumbler stir 1 part pepper vodka, 1 tomato juice.

Küchenmeister vineyard at Rödelsee in Franken region, Germany.

Kuentz-Bas wine producer est 1795 Husseren-les-Châteaux, Alsace, France. Famed Gewürztraminer wines including Cuvée Caroline, and many others.

Kugel, Christian wine producer in Südsteiermark, Austria.

Kugelspiel vineyard at Castell in Franken region, Germany.

Kuhberg vineyard at Schriesheim in Baden region, Germany.

Kuhnchen vineyard at Riveris in Mosel-Saar-Ruwer region, Germany.

Kuhstall vineyard at St Goar in Mittelrhein region, Germany.

Kulmbacher Mönchshof brewery with monastic origins (est 1349) in Kulmbach, Germany. Famed for beers including dark Kloster Schwarz-Bier.

Kulmbacher Reichelbräu brewery in Kulmbach, Germany, known for Eisbock Bayrisch G'frorns (Bavarian ice beer).

Kulmbacher Schweizerhof brewery in Kulmbach, Germany, known for **Kulmbacher Schweizerhof-Bräu** Pilsener beer.

Kulminator 28 *bock* beer by EKU brewery, Kulmbach, Germany. So called because beer is made to minimum gravity of 28 degrees, the highest for beer worldwide.

Kumala popular wine brand of South Africa. *see label opposite* ➡

Kumeu-Huapai-Waimauku wine region of Auckland province, North Island, New Zealand.

Kumeu River wine producer in Kumeu, New Zealand.

kümmel caraway-seed flavoured liqueur. Said to originate 1575 in distillery of Lucas Bols, Amsterdam, Netherlands. Bols, Mentzendorff and Wolfschmidt are among the international producers.

Kummerling after-dinner liqueur brand, Germany. Owned by Allied Domecq, UK.

Kummer-Schuster wine producer in Neusiedlersee, Burgenland, Austria.

Kunigunda Leicht small brewery at Pferdsfeld, Germany.

Kupferflöz vineyard at Dörscheid in Mittelrhein region, Germany.

Kupfergrube vineyard at Schlossböckelheim in Nahe region, Germany.

Kupferhalde vineyard at Oberderdingen mit Grossvillars in Württemberg region, Germany.

Kupp vineyards at Ayl mit Orsteil Biebelhausen, Ockfen, Saarburg, Serrig, Trier, Wiltingen and

Wittlich in Mosel-Saar-Ruwer region, Germany.

Küppers major brewery in Cologne, Germany. *Kölschbier*.

Kup's Indispensable Cocktail. Over ice shake five parts dry gin, 2 dry vermouth, 1 sweet vermouth, 1 dash pastis. Strain and squeeze orange peel over.

Kurfürst vineyards at Ellenz-Poltersdorf in Mosel-Saar-Ruwer region and Neustadt an der Weinstrasse in Rheinpfalz region, Germany.

Kurfürstenberg vineyard at Waldrach in Mosel-Saar-Ruwer region, Germany.

Kurfürstenhofberg vineyard at Trier in Mosel-Saar-Ruwer region, Germany.

Kurfürstenstück *Grosslage* incorporating vineyards at Gau-Bickelheim Gau-Weinheim, Gumbsheim, Vendersheim, Wallertheim and Wöllstein in Rheinhessen region, Germany.

Kurfürstlay *Grosslage* incorporating vineyards in Mosel-Saar-Ruwer region, Germany at, respectively: Bernkastel-Kues (Andel), Bernkastel-Kues (Bernkastel), Bernkastel (Kues), Brauneberg, Brauneberg (Filzen), Burgen, Kesten, Maring-Noviand, Mülheim, Osann-Monzel (Monzel), Osann-Monzel (Osann), Veldenz, Wintrich.

Kurz wine producer in Thermenregion, Niederösterreich, Austria.

Kuss mit Liebe combination liqueur (in divided, two-necked bottle) of kakao coffee liqueur and bramble-flavoured *Kroatzbeere* liqueur by Thienelt distillery, Düsseldorf, Germany.

Kutman wine producer at Mürefte, Turkey. Villa Doluca brand.

Kwak Pauwel brewery and beer brand of Flanders, Belgium.

Kwartier na Vijven liqueur by Van Zuylekom distillery, Amsterdam, Netherlands.

KWV Kooperatieve Wijnbouwers Vereniging (Co-operative Winegrowers' Assocation) of South Africa. Major wine producer and distributor est 1918 Paarl, South Africa. Said formerly to control 80 per cent of wine and spirit sales in South Africa. Now a co-operative only in name, following the KWV's conversion into a private company in 1997.

L

'L' Chardonnay *vin de pays d'Oc* brand of Domaine Laroche, Chablis, France.

Laacherberg vineyard at Mayschoss in Ahr region, Germany.

Labat, Château de wine estate of AC Haut-Médoc, Bordeaux, France.

Labatt major brewing company based in London, Ontario, Canada. Brands include **Labatt's Blue**, **Labatt's Classic**. Other beers are Duffy's and Velvet Cream Porter. **Labatt Ice Premium** lager (5.0% alc) is brewed in UK by Whitbread.

Labégorce, Château wine estate of AC Margaux, Médoc, Bordeaux, France. Classified *Cru Bourgeois Supérieur*.

Labégorce-Zédé, Château wine estate of AC Margaux, Médoc, Bordeaux, France. Classified *Cru Bourgeois Supérieur*.

Labère, Clos second wine of Château Rieussec, Bordeaux, France.

Laberstall vineyard at Ockenheim in Rheinhessen region, Germany.

Labord, Château wine estate of AC Lalande-de-Pomerol, Bordeaux, France.

Labottière, Château wine brand of Domaines Cordier, Bordeaux, France.

Labouré Roi well-known *négoçiant-éleveur* and winegrower of Nuits-St-Georges, Burgundy, France.

Lachesnaye, Château wine estate of AC Haut-Médoc, Bordeaux, France. Classified *Cru Bourgeois Supérieur*.

Lachryma Vitis white wine by Emmanuel Delicata, Marsa, Malta.

Lackner-Tinnacher, Fritz wine producer in Südsteiermark, Austria.

Lacoste-Borie second wine of Château Grand-Puy-Lacoste, Bordeaux, France.

Lacrima red grape variety, Marches, Italy.

Lacrima di Morro DOC for red wines from Lacrima grapes, Ancona, Marches region, Italy.

Lacryma Christi del Vesuvio red, *rosato* and white wines of DOC Vesuvio, Campania, Italy. Named after the legend of Christ's tears, shed on Mount Vesuvius.

Lacto Milk Stout beer by Farsons Brewery, Malta.

Ladies Cocktail. Over ice stir 1 part rye whisky, 1 dash Angostura bitters, 1 dash Anisette, 1 dash pastis.

Ladoix Serrigny wine village of Burgundy, France.

Ladoucette, Patrick de wine producer of ACs Pouilly-Fumé and Sancerre, Loire Valley, France.

Lady Be Good Cocktail. Over ice stir 2 parts brandy, 1 crème de menthe, 1 sweet vermouth. Strain.

Ladyburn ephemeral Lowland malt whisky distillery, Girvan, Ayrshire, Scotland. In production only from 1966–76.

Lady Macbeth Cocktail. Over ice shake 4 parts Scotch whisky, 1 lemon juice, 1 teaspoon amaretto, 1 teaspoon curaçao, 1 teaspoon sugar. Strain.

Lady of the Lake beer brand (4.2% alc) of Glastonbury Ales, Somerton, Somerset, England.

Lady's Finger Cocktail. Over ice stir 2 parts dry gin, 1 cherry brandy, 1 kirsch. Strain.

Lafaurie, Château wine estate of AC Premières Côtes de Bordeaux, France.

Lafaurie-Peyraguey, Château great wine estate of AC Sauternes, Bordeaux, France. Classified *1er Cru Classé*. This was the sweet wine shared by Sebastian Flyte and his guest Charles Ryder en route to Brideshead on their idyllic outing from Oxford in the immortal pages of *Brideshead Revisited*, the novel by Evelyn Waugh published 1945.

Lafayette wine brand of Nathaniel Johnston, Bordeaux, France.

Laffitte-Carcasset, Château wine estate of AC St-Estèphe, Médoc, Bordeaux, France. Classified *Cru Bourgeois*.

Laffitte-Laujac, Château second wine of Château Laujac, Bordeaux, France.

Lafite, Château wine estate of AC Premières Côtes de Bordeaux, France.

Lafite-Canteloup, Château wine estate of AC Haut-Médoc, Bordeaux, France. Classified *Cru Bourgeois*.

Lafite-Rothschild, Château great wine estate of AC Pauillac, Médoc, Bordeaux, France. Classified first among the *1ers Grands Crus Classés* in 1855, purchased by the Rothschilds in 1868 and still of pre-eminent reputation in many but not all vintages.

Lafite Très Vieille Réserve cognac blended from spirits up to 80 years old. A brand of Société Civile du Château Lafite-Rothschild.

Lafleur, Château great wine estate of AC Pomerol, Bordeaux, France.

Lafleur-Gazin, Château wine estate of AC Pomerol, Bordeaux, France.

Lafleur-du-Roy, Château wine estate of AC Pomerol, Bordeaux, France.

Lafon, Château wine estate of AC Listrac, Médoc, Bordeaux, France. Classified *Cru Grand Bourgeois*.

Lafon-Rochet, Château wine estate of AC St-Estèphe, Médoc, Bordeaux, France. Classified *4ème Grand Cru Classé*.

Lafüe, Château wine estate of AC Ste-Croix-du-Mont, Bordeaux, France.

lagar large stone trough formerly used for treading grapes by foot. Still in use on certain Douro estates for port, eg at Taylors' Quinta de Vargellas. Portuguese.

Lagarosse, Château wine estate of AC Premières Côtes de Bordeaux, France.

Lagavulin Island malt whisky distillery est 1816, Port Ellen, Islay, Scotland. Single malts: 12- and 16-year-old.

lager beer fermented and matured at low temperature. See box.

Lagler, Karl wine producer in Wachau, Niederösterreich, Austria.

lago Spanish for *lagar*.

Lagos brewery at Apapa, Lagos, Nigeria.

Lago di Caldaro DOC for red wines from Gentile, Grigia and Schiava grapes, lake Caldaro, Trentino-Alto Adige, Italy.

Lagrange, Château wine estate of AC Pomerol, Bordeaux, France.

Lagrange, Château wine estate of AC St Julien, Médoc, Bordeaux, France. Classified *3ème Grand Cru Classé*.

Lagrange, Gaston de cognac house est 1961 by Martini & Rossi, Cognac, France. XXX, VSOP, XO (40-year-old) etc.

Lagrange-de-Lescure, Château wine estate of AC St Emilion, Bordeaux, France. Classified *Grand Cru*.

Lagrave, Château wine estate of AC Ste-Croix-du-Mont, Bordeaux, France.

Lagrein red grape variety of Trentino-Alto Adige region, Italy.

Lágrima finest quality of Malaga wine, Spain.

Laguardia wine-producing town of Rioja Alavesa, Spain.

Lagüe, Château wine estate of AC Fronsac, Bordeaux, France.

Lagune, Château La wine estate of AC Haut-Médoc, Bordeaux, France. Classified *3ème Grand Cru Classé*.

Lahntal *Grosslage* at Bad Elms, Dausenau, Fachbach, Nassau, Obernhof and Weinäher in Mittelrhein region, Germany.

L'Aiglon Cocktail. Pour 1 part Mandarine Napoléon into a champagne glass and top with chilled champagne.

Lager

pale beer with a dark past

Brewers in Bavaria are credited with making the first lager. The name is the German word for a storage place, and thus identifies what distinguishes lager from beer. Lager is a beer that can be stored. Originally, it was beer 'laid down' in dark caves in the Alps where the cold conditions slowed the process of souring. This ensured a supply of drinkable beer in the summer − a time when warmer weather made it problematic to produce good, fresh new beer.

By the 19th century, commercial brewers had refined methods of fermenting the beer in near-freezing conditions. This 'bottom fermenting' process employed yeasts which were active even at very low temperatures, and remained in the bottom of the fermenting vessel throughout the lengthy duration of fermentation. This was originally up to 12 days − three or four times longer than for other beers − but can now be considerably quicker. Similarly, the period of cold maturation in storage vessels − originally between six weeks and six months − is now usually less than a month.

Lagers are ready to drink when bottled or barrelled. They do not improve, and will deteriorate if kept too long. The cold fermenting process induces not just a higher level of alcohol than other beers, but a greater retention of carbonic acid. This is what makes naturally made lagers relatively fizzy. Once these beers are opened, they lose their freshness and sparkle if not consumed immediately.

The first 'branded' lagers are claimed to be those of the Czech town of Pilsen, where in 1842 the lager process was applied to brewing a pale, clear beer of what was then a wholly new type. Previous lagers had been just as dark and cloudy as other beers. Pilsner-type lagers now dominate production throughout the world.

Laird O'Cockpen ten-year-old blended scotch whisky by Cockburn & Campbell, London, England. Commemorates Sir Alex Ramsay, hero of the battle of Otterburn, 1388.

Laird's Applejack apple-flavoured liqueur, USA. Said to have been devised by William Laird in Monmouth, New Jersey, 1698. The story goes that in 1760, George Washington obtained the recipe from Laird's descendants and the drink subsequently went into production in the Virginia colony.

La Jolla Cocktail. Over ice shake 3 parts brandy, 1 banana liqueur, 1 equal mix lemon and orange juice. Named after a Californian town, it is correctly pronounced 'La Hoya'.

Lake County vineyard district of California, USA. Includes AVAs Clear Lake and Guenoc Valley.

Lakefront brewery in Milwaukee, Wisconsin, USA.

Lakeland brew pub (Masons Arms) at Cartmell Fell, Cumbria, England.

Lakeview Cellars Estate wine producer in Vineland, Ontario, Canada.

Lakka cloudberry liqueur by Chymos, Finland.

Lalande, Château wine estate of AC Listrac, Médoc, Bordeaux, France. Classified *Cru Bourgeois*.

Lalande, Château wine estate of AC St Julien, Médoc, Bordeaux, France.

Lalande-Borie wine brand of Château Ducru Beaucaillou, Bordeaux, France.

Lalande de Pomerol AC adjacent to AC Pomerol, Bordeaux, France.

Lalanne, Jacques wine producer of AC Quarts de Chaume, Loire Valley, France.

La Leyenda brand of Pernod-Ricard.

Lalibarde, Château wine estate of AC Côtes de Bourg, Bordeaux, France.

Lamarque, Château wine estate of AC Ste-Croix-du-Mont, Bordeaux, France.

Lamarque, Château de wine estate of AC Haut-Médoc, Bordeaux, France. Classified *Cru Grand Bourgeois*.

Lamartine, Château second wine of Château Cantenac-Brown, Bordeaux, France.

Lamberhurst vineyard and winery est 1972 near Tunbridge Wells, Kent, England.

lambic wheat beer fermented with wild yeasts and from one third or more unmalted wheat (malted barley making up the balance). Lambic beer is still, and characterised by wine-like smell and flavour. Name is believed to derive from the brewing town of Lembeek, south of Brussels, Belgium, in the Zenne river valley, the traditional zone of production.

lambiek alternative spelling of lambic.

Lamblin & Fils *négociant-éleveur* of Chablis, France.

Lambrays, Clos des *Grand Cru* vineyard in Morey-St-Denis, Burgundy, France.

Lambrini 'slightly sparkling' perry brand of Halewood Vintners, Liversedge, England.

Lambrusco grape variety and *frizzante* (slightly sparkling) wine of Emilia-Romagna region, Italy. Produced on an industrial scale for worldwide export, particularly to UK and USA, in non-DOC forms including pink and white versions of varying sweetness. Authentic wine continues to be made, mostly for local consumption in four DOCs.

Lambrusco di Sorbara DOC for wine from Lambrusco di Sorbara grapes, region of Modena, Italy. Dry wines have best reputation for authentic quality.

Lambrusco Grasparossa di Castelvetro DOC for wine from Lambrusco Grasparassa grapes, region south of Modena, Italy. Mostly dry wines.

Lambrusco Reggiano DOC for commercial light wines from a blend of Lambrusco varieties. Emilia-Romagna, Italy.

Lambrusco Salamino di Santa Croce DOC for wine from Lambrusco Salamino grapes, region of Modena including Santa Croce, Italy.

L'Amesinthe absinthe brand of France.

Lamezia DOC for light red wines of Lamezia Terme, Catanzaro, Calabria, Italy.

Lammin Sahti rye beer of Häme, Finland.

Lämmler vineyard at Fellbach in Württemberg region, Germany.

Lamot brewery at Mechelen, Antwerp, Belgium.

Lamothe, Château wine estate of AC Côtes de Bourg, Bordeaux, France.

Lamothe, Château wine estate of AC Premières Côtes de Bordeaux, France.

Lamothe, Château wine estate of AC Sauternes, Bordeaux, France.

Lamothe-Bergeron, Château wine estate of AC Haut-Médoc, Bordeaux, France. Classified *Cru Bourgeois*.

Lamothe-Cissac, Château wine estate of AC Haut-Médoc, Bordeaux, France.

Lamothe-Guignard, Château wine estate of AC Sauternes, Bordeaux, France.

Lancaster Bomber bottled ale by Thwaites brewery, Blackburn, Lancashire, England.

Lancelot champagne brand of Vinicole de Mancy co-operative, Champagne, France.

Lancers popular branded wine by JM da Fonseca of Portugal. Mostly original pink, carbonated version, plus some red and white.

Landat, Château wine estate of AC Haut-Médoc, Bordeaux, France. Classified *Cru Bourgeois*.

Landesweingut Retz wine producer in Weinviertel, Niederösterreich, Austria.

Landier, Remi cognac house, Jarnac, France.

Landiras, Château wine estate of AC Graves, Bordeaux, France.

Landlord strong pale ale (4.1% alc) by Timothy Taylor brewery, Keighley, West Yorkshire, England.

La Landonne Côte Rôtie wine by Guigal, Rhône Valley, France.

Landsknecht vineyards at Volkach (Obervolkach) and Volkach (Rimbach) in Franken region, Germany.

Landskrone vineyards at Bad Neuenahr-Ahrweiler (Heimersheim) and

Bad Neuenahr-Ahrweiler (Lohrsdorf) in Ahr region, Germany.

Landskroon wine estate of Paul & Hugo De Villiers, Paarl, South Africa.

Landwein 'country wine' of Germany. Broadly similar to *vin de pays* of France. Must be from one of 15 defined regions, and have a higher alcohol level and maximum permitted sweetness than ordinary *Tafelwein*.

Lanessan, Château wine estate of AC Haut-Médoc, Bordeaux, France. Classified *Cru Bourgeois Supérieur*.

Lang wine producer in Neusiedlersee, Burgenland, Austria.

Längberg vineyard at Hammelburg in Franken region, Germany.

Lange Els vineyard at Hessheim in Rheinpfalz region, Germany.

Langenbach Liebfraumilch producer, Worms, Germany. Crown of Crowns brand.

Langenberg vineyards at Eltville in Rheingau region, Odernheim am Glan in Nahe region and Retzstadt in Franken region, Germany.

Langenlonsheim wine town of Nahe region, Germany. *Grosslage*: Sonnenborn.

Langenmorgen vineyard at Deidesheim in Rheinpfalz region, Germany.

Langenstein vineyards at Martinsheim in Franken region and Neustadt an der Weinstrasse in Rheinpfalz region, Germany.

Langenstück vineyards at Eltville, Eltville (Rauenthal) and Walluf in Rheingau region, Germany.

Langgarten vineyard at Manubach in Mittelrhein region, Germany.

Langhe hill region of Piedmont, Italy. Includes famed Barbaresco and Barolo vineyards, and many good-quality wines of the region not covered by those DOCs are sold as Langhe *vino da tavola*.

Langhölle vineyard at Obermoschel in Nahe region, Germany.

Langhorne Creek vineyard district south of Adelaide, South Australia.

Langlois Château leading wine producer in Saumur, Loire Valley, France. Sparkling Saumur wines.

Langoa-Barton, Château wine estate of AC St Julien, Médoc, Bordeaux, France. Classified *3ème Grand Cru Classé*.

Langs Supreme blended scotch whisky by Robertson & Baxter, Glasgow, Scotland. Also, **Langs Select** (12-year-old).

Langwerth von Simmern'sches Rentamt, Freiherrlich wine estate in Rheingau region, Germany. Noted Riesling wines from vineyards including Erbacher Marcobrunn, Hattenheimer Nussbrunnen etc.

Laniote, Château wine estate of AC St-Emilion, Bordeaux, France. Classified *Grand Cru Classé*.

Lanique vodka brand of Polmos Lancut, Poland.

Lannes, Domaine Les armagnac by Christian Domange, Bezolles, Gascony, France.

lanolin in winetasting, a soft, unctuous smell characterising ripe white wines especially those from Chenin Blanc grapes.

Lanson Père & Fils *Grande Marque* champagne house est 1760, Reims, France. Well-known Black Label NV and well-regarded 'Red Label' vintage.

Lapelletrie, Château wine estate of AC St-Emilion, Bordeaux, France. Classified *Grand Cru*.

Laphroaig Island malt whisky distillery est 1820, Port Ellen, Islay, Scotland. Single malts: ten- and 15-year-old. Name is pronounced la-froyg.

Lapin Kulta brewery in Lapland, Finland.

Larcis-Ducasse, Château wine estate of AC St-Emilion, Bordeaux, France. Classified *Grand Cru Classé*.

Lardit, Château wine estate of AC Côtes de Castillon, Bordeaux, France.

Larios leading gin brand of Spain. Also schnapps.

Larkins brewery est 1986 at Chiddingstone, Kent, England.

Larmande, Château wine estate of AC St-Emilion, Bordeaux, France. Classified *Grand Cru Classé*.

Laroche, Domaine leading wine producer est 1850 at Obédiencerie, Chablis, France. Wines of AC Chablis, Chablis Premiers Crus and Chablis Grands Crus plus branded wines of Languedoc.

Laroche, Michel *récoltant manipulant* champagne producer, Vauciennes, Champagne, France.

La Roche vineyard at Flonheim in Rheinhessen region, Germany.

Laroche-Bel-Air, Château wine estate of AC Premières Côtes de Bordeaux, France.

Laroque, Château wine estate of AC St-Emilion, Bordeaux, France. Classified *Grand Cru Classé* (1996).

Larose-Trintaudon, Château wine estate of AC Haut-Médoc, Bordeaux, France. Classified *Cru Grand Bourgeois*.

Laroze, Château wine estate of AC St-Emilion, Bordeaux, France. Classified *Grand Cru Classé*.

Larresingle leading armagnac producer, Condom, Gascony, France.

Larrivaux, Château wine estate of AC Haut-Médoc, Bordeaux, France. Classified *Cru Bourgeois*.

Larrivaux-Hanteillan, Château second wine of Château Hanteillan, Bordeaux, France.

Larrivet-Haut-Brion, Château wine estate of AC Pessac-Léognan, Bordeaux, France.

Larsen cognac house, Cognac, France. VSOP Viking, Golden Viking Hors d'Age etc.

Lartigue, Château wine estate of AC St-Estèphe, Médoc, Bordeaux, France.

Lartigue-de-Brochon second wine of Château Sociando-Mallet, Bordeaux, France.

Lasala absinthe brand of Philip Lasala, Spain.

Lascombes, Château wine estate of AC Margaux, Médoc, Bordeaux, France. Classified 2ème *Grand Cru Classé*.

Lasenberg vineyard at Bötzingen in Baden region, Germany.

Laski Rizling white grape variety and popular medium wine of Slovenia. Synonymous with Welschriesling. Once better known as 'Yugoslav Laski Riesling' and the top-selling individual wine brand in the UK.

Lasky Cocktail. Over ice shake 1 part dry gin, 1 grape juice, 1 Swedish Punsch. Strain.

Lassaubatju, Domaine de armagnac producer, Villeneuve-de-Marsan, France.

Lassalle, Château second wine of Château Potensac, Bordeaux, France.

Lassalle, J *récoltant manipulant* champagne producer, Chigny-les-Roses, Champagne, France.

Lassèque, Château wine estate of AC St-Emilion, Bordeaux, France. Classified *Grand Cru*.

Lass O'Gowrie brew pub in Manchester, England.

Last Resort bitter ale (4.2% alc) by Willys Brewery, Cleethorpes, England.

La Stupenda Cocktail. Over ice shake 2 parts vodka, 1 fresh cream, 1 raspberry liqueur. Strain. Said to be named in honour of Australia's stupendous soprano, Dame Joan Sutherland.

La Taberna brand of Pernod-Ricard.

late-bottled vintage port from one year's harvest (sometimes from declared vintages) matured in cask for four to five years then bottled, ready to drink. Commonly abbreviated by the plethora of shippers who produce it, to LBV. Portugal.

late harvest in English-speaking wine-producing countries, the term for sweet wine made from grapes picked after the main harvest. Extra ripening means higher concentrations of sugar.

Latisana DOC for red and white wines, Friuli-Venezia Giulia, Italy.

Latium wine-producing region of Italy, including Rome.

Latour, Château great wine estate of AC Pauillac, Médoc, Bordeaux, France. Classified *1er Grand Cru Classé*.

Latour, Louis leading wine producer and *négociant-éleveur* of Beaune, Burgundy, France. Many *Grand Cru* and *Premier Cru* holdings producing red and white wines of famed quality.

Latour à Pomerol, Château wine estate of AC Pomerol, Bordeaux, France.

La Tour Blanche wine estate of AC Sauternes, Bordeaux, France. The wine is made by the Ecole de Viticulture et d'Oenologue at Bommes.

Latour de France village and AC of Côtes du Roussillon, Midi, France.

Latricières-Chambertin *Grand Cru* vineyard adjacent to Chambertin, Côte d'Or, Burgundy, France.

Latt vineyard at Albersweiler in Rheinpfalz region, Germany.

Latzenbier 'beer from wood' – a style of strong *Altbier* brewed in Düsseldorf, Germany.

Laudamusberg vineyard at Neumagen-Dhron in Mosel-Saar-Ruwer region, Germany.

Laudun designated village of AC Côtes du Rhône Villages, France.

Lauder's blended scotch whisky by MacDuff International, Glasgow, Scotland.

Lauerburg wine estate of Mosel-Saar-Ruwer region, Germany. Part-owner of Bernkastel Doctor vineyard.

Lauerweg vineyard at Langenlonsheim in Nahe region, Germany.

Laugel wine producer at Marlenheim, Alsace, France. Leading producer of Crémant d'Alsace sparkling wine.

Laujac, Château wine estate of AC Médoc, Bordeaux, France. Classified *Cru Grand Bourgeois*.

Launay, Château wine estate of AC Entre-Deux-Mers, Bordeaux, France.

Launois Père & Fils *récoltant manipulant* champagne producer, le Mesnil-sur-Oger, Champagne, France.

Laurentiusberg vineyards at Altenbamberg and Wallhausen in Nahe region, Bremm, Saarburg mit Ortsteil Krutweiler and Waldrach in Mosel-Saar-Ruwer region and Königswinter in Mittelrhein region, Germany.

Laurentiuslay vineyards at Köwerich and Leiwen in Mosel-Saar-Ruwer region.

Laurent-Perrier *Grande Marque* champagne house est 1812 by Emile Laurent. His widow Mathilde added her maiden name, Perrier, in 1887 on his death. Tours-sur-Marne, France.

Laurenziweg vineyard at Dorsheim in Nahe region, Germany.

Laurétan, Château wine estate of AC Premières Côtes de Bordeaux, France.

Laurets, Château des wine estate of AC Puisseguin-St-Emilion, Bordeaux, France.

Laurette, Château wine estate of AC Ste-Croix-du-Mont, Bordeaux, France.

Lavalière, Château wine estate of AC Médoc, Bordeaux, France. Classified *Cru Bourgeois*.

Lavaux wine region of the Vaud, Switzerland.

Lavilledieu village VDQS of SW France. Co-operative-made red and rosé wines from Cabernet Franc, Gamay, Negrette, Syrah and Tannat grapes.

Laville-Haut-Brion, Château wine estate of AC Pessac-Léognan, Bordeaux, France. Classified *Cru Classé*.

Lavillotte, Château wine estate of AC St-Estèphe, Médoc, Bordeaux, France. Classified *Cru Bourgeois*.

Lawhill Cocktail. Over ice shake 2 parts rye whisky, 1 dry vermouth, 1 dash Angostura bitters, 1 dash maraschino, 1 dash pastis. Strain.

Lay vineyards at Bernkastel-Kues, Lehmen, Palzem, Senheim and Wittlich in Mosel-Saar-Ruwer region, Germany.

Layenberg vineyards at Bruttig-Fankel in Mosel-Saar-Ruwer region and Niedermoschel in Nahe region, Germany.

Laykaul vineyard at Korlingen in Mosel-Saar-Ruwer region, Germany.

Lazarus, Josef wine producer in Weststeiermark, Austria.

LBV see late-bottled vintage.

Leacock madeira house est 1741, now a brand of Madeira Wine Co, Funchal, Madeira.

Leányka white grape variety of Hungary.

Leap-Frog Cocktail. Over ice pour 4 parts dry gin, 1 lemon juice. Top up with dry ginger ale.

Leap Year Cocktail. Over ice shake 4 parts dry gin, 1 Grand Marnier, 1 sweet vermouth, 1 dash lemon juice. Strain and squeeze lemon peel over.

Leatherbritches brewery at Fenny Bentley, Ashbourne, Derbyshire, England.

Leave It To Me Cocktail. Over ice shake 2 parts dry gin, 1 apricot brandy, 1 dry vermouth, 1 dash grenadine, 1 dash lemon juice. Strain.

Lebanon not a country with a wine or spirit tradition, but home to famed vineyard of Château Musar and arrack-producing Ksara distillery, both in Bekaa Valley.

Leberl, Josef wine producer in Neusiedlersee Hügelland, Burgenland, Austria.

LeBlanc Estate wine producer at Harrow, Ontario, Canada.

Le Chanticleer Cocktail. Over ice shake 2 parts dry gin, 2 lemon juice, 1 Bénédictine, 1 crème de noyaux. Strain.

Leckerberg vineyards at Armsheim and Dittelsheim-Hessloch in Rheinhessen region, Germany.

Leckmauer vineyard at Müden in Mosel-Saar-Ruwer region, Germany.

Leckzapfen vineyard at Osthofen in Rheinhessen region, Germany.

Leconfield estate for high-quality wines from Cabernet Sauvignon and Riesling grapes, est 1974 Coonawarra, South Australia.

Ledaig single malt whisky (1974, 1975 vintage bottlings) by Tobermory distillery (formerly named Ledaig distillery), Isle of Mull, Scotland.

Ledbury brewery at Ledbury, Herefordshire, UK.

lees sediment thrown by wine after fermentation.

Lees, JW brewery at Middleton, Manchester, England. Bottled beers include Archer Stout, Harvest Ale, Tulip Lager.

Leeuwin Estate vineyard of Margaret River region, Western Australia. Famed Cabernet Sauvignon and Pinot Noir red wines and Chardonnay and Riesling whites.

Leeward Cocktail. Over ice stir 3 parts rum, 1 apple brandy, 1 sweet vermouth, 1 dash grenadine. Strain.

Leffe beer brand (6.6% alc) of Abbaye de Leffe (owned by Interbrew), France. Claims descent from ale of original Abbaye de Abdij van Leffe, est 1240.

Leflaive, Domaine Vincent great wine domain of Puligny-Montrachet, Côte d'Or, Burgundy, France. White wines from *Grand Cru* vineyards Le Montrachet, Bâtard-Montrachet, Bienvenues-Bâtard-Montrachet, Chevalier-Montrachet and *Premiers Crus* of Puligny-Montrachet Clavoillon, Les Combettes, Les Pucelles. Also branded red and white burgundies.

Leflaive Frères, Olivier wine domain and *negoçiants-éleveurs*, Puligny-Montrachet, Côte d'Or, France. *Premier Cru* vineyards Chassagne-Montrachet Chaumées, Meursault Poruzots. Well-known village and regional burgundies.

Lefranc, Charles pioneer wine-producer commemorated in Charles Lefranc brand of Almadén Winery, founded by him 1852, San Joaquin, California, USA.

Legendary 18-year-old scotch blended whisky brand of Clan Campbell distillers, UK.

legs in winetasting, the trails or 'tears' lingering on the sides of the bowl after swirling the wine in the glass. Long-lasting legs indicate glyceriney, rich wine.

Lehrner, Paul wine producer in Mittelburgenland, Austria.

Leidhecke vineyard at Bodenheim in Rheinhessen region, Germany.

Leiersberg vineyard at Leingarten in Württemberg region, Germany.

Leikaul vineyard at Trier in Mosel-Saar-Ruwer region, Germany.

Leinenkugel brewery at Chippewa Falls, Wisconsin, USA.

Leinhöhle vineyard at Deidesheim in Rheinpfalz region, Germany.

Leistenberg vineyard at Oberhausen an der Nahe in Nahe region, Germany.

Leiterchen vineyards at Nittel and Trittenheim in Mosel-Saar-Ruwer region, Germany.

Leitner, Herbert wine producer in Neusiedlersee, Burgenland, Austria.

Leitner, Matthias wine producer in Neusiedlersee, Burgenland, Austria.

Leiwen wine village of Mosel-Saar-Ruwer region, Germany. *Grosslage*: St Michael.

Lemnos island of Aegean known for rich white wine from Muscat grapes.

Lemoine-Nexon, Château second of Château Malleret, Bordeaux, France.

Lemon Pie Cocktail. Pour a measure of scotch whisky over ice in tumbler glass and top with lemonade.

Lenchen vineyards at Oestrich-Winkel in Rheingau region and Stadecken-Elsheim in Rheinhessen region, Germany.

length in winetasting, the time the flavour remains discernible in the mouth. The longer it lingers, the better it is.

Lennenborn vineyard at Bacharach in Mittelrhein region, Germany.

Lenzenberg vineyards at Stuttgart (Hedelfingen) and Stuttgart (Rohracker) in Württemberg region, Germany.

Léognan commune of Graves region, Bordeaux, France. Part of Pessac-Léognan AC.

Léon wine-producing region of northern Spain.

Léon, Château wine estate of AC Premières Côtes de Bordeaux, France.

León, Jean leading wine producer of Penedès region, Spain. Notable Cabernet Sauvignon and Chardonnay wines.

Leone de Castris wine producer at Salice Salentino, Apulia, Italy.

Leopard lager brand of Lion brewery, New Zealand.

Leopoldsberg vineyard at Bermatingen in Baden region, Germany.

Léoville-Barton, Château wine estate of AC St Julien, Médoc, Bordeaux, France. Classified *2ème Grand Cru Classé*.

Léoville-Las-Cases, Château great wine estate of AC St Julien, Médoc, Bordeaux, France. Classified *2ème Grand Cru Classé*.

Léoville-Poyferré, Château wine estate of AC St Julien, Médoc, Bordeaux, France. Classified *2ème Grand Cru Classé*.

Lepanto brandy by Gonzalez Byass, Jerez de la Frontera, Spain.

Lerchelsberg vineyard at Worms in Rheinhessen region, Germany.

Lerchenberg the name of 15 individual vineyards in Germany. Region by region, as follows: in Baden at Bretten, Eichstetten, Eppingen, Eppingen (Mühlbach), Eppingen (Rohrbach a G), Kraichtal, Kümbach, Meersburg, Oberderdingen, Stetten, Sulzfeld and Zaisenhausen; in Rheinpfalz at Kapsweyer; in Württemberg at Bönnigheim, Erligheim, Esslingen and Esslingen (Mettingen).

Lerchenböhl vineyard at Neustadt an der Weinstrasse in Rheinpfalz region, Germany.

Lerchenspiel vineyard at Gerolsheim in Rheinpfalz region, Germany.

Leroux liqueur brand formerly of Seagram, USA.

Leroy wine grower and *négociant-éleveur* of Auxey-Duresses, Burgundy, France. *Grand Cru* holdings in Chambertin, Clos de Vougeot and Musigny.

Lessona DOC for red wines mainly from Nebbiolo grapes grown in Vercelli hills, Piedmont, Italy.

Lestage, Château wine estate of AC Listrac, Médoc, Bordeaux, France. Classified *Cru Bourgeois Supérieur*.

Lestage-Darquier, Château wine estate of AC Moulis, Médoc, Bordeaux, France. Classified *Cru Bourgeois Supérieur*.

Lestage-Simon, Château wine estate of AC Haut-Médoc, Bordeaux, France. Classified *Cru Bourgeois*.

Leth, Franz wine producer in Donauland, Niederösterreich, Austria.

Letourt, Château second wine of Château Hauterive, Bordeaux, France.

Letten vineyards at Auggen in Baden region and Deidesheim and Hainfeld in Rheinpfalz region, Germany.

Letterlay vineyard at Kröv in Mosel-Saar-Ruwer region, Germany.

Levante regional name for ordinary wines of SE Spain.

Leverano DOC for red and *rosato* wines from Negroamaro grapes and whites from Malvasia. Apulia, Italy.

Levert *genever* distillery, Netherlands.

Lexia regional name for Muscat d'Alexandrie grape variety, Australia.

Leyland brewery at Wellingborough, Northamptonshire, England.

Lhéraud cognac growers and distillers, Lasdoux, Châteauneuf, Cognac. Réserve du Templier 10-year-old, Vieille Réserve du Templier 25-year-old, Très Vieille Réserve du Paradis 50-year-old.

Lia Fail beer (4.7% alc) by Inveralmond Brewery, Perth, Scotland. Name is Gaelic for Stone of Destiny – the coronation stone of the Kings of Scotland kept at Scone Palace, near the brewery.

Liaoming vineyard region of Manchuria, People's Republic of China.

Liatiko red grape variety of Aegean island of Crete.

Liberation commemorative bitter ale (4.8% alc) by Eldridge Pope Brewery, Dorset, England. First produced 1995 to mark 50th anniversary of the conclusion of the Second World War in Europe.

see label over ➠

Liberty Ale beer brand of Anchor Brewing Co, San Francisco, California, USA.

Liberty Cocktail. Over ice shake 2 parts apple brandy, 1 rum, 1 dash sugar syrup. Strain.

Lichfield Breweries brewery at Boley Park, Lichfield, Staffordshire, England.

Lichfield Gin brand of Lichfield Gin Co (founder Earl of Lichfield), distilled by W. Grant & Sons, UK.

Lichtenberg vineyards at Grossbottwar, Grossbottwar (Hof und Lembach), Grossbottwar (Winzerhausen), Ilsfeld, Oberstenfeld, Remshalden (Geradstetten), Remshalden (Hebsack), Steinheim and Steinheim (Kleinbottwar) in Württemberg region and Karlsruhe in Baden region, Germany.

lie 'lees' in French. The term is commonly seen on labels of AC Muscadet wines as 'Muscadet Sur Lie'. Signifies wine was kept 'on its lees' (in cask or vat) until bottling, rather than being racked immediately after fermentation. Contact with the lees supposedly enhances flavour.

Liebehöll vineyard at Münster-Sarmsheim in Nahe region, Germany.

Liebenberg vineyards at Osthofen in Rheinhessen region and Sachsenheim (Ochsenbach) and Sachsenheim (Spielberg) in Württemberg region, Germany.

Liebeneck-Sonnerlay vineyard at Osterspai in Mittelrhein region, Germany.

Liebenstein-Sterrenberg vineyards at Kamp-Bornhofen and Kestert in Mittelrhein region, Germany.

Liebesbrunnen vineyards at Dackenheim in Rheinpfalz region and Hochstätten in Nahe region, Germany.

Liebfrau vineyard at Volxheim in Rheinhessen region, Germany.

Liebfrauenberg vineyards at Bittelsheim-Hessloch in Rheinhessen region, Konz in Mosel-Saar-Ruwer region and Meddersheim in Nahe region, Germany.

Liebfraumilch 'Milk of Our Lady'. The name of Germany's largest-selling wine. It is a national rather than a regional wine, though produced mostly in Rheinhessen and Rheinpfalz regions, from Müller-Thurgau, Kerner, Silvaner and Riesling grapes to *QbA* standards. Name appears to have arisen from the soubriquet given to wines of the historic Liebfrauen Kirche vineyard at Worms in Rheinhessen region in the 17th century; the name was adopted by neighbouring growers and spread to other areas. Formalised under the German wine laws of 1971.

Liebfrauenmorgen *Grosslage* incorporating vineyards in Rheinhessen region, Germany at, respectively: Worms, Worms (Abenheim), Worms (Heppenheim), Worms (Herrnsheim), Worms (Hochheim), Worms (Horchheim), Worms (Leiselheim), Worms (Pfeddersheim), Worms (Pfiffligheim), Worms (Weinsheim), Worms (Wiesoppenheim).

Liebfrauenstift-Kirchenstück vineyard at Worms in Rheinhessen region, Germany. Said the be the origin of 'Liebfraumilch'.

Liebfrauenthal vineyard at Gimbsheim in Rheinhessen region, Germany.

Lieblich sweet (up to 45 g/l residual sugar) wine style, Austria.

Liefmans brewery in Oudenaarde, Belgium. Ales include Frambozen (4.5% alc), Kriekbier (6.0% alc).

Lieseberg vineyard at Waldlaubersheim in Nahe region, Germany.

Lieser wine village of Mosel-Saar-Ruwer region, Germany. *Grosslagen*: Beerenlay, Kurfürstlay and, respectively, vineyards of Niederburg-Herden and Schlossberg.

Lieth vineyard at Harxheim in Rheinhessen region, Germany.

lieu dit an individually identified, but officially unclassified, vineyard. Mainly Alsace and Rhône regions of France. Synonymous with *climat* (mainly Burgundy).

Lieutenant Cocktail. Over ice shake 2 parts bourbon, 1 apricot brandy, 1 grapefruit juice, 1 teaspoon sugar. Strain.

light ale in England, the bottled version of bitter ale; in Scotland, draught ale of low gravity.

light and bitter in UK, a pub pint made up of a half-pint of bottled light ale plus a half of draught bitter. Seasoned drinkers insist on the draught-bitter being dispensed first, in the hope (usually fulfilled in the best pubs) of more than an exact half.

light beer in USA, low-calorie beer.

light wine for excise duty purposes in UK, a wine of 14% alc or less – as distinct from fortified wines. In USA, a wine with low alcohol.

Lignell & Piispanen distilling company of Finland. Karpi, Tapio and other liqueur brands.

Ligondras, Château wine estate of AC Margaux, Médoc, Bordeaux, France.

Lilasons brewery at Govindpura, Bhopal, Madhya Pradesh, India.

Lilbert Fils *récoltant manipulant* champagne producer, Cramant, Champagne, France.

Lilian Ladouys, Château wine estate of AC St-Estèphe, Médoc, Bordeaux, France. Classified *Cru Bourgeois*.

Lillet herbal liqueur first made 1887 by brothers Paul and Raymond Lillet at Podensac, Bordeaux, France. Bordeaux wine and armagnac base. Red and white styles.

Lillet Cocktail. Over ice stir 2 parts Lillet, 1 gin. Strain and add a lemon peel twist.

Lilliput Cocktail. Over ice shake 1 part brandy, 1 lemon juice, 1 Lillet, 1 dash white curaçao. Strain.

Lily Cocktail. Over ice shake 1 part dry gin, 1 crème de noyaux, 1 Lillet, 1 dash lemon juice. Strain.

Limburg vineyard at Sasbach in Baden region, Germany.

Limekiln AVA of San Benito County, California, USA.

Limey Cocktail. Over ice shake 2 parts rum, 2 Rose's Lime Juice cordial, 1 Cointreau, 1 fresh lime juice. Strain into ice-filled wine glasses, adding a lime slice to each.

Limmonaya leading lemon vodka brand, Russia.

Limosin brandy by Castle Wine & Green, South Africa.

limoncello lemon-based liqueur of Italy. Many brands.

Limousin French oak valued for wine barrels.

Limoux AC for still white wine from Limoux, Pyrenees region, SW France. Limoux is better known for sparkling Blanquette wines.

Lind brewery at San Leandro, California, USA.

Lindauer leading sparkling wine brand of Montana Wines, Auckland, New Zealand.

Lindauer Seegarten *Grosslage* incorporating vineyards at Bodolz, Lindau, Nonnenhorn and Wasserburg in Württemberg region, Germany.

Lindeboom brewery in Limburg, Netherlands.

Lindelberg *Grosslage* incorporating vineyards in Württemberg region, Germany at, respectively: Bretzfeld, Bretzfeld (Adolzfurt), Bretzfeld (Dimbach), Bretzfeld (Geddelsbach), Bretzfeld (Schwabbach), Bretzfeld (Siebeneich), Bretzfeld (Unterheimbach), Bretzfeld (Waldbach), Langenbrettach (Langenbeutlingen),

Neuenstein (Eschelbach), Neuenstein (Kesselfeld), Neuenstein (Obersöllbach), Ohringen (Michelbach am Wald), Ohringen (Verrenberg), Pfedelbach, Pfedelbach (Harsberg), Pfedelbach (Heuholz), Pfedelbach (Oberohrn), Pfedelbach (Untersteinbach), Pfedelbach (Windischenbach), Wüstenrot (Maienfels).

Lindemans brewery at Vlezenbeek, Belgium. Lambic beers.

Lindemans major wine producer of Australia. Est 1870 in Hunter Valley, New South Wales and now with further vineyards in Coonawarra and Padthaway, South Australia and Murray River, Victoria. Lindemans' hi-tech winery at Karadoc, Victoria, is the largest in Australia. Brands include Ben Ean, Leo Buring, Rouge Homme and Lindemans' own proliferating Bin-numbered wines. Numerous top-quality and popular wines.

Linden popular lager brand, Germany.

Lindener Gilde brewery at Hanover, Germany, known for brands including Broyan Alt, Gilde Pilsener, Ratskeller Edel-Pils.

Lindhälder vineyard at Kernen in Württemberg region, Germany.

Lindisfarne Mead 'The world's finest mead' made on Holy Island, Berwick, England, described as a 'unique alcoholic fortified wine from fermented white grapes, honey, herbs, the pure freshwater from the island's artesian well and fortified with fine spirits'.

Linfit pub brewery (Sair Inn) at Linthwaite, Huddersfield, West Yorkshire, England.

Lingenfelder, Karl leading wine producer at Grosskarlbach in Pfalz region, Germany. Renowned wines from Riesling grapes and also Pinot Noir.

Linie Aquavit renowned aquavit of Løiten Braenderis, part of Norway's state alcohol monopoly. The 'line' in the name is the Equator, across which the spirit is shipped in cask to Australia and back in the belief that the climate changes, sea air and rolling of the ship contribute unique properties to the maturing spirit.

Linkwood Speyside malt whisky distillery est 1821, Elgin, Morayshire, Scotland. Single malts: 12-year-old, 15-year-old.

Linsenbusch vineyard at Ruppertsberg in Rheinpfalz region, Germany.

Linstead Cocktail. Over ice shake 1 part Scotch whisky, 1 sweetened pineapple juice, 1 dash pastis. Strain and squeeze lemon peel over.

Lion brewery in Auckland, New Zealand.

Lion brewery in Biyagama, Sri Lanka.

Lion brewery in Wilkes-Barre, Pennsylvania, USA. Beers include Stegmaier 1857, Stegmaier Porter.

Lion Nathan leading brewing and drinks company of New Zealand.

Liot, Château wine estate of AC Sauternes, Bordeaux, France.

Liouner, Château wine estate of AC Listrac, Médoc, Bordeaux, France. Classified *Cru Bourgeois*.

liqueur de tirage in champagne production, the sugar, wine and yeast mixture added to the new wine to promote second fermentation, and thus carbonation, in bottle.

liqueur d'expédition in champagne production, the cane sugar and wine mixture for topping up bottles following *dégorgement*. Quantity of sugar determines sweetness. The *liqueur* sometimes includes grape spirit.

Liqueur Muscat fortified dessert wine from Muscat grapes, Victoria state, Australia.

liquor any liquid, but especially alcoholic drinks, as in intoxicating liquor. Latin.

liquoroso style of fortified sweet wine, Italy.

Lirac village and AC of southern Rhône Valley, France. Red and rosé wines from Cinsaut, Grenache and Syrah grapes and white from Clairette.

Lisini wine estate of Montalcino, Tuscany, Italy. Noted Brunello di Montalcino wines.

Lismore blended scotch whisky brand of William Lundie, Glasgow, Scotland. Five-, eight-, 12-, 15- and 18-year-old blends.

Listan white grape variety of Midi, France. Synonymous with Palomino.

Listel brand of major commercial wine producer of southern France, Les Salins du Midi.

Listrac AC of Médoc region, Bordeaux, France. Prominent estates include Chx Fourcas Dupré, Fourcas Hosten.

Litana, wine estate in Donauland, Niederösterreich, Austria.

Litanies, Clos des wine estate of AC Pomerol, Bordeaux, France.

Little Devil Cocktail. Over ice shake 2 parts dry gin, 2 rum, 1 Cointreau, 1 lemon juice. Strain.

Littlemill Lowland malt whisky distillery, Bowling, Dumbartonshire,

Scotland. Est 1772, a contender as Scotland's oldest distillery. Single malts: eight- and 12-year-old.

Little Princess Cocktail. Over ice shake 1 part rum, 1 sweet vermouth. Strain.

Livermore Valley AVA of Alameda County, California, USA.

Liversan, Château wine estate of AC Haut-Médoc, Bordeaux, France. Classified *Cru Grand Bourgeois*.

Livran, Château wine estate of AC Médoc, Bordeaux, France. Classified *Cru Bourgeois*.

Ljaskovetz Controliran wine region of Bulgaria.

Ljutomer wine-producing area of Drav region, Slovenia. Home of Lutomer Laski Rizling.

Lobkowicz popular lager brand, Czech Republic.

Lochan Ora Scotch whisky liqueur brand of Pernod-Ricard, UK.

Loch Lomond Cocktail. Over ice stir 2 parts scotch whisky, 1 teaspoon sugar, 1 dash Angostura bitters. Strain.

Lochmühlerlay vineyard at Mayschoss in Ahr region, Germany.

Lochranza blended and single malt scotch whisky brands of Lochranza Whisky Distillery, Isle of Arran, Scotland.

Lochside East Highland malt whisky distillery, Montrose, Angus, Scotland. Est 1957, closed 1995.

Locke's brand of blended and single malt Irish whiskeys of Cooley Distillery, Riverstown, Dundalk, County Louth, Republic of Ireland. Originally the brand of John Locke & Co, est 1757 and claimed to be 'the oldest licensed whiskey distillery in the world.'

Locomotief *genever* brand of P Melcher distillery, Schiedam, Netherlands.

Locorotondo DOC for white wine from Bianco d'Alessano and Verdeca grapes, Locorotondo, Apulia, Italy.

lodges name given to the premises of port shippers in Vila Nova de Gaia, Portugal. From Portuguese *lojas* (storehouse).

Lodi wine region of San Joaquin Valley, California, USA.

Loel fortified wine producer, Cyprus.

Loges, Les wine village of AC Pouilly Fumé, Loire Valley, France.

Logis de la Montaigne cognac brand of Bonnin & Cie, Challignac, Barbezieux, France. XXX, VSOP, Vieille Réserve.

Logis de Montifaud cognac brand of Pierre Landreau, Segonzac, France. XXX, Réserve, Vieux Cognac 50-year-old.

Lognac, Château second wine of Château Ferrande, Bordeaux, France.

Loggerhead pub-brewery at Greensboro, North Carolina, USA.

Logrono administrative capital and important winemaking centre of Rioja region, Spain.

Lohrberger Hang vineyard at Frankfurt in Rheingau region, Germany.

Loimer, Fred wine producer in Kamptal, Niederösterreich, Austria.

Loire Valley great wine region of France with vineyards planted along the length of the river and its tributaries. Eastwards from central France, renowned ACs are Pouilly-Fumé, Sancerre, Menetou Salon, Quincy, Reuilly, Jasnières, Vouvray,

Montlouis, Bourgueil, Chinon, Saumur, Coteaux de Layon, Bonnezeaux, Quarts de Chaume, Savennières, and at the river's Atlantic estuary, Muscadet.

Løiten aquavit brand of state alcohol monopoly, Kristiania, Norway.

Lombard's blended scotch whisky by Lombard Scotch Whisky, Ramsay, Isle of Man, UK.

Lomelino Tarquinio madeira shipper, Funchal, Madeira.

Lomond Lowland single malt whisky of closed Inverleven distillery, Dumbarton, Scotland.

Londino Cocktail. Over ice shake 2 parts dry gin, 2 dry vermouth, 2 orange juice, 1 apricot brandy, 1 Campari. Strain.

London Beer Co brewery in Hoxton, London, England.

London Cocktail. Over ice shake 1 part dry gin, 2 dashes orange bitters, 2 dashes pastis, 2 dashes sugar syrup. Strain.

London gin style of dry gin, as distinct from fuller *genever* gin of Netherlands.

London Pride bitter ale (4.7% alc) by Fuller, Smith & Turner, Chiswick, London, England.

London Stout beers by, respectively, London Pilsener brewery, Bangalore, India and Moosehead brewery, New Brunswick, Canada.

London Winery wine producer at Blenheim, Ontario, Canada.

London Winery wine producer in London, Ontario, Canada. Brands include **London Cream** 'sherry' and even **London Chablis**.

Lone Star brewery and beer brand. San Antonio, Texas, USA.

Lone Tree Cocktail. Over ice shake 1 part dry gin, 1 dry vermouth, 1 sweet vermouth, 2 dashes orange bitters. Strain.

Lone Tree Cooler Cocktail. In a tall glass stir 1 part soda water and 1 pinch caster sugar. Add ice cubes. Add 1 part dry gin and 1 teaspoon dry vermouth. Top with soda, stir and add orange slice.

long in winetasting, a flavour that lingers discernibly in the mouth.

Longenburgerberg vineyard at Königswinter in Mittelrhein region, Germany.

Long Island small-scale wine-producing region of New York State, USA.

Long John blended scotch whisky by Allied Distillers, Dumbarton, Scotland.

Longland pear variety traditionally valued for perry-making. English.

Longleat bottle-conditioned beer (4.5% alc) by Ash Vine Brewery, Frome, Somerset, England. 'Developed exclusively for Lord Bath from an old Longleat House recipe using brandy and raisins to give a sumptuous, rich and fruity taste.'

Longmorn Speyside malt whisky distillery est 1894, Elgin, Morayshire, Scotland. Single malt: 15-year-old. Single malt: 15-year-old. Owned by Pernod-Ricard.

Long Pond rum distillery at Clark's Hill, Falmouth, Jamaica.

Longrow Campbeltown malt whisky distillery est 1973, within Springbank distillery, Campbeltown, Scotland. Single malts: 16- and 17-year-old.

long ship once a common phrase in the parlance of the British saloon bar. If a drinker in a group refers to this style of Viking warship, the implication is that one or more members of the party is being inexcusably slow to offer to buy a round. Reference may be subtly oblique, but in extreme cases, the accuser fixes the alleged jibber with a gimlet glare and declares outright that 'it's a long ship'.

Long Shot Cocktail. Into an ice-filled tall glass pour 3 parts blackberry liqueur, 1 orange juice, 1 teaspoon lemon juice, 1 dash orage bitters. Top with chilled dry ginger ale and stir.

Long Slow Comfortable Screw Cocktail. Over ice shake 1 part Southern Comfort, 1 vodka, 2 orange juice. Strain into tall ice-filled glass and add orange slice. An indelicately named variation on the Screwdriver cocktail.

Lontué wine region south of Santiago, Chile.

Loong Yan white grape variety of China. Name means 'eye of the dragon'.

Loose Moose Cocktail. Over ice stir 2 parts Canadian rye whisky, 1 dry vermouth, 1 dash each of Angostura bitters, maraschino, pastis. Strain.

Loosen, Dr see Dr Loosen.

López de Heredia Viña Tondonia *bodega* est 1877, Rioja, Spain. Todonia red wines and Bosconia whites.

Lorch wine village of Rheingau region, Germany. *Grosslage*: Burgweg.

Lorchhausen wine village of Rheingau region, Germany. *Grosslage*: Burgweg.

Lord Calvert Canadian whisky brand of Canadian Distillers, Canada.

Lord Suffolk Cocktail. Over ice shake 5 parts dry gin, 1 Cointreau, 1 maraschino, 1 sweet vermouth. Strain.

Lord Wisdom Solera Reserva brandy by Wisdom & Warter, Jerez de la Frontera, Spain.

Loreley Edel vineyard at St Goarshausen in Mittelrhein region, Germany.

Loreleyfelsen Grosslage incorporating vineyards at Bornich, Kamp-Bornhofen, Kestert, Nochern, Patersberg and St Goarshausen in Mittelrhein region, Germany.

Lorentz, Gustav wine producer in Berheim, Alsace, France.

Lorettoberg *Grosslage* incorporating vineyards in Baden region, Germany at, respectively: Au, Bad Krozingen, Bad Krozingen (Biengen), Bad Krozingen (Schlatt), Bad Krozingen (Tunsel), Bollschweil, Buggingen, Buggingen (Seefelden), Ebringen, Ehernkirchen (Ehrenstetten), Ehrenkirchen (Kirchofen), Ehrenkirchen (Norsingen), Ehrenkirchen (Scherzingen), Eschbach, Freiburg, Freiburg (St Georgen), Heitersheim, Merzhausen, Pfaffenweiler, Schallstadt, Schallstadt (Mengen), Schallstadt (Wolfenweiler), Staufen im Breisgau, Staufen im Breisgau (Grunern), Staufen im Breisgau (Wellelbrunn), Wittnau.

Loretto Lemonade Cocktail. Over ice shake 1 part Maker's Mark bourbon, 1 Midori, 2 apple juice. Strain into an ice-filled tumbler and top with chilled ginger beer. Stir and garnish with star fruit.

Loretto's Lady in a tall, ice-filled glass stir 2 parts Maker's Mark bourbon, 1 Cointreau. Top with chilled dry ginger ale. Add strawberry slices and mint.

Loriot, Henri *récoltant manipulant* champagne producer, Festigny, Champagne, France.

Loron & Fils wine grower and *négociant-éleveur* of Beaujolais, France.

Lorraine Cocktail. Over ice stir 2 parts dry gin, 1 Grand Marnier, 1 Lillet. Strain.

Los Angeles Cocktail. Over ice stir 1 egg, 4 parts rye whisky, 1 lemon juice, 1 dash sweet vermouth, 4 teaspoons sugar. Strain.

Los Infideles brand of Pernod-Ricard.

Los Llanos leading *bodega* of DO Valdepeñas, Spain. Innovative wines including red Señorío de Los Llanos.

Los Oteros wine region of Leon, Spain.

Los Ruiz brand of Pernod-Ricard.

Lost Coast pub-brewery in Eureka, California, USA.

lota in port trade, Portugal, a lot or consignment of wine from a given vineyard.

Lotberg vineyard at Ihringen in Baden region, Germany.

Lottenstück vineyard at Ingelheim in Rheinhessen region, Germany.

Loubens, Château wine estate of AC Ste-Croix-du-Mont, Bordeaux, France.

Loudenne, Château wine estate of AC Médoc, Bordeaux, France. Classified *Cru Grand Bourgeois*.

Louisa Cocktail. Into a tall, ice-filled tumbler, stir 1 part vodka, 2 tomato juice, 4 dashes Worcestershire sauce, 1 pinch freshly ground black pepper. Top with chilled sparkling water; add a cocktail olive.

Louis XIV brandy by Oude Meester, South Africa.

Louloumet, Château second wine of Château Chicane, Bordeaux, France.

Lounge Lizard Cocktail. In an ice-filled tall glass stir 1 part dark rum, 1 amaretto. Top with chilled cola.

Loupiac AC for sweet white wines, Bordeaux, France.

Loureiro white grape variety important in vinho verde wine of Minho region, Portugal.

Louvière, Château La wine estate of AC Pessac-Léognan, Bordeaux, France.

Love Cocktail. Over ice shake 2 parts sloe gin, 2 dashes lemon juice, 2 dashes orange juice, 1 egg white. Strain.

Löwenbräu renowned brewery in Munich, Germany. Beer is exported or brewed under licence, worldwide.

Lowrie's blended scotch whisky by WP Lowrie, Glasgow, Scotland.

Loyac, Château de second wine of Château Malescot-St-Exupéry, Bordeaux, France.

Lozitza Controliran wine region of Bulgaria. Cabernet Sauvignon wines.

LP non-vintage *brut* champagne of renowned quality by Laurent-Perrier, France.

Lucas, Château second wine of Château Dillon, Bordeaux, France.

Lucifer strong ale (8.0% alc) by Riva brewery, Belgium.

Lucifer Live Beer brewery in Clifton, Bristol, England.

Ludon commune of AC Haut-Médoc, Bordeaux, France.

Ludon-Pomiés-Agassac, Château second wine of Château La Lagune, Bordeaux, France.

Lugana DOC for dry white wine from Trebbiano di Lugana grapes, Lake Garda, Lombardy, Italy.

Lugger Cocktail. Over ice stir 1 part brandy, 1 apple brandy, 1 dash apricot brandy. Strain.

Luginsland vineyards at Aichwald in Württemberg region and Wachenheim in Rheinpfalz region, Germany.

Lugny wine village and AC (Mâcon-Lugny) of Mâconnais, Burgundy, France.

Lugton Inn pub-brewery at Lugton, Strathclyde, Scotland.

Luhmännchen vineyard at Alzenau in Franken region, Germany.

Luigi Cocktail. Over ice shake 2 parts dry gin, 2 dry vermouth, 1 tangerine juice, 1 dash Cointreau, 2 dashes grenadine. Strain.

Luisengarten vineyard at Bad Münster am Stein-Ebernburg in Nahe region, Germany.

Luis Felipe Edwards wine producer in Colchagua Valley, Rapel, Chile.

Luksusowa leading brand of potato vodka, Poland.

Lulu Cocktail. Over ice shake 2 parts Cointreau, 1 melon juice, 1 orange juice. Strain.

Lump vineyards at Kirschroth in Nahe region and Volkach in Franken region, Germany.

Lundetangens brewery at Skien, Norway.

Lungarotti great wine estate of DOCG Torgiano, at Perugia, Umbria, Italy. Lungarotti wines include red Rubesco and white Torre di Giano, plus Cabernet Sauvignon, Chardonnay and others. Also producer of distinguished grappa.

see label over➡

LUNGAROTTI
GRAPPA DI RUBESCO

ℓ.0,75e   45% Vol.
PRODOTTA IN ITALIA

Lupé Cholet wine grower and *négoçiant-éleveur*, Nuits-St-Georges, Burgundy, France. Owner of Château Gris vineyard.

Lur-Saluces, Comte Alexandre proprietor until 1999 of great sweet wine estate of Château d'Yquem, Sauternes, Bordeaux, France. An ancestor acquired Yquem by marriage to Josephine Sauvage d'Yquem, 1785.

Lurton, Jacques international winemaker responsible for numerous brands in France and South America, notably wines of Bodegas Lurton in Mendoza, Argentina.

Luscombes cider producer, Buckfastleigh, Devon, England.

Lusitania Cocktail. Over ice shake 2 parts dry vermouth, 1 brandy, 1 dash orange bitters, 1 dash pastis. Strain and sink.

Lussac satellite AC of St-Emilion, Bordeaux, France. Wines are designated AC **Lussac-St-Emilion**.

Lust, Joseph & Martha wine producer in Weinviertel, Niederösterreich, Austria.

Lustau, Emilio major independent sherry producer, Jerez de la Frontera, Spain. Leading shipper of *almacenista* sherries.

Lutèce *bière de garde* brand of Enfants de Gayant brewery, Douai, France.

Lützelberg vineyard at Sasbach in Baden region, Germany.

Lützeltalerberg vineyard at Grosswallstadt in Franken region, Germany.

Luxardo leading liqueur brand of Italy. Products include Amaretto, Limoncello, Maraschino, Sambuca.

Luxembourg small-scale wine-producing nation known particularly for sparkling wines of Bernard Massard. Vineyards of the Grand Duchy's Mosel river valley also produce white wines principally from Rivaner grapes.

Lychee Chiew lychee wine of People's Republic of China.

lychees in winetasting, a smell characterising the grape variety Gewürztraminer.

lyhing rice wine of Malaysia.

Lyme Bay Cider Co cider producer, Seaton, Devon, England.

Lynch-Bages, Château great wine estate of AC Pauillac, Médoc, Bordeaux, France. Classified *5ème Grand Cru Classé*.

Lynch-Moussas, Château wine estate of AC Pauillac, Médoc, Bordeaux, France. Classified *5ème Grand Cru Classé*.

Lynesack Porter ale brand of Butterknowle Brewery, Newcastle-upon-Tyne, England.

Lyonnat, Château du wine estate of AC Lussac-St-Emilion, Bordeaux, France.

Lysholm brand name of Vinmonopolet, Norway's state alcohol monopoly.

M

Macallan, The Speyside malt whisky distillery of Macallan-Glenlivet, Craigellachie, Scotland. Est 1824 and now the only malt distillery to age all its whisky in sherry casks. Independent until 1996 takeover by Highland Dstilleries and Suntory of Japan. Single malts: seven-, ten-, 12-, 18- and 25-year-old; vintage bottlings.

MacAndrew's beer brand of Caledonian brewery, Edinburgh, Scotland.

MacAndrew's blended scotch whisky by Alastair Graham, Leith, Edinburgh, Scotland.

Macardle brewery and beer brand, Dundalk, Eire. Owned by Guinness.

Macarena brand of Pernod-Ricard.

Macaroni Cocktail. Over ice shake 2 parts pastis, 1 sweet vermouth. Strain.

MacArthur's Select blended scotch whisky by Inver House Distillers, Airdrie, Lanarkshire, Scotland. Also, **MacArthur's 12 Years Old**.

Macau commune of AC Haut-Médoc, Bordeaux, France. Home of Château Cantemerle.

Macbeth's Red beer by Shakespeare brewery, Auckland, New Zealand.

Maccabeo white grape variety mainly of Penedès and Rioja regions, Spain, for *cava* and white Rioja wines respectively.

MacCarthy, Château wine estate of AC St-Estèphe, Médoc, Bordeaux, France. Classified *Cru Grand Bourgeois*.

MacCarthy-Moula, Château wine estate of AC St-Estèphe, Médoc, Bordeaux, France. Classified *Cru Bourgeois*.

Maceira 5 Estrellas spirit brand of Pernod-Ricard.

Machiavelli Chianti Classico by Conti Serristori, St Andrea in Percussina, Italy. Commemorates exile of Italian statesman-philosopher Niccolo Machiavelli (1469–1527) to the Serristori Estate.

Macduff East Highland malt whisky distillery, Banff, Scotland. Name is used only by independent bottlers for the single malts. Proprietors bottle under Glen Deveron name.

MacDuff, The blended scotch whisky by MacDuff International, Glasgow, Scotland.

macération carbonique accelerated winemaking method in which grapes are put uncrushed into carbondioxide filled fermenting vats. CO_2 causes fermentation to begin inside the grapes and a natural fermentation begins lower down in the vat as yeasts and sugars mingle in fruit crushed by the weight of that above. Extract is improved by this process, which enables wines such as Beaujolais to be made in a matter of weeks. French, but now used elsewhere in Europe.

Machard de Gramont wine estate of Nuits-St-Georges, Burgundy, France. *Premier Cru* vineyards in Pommard, Savigny-lès-Beaune.

Macharnudo most-esteemed *albariza* vineyard district of Jerez de la Frontera, Spain.

Machuraz village and *cru* of Vin du Bugey, Savoie, France.

Mack brewery and lager brand at Tromsø, Norway. Reputedly the world's northernmost brewery.

Mackenzie port shipper late of Vila Nova de Gaia, Portugal. Vintages: 1955, 57, 58, 60, 63, 66, 70, 75.

Mackeson renowned stout (3% alc) by Whitbread, Samlesbury Brewery, Preston, Lancashire, England. Mackeson was first brewed at Hythe, Kent in 1669.

Mackinlay five-, 12- and 21-year-old blended scotch whiskies by Charles Mackinlay, Edinburgh, Scotland. Now known as The Original Mackinlay.

Maclay brewery in Alloa, Clackmannanshire, Scotland. Export Ale (4.0% alc), Honey Weizen (4.0% alc), Oat Malt Stout (4.5% alc), Scotch Ale (5.0% alc), 60/- Light Ale.

Mâcon red, rosé and white wine of Mâconnais region of Burgundy, France. Gamay grapes for red and rosé, Chardonnay for white. **Mâcon Supérieur** wines have 1% higher alcohol level.

PRODUCE OF FRANCE   75 cl   MISE EN BOUTEILLE À LA PROPRIÉTÉ

MACON SUPERIEUR BLANC

APPELLATION MACON SUPÉRIEUR CONTROLÉE

CAVE DES VIGNERONS DE BUXY - 71390 BUXY - FRANCE

Mâconnais southern vineyard district of Burgundy region, France. Centred on town of Mâcon. ACs for red, rosé and white wines are Mâcon, Mâcon Supérieur, Mâcon-Villages and individual village ACs of Pouilly-Fuissé, Pouilly-Loché, Pouilly-Vinzelles, St-Véran. Wines for regional ACs of Bourgogne, Bourgogne Grand Ordinaire, Bourgogne Passe-Tout-Grains.

Mâcon-Villages AC for superior red and, particularly, white wines from vineyards of 43 nominated villages of Maconnais region, Burgundy, France. The villages may append their name to the wine's description, eg Mâcon-Lugny, Mâcon-Prissé.

The former Mâcon-Clessé and Mâcon-Viré village appellations were combined into one, Viré-Clessé, from the 1999 vintage.

MacPhail's Speyside single malt whisky brand of Gordon & MacPhail, Elgin, Scotland. Many ages and single vintage bottlings.

Macquin-St-Georges, Château wine estate of AC St Georges-St-Emilion, Bordeaux, France.

Mac's microbrewery at Stoke, Nelson, New Zealand.

Maculan wine producer in Breganze, Veneto, Italy. Red wine and whites including Torcolato dessert brand.

Macvin grape-based apéritif of Jura region, France. Unfermented grape juice and *marc* spirit.

Madame Geneva soubriquet for English gin from 18th century. Geneva is a corruption of original Dutch *genever*.

Madargues wine-producing *cru* of Côtes d'Auvergne, France.

madeira fortified wine of island of Madeira, Portugal. Wine undergoes unique 'cooking' process in heated vats called *estufas* to reproduce the effects that originally gave the wine its 'burnt' character – namely storage in casks in the broiling holds of Portuguese merchant vessels en route to India in the 1500s. Four styles of madeira wine are named after their constituent grapes: dry Sercial, medium Verdelho, sweet Bual, nectareous Malmsey. Longest-lived of all wines, peaking at 100-150 years old.

Madeira Mint Flip Cocktail. Over ice shake 2 parts madeira, 1 chocolate mint liqueur, 1 egg. Strain and sprinkling grated plain chocolate over.

Madeira Wine Company principal producer of madeira wines, Funchal, Madeira. An incorporation of numerous old shippers including Blandy Brothers (est 1811), Cossart Gordon (est 1745), Leacock (est 1741), Lomelino (est 1820), Rutherford & Miles (est 1814), Shortridge Lawton (est 1757). Majority stockholder is Symington of Oporto.

Madeleine, Clos La wine estate of AC St-Emilion, Bordeaux, France. Classified *Grand Cru Classé*.

Madeleine Angevine white grape variety principally of England.

Madera AVA of San Joaquin Valley, California, USA.

maderised in winetasting, a white wine past its best, as indicated by a browning colour (resembling madeira) caused by oxidation.

Mad Ferret seasonal (spring) brown ale (5.0% alc) by Hydes brewery, Manchester, England. 'Deliciously hopped with fine English Fuggles this ale is silky smooth and very moorish (*sic*).'

Madiran AC and village of Gascony, SW France. Tough red wines from Tannat grapes plus Cabernet Franc and Cabernet Sauvignon.

Madonnenberg vineyard at Schriesheim in Baden region, Germany.

maduro a wine for drinking in its maturity, Portugal. *Vinho maduro* as distinct from *vinho verde*.

Maes brewery at Waarloos, Mechelen, Belgium. Maes Pils beer.

Maeve's 'Crystal Wheat' beer brand (4.7% alc) of Dublin Brewing Company, Eire.

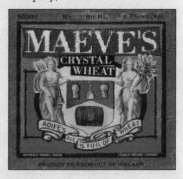

Mafia *sahti* (rye beer) brand and brewery of Lappland, Northwest Finland.

Maffini, Luigi Leading wine producer at San Marco di Castellabate, Italy. Aglianico di Cilento and other regional DOC wines.

Magaratch Ruby red grape variety of Crimea region, Black Sea.

Magdalenenkreuz vineyard at Rüdesheim in Rheingau region, Germany.

Magdelaine, Château wine estate of AC St-Emilion, Bordeaux, France. Classified *1er Grand Cru Classé*.

Magence, Château wine estate of AC Graves, Bordeaux, France.

Magna Carta Cocktail. Over ice stir 2 parts tequila, 1 Cointreau. Strain into a wine glass and top with chilled sparkling wine.

Magneau, Château wine estate of AC Graves, Bordeaux, France.

Magnet bitter ale brand of John Smith's brewery, Tadcaster, North Yorkshire, England.

Magno solera brandy by Osborne, Puerto de Santa Maria, Spain.

Magnol, Château wine estate of AC Haut-Médoc, Bordeaux, France. Classified *Cru Bourgeois*.

Magnolia Blossom Cocktail. Over ice shake 2 parts dry gin, 1 cream, 1 lemon juice. Strain.

Magnotta Cellars wine producer in Beamsville, Ontario, Canada.

Magnotta Vineyards wine producer in Mississauga, Ontario, Canada.

Magnotta Winery wine producer in Vaughan, Ontario, Canada.

Magnotta Wines wine producer in Scarborough, Ontario, Canada.

magnum wine-bottle format of 1.5 litres. Equivalent to two standard wine bottles.

Magon red wine from Cinsaut and Mourvèdre grapes, Tébourda, Tunisia.

Mah-jongg Cocktail. Over ice shake 4 parts dry gin, 1 Cointreau, 1 rum. Strain.

Mähler-Besse wine grower and négoçiant of Bordeaux, France. Part-owner of great Château Palmer estate of Médoc.

Mahou brewery and lager brand, Spain.

Maiberg vineyards at Heppenheim, Heppenheim (Hambach) and Heppenheim (Erbach) in Hessische Bergstrasse region, Germany.

maibock style of pale, high-quality bock lager. Originally Bavarian, brewed seasonally to mark May festivals.

Maiden's Blush Cocktail. Over ice shake 2 parts dry gin, 1 pastis, 2 dashes grenadine. Strain. Alternatively, over ice shake 4 parts dry gin, 1 grenadine, 1 orange curaçao, 1 dash lemon juice. Strain.

Maiden's Prayer Cocktail. Over ice shake 3 parts Cointreau, 3 gin, 1 lemon juice, 1 orange juice. Strain.

Maien vineyard at Winnenden in Württemberg region, Germany.

Maillac, J de great armagnac estate, Montréal-du-Gers, Gascony, France. Bertholon family owners introduced Hors d'Age and single vintage armagnacs. Brands include Hors d'Age blended from armagnacs five-20 years old, Hors d'Age Extra and famed Bas Armagnac Folle Blanche.

Maillard, Château wine estate of AC Premières Côtes de Bordeaux, France.

Mailly-Champagne champagne brand of Société des Producteurs Mailly-Champagne, France.

Maindreieck *Bereich* of Franken region, Germany. Vineyards include Escherndorf, Nordheim, Randersacker, Volkach, Wurzburg.

Mainhölle vineyard at Bürgstadt in Franken region, Germany.

Mainleite vineyards at Schweinfurt, Waigolshausen (Hergolshausen) and Waigolshausen (Theilheim) in Franken region, Germany.

Mainzerweg vineyard at Bingen in Rheinhessen region, Germany.

Mainviereck *Bereich* of Franken region, Germany.

Mainz city of Rheinhessen wine region and wine-industry centre of Germany.

Maipo longest-established major wine-producing region of Chile. South of Santiago.

Maire, Henri leading wine grower and *négoçiant* of Arbois, Jura region, France.

Maisach brewery in Munich, Bavaria, Germany.

Maisel largest of several breweries with this name in Bavaria, Germany. Situated in Bayreuth, known for **Maisel Dampfbier**.

Maison-Blanche, Château wine estate of AC Montagne-St-Emilion, Bordeaux, France.

Maison Blanche, Château wine estate of AC Pomerol, Bordeaux, France.

Maison-Rose, Château second wine of Château des Laurets, Bordeaux, France.

Mai Tai Cocktail. Over ice shake 3 parts rum, 1 apricot brandy, 1 curaçao, 1 fresh lime juice, 1 teaspoon grenadine. Strain and add a maraschino cherry to each glass.

Maître d'Estournel wine brand of Le Cercle d'Estournel, Bordeaux, France.

Maitz, Wolfgang wine producer in Südsteiermark, Austria.

Maiwein 'May Wine'. Seasonal drink of Rhine wine aromatised with leaves of woodruff and decorated with fruit. Germany.

Major Gunn's blended scotch whisky by Andrew MacLagan, Leith, Edinburgh, Scotland.

Maker's Mark Bourbon brand est 1953 by Bill Samuel Sr of Kentucky, USA. Owned by Allied Domecq, UK.

málaga fortfied wine from vineyards of resort town of Málaga, Spain. Medium to extra-sweet wines from Moscatel and Pedro Ximenez grapes.

Malagar, Château wine estate of AC Premières Côtes de Bordeaux, France.

Malartic-Lagravière, Château wine estate of AC Graves, Bordeaux, France. Classified *Cru Classé*.

Malat wine producer in Kremstal, Niederösterreich, Austria.

Malayan Breweries producer of Tiger lager, Singapore.

Malbec red grape variety principally of Bordeaux and Cahors regions, France. Increasing, also, in Australia and Latin America. Synonymous with Auxerrois and Cot.

Malescasse, Château wine estate of AC Haut-Médoc, Bordeaux, France. Classified *Cru Bourgeois*.

Malescot-St-Exupéry, Château wine estate of AC Margaux, Médoc, Bordeaux, France. Classified *3ème Grand Cru Classé*.

Malibu coconut-flavoured liqueur brand based in Jamaican rum. Former Seagram brand purchased 2002 by Allied Domecq, UK.

Maligny wine village of Chablis, France.

Mallard brewery at Carlton, Nottingham, England.

Malle, Château de wine estate of AC Sauternes, Bordeaux, France. Classified *2ème Cru Classé*.

Malleret, Château de wine estate of AC Haut-Médoc, Bordeaux, France. Classified *Cru Grand Bourgeois*.

Mallorca island of Balearics, Spain, with vineyards in Binisalem and Fenalito. Co-operative-produced red and *rosado* wines for local consumption.

Mallorca Cocktail. Over ice stir 2 parts rum, 1 banana liqueur, 1 Drambuie, 1 dry vermouth. Strain.

Malmaison, Château second wine of Château Clarke, Bordeaux, France.

Malmaison Cocktail. Over ice shake 2 parts rum, 1 sweet sherry, 1 lemon juice, 1 dash Anisette. Strain.

malmsey sweetest style of madeira wine, from Malmsey (Malvasia) grapes. Fortified with grape spirit during fermentation to retain natural sugar.

malolactic fermentation in winemaking, natural secondary fermentation following alcoholic fermentation, converting malic ('apple') acid into lactic ('milk') acid.

malt in brewing and distilling, grain steeped in water to activate sugars associated with germination. Sprouting is prevented by drying the grain.

Malta the Mediterranean island republic has small-scale wineproduction. Mostly ordinary wines from Marsovin company for local consumption.

Maltesergarten vineyards at Bad Krozingen (Biengen), Bad Krozingen (Schlatt), Bad Krozingen (Tunsel), Buggingen, Buggingen (Seefelden), Eschbach, Heitersheim and Staufen im Breisgau in Baden region, Germany.

Malteserkreuz aquavit distiller, Munich, Germany.

malt liquor style of strong lager commonly and loosely used in USA.

Malton hotel-brewery (Crown) at Malton, North Yorkshire, England.

Malvasia white grape mainly of southern Europe. In Italy, grown in Emilia-Romagna, Sardinia and Tuscany, and in Latium for wines such as Frascati; in Portugal for table wines and white port and on island of Madeira for Malmsey; also in France, Spain etc. Malvasia Rosso is an associated red grape variety.

Malvasia delle Lipari DOC for dessert wine from Malvasia grapes, Lipari (Aeolian) islands, Sicily, Italy.

Malvasia di Bosa DOC for dessert and fortified (*liquoroso*) white wines from Malvasia di Sardegna grapes of Bosa, Sardinia, Italy.

Malvasia di Cagliari DOC for dessert and fortified (*liquoroso*) white wines from Malvasia di Sardegna grapes of Campidano district, Sardinia, Italy.

Malvasia di Casorzo d'Asti DOC for light red sweet sparkling wine from Malvasia Rosso grapes, Casorzo, Piedmont, Italy.

Malvasia di Castelnuovo Don Bosco DOC for light red sweet sparkling wine from Malvasia Rosso grapes, Castelnuovo Don Bosco, Piedmont, Italy.

Malvern Hill pear variety traditionally valued for perry-making. English.

Malvern Hills brewery at Great Malvern, Worcestershire, England.

Malvoisie regional name for several different grape varieties. In Languedoc, SW France for Bourboulenc; in Limoux, SW France for Maccabeo; in Loire Valley, France and in Switzerland for Pinot Gris.

Malvoisie sweet white wine from Pinot Gris grapes, Valais, Switzerland.

Malzmühl restaurant-brewery in Cologne, Germany.

Mamartine historic wine of ancient Rome. Julius Caesar was an *aficionado*. Commemorated in modern sweet **Mamertino**, from sun-dried Cataratto, Grillo and Inzolia grapes, Sicily, Italy.

Mamie Taylor Cocktail. Over ice in a tall glass pour 2 parts whisky, 1 fresh lime juice. Top with dry ginger ale.

Mammolo red grape variety of Tuscany, Italy.

Mampe liqueur distiller, Berlin, Germany.

Mañana Cocktail. Over ice shake 3 parts rum, 1 apricot brandy, 1 teaspoon lemon juice. Strain.

Mancha, La extensive DO of central Spain. Principally Airén white grapes for ordinary wines. Pockets of quality winemaking are appearing.

Manchuela DO of central Spain. Ordinary wines.

Mandarine Napoléon liqueur from mandarin peel macerated in old brandy. Claimed to be a recipe of Napoleon Bonaparte. Produced by Fourcroy, Belgium.

Mandarine Sour Cocktail. In an ice-filled cocktail glass stir 1 part Mandarine Napoléon, 1 lemon juice, 1 dash triple sec.

Mandelbaum vineyard at Praffen-Schwabenheim in Rheinhessen region, Germany.

Mandelberg vineyards at Alzey, Lonsheim and Offenheim in Rheinhessen region, Birkweiler, Kirrweiler, Laumersheim and Neustadt an der Weinstrasse in Rheinpfalz region and Wertheim in Baden region, Germany.

Mandelbrunnen vineyard at Gundheim in Rheinhessen region, Germany.

Mandelgarten vineyards at Neustadt an der Weinstrasse, Obrigheim, Wachenheim and Weisenheim am Berg in Rheinpfalz region, Germany.

Mandelgraben vineyards at Brauneberg and Brauneberg (Filzen) in Mosel-Saar-Ruwer region, Germany.

Mandelhang vineyard at Edesheim in Rheinpfalz region, Germany.

Mandelhöhe *Grosslage* incorporating vineyards at Kirrweiler, Maikammer and Maikammer-Asterweiler in Rheinpfalz region, Germany.

Mandelpfad vineyards at Billigheim-Ingenheim, Dirmstein, Obrigheim and Rohrbach in Rheinpfalz region, Germany.

Mandelring vineyard at Neustadt an der Weinstrasse in Rheinpfalz region, Germany.

Mandelröth vineyard at Dackenheim in Rheinpfalz region, Germany.

Mandelstein vineyard at Boppard in Mittelrhein region, Germany.

Mandement vineyard district of Geneva canton, Switzerland.

Mandilaria red grape variety of Aegean islands, Greece.

Mandrolisai DOC for red and *rosato* wines from Bovale Sardo, Cannonau and Monica grapes grown around Sorgono, Sardinia, Italy.

Manduria DOC for red wines from Primitivo grapes, Taranto, Apulia, Italy.

Manhasset Cocktail. Over ice shake 2 parts rye whisky, 1 equal mis dry and sweet vermouth, 1 lemon juice. Strain.

Manhasset Mauler Cocktail. Over ice stir 2 parts dry gin, 1 sloe gin. Strain and squeeze lemon peel over.

Manhattan Brewing Company pub-brewery in SoHo, New York City, USA.

Manhattan Cocktail. Over ice stir 2 parts rye whisky, 1 sweet vermouth, 1 dash Angostura bitters. Strain and add cocktail cherry to glass. **2** Alternatively, for a 'dry' Manhattan, over ice stir 1 part rye whisky, 1 dry vermouth. Strain. **3** ('sweet') over ice stir 1 part rye whisky, 1 sweet vermouth. Strain.

Manhattan Cooler Cocktail. Over ice stir 4 parts claret, 1 lemon or lime juice, 2 dashes rum, 1 teaspoon sugar. Strain and add fruit slices to glass.

Manicle wine *cru* of Vin du Bugey, Savoie, France.

Man in the Moon brewery at Ashby Magna, Leicestershire, England.

Mannaberg *Grosslage* incorporating vineyards in Baden region, Germany at, respectively: Bad Schönborn, Bruchsal, Bruchsal (Heidelsheim), Bruchsal (Helmsheim), Bruchsal (Obergrombach), Bruchsal Untergrombach), Dielheim, Dielheim (Horrenberg), Heidelberg, Kraichtal, Leimen, Malsch, Mühlhausen, Mühlhausen (Rettigheim), Mühlhausen (Tairnbach), Nussloch, Ostringen, Rauenberg, Rauenberg (Malschenberg), Rauenberg (Rotenberg), Ubstadt-Weiher (Stettfeld), Ubstadt-Weiher (Ubstadt), Ubstadt-Weiher (Zeutern), Wiesloch.

Mannberg vineyard at Eltville in Rheingau region, Germany.

Mannochmore Speyside malt whisky distillery est 1971, Elgin, Scotland. Single malt: 12-year-old.

Mann's Brown Ale beer brand of former **Mann, Crossman & Paulin** brewery of Whitechapel, London, England. Successively taken over, but continuously produced, by brewers Watney, Courage and Scottish & Newcastle.

Manor House Canadian whisky brand of Palliser Distillers, Canada.

Manseng white grape variety of two distinct types, Gros Manseng and Petit Manseng. Both are used for AC Jurançon wines of SW France and elsewhere in the region.

Mansfield brewery at Littleworth, Mansfield, Nottinghamshire, England.

Mansfield Arms brewery at Sauchie, Alloa, Scotland.

Mansion House brand of Pernod-Ricard.

Mantinia dry white wine from Moschofilero grapes, Peloponnese, Greece.

Mantler, Josef wine producer in Donauland, Niederösterreich, Austria.

Mantlerhof, Josef & Margit wine producer in Kremstal, Niederösterreich, Austria.

Mantonico di Bianco heavy white wine from dried Mantonico grapes, town of Bianco, Calabria, Italy.

Manyann Cocktail. Over ice shake 2 parts Caperitif, 2 dry gin, 1 lemon juice, 2 dashes curaçao. Strain.

manzanilla bone-dry sherry style reputed to acquire a salty tang from proximity of *bodegas* to seaside at Sanlucar de Barrameda, Spain. **Manzanilla pasada** is a mature version, approaching *amontillado* in style. Manzanilla is the original pale, dry sherry and pre-dates the better-

Maple

known fino sherry of Jerez. It was
first produced at Sanlucar in the early
20th century when the solera system,
based on a series of casks which could
be constantly 'refreshed' with successive batches of younger wine, was devised. Manzanilla is typically 15% alc
and the producers claim that it accounts for fifty-five per cent of all the
sherry drunk in Spain. Leading producers include Argüeso, Barbadillo,
Hidalgo. Manzanilla is the Spanish
word for Chamomile, but some
sherry producers claim the name
means 'little apple' – personifying the
crisp, fresh style of the wine.

Maple liqueur produced by Rieder,
Ontario, Canada.

Maraca Puerto Rico rum brand of
Hiram Walker & Sons, Canada.

Maranges, Les AC covering three
wine villages (Cheilly, Dezize, Sam-
pigny) of Côte de Beaune, Burgundy,
France.

maraschino Italian cherry-based
sweet liqueur. Usually white, but a
few brands are coloured red.

Marastina white grape variety and
wine of Dalmatian coast and islands,
Croatia.

Marbach vineyard at Sobernheim in
Nahe region, Germany.

Marbuzet, Château de wine estate of
AC St-Estèphe, Médoc, Bordeaux,
France. Classified *Cru Grand Bour-
geois Exceptionnel*.

Marbuzet, Château de second wine of
Château Cos d'Estournel, Bordeaux,
France.

marc detritus of grape pressing:
pips, skins and stalks. The name
given to spirit distilled from this
material. French. *see label opposite* ➤

Marches wine region of eastern-
central Italy. DOCs for white
Verdicchio, red Rosso Conero etc.

Marches Ales brewery at Leominster, Herefordshire, England.

Marchive cognac grower and distiller, Logis de Scée, Vars, St Amant
de Boixe, France.

Marcillac VDQS for red and rosé
wines from (mainly) Fer Servadou
grapes of Lot Valley, SW France.

Marcobrunn vineyards at Eltville
(Erbach) and Eltville (Hattenheim)
in Rheingau region, Germany.

Mardi Gras popular brand name for
seasonal pre-Lenten beers brewed
in northern Europe.

Mardi Gras Bock seasonal beer by
Abita brewery, New Orleans, USA.

Maréchal Foch red grape variety of
Canada.

Maremma *vino da tavola* wines of
Tuscany, Italy. Red and *rosato* from
Sangiovese grapes and white from
Trebbiano and other varieties.

Margarete vineyards at Neuenstein
and Ohringen in Württemberg
region, Germany.

Margaret River wine district of
Western Australia.

Margaret Rose Cocktail. Over ice
shake 2 parts calvados, 2 dry gin, 1
Cointreau, 1 lemon juice, 1 dash
grenadine. Strain.

Margarita Cocktail. Over ice shake 2 parts tequila, 2 lemon juice, 1 Cointreau. Strain into glass with rim frosted by dipping first into fruit juice and then into sugar.

Margarita Impériale Cocktail. Over ice shake 1 part Mandarine Napoléon, 1 tequila, 1 lemon juice, 1 dash curaçao.

Margaux famed wine village and AC of Médoc, Bordeaux, France. AC also covers wine of villages of Arsac, Cantenac, Labarde, Soussans. Wines from great properties including Châteaux Margaux, Palmer, Rausan-Ségla etc are particularly known for their bouquet.

Margaux, Château great wine estate of AC Margaux, Médoc, Bordeaux, France. Classified *1er Grand Cru Classé*.

Mariachi brand of Pernod-Ricard.

Mariage Parfait lambic beer brand of Boon brewery, Lembeek, Belgium.

Maria Magdalena vineyard at Klingenmünster in Rheinpfalz region, Germany.

Marie Brizard major distillery and liqueur-producing company of France. Founded by Marie Brizard, b 1714.

marie jeanne regional name for magnum wine bottle, Loire Valley, France.

Marienberg vineyards at Koblenz (Güls), Koblenz (Metternich) and Perl in Mosel-Saar-Ruwer region, Germany.

Marienburg vineyard at Pünderich in Mosel-Saar-Ruwer region, Germany.

Marienburger vineyard at Zell in Mosel-Saar-Ruwer region, Germany.

Mariengarten *Grosslage* incorporating vineyards at Deidesheim, Forst an der Weinstrasse and Wachenheim in Rheinpfalz region, Germany.

Mariengarten vineyard at Prichsenstadt in Franken region, Germany.

Marienholz vineyards at Trier (Eitelsbach) and Trier (Ruwer) in Mosel-Saar-Ruwer region, Germany.

Marienpforter Klosterberg vineyard at Waldböckelheim in Nahe region, Germany.

Mariensteiner white grape variety of Germany.

Marignan wine-producing *cru* of AC Vin de Savoie, France.

Marimar Torres wine producer in Sonoma County, California, USA. Renowned wines from Chardonnay and Pinot Noir grapes.

Marin Brewing Co wheat beer producer, Larkspur Landing, California, USA.

Mariner's Gold beer by Willys Brewery, Cleethorpes, England.

Mariner's Mild beer by Pacific Coast brewery, Oakland, California, USA.

Maris Otter barley variety much valued for malting in the brewing process.

Markgraf Babenburg collective vineyard (*Grosslage*) at Frickenhausen in Franken region, Germany.

Marksburg *Grosslage* incorporating vineyards at Braubach, Filsen, Koblenz, Koblenz (Ehrenbreitstein und Niederberg), Lahnstein, Osterspai, Urbar and Vallendar in Mittelrhein region, Germany.

Marin wine village and *cru* of AC Vin de Savoie, France.

Marino DOC for white wines from Malvasia and Trebbiano grapes, Latium, Italy. Notably similar to Frascati.

Maris seasonal (summer) beer (4.0% alc) by Hydes brewery, Manchester, England. 'Mashed with an all malt Maris Otter grist, this beer is light, very drinkable and extremely refreshing.'

Markgräflerland *Bereich* of Baden region, Germany. *Grosslagen*: Burg Neuenfels, Lorettoberg, Vogtei Rötteln.

Markowitsch, Johann wine producer in Carnuntum, Niederösterreich, Austria.

Markowitsch, Gerhard wine producer in Carnuntum, Niederösterreich, Austria.

marl clay-and-lime soil type particularly ideal for vineyards. Chablis, France, is a famous example.

Marlborough major wine region of South Island, New Zealand.

Marli cider and liqueur producer, Finland.

Marmalade Cocktail. Over ice gently shake 6 parts dry gin, 3 lemon juice, 1 marmalade. Strain and squeeze orange peel over glass.

Marmorberg vineyard at Braubach in Mittelrhein region, Germany.

Marne & Champagne major producer of 'Buyer's Own Brand' champagnes for sale under retailers' labels worldwide. Epernay, France.

Marnique brandy-based liqueur. Australia.

Marny Cocktail. Over ice stir 2 parts dry gin, 1 Grand Marnier. Strain.

Marondera export wine brand of Zimbabwe.

Marquerite Cocktail. Over ice stir 2 parts Plymouth gin, 1 dry vermouth, 1 dash orange bitters. Strain. This recipe, first made public in 1896 by Thomas Stuart in his *Stuart's Fancy Drinks and How to Mix Them*, is said to be the first documented Dry Martini cocktail.

Marques del Real Tesoro sherry producer est 1780, Jerez de la Frontera, Spain.

Marqués de Monistrol wine producer of Penedès, Spain, noted for *cava* sparkling wines.

Marqués de Murrieta great *bodega* est 1870 Rioja, Spain. Wines include *reserva* red Castillo de Ygay and famously old-fashioned oxidised white.

Marqués de Riscal oldest *bodega* est 1860 of Rioja, Spain. Long-aged red wines and renowned white.

Marquis-d'Alesme-Becker, Château wine estate of AC Margaux, Médoc, Bordeaux, France. Classified *3ème Grand Cru Classé*.

Marquis-de-Bressane, Château second wine of Château Hauterive, Bordeaux, France.

Marquis, Clos de second wine of Château Léoville-Las-Cases, Bordeaux, France.

Marquis de St-Estèphe, wine brand of Caves-Co-opérative de Marquis de St-Estèphe, Bordeaux, France.

Marquis de St Maigrin cognac producer, Archiac, France.

Marquis-de-Terme, Château wine estate of AC Margaux, Médoc, Bordeaux, France. Classified *4ème Grand Cru Classé*.

Marrano white wine brand from Grechetto grapes by Bigi, Umbria, Italy.

Marsac-Séguineau, Château wine estate of AC Margaux, Médoc, Bordeaux, France. Classified *Cru Bourgeois*.

marsala fortified wine of Sicily, Italy. See box.

Marsannay village and AC of Dijon, Burgundy, France. Red, rosé and white wines.

Marsanne white grape variety of northern Rhône Valley, France. The grape, with Roussanne, of white Hermitage and Crozes-Hermitage, St-Joseph and St-Péray. Also grown successfully in Victoria, Australia.

Marsberg vineyard at Randersacker in Franken region, Germany.

Marschall vineyard at Wiesbaden in Rheingau region, Germany.

Marsens wine region of Lavaux, Switzerland.

Marsovin wine producer at Marsa, Malta. 'Fine vintage wines'.

Marston, Thompson & Evershed brewery at Burton upon Trent, England. Brands including Burton SPA (6.2% alc), Merrie Monk, Owd Roger, Oyster Stout (4.5% alc), Pedigree, Single Malt (4.2% alc).

Marston Moor brewery in Kirk Hammerton, North Yorkshire, England.

Martell leading cognac producer, Cognac, France. Founded by Jersey, Channel Islands, merchant Jean Martell, 1715. Brands: XXX, Médaillon, Cordon Rubis, Cordon Noir Napoléon, Cordon Bleu (20-30 year-old), Cordon Argent (50 or more years old). Martell was renowned as the sponsor from 1990 to 2004 of Britain's Grand National, the world's premier steeplechase – an event with an estimated worldwide television audience of around 500 million. Sold by Seagram to Pernod-Ricard in 2001.

Marsala

wine and history in the making

Even though Sicily's winemaking traditions date back several millennia, the island's most famous sweet wine lacks ancient, or even strictly indigenous, provenance. Marsala is a confection created as recently as 1773 by Liverpool-born John Woodhouse, who exploited the island's underdeveloped vineyards, and underemployed population, to make wines that would rival costlier port and malaga – then in great demand in England. The wine takes its name from Marsala, the seaport at the island's westernmost point.

Woodhouse was fortunate in the timing of the Napoleonic wars. French occupation of Italy drove the King of Naples into exile in Sicily, where he received the support of a large British garrison, fortified by the presence of Admiral Nelson's Mediterranean fleet. The Royal Navy stocked its ships with marsala in place of rum and the drink consequently enjoyed loyal popularity in Britain. It soon became the principal export of western Sicily. The port became a British *entrepot* comparable with Vila Nova de Gaia in Portugal. It continued a long tradition of British presence here. The 16 great grey marble columns of the town's medieval basilica, for example, are said to have been destined for Canterbury Cathedral, but were salvaged from the ship which, bound for England, foundered off Marsala.

Marsala, formerly Lilybaeum, was the principal stronghold of Carthage in Sicily until it was surrendered to the Romans in 241 BC at the conclusion of the First Punic War. The origin of the present name is Saracen, from *Marsa Ali*, port of Ali. Garibaldi began his campaign at Marsala when he landed here with 1,000 men in 1860.

Under quality regulations of 1984 basic marsala wine is fortified with *cotto*, a caramelised grape syrup, and grape spirit to make two styles: *Fine*, aged four months or more at a minimum 17% alc (formerly called Italy Particular or IP); *Superiore*, aged two years at a minimum 18% alc (formerly Superior Old Marsala or SOM, London Particular or LP and Garibaldi Dolce or GD). *Vergine* and *Vergine Stravecchio* are different, usually unfortified and reaching the required 18% alc through evaporation during long ageing (minimum five and ten years respectively) in cask.

Popular 'cooking' marsala, especially for zabaglione dessert, with added egg, or flavoured with banana, chocolate, coffee etc seriously diminished wine-drinkers' interest in the authentic marsala, prompting new regulations in 1969 as well as 1984. Under these, the cooking brands are now labelled *Cremoso Zabaione Vino Aromatizzato* or annotated *preparato con l'Impiego di vino Marsala*. 🍃

Martens brewery in Limburg, Belgium. Known for Sezoens beer.

Martillac wine-producing commune of AC Graves, Bordeaux, France.

Martina Franca DOC for white wine of Apulia region, Italy.

Martinborough wine estate of Marlborough region, New Zealand. Pinot Noir red wine of outstanding quality and noted whites.

Martinens, Château wine estate of AC Margaux, Médoc, Bordeaux, France. Classified *Cru Bourgeois Supérieur*.

Martinez Cocktail. Over ice shake 4 parts dry gin, 1 curaçao, 2 dashes orange bitters. Strain and add cocktail cherry and lemon peel to glass.

Martinez Gassiot port house est 1790 by Spaniard Sebastian Gonzalez Martinez, Vila Nova de Gaia, Portugal. Many brands and vintages: 1955, 60, 63, 67, 70, 75, 78, 82, 83, 85, 87, 91, 92, 94, 97, 2000, 03.

Martini gin-and-vermouth cocktail named after its deviser, Martini de Arma de Taggia, barman at the Knickerbocker Hotel, New York City, USA in early 1900s. Original recipe was equal measures gin and dry vermouth (possibly, but coincidentally, a Martini & Rossi brand).

Recipes have included progressively diminishing proportions of vermouth since the First World War. For a **Dry Martini** stir 4 parts dry gin and 1 dry vermouth over ice then strain and squeeze lemon peel over. For an **Extra Dry Martini** stir 8 parts dry gin, 1 dry vermouth over ice then strain and squeeze lemon peel over. For an **Ultra Dry Martini** shake 1 part dry vermouth over ice, drain the liquid off and discard, then stir 4 parts dry gin over same ice and strain. Squeeze lemon peel over.

Martini, Louis wine producer in Napa Valley and Sonoma Valley, California, USA. Red wines from Barbera and other grape varieties.

Martini & Rossi world-renowned vermouth producer est 1863 at Pessione, Turin, Italy. Martini Bianco and Martini Rosso. Also a major producer of Asti Spumante and with international wine and spirit interests. Now merged as Bacardi-Martini.

Martinon, Château wine estate of AC Entre-Deux-Mers, Bordeaux, France.

Martinsberg vineyards at Siefersheim and Wonsheim in Rheinhessen region, Germany.

Martinsborn vineyard at Bruttig-Fankel in Mosel-Saar-Ruwer region, Germany.

Martinshöhe vineyard at Gönnheim in Rheinpfalz region, Germany.

Martouret, Château de wine estate of AC Entre-Deux-Mers, Bordeaux, France.

Marvel Cocktail. Over ice shake 6 parts rum, 1 grenadine, 1 sirop-de-citron. Strain.

Marynissen Estates wine producer in Niagara-on-the-Lake, Ontario, Canada.

Mary Pickford Cocktail. Over ice shake 1 part rum, 1 pineapple juice, 2 dashes grenadine. Named after the American actress and film producer Mary Pickford (1893-1979).

Marzelle, Château La wine estate of AC St-Emilion, Bordeaux, France. Classified *Grand Cru Classé*.

Marzemino red grape variety of Trentino, Italy.

Märzen(bier) seasonally brewed, dark style of lager. Said to have been devised by brewer Anton Dreher in Vienna, Austria, in 1841, and thereafter widely imitated in Bavaria. The beer was brewed in March (*Märzen*) – the last month in which wild yeasts posed no problems in the unrefrigerated premises of the time – then lagered (stored) for summer consumption. The remaining casks were traditionally finished off in autumn beer festivals. The term **Märzen-Oktoberfest** (a metaphorical translation might be 'Last of the Summer Beer') is still common for seasonal beers made for the famous Munich event and other German beer festivals. Beer in this style is also produced in Scandinavia and north America.

Mascarello, Bartolo wine producer of DOCG Barolo and other wines of Piedmont, Italy.

Mascarello & Figli, Giuseppe wine producer of DOCG Barolo and other wines of Piedmont, Italy.

mash in brewing and distilling, the activating of malt sugars through steeping grain in water. The term is also applied to the mixture itself.

mash tun in brewing, vessel for mashing.

Masi wine producer of Veneto, Italy. Bardolino and Valpolicella red wines, Soave white and others. Branded wine Campo Fiorin.

Masia Bach wine estate of Penedès region, Spain.

Masianco white wine brand of Masi, Valpolicella, Veneto, Italy.

Masi Tupungato Wine producer of Argentina, owned by Masi of Italy. Famed Paso Doble red.

maso vineyard holding, Italy.

Mason's Arms pub-brewery at Cartmel Fell, Cumbria, England.

Massandra traditional name for Moscatel wines of state co-operative of Crimea, Black Sea. Originally the Massandra Winery, built to supply wines for the summer palace of Tsar Nicholas II at Lividia. Old wine stocks which had, almost incredibly, survived both the Revolution and the Second World War, were auctioned in 1990, creating a new interest in Massandra.

Massard, Bernard renowned sparkling wine producer of Grand Duchy of Luxembourg est 1921 Grevenmacher. Cuvée de L'Ecusson Brut and other brands by *méthode champenoise*.

Massawippi pub-brewery of Quebec, Canada.

Mass Bay brewery in Boston, Massachusetts, USA.

Massé *Grande Marque* champagne house est 1853 Rilly-la-Montagne, France.

Massenez, GE distiller est 1870, Bassemberg, Ville Valley, Alsace, France. Renowned *eaux de vie*.

masseria farm or estate producing wine. Italy.

Massimo Cocktail. Over ice in a tall glass, pour 2 parts marsala and 1 dry gin. Stir and top with lemonade. Add mint sprig and slices of lemon, lime and orange.

Masson, Paul major wine company at Gonzalez, California, USA. Est by Frenchman Paul Masson, 1878.

Master Blend brand of Pernod-Ricard.

Masterbrew Bitter ale brand of Shepherd Neame brewery, Faversham, Kent, England.

Master of Wine accolade of UK wine trade open to wine professionals able to pass rigorous examinations. Arguably the most prestigious wine-trade qualification worldwide.

Masterpiece Canadian whisky brand formerly of Seagram, Canada.

masticha alternative spelling of mastika.

mastika resinated colourless grape spirit of island of Chios, Greece.

Mastroberardini leading wine producer of Campania region, Italy. DOC wines include Fiano di Avellino, Greco di Tufo, Lacrima Christi etc.

Matanzas Creek wine producer in Sonoma, California, USA. Chardonnay and others.

Matador Cocktail. Over ice shake 1 part tequila, 2 pineapple juice, 1 fresh lime juice. Strain.

Mataro regional name for Mourvèdre grape variety, Australia.

Matawhero wine producer in Poverty Bay, New Zealand.

Mateus Rosé leading wine brand since 1950s, from Minho region,

Portugal, by Sogrape. Still or very slightly sparkling according to market: eg still in US, sparkling in UK.

Matheisbildchen vineyard at Bernkastel-Kues in Mosel-Saar-Ruwer region, Germany.

Mather & Sons brewery in Leeds, Yorkshire, England. Known for **Mather's Black Beer**, a high-strength (8%) 'malt liquor' first produced 1903.

Mathias Weingarten vineyard at Bacharach in Mittelrhein region, Germany.

Matilda Bay brewery in Fremantle, Western Australia. Known for Red Back wheat beer.

Matinee Cocktail. Over ice shake 2 parts dry gin, 1 Sambuca, 1 fresh cream, 1 teaspoon fresh lime juice, 1 egg white. Strain.

Matino DOC for red and *rosato* wines from Negroamaro grapes, Apulia, Italy.

Matras, Château wine estate of AC St-Emilion, Bordeaux, France. Classified *Grand Cru Classé*.

Matt, FX brewery of Francis Xavier Matt in Utica, New York, USA.

Matthew Clark Taunton cider (Gaymer and Taunton), liqueur, perry (Babycham) and wine producer, Bristol, Shepton Mallet and Taunton, Somerset, England.

Mattingley & Moore whiskey brand formerly of Seagram, USA.

Matua Valley wine producer in Huapai, New Zealand.

mature in winetasting, the character of a wine that has spent the optimum time in bottle or cask – long enough for the fruit, alcohol, acid and tannin to 'marry', forming ideal colour, bouquet and flavour.

Matusalem *oloroso muy viejo* sherry by Gonzalez Byass, Jerez de la Frontera, Spain.

Maucaillou, Château wine estate of AC Moulis, Médoc, Bordeaux, France. Classified *Cru Bourgeois*.

Maucamps, Château wine estate of AC Haut-Médoc, Bordeaux, France. Classified *Cru Bourgeois*.

Mauerberg vineyard at Baden-Baden in Baden region, Germany.

Mäuerchen vineyards at Geisenheim in Rheingau region and Mertesdorf in Mosel-Saar-Ruwer region, Germany.

Mauget liqueur brand of Halewood International, Huyton, Merseyside, England.

Mauldon's brewery at Sudbury, Suffolk, England.

Mauler sparkling wine brand of Mauler & Cie, est 1829, Neuchatel, Switzerland.

Maupas, Domaine de armagnac producer, Mauleon d'Armagnac, France.

Maurer, Alfred wine producer in Weinviertel, Niederösterreich, Austria.

Maurer, Martin wine producer in Weinviertel, Niederösterreich, Austria.

Maurice Cocktail. Over ice shake 2 parts dry gin, 1 dry vermouth, 1 sweet vermouth, 1 orange juice, 1 dash pastis.

Maury *vin doux naturel* sweet wine from Grenache and Muscat grapes, Maury, Pyrenees region, SW France.

Mäushöhle vineyard at Deidesheim in Rheinpfalz region, Germany.

Mausse, Château wine estate of AC Canon-Fronsac, Bordeaux, France.

Maustal vineyard at Sulzfeld in Franken region, Germany.

Mauvesin, Château wine estate of AC St-Emilion, Bordeaux, France. Classified *Grand Cru* (1996).

Mauvezin, Château wine estate of AC Moulis, Médoc, Bordeaux, France. Classified *Cru Bourgeois Supérieur*.

Mauzac Blanc white grape variety of SW France. Main variety for Blanquette de Limoux.

Mavrodaphne red grape variety of Greece.

Mavron black grape variety of island of Cyprus.

Mavrud black grape variety of Bulgaria.

Max Ferd Richter leading wine estate of Mülheim, Mosel-Saar-Ruwer region, Germany.

Maxim brewery at Greymouth, New Zealand.

Maximator bock beer brand by Augustiner brewery, Bavaria, Germany.

Maximilian pub-brewery in Amsterdam, Netherlands.

Maximiner vineyard at Trier in Mosel-Saar-Ruwer region, Germany.

Maximiner Burgberg vineyard at Fell (mit Orsteil Fastrau) in Mosel-Saar-Ruwer region, Germany.

Maximiner-Herrenberg vineyard at Longuich in Mosel-Saar-Ruwer region, Germany.

Maximiner Hofgarten vineyard at Kenn in Mosel-Saar-Ruwer region, Germany.

Maximiner Klosterlay vineyard at Detzem in Mosel-Saar-Ruwer region, Germany.

Maximiner Prälat vineyard at Kastel-Staadt in Mosel-Saar-Ruwer region, Germany.

Mayacamas Vineyards wine producer in Napa Valley, California, USA.

Mayer am Pfarrplatz wine producer in Wien (Vienna), Austria.

Mayfair Cocktail. Over ice shake 2 parts dry gin, 1 apricot brandy, 1 orange juice, 1 dash clove syrup. Strain.

Mayhems brewery at Lower Apperley, Gloucestershire, England.

Mayne, Château du wine estate of AC Sauternes, Bordeaux, France.

Mayne d'Anice, Château second wine of Château Chantegrive, Bordeaux, France.

Mayne-Binet, Château wine estate of AC Cérons, Bordeaux, France.

Mayne-Lévêque, Château second wine of Château de Chantegrive, Bordeaux, France.

Mayne-Vieil, Château wine estate of AC Fronsac, Bordeaux, France.

Maypole brewery at Eakring, Nottinghamshire, England.

Mayr, Anton wine producer in Kremstal, Niederösterreich, Austria.

Mazarin, Château wine estate of AC Loupiac, Bordeaux, France.

Mazeris, Château wine estate of AC Canon-Fronsac, Bordeaux, France.

Mazeris-Bellevue, Château wine estate of AC Canon-Fronsac, Bordeaux, France.

Mazeyres, Château wine estate of AC Pomerol, Bordeaux, France.

Mazeyres, Clos wine estate of AC Pomerol, Bordeaux, France.

Mazis-Chambertin *Grand Cru* vineyard, Gevrey-Chambertin, Burgundy, France.

Mazouna wine district of Dahra, Algeria.

Mazuela red grape variety of Spain. Synonymous with Carignan.

McAuslan brewery at St Henri, Montreal, Canada.

McCallum brewery at Colombo, Sri Lanka. Known for Three Coins pilsener and Sando Stout.

McCallum's Perfection blended scotch whisky by D & J McCallum, Edinburgh, Scotland.

McClelland Cocktail. Over ice shake 2 parts sloe gin, 1 curaçao, 1 dash pastis. Strain.

McDowell Valley AVA of Mendocino County, California, USA.

McEwans range of ale brands of Scottish Courage, produced in Edinburgh, Scotland and in northern England and Wales. Brands include Champion Ale (7.3% alc), 80/- Traditional Ale (4.5% alc), 90/- Traditional Ale, Export (for UK market) and McEwan's Scotch Ale (for export).

McGibbon's Special Reserve blended scotch whisky by Douglas Laing, Glasgow, Scotland. Along with **McGibbon's Premium Reserve**, is bottled in a ceramic golf-bag-shaped decanter.

McGuire's pub-brewery in Pensacola, Florida, USA. Beers include **McGuire's Irish Red**.

McLaren Vale town and wine district south of Adelaide, South Australia.

McMullen & Sons brewery est 1827 in Hertford, Hertfordshire, England. Famed for AK Original ale.

McTarnahan's ale brand of Portland Brewing Co, Oregon, USA.

McWilliam's wine company est 1877 Murray River, and now in Hunter Valley and Riverina regions, Australia. Well-known Mount Pleasant wines and others.

mead fermented drink from honey and water. Said to be the earliest manmade alcoholic beverage. See box.

Meadowbrook American straight rye whiskey brand, USA.

Meadow Cream liqueur brand of Halewood International, Huyton, Merseyside, England.

Mead

a taste of honey

There is a reasonable argument that mead is the oldest of all alcoholic drinks. It is made by adding honey to water, boiling it, skimming off the froth until the mix is reasonably clear, then adding yeast prior to a few days' fermentation. Given that honey is acknowledged as early man's first source of sugar and that all alcohol is obtained from the fermentation of sugar, it seems likely that liquid wild honey, diluted or not, spontaneously fermented by the attentions of wild yeasts, might well have been our ancestors' first experience of a mind-altering substance.

The earliest Greek writers, including Hesiod in the eighth century BC, mention honey as the 'nectar of the gods' – imputing to it supernatural properties that were undoubtedly more to do with its fermented form, as an intoxicating liquor, than to its mere sweetness. The 'ambrosia' of Olympus was certainly mead, but it was not immortal. Wine, from grapes cultivated in Oenotria – the name the Greeks gave to their Italian colony – had displaced mead by the time of Aristotle.

Nevertheless, mead remained a prized and expensive source of alcohol across the known world right up to the Reformation. Where wine could not be made, in northern Europe, the honey drink, named *meodu* in Old English after Saxon *met*, was a valued alternative to ale and cider, and could be made as a by-product, the remains of the comb after the honey was run off and wax extracted.

But as the rituals of the Catholic church gave way to plain Protestant observations, demand for beeswax candles in monasteries and abbeys, churches and cathedrals melted away. By the 17th century, beekeeping, once a major branch of agriculture in Britain, Germany and Scandinavia had all but withered.

Sugar soon became available from other sources. The

'agricultural revolution' of the 18th century brought sugar beet into production in Europe and sugar cane had already become the principal crop of colonies and nations in Asia, the Caribbean and the Americas.

Mead has survived as a specialist drink, and clings to its reputation as an aphrodisiac. One version of the meaning of 'honeymoon' derives from a reputed Old Norse tradition of newlyweds drinking mead daily for the first moon (month) of their marriage to promote fertility and fulfilment.

To make a gallon of mead, boil eight pints of water with 2.5lbs of honey. Skim until no more froth appears on the surface. Add the juice of one lemon and half a pint of strong tea. Let the mix cool to blood temperature before adding a wine yeast. Rack off into a fermenting jar and stop with a fermenting trap. Allow to ferment up to 14 days. Rack off into bottles. Optional flavourings to add prior to fermenting are cinnamon, fresh ginger or cloves.

Méaume, Château wine estate of AC Bordeaux Supérieur, Bordeaux, France.

Médaille d'Or apple variety traditionally valued for cider-making. French.

Medea wine zone of Alger, Algeria.

medium in wine designation, usually means sweet.

medium dry in wine designation, a style with some residual sugar.

medium-sweet in wine designation, a style with obvious residual sugar and tasting noticeably sweet.

Medley's Mellow Corn American straight corn whiskey brand, USA.

Médoc the major quality wine region of Bordeaux, France, and an AC within which lie the famed commune ACs of Margaux, Pauillac, St-Estèphe, St Julien etc. Contrarily, the Bas-Médoc is the northern part of the region and the Haut-Médoc the southern part. The highest-priced wines of the region were classified in five ranks in 1855 (see box), and continue to be among the world's most-valued red wines. For reds, Cabernet Sauvignon grapes predominate, followed by Merlot and small quantities (if any) of Cabernet Franc, Malbec and Petit Verdot.

Médoc Noir red grape variety of Hungary, believed related to Merlot of Bordeaux.

Meerendal wine producer of Durbanville, South Africa.

Meerlust great wine estate of Stellenbosch, South Africa. Bordeaux-style reds including famed Rubicon, and a renowned Pinot Noir.

The Médoc's

'Classed Growths'

The *Grand Cru Classé*s of the Médoc in Bordeaux include many of the most famous wine names in the world. The 60 estates on the list were those selected by the Bordeaux Chamber of Commerce in 1855 as representing the best of the region, each worthy to have its wines on show at the Great Exhibition held in Paris that year. The properties were classed in five sub-divisions as *crus* – meaning, literally, 'growths' – in other words, grape-growing farms. Seniority in the list accorded with the price being fetched on the Bordeaux market at the time. It is a tribute to the stability of the Bordeaux trade that all the wines mentioned are still in production – although a couple of the estates have amalgamated – and most today occupy a level of prestige much in line with their respective positions a century and a half ago.

The list is as first issued. The names in brackets are the communes (parishes) in which each estate lies. All are in the Médoc except Haut-Brion, the Graves estate which was recognised as a *grand cru* in its own right long before the name of any Médoc château became widely known. The rest of the Graves, and the vineyards of St Emilion, were later classified separately.

Premiers Crus
Château Lafite (Pauillac)
Château Latour (Pauillac)
Château Margaux (Margaux)
Château Haut-Brion (Pessac, Graves)
Deuxièmes Crus
Château Mouton-Rothschild (Pauillac) (promoted to 1*er Cru*, 1973)
Château Rausan-Ségla (Margaux)

Château Rauzan-Gassies (Margaux)
Château Léoville-Las-Cases (St Julien)
Château Léoville-Poyferré (St Julien)
Château Léoville-Barton (St Julien)
Château Durfort-Vivens (Margaux)
Château Lascombes (Margaux)
Château Gruaud-Larose (St Julien)
Château Brane-Cantenac (Cantenac-Margaux)

Château Pichon-Longueville-Baron (Pauillac)

Château Pichon-Lalande (Pauillac)

Château Ducru-Beaucaillou (St Julien)

Château Cos d'Estournel (St Estèphe)

Château Montrose (St Estèphe)

Troisièmes Crus

Château Giscours (Margaux)

Château Kirwan (Cantenac-Margaux)

Château d'Issan (Cantenac-Margaux)

Château Lagrange (St Julien)

Château Langoa-Barton (St Julien)

Château Malescot-St-Exupéry (Margaux)

Château Cantenac-Brown (Cantenac-Margaux)

Château Palmer (Cantenac-Margaux)

Château La Lagune (Ludon)

Château Desmirail (Margaux)

Château Calon-Ségur (St Estèphe)

Château Ferrière (Margaux)

Château Marquis-d'Alesme (Margaux)

Château Boyd-Cantenac (Margaux)

Quatrièmes Crus

Château Saint-Pierre-Sevaistre (St Julien)

Château Branaire (St Julien)

Château Talbot (St Julien)

Château Duhart-Milon (Pauillac)

Château Pouget (Cantenac-Margaux)

Château La Tour Carnet (St Laurent)

Château Lafon-Rochet (St Estèphe)

Château Beychevelle (St Julien)

Château Prieuré-Lichine (Cantenac-Margaux)

Château Marquis de Terme (Margaux)

Cinquièmes Crus

Château Pontet-Canet (Pauillac)

Château Batailley (Pauillac)

Château Grand-Puy-Lacoste (Pauillac)

Château Grand-Puy-Ducasse (Pauillac)

Château Haut-Batailley (Pauillac)

Château Lynch-Bages (Pauillac)

Château Lynch-Moussas (Pauillac)

Château Dauzac (Labarde-Margaux)

Château D'Armailhacq (Pauillac)

Château de Tertre (Arsac-Margaux)

Château Haut-Bages-Libéral (Pauillac)

Château Pédesclaux (Pauillac)

Château Belgrave (St Laurent)

Château Camensac (St Laurent)

Château Cos Labory (St Estèphe)

Château Clerc-Milon (Pauillac)

Château Croizet-Bages (Pauillac)

Château Cantemerle (Macau)

Meerspinne *Grosslage* incorporating vineyards at Neustadt an der Weinstrasse on four sites: Gimmeldingen an der Weinstrasse, Haardt an der Weinstrasse, Königsbach an der Weinstrasse and Mussbach an der Weinstrasse.

Meffre, Gabriel large-scale wine producer of Rhône Valley, France.

Mehana wine category and brand of Bulgaria. Name means 'bistro'. Lately superseded by the 'Country Wine' designation for export markets.

Mehrhölzchen *Grosslage* incorporating vineyards at Eltville, Oestrich-Winkel (Hallgarten) and Oestrich-Winkel (Oestrich) in Rheingau region, Germany.

Mehring wine village of Mosel-Saar-Ruwer region, Germany. *Grosslagen*: Probstberg, St Michael.

Meknès-Fez major wine region of Morocco incorporating quality zones of Beni m'Tir, Beni Sadden, Guerrouane, Sais, Zerkhoun.

Meisenberg vineyard at Waldrach in Mosel-Saar-Ruwer region, Germany.

Melba Cocktail. Over ice shake 4 parts rum, 4 Swedish Punsch, 1 lemon juice, 2 dashes grenadine, 2 dashes pastis. Strain.

Melbourne Bitter lager brand of Carlton & United Breweries, Melbourne, Australia.

Melcher, P distillery for *genever* and other spirits, Schiedam, Netherlands.

Melcher's Rat brandy by Racke distillers, Bingen, Germany.

melchior largest standard bottle size for port. Holds 18 litres.

Melini major wine producer in Poggibonsi, Tuscany, Italy. Chianti Classico wines and many others.

Mélinots *Premier Cru* vineyard of Chablis, Burgundy, France.

Melissa DOC for red wines from Gaglioppo grapes and whites from Greco Bianco, district around town of Melissa, Calabria, Italy.

Mellot, Alphonse wine grower (Domaine la Moussière) and *négociant* of AC Sancerre, Loire Valley, France.

Mellowwood brandy by Sedgewick Tayler distillery, South Africa.

Melnik town, grape variety and red wine of SW Bulgaria.

Melon Balls Cocktail. Over ice shake 1 part Midori (melon liqueur), 1 vodka, 1 pineapple juice. Strain.

Melon de Bourgogne white grape variety of Loire Valley, France. The sole constituent of Muscadet wine.

Melon State Balls Cocktail. Over ice shake 2 parts vodka, 1 Midori (melon liqueur), 2 orange juice. Strain.

Menada Stara Zagora winery est 1947, Sredna Gora, Bulgaria. Oriachovitza Cabernet Sauvignon and Merlot wines. Name Menada is that of the handmaiden of Dionysus in Thracian mythology.

Ménard cognac producer, St-Même-les-Carrières, France.

Mendocino wine region of California, USA. Includes **Mendocino County** AVA and others.

Mendocino Brewing Co brewery at Hopland, Mendocino, California.

Mendoza principal wine region of Argentina.

Ménétou-Salon AC for red and rosé wines from Pinot Noir grapes and whites from Sauvignon Blanc, Loire Valley, France.

Menjucq major *négociant-éleveur* at Pau, SW France.

Menota, Château wine estate of AC Sauternes, Bordeaux, France.

Menotat, Château Le wine estate of AC Premières Côtes de Blaye, Bordeaux, France.

Méntrida wine region of central Spain. Ordinary red wines.

Menuet cognac producer, St-Mêmeles-Carrières, France.

Menuts, Clos des wine estate of AC St-Emilion, Bordeaux, France. Classified *Grand Cru*.

Meranese di Collina DOC for red wines from Schiava grapes, Trentino-Alto Adige region, Italy.

mercaptan in winetasting, a sour, unhealthy odour from hydrogen sulphide; the wine will be undrinkable.

Mercian leading wine-producing company, Japan.

Mercier *Grande Marque* champagne house est 1858, Epernay, France. Owned by Moët-Hennessy.

Mercurey AC and wine village of Côte Chalonnaise, Burgundy, France. Red wines from Pinot Noir grapes and whites from Chardonnay by producers including Château de Chamirey, Domaine Saier. Village is site of Roman temple to god Mercury.

Merlin's Ale beer (4.2% alc) by Broughton Ales, Peeblesshire, Scotland. Named after wizard of Arthurian legend said to have lived near the site of the brewery. 'Close by at Stobo Kirk stands a stained glass window showing St Mungo baptising Merlin in the River Tweed.'

Merlin's Magic beer (4.3% alc) by Moor Beer Co, Somerset, England. Named in honour of brewery's proximity to Arthurian Glastonbury.

Merlot most widely planted grape variety of Bordeaux, France. Now increasingly cultivated in many other parts of France, Europe and the New World. The principal variety of Bordeaux ACs Pomerol and St Emilion, where it is usually blended on a ratio around two to one with Cabernet Franc, and in ACs of Médoc and Graves in second place only to Cabernet Sauvignon (Merlot typically constitutes a quarter of the cépage in red wines of these appellations). Widespread in SW France, Italy, Spain, Bulgaria, Hungary etc. Important in Argentina and Chile, Australia, South Africa and the USA.

Merlot Colli Orientali del Friuli DOC for red wines from Merlot grapes, Friuli-Venezia Giulia region, Italy.

Merlot Colli Goriziano DOC for red wines from Merlot grapes, Gorizio, Friuli-Venezia Giulia region, Italy.

Merlot del'Alto Adige DOC for red wines from Merlot grapes, Alto Adige region, Italy.

Merlot del Piave DOC for red wines from Merlot grapes, Veneto region, Italy.

Merlot Isonzo DOC for red wines from Merlot grapes, Gorizio, Friuli-Venezia Giulia region, Italy.

Merlot Lison-Pramaggiore DOC for red wines from Merlot grapes, Veneto region, Italy.

Merlyn whisky-based liqueur brand of Welsh Whisky Co, Penderyn, Brecon, Wales.

Merman Scottish ale brand (4.8% alc) of Caledonian Brewing Co, Edinburgh, Scotland. *see label opposite* ➡

Merret, Dr possibly the originator of sparkling wine. An Englishman, he presented a paper to the Royal Society in London in 1662, explaining the principles under which part-fermented wine in bottles could be dosed with spirit and/or sugar, causing a new fermentation which rendered the wine fizzy. Because English bottles were by then more advanced, and more robust, than others, they were less likely to explode from the pressure built up within. Merret's paper preceded the introduction of sparkling champagne by some decades.

Merrie Monk dark ale by Marston's brewery, Burton upon Trent, England.

Merriman's brewery operated by Old Fart Ltd at Leeds, Yorkshire, England.

Merrit Island AVA of Yolo County, California, USA.

Merry Widow Cocktail. Over ice shake 1 part dry gin, 1 dry vermouth, 2 dashes Angostura bitters, 2 dashes Bénédictine, 2 dashes pastis. Strain.

Mersin Turkish liqueur similar to curaçao.

Merzeguera white grape variety of Alicante region, Spain.

mescal incorrect, but common, misspelling of mezcal, Mexico's spirit from maguey cactus. This erroneous rendering has given rise to a myth that mezcal is related to the hallucinogenic and dangerous alkaloid mescalin derived from the peyote cactus mescal.

Mesimarja liqueur from Arctic bramble. Finland.

Messias port shipper and wine producer in Bairrada, Portugal. Port vintages: 1950, 52, 58, 60, 63, 66, 67, 70, 75, 77, 79, 80, 82, 83, 84, 85, 87, 89, 91, 94, 97, 2000, 03.

Messina beer brand of Italy.

Mestreechs Aajt lambic beer of Zwarte Ruiter brewery, Maastricht, Belgium.

Métaireau, Louis wine grower and quality-wine brand used by other producers, AC Muscadet, Loire Valley, France.

metallic in winetasting, a flavour indicating metallic contamination. A serious fault.

Metaxa principal spirit distiller of Greece. Brandies include three, five and seven star brands (each star indicating minimum years' ageing) and a drier VSOP. Est by Spyros Metaxa at Kifissia, Greece, 1888. Formerly owned by Diageo of UK but sold to Dutch liqueur company Bols in 1999.   *see label opposite* ➡

Meteor brewery in Alsace, France.

méthode champenoise 'champagne method'. The technique of producing sparkling wine by bottling new-made wine, adding sugar and yeast and sealing the bottle so that the ensuing second fermentation carbonates the wine. The method originates in Champagne, France, but is now employed widely elsewhere. Use of the term *méthode champenoise*, according to European Union regulations, is restricted to wine made within AC Champagne.

méthode traditionelle synonym for *méthode champenoise* used in Europe to circumvent restriction of 'champagne method' description to AC Champagne, France.

methusaleh champagne bottle format of six litres. Equal to eight bottles of standard size. Named after Old Testament patriarch Methusaleh, credited with living 969 years.

methyl radical of wood alcohol used in spirit manufacture to make products unpalatable. This has not proved an infallible method of deterring all problem drinkers. Methyl shares its etymological derivation between the Ancient Greek words *hyle* (wood) and *methu* (wine). The pathological condition **methysis** is that of drunkenness.

metodo Charmat Italian sparkling wine made by the tank method.

metodo classico describes Italian sparkling wine made by the erstwhile nomenclature of the *méthode champenoise*.

metodo friuliano winemaking technique of producing white wines in closed vats by cooled (and thus protracted) fermentation. Resulting wines have maximum freshness and minimum oxidation. The method has been widely adopted in Italy but originated in the Friuli region.

metodo tradizionale the same as *metodo classico*.

Metro Cocktail. Over ice shake 1 part brandy, 1 sweet vermouth, 1 dash Angostura bitters, sprinkling of sugar. Strain.

Metsovo red wine from Cabernet Sauvignon grapes, Epirus, Greece.

Metternich-Sandor wine producer in Kamptal, Niederösterreich, Austria.

Metz schnapps-based brand of Martini & Rossi, Italy.

Meulière, Château de la wine estate of AC Premières Côtes de Bordeaux, France.

Meunier grape variety important in Champagne region, France. From Pinot Meunier vine, a relative of Pinot Noir.

Meursault wine village/town and AC of Côte de Beaune, Burgundy, France. Famed white wines from Chardonnay grapes sold under village name, AC Meursault, or from the *Premier Cru* vineyards with their respective names appended to that of the village: les Bouchères, les Caillerets, les Charmes, les Crats, les Gouttes d'Or, les Perrières, les Pêtures, le Poruzot, les Santenots etc. Small quantities of red wine are made. Important growers include Ampeau, Germain, Lafon, Michelot, Prieur-Brunet, Ropiteau.

Meursault, Château de leading producer of AC Meursault wine, Burgundy, France.

Meursault-Blagny adjacent AC for white wines of Meursault, Burgundy, France. Includes *Premiers Crus* le Dos de l'Ane, les Genevrières, la Jennelotte, la Pièce sous le Bois.

Mexican Cocktail. Over ice shake 1 part tequila, 1 pineapple juice, 1 dash grenadine.

Mexicila tequila brand of Pernod-Ricard, Mexico.

Mexico important brewing nation since 1544, with the establishment of the first commercial brewery in the New World. Spirit production is centred on brandy and tequila. Wines are produced in Baja California and other regions.

Mexicola Cocktail. In a tall, ice-filled glass stir 2 parts tequila, 1 fresh lime juice. Top with chilled cola.

Meyer, Jos wine producer in Wintzenheim, Alsace, France.

Meyney, Château wine estate of AC St-Estèphe, Médoc, Bordeaux, France. Classified *Cru Grand Bourgeois Exceptionnel*.

Meynieu, Château Le wine estate of AC Haut-Médoc, Bordeaux, France. Classified *Cru Grand Bourgeois*.

mezcal spirit distilled from extract of cactus plants of the maguey family, Mexico. San Louis Potosi and Pacific Coast regions are principal zones of production. The spirit, usually colourless, is commonly bottled with the dried body a worm (*gusano*).

Mézesféher white grape variety of Hungary. Sweet wines of Lake Balaton area.

Miami Cocktail. Over ice shake 2 parts rum, 1 crème de menthe, 1 dash lemon juice. Strain.

Miami Beach Cocktail. Over ice shake 1 part scotch whisky, 1 dry vermouth, 1 grapefruit. Strain.

Michaeliskapelle vineyard at Braunweiler in Nahe region, Germany.

Michaelsberg vineyards at Bruchsal in Baden region and at Cleebronn, Güglingen, Güglingen (Eibensbach) and Güglingen (Frauenzimmern) in Württemberg region, Germany.

Michel Barlaam Cognac producer. France.

Michel, Louis leading wine producer of Chablis, Burgundy, France.

Michel Lynch brand of good-quality AC Bordeaux red, rosé and white wines by Jean-Michel Cazes. M Cazes owns famed Château Lynch-Bages of Médoc region, Bordeaux, France.

Michelmark vineyard at Eltville in Rheingau region, Germany.

Michelob beer brand of Anheuser-Busch brewing company, Missouri, USA. Products include **Michelob** beer (5.0% alc) and **Michelob Golden Draught** (5.0% alc), also **Michelob Ultra** low-carbohydrate beer.

Michelsberg *Grosslage* incorporating vineyards in Mosel-Saar-Ruwer region, Germany at, respectively: Hetzerath, Kalusen. Minheim, Neumagen-Dhron (Dhron), Neumagen-Dhron (Neuman), Piesport, Piesport (Niederemmel), Rivenich, Sehlem, Trittenheim.

Michelsberg vineyards at Bad Dürkheim, Bad Dürkheim (Ungstein) and Weyer in der Pfalz in Rheinpfalz region and Mettenheim in Rheinhessen region, Germany.

Michigan wine-producing state of USA. Vineyards centre around Chicago and Lake Michigan.

Mickey Finn a drugged drink. USA.

Mickey's Big Mouth beer brand of Heileman Brewing Co, Wisconsin, USA.

Mickie Walker Cocktail. Over ice shake 3 parts scotch whisky, 1 sweet vermouth, 1 dash grenadine, 1 dash lemon juice. Strain.

Middelvlei wine producer in Stellenbosch, South Africa. Red wines from Cabernet Sauvignon and Pinotage grapes.

Middleton brewery at Barnard Castle, County Durham, England.

Midi wine-producing region of southern France extending from Pyrenees to Rhône Valley. Formerly the source of industrial quantities of *vin ordinaire*, but since grubbing up of large areas of poor vineyards now a region with growing numbers of quality sub-regions including ACs Corbières, Costières de Nîmes, Côtes du Roussillon etc and numerous *vin de pays* zones.

Midnight Express Cocktail. Over ice shake 2 parts dark rum, 1 Cointreau, 2 fresh lime juice. Strain.

Midori green-coloured melon liqueur by Suntory, Japan.

Mighty Oak brewery at Brentwood, Essex, England.

Mignon, Yves *récoltant manipulant* champagne producer, Cumières, Champagne, France.

Mignon & Pierrel *négoçiant-manipulant* champagne house, Epernay, Champagne, France. Brands include Cuvée Bagatelle, Cuvée Florale, Marquis de La Fayette.

Migraine former vineyard name of Auxerrois district of northern Burgundy, France. Now used informally for some wines of the region.

Migsich wine producer in Neusiedlersee Hügelland, Burgenland, Austria.

Mikado Cocktail. Over ice shake 1 part brandy, 2 dashes Angostura bitters, 2 dashes Crème de noyaux, 2 dashes curaçao, 2 dashes Orgeat Syrup. Strain.

mild ale style of English beer with mild hop-flavouring; usually dark in colour and low (3%) in alcohol.

Mildara major wine producer in Mildura, Victoria, Australia and Coonawarra, South Australia.

Milenario solera gran reserva brandy by Luis Caballero, Puerto de Santa Maria, Spain.

milk stout style of sweet stout made with lactose (milk sugars) in a process first patented in London, England, 1875.

Milk Street microbrewery in Frome, Somerset, England. Ales include, Bison, Gulp, Nick's (after proprietor Nick Bramwell) and one called Beer.

Millars blended Irish whiskey brand of Cooley Distillery, Riverstown, Dundalk, County Louth, Republic of Ireland.

Millburn North Highland malt whisky distillery, Inverness, Scotland. Est 1807, closed 1988.

Millefiori yellow liqueur flavoured with Alpine flowers. Bottles contain twig to which sugar adheres and crystallises. Italy.

Millennium champagne brand of 'EastEnders' drink retailer, Calais, France.

Miller major USA brewer known for **Miller Lite** beer. **Miller Genuine Draught** (4.7% alc) is brewed in UK by Scottish Courage.

millerandage vine ailment: inauspicious flowering conditions result in poor setting of fruit and grapes remain underdeveloped. French.

Miller's Burgundy regional name for Pinot Meunier grape variety, Australia.

Mille-Sescousses, Château wine estate of AC Bordeaux Supérieur, France.

millésime 'vintage year', French.

Millet, Château wine estate of AC Graves, Bordeaux, France.

Millgate brewery at Failsworth, Manchester, England.

Millionaire Cocktail. Over ice shake 1 part apricot brandy, 1 rum, 1 sloe gin, 1 fresh lime juice, 1 dash grenadine. Strain.

Million Dollar Cocktail. Over ice shake 1 egg white, 4 parts dry gin, 2 sweet vermouth, 1 pineapple juice, 2 dashes grenadine. Strain.

Millstream small brewery at Amana Church, Iowa, USA.

Millton wine producer of Gisborne, New Zealand. Organic and biodynamic methods.

Millwood liqueur brand of Halewood International, Huyton, Merseyside, England.

Milner's Brown Label blended scotch whisky of W H Milner, wine and spirit arm of Marston's brewery, Burton upon Trent, England.

Milord's twelve-year-old blended scotch whisky by Macdonald Martin Distilleries, Leith, Edinburgh, Scotland.

Miltonduff Speyside malt whisky distillery est 1824, Elgin, Morayshire, Scotland. Single malt: 12-year-old.

Milwaukee Weiss beer by Sprecher Brewing Co, Milwaukee, USA.

Mimosa Cocktail. In an ice-filled wine glass stir 1 part sparkling wine, 1 fresh orange juice.

Mine Beer ale brand of Blind Man's Bewery, Leighton, Somerset, England.

Miner's Arms pub-brewery in Westbury-sub-Mendip, Somerset, England.

Minerva pub-hotel-brewery at Hull, Humberside, England.

Minervois AC for (mainly) red wines from Carignan, Cinsaut, Grenache, Mourvèdre and Syrah grapes grown around village of Minerve, Midi, France.

Minho wine region of northern Portugal for *vinho verde*.

Minnesota Brewing Co brewery in St Paul, Minnesota, USA.

Minöségi Bor quality mark of wines of Hungary.

Minsterley Ale beer by The Salopian Brewery, Shrewsbury, Shropshire, England.

Mint Cocktail. In shaker, soak sprigs of garden mint in 3 parts white wine for two hours. Add ice, 4 parts dry gin, 3 white wine, 1 crème de menthe and shake. Strain and add fresh mint sprig to each glass.

Mint Cooler Cocktail. Into a tumbler glass with ice add 2 parts Scotch whisky, 2 dashes crème de menthe. Top with soda water.

Mint Julep Cocktail. In a wine glass, place 4 mint leaves and a teaspoon of sugar. Add a dash of soda. Stir to mix and release the mint flavour. Add a shot of bourbon whisky, and ice and top with soda.

mirabelle *eau de vie* distilled from yellow mirabelle plums. France and Switzerland.

Miralduolo estate owned by Lungarotti of Torgiano, Umbria, Italy. Cabernet Sauvignon and Chardonnay wines.

Miramar wine producer of Mudgee, New South Wales, Australia.

Mirassou Vineyards wine producer of Monterey, California, USA.

Mireille, Clos wine estate of Domaines Ott near St Tropez, Provence, France.

mis en bouteille 'bottled'. French, past participle of *mettre*, to put. As in *mis en bouteille au château* for 'bottled at the château'.

mise en bouteille 'the bottling'. French, gerund of *mettre*, to put. As in *mise en bouteille au château* for 'bottling [took place] at the château'.

Misket white wine from red **Misket** grape, Bulgaria.

Mission red grape variety of California, USA. So named after tradition that it was the first variety planted in the state, by a Jesuit, in 1697.

Mission revival of brewery closed 1917 in San Diego, California, USA, now with restaurant attached.

Mission wine producer of Hawkes Bay, New Zealand. Est by Society of Mary, 1851, and NZ's oldest working vineyard.

Mission-Haut-Brion, Château La great wine estate of AC Pessac-Léognan, Bordeaux, France. Classified *Cru Classé*.

Mission Hill Vineyards wine producer in British Columbia, Canada.

Mississippi Mule Cocktail. Over ice shake 4 parts dry gin, 1 crème de cassis, 1 lemon juice. Strain.

mistelle grape must used in production of wine-based beverages, particularly vermouth. Addition of spirit halts fermentation, so sugars are retained. French.

Mitchell leading wine producer in Clare Valley, Australia. Distinguished wines from Grenache, Riesling, Shiraz and other grape varieties.   *see label opposite* ➡

Mitchell's brewery at Lancaster, Lancashire, England.

Mittelbach, Gottfried & Ingrid wine producer in Kremstal, Niederösterreich, Austria.

Mittelberg vineyard at Bayerfeld-Steckweiler in Nahe region, Germany.

Mittelburgenland wine district of Burgenland region, Austria. Principally red wines.

Mittelhardt Deutsche Weinstrasse *Bereich* of Rheinpfalz region, Germany.

Mittelheim wine village of Rheingau region, Germany. *Grosslagen*: Erntebringer, Honigberg.

Mittelhölle vineyard at Geisenheim in Rheingau region, Germany.

Mittelmosel central and highest-rated vineyard area of Mosel-Saar-Ruwer region, Germany.

Mittelrhein wine region of Germany comprising three *Bereichen*: Bacharach, Rheinburgengau and Siebengebirge.

MITCHELL

CLARE VALLEY

1996

THE GROWERS
GRENACHE

750ML

Miura brandy-based liqueur by Luis Caballero, Puerto de Santa Maria, Spain.

Mocha Mint Cocktail. Over ice stir 1 part crème de cacao, 1 crème de menthe, 1 Tia Maria. Strain.

Moctezuma major brewing company in Vera Cruz, Mexico, known for widely exported beer brands Dos Equis and Sol.

Modelo largest brewing company of Mexico. Brands include Negra Modelo and Victoria.

Modder River Cocktail. Over ice stir 2 parts dry gin, 1 Caperitif, 1 dry vermouth. Strain.

Modesto winemaking centre of E&J Gallo, California, USA. The largest winery in the world.

moëlleux style of white wine of rich 'marrowy' softness, particularly AC Vouvray and neighbours in Loire Valley, France.

Moët & Chandon *Grande Marque* champagne house est 1743 by Claude Moët, Epernay, France. Pierre-Gabriel Chandon was grandson-in-law of founder. Wines are labelled Brut Imperial (after avid patron, Emperor Napoleon Bonaparte) or Première Cuvée. The name Dom Pérignon for famed vintage wine was purchased from Mercier 1930.

Mohan major brewing company of India with production centres at Bangalore, Himachal, Lucknow, Madras, New Delhi etc.

Moillard major wine grower and *négociant-éleveur* in Nuits-St-Georges, Burgundy, France.

Moines, Château des wine estate of AC Lalande-de-Pomerol, Bordeaux, France.

Moines, Château Les wine estate of AC Médoc, Bordeaux, France.

Moinette *saison* beer of Dupont brewery, Tourpes, Belgium.

Mojito Cocktail. Over ice shake 2 parts rum, 1 fresh lime juice, 1 dash Angostura bitters, teaspoon sugar, 1 mint sprig. Strain.

Mojito Club rum-based liqueur brand of Pernod-Ricard.

molasses sugar-cane-processing residue fermented to form 'wash' from which rum is distilled. From Spanish *melaza*, perhaps derived from French *miel* (honey).

Molasses Act rum distilling was a major industry in the New England of the early 18th century, until Parliament in London passed a Molasses Act in 1733, imposing high taxes on sugar imports from outside the British empire. The first rebellions by American colonists protesting 'No taxation without representation,' were in response to the Act and, in effect, the beginnings of the struggle for independence.

Moldova 'confederated independent state' formerly of Soviet Union, with extensive vineyards. An emerging quality-wine producer from French grape varieties.

Mole's brewery in Melksham, Wiltshire, England.

Molette white grape variety of Savoie region, France. Seyssel sparkling wines.

Molinara red grape variety, Veneto, Italy. Bardolino and Valpolicella wines.

Molise wine region of southern Italy including DOCs Biferno and Pentro di Isernia.

Moll Cocktail. Over ice shake 1 part dry gin, 1 dry vermouth, 1 sloe gin, 1 dash orange bitters, sprinkle of sugar. Strain.

Mollenbrunnen vineyards at Bad Kreuznach and Hargesheim in Nahe region, Germany.

Mollner-Titz wine producer in Neusiedlersee, Burgenland, Austria.

Molotov Cocktail. Over ice stir 2 parts vodka, 1 Sambuca. Strain.

Molotov Cocktail the incendiary device commemorates Vyacheslav Mikhailovich Skriabin, the Russian known by his fellow revolutionaries as Molotov, 'the Hammer'. The eponymous petrol bomb was neither invented nor employed by Molotov. It was first used as a weapon by Finnish resistance fighters in 1940 – against Russian tanks. Molotov's more permanent achievements included the division of post-war Germany and the dangerous exacerbation of the Cold War. Expelled by Kruschev from the Communist party in 1957 as 'a saboteur of peace' and sent to Outer Mongolia, this persistent man nevertheless survived to be reinstated as a party member in 1984, aged ninety-three. He died two years later.

Molson major brewing company of Montreal, Canada, now amalgamated with Carling. Brands include **Molson Canadian** lager, **Molson Golden** ale, **Molson Porter**. **Molson Dry** (5.1% alc) is brewed in UK by Scottish Courage.

Mombasa brewery at Mombasa, Kenya. Tusker beer.

Mommessin wine producer principally of Beaujolais, but also of famed Clos de Tart *Grand Cru* vineyard, Morey-St-Denis, Burgundy, France.

Mona Lisa Cocktail. Over ice stir 3 parts crème de cacao, 1 dry vermouth. Strain into a cocktail glass with rim frosted by dipping it first in lemon juice and then in sugar.

Monarch, The ten-year-old blended scotch whisky of Lambert Bros, Edinburgh, Scotland.

Monastrell red grape variety of Spain. Catalonia, Levante and other regions.

Monbazillac AC for sweet white wines from Sémillon, Sauvignon and Muscadelle grapes, Dordogne region, SW France.

Monbazillac, Château leading wine producer of AC Monbazillac, Dordogne, France.

Monbousquet, Château wine estate of AC St-Emilion, Bordeaux, France. Classified *Grand Cru*.

Monbrison, Château wine estate of AC Margaux. Médoc, Bordeaux, France. Classified *Cru Bourgeois*.

Moncabon, Enclos de second wine of Château Rauzan-Gassies, Bordeaux, France.

Monção vineyard region in northern Minho Valley, Portugal. Superior *vinho verde* wines.

Monceau St Waast brewery in the Avenois region, northern France. Known for L'Avenoise beer and *bière de garde* brands labelled either Vieille Garde or Old Garde.

Moncets, Château wine estate of AC Lalande-de-Pomerol, Bordeaux, France.

Mönchbäumchen vineyard at Zornheim in Rheinhessen region, Germany.

Mönchberg the name of 11 individual vineyards in Germany. Region by region, as follows: in Ahr at Mayschoss; in Franken at Sulzheim; in Nahe at Bad Kreuznach, Hergenfeld, Hüffelsheim; in Rheinhessen at Volxheim; in Württemberg at Fellbach, Kernen (Rommelshausen), Kerner (Stetten), Stuttgart (Bad Cannstatt), Stuttgart (Untertürkheim).

Mönchgarten vineyard at Neustadt an der Weinstrasse in Rheinpfalz region, Germany.

Mönchhhalde vineyards at Stuttgart, Stuttgart (Bad Cannstatt) and Stuttgart (Zuffenhausen) in Württemberg region, Germany.

Mönchhube vineyard at Dittelsheim-Hessloch in Rheinhessen region, Germany.

Mönchpforte vineyards at Nieder-Hildersheim and Ober-Hilbersheim in Rheinhessen region, Germany.

Mönchsberg vineyards at Bad Mergentheim, Brackenheim, Brackenheim (Dürrenzimmern) and Weikersheim in Württemberg region, Germany.

Mönchsbuck vineyard at Sugenheim in Franken region, Germany.

Mönchsgewann vineyard at Flörsheim in Rheingau region, Germany.

Mönchshang vineyard at Zeil am Main in Franken region, Germany.

Mönchsleite vineyard at Eibelstadt in Franken region, Germany.

Mönchspfad vineyards Geisenheim in Rheingau region, Schornsheim in Rheinhessen region and Siebeldingen in Rheinpfalz region, Germany.

Mönchwingert vineyard at Manubach in Mittelrhein region, Germany.

Monconsel-Gazin, Château wine estate of AC Premières Côtes de Blaye, Bordeaux, France.

Moncrieffe eight- and 15-year-old blended scotch whiskies of Moncreiffe & Co, Perthshire, Scotland. Full name Sir Iain's Special Moncreiffe – in memory of Sir Ian Moncreiffe of that Ilk, 23rd Laird, d 1985.

Mondavi, Robert leading winemaker of California, USA. Founder of Robert Mondavi Winery, Woodbridge, Napa Valley 1966. Noted wines include Cabernet Sauvignon Reserve, Chardonnay, Fumé Blanc, Pinot Noir Reserve and joint-venture (with late Baron Philippe Rothschild) Opus One.

Monday Blues Cocktail. Over ice stir 1 part vodka, 1 teaspoon blue curaçao, 1 teaspoon Cointreau. Strain.

Mondeuse red grape variety mainly of Savoie region, France. Synonymous with Refosco of Italy.

Mondschein vineyard at Dittelsheim-Hessloch in Rheinhessen region, Germany.

Monica di Cagliari DOC for strong and mostly sweet red wines from Monica grapes, Cagliari, Sardinia, Italy.

Monica di Sardegna DOC for dry red wines from Monica grapes, Sardinia, Italy.

Monkey Gland Cocktail. Over ice shake 3 parts dry gin, 1 orange juice, 2 dashes pastis, 2 dashes grenadine. Strain.

Monkey Wrench ale brand (5.3% alc) of Daleside Brewery, Harrogate, Yorkshire, England. 'Revives the old legend in Hartlepool of a shipwrecked monkey accused of being a spy.'

Monkey Wrench Cocktail. Add 2 parts white rum to a tall, ice-filled glass. Top with pineapple juice and stir.

Monnet cognac house, Cognac, France. Brands include Le Club,

XO 25–30 year-old, Josephine 40–45 year-old. Est by father of Jean Monnet, founder of the Franco-German Coal & Steel Union, forerunner of the European Union, the firm is now, appropriately, owned by Scharlachberg of Germany.

Monsanto wine producer (Il Poggio estate) of DOCG Chianti Classico, Tuscany, Italy.

Monsecco red wine brand of DOCG Gattinara, Piedmont, Italy. By Conte Ravizza.

Monster's Choice blended scotch whisky by Strathnairn Whisky, Inverness, Scotland. Purports to be 'Nessie's Favourite Dram'.

Montado Solera brandy by Wisdom & Warter, Jerez de la Frontera, Spain.

Montagne satellite AC of St-Emilion, Bordeaux, France. Wines are designated AC **Montagne-St-Emilion**.

Montagne de Reims vineyard region of AC Champagne, France.

Montagnieu wine *cru* of AC Vin de Bugey, Savoie, France.

Montagny AC for white wines from Chardonnay grapes, Côte Chalonnaise, Burgundy, France.

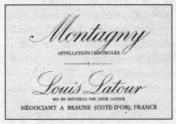

Montagny 1er Cru wines have higher alcohol level and are produced by the well-known Cave Coopérative de Buxy.

Montalbano

Montalbano wine zone of Chianti Putto, Tuscany, Italy.

Montalbert, Château wine estate of AC St-Emilion, Bordeaux, France. Classified *Grand Cru*.

Montalcino hill town home of famed DOCG Brunello di Montalcino, Tuscany, Italy. See Brunello.

Montalivet, Château wine estate of AC Graves, Bordeaux, France.

Montana major wine-producing company of New Zealand with vineyards and wineries in Gisborne and Marlborough and HQ in Auckland. Said to produce half of all the wine made in NZ. Previously owned by Seagram and acquired by Allied Domecq, 2001.

Montana Cocktail. Over ice shake 2 parts brandy, 1 port, 1 dry vermouth, 2 dashes Angostura bitters. Strain.

Montanchez village and sherry-style red aperitif wine of Extremadura, Spain.

Montaudon champagne house, Reims, France.

Montbrun, Château wine estate of AC Margaux, Médoc, Bordeaux, France. Classified *Cru Bourgeois*.

Mont de Milieu *Premier Cru* vineyard of Chablis, Burgundy, France.

Mont d'Or, Domaine du noted wine producer in Sion, Valais, Switzerland.

Montebello *Grande Marque* champagne house, Mareuil-sur-Aÿ, France.

Montecarlo DOC for red and (more notably) white wines, Tuscany, Italy.

Monte Carlo Imperial Cocktail. Over ice shake 2 parts dry gin, 1 white crème de menthe, 1 lemon juice. Strain into wine glass and top with champagne.

Montecillo renowned *bodega* of Rioja, Spain. Brands include Viña Monty reserva Rioja.

Montecompatri Colonna DOC for Frascati-style white wines from Malvasia and Trebbiano grapes, Latium, Italy.

Monte Cristo wine producer of Montilla-Moriles, Spain.

Montée de Tonnerre *Premier Cru* vineyard of Chablis, Burgundy, France.

Montefalco Rosso DOC for red wine from Sangiovese, Sagrantino and Trebbiano grapes grown at Montefalco, Umbria, Italy.

Montego Bay Cocktail. Over ice shake 1 part Jamaican rum, 1 equal mix fresh lime and pineapple juice, 1 dash grenadine. Strain.

Monteil-d'Arsac, Château second wine of Château d'Arsac, Bordeaux, France.

Monteith's lager brand of Dominion brewery, Greymouth, New Zealand.

Monte Jup vineyard at Rheinbrohl in Mittelrhein region, Germany.

Montelena, Château wine estate est 1882 at Calistoga, Napa Valley, California, USA.

Montello e Colli Asolani DOC for red wines from Bordeaux grape varieties, Veneto region, Italy.

Monteneubel vineyard at Enkirch in Mosel-Saar-Ruwer region, Germany.

Montepulciano red grape variety of Italy.

Montepulciano d'Abruzzo DOC for red and *rosato* wines from Montepulciano grapes, Abruzzi region, Italy. *see label opposite* ➡

Monterey wine-producing county of California, USA.

Monterey Vineyard major wine producer of Monterey County, California, USA. Classic and Limited Release wine brands.

Monterrey wine region of Galicia, Spain.

Montescudaio DOC for red wines from (mostly) Sangiovese grapes, whites from Trebbiano. Also, Vin Santo wine.

Montesodi noted Chianti Rufina riserva red wine by Frescobaldi at Nippozzano, Tuscany, Italy.

Montez Champalimaud port shipper, Vila Nova de Gaia, Portugal. Vintages: 1982, 91.

Montezuma tequila brand of Pernod-Ricard. Mexico.

Montfort vineyard at Odernheim am Glan in Nahe region, Germany.

MontGras leading wine producer at Colchagua, Chile.

Monthélie wine village and AC of Côte de Beaune, Burgundy, France. *Premier Cru* vineyards: Champs Fulliot, Lavalle, le Meix Bataille, les Riottes, la Taupine, les Vignes Rondes etc.

Monthélie, Château de leading wine estate of AC Monthélie, Burgundy, France. Property of Suremain.

Monthil, Château du wine estate of AC Médoc, Bordeaux, France. Classified *Cru Bourgeois*.

Montilla sherry-like wine of DO Montilla-Moriles, Andalucia, Spain. Mainly from Pedro Ximenez grapes, wines are fermented to high natural levels of alcohol and are (usually) unfortified. Maturing is similar to sherry, in a *solera* system. Styles are dry to sweet.

Montlouis AC for white wines from Chenin Blanc grapes, Loire Valley, France. Styles include dry, medium and *moelleux* (rich, soft) and plus semi-sparkling and sparkling.

Montmains *Premier Cru* vineyard of Chablis, Burgundy, France.

Montmélian wine *cru* of Savoie, France.

Montpeyroux wine zone north of Béziers of AC Coteaux du Languedoc, Midi, France.

Montrachet, Le great vineyard and greatest white wine of Burgundy, France. Straddles boundary between villages of Chassagne-Montrachet and Puligny-Montrachet, covering 19 acres. Chardonnay grapes and white wines only. Ownership is divided largely between Bouchard Père & Fils, Fleurot-Larose, Marquis de Laguiche, Domaine de la Romanée Conti, Baron Thénard, Roland Thévenin.

Montravel AC for white wines of Bergerac region, SW France.

Mont Redon, Château major wine estate of AC Châteauneuf-du-Pape, Rhône Valley, France.

Montrose, Château wine estate of AC St-Estèphe, Médoc, Bordeaux, France. Classified *2ème Grand Cru Classé*.

Monts du Tessalah wine zone of NE Algeria.

Mony, Château wine estate of AC Premières Côtes de Bordeaux, France.

Monymusk sugar estate and rum distillery at St Catherine's Town, Jamaica. Renowned pot still rums for long ageing.

Mooiuitsig table- and fortified-wine producer, Breede River Valley, South Africa.

Moonlight Cocktail. Over ice shake 4 parts dry gin, 4 white wine, 3 grapefruit juice, 1 kirsch. Strain and add lemon peel twist to glass.

Moonlight Cooler Cocktail. Over ice shake 2 parts apple brandy, 1 lemon juice, 1 teaspoon sugar. Strain into tall glass. Top with soda water and add fruit slices.

Moonraker Cocktail. Over ice shake 1 part brandy, 1 peach brandy, 1 quinquina, 1 dash pastis. Strain.

moonshine colloquial term for illicit liquor, USA. Said to originate from the nocturnal activities of unlicensed distillers (moonshiners) in Florida, 1785.

Moonshine strong (7.5% alc) cider brand of Broadoak Brewery, England.

Moonshine Extra Strong barley wine brand of Grand Ridge brewery, Victoria, Australia.

Moonshot Ephemeral UK 'alcopop' brand in a bottle resembling a hypodermic syringe but quickly withdrawn after protests from anti-alcohol-abuse campaigners.

Moor Beer Co microbrewery est 1996 by Arthur and Annette Frampton at Ashcott, Somerset, England. Ales include Withy Cutter (3.8% alc), Peat Porter (4.5%), Avalon Springtime (4%), Merlin's Magic (4.3%), Old Freddy Walker (7.3%).

Moorcroft pear variety traditionally valued for perry-making. English.

Moorhouse's brewery in Burnley, Lancashire, England.

Moortgat brewery in Breendonk, Mechelen/Malines, Belgium is renowned for Duvel, Lucifer and Maredsous beer brands.

Moosberg vineyards at Hahnheim and Sörgenloch in Rheinhessen region, Germany.

Moosehead brewing company in New Brunswick and Nova Scotia, Canada. Brands include **Moosehead Canadian Lager** and **Moosehead Export**.

mops and brooms drunk. Idiomatic English of doubtful origin.

Morange, Château wine estate of AC Ste-Croix-du-Mont, Bordeaux, France.

Moravia principal vineyard region of Czech Republic. Improving wines from imported grape varieties.

Moravia Pils beer brand of Holsten brewery, Lüneburg, Germany.

morbido 'soft' (wine). Italian.

Mordue brewery at North Shields, Tyne & Wear, England.

Moreau & Fils, J major wine grower and *négoçiant-éleveur* of Chablis, France.

Morellino di Scansano DOC for red wine from Sangiovese grapes grown near Grosseto, Tuscany, Italy.

Moretti Baffo D'Oro beer (4.8% alc) by CDB Milan brewery, Italy.

Morey, Albert wine domaine in Chassagne-Montrachet, Burgundy, France.

Morey St-Denis wine village and AC of Côte de Nuits, Burgundy, France. *Grand Cru* vineyards are Bonnes Mares, Clos de la Roche, Clos de Tart, Clos St-Denis. *Premier Cru* vineyards: Clos Baulet, les Bouchots, Clos de la Bussière, Calonères, les Chabiots, les Chaffots, aux Charmes, les Chénevery, Côte Rôtie, les Fremières, les Froichots, les Gruenchers, Clos des Lambrays, Maison Brûlée, Meix Rentiers, les Millandes, les Mochamps, Monts-Luisants, Clos des Ormes, la Riotte, les Ruchots, Clos Sorbés, les Sorbés.

Morgadio de Torre noted *vinho verde* by Sogrape, Minho, Portugal.

Morgan cider (5.5% alc) from Morgan Sweet apples by Thatcher's Cider, Sandford, Somerset, England.

Morgenhof wine estate in Stellenbosch, South Africa. French grape varieties. Owned by Huchon family, new proprietors of Gosset, oldest *maison* of Champagne, France.

Morgon wine village and *cru* of Beaujolais region, Burgundy, France.

Móri Ezerjó white wine of Mór, west of Budapest, Hungary.

Moretti brewery and beer brand, Udine, Italy.

Morgan port brand of Croft, Vila Nova de Gaia, Portugal. Vintages: 1960, 63, 66, 70, 77, 82, 85, 91, 94, 97, 2000, 03.

Morgenbachtaler vineyard at Trechtingshausen in Mittelrhein region, Germany.

Morin, Château wine estate of AC St-Estèphe, Médoc, Bordeaux, France. Classified *Cru Grand Bourgeois*.

Morio-Muscat white grape variety mainly of Rheinhessen region, Germany.

Morland brewery est 1711, Abingdon, Oxfordshire, England. Hen's Tooth ale (6.6% alc), Old Speckled Hen Pale Ale (5.2% alc), Ruddles County Ale (4.7% alc). Taken over by Greene King 1999. Some Morland brands are now being subsumed.

Mornag, Château red and rosé wine brand of UCCVT, Tunisia.

Morey-Saint-Denis
APPELLATION MOREY-SAINT-DENIS CONTRÔLÉE

1985

MIS EN BOUTEILLE À SAVIGNY-LES-BEAUNE (CÔTE D'OR)
PAR DE LUZE & FILS

Morning Cocktail. Over ice shake 1 part brandy, 1 dry vermouth, 2 dashes curaçao, 2 dashes maraschino, 2 dashes orange bitters, 2 dashes pastis. Strain and add cocktail cherry to glass.

Morning Glory Cocktail. Over ice shake 1 part whisky, 1 lemon juice, 2 dashes pastis, 1 egg white, 1 teaspoon sugar. Strain into a tall, ice-filled glass and top with chilled sparkling water.

Morocco wine-producing nation since French immigration of 1920s but now in decline. Residual quality-wine system imitates AC. Main vineyard regions centre on Berkane-Oudja, Casablanca, Meknès-Fez, Rabat. Southern French grape varieties for largely red wines.

Morocco Ale beer (5.5% alc) by Daleside Brewery, Harrogate, Yorkshire, England. 'Spiced beer full of intriguing flavours ... said to originate from Tangiers.'

Morrells brewery in Oxford, England. Beers include College Ale and Varsity bitter.

Morris, JW 'port' wine producer of California, USA.

Morris Wines wine producer in Rutherglen, Victoria, Australia, renowned for Liqueur Muscat wines.

Morro Cocktail. Over ice shake 2 parts dry gin, 1 rum, 1 fresh lime juice, 1 pineapple juice. Strain.

Morstein vineyard at Westhofen in Rheinhessen region, Germany.

Mortlach Speyside malt whisky distillery est 1823, Dufftown, Banffshire, Scotland. Single malts 15-,: 16-, 21-, 22-year-old.

Morton Estate wine producer at Waikato, New Zealand.

Mort Subite beer brand (name translates as 'Sudden Death') of De Keersmaecker brewery, Payottenland, Belgium.

Mosaic fortified wine brand of Keo, island of Cyprus.

Moscadello di Montalcino DOC for sweet sparkling wine from Moscadello grapes, Montalcino, Tuscany, Italy.

Moscatel regional name for Muscat d'Alexandrie grape variety, Portugal and Spain.

Moscato Bianco white grape variety widely grown throughout Italy. Synonymous with Muscat Blanc à Petits Grains.

Moscato d'Asti DOC for fruity sparkling wines from Moscato grapes grown around Asti, Piedmont, Italy.

Moscato di Cagliari DOC for dessert wines from Moscato grapes, Cagliari, Sardinia, Italy. Sweet wine at 15% alc and sweet fortified at 17.5%.

Moscato di Noto DOC for dessert wine from Moscato Bianco grapes, Noto, Sicily, Italy. Still and *spumante* wines plus fortified at 22% alc.

Moscato di Pantelleria DOC dessert wine in several variations from Zibibbo grapes grown on island of Pantelleria, Sicily, Italy.

Moscato di Sardegna DOC for *spumante* wine from Moscato Bianco grapes, island of Sardinia, Italy.

Moscato di Siracusa DOC for dessert wine from Moscato grapes, Siracusa, Sicily, Italy.

Moscato di Sorso Sennori DOC for dessert wines from Moscato grapes of vineyards around Sorso and Sennori, island of Sardinia, Italy.

Moscato di Strevi DOC for (mainly) sparkling wines from Moscato grapes, Strevi, Piedmont, Italy.

Moscato di Trani DOC for dessert wines from Moscato Reale grapes, Trani, Apulia, Italy.

Moscato Giallo white grape variety of NE Italy. Related to Muscat Blanc à Petits Grains. Synonymous with Goldenmuskateller.

Moscato Rosa white grape variety of NE Italy. Related to Muscat Blanc à Petits Grains. Synonymous with Rosenmuskateller.

Moscophilero white grape variety of Peloponnese, Greece.

Moscow Mule a mixed drink of vodka and ginger ale. Said to originate from Los Angeles, USA, 1964.

Mosel under Germany wine law, correct generic term for ordinary *Tafelwein* of Mosel-Saar-Ruwer region, Germany.

Moselland largest wine-producing co-operative (Winzergenossenschaft) of Mosel-Saar-Ruwer region, Germany.

Moselle popularly, a generic name for all qualities of wine from Mosel-Saar-Ruwer region, Germany. From French spelling of river Mosel.

Mosel-Saar-Ruwer wine region of Germany extending southwest from Koblenz along the valleys of the river Mosel and its tributaries the Saar and Ruwer rivers to the Vosges mountains. Comprises *Bereichen* (sub-regions), Zell, Bernkastel, Saar-Ruwer and Obermosel and 20 *Grosslagen* (collective vineyards), with 525 *Einzellagen* (individual vineyards). Many of Germany's greatest wines, especially from Riesling grapes, sold in green bottles to distinguish them from brown-bottled Rhine wines.

Moser, Dr Lenz principal wine producer of Austria. Estate wines plus popular branded white Schluck.

Moser, Hans wine producer in Neusiedlersee Hügelland, Burgenland, Austria.

Moser, Hermann wine producer in Kremstal, Niederösterreich, Austria.

Moser, Sepp wine producer in Kremstal, Niederösterreich, Austria.

Moshi brewery at Moshi, Tanzania.

Moskovskaya grain vodka brand, Moscow, Russia.

Mosstowie Speyside single malt whisky formerly made by Miltonduff distillery, Elgin, Scotland.

Moss Wood wine producer of Margaret River, Western Australia.

mother's ruin nickname for gin. Originally early 18th century and revived in 20th century.

mou in winetasting, French for 'flabby' – lacking acidity.

Mouchão, Herdade de revived and renowned wine estate of Alentejo region, Portugal.

Moueix, JP leading wine grower and *négociant* of Pomerol and St-Emilion, Bordeaux, France. Interests include top Pomerol châteaux Pétrus and Trotanoy, and Magdelaine in St-Emilion.

Moulin brewery-hotel at Moulin, Pitlochry, Perthshire, Scotland.

Moulin à Vent wine *cru* and AC of Beaujolais region, Burgundy, France. Covers 650 hectares of vineyards of villages of Chénas and

Romanèche-Thorins. Named (in 1936) after last working windmill of Beaujolais. The windmill, employed to grind grain, had ceased production in 1910 after losing its sails to a storm. It was finally restored, to some local dismay, as a visitor attraction in 1999.

Moulin-à-Vent, Château wine estate of AC Lalande-de-Pomerol, Bordeaux, France.

Moulin-à-Vent, Château wine estate of AC Moulis, Bordeaux, France. Classified *Cru Grand Bourgeois*.

Moulin-d'Arvigny, Château second wine of Château Beaumont, Bordeaux, France.

Moulin-de-Laborde, Château wine estate of AC Listrac, Bordeaux, France.

Moulin-de-la-Roque, Château second wine of Château La Tour de By, Bordeaux, France.

Moulin de la Rose, Château wine estate of AC St Julien, Médoc, Bordeaux, France. Classified *Cru Bourgeois*.

Moulin-de-Launay, Château wine estate of AC Entre-Deux-Mers, Bordeaux, France.

Moulin-des-Carruades second wine of Château Lafite-Rothschild, Bordeaux, France.

Moulin-de-St-Vincent, Château second wine of Château Moulin à Vent, Bordeaux, France.

Moulin de Taffard, Château wine estate of AC Médoc, Bordeaux, France.

Moulin du Cadet, Château wine estate of AC St-Emilion, Bordeaux, France. Classified *Grand Cru Classé*.

Moulin-Duhart second wine of Château Duhart-Milon, Bordeaux, France.

Mouline, La vineyard and brand name of AC Côte Rôtie by Guigal, Rhône Valley, France.

Moulinet, Château wine estate of AC Pomerol, Bordeaux, France.

Moulinet-Lasserre, Château second wine of Clos René, Bordeaux, France.

Moulin-Haut-Laroque, Château wine estate of AC Fronsac, Bordeaux, France.

Moulin-Haut-Villars, Château wine estate of AC Fronsac, Bordeaux, France.

Moulin-Pey-Labrie, Château wine estate of AC Canon-Fronsac, Bordeaux, France.

Moulin-Riche, second wine of Château Léoville-Poyferré, Bordeaux, France.

Moulin Rouge, Château wine estate of AC Côtes de Castillon, Bordeaux, France.

Moulin Rouge, Château du wine estate of AC Haut-Médoc, Bordeaux, France.

Moulin Rouge Cocktail. Over ice shake 2 parts apricot brandy, 1 lemon juice, 1 orange gin, 3 dashes grenadine. Strain.

Moulin Touchais famed wine producer of AC Anjou Blanc, Loire Valley, France. Rich white wines from Chenin Blanc grapes.

Moulis AC of Médoc, Bordeaux, France.

Moulis, Château wine estate of AC Moulis, Médoc, Bordeaux, France. Classified *Cru Bourgeois Supérieur*.

Moullay-Hofberg vineyard at Reil in Mosel-Saar-Ruwer region, Germany.

mountain former name for wine of Málaga, Spain.

Mountain Brewers small brewery at Bridgewater, Vermont, USA. Known for Long Trail Ale.

Mountain Cocktail. Over ice shake 1 egg white, 3 parts rye whisky, 1 dry vermouth, 1 sweet vermouth, 1 lemon juice. Strain.

Mountain Wheat wheat beer by Breckenridge brewery Colorado, USA.

Mount Eden wine producer in Santa Clara, California, USA.

Mount Gay rum distiller, Barbados, said to have been established 1703 and claiming to be the oldest in the world. The estate, now owned jointly by Rémy-Cointreau and the Ward family, has been so-called since 1801 when its former name, Mount Gilboa, was given up in commemoration of Sir John Gay Alleyne, its administrator, who died in that year. The owners were then a family called Sober, who sold out to the Wards in 1860. Principal brand is Mount Gay Eclipse.

Mount Hurtle wine brand of Stratmer Vineyards, Reynella, South Australia.

Mount Konocti wine estate at Kelseyville, Clear Lake, California, USA.

Mount Murray brewery at Braddan, Isle of Man, UK.

Mount Rufus vintage tawny 'port' brand of Seppelt, South Australia.

Mount Tolmie Dark beer by Spinnakers brewery, Canada.

Mourisco Tinto red grape variety of Douro Valley, Portugal.

Mourlet, Château second wine of Château d'Archambeau, Bordeaux, France.

Mourvèdre red grape variety of growing significance in southern France. Major constituent of red wines of Provence, Rhône and Midi. Known as Mataro in Australia and Monastrell in Spain.

Mousel et Clausen brewery of the Grand Duchy of Luxembourg. Beers under the brand name Royal-Altmünster.

mousse the effervescence of sparkling wine. French.

mousseux 'sparkling' (wine). French.

Moutai Chiew grain spirit distilled from millet and wheat, and China's 'national spirit'. Produced in town of Mou-Tai Chen, Kweichow province of People's Republic of China.

Moutardier, Jean *récoltant manipulant* champagne producer, le Breuil, Champagne, France.

Mouton-Baron-Philippe, Château former name (1956–76) of Château Mouton-Baronne-Philippe, Bodeaux, France.

Mouton-Baronne-Philippe, Château former name (1976–91) of Château d'Armailhac, Bordeaux, France.

Mouton-Cadet wine brand of La Baronnie, Bordeaux, France.

Moutonne, La important but unclassified vineyard of Chablis, Burgundy, France.

Mouton-Rothschild, Château great wine estate of AC Pauillac, Médoc, Bordeaux, France. Classified (since 1973) *1er Grand Cru Classé.*

moutwijn neutral alcohol from barley maltings prepared for distillation with botanicals (principally juniper) for production of *genever*. Netherlands.

moutwijnjenever double-distilled all-malt *genever*. Netherlands.

Moyet cognac house, Cognac, France.

Mozart Chocolate Nougat liqueur brand of Halewood International, Huyton, Merseyside, England.

MQS Cocktail. Over ice stir 2 parts scotch whisky, 1 Drambuie, 1 green Chartreuse. Strain. Initials are for Mary, Queen of Scots.

Mr Harry winter ale by Fuller's brewery, London, England.

Mtsvane white grape variety of Black Sea region, particularly Crimea and Georgia.

Muckerhöhle vineyard at Waldböckelheim in Nahe region, Germany.

Mudgee wine region of New South Wales, Australia.

'mud in your eye' the toast commemorates an unlucky American doctor. Samuel Mudd had a country practice near Washington, and one night in April 1865 was visited by a very excitable patient in his mid-fifties with a broken shin. He treated the man and thought no more of it until discovering the next day that President Abraham Lincoln had been assassinated. The killer's description matched that of his patient. Dr Mudd contacted the authorities at once, but to his dismay was accused of conspiring with the assassin, John Wilkes Booth. Mudd was imprisoned for life. His pleas of innocence were widely publicised (and ignored) and his name came to symbolise anyone who vigorously denied involvement in a crime, innocent or otherwise.

Mudslide cream-based Kahlua liqueur brand of Allied Domecq, UK.

Muga wine grower and producer of Rioja, Spain.

Mühlbächer vineyard at Mundelsheim in Württemberg region, Germany.

Mühlberg vineyards at Boxberg and Lauda Königshofen in Baden region, Braubach in Mittelrhein region,

Edenkoben in Rheinpfalz region, Schlossböckelheim, Sponheim and Waldböckelheim in Nahe region and Veldenz in Mosel-Saar-Ruwer region, Germany.

Mühlenberg vineyards at Hensch in Mosel-Saar-Ruwer region and Roxheim and Wallhausen in Nahe region, Germany.

Muirhead's eight- and 12-year-old blended scotch whiskies by Gibson International, London, England.

Mulderbosch wine estate of Stellenbosch, South Africa, Legendary Sauvignon Blanc white wine.

Mule's Hind Leg Cocktail. Over ice shake 1 part apple brandy, 1 apricot brandy, 1 Bénédictine, 1 dry gin, 1 maple syrup. Strain.

Mülheim wine village of Mosel-Saar-Ruwer region, Germany. *Grosslage*: Kurfürstlay. Known for wines of Max Ferdinand Richter estate.

mulled wine drink of spiced wine, traditionally warmed by immersion of a hot fire poker. English answer to *Glühwein* of Germany.

Müller, Günter wine producer in Weststeiermark, Austria.

Müller, Rudolph wine producer and shipper in Mosel-Saar-Ruwer region, Germany.

Müller, Walter wine producer in Süd-Oststeiermark, Austria.

Müller-Grossmann wine producer in Kremstal, Niederösterreich, Austria.

Müller-Scharzhof, Weingut Egon great wine estate of Saar *Bereich* of Mosel-Saar-Ruwer region, Germany. Holdings include part of Scharzhofberg vineyard.

Müller-Thurgau white grape variety of Germany. A cross between Riesling and Sylvaner varieties, originally by oenologist Dr Müller (born Thurgau, Switzerland) in 1883. Major constituent of Liebfraumilch and Germany's most widely planted grape variety. Also grown in England, Italy, New Zealand, Switzerland etc.

Müllner wine producer in Kremstal, Niederösterreich, Austria.

mum style of beer originally brewed in Brunswick, Germany.

Mumm, GH & Co *Grande Marque* champagne house est 1827 Reims, France. Well-known Cordon Rouge NV Brut and admired Mumm de Cramant (softly sparkling champagne from the firm's vineyards at Cramant, previously known as Crémant de Cramant). Sold by Seagram to Allied Domecq, 2001.

Mumm VSOP cognac sold exclusively in USA. Named after champagne house, GH Mumm, formerly owned by Seagram.

Mumme style of dark beer first brewed in Germany, 15th century. See Braunschweige Mumme.

Mundklingen vineyard at Seeheim in Hessliche Bergstrasse region, Germany.

Munslow brewhouse of The Crown Inn, Munslow, Shropshire, England.

Münsterberg vineyard at Treis-Karden in Mosel-Saar-Ruwer region, Germany.

Münster-Sarmsheim wine village of Nahe region, Germany. *Grosslage*: Schlosskapelle.

Münsterstatt vineyard at Temmels in Mosel-Saar-Ruwer region, Germany.

Münzberg vineyard at Landau in der Pfalz in Rheinpfalz region, Germany.

Münzenrieder, Johann wine producer in Neusiedlersee, Burgenland, Austria.

Münzlay *Grosslage* incorporating vineyards at Bernkastel-Kues, Graach, Zeltingen-Rachtig and Zeltingen-Rachtig (Zeltingen) in Mosel-Saar-Ruwer region, Germany.

Murças port shipper, Vila Nova de Gaia, Portugal. Vintages: 1987, 91.

Muré wine producer in Rouffach, Alsace, France. Wines from Clos St Landelin estate of *Grand Cru* Vorbourg.

mûre sauvage *eau de vie* distilled from blackberries. France and Switzerland.

Murfatlar wine region of SE Romania.

Murphy's Irish stout brand (4.0% alc) originally of **Murphy** brewery, est 1856, Cork, Eire. Owned by Heineken.

Murray River wine region of Victoria, Australia.

Murrumbidgee Irrigation Area extensive wine-growing area of New South Wales more usually known as abbreviated MIA or as Riverina.

Musar, Château famed wine estate of Hochar family in Bekáa Valley, Lebanon. Mainly red wine from Cabernet Sauvignon, Cinsaut and Syrah grapes.

Muscadelle white grape variety of Bordeaux, France. Minor constituent of sweet wines of Sauternes. Also grown in nearby Bergerac region, and in Australia (under name Tokay).

Muscadet white grape variety and dry white wine of estuarial Loire Valley, France. Three ACs: Muscadet (for simplest wines of vineyards south of Nantes), Muscadet de Sèvre et Maine (grapes from lower-yielding vineyards of Sèvre et Maine, east of Nantes), Muscadet des Coteaux de La Loire (also from lower-yield vineyards, east of Nantes). Best wines are unfiltered, bottled direct from vats *sur lie* (on the lees). **Muscardin** rare red grape variety of Châteauneuf-du-Pape, Rhône Valley, France.

Muscat d'Alexandrie white grape variety of southern Europe for sweet wines including *vin doux naturel* of SW France. In Portugal and Spain known as Moscatel and in Italy as Moscato di Pantellaria. Also grown in Australia as Gordo Blanco and South Africa as Hanepoot.

Muscat d'Alsace dry (but exotic) style of wine of Alsace region, France, from Muscat Blanc à Petits Grains and Muscat Ottonel grapes.

Muscat Blanc à Petits Grains white grape variety for sweet wines of France including **Muscat de Beaumes de Venise** and Clairette de Die of Rhône Valley and *vin doux naturel* of Midi. Synonymous with Moscato Bianco of Italy and Muscat Canelli of California, USA.

Muscat de Frontignan *vin doux naturel* from Muscat Blanc à Petits Grains grapes of Frontignan, Midi, France.

Muscat de Kelibia dry white wine from Muscat grapes, Cap Bon, Tunisia.

Muscat de Lunel *vin doux naturel* from Muscat Blanc à Petits Grains grapes of Lunel, Montpellier, Midi, France.

Muscat de Mireval *vin doux naturel* from Muscat Blanc à Petits Grains grapes of Mireval, Montpellier, Midi, France.

Muscat de Rivesaltes *vin doux naturel* from Muscat Blanc à Petits Grains and Muscat d'Alexandrie grapes of Rivesaltes, Midi, France.

Muscat de St-Jean-de-Minervois *vin doux naturel* from Muscat Blanc à Petits Grains grapes of St Jean de Minervois, Midi, France.

Muscat Ottonel white grape variety grown in Alsace, France and also in Austria and eastern Europe. Dry as well as sweet wines.

muselage or **muselet** the wire cage securing cork in sparkling wine bottles. French.

Musenhang vineyard at Forst an der Weinstrasse in Rheinpfalz region, Germany.

Museum Ale beer by Samuel Smith brewery, Tadcaster, Yorkshire, England.

Musigny, Le *Grand Cru* vineyard at Chambolle-Musigny, Côte de Nuits, Burgundy, France. Renowned red (and some white) wines from producers including Drouhin, Jadot, Roumier, De Vogue.

Musikantenbuckel vineyard at Freinsheim in Rheinpfalz region, Germany.

must in winemaking, the newly pressed juice of the grapes, before fermentation.

must weight measure of the natural sugar content of grape juice, according to ripeness at time of harvest. Must weights are calibrated according to systems including Balling, Baumé, Brix, Oechsle.

musty in winetasting, a cobwebby, stale smell. May indicate diseased cork.

mutage in French winemaking, the 'silencing' of fermentation by adding yeast-killing spirit to must. Used in producing *vin doux naturel*.

Mütterle vineyard at Landau in der Pflaz in Rheinpfalz region, Germany.

Myers dark rum brand of Jamaica, owned by Diageo.

My Fair Lady Cocktail. Over ice shake 1 egg white, 2 parts dry gin, 1 lemon juice, 1 orange juice, 3 dashes strawberry liqueur. Strain.

Myr mixed drink of Gabriel Boudier Crème de Myrtilles (bilberry liqueur) topped with dry white Loire wine. A variation on Kir, suggested to Robin Yapp, wine merchant of Mere, Wiltshire, England, by composer Sir Harrison Birtwistle.

Myra Cocktail. Over ice stir 2 parts red wine, 1 dry vermouth, 1 vodka. Strain.

Myrat, Château dormant wine estate of AC Sauternes, Bordeaux, France. Classified *2ème Cru Classé*.

myrtille *eau de vie* distilled from bilberries. France and Switzerland.

Mysore brewery at Yeshwanthpur, Bangalore, India.

Mythos beer brand of Boutaris wine company of Thessaloniki, Greece, produced as a joint venture with Guinness.

N

Nachbaur, Franz wine producer in Vorarlberg, Austria.

Nackenheim wine town of Rheinhessen region, Germany. *Grosslagen*: Gutes Domthal and Spiegelberg.

Nacktarsch *Grosslage* incorporating vineyards at Kröv and Kröv (Kövenig) in Mosel-Saar-Ruwer region, Germany.

Nags Head pub-brewery at Abercych, Boncath, Pembrokeshire, Wales.

Nagyburgundi regional name for Pinot Noir grape variety, Hungary.

Nahe wine region of Germany. Named after Rhine tributary. Two *Bereichen*, Kreuznach and Schlossböckelheim, and seven *Grosslagen*.

Nairac, Château wine estate of AC Barsac, Bordeaux, France. Classified *2ème Cru Classé*.

Naltrexone ethical drug developed by pharmacologists in Helsinki, Iceland, for treatment of alcoholism. First papers published 1999. Effective action on endorphins, but a controversial therapy because patients are expected to continue to drink alcohol during treatment, in which psychological management plays an important role.

Namibia Breweries brewing company of Namibia, SW Africa.

Nanok beer by Wiibroe brewery, Elsinore, Denmark.

Naoussa red wine from Xynomavro grapes, Mount Velia, Thessalonika, Greece. *see label opposite* ➡

Napa wine town, county, valley and AVA of northern California, USA.

Napobitter Cocktail. Pour 1 part Mandarine Napoléon into a tall, ice-filled glass. Top with chilled bitter lemon.

Napoléon in cognac descriptions, a brandy blended from spirits which have aged in oak for at least six years and up to 15 years or, sometimes, more before bottling. Also applied to armagnac. French. Bottles of the original 'Napoleon' brandy, produced for Napoléon Bonaparte and branded with the imperial 'N' in 1811, are said still to exist, but are unlikely to make pleasant drinking today.

Napoléon *Grande Marque* champagne house est 1825 Vértus, Marne, France.

Napoleon Cocktail. Over ice shake 1 part dry gin, 1 dash curaçao, 1 dash Dubonnet, 1 dash Fernet Branca. Strain and squeeze lemon peel over.

Napoleon's Redemption Cocktail To a tall ice-filled glass pour in 1 part Mandarine Napoléon, 1 vodka. Top with chilled tonic water.

Narbag sweet white wine from Narince grapes grown at Tokat, Anatolia, Turkey.

Nardo red wine from Malvasia Nera and Negroamaro grapes, Lecci, Apulia, Italy.

Narrenberg vineyards at Hergersweiler, Römerberg (bei Speyer) (Berghausen), Römerberg (bei Speyer) (Heiligenstein) and Winden in Rheinpfalz region, Germany.

Narrenkappe vineyard at Bad Kreuznach in Nahe region, Germany.

Nasco di Cagliari DOC for white wines from part-dried Nasco grapes, Cagliari, Sardinia, Italy. Dry, sweet and fortified *liquoroso* (both *secco* and dolce *naturale*).

Nastro Azzurro beer brand (5.2% alc) of Birra Peroni, Italy.

Natasha vodka brand formerly of Seagram, Canada.

Nathaniel Johnston merchant company est 1734, Bordeaux, France. Now an important *négoçiant*.

Nathaniel's Special ale brand of Fox & Hounds pub-brewery, Barley, Hertfordshire, England.

Natch cider brand of Matthew Clark, Shepton Mallet, Somerset, England.

Natu Nobilis spirit brand of Pernod-Ricard.

naturwein wine made without addition of sugar, Austria.

Naudin, Clos wine estate of AC Vouvray, Loire Valley, France.

Navajo Trail Cocktail. Over ice shake 2 parts tequila, 1 triple sec, 1 fresh lime juice, 1 cranberry juice. Strain.

Navarra wine region of northern Spain neighbouring Rioja, including DO Navarra south of Pamplona. Sub-regions are Baja Montaña, Ribera Alta, Ribera Baja, Tierra de Estella, Valdizarbe. Red wines comparable with those of Rioja.

Naveltje Bloot liqueur by van Zuylekom distillery, Amsterdam, Netherlands. Name means 'bare navel'.

Navip slivovitz brand popular in former Yugoslav states.

Navy Cocktail. Over ice shake 3 parts rum, 1 sweet vermouth, 1 orange juice. Strain.

Nawlins Cocktail. Over ice shake 2 parts rum, 1 equal mix of fresh lime and orange juice. Strain into an ice-filled tumbler and top with chilled dry ginger ale.

nazdorovia 'cheers' in Russian.

Néac wine commune next to, and in reputation overwhelmed by, commune and AC Lalande de Pomerol, Bordeaux, France.

Nebenführ wine producer in Weinviertel, Niederösterreich, Austria.

Nebbiolo black grape variety of northern Italy. In Piedmont region, sole constituent of great wines of Barbaresco, Barolo, Gattinara, Ghemme etc. Also called Spanna. In Valtelline region, makes Grumello, Inferno, Sasello Valgello. Name derives from Latin *nebula*, fog – after mists which commonly cover hills of Piedmont.

Nebbiolo d'Alba DOC for red wines from Nebbiolo grapes grown around town of Alba, Piedmont, Italy.

Nebbiolo delle Langhe red wine from Nebbiolo grapes, Langhe hills, Piedmont, Italy.

Nebbiolo del Piemonte red wine from Nebbiolo grapes of Piedmont, Italy.

Nebbiolo del Roero DOC for red wine from Nebbiolo grapes of Roero, Piedmont, Italy.

Nebiker, H distiller of *eau de vie*, Sissbach, Switzerland.

nebuchadnezzar large-format champagne bottle of 15 litres. Equals 20 standard bottles. Named after King of Babylon of 6th century BC.

Neckarhälde vineyards at Affalterbach, Benningen, Erdmannshausen, Freiberg/Neckar, Ludwigsburg (Hoheneck), Ludwigsburg (Neckarweihingen), Ludwigsburg (Poppenweiler), Marbach and Murr in Württemberg region, Germany.

Nederburg great wine estate of Paarl, South Africa. Many branded and varietal wines including 'Private Bin' range and Nederburg Auction Wines from annual auction, first held 1975 and now claimed to be 'South Africa's wine event of the year'.

Ned Kelly whisky brand, Australia.

nèfle *eau de vie* distilled from medlars. France and Switzerland.

négociant wine dealer, buying grapes, must or made wine for blending and/or bottling under his or her own name. France.

négociant-éleveur wine dealer also carrying out *élevage* ('bringing-up') of wine in cellars prior to bottling and sale under own brand. France.

Negra Modelo lager brand of Modelo brewery, Mexico City, Mexico.

Negroni Cocktail. Over ice stir 1 part Campari, 1 dry gin, 1 sweet vermouth. Strain and add orange slice to glass.

Negus mixed sherry-based hot drink devised by Francis Negus (d. 1732). Warm 1 bottle dark sherry in a saucepan and add 2 pints (1 litre) boiling water and 1 lemon, sliced. Remove from heat and add 1 small glass brandy. Add sugar and freshly grated nutmeg to taste.

Nekowitsch wine producer in Neusiedlersee, Burgenland, Austria.

Nelson's Creek wine producer of South Africa noted for Klein Begin, meaning 'small beginnings', the first wine brand made and owned by black workers on 25 acres of vineyard given by the estate's owner, Alan Nelson. First vintage made in 1998.

Nelson's Revenge ale brand (4.5% alc) of Woodforde's brewery, Woodbastwick, Norfolk, England.

Nemea red wine from Agiorgitiko grapes of Corinth, Peloponnese, Greece.

Nenin, Château wine estate of AC Pomerol, Bordeaux, France.

Nenin, Château wine estate of AC Premières Côtes de Bordeaux, France.

Neptun brewery in Jutland, Denmark, known for green-coloured Pinsebryg ('Whitsun brew') beer.

Nerello red grape variety of Sicily, Italy.

Neroberg vineyard at Wiesbaden in Rheingau region, Germany.

Nerte, Château de la leading wine estate of AC Châteauneuf-du-Pape, Rhône Valley, France.

Ness brewery at Foyers, Inverness, Scotland.

Nessie 'Whisky Malz Bier' produced by Eggenberg brewery, Salzburg, Austria. Named after the monster said to inhabit Loch Ness, Scotland.

Nessie Ale 'monster mash' ale (4.5% alc) by Tomintoul Brewery, Ballindalloch, Banffshire, Scotland.

Nethergate brewery at Clare, Suffolk, England.

Netherland Cocktail. Over ice stir 1 part brandy, 1 triple sec, 1 dash orange bitters. Strain.

Nettelback brewery in Brunswick, Germany, known for Braunchweiger Mumme tonic beer.

Netzl wine producer in Carnuntum, Niederösterreich, Austria.

Neuberg vineyards at Bornheim and Meckenheim in Rheinpfalz region and Osthofen in Rheinhessen region, Germany.

Neuberger white grape variety of Austria.

Neuchâtel wine-growing canton of Switzerland. White wines from Chasselas grapes, reds from Pinot Noir.

Neumagen wine village of Mittelmosel, Mosel-Saar-Ruwer region, Germany. *Grosslage*: Michelsberg. Vineyards include Engelgrube, Laudamusberg, Rosengärtchen.

Neumayer wine producer in Traisental, Niederösterreich, Austria.

Neumeister, Albert wine producer in Süd-Oststeiermark, Austria.

Neusiedlersee wine-producing area of Burgenland region, Austria.

Neustadt brewery at Neustadt, Bavaria, Germany, known for Rauchenfels Steinbier 'stone beer'.

Neustadt wine town of Rheinpfalz region, Germany.

Neuwies vineyard at Ockfen in Mosel-Saar-Ruwer region, Germany.

Neuwingert vineyard at Brodenbach in Mosel-Saar-Ruwer region, Germany.

Nevada City brewery in Nevada City, California, USA.

Nevada Cocktail. Over ice shake 3 parts Bacardi rum, 2 grapefruit juice, 1 fresh lime juice, 1 dash Angostura bitters. Strain.

Nevers French oak valued for making of wine barrels.

Nevins Cocktail. Over ice shake 3 parts bourbon, 1 equal grapefruit and lemon juice, 1 teaspoon apricot brandy, 2 dashes Angostura bitters. Strain.

New Amsterdam Ale beer brand by FX Matt brewery, Utica, New York, USA.

New Arrival Cocktail. Over ice stir 1 part dry gin, 1 orange bitters, 2 dashes Crème Yvette, 2 dashes Lillet. Strain.

New Belgium Brewing Co brewery est 1992 in Fort Collins, Colorado, USA.

Newbury Cocktail. Over ice shake 1 part dry gin, 1 sweet vermouth, 3 dashes curaçao, 1 piece lemon rind, 1 piece orange rind. Strain.

Newcastle Brown famed bottled beer by Scottish Courage of Newcastle-upon-Tyne, England. First made in 1927, is strong by reputation, but less so (4.7%) by volume. Made at the Tyne brewery in Newcastle until 2005, when production was moved to the Federation Brewery in nearby Gateshead. The original label name was changed by the dropping of the word 'Ale' in 2000.

New England Brewing Co brewery in Danbury, Connecticut, USA. Beer brands include **New England Atlantic Amber**.

New Haven Brewing university-town (Yale) brewery in Connecticut, USA famed for beers including Blackwell Stout and Elm City Connecticut Ale.

Newman's Brand Saratoga Lager Dortmunder-style beer by Catamount brewery, White River Junction, Vermont, USA.

New Orleans Gin Fizz Cocktail. Over ice shake 2 parts dry gin, 1 fresh lime juice, 1 lemon juice, 1 egg white, 1 tablespoon cream, 1 teaspoon sugar. Strain into ice-filled glasses and top with chilled sparkling water.

Newquay Steam Beer range of brands reviving style of steam beers once made in Cornwall, England and exported via the Cornish port of Newquay. Owned by Whitbread.

New South Wales wine-producing state of Australia. Vineyard districts include Corowa, Hunter Valley, Mudgee, Riverina etc.

Newton's Special Cocktail. Over ice shake 3 parts brandy, 1 Cointreau, 1 dash Angostura bitters. Strain.

New York Cocktail. Over ice shake 2 parts rye whisky, 1 fresh lime juice, 2 dashes grenadine, 1 piece orange peel, 1 sugar lump. Strain.

New York Sour Cocktail. Over ice shake 2 parts rye whisky, 1 lemon juice, 1 teaspoon sugar. Strain into wine glasses and top with chilled dry white wines.

New York State principal wine-producing state of eastern USA.

New Zealand emerging wine-producing nation already making world-class wines from Chardonnay, Sauvignon and Pinot Noir grapes and adding new varieties including Riesling. Established North Island vine districts include Hawkes Bay and Poverty Bay and South Island districts of Canterbury and Marlborough.

Niagara white grape variety of eastern USA.

Niagara County wine-producing region of New York State, USA.

Niagara Falls Brewing brewery at Niagara, Canada, noted for Eisbock beer and other specialities.

Nicastro *vino da tavola* of Nicastro, Calabria, Italy. Red from Nerello and Gaglioppo grapes and white from Malvasia.

Nice Pair Cocktail. Over ice shake 1 part dry sherry, 1 cream sherry, 1 rum, 2 dashes orange bitters. Strain into a small wine glass.

Nick's Own Cocktail. Over ice shake 1 part brandy, 1 sweet vermouth, 1 dash Angostura bitters, 1 dash pastis. Strain, add cocktail cherry to glass and squeeze lemon peel over.

Nicollet Island Ale

Nicollet Island Ale beer by Taps brewery, Minneapolis, USA.

Niederberg vineyard at Rivenich in Mosel-Saar-Ruwer region, Germany.

Niederberg-Helden vineyard at Lieser in Mosel-Saar-Ruwer region, Germany.

Niederhausen wine village of Nahe region, Germany. *Grosslage*: Burgweg. Vineyards include Hermannsberg, Hermannshöhle, Steinberg.

Niederkirchen wine estate of Deidesheim, Rheinpfalz, Germany. Originally property of church on ther site founded 1100.

Niederösterreich Lower Austria, the region of the Danube plain producing more than 80 per cent of the country's wine. Principal appellations are Carnuntum, Donauland, Kamptal, Kremstal, Thermenregion, Traisental, Wachau, Weinviertel.

Nielluccio red grape variety of island of Corsica.

Niepoort & Co family port house est by Dutchman Eduard Kebe 1842 Vila Nova de Gaia, Portugal. Old tawnies and vintages: 1955, 60, 63, 66, 70, 75, 77, 78, 80, 82, 83, 85, 87, 91, 92, 94, 97, 2000, 03.

Nierstein wine town of Rheinhessen region, Germany. Name, too, of an extensive *Bereich* including *Grosslagen* Auflangen, Gutes Domtal, Rehbach and Spiegelberg.

Nies'chen vineyard at Kasel in Mosel-Saar-Ruwer region, Germany.

Night Cap Cocktail. Over ice shake 1 egg yolk, 1 part Anisette, 1 brandy, 1 curaçao. Strain.

Night Owl Cocktail. Over ice shake 2 parts bourbon, 1 teaspoon Cointreau, 1 teaspoon lemon juice. Strain into an ice-filled tumbler and top with chilled soda water.

Nigl, Martin wine producer in Kremstal, Niederösterreich, Austria.

Nikka Distilleries whisky producer, Japan. Brands include Black Nikka.

Nikolai vodka brand formerly of Seagram, USA.

Nikolaihof Wachau wine producer in Wachau, Niederösterreich, Austria.

Nikolausberg vineyard at Cochem in Mosel-Saar-Ruwer region, Germany.

Nile brewery at Jinja, Uganda.

Nill vineyard at Kallstadt in Rheinpfalz region, Germany.

Nimrod tawny port by Warre & Ca, Vila Nova de Gaia, Portugal.

909 Canadian whisky brand of Canadian Gibson Distilleries, Canada.

Nine-Pick Cocktail. Over ice shake 2 parts pastis, 1 dry gin, 1 dash Angostura bitters, 1 dash orange bitters, 1 dash sugar syrup. Strain.

Nineteen Cocktail. Over ice shake 4 parts dry vermouth, 1 dry gin, 1 kirsch, 4 dashes sugar syrup, 1 dash pastis. Strain.

Nineteenth Hole Cocktail. Over ice stir 3 parts dry gin, 2 dry vermouth, 1 sweet vermouth, 2 dashes Angostura bitters. Strain.

Ninkasi Beer revival of ancient Sumerian bread beer (made from about 10,000 BC by steeping barley bread in water) by Anchor brewery,

San Francisco, USA. Named after Sumerian goddess of brewing.

Ninotchka over ice shake 3 parts vodka, 1 crème de cacao, 1 lemon juice. Strain.

Nipozzano, Castello di great wine estate of Chianti Montesodi, Tuscany, Italy. Property of Frescobaldi.

Nittardi Chianti Classico and Vin Santo producer of Castellina in Chianti, Tuscany, Italy.

Nittnaus, Christine & Hans wine producer in Neusiedlersee, Burgenland, Austria.

Nittnaus, Hans & Anita wine producer in Neusiedlersee, Burgenland, Austria.

Nixenberg vineyard at Dorsheim in Nahe region, Germany.

Nobilo major wine producer of Huapai, New Zealand.

noble rot English for benificent grape mould *pourriture noble*.

Noblessa white grape variety principally of Baden region, Germany.

Noblesse Canadian whisky brand of Canadian Gibson Distilleries, Canada.

Nobling white grape variety principally of Baden region, Germany.

Noche Buena Christmas beer by Moctezuma brewery, Mexico.

nocivo harmful, Spanish. As in the official health warning on all spirit labels in Mexico: *El abuso en el consumo de este producto es nocivo para la salud* – abuse in the consumption of this product is harmful to health.

Noddy Cocktail. Over ice stir 3 parts dry gin, 2 bourbon, 1 pastis. Strain.

Noë, Château La wine estate of AC Muscadet de Sèvre et Maine, Loire Valley, France.

Noël-Bouton wine producer in AC Rully, Burgundy, France.

Noggins café-brewery in Seattle, Washington, USA.

Noilly Prat French vermouth created 1813 by herbalist Louis Noilly and sold under present brand since Noilly entered a partnership with his son-in-law, salesman Claudius Prat, in 1843. Wine base is from Picpoul (80%) and Clairette (20%) grapes of vineyards close to the manufacturing centre of Marseillan on the Mediterranean coast southwest of Montpellier. Wines are aged 18 months in oak casks, with a year outdoors exposed to high summer temperatures and occasional frosts. This policy derives from the discovery in the 19th century that the wines, shipped in casks to the Caribbean (always an important market for the vermouth) on deck and thus exposed to extreme changes in temperature and humidity, arrived at their destination not only none the worse, but with 'a significant improvement in colour, flavour and bouquet.' At blending, *mistelle* – unfermented grape juice – is added, along with small measures of lemon and raspberry *eaux de vie*. Final flavouring is with what the company says is '20 different plants and herbs, the majority natural calmatives, helping to soothe tension and stress. Chamomile makes up the largest proportion and is joined by cloves (another calmative), black elder and nutmeg (known to help induce soporific sleep), coriander, holy thistle and common cenraury (helps calm upset stomachs) and yellow gentian (one of the best-known natural tonics known to science.'

Nolet distiller of *genever* and other spirits, Schiedam, Netherlands.

Nollenköpfle vineyard at Gengenbach in Baden region, Germany.

Nonnberg vineyard at Flörsheim in Rheingau region, Germany.

Nonnenberg vineyards at Bernkastel-Kues in Mosel-Saar Ruwer region, Ebelsbach In Franken region, Eltville in Rheingau region, Lauda-Königshofen (Beckstein), Lauda-Königshofen (Lauda) in Baden region and Weinstadt in Württemberg region, Germany.

Nonnengarten vineyards at Bad Kreuznach and Traisen in Nahe region, Briedel and Pünderich in Mosel-Saar-Ruwer region and Mörstadt in Rheinhessen region, Germany.

Nonnenstück vineyard at Deidesheim in Rheinpfalz region, Germany.

Nonnenwingert vineyards at Worms (Hocheim), Worms (Leiselheim), Worms (Preddersheim) and Worms (Pfiffligheim) in Rheinhessen region, Germany.

non-vintage wine made from grapes of more than one year's harvest, or without reference to year of harvest. Applies to ordinary wines for drinking young, but also to quality wines such as champagne, made from blends of different years' grapes in order to maintain consistency of style.

Norfolk Nog old dark ale (4.6% alc) by Woodforde's brewery, Woodbastwick, Norfolk, England.

Norfolk Wherry bitter ale (3.8% alc) by Woodforde's brewery, Woodbastwick, Norfolk, England.

Norheim wine village of Nahe region, Germany. *Grosslage*: Burgweg.

Norkie strong (5.0% alc) ale by Woodforde's brewery, Woodbastwick, Norfolk, England.

Norman apple variety traditionally valued for cider-making. Synonymous with White Bache. Anglo-French.

Normandin-Mercier cognac house, Dompierre, France.

Norman's Conquest Ale brand of strong (7.0% alc), dark bottled beer launched 1995 by Christopher Norman of Cottage Brewery, West Lydford, Somerset, England. Currently sold only as a cask-conditioned ale at 5.% alc.

Northampton brewery in Northampton, Massachusetts, USA.

North Coast Brewing brewery at Fort Bragg, California, USA.

Northern brewery at Sault Ste Marie, Ontario, Canada.

Northern Clubs' Federation brewery at Dunston, Tyne & Wear, England.

Northgate Bitter ale by Wadworth, Northgate Brewery, Devizes, Wiltshire, England.

North Lodge brewery at Langley, Maidstone, Kent, England.

North Pole Cocktail. Over ice shake 3 parts dry vermouth, 1 pineapple juice. Strain into glass with rim frosted by dipping first into fruit juice and then into sugar.

North Port-Brechin East Highland malt whisky distillery, Brechin, Angus, Scotland. Est 1820, closed 1983.

Northumberland brewery at Ashington, Northumberland, England.

Norton leading wine producer in Mendoza, Argentina.

nose in winetasting, the smell of the wine.

Nostrano red wine of Ticino, Austria.

Notton, Château second wine of Château Brane-Cantenac, Bordeaux, France.

Nourishing Strong Stout beer by Samuel Smith brewery, Yorkshire, England.

nouveau term defining wine produced and marketed within a few weeks of the grape harvest. First such wines were those of Beaujolais, as defined under decree by the government of France, 9 November, 1951.

Nouveau winter beer by Harviestoun brewery, Dollar, Scotland.

Novi Pazar Controliran wine region of Bulgaria.

Novo Selo Controliran wine region of Bulgaria.

Nowell, Alexander English cleric credited with the introduction of bottle-conditioned beer. While angling on the Thames at Battersea in the 1550s Nowell received a message that the Bishop of London had ordered him arrested on a charge of heresy. He had to flee the country at once (for Strasbourg), leaving behind him his lunch, including a stone bottle newly filled with ale from the cask. With the end of Queen Mary Tudor's reign, Nowell returned to London and to his favourite place on the riverbank, where he was astonished to find 'no bottle but a gun, such was the sound at the opening thereof: and this is believed ... the original bottled ale in England'. Nowell later became Dean of St Paul's and a Fellow of Brasenose (so-called from Old Flemish *brazenhuis*, a brewhouse) College, Oxford.

Nozet, Château du wine property of AC Pouilly-Fumé, Loire Valley, France. White wine under Patrick de Ladoucette label.

Nozzole wine estate, Tuscany, Italy.

Nuits St-Georges AC, town and wine centre of Côte de Nuits, Burgundy, France. The name has long been synonymous with the fullest-flavoured style of 'old-fashioned' burgundy in England, where it has the twin attractions of pronouncability and a tenuous association with the patron saint. AC Nuits St-Georges wines include those of neighbouring Prémaux. *Premier Cru* vineyards wholly or partially within Nuits AC are: aux Argillats, les Argillats, aux Boudots, aux Bousselots, les Cailles, les Chaboeufs, Chaînes Carteaux, aux Champs Perdrix, aux Chargnots, Clos des Corvées, aux Cras, aux Crots, aux Damodes, les Haut-Pruliers, aux Murgers, les St-Georges, la Perrière, Perrière Noblet, les Porets, les Poulettes, les Procès, les Pruliers, la Richemone, la Roncière, Rue de Chaux, aux Thorey, les Vaucrains, les Vallerots, aux Vignes-Rondes. Principal wine growers and *négoçiants-éleveurs* include Clos de l'Arlot, Chevillon, Faiveley, Geisweiler, Grivot, Leroy, Michelot, Rion.   *see label opposite* ➡

Nun Wiser ale brand (4.5% alc) of Cottage Brewing Co, Lovington, Somerset, England.

Nuragus di Cagliari DOC for white wine from Nuragus grape, Cagliari, Sardinia, Italy.

Nus village of Valle d'Aosta producing curious Malvoisie de Nus wine from part-dried Malvoisie grapes, slow-fermented and aged two or more years in cask.

Nussberg vineyard at Zell in Mosel-Saar-Ruwer region, Germany.

Nussbien vineyard at Ruppertsberg in Rheinpfalz region, Germany.

Nussbrunnen vineyard at Eltville in Rheingau region, Germany.

Nussdorf brewery of Bachofen von Echt family at Nussdorf, Vienna, Austria.

Nussriegel vineyard Bad Dürkheim in Rheinpfalz region, Germany.

Nusswingert vineyard at Neumagen-Dhron in Mosel-Saar-Ruwer region, Germany.

Nut Brown Ale beer by Samuel Smith brewery, Tadcaster, Yorkshire, England. Also sold as Old Brewery Brown Ale.

nutty in winetasting, a smell and flavour reminiscent of hazelnuts, particularly associated with dry *amontillado* sherries.

Nyala white wine brand of Philips Central Cellars, Harare, Zimbabwe.

Nyköping sweet aniseed, caraway and fennel *brannvin*. Sweden.

O

oak the preferred wood for barrels in distilling and winemaking. The characters of many of the world's most-valued wines and spirits are substantially formed by contact with oak of varying ages, and over differing periods. French oak, especially from Limousin and Nevers, is highly prized around the world as well as domestically. The great wines of Bordeaux, Burgundy, Rhône and other classic regions (with notable exceptions of Alsace and Champagne) are commonly aged in oak casks. Some producers renew these annually. Italy uses Croatian oak. Hungarian oak is also valued. The USA is a major oak grower, particularly in whiskey-producing centres such as Kentucky and Tennessee. Oak is expensive, and chestnut wood is among the acceptable substitutes.

Oak brewery in Heywood, Manchester, England.

Oak Cheshire brewery in Ellesmere Port, Cheshire, England.

oak chips in winemaking and (rarely) in brewing, loose oak chips may be added during the production process to impart flavours associated with fermenting or ageing wine or beer in oak casks.

Oaken Glow brand of Pernod-Ricard.

Oakham Ales brewery at Oakham, Rutland, England.

Oakhill brewery at Oakhill, Shepton Mallet, Somerset, England. Beers include Farmers Ale.

Oasis ESB ale brand by Boulder brewery, Colorado, USA.

oatmeal stout style of beer in which oats are added to the barley mash. Renowned English brands include Young's of London and McMullen's of Hertford.

Oban West Highland malt whisky distillery, Oban, Argyll, Scotland. Est 1794 by Stevenson family. Single malt: 14-year-old.

Oberberg vineyards at Norheim in Nahe region and Walluf in Rheingau region, Germany.

Oberdürrenberg vineyard at Pfaffenweiler in Baden region, Germany.

Obere Heimbach vineyard at Meisenheim in Nahe region, Germany.

Oberemmel wine willage on Saar river in Mosel-Saar-Ruwer region, Germany. *Grosslage*: Scharzberg. Vineyards include Agritiusberg, Artenberg, Karlsberg, Hütte. Growers include Friedrich Wilhelm Gymnasium, Kesselstatt, von Hövel.

Oberer‑ Berg vineyards at Ludwigsburg and Steinheim in Württemberg region, Germany.

Obermosel *Bereich* of Mosel-Saar-Ruwer region, Germany.

Oberrot vineyard at Triefenstein in Franken region, Germany.

Oberscholss vineyard at Kirrweiler in Rheinpfalz region, Germany.

Obidos undesignated white-wine region of western Portugal.

Ochsenberg vineyard at Brackenheim in Württemberg region, Germany.

Ockfen wine village on Saar river in Mosel-Saar-Ruwer region, Germany. *Grosslage*: Scharzberg. Vineyards include Bockstein, Geisberg, Herrenberg, Kupp etc. Growers include Dr Fischer and Friedrich Wilhelm Gymnasium.

O'Connell Street Ale (5.5% alc) brewed in Cork, Ireland, by Scottish Courage of Edinburgh, Scotland.

Oddero wine brand of Fratelli Oddero, La Morra, Piedmont, Italy. Barolo and other regional wines.

Okhotnichaya Hunter's vodka flavoured with port, ginger, herbs, pepper, coffee, citrus etc. Russian.

Odakra Taffel aquavit flavoured with caraway, coriander and fennel. Sweden.

Odd McIntyre Cocktail. Over ice shake 1 part brandy, 1 Cointreau, 1 Lillet, 1 lemon juice. Strain.

Odell Brewing Co brewery in Fort Collins, Colorado, USA. Beers include 90/- Ale.

Odinstal vineyard at Wachenheim in Rheinpfalz region, Germany.

Oechsle system for determining must weight (sugar content) and potential alcohol in grape juice, Germany. Wines must reach statutorily fixed points on the scale to qualify for the various quality designations allowed under German wine laws of 1971. The points vary according to grape variety and region.

Oelberg vineyards at Efringen-Kirchen and Ehrenkirchen in Baden region, Germany.

oeil de perdrix in winetasting, 'partridge eye' – a copper-gold colour associated with certain table and fortified wines. French.

oenology the study of wine. Greek *oinos* (wine) and *logos* (word).

Oeste regional name covering western Portugal's wine districts.

Oestrich important wine village of Rheingau region, Germany. *Grosslage*: Gottesthal. Renowned vineyard of Lenchen. Main grower is Wegeler-Deinhard.

OFC Canadian whisky brand of Canadian Schenley Distilleries, Canada.

Offley port brand of Forrester & Cia (formerly Offley Forrester), Vila Nova de Gaia, Portugal. Also, **Offley Boavista** LBV and vintage ports.

off-licence permit, or retail outlet with such permit, to sell alcohol for consumption other than at the point of sale. UK.

OG original gravity.

Ogba brewery at Ogba, Ikeja, Lagos State, Nigeria.

Ognoas, Domaine d' armagnac estate, Villeneuve-de-Marsan, France.

O'Hanlon's brewery at Vauxhall, London, England. **O'Hanlon's Wheat Beer** (4.0% alc) bottle-conditioned ale.

Oh, Henry! Cocktail. Over ice stir 1 part Bénédictine, 1 whisky, 1 ginger ale.

Ohio wine-producing state of USA.

Ohlenberg vineyard at Boppard in Mittelrhein region, Germany.

Ohligsberg vineyard at Wintrich in Mosel-Saar-Ruwer region, Germany.

Ohligpfad vineyard at Bobenheim am Berg in Rheinpfalz region, Germany.

oidium common 'powdery mildew' disease attacking vines, and prevented by spraying with sulphur preparations.

Oisly & Thesée co-operative wine producer in Touraine, Loire Valley, France.

Ojo de Liebre regional name for Tempranillo grape variety, Catalonia, Spain.

Okanagan Riesling white grape variety of Okanagan Valley, British Columbia, Canada.

Okanagan Spring brewery in Vernon, British Columbia, Canada.

Okelehao spirit distilled from fermented ti-plant roots. Hawaii.

Okell & Son brewery at Douglas, Isle of Man, UK.

Okocim popular lager brand, Poland.

okole maluna hauoli maoli oe 'cheers' in Hawaii.

Oktoberfestbier term for beers brewed specially for Oktoberfest, the annual beer festival held in Munich, Germany.

Oland brewery at Halifax, Nova Scotia, Canada.

Olarra major *bodega* of Rioja, Spain.

Olaszriesling regional name for Welschriesling grape variety, Hungary.

Ölbaum vineyards at Malsch, Mühlhausen and Rauenberg in Baden region, Germany.

Ölberg vineyards at Dossenheim, Durbach, Endingen and Hohentengen in Baden region, Gau-Odernheim, Grolsheim, Nierstein and Wöllstein in Rheinhessen region and Neustadt an der Weinstrasse in Rheinpfalz region, Germany.

Oldacre's spritzer brand of Three Choirs Vineyard, Gloucestershire, England.

old ale loosely defining term for traditionally made strong, dark and richly flavoured beers. Mainly English. Famous English brands include Adnams Old Ale, Gale's Prize Old Ale and Theakston's Old Peculier.

Old Angus blended scotch whisky of RH Thompson, Edinburgh, Scotland.

Old Arnold 'Strong Old Beer' (4.8% alc) by Wickwar Brewing, Gloucestershire, England. Commemorates brewery's founder (1800).

Old Bawdy barley wine by Pike Place brewery, Seattle, USA. The brewery occupies the site of an erstwhile brothel.

Old Bear brewery at Keighley, West Yorkshire, England.

Old Black 'old ale' brand of Tooheys brewery, New South Wales, Australia.

Old Bob ale by Ridley's brewery, Chelmsford, England.

Old Brewery Brown Ale beer by Samuel Smith brewery, Tadcaster, Yorkshire, England. Also sold as Nut Brown Ale.

Old Bushmills Distillery the oldest working distillery in the world, producing Bushmills pot still whiskey. Co Antrim, Northern Ireland. First licensed 1608.

Old Buzzard 'old ale' brand (4.8% alc) of Cotleigh brewery, Somerset, England.

Old Chalet brandy by Uniewyn, South Africa.

Old Charlie dark rum brand originally of Seagram, UK.

Old Charter bourbon whiskey brand, USA.

Old Chimneys brewery at Diss, Norfolk, England.

Old Colorado pub-brewery in Fort Collins, Colorado, USA.

Old Cottage Beer Co brewery at New Hutton, Kendal, Cumbria, England.

Old Court blended scotch whisky by Gibson International, London, England.

Old Court Brewhouse brewery at Huddersfield, West Yorkshire, England.

Old Crow bourbon whiskey brand, USA.

Old Dan ale by Thwaites brewery, Blackburn, England.

Old Decanter twelve-year-old blended scotch whisky by Cockburn & Co, Leith, Scotland.

Old Ebenezer barley wine brand of Butterknowle Brewery, Newcastle-upon-Tyne, England.

Old England 'British wine' brand of Matthew Clark, Bristol, England.

Olde Heuriche beer by FX Matt brewery, New York, USA.

Old Elgin eight- and 15-year-old vatted malt whiskies by Gordon & MacPhail, Elgin, Scotland. Also vatted malt bottlings from 1938, 1939, 1940, 1947, 1949.

Old Elk Brown Ale beer by Walnut Brewing, Colorado, USA.

Oldenberg brewery in Fort Mitchell, Kentucky, USA.

Oldershaw brewery at Grantham, Lincolnshire, England.

Old Etonian Cocktail. Over ice shake 1 part dry gin, 1 Lillet, 2 dashes Crème de noyaux, 2 dashes orange bitters. Strain and squeeze orange peel over.

Old Fart notably pungent 'old ale' brand of Robinwood brewery, Todmorden, Yorkshire, England.

Old Fashioned Cocktail. Crush ice cubes with a sugar lump and 2 dashes Angostura bitters to fill tumbler glass. Add measure of preferred spirit (Bourbon whiskey was the original) plus slices of orange and lemon. Stir.

Old Fettercairn Highland malt whisky distillery est 1824, Kincardine, Scotland. Single malt: 10-year-old.

Oldfield pear variety traditionally valued for perry-making. English.

Old Foghorn exceptionally strong (8.7% alc) and renowned barley wine by Anchor Brewing Co, San Francisco, California, USA.

Old Forester bourbon whiskey brand, USA.

Old Foxwhelp apple variety traditionally valued for cider-making. English.

Old Freddy Walker strong (7.3% alc) old ale brand of Moor Beer Co, Somerset, England.

Old Glasgow blended scotch whisky by Donald Hart, Glasgow, Scotland.

Old Glomore blended scotch whisky by James Williams, Dyfed, Wales.

Old Grand-Dad bourbon whiskey brand, USA.

Old Groyne strong ale (6.2% alc) by Willys Brewery, Cleethorpes, England. A groyne (groin in US), in nautical parlance, is a protective wall built out from the shore to limit beach erosion.

Old Hickory bourbon whiskey brand, USA.

Old Highland Blend blended scotch whisky by Eldridge Pope, Dorchester, Dorset, England.

Old Inverness blended scotch whisky of JG Thomson, Inverness, Scotland.

Old Jock 'old ale' (6.7% alc) brand of Broughton brewery, Peeblesshire, Scotland. 'For centuries the soldiers of the Highlands and Lowlands of Scotland have been familiarly referred to as the Jocks – powerful fighting men who have enjoyed strong beers in their off-duty hours.'

Old Knucklehead barley wine by BridgePort brewery, Portland, Oregon, USA.

Old Legover Yorkshire beer brand of Daleside Brewery, Starbeck, Harrogate, England. Name is dedicated to fell-runners, who 'have to leg over thousands of stiles, stone walls and streams in pursuing this traditional sport.'   *see label over* ➡

Old Lodge tawny port by Smith Woodhouse, Vila Nova de Gaia, Portugal.

Old Luxters farm-brewery at Hambleden, Oxfordshire, England.

Old Matured blended scotch whisky by Daniel Crawford, Leith, Scotland.

Old Mill brewery at Snaith, Humberside, England.

Old Mull blended scotch whisky by Whyte & Mackay, Glasgow, Scotland.

Old Mulled Ale beer by Tisbury Brewery, Wiltshire, England.

Old Nick barley wine brand of Young & Co of Wandsworth, London, England. Noted for dark red colour and fiery alcohol (7.25%) level.

Old Nick white rum by Bardinet, Dillon Distillery, Martinique.

Old No. 38 dry stout by North Coast Brewing, Fort Bragg, California, USA.

Old Oporto port brand of Smith Woodhouse, Vila Nova de Gaia, Portugal.

Old Original Strong Traditional Ale brand of Everards brewery, Leicester, England

Old Orkney blended scotch whisky by Gordon & MacPhail, Elgin, Scotland.

Old Overholt American straight rye whiskey brand, USA.

Old Pal Cocktail. Over ice stir 1 part Campari, 1 dry vermouth, 1 rye whisky. Strain.

"A RIGHT GRAND YORKSHIRE BEER"

Old Pale Cocktail. Over ice stir 2 parts bourbon, 1 Campari, 1 dry vermouth. Strain and squeeze lemon peel over.

Old Parr twelve-year-old blended scotch whisky by Macdonald Greenlees, Edinburgh, Scotland. Also, **Old Parr Elizabethan**, **Old Parr Superior**, **Old Parr Tribute**.

Old Peculier famous 'old ale' brand of T & R Theakston, Masham, Yorkshire, England. Name commemorates the town of Masham's medieval entitlement to a local ('peculier') ecclesiastical court.

Old Pig Squeal cider by Whitestone Cider Co, Devon, England. Slogan: 'The Cider Your Grandparents Warned You About'.

Old Pint Pot brewery at Salford, Manchester, England.

Old Pulteney Highland malt whisky distillery est 1826, Wick, Caithness, Scotland. The northernmost distillery of mainland Scotland. Single malt: eight-year-old.

Old Rascal cider (6.0% alc) by Thatcher's Cider, Sandford, Somerset, England.

Old Rascal 'original Devonshire Scrumpy cider' by Farmer John Cligg of Newton Poppleford, Devon, England. Farmer John's motto is enshrined in an immortal verse: *see label opposite* ➡

> Me Grandad drunk this special brew
> And lived till 'e was ninety-two.
> 'E said, 'Me lad you do like I,
> Then you will live until you die.'

Old Rats' Tale cider by Gwatkin's, UK.

Old Red Fox Kentucky straight bourbon whiskey brand, USA.

Old Redwood Rye 'light spirit' brand of Halewood International, Huyton, Mereyside, England.

Old Rogue Ale golden bitter ale (4.5% alc) by Daleside Brewery, Harrogate, Yorkshire, England.

Old Rosdhu eight-year-old South Highland single malt whisky by Loch Lomond distillery, Alexandria, Dumbartonshire, Scotland.

Old Royal twenty-one-year-old blended scotch whisky by Burn Stewart Distillers, Glasgow, Scotland.

Old Slug bottle-conditioned porter (4.5% alc) by RCH Brewery, Weston-Super-Mare, Somerset, England.

Old St Andrews four-, eight- and 12-year-old blended scotch whiskies by Old St Andrews Ltd, Biggin Hill, Kent, England. Golf-associated packaging.

Old Smuggler blended scotch whisky by J&G Stodart, Dumbarton, Scotland.

Old Somerset cider brand of Matthew Clark, Shepton Mallet, Somerset, England.

Old Southwark Stout beer by South Australia Brewing, Adelaide.

Old Speckled Hen strong pale ale by Morland brewery, Abingdon, Oxfordshire, England.

Old Slug Porter beer brand of Wessex Craft Brewers, England.

olu beer. Estonian.

Old Spot Prize Ale beer by Uley brewery, Gloucestershire, England.

Old Stagg bourbon whiskey brand, USA.

Old Sunny Brook bourbon whiskey brand, USA.

Old Suntory blended whiskey brand of Suntory, Japan.

Old Tankard Ale beer by Pabst brewery, Milwaukee, USA.

Old Taylor bourbon whiskey brand, USA.

Old Thumper extra strong ale by Ringwood Brewery, Hampshire, England.

Old Timer ale by Wadworth brewery, Devizes, Wiltshire, England.

Old Tom very strong (8.5% alc) 'old ale' brand by Robinson's brewery, Stockport, Cheshire, England.

Old Triangle vineyard of Hill-Smith Estate, Barossa Valley, Australia. Famed Riesling wine.

Old Trout Cocktail. Into an ice-filled tall glass pour 1 part Campari, 2 fresh orange juice. Top with Perrier and add orange slice.

Old Vienna lager brand of Carling O'Keefe brewery, Canada.

Old Woolly barley wine brand of Big Time brewery, Seattle, Washington, USA.

Olgaberg vineyard at Singen in Baden region, Germany.

Ölgässel vineyard at Neustadt an der Weinstrasse in Rheinpfalz region, Germany.

Ölgild vineyard at Lörzweiler in Rheinhessen region, Germany.

Olifant *genever* by Allied-Domecq (UK), Netherlands.

Olifantsrivier wine district of South Africa.

Olive Farm oldest working wine estate of Australia, est 1829 South Guildford, Western Australia. Noted varietal wines.

Olivette Cocktail. Over ice shake 3 parts dry gin, 1 pastis, 2 dashes orange bitters, 2 dashes sugar syrup. Strain and add cocktail olive to glass.

Olivier, Château wine estate of AC Pessac-Léognan, Bordeaux, France. Classified *Cru Classé*.

Ölkuchen vineyard at Tauberbischofsheim in Baden region, Germany.

Ollauri wine village of Rioja, Spain.

Ollioules wine-producing commune of AC Bandol, Provence, France.

Olly's Cocktail. Over ice shake 2 parts vodka, 2 Cointreau, 1 lemon juice, 1 small scoop vanilla ice cream. Add 2 parts chilled sparkling wine before straining into chilled, frosted wine glasses.

Olmeca tequila brand of Pernod-Ricard, Mexico.

Ol' Moe's Porter beer by Rubicon brewery, Sacramento, USA.

oloroso 'fragrant' in Spanish. The darkest and most intense style of sherry, Jerez de la Frontera, Spain. In traditional sherry-making, colour and flavour result from oxidation during ageing in *solera*. Unlike *fino* and its derivative *amontillado*, *oloroso* sherry does not form *flor*, the surface crust which minimises the effects of oxidation. Wine is naturally dry but is often blended with PX wines to produce sherries (including 'cream' brands) of varying sweetnesses. Some *olorosos* are darkened with *vino de color*.

Ölsberg vineyard at Oberwesel in Mittelrhein region, Germany.

Ölschnabel vineyard at Zeil am Main in Franken region, Germany.

Ölspiel *Grosslage* incorporating vineyards at Eibelstadt and Sommerhausen in Franken region, Germany.

Oltrepò Pavese wide-ranging DOC for red, *rosato*, *spumante* and white wines of Pavia, Po Valley, Lombardy, Italy.

Olvi brewery in Iisalmi, Finland.

Olympic Cocktail. Over ice shake 1 part brandy, 1 curaçao, 1 orange juice. Strain.

Omar Khayyam sparkling wine brand by Royal Maharashtra winery, India. Wines are made from Chardonnay grapes planted 750

metres above sea level in the Sahyadri Mountains (180 kilometres east of Bombay), a region the producers like to refer to as the 'California of India'. The wine is made by a Champagne-trained, French-born maker on equipment provided by Laurent-Perrier in Epernay. Name commemorates bibulous Indo-Persian polymath Omar Khayyam (*c.*1048–1122).

Ondenc white grape variety of SW France.

Onder de Linden brewery at Wageningen, Gelderland, Netherlands.

One Exciting Night Cocktail. Over ice shake 1 part dry gin, 1 dry vermouth, 1 sweet vermouth, 1 orange juice. Strain into glass with rim frosted by dipping first into fruit juice and then into sugar.

100 Pipers Scotch whisky brand of Pernod-Ricard.

103 brandy by Bobadilla, Jerez de la Frontera, Spain. **103 Etiqueta Negra** (Black Label) is the solera reserva brand.

Onkelchen vineyard at Norheim in Nahe region, Germany.

on-licence permit, or premises with such permit, to sell alcohol for consumption at the point of sale. UK.

Ontario wine-producing state of Canada.

On the Tiles bottle-conditioned bitter ale (4.0% alc) by RCH Brewery, Weston-Super-Mare, Somerset, England.

oogy Wawa 'cheers' in Zululand.

Oom Paul Cocktail. Over ice shake 1 part apple brandy, 1 Caperitif. Strain.

Op-Ale beer by De Smedt brewery, Opwijk, Belgium.

Opal Ridge wine brand of Miranda winery, Australia.

Opening Cocktail. Over ice shake 2 parts rye whisky, 1 sweet vermouth, 1 grenadine. Strain.

Opera Cocktail. Over ice shake 4 parts dry gin, 1 Dubonnet, 1 maraschino. Strain and squeeze orange peel over.

Opimian wine of ancient Rome.

Opitz, Willi wine producer in Neusiedlersee, Burgenland, Austria. Famed late-harvested wines including **Opitz One**.

Opol pale red wine mainly from Plavac grapes, Dalmatia, Croatia.

Oporto city of Portugal. Its local name, Porto, was first used by British merchants in the 1670s for the fortified wine they shipped from the city.

Oppenheim important wine village of Rheinhessen region, Germany. *Grosslagen*: Guldenmorgen and Krötenbrunnen. Wine growers include Dahlem and Guntrum.

Oppenheim Cocktail. Over ice stir 2 parts scotch whisky, 1 sweet vermouth, 1 grenadine. Strain.

Opthalmo red grape variety of island of Cyprus.

Optima white grape variety of Germany. Chiefly Mosel and Rheinhessen regions.

Optimator bock beer brand of Spaten brewery, Bavaria, Germany.

Opus One 'prestige' Bordeaux-style Californian red wine brand from Cabernet Sauvignon grapes created jointly by Robert Mondavi Winery, California, USA and late Baron

Philippe de Rothschild of Château Mouton-Rothschild, Bordeaux, France.

OPW Oporto Partners' Wine, a 'house port' of Taylor, Fladgate & Yeatman, Vila Nova de Gaia, Portugal. Affectionately known by the directors of the family-owned company as Old Piss and Wind.

Oragnac cognac and triple sec liqueur brand of Bols, Netherlands.

Orange Bloom Cocktail. Over ice shake 2 parts dry gin, 1 Cointreau, 1 sweet vermouth. Strain and add cocktail cherry to glass.

Orange Blossom Cocktail. Over ice shake 1 part dry gin, 1 orange juice. Strain. Alternatively, over ice shake 1 part dry gin, 1 orange juice, 1 dash grenadine, 1 dash orange bitters. Strain.

Orange Brewery pub-brewery est 1984 in Pimlico, London, England. Beers include Pimlico Light and Pimlico Porter.

Orange Fizz Cocktail. Over ice shake 2 parts dry gin, 1 Cointreau, 1 lemon juice, 1 orange juice, 1 teaspoon sugar. Strain into tall ice-filled glasses and top with chilled sparkling wine.

Orange Martini Cocktail. In shaker soak stripped peel of 1 orange for 2 hours in 5 parts dry gin, 4 dry vermouth, 2 sweet vermouth. Add ice and 2 dashes orange bitters, shake and strain.

Orange Oasis Cocktail. Over ice shake 2 parts dry gin, 1 cherry brandy, 3 orange juice. Strain into tall, ice-filled glasses and top with chilled dry ginger ale.

oranjebitter orange liqueur traditionally drunk in toasts to the Dutch monarch. Netherlands.

Oranjeboom lager (5.0% alc) brand of Allied Breweries, Brabant, Netherlands. Original Oranjeboom brewery is said to have been opened in 1671.

oranjejenever orange-flavoured 'London Dry'-style *genever* gin. Netherlands.

Oratoire, Clos de L' wine estate of AC St-Emilion, Bordeaux, France. Classified *Grand Cru Classé*.

Orbel vineyard at Nierstein in Rheinhessen region, Germany.

Orbello red wine principally from Nebbiolo grapes by Fabrizio Sella, Bramaterra, Piedmont, Italy.

Orca Pilsner beer by Sunshine Coast brewery, British Columbia, Canada.

Ordensgut *Grosslage* incorporating vineyards at Edesheim, Hainfeld, Rhodt unter Rietburg and Weyher in der Pfalz in Rheinpfalz region, Germany.

Order of Merit Canadian whisky brand of Canadian Schenley Distilleries, Canada.

Oregon wine-producing state of USA. Willamette Valley is principal region.

Oregon Trail brewery in Corvalis, Oregon, USA.

Oremus white grape variety (crossing of Furmint and Bouvier) of Tokaji, Hungary.

organic methods in winemaking, a burgeoning trend towards avoiding use of chemicals in vineyard and winery. Australia, France, Germany, Italy and the USA all have increasing numbers of such wine producers.

Orgeat almond-flavour liquor, France.

Oriachovitza Controliran wine region of Bulgaria. Cabernet Sauvignon and Merlot wines.

Oriental Cocktail. Over ice shake 2 parts rye whisky, 1 sweet vermouth, 1 white curaçao, 1 fresh lime juice. Strain.

Orient Express Cocktail. Over ice stir 1 part dry gin, 1 bourbon, 1 brandy. Strain.

Original Brewing Co brewery at Braunstone, Leicester, England.

Original Dark Ruby Mild famed, strong (6.0% alc) ale by Sarah Hughes Brewery, Beacon Hotel, Sedgley, West Midlands, England.

original gravity in brewing, the density level of sugars present in the mash at the onset of fermentation; the measure of strength historically preceding those of alcohol by volume or weight. 'Plato' original gravity scale devised by Carl Joseph Balling, 1843, and refined by Dr Fritz Plato is still in use. British original gravity scale or o.g. has a base figure of 1000 plus a multiple of four times the Plato measure. Thus, a beer such as American Budweiser has a Plato of 11.25 and an o.g. of 1045. The latter two digits express approximately the alcoholic strength by volume, namely 4.5% for American Budweiser.

Orkney Brewery small brewery est 1988 in Quoyloo, Orkney, Scotland. Ales include Dark Island, Raven, Skullsplitter.

Orlando major wine producer based at Jacob's Creek, Barossa Valley, South Australia. Founded as G Gramp company 1847 but now a brand of Pernod-Ricard of France. Many brands including worldwide bestseller Jacob's Creek.

Orlenberg vineyard at Bissersheim in Rheinpfalz region, Germany.

Orloff vodka brand of Pernod-Ricard.

Ormarins, L' noted wine estate in Franschhoek, Paarl, South Africa. Optima Reserve Cabernet-Merlot red and other wines from French grape varieties.

Ormes-de-Pez, Château Les wine estate of AC St-Estèphe, Médoc, Bordeaux, France. Classified *Cru Grand Bourgeois*.

Ormes-Sorbet, Château Les wine estate of AC Médoc, Bordeaux, France. Classified *Cru Grand Bourgeois*.

Oropilla brandy of distillers Pilla, Castel Maggiore, Italy.

Orta Nova DOC for red and *rosato* wines from Sangiovese and other grape varieties, Foggia, Apulia, Italy.

Ortega white grape variety of Germany, and England.

Ortelberg vineyard at Böbingen in Rheinpfalz region, Germany.

Ortenau *Bereich* of Baden region, Germany. *Grosslagen*: Fürsteneck and Schloss Rodeck.

Ortlieb former brewery and current beer brand by Schmidt brewery, Philadelphia, Pennsylvania, USA.

Orval monastery-brewery and Trappist beer of the Abbaye de Notre Dame d'Orval, Villers-devant-Orval, Belgium.

Orvieto DOC for white wines from Grechetto, Malvasia, Trebbiano, Verdello and other grape varieties grown around Orvieto hilltown, Umbria, Italy. Orvieto Classico wines are from a defined zone close to the town. Two styles: *abboccato* (medium dry) and *secco* (dry).

Osborne major sherry producer and brandy distiller est 1772, Puerto de Santa Maria, Spain, and port shipper of Vila Nova de Gaia, Portugal. Fino Quinta, Coquinero *amontillado* and 10RF *oloroso* sherries; Conde de Osborne, Independencia, Magno and Veterano brandies; ports:

vintages 1960, 70, 75, 82, 85, 91, 92, 94, 97, 2000, 03.

Osborne House Cocktail. In a wine glass mix 3 parts red wine, 1 scotch whisky. The drink is so-called after the Isle of Wight home of Queen Victoria, who liked her claret reinforced. She died at Osborne House in 1901, aged 82.

Oschelskopf vineyard at Freinsheim in Rheinpfaz region, Germany.

Oslo Mikro Bryggeri pub-brewery in Oslo, Norway.

Ossian's Ale pale ale (4.1% alc) by Inveralmond Brewery, Perth, Scotland. Commemorates Ossian, son of Fingal, legendary 3rd century bard and warrior.

Ostend Fizz Cocktail. Over ice shake 1 part crème de cassis, 1 kirsch, 1 lemon juice. Strain into an ice-filled glass and top with chilled sparkling water.

Osterberg vineyards at Bad Dürkheim, Essingen and Grosskarlbach in Rheinpfalz region, Bingen, Mommenheim, Selzen, Spiesheim and Wolfsheim in Rheinhessen region and Dielheim in Baden region, Germany.

Osterbrunnen vineyard at Niederkirchen in Rheinpfalz region, Germany.

Osterholl vineyard at Bad Kreuznach in Nahe region, Germany.

Osterlämmchen vineyard at Ediger in Mosel-Saar-Ruwer region, Germany.

Ostertag wine estate of Epfig, Alsace, France.

Ostuni DOC for red wine from Ottavianello grapes and white from Francavilla and Impigno grapes, Apulia, Italy.

Oswald, Eduard wine producer in Weststeiermark, Austria.

Otard major cognac producer est 1799 and now headquartered in ancient Château de Cognac, Cognac, France. Brands: XXX, Baron Otard VSOP, Napoléon, Princes de Cognac.

Othello red wine brand of Keo, island of Cyprus.

Ott, Bernhardt wine producer in Donauland, Niederösterreich, Austria.

Ott, Domaines leading wine producer of Provence, France. Properties include Clos Mireille in AC Côtes de Provence, Château Romassan in AC Bandol, Château de Selle in AC Côtes de Provence. Organic methods.

Ottakringer brewery est 1837 in Vienna, Austria.

Ottawa Valley brewery in Nepean, Ontario, Canada.

Otter brewery and ale brand, Luppitt, Devon, England.

Otterberg vineyard at Waldlaunersheim in Nahe region, Germany.

Oud advocaat brand, Netherlands.

Oud Beersel brand for lambic beers of Vandervelden brewery, Beersel, Belgium.

Oud Bruin 'Old Brown' ale by Liefmans brewery, Oudenaarde, Belgium.

oude 'old' in Dutch. Commonly asserted on labels of *genever* and other spirits. Netherlands and South Africa.

Oude Meester leading wine, brandy and liqueur producer of South Africa.

Oudenaards ale by Roman brewery, Oudenaarde, Belgium.

Oudenaards Wit Tarwebier wheat beer by Clarysse brewery, Oudenaarde, Belgium.

Ouden Tripel 'red ale' by Bockor brewery, Kortrijk, Belgium.

Oudinot champagne house, Epernay, France.

ouillage in winemaking, the practice of topping up barrels as wine level drops through cask-absorption or evaporation. French.

Our Brewery microbrewery in Johannesburg, South Africa.

ouzo national aniseed-flavoured spirit of Greece. Production is widespread on the mainland and among the islands of Aegean.

OV8 eight-year-old blended scotch whisky by Cockburn & Co, Leith, Scotland.

Ovens Valley wine district of northern Victoria, Australia.

Overberg Wine of Origin district of the Cape, South Africa.

Overgaauw wine estate of Stellenbosch, South Africa. 'Port' and noted table wines from classic French grape varieties.

Owd Roger strong ale by Marston's brewery, Burton upon Trent, England.

oxidation in wine, the effect of exposure to oxygen in air. Controlled oxidation is beneficial especially in producing fortified wines such as sherry, but extended exposure to air causes all wines (including sherry) to lose freshness and flavour and become stale.

Oy Alko Ab the state alcohol monopoly of Finland.

Oyster Stout beer (4.5% alc) by Wolverhampton & Dudley brewery, Wolverhampton, England.

Oy Suomen Marjat Ab liqueur producer (Tyrni brand), Finland.

P

Paarl town 30 miles north of Cape Town and important Wine of Origin district of Coastal Region, South Africa. Numerous improving wine producers including long-established KWV and Nederburg estate.

Paarl Riesling regional name for Cruchen Blanc grape variety, South Africa.

Pabst brewery in Milwaukee, Wisconsin, USA. Beers include **Pabst Blue Ribbon** and Ballantine brands.

Pabst & Richarz brandy distiller est 1861 Elsfeth, Germany.

pacari fermented drink from preparation of roots, Guyana.

Pacherenc de Vic Bihl AC for dry and sweet white wines from Arruffiac, Gros Manseng, Petit Courbu and Gros Manseng grapes, Madiran district, Gascony, SW France. Producers include Domaine Damiens.

Pacific Coast Brewing pub-brewery in Oakland, California, USA.

Pacific Northwest encompassing term for the vine-growing areas of the three US states of Idaho, Oregon and Washington.

Pacifico beer brand (6.0% alc) of Cerveceria del Pacifico, Mazatlan, Mexico. *see label opposite* ➡

Pacific Sunrise Cocktail. Over ice shake 1 part tequila, 1 blue curaçao, 1 fresh lime juice, 1 dash Angostura bitters. Strain.

Pacific Western brewery with production at Prince George's, British Columbia and St Catherine's, Ontario, Canada.

Paddy Irish whiskey brand of Cork Distilleries, Cork, Eire. Owned by Irish Distillers.

Paddy Cocktail. Over ice stir 1 part Irish whiskey, 1 sweet vermouth, 1 dash Angostura bitters.

Padouen, Château wine estate of AC Sauternes, Bordeaux, France.

Padthaway Estate wine-producer (mostly sparkling) of Padthaway district, South Australia.

Päffgen restaurant brewery in Cologne, Germany, known for **Päffgen Kölsch**.

Pagadebit white wine from Pagadebit Gentile grapes by Bertinoro, Emilia-Romagna, Italy.

Paicines AVA of San Benito County, California, USA.

Paillard, Bruno champagne house est 1981 by Bruno Paillard, Murigny, Champagne, France.

Paillard, Pierre *récoltant manipulant* champagne producer, Bouzy, Champagne, France.

Pais red grape variety of Chile since 1500s. Bulk-wine production.

Palais-Cardinal-La-Fuie, Château wine estate of AC St-Emilion, Bordeaux, France. Classified *Grand Cru*.

Palatinate English term for Rheinpfalz wine region, Germany.

pale ale broad term for beer closer in colour to tea than to coffee. Sometimes used to described bottled premium ales.

pale cream sherry style having the pale colour of *fino* but the sweetness of 'cream' sherry.

Palette AC of Aix-en-Provence, southern France, dominated by estate of Château Simone. Renowned red wine from Grenache, Cinsault and Mourvèdre grapes supplemented by what UK importer Robin Yapp calls 'antique grape varieties that were once ubiquitous here in Provence ... curiosities such as Monosquan, Branforquas, Teoulier and Castet.' White wine from Ugni Blanc grapes with Grenache and Clairette. Also rosé.

palinka grape spirit of Hungary.

Palliser Estate leading wine producer in Martinborough, New Zealand.

Pall Mall Cocktail. Over ice shake 1 part dry gin, 1 dry vermouth, 1 sweet vermouth, 4 dashes white crème de menthe, 1 dash orange bitters. Strain.

Palm ale brand and brewery est 1747 in Steenhuffel, Belgium. Name dates from 1918, marking the peace brought about by the Armistice of that year.

palma in sherry trade, a *fino* of particular quality. With age, the wine can be promoted to *dos*, *tres* and, ultimately, *cuatro* palmas. Jerez de la Frontera, Spain.

Palm Beach Cocktail. Over ice shake 1 part Bacardi rum, 1 dry gin, 1 pineapple juice. Strain.

Palmberg vineyard at Valwig in Mosel-Saar-Ruwer region, Germany.

Palmberg Terrassen vineyard at St Aldegund in Mosel-Saar-Ruwer region, Germany.

Palmela wine region of Arrábida, Portugal.

Palmengarten vineyard at Mandel in Nahe region, Germany.

Palmenstein vineyard at Bingen in Rheinhessen region, Germany.

Palmer, JC & RH brewery in Bridport, Dorset, England. **Palmer's Bitter**, IPA and Tally Ho.

Palmer champagne brand of Société Coopérative de Producteurs des Grands Terroirs de Champagne, Reims, France.

Palmer, Château great wine estate of AC Margaux, Médoc, Bordeaux, France. Classified *3ème Grand Cru Classé*.

Palmer Cocktail. Over ice shake 1 part rye whisky, 1 dash Angostura bitters, 1 dash lemon juice. Strain.

Palmetto Cocktail. Over ice shake 1 part rum, 1 sweet vermouth, 2 dashes orange bitters. Strain.

palo cortado rare and valued sherry style, deeper in colour than *fino-amontillado* but lighter than an *oloroso*. Jerez de la Frontera, Spain.

Palomino the grape variety of sherry. Spain.

Palomino & Vergara sherry producer est 13th century in, and possibly oldest of, Jerez de la Frontera, Spain. Tio Mateo fino sherry.

Palo Viejo white rum brand formerly of Seagram, Puerto Rico.

Pamid red grape variety and pale red wine of Bulgaria.

Panama Cocktail. Over ice shake 1 part rum, 1 crème de cacao, 1 fresh cream. Strain.

Panama Hat Cocktail. Over ice shake 3 parts rum, 2 banana liqueur, 1 curaçao, 1 teaspoon lemon juice. Strain.

Pando fino sherry brand of Williams & Humbert, Jerez de la Frontera, Spain.

Pandoer red ale brand of Verhaeghe brewery, Vichte, Belgium.

Panigon, Château wine estate of AC Médoc, Bordeaux, France. Classified *Cru Bourgeois*.

Pannonian Plain the Great Plain of Hungary. Major wine-growing region.

Pansy Cocktail. Over ice shake 2 parts pastis, 1 grenadine, 1 dash Angostura bitters. Strain.

Pansy Blossom Cocktail. Over ice shake 4 parts Anisette, 1 grenadine, 2 dashes Angostura bitters. Strain.

Papa Doble Cocktail. Over ice shake 6 parts rum, 1 fresh lime juice. Strain. A version of the Daiquiri cocktail (*qv*) devised by Ernest 'Papa' Hemingway (1899–1961).

The proportion of rum is doubled, and the sugar withheld.

Pape, Château Le wine estate of AC Pessac-Léognan, Bordeaux, France.

Pape-Clément, Château wine estate of AC Pessac-Léognan, Bordeaux, France. Classified *Cru Classé*.

Papillon, Clos du wine estate of AC Savennières, Loire Valley, France.

Paradies vineyards at Bad Kreuznach in Nahe region, Ippesheim in Franken region, Kröv in Mosel-Saar-Ruwer region, Müllheim in Baden region, Neustadt an der Weinstrasse in Rheinpfalz region and Obersulm in Württemberg region, Germany.

Paradiesgarten *Grosslage* incorporating vineyards in Nahe region, Germany at, respectively: Alsenz, Auen, Bayfeld-Steckweiler, Boos, Desloch, Feilbingert, Gaugrehweiler, Hochstätten, Kalkhofen, Kirschroth, Lauschied, Lettweiler, Mannweiler-Cölln, Martinstein, Meddersheim, Meisenheim, Merxheim, Monzingen, Münsterappel, Niederhausen an der Appel, Niedermoschel, Nussbaum, Oberhausen an der Appel, Obermoschel, Oberndorf, Oberstreit, Odernheim am Glan, Raumbach/Glan, Rehborn, Sobernheim, Sobernheim (Steinhard), Staudernheim, Unkenbach, Waldböckelheim, Weiler bei Monzignen, Winterborn.

Paradiesgarten vineyard at Deidesheim in Rheinpfalz region, Germany.

paradis in Cognac, France, a storing place for casks and jars of the oldest brandies.

Paradise Cocktail. Over ice shake 2 parts dry gin, 1 apricot brandy, 1 orange juice, 1 dash lemon juice. Strain.

Parc, Château du wine estate of AC Haut-Médoc, Bordeaux, France.

Pardaillan, Château wine estate of AC Premières Côtes de Blaye, Bordeaux, France.

Parde de Haut-Bailly, Château La second wine of Château Haut-Bailly, Bordeaux, France.

Parducci Wine Cellars wine producer in Mendocino, California, USA.

Parellada white grape variety of Catalonia, Spain. Sparkling wines, and the grape variety for Viña Sol white wine brand of Miguel Torres, Penedés, Spain.

Pares vineyard at Ingelheim in Rheinhessen region, Germany.

Parfait (d')Amour citrus liqueur flavoured with almonds, rose petals and vanilla. France, Netherlands etc.

parfum in winetasting, the characteristic aroma of a particular grape variety. French.

Paris Cocktail. Over ice stir 1 part dry gin, 1 crème de cassis, 1 dry vermouth. Strain.

Parish brewery at Somerby, Leicestershire, England.

Parisian Cocktail. Over ice shake 1 part crème de cassis, 1 dry vermouth, 1 dry gin. Strain.

Parisian Blonde Cocktail. Over ice shake 1 part curaçao, 1 rum, 1 sweetened cream. Strain.

Parker & Son brewery at Wellingborough, Northamptonshire, England.

Park Royal west London brewery of Guinness, closed 2004.

Paroisse, Château La wine brand of Cave-Co-opérative of Haut-Médoc, Bordeaux, France.

Parrina DOC for red wines from Sangiovese grapes and white wines from Trebbiano, southern Tuscany, Italy.

Parsac lost appellation of St-Emilion, Bordeaux, France.

Parson's Choice cider by Parsonage Farm, West Lyng, Somerset, England.

Pasado top-quality designation for *fino* and *amontillado* sherries, Jerez de la Frontera, Spain.

Pascal Frères important wine producer in the villages of southern Côtes du Rhône, France. Renowned wines of village ACs Gigondas (Domaine du Grand Montmirail) and Vacqueyras as well as AC Côtes du Rhône and AC Côtes du Rhône Villages wines.

Pasha coffee liqueur brand formerly of Seagram, Turkey.

Pasmados noted red wine brand of JM da Fonseca, Alentejo, Portugal.

Pasqua leading wine producer in Verona, Italy. Valpolicella and other regional wines.

Pasquier Desvignes *négociant-éleveur* of Beaujolais region, Burgundy, France.

Passageway brewery at Queen's Dock, Liverpool, England.

passerillage sweet-wine-producing method in Jurançon, SW France. Grapes are left on vines until late autumn to allow sugars to concentrate.

Passionate Mangorita Cocktail. Over ice shake 3 parts Sauza Hornitos (or other) tquila, 1 passion fruit liqueur, 1 mango purée, 1 fresh lime juice. Strain.

passito semi-dried grapes for making strong, sweet *passito* wine. Italy.

Passover Slivovitz vodka flavoured with plum spirit and bottled at natural strength of 70% alc. Poland.

Passport blended scotch whisky formerly of Seagram, Montreal, Canada.

pasteurisation in brewing and wine-making, a process of sterilisation in which the liquid is heated to a temperature up to 79° centigrade (174F). Devised by Louis Pasteur (1822–1895).

pastis aniseed-flavoured spirit of France. Brands include **Pastis 51**, Pernod, Ricard, Rivanis. Synonymous with anis.

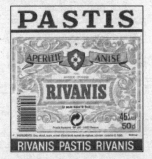

Pastorei vineyard at Bretzenheim in Nahe region, Germany.

Pastorenberg vineyard at Wallhausen in Nahe region, Germany.

Patache, Château La wine estate of AC Pomerol, Bordeaux, France.

Patache-d'Aux, Château wine estate of AC Médoc, Bordeaux, France. Classified *Cru Grand Bourgeois*.

Pata de Galina naturally sweet style of *oloroso* sherry. Jerez de la Frontera, Spain.

Paterberg vineyard at Nierstein in Rheinhessen region, Germany.

Paterhof vineyards at Dienheim and Oppenheim in Rheinhessen region, Germany.

Paternina, Federico major *bodega* of Rioja, Spain. Well-known Banda Azul red and Banda Dorada white wines.

Pater Noster abbey beer by Bios brewery, Ertvelde, Belgium.

Patras principal wine region of Peloponnese, Greece. Within lie designated wine areas for Mavrodaphne sweet wine, Muscat of Rion, Muscat of Patras and **Patras** red wine from Rhoditis grapes.

Patriarche Père et Fils wine growers and *négociants-éleveurs* of Beaune, Burgundy, France. Vineyards include Château de Meursault and holdings in *Premiers Crus* of Beaune. Also producer, on an industrial scale, of Kriter sparkling wine.

Patrimonio AC for red, rosé and white wines of NW Corsica, France.

Patris, Château wine estate of AC St-Emilion, Bordeaux, France. Classified *Grand Cru*.

Paulaner

Paulaner brewery in Munich, Germany, renowned for strong seasonal Salvator beer.

Pauline Cocktail. Over ice shake 1 part rum, 1 lemon juice, 2 dashes pastis, sprinkling of sugar, pinch of grated nutmeg. Strain.

Paulinsberg vineyards at Kasel and Kesten in Mosel-Saar-Ruwer region, Germany.

Paulinshofberger vineyard at Kesten in Mosel-Saar-Ruwer region, Germany.

Paulinslay vineyard at Osann-Monzel in Mosel-Saar-Ruwer region, Germany.

Paul Jones whiskey brand formerly of Seagram, USA.

Pauillac estuarial town, wine commune and AC of Médoc, Bordeaux, France. Location of three of the four *premier grand cru classé* châteaux of the Médoc, Lafite, Latour and Mouton-Rothschild and many other great properties.

Paulus red ale by Leroy brewery, Boezinge, Belgium.

Paulus vineyard at Bensheim in Hessliche Bergstrasse region, Germany.

Paveil-de-Luze, Château wine estate of AC Margaux, Médoc, Bordeaux, France. Classified *Cru Bourgeois*.

Pavichevich Brewing Co microbrewery at Elmhurst, Chicago, Illinois, USA. Baderbrau pilsner beer.

Pavie, Château great wine estate of AC St-Emilion, Bordeaux, France. Classified *1er Grand Cru Classé*.

see label opposite ➡

Pavie-Decesse, Château wine estate of AC St-Emilion, Bordeaux, France. Classified *Grand Cru Classé*.

Pavie-Macquin, Château wine estate of AC St Emilion, Bordeaux, France. Classified *Grand Cru Classé*.

Pavillon, Château du wine estate of AC Ste-Croix-du-Mont, Bordeaux, France.

Pavillon Blanc white wine of Château Margaux, Bordeaux, France.

Pavillon-de-Boyrein, Château wine estate of AC Graves, Bordeaux, France.

Pavillon-Cadet, Château wine estate of AC St-Emilion, Bordeaux, France. Classified *Grand Cru* (1996).

Pavillon Rouge second wine (red) of Château Margaux, Bordeaux, France.

Pavlikeni Controliran red-wine region of Bulgaria.

Paxarete sweet blending wine for sherry production. PX grapes. Jerez de la Frontera, Spain.

Pazo de Barrantes strong (48%) *aguardiente* brand of Marques de Murrieta. Distilled from Albariño grapes in Rias Baixas, Galicia, Spain.

Peach Buck Cocktail. Over ice shake 3 parts vodka, 1 peach brandy, 1 fresh lime juice. Strain into ice-filled tumblers and top with chilled dry ginger ale.

SAINT-ÉMILION 1er GRAND CRU CLASSÉ

Château Pavie

Appellation St-Émilion 1er Grand Cru Classé Contrôlée

1982

VALETTE
PROPRIÉTAIRES A St-ÉMILION (GIRONDE)

PRODUCE OF FRANCE

75 cl

Peaches and Cream Cocktail. Over ice shake 2 parts rum, 1 peach brandy, 1 tablespoon fresh cream.

Pearl beer by Pabst brewery, San Antonio, Texas, USA.

Pearl River rum brand of state trading monopoly, Kwantung, People's Republic of China.

Peatling's blended scotch whisky by Mcdonald & Muir for Thos Peatling, Bury St Edmunds, Suffolk, England.

Peat Porter ale brand (4.5% alc) of Moor Beer Co, Ashcott, Somerset. The brewery stands on the Somerset Levels, where peat continues to be cut for horticultural purposes.

Pecan Street beer by Shiner brewery, Texas, USA.

Pécharmant AC for red wines of Bergerac region, SW France.

Pêcheur, Blanc du wine brand of Borie-Manoux, Bordeaux, France.

Pechstein vineyard at Forst an der Weinstrasse in Rheinpfalz region, Germany.

Péconnet, Château wine estate of AC Premières Côtes de Bordeaux, France.

Pécs wine district south of Lake Balaton, Hungary. Simple white wines from Olaszriesling grapes. Name is pronounced 'paysh'.

Pedavena beer brand of Italy.

Pédesclaux, Château wine estate of AC Pauillac, Médoc, Bordeaux, France. Classified *5ème Grand Cru Classé*.

Pedigree Bitter ale by Marston brewery, Burton upon Trent, England.

Pedro Ximenéz grape variety for sherry and wines of Montilla, and for table wines in several regions of Spain. Sole constituent of rare sweet sherries, more usually sun-dried and used for colouring and sweetening blends. Commonly abbreviated to PX.

Peggy Cocktail. Over ice shake 2 parts dry gin, 1 dry vermouth, 1 dash Dubonnet, 1 dash pastis. Strain.

Pegu Club Cocktail. Over ice shake 4 parts dry gin, 2 curaçao, 1 fresh lime juice, 1 dash Angostura bitters, 1 dash orange bitters. Strain.

Peizer Hopbel brewery and beer brand, Peizen, Groningen, Netherlands.

peket Flemish name for *jenever*, Belgium. Also **pequet**.

Pelee Island winery at Kingsville, Ontario, Canada.

Pelforth brewery in Lille, France. Beers include Blonde, Brune, Irish Red, Pelforth Porter. Owned by Heineken.　　*see label over* ➡

pelure d'oignon in winetasting, a colour description: 'onion skin'. Applies to pale rosé and *vin gris*. French.

Pelzerberger vineyard at Beuren in Mosel-Saar-Ruwer region, Germany.

Pembroke brewery at Pembroke, Dyfed, Wales.

Peñaflor major wine producer of Mendoza region, Argentina. Brands include Trapiche.

Penderyn whisky brand of the Welsh Whisky Company at Penderyn, Brecon, Wales. The company's first whisky product, a four-year-old single malt, went on sale on St David's Day (March 1) 2004.

Pendle Witches' Brew bitter ale by Moorhouse's brewery, Lancashire, England.

Penedés DO wine region of Catalonia, Spain, SW of Barcelona. Known for sparkling *cava* wines, but also home to famed Miguel Torres company.

Penfolds leading wine company est 1844 Adelaide, South Australia. Now with interests in most of Australia's wine-growing regions including Barossa Valley, Coonawarra, Riverina etc. Brands from popular Bin Number varietals to Australia's premier red wine, Grange Hermitage.

Penguin Porter bottle-conditioned beer (4.2% alc) by Ash Vine brewery, Trudoxhill, Somerset, England.

Penley Estate wine producer of Coonawarra, South Australia. Noted Cabernet Sauvignon, Chardonnay and other wines.

Pennard cider producer at East Pennard, Shepton Mallet, Somerset, England.

Penn Dark lager by Pennsylvania Brewing, Allegheny brewery, Pittsburgh, Pennsylvania, USA.

Pennsylvania Brewing restaurant-brewery at Allegheny, Pittsburgh, Pennsylvania, USA.

Penshurst vineyard near Tunbridge Wells, Kent, England.

Pentro di Isernia DOC for red and rosato wines from Montepulciano and Sangiovese grapes and whites from Trebbiano and Bombino Bianco grapes, Molise, Isernia, Italy.

Père Blanc traditional herbal liqueur of Luxembourg.

Père Magloire calvados brand of Debrise Dulac, Pont L'Evêque, Normandy, France. Est 1821.

Perenne, Château wine estate of AC Premières Côtes de Blaye, Bordeaux, France.

Perfect Cocktail. Over ice shake 1 part dry gin, 1 dry vermouth, 1 sweet vermouth. Strain.

Perfect Lady Cocktail. Over ice shake 2 parts dry gin, 1 peach brandy, 1 lemon, 1 teaspoon egg white. Strain.

Periquita red grape variety of southern Portugal and brand name of notable wine from the variety by J M da Fonseca of Alentejo.

Perlan regional name for Chasselas grape variety, Geneva canton, Switzerland.

perlant synonym for *pétillant* (slightly sparkling). French.

perlé synonym for *pétillant*. French.

Perle white grape variety, a crossing of Gewürztraminer and Müller-Thurgau, chiefly of Franken region, Germany.

Perlwein cheap semi-sparkling style of *Tafelwein* of Germany.

Pernand-Vergelesses village and AC of Côte d'Or, Burgundy, France. *Grand Cru* vineyards: Corton, Corton-Charlemagne. *Premiers Crus*: les Basses Vergelesses, en Caradeux, Creux de la Net, les Fichots, Ile de Vergelesses.

Pernaud, Château wine estate of AC Sauternes, Bordeaux, France. Classified *Cru Bourgeois*.

Pernod leading pastis brand, by drinks giant **Pernod-Ricard**, of France. The founder, Henri-Louis Pernod, was the son-in-law of Henri Dubied, the first commercial producer of absinthe (in Switzerland). Pernod opened his own absinthe factory in France in 1805.

Pernod Frappé Cocktail. Over ice shake 3 parts Pernod, 1 Anisette, 1 fresh cream, 1 egg white. Strain into small wine glasses filled with crushed ice.

Peroni largest brewery company of Italy. Brands include Grand Riserva, Nastro Azzuro and Raffo. Peroni is said to account for more than three-quarters of all Italian beer sales in the UK, largely thanks to their introduction through the Pizza Express restaurant chain from 1965.

Perpetum ancient name for Sicilian wine now known as Marsala. In Roman myth, the wine was associated with the goddess Venus.

Perrier Fils & Co, Joseph *Grande Marque* champagne house est 1825 by Joseph Perrier, nephew of Pierre-Nicolas-Marie Perrier, founder of Perrier-Jouët. Châlons-sur-Marne, France.

Perrier-Jouët *Grande Marque* champagne house est 1811 by Pierre-Nicolas-Marie Perrier, who married Adèle Jouët. Epernay, France. Sold by Seagram to Allied-Domecq 2001.

Perron, Château wine estate of AC Lalande-de-Pomerol, Bordeaux, France.

perry still or sparkling alcoholic drink made from the fermented juice of pears. Production methods are similar to those for cider. Mainly English.

Perry's Cider Mills cider producer, Dowlish Wake, Ilminster, Somerset, England. Range includes single vintage and farmhouse ciders, and the farm has a renowned museum of rural life.

persico liqueur flavoured with almonds, peach stones and spice. Netherlands.

Pertotale faro lambic beer by Frank Boon brewery, Lembeek, Belgium.

Pertsovka red-pepper-flavoured vodka brand. Russia.

Peru small-scale vine-growing nation with much of the harvest distilled for *pisco*. Tacama Vineyards in Ica produces table and sparkling wines from French grape varieties.

Peru Gold beer brand (5.0% alc) of Cervecera del Sur del Peru, Arequipa, Peru.

Perushtitza winery est 1934 at Plovdid, southern Bulgaria. Renowned Brestnik wines plus varietals from local grape varieties including Rubin, and imported varieties.

Pesquera red wine from Tempranillo grapes by Alejandro Fernandez in DO Ribera del Duero, NW Spain.

Pessac-Léognan AC of Graves region, Bordeaux, France, covering all *crus classés* of the region.

Pessan-St-Hilaire, Château wine estate of AC Graves, Bordeaux, France.

Petaluma major wine producer of Australia, based in Adelaide Hills, South Australia. Red wines of Coonawarra, Rhine Riesling of Clare Valley, exceptional sparkling wines from classic Champagne grape varieties by Brian Croser.

Peter Dawson blended scotch whisky by Peter Dawson, Glasgow, Scotland.

Peter Pan Cocktail. Over ice shake 1 part dry gin, 1 dry vermouth, 1 peach bitters, 1 orange juice. Strain.

Peters, Pierre *récoltant manipulant* champagne producer, le Mesnil-sur-Oger, Champagne, France.

Petersberg *Grosslage* incorporating vineyards at Albig, Alzey, Bechtolsheim, Biebelnheim, Framersheim, Gau-Heppenheim, Gau-Odernheim, Gau-Odernheim (Gay Köngernheim) and Spiesheim in Rheinhessen region and Bad Honnef, Königswinter, Königswinter (Niederdollendorf) and Königswinter (Oberdollendorf) in Mittelrhein region, Germany.

Petersberg vineyards at Neef in Mosel-Saar-Ruwer region and Weingarten in Baden region, Germany.

Petersborn-Kabertchen vineyard at Zell in Mosel-Saar-Ruwer region, Germany.

Peterstim vineyard at Schweinfurt in Franken region, Germany.

Pete's Brewing Co brewery at Palo Alto, California, USA, known for **Pete's Wicked Ale** brown ale. Prop Pete Slosberg.

pétillant 'slightly sparkling' wine usually self-carbonated after bottling due to residual sugar causing secondary fermentation. French.

pétillant de raisin regional part-fermented grape-juice drink of Gaillac, France.

Petit Chablis AC for wine of Chablis, Burgundy, France, of simplest quality.

petit château informal term for un-classified minor estates of Bordeaux region, particularly those of less-fashionable ACs such as Blaye, Bourg, Premières Côtes de Bordeaux etc.

Petite Fleur Cocktail. Over ice shake 1 part rum, 1 Cointreau, 1 grape-fruit, 1 dash grenadine. Strain.

Petite Montagne minor vineyard district of AC Champagne, France.

Petite Sirah red grape variety originally of but now rare in southern Rhône Valley, France. Grown successfully in California, USA, and in Mexico, where it has found fame in the eponymous wine of LA Cetto winery of Baja California.

Petit-Faurie-de-Soutard, Château wine estate of AC St-Emilion, Bordeaux, France. Classified *Grand Cru Classé*.

Petit Verdot red grape variety of Médoc, Bordeaux, France. Plays a small part in *encépagement* of many great wines of the region, imparting colour and body.

Petit-Village, Château wine estate of AC Pomerol, Bordeaux, France.

Peto Cocktail. Over ice shake 2 parts dry gin, 1 dry vermouth, 1 sweet vermouth, 1 orange juice, 2 dashes maraschino. Strain.

Petrus red ale by Bavik-De Braban-dere brewery, Bavikhove, Belgium.

Pétrus, Château greatest wine estate of AC Pomerol, Bordeaux, France. Relatively small 11.5-hectare vine-yard of Merlot vines produces about 4,000 cases of Bordeaux's second-most-expensive red wine after Le Pin.

Pettenthal vineyard at Nierstein in Rheinhessen region, Germany.

Pewsey Vale vineyard in Adelaide Hills, South Australia.

Peychaud, Château wine estate of AC Côtes de Bourg, Bordeaux, France.

Peymartin, Château second wine of Château Gloria, Bordeaux, France.

Pey-Martin, Château wine estate of AC Médoc, Bordeaux, France. Classified *Cru Bourgeois*.

Peyrabon, Château wine estate of AC Haut-Médoc, Bordeaux, France. Classified *Cru Grand Bourgeois*.

Peyrat, Château wine estate of AC Premières Côtes de Bordeaux, France.

Peyrat, Château du wine estate of AC Premières Côtes de Bordeaux, France.

Peyraud, Château second wine of Château Bonnet, Bordeaux, France.

Peyreau, Château wine estate of AC St-Emilion, Bordeaux, France. Classified *Grand Cru*.

Peyredon-Lagravette, Château wine estate of AC Listrac, Médoc, Bordeaux, France. Classified *Cru Bourgeois*.

Peyredoulle, Château wine estate of AC Premières Côtes de Blaye, Bordeaux, France.

Peyrelongue, Château de wine estate of AC St-Emilion, Bordeaux, France. Classified *Grand Cru*.

Pez, Château de wine estate of AC St-Estèphe, Médoc, Bordeaux, France. Classified *Cru Bourgeois Supérieur*.

Peza sweet red wine of island of Crete, Greece.

Pfaffenberg vineyards at Ammerbuch in Württemberg region, Bad Neuenahr-Ahrweiler in Ahr region, Billigheim-Ingenheim and Landau in der Pfalz in Rheinpfalz region, Burgsponheim in Nahe region, Ediger-Eller in Mosel-Saar-Ruwer region, Eltville in Rheingau region, Flonheim in Rheinhessen region and Würzburg and Würzburg (Unterdürrbach) in Franken region, Germany.

Pfaffengarten vineyard at Saulheim in Rheinhessen region, Germany.

Pfaffengrund *Grosslage* incorporating vineyards at Neustadt an der Weinstrasse (Deidesfeld an der Weinstrasse), Neustadt an der Weinstrasse (Duttweiler), Neustadt an der Weinstrasse (Geinsheim), Neustadt an der Weinstrasse (Hambach an der Weinstrasse) and Neustadt an der Weinstrasse (Lachen/Speyerdorf) in Rheinpfalz region, Germany.

Pfaffenhalde vineyard at Alzey in Rheinhessen region, Germany.

Pfaffenkappe vineyard at Nierstein in Rheinhessen region, Germany.

Pfaffenmütze vineyard at Dittelsheim-Hessloch in Rheinhessen region, Germany.

Pfaffenpfad vineyard at Alsenz in Nahe region, Germany.

Pfaffenstein vineyard at Niederhausen an der Nahe in Nahe region, Germany.

Pfaffenstück vineyard at Müllheim in Baden region, Germany.

Pfaffenweg vineyard at Gau-Bischofsheim in Rheinhessen region, Germany.

Pfaffenwies vineyard at Lorch in Rheingau region, Germany.

Pfaffl, Roman & Adelheid wine producer in Weinviertel, Niederösterreich, Austria.

Pfalzgrafenstein vineyard at Kaub in Mittelrhein region, Germany.

Pfarrberg vineyard at Kappelrodeck in Baden region, Germany.

Pfarrgarten *Grosslage* incorporating vineyards at Dalberg, Gutenberg, Hergenfeld, Schöneberg, Sommerloch, Spabrücken and Wallhausen in Nahe region, Germany.

Pfarrgarten vineyards at Bingen (Gaulsheim), Bingen (Kempten) and Gau-Heppenheim in Rheinhessen region, Bruttig-Fankel in Mosel-Saar-Ruwer region and Filsen in Mittelrhein region, Germany.

Pfarrwingert vineyard at Dernau in Ahr region, Germany.

Pfingstweide vineyard at Niederhausen an der Nahe in Nahe region, Germany.

Pfirsichgarten vineyard at Ediger-Eller in Mosel-Saar-Ruwer region, Germany.

Pforte vineyard at Volkach in Franken region, Germany.

Pflumli *eau de vie* distilled from plums. Switzerland.

Pfülben vineyard at Igel in Franken region, Germany.

pH measure of acidity in alcoholic drinks.

Phantom & Firkin pub-brewery at Loughborough, Leicestershire, England.

Pharaoh & Firkin pub-brewery in Fulham, London, England.

Pheasant Plucker cider (6.2% alc) by Broadoak Brewery, England.

Phélan-Ségur, Château wine estate of AC St-Estèphe, Médoc, Bordeaux, France. Classified *Cru Grand Bourgeois Exceptionnel*.

Phelps, Joseph wine producer in Napa Valley, California, USA. Renowned varietal wines and prestige Insignia brand.

Philanthropist & Firkin pub-brewery at St Albans, Hertfordshire, England.

Philadelphia Cocktail. Over ice stir 2 parts brandy, 1 curaçao, 1 dash pastis.

Philadelphia Scotchman Cocktail. Into tumbler glass with ice pour 1 part apple brandy, 1 port, 1 orange juice. Top with ginger ale.

Philiponnat champagne house est 1912 Mareuil-sur-Aÿ, France.

Philippe de Castaigne cognac house, Jarnac, France.

Philips Old English alcoholic cordial brand of Allied Domecq, UK. Includes aniseed, grenadine, lovage, peppermint and shrub.

Phillips brewery at Norton, Shifnall, Shropshire, England.

Philomel Cocktail. Over ice shake 5 parts dry sherry, 3 orange juice, 2 quinquina, 2 rum, sprinkle of ground pepper. Strain.

Philosopher & Firkin pub-brewery in Oxford, England.

Phoebe Snow Cocktail. Over ice shake 1 part brandy, 1 Dubonnet, 1 dash pastis. Strain.

Phoenix & Firkin pub-brewery at Denmark Hill, London, England.

Phoenix brewery at Heywood, Greater Manchester, England.

Phoenix Beer ale by Macardle brewery, Dundalk, Eire.

Phylloxera dread disease of vines. An infestation by grub of aphid *phylloxera vastatrix* kills roots and spreads with devastating effect. Vineyards of France and subsequently all of Europe were obliterated by the disease in the 1860s–70s. It can be remedied only by grafting vines on to resistant American rootstocks. Apart from a few immune pockets, the disease is still present throughout the world, including America.

Physician & Firkin pub-brewery in Edinburgh, Scotland.

Piada, Château wine estate of AC Sauternes, Bordeaux, France. Classified *Cru Bourgeois*.

Piast popular lager brand, Poland.

Piat Père et Fils wine grower and major *négociant* of Mâcon, Burgundy, France. Vineyards in Beaujolais and Mâconnais and originator of an enduring table wine brand, **Piat d'Or**.

Piave DOC zone of Veneto region, Italy. Wines are red Cabernet del Piave (Cabernet Franc or Cabernet Sauvignon grapes, or both), red Merlot del Piave (Merlot grapes), white Tocai del Piave and Verduzzo del Piave from respective grape varieties.

Pibran, Château wine estate of AC Pauillac, Médoc, Bordeaux, France. Classified *Cru Bourgeois*.

Pic, Albert Chablis brand of Ladoucette, Chablis, France.

Picardin white grape variety of AC Châteauneuf-du-Pape, France.

Piccad Cocktail. Over ice shake 1 part dry gin, 1 Caperitif, 2 dashes Angostura bitters. Strain and add lemon slice to glass.

Piccadilly Cocktail. Over ice shake 2 parts dry gin, 1 dry vermouth, 1 dash grenadine, 1 dash pastis. Strain.

Piccone red wine from Nebbiolo, Vespolina and Bonarda grapes by Fabrizio Sella, Vercelli Hills, Piedmont, Italy.

pichet wine carafe, traditionally of pottery, France.

Pichler, Rudi wine producer in Wachau, Niederösterreich, Austria.

Pichon, Château wine estate of AC Haut-Médoc, Bordeaux, France.

Pichon-Longueville Baron, Château great wine estate of AC Pauillac, Bordeaux, France. Classified 2ème *Grand Cru Classé.*

Pichon-Longueville Comtesse-de-Lalande, Château great wine estate of AC Pauillac, Médoc, Bordeaux, France. Classified 2ème *Grand Cru Classé.*

Pickwick's gin brand formerly of Seagram, Canada.

Pickwick's Porter beer by Malton brewery, North Yorkshire, England.

Picolit rich and alcoholic (minimum 15%) sweet wine from Picolit grapes of DOC Colli Orientali del Friuli, Friuli-Venezia Giulia, Italy.

Picon Cocktail. Over ice shake 1 part Amer Picon, 1 sweet vermouth. Strain.

Picon & Grenadine Cocktail. Over ice shake 2 parts Amer Picon, 1 grenadine. Strain and top with soda water.

Picorneau, Château second wine of Château Le Bourdieu, Bordeaux, France.

Picpoul de Pinet white wine from (mainly) Picpoul grapes of Pinet in AC Coteaux du Languedoc, France.

Picque-Caillou, Château wine estate of AC Pessac-Léognan, Bordeaux, France.

pièce traditional wine cask of Burgundy, France. Capacity is 228 litres, as distinct from Bordeaux *barrique* of 225 litres. In other regions of France a *pièce* ranges from 205 litres upwards.

Piedmont major wine-producing region of NW Italy.

Pieprzowka twice-rectified pepper vodka of Poland.

Pieropan leading wine producer of DOC Soave, Veneto, Italy.

Pierredon, Château wine estate of AC Bordeaux Supérieur, France.

Piesport important wine village of Mosel-Saar-Ruwer region, Germany. *Grosslage*: Michelsberg. Vineyards include Goldtröpfchen, Gunterslay, Treppchen etc. Producers include Bischöfliches Konvikt and von Kesselstatt.

Pigato white grape variety of Liguria, Italy.

pigeage in winemaking, method of steeping and agitating grape skins in must to improve extract. Traditionally, by foot. French.

Pig Rye beer (5% alc) by Pig Breweries, UK.

Pig's Nose blended scotch whisky by Invergordon Distillers for Sheep Dip Whisky Co, Oldbury on Severn, Bristol, England. 'Scotch ... as soft and smooth as a pig's nose'.

Pikantus strong (7.3% alc) wheat beer by Erdinger brewery, Bavaria, Germany.

Pike Place brewery in Seattle, Washington, USA.

Piketberg Wine of Origin district of the Cape, South Africa.

Pilgerpfad *Grosslage* incorporating vineyards at Bechteim, Dittelsheim-Hessloch (Dittelheim), Dittelsheim-Hessloch (Hessloch), Frettenheim, Monzernheim and Osthofen in Rheinhessen region, Germany.

Pilgerpfad vineyard at Kamp-Bornhofen in Mittelrhein region, Germany.

Pilgerstein vineyard at Biebelnheim in Rheinhessen region, Germany.

Pilgerweg vineyard at Zornheim in Rheinhessen region, Germany.

Pilgrim brewery at Reigate, Surrey, England.

Pillitteri Estate wine producer at Niagara-on-the-Lake, Ontario, Canada.

pils short form of **pilsner**. See Diat Pils.

pils(e)ner style of lager deriving from a beer first brewed in Pilsen, Bohemia, in 1842 and having a golden colour, complete clarity and around 4 to 5% alc.

Pilsner Urquell famed beer (4.4% alc) of the Plzensky Prazdroj brewery in Pilsen, Czech Republic – where the first 'Pilsen' beer was produced in 1842.

Pilton Manor former vineyard of manor house in Pilton near Shepton Mallet, Somerset, England. White wines and grape spirit.

Pimlico brand name for beers of Orange Brewery, Pimlico, London, England.

Pimm's bitter-sweet fruit cup mix based on gin (**Pimm's No. 1**) or vodka (**Pimm's Vodka Cup**). Devised by

James Pimm around 1823 as a house cup for his oyster bar in City of London, England. First bottled for sale 1859, there have been six different versions.

Pimm's Cooler Cocktail. Over ice shake 2 parts Pimm's No. 1, 2 fresh lime juice, 1 lemon juice, 1 dash Cointreau, 1 pinch caster sugar. Strain into an ice-filled glass and top with soda water. Add lime slice.

Pimpeltjens herbal curaçao by De Kuyper, Schiedam, Netherlands.

Pin renowned red wine brand of La Spinetta estate, Piedmont, Italy. Blend of Nebbiolo, Barbera and Cabernet Sauvignon grapes by maker Giorgio Rivetti.

pin small wooden cask for ale. Equivalent to half a firkin, or 4½ gallons.

Pin, Château Le great wine estate of AC Pomerol, Bordeaux, France. Routinely, the world's most expensive annually harvested wine.

Piña Colada Cocktail. Over ice shake 1 part rum, 1 coconut liqueur (or milk), 2 pineapple juice. Strain into ice-filled tumblers and add fresh pineapple slices.

pinard informal term for simple red wine. French.

Pinch brand name in USA of Dimple blended whisky by John Haig, Markinch, Scotland.

Pine pear variety traditionally valued for perry-making. English.

Pineau d'Aunis red grape variety of Loire Valley, France. Rosé wines of Anjou and Touraine.

Pineau de la Loire regional name for Chenin Blanc grape variety, Loire Valley, France.

Pineau des Charentes regional aperitif of Cognac, France. Made since the 16th century, it is produced by blending unfermented grape juice from the Charentais with cognac. Slightly sweet and typically 17–18% alc. Production is regulated under an *appellation contrôlée*.

Pinenc regional name for Fer Servadou grape, Madiran, SW France.

Ping-Pong Cocktail. Over ice shake 2 parts Crème Yvette, 2 sloe gin, 1 lemon juice. Strain.

Pinhel quality wine region of Beiras, Portugal. Red and (more significantly) white wines.

Pink Baby Cocktail. Over ice shake 1 egg white, 2 parts dry gin, 1 grenadine, 1 lemon syrup. Strain.

Pink Gin Cocktail. Over ice shake 1 part dry gin, 1 dash Angostura bitters. Strain.

Pink Heather Cocktail. Into a champagne glass pour 1 part Scotch whisky, 1 strawberry liqueur. Top with chilled sparkling wine.

Pink Lady perry brand of Matthew Clark, Shepton Mallet, Somerset, England.

Pink Lady Cocktail. Over ice shake 1 egg white, 2 parts dry gin, 1 grenadine. Strain.

Pink Planter Cocktail. Over ice shake 1 part white rum, 1 coconut liqueur, 1 amaretto, 3 cranberry juice, 1 pineapple juice. Strain into tall ice-filled glasses.

Pink Rose Cocktail. Over ice shake 1 egg white, 4 parts dry gin, 1 grenadine, 1 lemon juice, 1 sweetened cream. Strain.

Pink Squirrel Cocktail. Over ice shake 1 part crème to noyaux, 1 crème de cacao, 1 fresh cream. Strain.

Pinkus Müller inn and brewery in Münster, Westphalia, Germany. **Pinkus Organic** beer (5.0% alc).

Pink Whiskers Cocktail. Over ice shake 2 parts apricot brandy, 2 orange juice, 1 dry vermouth, 2 dashes grenadine. Strain.

Pinky Cocktail. Over ice shake 1 egg white, 2 parts dry gin, 2 grenadine. Strain.

Pinnacle Pale Ale beer by Triple Rock brewery, Berkeley, California, USA.

Pinnerkreuzberg vineyard at Cochem in Mosel-Saar-Ruwer region, Germany.

Pinot Auxerrois regional name for Auxerrois grape variety, Alsace, France.

Pinot Beurot regional name for Pinot Gris grape variety, Côte d'Or, Burgundy, France.

Pinot Bianco Italian name for Pinot Blanc grape variety.

Pinot Bianco Alto Adige DOC for white wines from Pinot Bianco grapes, Trentino-Alto Adige region, Italy.

Pinot Bianco dei Colli Berici DOC for white wines from Pinot Bianco grapes, Colli Berici, Veneto, Italy.

Pinot Bianco Colli Orientali del Friuli DOC for white wines from Pinot Bianco grapes, Colli Orientali, Friuli-Venezia Giulia, Italy.

Pinot Bianco Collio Goriziano DOC for white wines from Pinot Bianco grapes, Colli Goriziano, Friuli-Venezia Giulia, Italy.

Pinot Bianco Grave del Friuli DOC for white wines from Pinot Bianco grapes, Grave del Friuli, Friuli-Venezia Giulia, Italy.

Pinot Blanc white grape variety of France, chiefly in Alsace region. Widely planted in Germany under Weissburgunder name and in Italy as Pinot Bianco. Pinot Blanc is a common synonym for Chardonnay in Australia, while in South Africa, 'Chardonnay' wines are frequently made from Pinot Blanc grapes.

Pinot Chardonnay grape description common on labels of wines from Maconnais region, Burgundy, France. Not a grape variety but an allusion to the two quite separate varieties permissible for the wine: Pinot Blanc and Chardonnay.

Pinot Droit black grape variety related to Pinot Noir, Burgundy, France.

Pinot Grigio grape variety (synonymous with Pinot Gris) and popular white wine of northern Italy.

Pinot Grigio Collio Goriziano DOC for white wines from Pinot Grigio grapes, Colli Goriziano, Friuli-Venezia Giulia, Italy.

Pinot Grigio Grave del Friuli DOC for white wines from Pinot Grigio grapes, Grave del Friuli, Friuli-Venezia Giulia, Italy.

Pinot Grigio Oltrepò de Pavese DOC for white wines from Pinot Grigio grapes, Oltrepò de Pavese, Lombardy, Italy.

Pinot Gris grape variety principally of Alsace, France. Also known as Tokay d'Alsace.

Pinot Meunier synonym for Meunier grape variety.

Pinot Nero Italian name for Pinot Noir grape variety.

Pinot Noir black grape variety of France. The sole constituent of all the great red wines of the Côte d'Or, Burgundy. Important in all other Burgundy red wines except Beaujolais. Also, one of the three permitted varieties, along with Pinot Meunier and Chardonnay, for the wines of Champagne. Elsewhere in France and throughout the world the variety produces still red and sparkling white wines with greatly varying degrees of success.

Pinotage black grape variety of South Africa. Cross between Pinot Noir and Cinsaut, the latter being locally known as Hermitage, thus

the portmanteau name. Makes some of South Africa's best red wines.

Pinto Ferreira port shipper late of Vila Nova de Gaia, Portugal. Vintages: 1963, 66, 75, 79.

Pint Pot brewery at Preston, Lancashire, England.

Pinwinnie blended scotch whisky by Inver House Distilleries, Airdrie, Lanarkshire, Scotland.

pipe large cask for port, from Portuguese word *pipa*. Sizes vary between 550 and 620 litres.

Pipeau, Château wine estate of AC St-Emilion, Bordeaux, France. Classified *Grand Cru*.

Piper-Heidsieck *Grande Marque* champagne house est 1834 by Christian Heidsieck (who died within a year and whose widow married a Monsieur Piper) Reims, France.

Piper's Brook wine estate in Tamar Valley, Tasmania, Australia. Noted Chardonnay and Pinot Noir wines.

Piper's Pride 'Scottish ale' by Sherlock's Home pub-brewery, Minnesota, USA.

pipette in winemaking, a glass tube used for extracting samples from casks by suction. French.

piquette informal term for cheap wine, particularly if watered. French.

Piranha 'alcoholic lemonade' (4.3% alc) by J Sainsbury supermarkets, UK.

Pirassununga 51 leading *cachaca* brand, Brazil.

pisco colourless grape brandy of Chile and Peru.

Pisco Capel leading producer of pisco, Chile.

Pisco Control leading producer of pisco, Chile.

Pisco Sour Cocktail. Over ice shake equal parts Pisco and lemon juice with one egg white per two servings. Strain.

Pisco Special Cocktail. Over ice shake 2 parts Pisco, 1 lemon juice, 1 teaspoon sugar, 1 egg white, 1 dash Angostura bitters. Strain.

Piscy Bishop Cocktail. Over ice shake 2 parts scotch whisky, 1 dry vermouth, 1 teaspoon triple sec, 1 teaspoon orange juice, sprinkling caster sugar. Strain.

Pisse Vieille unappetising name for a wine of the *cru* village of Brouilly in the Beaujolais region of France has a curious story behind it. Long ago in the village, we are told, an old woman went to church to make her confession. Giving her absolution, the priest enjoined the sinner, as always, '*ne piche plus,*' local dialect for *ne péche plus* – sin no more. But with age she had lately grown hard of hearing. Although mystified by the misheard instruction, she took the priest at his word. She returned home and after a day or so started to behave oddly. Her husband, anguished by her growing desperation, demanded an explanation. On receiving it, he made haste to the church – and was soon on his way back, bellowing through the streets as he came, '*Pisse, vieille, pisse!*' The phrase became a motto of the village.

Pitchfork bottle-conditioned beer (4.3% alc) by RCH Brewery, Weston-Super-Mare, Somerset, England. Commemorates Somerset's Pitchfork Rebellion of 1685 in which local people, armed with little besides, rose against the Crown in support of pretender to the throne, James Scott, Duke of Monmouth. The rebellion was put down with extreme prejudice.

Pitnauer, Hans leading wine producer in Carnuntum, Niederösterreich, Austria.

Pitron, Château wine estate of AC Graves, Bordeaux, France.

Pitray, Château wine estate of AC Côtes de Castillon, Bordeaux, France.

Pittermännchen vineyard at Dorsheim in Nahe region, Germany.

Pittersberg vineyard at Münster-Sarmsheim in Nahe region, Germany.

Pittnauer, Helmut & Erich wine producer in Neusiedlersee, Burgenland, Austria.

Pittsburgh Brewery producer of popular Iron City Beer brand, Pittsburgh, Pennsylvania, USA.

Pittyvaich Speyside malt whisky distillery est 1975 by Arthur Bell & Sons, Dufftown, Banffshire, Scotland. Single malts: 12-year-old, 13-year-old.

Pitú leading *cachaca* brand of Brazil.

pivovar brewery, Czech.

Plagnac, Château wine estate of AC Médoc, Bordeaux, France. Classified *Cru Bourgeois*.

Plain-Point, Château wine estate of AC Fronsac, Bordeaux, France.

Plains Brewery producer of Hog's Head Dark ale, Christchurch, New Zealand.

Plaisance, Château wine estate of AC Premières Côtes de Bordeaux, France.

Plaisir de Merle vineyard est 1693 at Drakenstein, South Africa. Owned by Stellenbosch Farmers' Winery since 1964. Notable Cabernet Sauvignon and Chardonnay.

Plantagenet wine producer in Mount Barker, Western Australia.

Plantation Punch Cocktail. Over ice shake 1 part Southern Comfort, 1 rum, 1 lemon juice, 1 teaspoon sugar. Strain into ice-filled tumblers and top with chilled sparkling water.

Planter's Cocktail. Over ice shake 1 part rum, 1 orange juice, 1 dash lemon juice. Strain.

Planter's Punch Cocktail. Over ice shake 4 parts Jamaica rum, 2 fresh lime juice, 1 sugar syrup, 1 dash Angostura bitters. Pour into tall glass and add fruit slices.

Plantey, Château wine estate of AC Pauillac, Médoc, Bordeaux, France.

Plantey-de-Croix, Château second wine of Château Verdignan, Bordeaux, France.

Plassan, Château wine estate of AC Premières Côtes de Bordeaux, France.

Plassey brewery at Eyton, Clwyd, Wales.

Platinum Blonde Cocktail. Over ice shake 1 part rum, 1 Cointreau, 1 fresh cream. Strain.

Plato in brewing, a scale of original gravity; based on Balling system. See original gravity.

Platzer Weinhof wine producer in Süd-Oststeiermark, Austria.

Plauelrain vineyard at Durbach in Baden region, Germany.

Plavac everyday red wine of Dalmatian coast, Croatia. From **Plavac Mali** grape variety.

Playa Del Mar Cocktail. Over ice shake 4 parts Sauza Hornitos (or other) tequila, 2 cranberry juice, 2 pineapple juice, 1 fresh lime juice. Strain into tall glass and float a teaspoon of Grand Marnier on top of each.

Playing Fields Cocktail. Fill a tumbler glass with crushed ice and stir in 4 parts dry gin, 1 crème de menthe, 1 dash Angostura bitters. Top with ginger beer and add cocktail cherry, slice of apple and sprig of mint.

Plaza Cocktail. Over ice shake 1 part dry gin, 1 dry vermouth, 1 sweet vermouth, 1 slice pineapple. Strain.

Pleil, Josef wine producer in Weinviertel, Niederösterreich, Austria.

Plessis, Château second wine of Château Moulin-de-Launay, Bordeaux, France.

Plettenberg'sche Verwaltung, Reichgräflich von wine estate with vineyards at Bad Kreuznach and Schlossböckelheim, Nahe region, Germany.

Plince, Château wine estate of AC Pomerol, Bordeaux, France.

Ploder, Alfred wine producer in Süd-Oststeiermark, Austria.

plonk cheap wine. Name derives from Cockney rhyming interpretation of *petit blanc*, the small glass of ordinary white wine enjoyed by French drinkers with a frequency that impressed British servicemen during the First World War (1914-18). Shortened from onomatopoeic rhyming slang 'plink plonk'.

Ployez-Jacquemart champagne house, Ludes, France.

Plymouth Cape Cocktail. Over ice shake 2 parts Plymouth gin, 1 cranberry juice. Strain.

Plymouth Gin distiller est 1793 at Plymouth, England. See box.

Plzensky Prazdroj brewery of Pilsner Urquell, Pilsen, Czech Republic.

PM Blended American blended whiskey brand, USA.

PM Canadian whisky brand of Canadian Gibson Distilleries, Canada.

Poças Junior family port house est 1918, Vila Nova de Gaia, Portugal. Old tawnies including colheitas and vintages: 1960, 63, 70, 75, 85, 91, 97, 2000, 03.

Pöckl, Josef wine producer in Neusiedlersee, Burgenland, Austria.

Podensac wine commune of AC Cérons, Bordeaux, France.

podere small farm or estate producing wine. Italy.

Poet's Dream Cocktail. Over ice shake 2 parts dry gin, 2 dry vermouth, 2 dashes Bénédictine, 2 dashes orange bitters. Strain.

Point brewery in Stevens Point, Wisconsin, USA. Brands include **Point Genuine Bock** and **Point Special**.

Pointe, Château La wine estate of AC Pomerol, Bordeaux, France.

Poire Williams *eau de vie* distilled from Williams pears. France and Switzerland.

Poit Dhubh twelve- and 21-year-old vatted malt scotch whiskies by Sir Iain Noble's Praban na Linne Ltd, Isle Ornsay, Skye, Scotland. Gaelic Poit Dhubh is pronounced Pot-Doo and means black pot.

Poker Cocktail. Over ice shake 1 part Bacardi rum, 1 sweet vermouth. Strain.

Polar rum brand formerly of Seagram, Germany.

Polar Beer export brand of Egill Skallagrimsson Brewery, Iceland.

Polignac, Prince Hubert de cognac producer, Cognac, France.

Plymouth Gin

challenging the big city brands

The original Plymouth distillery was established in the Devon seaport in 1793. Its home was a former Dominican friary founded in 1431, dissolved in 1539 and subsequently adapted as an inn. It is said that a number of the emigrants known as the Pilgrim Fathers, whose ship from Portsmouth had been blown by a storm into the Plymouth Sound, stayed at the inn prior to resuming their voyage to America aboard the *Mayflower* in 1620.

Established by Coates & Co, the Black Friars Distillery (named in commemoration of the erstwhile Dominicans) is now the only English gin being produced on its original site. At the time of its takeover by the multinational Allied Breweries company (later Allied Domecq) in the 1970s, Plymouth was a successful brand selling more than half a million bottles a year in the USA alone. But the brand subsequently lost market share and is said to have faced oblivion before Coates & Co was bought by an independent syndicate in 1996. Half the equity was acquired in 2000 by Vin & Sprit AB of Sweden and the takeover was gradually completed in ensuing years.

Plymouth gins were relaunched in three brands at strengths of 41.2%, 47.3% and 57% 'Navy Strength'. There are also also two liqueur gins, Plymouth Sloe and Plymouth Damson. Coates executive Charles Rolls, credited with taking sales of the gin from 5,000 cases to 100,000, was emphatic in his claim that Plymouth 'has long been considered to be the best in the world.' In addition to the 'usual' gin botanicals of juniper and coriander, he said, 'Plymouth derives its uniquely dry taste from a large proportion of root botanicals including orris from Italy and sweet angelica from Saxony. The resulting gin is smoother and 'rootier' making it the perfect dry base for cocktails and mixers.'

Polish Pure Spirit rectified neutral spirit as basis for Polish vodka.

Pollak, Walter wine producer in Weinviertel, Niederösterreich, Austria.

Pollino DOC for red wines from Gaglioppo and Greco Nero grapes of Monte Pollino, Calabria, Italy.

Pollyanna Cocktail. Over ice shake 2 parts dry gin, 1 sweet vermouth, 2 dashes grenadine, 1 slice of orange, 1 slice of pineapple. Strain.

Polmos brand of Polish spirit producer, Pabstwowy Monopol Spirytusowy.

Polo Cocktail. Over ice shake 1 part dry gin, 1 dry vermouth, 1 sweet vermouth, 4 dashes fresh lime (or lemon) juice. Strain.

Polonaise Cocktail. Over ice shake 3 parts brandy, 1 blackberry liqueur, 1 dry sherry, 1 teaspoon lemon juice. Strain

Pol Roger *Grande Marque* champagne house est 1849, Epernay, France, by Pol Roger whose heirs, now known by the surname Pol-Roger, still run the company. The favourite champagne of Sir Winston Churchill (1874–1965), an honour commemorated in the name of the 'prestige' wine Cuvée Sir Winston Churchill.

Polz, Erich & Walter wine producer in Südsteiermark, Austria.

pomace in cider-making, the pulp from milled apples.

pomace in winemaking, the pips, skins and stalks remaining from the pressing.

Pomerell vineyard at Zell in Mosel-Saar-Ruwer region, Germany.

Pomerol village and AC zone of the Libournais, Bordeaux, France. Until 1900 recognised only as a wine-producing satellite of St Emilion but since 1960s of growing prestige as a wine region in its own right. Vineyards are planted predominantly with Merlot and relatively small plots of Cabernet Franc grapes. Châteaux such as Pétrus, Le Pin and Trotanoy have reputations – and prices – which in some vintages eclipse even the greatest estates of St-Emilion and the Médoc. Nevertheless, there has been no formal classification of the region to date.

Pomeys, Château wine estate of AC Moulis, Médoc, Bordeaux, France. Classified *Cru Bourgeois Supérieur*.

Pomino DOC for red wines from Canaiolo, Sangiovese and several Bordeaux varieties of grapes, and whites from Pinot Bianco and Pinot Grigio. Wines are chiefly made by Frescobaldi.

Pommard wine village and AC of Côte de Beaune, Burgundy, France. Popular village red wines and many *premier cru* vineyards: les Argillières, les Arvelets, Clos Blanc, les Boucherottes, la Chanière, les Chanlins Bas, les Chaponnières, les Charmots, les Combes Dessus,

Clos de la Commaraine, les Croix Noirs, Derrières St Jean, les Epenots, les Fremiers, le Clos Micot, les Petits Epenots, les Pézerolles, la Platière, la Refène, les Rugiens, les Rugiens Haut, les Saucilles, Clos de Verger. Leading producers include Comte Armand, de Courcel, Leroy, Machard de Gramont, Château de Pommard etc.

Pommery & Greno *Grande Marque* champagne house est 1836 by Louis Pommery (d 1856) and made famous by his widow Louise. Reims, France.

Pompejaner vineyard at Aschaffenburg in the Franken region, Germany.

Pomys, Château wine estate of AC St-Estèphe, Médoc, Bordeaux, France. Classified *Cru Bourgeois Supérieur*.

Poncet, Château de wine estate of AC Premières Côtes de Bordeaux, France.

ponche brandy- and sherry-based herbal digestive spirit flavoured with orange. First made by José de Soto, Jerez de la Frontera, Spain. Moonshine versions proliferate in Iberia.

Ponche Caballero brandy-based sweet liqueur brand of Luis Caballero, Puerto de Santa Maria, Spain.

Ponnelle, Pierre wine grower of Beaune, Burgundy, France. Vineyards in Beaune Grèves, Bonnes Mares, Charmes-Chambertin, Corton, Clos Vougeot.

Pontac disappearing red grape variety of South Africa.

Pontac-Lynch, Château wine estate of AC Margaux, Médoc, Bordeaux,

France. Classified *Cru Bourgeois Supérieur*.

Pontac-Monplaisir, Château wine estate of AC Pessac-Léognan, Bordeaux, France.

Pontet, Château wine estate of AC Médoc, Bordeaux, France. Classified *Cru Bourgeois*.

Pontet-Canet, Château wine estate of AC Pauillac, Médoc, Bordeaux, France. Classified *5ème Grand Cru Classé*.

Pontet-Chappaz, Château wine estate of AC Margaux, Médoc, Bordeaux, France.

Pontet-Clauzure, Château wine estate of AC St-Emilion, Bordeaux, France. Classified *Grand Cru*.

Pontoise-Cabarrus, Château wine estate of AC Haut-Médoc, Bordeaux, France. Classified *Cru Bourgeois*.

Poole brewery at Poole, Dorset, England.

Poop Deck Cocktail. Over ice shake 2 parts blackberry liqueur, 1 brandy, 1 port. Strain.

Pope Valley wine region of Napa Valley, California, USA.

Poppy Cocktail. Over ice shake 2 parts dry gin, 1 crème de cacao. Strain.

Poretti brewing company of Italy.

port fortified wine of Portugal. Wine from grapes (principally Bastardo, Donzelinho Tinto, Mourisco, Tinta Cão, Tinta Francisca, Tinta Roriz, Touriga Francesca, Touriga Nacional varieties) of Douro Valley is part fermented before addition of grape spirit (ratio 4 wine to 1 spirit) to end fermentation, retain sweetness of unfermented sugars and produce wine fortified to around 20% alc. Port is aged in cask for very variable periods. Wine long-aged in wood changes in colour from dark ruby to lightening copper and is marketed as 'tawny' – the best of it at 10 or 20 years old or older. Ordinary ports aged briefly in cask are bottled and sold as 'ruby' or 'tawny' (for the latter, the colour comes from blending with young white wine). Longer-aged ports are sold as 'LBV' (late-bottled vintage), 'Vintage Character' etc. Finest ports are single vintage or *colheita* wines intended for long-ageing (decades) in bottle. Some white port is made from Malvasia Fina, Verdelho and other grapes. Port trade has been dominated by British shippers who initiated the business in the 1670s.

Porte Cochère Cocktail. Over ice shake 6 parts vodka, 2 apricot brandy, 2 orange juice, 1 grenadine, 1 egg yolk. Strain.

Port Ellen Island malt whisky distillery, Port Ellen, Islay, Scotland. Est 1825, closed 1929, reopened 1967, visited by HM Queen Elizabeth II 1980, closed 1983. Maltings supplies all Islay distilleries.

porter style of very dark beer originating in London, England, in 18th century; popularised particularly in Ireland, and later worldwide, since 1817 patenting of grain-roasting process producing dark malts and roasted flavours. Name may derive from first commercial breweries in London, whose beer deliveries to public houses were heralded with the cry 'Porter!'.

Porter Brewing brewery at Haslingden, Lancashire, England.

Portets wine commune of AC Graves, Bordeaux, France.

Portets, Château de wine estate of AC Graves, Bordeaux, France.

Port in a Storm Cocktail. Over ice stir 3 parts port, 1 brandy, 1 lemon juice. Strain into small wine glasses.

Portland Brewing Co pub-brewery in Portland, Oregon, USA, noted for **Portland Ale**.

Portland Lager beer brewed by FX Matt, Utica, New York, for Maine Coast Brewing, USA.

Port Mahon brewery at Sheffield, South Yorkshire, England.

Port Morant sugar estate est 1732 in Demerara, British Guyana and source of unique rum from last Demerara vat still in existence – currently operated by Guyana Distilleries. Noted 20-year-old rum from French oak casks (Bristol Spirits Co).

BRISTOL
CLASSIC RUM
PORT MORANT STILL
DEMERARA
20

Portnersberg vineyard at Wittlich in the Mosel-Saar-Ruwer region, Germany.

Portneuvoise, La brewery and beer brand, St Casimir, Quebec, Canada.

Porto Rico Cocktail. Over ice shake 1 egg white, 1 part port. Strain and grate nutmeg over glass.

Porto Vecchio town and wine district of Corsica, France. Red, rosé and white wines mainly from one property, Domaine de Torraccia.

Portugal wine-producing nation with vineyards from extreme north to extreme south: DOC (top-quality-rated) regions are Vinho Verde, Douro (port and table wines), Bairrada, Dão, Bucelas, Colares. Other regions, including Alentejo, Algarve, Estremadura, Ribatejo, Setubal and the nation's largest, Oeste, make many wines of great, if insular, quality. The island of Madeira is a Portuguese possession.

Port Wine Cocktail. Over ice stir 1 part port, 1 dash brandy. Strain and squeeze orange peel over. Alternatively, over ice stir 1 part port, 2 dashes curaçao, 1 dash Angostura bitters, 1 dash orange bitters. Strain.

Port Wine Flip Cocktail. Over ice shake 3 parts port, 1 egg, 1 teaspoon sugar. Strain into a wine glass and sprinkle a pinch of ground nutmeg over.

Posip white grape variety and wine of Dalmatian island of Korcula, Croatia.

Posten vineyard at Bacharach in Mittelrhein region, Germany.

pot traditional wine bottle of Beaujolais region, France. Originally 50cl and formerly adopted in 75cl size by Piat company.

Potcheen brand of 80% alc, colourless grain spirit of Bunratty Mead & Liquor, County Clare, Ireland. Bears the slogan 'Illegal in Ireland' (where home-distilled poteen is outlawed). From 1999 licences to make and sell potcheen in Eire became available for the first time since 1661.

poteen grain or potato spirit, said to have been distilled, widely and illicitly, in Ireland since the 6th century. Name means 'small pot' (as in pot still). Variously believed to be, as well as a potent intoxicant, an aphrodisiac, an explosive, an ointment for chest ailments and a remedy for underachieving racehorses.

Potensac, Château wine estate of AC Médoc, Bordeaux, France. Classified *Cru Grand Bourgeois*.

Pot Flamand *bière de garde* by Clerck brewery, Picardy, France.

Potheen an alternative spelling of **poteen**.

Potocki vodka of independent distiller Jan Potocki, Poland.

Potter Valley AVA of Mendocino County, California, USA.

Pouget, Château wine estate of AC Margaux, Médoc, Bordeaux, France. Classified *4ème Grand Cru Classé*.

Pouilly Fuissé AC for white wine from Chardonnay grapes of villages of Fuissé and Pouilly, among others, in Mâconnais region, Burgundy, France.

Pouilly-Fumé AC for white wine from Sauvignon Blanc grapes of seven communes surrounding town of Pouilly-sur-Loire, Loire Valley, France.

Pouilly-Loché AC for white wine from Chardonnay grapes of village of Loché, Mâconnais region, Burgundy, France.

Pouilly-Vinzelles AC for white wine from Chardonnay grapes of village of Vinzelles, Mâconnais region, Burgundy, France. Wine from village of Loché is commonly sold under this name.

Poujeaux, Château wine estate of AC Moulis, Médoc, Bordeaux, France. Classified *Cru Grand Bourgeois Exceptionnel*.

Poulsard red grape variety of Jura region, France.

pourriture grise 'grey rot'. Destructive effect of grape fungus *botrytis cinerea*, particularly in cold and humid conditions. French.

pourriture noble 'noble rot'. French. Beneficial effect of fungus *botrytis cinerea*, causing grapes remaining on vines during autumn when mornings are misty and days warm to shrivel and gain concentration of sugars. Fruit thus affected makes the great dessert wines of Barsac and Sauternes in Bordeaux and *vendange tardive* (late harvest) wines in Alsace, France. Similarly, in Mosel and Rhine Valleys, Germany, Tokay in Hungary and even in Australia.

Pousse d'Or, Domaine de La wine estate of Volnay, Côte de Beaune, Burgundy, France.

Poussie, Clos de La wine estate of AC Sancerre, Loire Valley, France.

Poverty Bay wine region of North Island, New Zealand.

Power's Irish whiskey brand of Irish Distillers, Midleton, Eire.

Power's Bitter popular beer brand, Australia.

PPS UK drinks trade acronym for premium-packaged spirits – usually branded gin, rum or vodka mixed with fruit juices in single-serving bottles or cans. Also known as RTDs (ready to drink), Fabs (flavoured alcoholic beverages) or, to the wider public, alcopops.

Prädikat see *Qualitätswein mit Prädikat*.

Pradines, Château Les wine estate of AC St-Estèphe, Médoc, Bordeaux, France.

Prado Cocktail. Over ice shake 3 parts tequila, 2 lemon juice, 1 maraschino, 4 dashes grenadine, 1 egg white. Strain and add a maraschino cherry.

Prager wine producer in Wachau, Niederösterreich, Austria.

Prairie Oyster Cocktail. Over ice shake 1 part brandy, 1 equal mix of wine vinegar and Worcestershire sauce, 1 teaspoon tomato ketchup. Strain into a tumbler and add an egg yolk. Sprinkle 1 pinch of cayenne pepper over.

Prälat vineyard at Erden in Mosel-Saar-Ruwer region, Germany.

Pramaggiore DOC for red wines either from Cabernet (Franc or Sauvignon) or from Merlot grapes, Pramaggiore, Veneto, Italy.

Pramian wine of ancient Greece.

Präsent vineyard at Medersheim in Nahe region, Germany.

precocious in winetasting, the smell or flavour of a young wine more developed than would be expected.

Predigtstuhl vineyard at Dorfpro-zelten in Franken region, Germany.

Pregartner, Alois wine producer in Süd-Oststeiermark, Austria.

Preignac wine village of AC Sau-ternes, Bordeaux, France.

Preiss Henny wine producer of Mittelwiher, Alsace, France.

Preiss Zimmer wine producer of Riquewihr, Alsace, France.

Prémeaux wine village of Côte de Nuits, Burgundy, France. Wines are sold under Nuits St-Georges name.

Premier Cru vineyard of the first quality, particularly in Bordeaux and Burgundy regions of France. In Bordeaux's Médoc classification of 1855, four great estates were ranked *Premier Grand Cru Classé*, and a fifth, Mouton-Rothschild, was pro-moted from *Deuxième* in 1971. In Barsac and Sauternes, Château Yquem is ranked *Premier Cru Supérieur* and several other great sweet white wine estates are desig-nated *Premiers Crus Classés*. St-Emilion has two classes of *Premier Grand Cru Classé* properties: two, Ausone and Cheval Blanc, rank 'A' and nine rank 'B'. In Burgundy, hundreds of vineyards are classed *Premier Cru*, and most of them are in multiple ownership. Burgundies from vineyards thus ranked are usually labelled with the village/AC name to which the name of the *Pre-mier Cru* vineyard is appended, eg Puligny-Montrachet Les Pucelles.

Premières Côtes de Blaye AC of Blaye, Bordeaux, France. Chiefly red wines from Merlot and Cabernet Franc grapes.

Premières Côtes de Bordeaux exten-sive AC for minor properties of Bordeaux region, France. Red and white wines.

premium much used on drinks labels to imply special quality. It may describe what a brewer, cidermaker or distiller deems a top-quality pro-duct, but has no significance under the laws governing food standards in Europe or in the US.

Premium Press dry cider (6.0% alc) by Thatcher's Cider, Sandford, Somerset, England.

Premium Verum lager by Oldenberg brewery, Kentucky, USA,

President Cocktail. Over ice shake 2 parts rum, 1 orange juice, 2 dashes grenadine. Strain.

Pressac regional name for Malbec grape variety, St-Emilion, Bordeaux, France.

Pressac, Château de wine estate of AC St-Emilion, Bordeaux, France. Classified *Grand Cru*.

Presto Cocktail. Over ice shake 4 parts brandy, 1 sweet vermouth, 1 orange juice, 1 dash pastis. Strain.

Preston brewery at Embudo, New Mexico, USA. Said to be the nation's smallest.

Preuillac, Château wine estate of AC Médoc, Bordeaux, France. Classified *Cru Bourgeois* but de-classified 2003.

Preuses *Grand Cru* vineyard of Chablis, Burgundy, France.

Priam's Daughter Cocktail. Over ice shake 2 parts vodka, 1 cherry brandy, 1 dash orange bitters. Strain.

pricked in winetasting, a wine with an unpleasant, tongue-twingeing taste indicating volatile acidity.

Pride of Islay twelve-year-old vatted malt scotch whisky of Gordon & MacPhail, Elgin, Scotland.

Pride of Orkney twelve-year-old vatted malt scotch whisky of Gordon & MacPhail, Elgin, Scotland.

Pride of Strathspey twelve-year-old vatted malt scotch whisky of Gordon & MacPhail, Elgin, Scotland. Also, 25 Years Old vatted malt and bottlings from 1938, 1940, 1946, 1950.

Pride of The Lowlands twelve-year-old vatted malt scotch whisky of Gordon & MacPhail, Elgin, Scotland.

Prieler, Engelbert wine producer in Neusiedlersee Hügelland, Burgenland, Austria.

Prieur, Domaine Jacques wine producer in Meursault, Burgundy, France. Also with vineyards in Chambertin, Montrachet, Volnay.

Prieur du Château Meyney second wine of Château Meyney, Bordeaux, France.

Prieuré, Château Le wine estate of AC St-Emilion, Bordeaux, France. Classified *Grand Cru Classé*.

Prieuré-Lichine, Château wine estate of AC Margaux, Médoc, Bordeaux, France. Classified *4ème Grand Cru Classé*.

Prieurs de la Commanderie, Château wine estate of AC Pomerol, Bordeaux, France.

primeur term defining wine produced and marketed within a few weeks of the grape harvest. First such wines were those of Beaujolais, as defined under decree by the government of France, 9 November, 1951.

priming in brewing, the addition of sugars to promote secondary fermentation.

Primitivo red grape variety chiefly of Apulia, Italy.

Primitivo di Manduria DOC for red wines from Primitivo grapes, Manduria, Apulia, Italy. Includes high-alcohol *liquoroso* styles.

Prince Charles Cocktail. Over ice stir 2 parts dry gin, 1 cherry brandy, 2 dashes curaçao. Strain and squeeze orange peel over.

Prince Charlie whisky brand of Pernod-Ricard.

Prince Hubert de Polignac cognac brand of Unicognac growers and distillers co-operative, Cognac, France. VS five-eight year-old, VSOP 12-15 year-old, Napoléon 18-20 year-old, XO 20-year-old.

Prince of Wales ten-year-old single malt Scotch whisky brand of former Welsh Whisky Co, Brecon, Wales.

Prince Poniatowsky leading wine producer in AC Vouvray, Loire Valley, France.

Princess Cocktail. Into port glass carefully pour 3 parts apricot brandy, 1 sweetened cream. Avoid mixing ingredients.

Princess Mary Cocktail. Over ice shake 1 part crème de cacao, 1 dry gin, 1 sweetened cream. Strain.

Prince's Smile Cocktail. Over ice shake 2 parts dry gin, 1 apple brandy, 1 apricot brandy, 1 dash lemon juice. Strain.

Princeton Cocktail. Over ice stir 2 parts dry gin, 1 port, 2 dashes orange bitters. Strain and squeeze lemon peel over.

Princetown brewery at Princetown, Devon, England.

Principe di Piemonte Blanc de Blancs brand of Asti Spumante wine by Cinzano. Piedmont, Italy.

Printemps seasonal ('Spring') beer by Duyck brewery, Jenlain, France.

Priorat wine DOCa of Catalonia, Spain since 2004. Fashionable red wines from Garnacha, Cariñena and Cabernet Sauvignon grapes by renowned producers including Alvaro Palacios, René Barbier, Cellers de Scala Dei, Mas Martinet. Some dry white wines.

Pripps brewery near Stockholm, Sweden. Brands include Carnegie Porter and Julöl lager.

prise de mousse in champagne-making, the second fermentation that takes place inside the closed bottle, producing the *mousse* (effervescence). French.

Privateer 'vintage character' port brand of Robertson Brothers, Vila Nova de Gaia, Portugal.

Prize Old Ale renowned strong (9% alc) beer by George Gale & Co, Horndean, England.

Probstberg *Grosslage* incorporating vineyards at Fell (mit Orsteil Fastrau), Kenn, Longuich, Riol and Schweich in Mosel-Saar-Ruwer region, Germany.

Probstberg vineyards at Bad Mergentheim and Weikersheim in Württemberg region, Germany.

Probsteilberg vineyard at Boppard in Mittelrhein region, Germany.

Probstey vineyard at Saulheim in Rheinhessen region, Germany.

Productions Réunis de Puisseguin et Lussac-St-Emilion wine co-operative of St-Emilion region, Bordeaux, France.

produttore producer (of wines etc). Italy.

prohibition risky branch of the black art of social engineering in which governments attempt to impose temperance upon entire populations. New Zealand and Scandinavian nations have been among the practitioners, but the most notorious attempt was that empowered by the Volstead Act of 1919 in the USA. Until revocation in 1933, the United States endured a period of drunkenness and lawlessness on a scale unparallelled before or since.

Proidl, Franz wine producer in Kremstal, Niederösterreich, Austria.

Prokupac red grape variety of Serbia.

Proosje van Schiedam quintuple-distilled *korenjenever* (*genever* without juniper) by Nolet distillery, Schiedam, Netherlands.

proost 'cheers' in Dutch.

Prosecco white grape variety of NE Italy and the name given to a range of *frizzante* (slightly sparkling) wines made in the region.

Prosecco di Conegliano-Valdobbiadene DOC for still and sparkling wines chiefly from Prosecco grapes, district of Cartizze, Veneto, Italy.

Prosek sweet wine of Dalmatian coast, Croatia.

pros(i)t 'cheers' in German.

Prosper Maufoux *négoçiant-éleveur* of Santenay, Burgundy, France.

Prosperity wine brand of Firestone Vineyard, Los Olivos, California, USA. Well known for red and white wines labelled in 1930s style symbolising industrial revival of the United States following the Great Depression. The Firestone Vineyard is the property of the famed tyre-manufacturing family.

Provence wine-producing region of southern France. Larger ACs include Côtes de Provence, Coteaux d'Aix-en-Provence, Côtes du Lubéron. Distinctive wines are produced in smaller ACs such as Bandol, Bellet, Cassis, Palette.

Proviar sparkling- and still-wine producer of Argentina.

Providence sugar estate and rum distillery at Chagunos, Trinidad. Famed light golden rums from the Providence Patent Still.

Providence, Château La wine estate of AC Bordeaux Supérieur, France.

Providence, Château La wine estate of AC Pomerol, Bordeaux, France.

Prüfnummer on Austrian wines, the registration number displayed on the red-and-white Banderole neck label. Confirms that the wine has passed analytical and sensory tests.

Prüfungsnummer on German wines, the registration number displayed on label confirming authenticity.

Prugnolo red grape variety of Montepulciano, Tuscany, Italy.

Pruimpje Prik In plum liqueur by van Zuylekom distillery, Amsterdam, Netherlands.

pruina film on grapeskins to which yeasts and other organisms adhere, forming a 'bloom'.

Prüm, JJ great wine producer based at Wehlen in Mosel-Saar-Ruwer region, Germany. Vineyard holdings include famed Wehlener Sonnenuhr.

Prüm Erben, SA wine estate at Wehlen in Mosel-Saar-Ruwer region, Germany. Quite separate from JJ Prüm.

Pruneaux Cocktail. Over ice shake 2 parts dry gin, 2 dry sherry, 1 orange juice, 1 prune syrup. Strain and serve in crushed-ice-filled glass.

Prunelle de Bourgogne liqueur from sloe kernels macerated in spirit, noted for 'liquid marzipan' flavour. Gabriel Boudier, Dijon, France.

see label over ➡

Prunier cognac house est 1701, Cognac, France. *see label over* ➡

pruning in winemaking, the noble art of training vines to produce optimum fruit, with the aid of secateurs. Techniques vary radically between regions.

Prünte, Klaus wine producer in Südsteiermark, Austria.

p'tit caribou a concocted winter-warming drink peculiar to the province of Quebec, Canada. Principal ingredients are high-strength spirit and sweetened red wine. Also known as *gros gin*, irrespective of use of gin.

puckering in winetasting, a characteristic of young wine in which tannin causes a desiccating, puckering sensation in the mouth.

Puerto Apple Cocktail. Over ice shake 2 parts apple brandy, 1 rum, 4 dashes fresh lime juice, 1 teaspoon sugar. Strain.

Puerto de Santa Maria sherry-producing city and port of Andalucia, Spain.

Puglia local name of Apulia wine region, Italy.

Puisseguin satellite AC of St-Emilion, Bordeaux, France. Wines are designated AC **Puisseguin-St-Emilion**.

Pujols sur Ciron white-wine commune of AC Graves, Bordeaux, France.

Pulchen vineyard at Konz in Mosel-Saar-Ruwer region, Germany.

Puligny-Montrachet famed wine village and AC of Côte de Beaune, Burgundy, France. Renowned white wines of village AC and *Grands Crus* Bâtard-Montrachet, Bienvenues-Bâtard-Montrachet, Chevalier-Montrachet and Le Montrachet. *Premiers Crus*: Clos du Cailleret, les Chalumeaux, Champ Chanet, Clavoillons, les Combettes, les Folatières, la Garenne, Hameau de Blagny, les Pucelles, les Referts, Sous les Puits.

Pulling & Co brand name of Tanners of Shrewsbury, England, for Hereford dry gin.

Pulling's Herefordshire cider brand of Tanners, Shrewsbury, England.

pulque fermented sap of maguey or mezcal cactus of Aztec Mexico. Now the base for distilling tequila.

Pulverberg vineyard at Ackern in Baden region, Germany.

Pulverbuck vineyard at Vogtsberg im Kaiserstuhl in Baden region, Germany.

Pulvermächer vineyard at Kernen in Württemberg region, Germany.

Pumphouse brewery in Sydney, New South Wales, Australia.

punch any mixed drink containing fruit juice, but not always alcohol. Term is said to have derived from mixed drinks comprising five ingredients in India, so-named from Hindi *panch* (five).

puncheon large cask for beer or wine.

punt the dimple in the base of a champagne bottle, to give strength.

Punt e Mes Italian vermouth brand by Carpano, Turin. Est by Antonio Benedetto Carpano, 1786. Dark brown with a bitter-sweet flavour based on quinine. The name means 'point and a half', a stock market term. Stockbrokers who patronised the original Signor Carpano's bar, next to the stock exchange in Turin's Piazza Castello, applied the term to the proportions for their preferred mixed version of the drink. Punt e Mes is customarily served chilled with ice and an orange slice, or mixed with fresh orange juice.

see label opposite ➡

Pupillin wine village of AC Arbois, Jura, France.

pupitre in champagne-making, the perforated hinged boards in which wine bottles are manipulated by the *remueur*, gradually to up-end them to manoeuvre sediment into the neck. Champagne, France.

Puritan Cocktail. Over ice shake 1 part dry gin, 1 Lillet, 2 dashes orange juice, 1 dash apricot brandy.

Purple Haze Cocktail. Over ice shake 1 part vodka, 1 grape juice, 1 grapefruit juice, 1 teaspoon sugar. Strain into an ice-filled glass.

Pusser's stong (54.5% alc) rum brand of Pusser's distillery, British Virgin Islands, West Indies.

Putachieside twelve-year-old blended scotch whisky by J&A Mitchell, Campbeltown, Scotland.

Puttonyos degree of sweetness of wines of Tokaji, Hungary. Sweet *aszu* grape must is stored in small 32-litre barrels called **putts** and each of these added to the dry base wine represents one puttonyo. Minimum is three, maximum six.

Puy-Blanquet, Château wine estate of AC St-Emilion, Bordeaux, France. Classified *Grand Cru*.

Puyblanquet-Carille, Château wine estate of AC St-Emilion, Bordeaux, France. Classified *Grand Cru*.

Puycarpin, Château wine estate of AC Côtes de Castillon, Bordeaux, France.

Puy-Castéra, Château wine estate of AC Haut-Médoc, Bordeaux, France. Classified *Cru Bourgeois*.

Puyguilhem, Château wine estate of AC Fronsac, Bordeaux, France.

Puymiran, Château wine estate of AC Entre-Deux-Mers, Bordeaux, France.

Puzzle Wheat Beer NRD beer (4.8% alc) by Salopian Brewery, Shropshire, England.

PX see Pedro Ximenéz.

Pyramid ten-year-old tawny port by Robertson Brothers, Vila Nova de Gaia, Portugal.

Pyramid Wheaten Ale noted wheat beer by Hart Brewing Co, Kalama, Washington, USA.

Pyramup red wine brand of Château Barker, Western Australia.

Q

QbA abbreviation of *Qualitätswein bestimmter Anbaugebiet*.

QC 'British wine' brand of Matthew Clark, Bristol, England.

QmP abbreviation of *Qualitätswein mit Prädikat*.

Quady, Andrew famed producer of fortified wines, Madera, Central Valley, Caifornia, USA. **Quady Essensia Orange Muscat, Quady's Starboard.**

Quail's Gate wine producer in Ontario, Canada.

Quaker's Cocktail. Over ice shake 2 parts brandy, 2 rum, 1 lemon juice, 1 raspberry syrup. Strain.

Qualitätswein bestimmter Anbaugebiet 'quality wine from designated areas'. A description introduced under German wine laws of 1971, covering areas of Ahr, Baden, Franken, Hessische Bergstrasse, Mittelrhein, Mosel-Saar-Ruwer, Nahe, Rheingau, Rheinhessen, Rheinpfalz, Württemberg. Wine must be from specified grape varieties with sufficient natural sugar content to elevate it above basic *Tafelwein*. *QbA* wines account for the bulk of German output, including Liebfraumilch.

Qualitätswein mit Prädikat the upper echelon of German quality wine. Wines must have higher natural sugar content (as determined on the Oechsle scale) than basic *QbA*. Within the *QmP* are five categories drawn according to rising sugar levels: *Kabinett, Spätlese, Auslese, Beerenauslese* and *Trockenbeerenauslese*, plus specialised *Eiswein*.

Quarles Harris port producer and shipper est 1680 by Devon-born Thomas Dawson, Vila Nova de Gaia, Portugal. Now Symington-owned. Old tawnies and vintages: 1960, 63, 66, 70, 75, 77, 80, 83, 85, 91, 94, 97, 2000, 03.

Quarter Deck Cocktail. Over ice shake 4 parts rum, 2 sherry, 1 fresh lime juice. Strain.

Quartet sparkling wine by Roederer Estate, Mendocino, California, USA.

Quarto Vecchio wine producer and red-wine brand from Bordeaux grapes, Po Valley, Veneto, Italy.

Quarts de Chaume vineyard and sweet white wine of Coteaux du Layon, Loire Valley, France. Highly prized wines from selected, 'noble rot'-affected Chenin Blanc grapes. Producers include Château de l'Echarderie, Château la Suronde.

quassia bitter-flavoured medicinal bark extract from Quassia genus of tropical American trees. Formerly used as an additive in strong ales. Now more common in insecticides.

Quatourze wine district of Coteaux du Languedoc, Midi, France.

Quattro Vicariati red wine brand from Cabernet Franc, Cabernet Sauvignon and Merlot grapes by Cavit, Trentino-Alto Adige, Italy.

Quay brewery at Weymouth, Dorset, England.

Queen Anne blended Scotch whisky brand formerly of Seagram, Montreal, Canada.

Queen Charlotte Cocktail. In a large wine glass combine 2 parts red wine, 1 grenadine, 1 teaspoon lemon juice. Add ice cubes, top with chilled sparkling water and stir.

Queen Diana three-, 15- and 21-year-old blended scotch whiskies by Glen Murray Blending, Harrow, Middlesex, England.

Queen Elizabeth blended scotch whisky by Burn Brae, Perth, Scotland.

Queen Elizabeth De Luxe blended scotch whisky by Avery's of Bristol, England.

Queen Elizabeth Cocktail. Over ice shake 2 parts dry gin, 1 Cointreau, 1 lemon juice, 1 dash pastis. Strain.

Queen Mary I five- and 12-year-old blended scotch whiskies by H Stenham, London, England.

Queen Mother Cocktail. In a cocktail glass combine 1 part chilled dry gin, 1 chilled Dubonnet.

Queen of Denmark Cocktail. Into a small wine glass pour 2 parts Cherry Heering and float a teaspoon of fresh cream on top.

Queen of Spades Cocktail. Over ice shake 2 parts rum, 1 Tia Maria, 1 fresh cream. Strain.

Queen's Choice blended scotch whisky by C&J Macdonald, Perth, Scotland.

Queen's Cocktail. Over ice shake 2 parts dry gin, 1 dry vermouth, 1 sweet vermouth, 1 slice pineapple. Strain.

Quelle Vie Cocktail. Over ice stir 2 parts brandy, 1 kümmel. Strain.

quentao cane-spirit-based spiced liquor of Brazil said to have been introduced by Portuguese colonists of the sixteenth century. Traditional drink of the festival of St João (St John).

Quentin, Château wine estate of AC St-Emilion, Bordeaux, France. Classified *Grand Cru*.

questch *eau de vie* distilled from Switzen plums. France, particularly Alsace, Germany and Switzerland.

Queyrats, Château Les wine estate of AC Graves, Bordeaux, France.

Quincy AC for white wines from Sauvignon Blanc grapes, upper Loire Valley, France.

quinine bark flavouring ingredient of vermouth.

Quinn's Scottish Ale brand of Wynkoop brewery, Colorado, USA.

quinquina wine-based apéritif with quinine flavouring. French.

Quinsac, Château de wine estate of AC Entre-Deux-Mers, Bordeaux, France.

quinta 'farm' or 'estate' in Portuguese. Widely used to label single-estate wines, particularly vintage ports from named vineyards.

Quinta da Agua Alta single-estate vintage port by Churchill-Graham, Vila Nova de Gaia, Portugal.

Quinta da Aveleda renowned single-estate *vinho verde* wine of Guedes family (Mateus) property, Douro Valley, Portugal.

Quinta da Cavadinha single-estate vintage port by Warre & Ca, Vila Nova de Gaia, Portugal.

Quinta da Ervamoira single-estate ten-year-old tawny port by Ramos-Pinto, Vila Nova de Gaia, Portugal.

Quinta da Ferradosa single-estate vintage port by Borges E Irmao, Vila Nova de Gaia, Portugal.

Quinta da Foz single-estate vintage port by AA Calem & Filho, Vila Nova de Gaia, Portugal.

Quinta da Griecha vineyard of upper Douro Valley, Portugal. Bought by Churchill's Port, 1999.

Quinta das Carvalhas single-estate tawny port by Royal Oporto Wine Co, Vila Nova de Gaia, Portugal.

Quinta de Bacalhõa wine brand and estate of Estremedura, Portugal. Cabernet Sauvignon red produced under contract by João Pires.

Quinta de Pacheca leading producer of Douro table wines, Trás-os-Montes, Douro Valley, Portugal.

Quinta de Panascal single-estate vintage port by Fonseca Guimaraens, Vila Nova de Gaia, Portugal.

Quinta de Pancas noted red-wine estate of Alenquer, Estredemura, Portugal.

Quinta de Vargellas renowned single-estate vintage port by Taylor Fladgate & Yeatman, Vila Nova de Gaia, Portugal.

Quinta do Bomfim single-estate vintage port by Dow's, Vila Nova de Gaia, Portugal.

Quinta do Bom-Retiro single-estate 20-year-old tawny port by Ramos-Pinto, Vila Nova de Gaia, Portugal.

Quinta do Cachão port brand of Messias, Mealhada, Portugal.

Quinta do Carmo noted estate of Alentejo region, Portugal. Fine red and white table wines. Owned by Rothschilds of Château Lafite, Bordeaux, France.

Quinta do Corval noted table-wine producer, Pinhão, Upper Douro Valley, Portugal.

Quinta do Côtto single-estate vintage port by Champalimaud & Cia, Vila Real, Portugal. Also known for high-quality table wines.

Quinta do Crasto port shipper and noted table-wine producer, Vila Nova de Gaia, Portugal. Vintages: 1978, 82, 89, 90, 91, 92, 94, 97, 2000, 03.

Quinta do Junço single-estate vintage port by Borges E Irmao, Vila Nova de Gaia, Portugal.

Quinta do Noval port estate est 1715, formerly of A J da Silva & Co, Vila Nova de Gaia, Portugal. Owned since 1991 by French insurer AXA. Famed wines of Naçional grapes from unique 1925-planted vineyard, Noval LB, Noval LBV, old tawnies, colheitas and vintages: 1960, 62, 63, 64, 66, 67, 70, 75, 78, 80, 82, 83, 84, 85, 87, 91, 94, 97, 2000, 03.

Quinta do Porto ten-year-old tawny port by Ferreira, Vila Nova de Gaia, Portugal.

Quinta do Roeda single-estate vintage port by Croft, Vila Nova de Gaia, Portugal. The vineyard, formerly owned by Taylor, Fladgate & Yeatman, was reacquired by Taylors as part of their purchase of Croft port in 2001.

Quinta do Roncão single-estate vintage port by Borges E Irmao, Vila Nova de Gaia, Portugal.

Quinta do Silval port estate acquired 1995 by Quinta do Noval, Portugal. Vintages: 1998, 2000, 01, 02, 03.

Quinta dos Malvedos single-estate vintage port by W & J Graham, Vila Nova de Gaia, Portugal.

Quinta do Soalheira single-estate vintage port by Borges E Irmao, Vila Nova de Gaia, Portugal.

Quinta do Valdoerio port brand of Messias, Mealhada, Portugal.

Quinta do Vao single-estate vintage port by Sandeman, Vila Nova de Gaia, Portugal.

Quinta do Vesuvio port shipper, Vila Nova de Gaia, Portugal. Vintages: 1989, 90, 91, 92, 97, 99, 2000, 03.

quintal measure of grape quantity (100 kg), Italy.

Quinta Roriz port estate of Douro Valley, Portugal.

Quinta São Luiz vintage-port brand of CN Kopke, Vila Nova de Gaia, Portugal.

Quinta Senhora da Ribeiro port vineyard of Dow, Portugal.

Quintine strong (8% alc) beer brand of Guinaumont Brasserie Ellezelloise. Ellezelles, Belgium.

Quirk winemaking dynasty of Kent, England. Noted Pinot whites and Triomphe d'Alsace red from Chiddingstone Vineyards, which were ploughed up in 2003.

Quitte *eau de vie* distilled from quince. Switzerland.

Quondyp white wine brand of Château Barker, Western Australia.

Qupé wine producer in Santa Barbara County, California, USA. Est 1982 by Bob Lindquist, who maintains he was thrust into self-employment when sacked from his job in a wine shop for going to a Kinks concert. Qupé is a 'modern Stone Age winery' run on traditional lines and renowned for wines from grapes indigenous to the Rhône Valley in France.

R

'R' dry white wine of Château Rieussec, Bordeaux, France.

Raaf brewery at Nijmegen, Netherlands, known for abbey ales.

Rabat wine-producing region of Morocco.

Rabaud-Promis, Château wine estate of AC Sauternes, Bordeaux, France. Classified *1er Cru Classé*.

Rabenkopf vineyards at Ingelheim and Wackernheim in Rheinhessen region, Germany.

Rabigato white grape variety of northern Portugal. *Vinho verde* and white port.

Rablay sur Layon wine village of Coteaux du Layon, Loire Valley, France.

Raboso del Piave DOC for red wines from Raboso grapes, Piave, Veneto, Italy.

RAC Cocktail. Over ice stir 2 parts dry gin, 1 dry vermouth, 1 sweet vermouth, 1 dash grenadine, 1 dash orange bitters. Strain and add cocktail cherry to glass. Squeeze orange peel over.

Racke brandy distiller, Bingen, Germany. Dujardin brand and Melcher's Rat.

racking in brewing and winemaking, running cleared beer or wine off its sediment into a clean cask or tank.

Racquet Club Cocktail. Over ice stir 1 part dry gin, 1 dry vermouth, 1 dash orange bitters.

racy in winetasting, the character of a white wine with lively fruit and acidity, especially Riesling.

Radeberger-Pils pilsner beer by the Radeberg brewery, Dresden, Germany.

Radetzky, Field Marshal Count wine producer in Weinviertel, Niederösterreich, Austria.

Raffault wine-producing dynasty of AC Chinon, Loire Valley, France. Several domaines under ownership of different members of the family.

Raffiat de Moncade white grape variety of SW France. Notable in Pacherenc de Vic Bilh.

Raffles Knockout Cocktail. Over ice shake 1 part Cointreau, 1 kirsch, 1 dash lemon juice. Strain and add cocktail cherry to glass.

Raffo beer by Peroni brewery, Italy.

Ragnaud Sabourin cognac producer, Ambleville, Barbezieux, France.

Rahoul, Château wine estate of AC Graves, Bordeaux, France.

Raimat distinguished wine producer of DO Costa del Segre, Catalonia, Spain. Branded red wine **Raimat Abadia** plus Cabernet Sauvignon, Chardonnay and *cava*.

Rain distiller and vodka brand of Kentucky, USA. 'The first organic vodka – quadruple distilled from organically grown American grain and pure Kentucky limestone water.'

Rainbow Cocktail. Into a liqueur glass, pouring gently to prevent ingredients mixing, put 1 part crème de cacao, 1 crème de violette, 1 yellow Chartreuse, 1 maraschino, 1 Bénédictine, 1 green Chartreuse, 1 brandy.

Rainbow Inn brewery at Coventry, West Midlands, England.

Rainbow Room Coffee Cocktail. Over ice shake 1 part port, 1 brandy, yolk of 1 small egg, 1 teaspoon sugar. Strain.

Rainbow's End Cocktail. Over ice shake 2 parts apricot brandy, 1 cherry brandy, 1 banana liqueur, 1 tablespoon fresh cream. Strain.

Rainbow Trout Stout beer by Hubcap Brewery, Vail, Colorado, USA.

Rainier Ale beer by Rainier brewery, Seattle, Washington, USA.

Rainwater light and medium-dry style of madeira wine. Madeira, Portugal.

Raker Bitter ale by Wadworth brewery, Devizes, Wiltshire, England.

raki fiery spirit of the Middle East (especially Turkey) and Far East, based variously in alcohol from wine or fermented dates, figs, palm sap or rice. Often flavoured with anis. Name comes from the Arabic for 'juice' or 'sweat'. Alternative names are arrack and arraki.

Rakovanka dark lager by **Rakovnik** brewery, est 1454, Czech Republic.

Rallo & Figli, Diego marsala and table-wine producer, Sicily, Italy.

Ramage-la-Bâtisse, Château wine estate of AC Haut-Médoc, Bordeaux, France. Classified *Cru Bourgeois*.

Ramandolo white wine from Verduzzo grapes of DOC Colli Orientali del Friuli, Friuli-Venezia Giulia, Italy.

Ramazotti brandy distiller of Lainate, Milan, Italy. Brandy Ramazotti 7-year-old and Brandy Riserva Ramazotti.

Ram Brewery famed brewery of Young & Co, Wandsworth, London, England.

Rame, Château La wine estate of AC Ste-Croix-du-Mont, Bordeaux, France.

Ramisco red grape variety of Colares, Portugal. Sole constituent of the strange red wine.

Ramitello red and white wine brand of Di Majo Norante, Molise, Abruzzi, Italy.

Ramondon, Château de wine estate of AC Premières Côtes de Bordeaux, France.

Ramonet-Prudhon wine producer in Chassagne-Montrachet, Côte de Beaune, Burgundy, France. Renowned white wines from *Grands Crus* Bâtard-Montrachet and Bienvenues-Bâtard-Montrachet.

Ramos-Pinto port shipper est 1880 by Adriano Ramos-Pinto and now French-owned, Vila Nova de Gaia, Portugal. Old tawnies, white ports and vintages: 1960, 63, 64, 70, 75, 77, 82, 83, 84, 85, 91, 94, 97, 2000, 03.

see label opposite ➡

Rampant Ram seasonal (spring) beer (4.3% alc) by Hydes brewery, Manchester, England. 'Brewed using choicest Pudge Fuggle bittering and aroma hops.'

RamRod bottled ale by Young's brewers, London, England.

Ram Tam 'old ale' by Timothy Taylor brewery, Keighley, Yorkshire, England.

rancio in winetasting, a smell and taste characterising old fortified wines. Also used to describe the 'burnt' flavour of fine old brandies, especially cognac. Spanish.

Randall, RW brewery on Guernsey, Channel Islands, UK.

Ranina regional name for Bouvier grape variety, Hungary.

Ranzenberg vineyards at Ellhofen and Weinsberg in Württemberg region, Germany.

Rapitalà wine producer of Sicily, Italy. Bianco Alcamo brand.

Raposeira sparkling-wine producer of Lamego, Portugal.

Rappen vineyard at Ilsfeld in Württemberg region, Germany.

Rapsani red wine of Mount Olympus, Thessaly, Greece.

Rasp-beret lager brand of the Paris Real Ale Brewery, France.

raspberries in winetasting, a smell indicating a young red wine of freshness and quality, especially from Pinot Noir grapes.

Rasteau village of AC Côtes du Rhône Villages. Red and white wines plus a *vin doux naturel*.

Rat and Ratchet brewery at Huddersfield, West Yorkshire, England.

ratafia wine-country aperitif from grape brandy added to grape juice. Burgundy and Champagne regions of France and under different names in other regions. Name allegedly comes from Roman *rata fiat*, a toast to the ratification of an agreement.

Rathausberg vineyard at Bruttig-Fankel in Mosel-Saar-Ruwer region, Germany.

Ratsgrund vineyard at Sommerloch in Nahe region, Germany.

Ratsherr vineyard at Volkach mit Orsteil Fahr in Franken region, Germany.

Ratti, Renato wine producer at Abbazia dell'Annunziata, Piedmont, Italy. Renowned Barbaresco, Barolo etc.

Rattler Cocktail. Over ice shake 4 parts rye whisky, 1 lemon juice, 2 dashes pastis, 1 teaspoon sugar, 1 egg white. Strain.

Rattlesnake Cocktail. Over ice shake 1 egg white, 4 parts rye whisky, 1 lemon juice, 2 dashes pastis, 1 teaspoon sugar. Strain.

Rauchbier 'smoked beer' in which malts have been kiln-dried over fire rather than conventional hot air. German.

Rauchenfels Steinbier 'stone beer' variation of smoke beer by Neustadt brewery, Bavaria, Germany. Companion brand is bottle-conditioned wheat beer **Rauchenfels Steinweizen**.

Rauenegg vineyard at Ravensburg in Würrtemberg region, Germany.

Rauenthal wine village of Rheingau region, Germany. *Grosslage*: Steinmächer. Vineyards include Baiken, Gehrn, Langenstuck etc. Producers include Lanwerth von Simmern, Schloss Schönborn.

Raul vineyard at Konz in Mosel-Saar-Ruwer region, Germany.

Rausan-Ségla, Château wine estate of AC Margaux, Médoc, Bordeaux, France. Classified *2ème Grand Cru Classé*.

Rausch vineyard at Saarburg in Mosel-Saar-Ruwer region, Germany.

Rauschelay vineyard at Kaub in Mittelrhein region, Germany.

Raux, Château du wine estate of AC Haut-Médoc, Bordeaux, France.

Rauzan-Gassies, Château wine estate of AC Margaux, Médoc, Bordeaux, France. Classified *2ème Grand Cru Classé*.

Ravello town and wine-producing district of Campania, Italy. Red and *rosato* wines from Aglianico, Pere Palummo and Merlot grapes, whites from Coda di Volpe, Greco and San Nicola.

Raven ale by Orkney Brewery, Scotland.

Raveneau, François wine producer of Chablis, Burgundy, France. Wines from *Grand Cru* vineyards Blanchots, Les Clos and Valmur as well as from *premiers crus*.

Ravensburg *Grosslage* incorporating vineyards at Erlabrunn, Günters-leben, Leinach, Thüngersheim, Veitshöchheim, Zellingen and Zellingen (Retzbach) in Franken region, Germany.

Rawhide 'bourbon-style' whiskey by Suntory, Japan.

Raw Passion vodka-based passion fruit 'cocktail' by Welsh Distillers Ltd, Brecon, Wales. Variations include Caribbean Passion, Tropical Passion, Wild Passion.

raya in sherry-making, a cask mark indicating the style of the developing wine. Butts with *flor*, and destined to produce *fino* and *amontillado* sherries, are marked with one *raya*; butts in which no *flor* is present and which are destined for *oloroso*, are marked with two *rayas*.

Rayas, Château leading wine estate of AC Châteauneuf-du-Pape, Rhône Valley, France.

Ray Long Cocktail. Over ice shake 2 parts brandy, 1 sweet vermouth, 4 dashes pastis, 1 dash Angostura bitters. Strain.

Raymond Ragnaud, Madame distinguished Grande Champagne cognac grower-producer at Le Château Ambleville, Barbezieux, France. Cognacs under Le Château Ambleville label.

Raymond, Château wine estate of AC Entre-Deux-Mers, Bordeaux, France.

Raymond Hitch Cocktail. Over ice shake 2 parts sweet vermouth, 1 orange juice, 1 dash orange bitters, 1 slice pineapple. Strain.

Raymond-Lafon, Château wine estate of AC Sauternes, Bordeaux, France. Classified *Cru Bourgeois*.

Rayne Sec dry white wine of Château de Rayne-Vigneau, Bordeaux, France.

Rayne-Vigneau, Château wine estate of AC Sauternes, Bordeaux, France. Classified *1er Cru Classé*.

RCH brewery at West Hewish, North Somerset, England. Initials are for Royal Clarence Hotel, the pub in Burnham on Sea, Somerset, that was the original brewery site. RCH beers include Ale Mary, East Street, Firebox, Hewish IPA, Old Slug Porter, PG Steam Bitter, Pitchfork.

RD *Récemment Dégorgé*. 'Recently disgorged' champagne brand of Bollinger, Aÿ, France.

Real Companhia Vinícola do Norte de Portugal formerly the state-run governing body of the port trade, long since evolved into the largest port shipper, Vila Nova de Gaia, Portugal. Trades as Royal Oporto Wine Co.

Real Mackay, The blended scotch whisky by Mackay & Co, Guernsey, Channel Is, UK.

Real Mackenzie, The blended scotch whisky by Peter Mackenzie, Perth, Scotland.

Real Nut Ale beer (4.5% alc) by Tisbury Brewery, Wiltshire, England. 'Brewed from four different hop varieties and from real chestnuts to give a complex, rich, earthy taste.'

Rebellion lager by Upper Canada brewery, Toronto, Canada.

Rebellion Beer brand of the Marlow Brewery, Marlow, Buckinghamshire, England.

Rebello Valente vintage port brand of Robertson brothers, Vila Nova de Gaia, Portugal.

Rebstöckel *Grosslage* incorporating vineyards at Neustadt an der Weinstrasse on two sites, Deidesfeld and Hambach in Rheinpfalz region, Germany.

Rebtal vineyard at Freiburg in Baden region, Germany.

Rechbächel vineyard at Wachenheim in the Rheinpfalz region, Germany.

Recioto specialised wine from dried grapes unique to white Soave and red Valpolicella of Veneto, Italy. Concentrated in flavour – sweet for the white wine, sweet or *amarone* (dry) for the red.

récoltant manipulant 'grower-producer'. In Champagne, France, a grape grower who makes and markets champagne from his own vineyard.

récolte (grape) harvest. French.

Rectory Ales parochial brewery of Plumpton, Novington and East Chiltington, East Sussex, England. Beers include **Rector's Revenge** and Parson's Porter.

Redback beer brand of Matilda Bay Brewing Co, Freemantle, Western Australia. Name evinces that of Australia's notoriously venomous arachnid. Wheat beers **Redback Light** and **Redback Original**.

Redback Brewery Foster's-owned brewery in Melbourne, Victoria, Australia, known for Matilda Bay Pils lager.

red biddy long-lost concocted drink of cheap red wine and brandy – a do-it-yourself 'port'.

Red Cluster apple variety traditionally valued for cider-making. English.

Red Cross brewery at Bromsgrove, Worcestershire, England.

Red Cuillin pale ale (4.2% alc) by Isle of Skye Brewery, Scotland. Named after the island's hill range.

Red Flag Cocktail. Over ice shake 1 part dry gin, 1 rum, 1 lemon juice, 1 pineapple juice, 1 dash grenadine. Strain.

Red Fox autumn 'tawny red' ale (4.3% alc), brewed with toasted oats, by Fuller's brewery, London, England.

Redhook brewery in Seattle, Washington, USA. Well-known ales include **Redhook Ale**, **Redhook ESB**.

Red Infuriator elusive red-wine brand of Coteau de Tlemcen, Algeria.

Red Lion brewery at Llandloes, Powys, England.

Red Lion Cocktail. Over ice shake 2 parts Grand Marnier, 1 dry gin, 1 lemon juice, 1 orange juice. Strain.

Red MacGregor beer (5.0% alc) by Orkney Brewery, Quoyloo, Sandwick, Orkney, UK.

Red Misket white grape variety of Bulgaria.

Red-pear pear variety traditionally valued for perry-making. English.

Red Rock cider by Taunton Cider, Somerset, England. Memorable 1990s advertising slogan: 'It isn't red, and it doesn't have any rocks in it.'

Red Rock Ale beer by Triple Rock brewery, Berkeley, California, USA.

Redruth brewery at Redruth, Cornwall, England.

Red Square Ready-to-drink brand based on a blend of Red Bull and vodka. Ingredients include citric acids, ginseng and caffeine and different flavourings include blueberry, cranberry, lemon, lime, loganberry, wolfberry.

Red Stripe lager brand (4.7% alc) of HP Bulmer, Hereford, England.

Red Trolley ale by Old Columbia brewery, California, USA.

Red Witch Cocktail. Over ice shake 2 parts Pernod, 1 blackcurrant cordial. Strain into small wine glasses and top with chilled dry sparkling cider.

Redwood Valley wine district of Mendocino County, California, USA.

Red Velvet Canadian whisky brand of Gilbey Canada.

Reepham brewery at Reepham, Norfolk, England.

Reform Cocktail. Over ice stir 2 parts dry sherry, 1 dry vermouth, 1 dash orange bitters. Strain.

Refresh UK Brewing company of Oxford, England, incorporating Wychwood Brewery.

Regaleali wine brand of Conte Tasca d'Almerita, Vallelunga, Sicily, Italy. White, red and rosato wines, but it is the Bianco that is best known, for its spritzy freshness.

Regency spirit brand of Pernod-Ricard.

Regent popular dark lager brand, Prague, Czech Republic.

Reggenhag vineyard at Müllheim in Baden region, Germany.

régisseur traditional title of wine-estate manager, Bordeaux, France.

Régnard & Fils, A *négociants-éleveurs* of Chablis, Burgundy, France.

Regner white grape variety chiefly of Rheinhessen region, Germany.

Régnié village and latest-created (1988) wine *cru* and AC of Beaujolais region, Burgundy, France.

Reh und Söhne, Franz wine grower and shipper of Mosel-Saar-Ruwer region, Germany.

Rehbach collective vineyard (*Grosslage*) at Nierstein in Rheinhessen region, Germany.

rehoboam champagne bottle format equal to six standard bottles. Named after regional king of Israel, 10th century BC.

Reichelbräu   Aktien-Gesellschaft brewery est 1846 and beer brand of Kulmbach, Germany. Famed for **Reichelbräu Eisbock** lager.

Reichensteiner white grape variety of Germany now also grown in England.

Reichesthal vineyards at Hochheim and Mainz in Rheingau region, Germany.

Reichsgraf von Kesselstatt leading wine producer of Mosel-Saar-Ruwer region, Germany. Noted Scharzhofberger Rieslings.

Reichshalde vineyards at Knittlingen, Knittlingen (Freudenstein) and Maulbronn in Württemberg region, Germany.

Reichskeller vineyard at Freilaubersheim in Rheinhessen region, Germany.

Reichsritterstift vineyard at Bodenheim in Rheinhessen region, Germany.

Reifenstein vineyard at Sommerhausen in Franken region, Germany.

Reifersley vineyard at Niederheimbach in Mittelrhein region, Germany.

Reif Estate wine producer at Niagara-on-the-Lake, Ontario, Canada.

Reil wine village of Mosel-Saar-Ruwer region, Germany. *Grosslage*: Vom Heissen Stein. Vineyards include Goldlay.

Reims historic capital of Champagne region, France.

reineclaude *eau de vie* distilled from greengages. France and Switzerland.

Reinheitsgebot German Beer Purity Law, originally of 1516. The forerunner of all brewing-standards legislation.

Reinig auf der Burg vineyard at Wasserliesch in Mosel-Saar-Ruwer region, Germany.

Reininghaus-Puntigam brewery and beer brand, Graz, Austria.

Reinisch, Johann & Johannes wine producer in Thermenregion, Niederösterreich, Austria.

Reinprecht, Hans wine producer in Neusiedlersee Hügelland, Burgenland, Austria.

Reinprecht, Hugo wine producer in Wien (Vienna), Austria.

Reischklingberg vineyard at Grossostheim in Franken region, Germany.

Reissdorf *Kölschbier* brand, Cologne, Germany.

Reiterer, Christian wine producer in Weststeiermark, Austria.

Reiterpfad vineyard at Neustadt an der Weinstrasse and Ruppertsberg in Rheinpfalz region, Germany.

Reitsteig vineyard at Castell in Franken region, Germany.

Reliance blended scotch whisky by Forbes, Farquarson & Co, Perth, Scotland.

Remeyerhof vineyard at Worms in Rheinhessen region, Germany.

Remoissenet Père et Fils wine growers and *négociants-éleveurs* of Beaune, Burgundy, France.

remontage in winemaking, the process of maximising the extraction of colour and tannin from grape skins by pumping the fermenting juice through the 'cap' that forms at the top of the fermenting vessel. French.

Remstal-Stuttgart *Bereich* of Württemberg region, Germany.

Remsen Cooler Cocktail. Carefully peel 1 lemon to form a continuous spiral of rind. Place, with ice, in a tall glass. Add generous measure gin and top with soda water.

remuage in champagne-making, the technique of gradually easing the detritus from the secondary fermentation into the neck of the bottle prior to expelling it. Bottles are put horizontally into *pupitres* in which they can be fractionally turned and tilted daily by a *remueur* until they are up-ended. Champagne, France. This laborious process is now commonly carried out by machines called *giropalettes*, within and without the Champagne region.

Remy, Château wine estate at Avoca, Victoria, Australia.

Rémy Martin renowned cognac house est 1724 Cognac, France. Brands include VSOP, XO Special, Extra and Louis XIII 50-year-old.

Remy Pannier wine growers and *négociants-éleveurs* of Anjou, Loire Valley, France.

Renaissance Cocktail. Over ice shake 1 part dry gin, 1 dry sherry, 1 tablespoon fresh cream, Strain and sprinkle a pinch of ground nutmeg over.

Renault cognac house est 1835, Cognac, France. Acquired by Pernod-Ricard, 2001.

Renchtäler the name of 12 individual vineyards in Baden region, Germany at, respectively: Appenweier, Lautenbach, Oberkirch (Bottenau), Oberkirch (Haslach), Oberkirch (Nussbach), Oberkirch (Ödsbach), Oberkirch (Ringelbach), Oberkirch (Stadelhofen), Oberkirch (Tiergarten), Renchen (Erlach), Renchen (Ulm).

rendement the yield (quantity of made wine) expected from a given vineyard. French.

René Briand brandy formerly of Seagram Italia, Segrate, Italy.

René, Clos wine estate of AC Pomerol, Bordeaux, France.

Renmano large-scale wine producer, Riverlands district, South Australia.

Renner, Helmut wine producer in Neusiedlersee, Burgenland, Austria.

reposado stored for maturing purposes, Spanish. Most tequila in Mexico is thus designated. The description is often elaborated as *reposado en barricas de roble blanco* (aged in oak barrels).

reserva wine-quality term of Portugal and Spain. In Rioja and other Spanish regions signifies wine of a good vintage which has had at least one year's ageing in oak cask and two in bottle. Portuguese *reservas* have fractionally higher alcohol content than their humbler counterparts, but age does not come into it.

Réserve de la Comtesse second wine of Château Pichon-Longueville Comtesse de Lalande, Bordeaux, France.

Réserve du Brasseur *bière de garde* by St Arnould brewery, Lille, France.

Réserve du Marquis d'Evry second wine of Château de Lamarque, Bordeaux, France.

residual sugar in winemaking, the unfermented fructose remaining after yeast-action has ceased. In sweet wines, residual sugar is commonly measured at 100 to 200 grammes per litre of the finished wine.

Resolute Cocktail. Over ice shake 2 parts dry gin, 1 apricot brandy, 1 lemon juice. Strain.

Respide, Château de wine estate of AC Graves, Bordeaux, France.

Respide-Médeville, Château wine estate of AC Graves, Bordeaux, France.

Ress, Balthasar wine estate and shipper of Rheingau region, Germany. Vineyards include Geisenheim, Oestrich, Rüdesheim.

Restalrig 'village brewery' in Edinburgh, Scotland.

Retout, Château de wine estate of AC Haut-Médoc, Bordeaux, France. Classified *Cru Bourgeois*.

retsina white wine of mainland and islands of Greece with characteristic aroma and flavour from Alep pine resin. Custom of flavouring the wine in this way is believed to derive from the pine-resin sealants used by ancient Greeks to keep amphorae of wine airtight.

Retzl, Erwin wine producer in Kamptal, Niederösterreich, Austria.

Reuilly village and AC of central Loire Valley, France. Red wine from Pinot Noir grapes, rosé from Pinot Gris, white from Sauvignon Blanc.

Reumann, Josef & Maria wine producer in Mittelburgenland, Austria.

Reumann Grenzlandhof wine producer in Mittelburgenland, Austria.

Reuschberg collective vineyard (*Grosslage*) at Alzenau in Franken region, Germany.

Revernz lager by Fischer/Ueli brewery, Basel, Switzerland.

Reverie Cocktail. Over ice shake 2 parts dry gin, 1 Dubonnet, 1 Van der Hum, 1 dash orange juice. Strain.

Reynella, Château first wine estate est 1838 by John Reynell in South Australia, in Southern Vales district. Table wines and 'Vintage Port'.

Reynier, Château wine estate of AC Entre-Deux-Mers, Bordeaux, France.

Reynon, Château wine estate of AC Premières Côtes de Bordeaux, France.

Reysson, Château wine estate of AC Haut-Médoc, Bordeaux, France. Classified *Cru Bourgeois*.

Rheinberg vineyards at Ehlberg in Rheingau region and Oberdiebach in Mittelrhein region, Germany.

Rheinblick *Grosslage* incorporating vineyards at Alsheim, Dorn-Dürkheim and Mettenheim in Rheinhessen region, Germany.

Rheinblick vineyards at Münster-Sarmsheim in Nahe region and Osthofen and Worms in Rheinhessen region, Germany.

Rheingarten vineyards at Eltville (Ehrbach) and Eltville (Hattenheim) in Rheingau region, Germany.

Rheingasse vineyard at Lettweiler in Nahe region, Germany.

Rheingau northernmost and arguably greatest Rhineland wine region of Germany. One *Bereich*, 'Johannisberg' which applies to the entire region, ten *Grosslagen* and many of Germany's most-renowned *Einzellagen* (individual vineyard sites) and producers, eg Schloss Johannisberg, Schloss Vollrads etc.

Rheingoldberg vineyard at Niederburg in Mittelrhein region, Germany.

Rheingrafenberg vineyards at Freilaubersheim and Wörrstadt in Rheinhessen region and Meddersheim in Nahe region, Germany.

Rheingrafenstein *Grosslage* incorporating vineyards in Rheinhessen region, Germany at, respectively: Eckelsheim, Freilaubersheim, Fürfeld, Hackenheim, Neu-Bamberg, Pleitersheim, Siersheim, Stein-Bockenheim, Tiefenthal, Volxheim, Wöllstein, Wonsheim.

Rheinhell vineyard at Eltville in Rheingau region, Germany.

Rheinhessen largest wine region of Germany. Three *Bereichen*: Bingen, Nierstein, Wonnegau. Much production of ordinary wines from Müller Thurgau grapes such as Liebfraumilch but fine Riesling wines from vineyards centred on riverside villages such as Dienheim, Nackenheim and Nierstein.

Rheinhöhle vineyard at Ingelheim in Rheinhessen region, Germany.

Rheinhöller vineyard at Linz in Mittelrhein region, Germany.

Rheinnieder vineyards at Urbar and Vallendar in Mittelrhein region, Germany.

Rheinpfalz southernmost and most-productive of the three major Rhineland wine regions of Germany. *Bereichen*: Mittelhaardt Deutscher Weinstrasse, Südliche Weinstrasse. Large-scale production of Liebfraumilch etc from Müller-Thurgau grapes but renowned Riesling wines from central Mittelhaardt region – villages include Deidesheim, Forst, Ruppertsberg.

Rheinpforte vineyard at Selzen in Rheinhessen region, Germany.

Rhenania *Altbier* by Krefeld brewery, Düsseldorf, Germany.

Rhine Wine Punch in punch bowl mix the following ingredients, all of which should be chilled beforehand: 3 litres German wine, 1 litre sparkling mineral water, 1 glass brandy, 1 glass maraschino. Immerse 1 teabag in mixture for 10 minutes before adding fruit slices and serving.

Rhodes wine-producing Aegean island of Greece. Red wines from Amorgiano grapes, whites from Athiri, sweet wines from Muscat.

Rhoditis white grape variety of Greece. Retsina.

Rhomberg lager by Dubuque brewery, Iowa, USA.

Rhône Valley great wine-producing region of France extending southwards from Vienne to Arles. Along the way, famed ACs include Côte Rôtie, Condrieu, Crozes-Hermitage, Hermitage, St-Joseph, Cornas, St Péray in northern part of the valley and in the south, Tricastin, Rasteau, Gigondas, Beaumes-de-Venise, Vacqueyras, Châteauneuf-du-Pape, Lirac, Tavel. The wines of ACs Côtes du Rhône and Côtes du Rhône Villages are from the southern part of the valley. For red wines of the north, Syrah grapes predominate, and for whites, Marsanne, Roussanne and Viognier. In the south, Grenache and several other varieties are grown alongside Syrah.

rhum vieux oak-aged rum intended for sipping undiluted as an apéritif. Examples include Rhum Vieux Agricole of island of Martinique. French.

Rias Bajas DO for white wines from Albarino grapes, Galicia, Spain.

Riband wheat variety valued for malting by brewers.

Ribatejo wine-producing province north of Lisbon, Portugal.

Ribeauvillé wine town of Alsace, France.

Ribeira Sacra DO for red and white wines of Lugo region, NW Spain.

Ribeiro DO for red and white wines of Galicia, Spain.

Ribera del Duero DO wine region of NW Spain. Rich red wines from Tinto Aragonés and Tinto Fino grapes. Renowned brands include costly Vega Sicilia.

Ribollo white grape variety and wine of DOC Orientali del Friuli, Friuli-Venezia Giulia, Italy.

Ricard leading pastis brand of France, launched 1932. Recipe is based on aniseed eau de vie, liquorice and herbs. See box.   *see label opposite* ➡

Ricasoli leading wine producer of Chianti Classico, Tuscany, Italy. Firm was est 1850s by Florentine Baron Bettino Ricasoli, prime minister of Italy. Ricasoli spent his retirement years on the family estate at Castello Brolio, formulating the method by which chianti is still made.

Ricaud, Château de wine estate of AC Loupiac, Bordeaux, France.

Riccadonna marsala, sparkling wine and vermouth producer of Italy.

Richebourg *Grand Cru* vineyard of Vosne-Romanée, Burgundy, France.

Richelieu, Château wine estate of AC Fronsac, Bordeaux, France.

Richlieu brandy by Oude Meester distillers, South Africa.

Richmond Cocktail. Over ice stir 2 parts dry gin, 1 Lillet. Strain and squeeze lemon peel over.

Rich's farmhouse cider producer at Watchfield, Somerset, England, est 1953 by Gordon Rich.

Ridge great wine estate on Monte Bello Ridge, Santa Cruz Mountains, California, USA. Famed Cabernet Sauvignon wines.

Ridley, TD brewery in Chelmsford, Essex, England. Bishop's Ale, Essex Ale, HE Bitter.

Riecine small but renowned wine estate at Gaiole, Chianti Classico, Tuscany, Italy.

Ried individual vineyard entitled to nomination on wine label. Austria.

Ricard

spirit of entrepreneurialism

The name on France's leading brand of pastis, and one of the world's biggest-selling spirits, is that of Paul Louis Marius Ricard, born into a family of wine merchants in Marseilles in 1909. For much of Paul's childhood, pastis was banned under French law, because of its alleged similarity to absinthe, but this did not discourage the enterprising young man from experimenting with a recipe he claimed to have obtained from an old Provençal peasant. By the time the ban on the liquor was repealed in 1932, Ricard was in full production – in the cellar beneath a hairdressing salon.

Sales, in competition with long-established Pernod, boomed until 1940 when the puppet Vichy government reinstated the interdict. After Liberation in 1945 it took four more years of vigorous campaigning by Ricard to lift the ban. Advertising remained proscribed, and Ricard set about a remarkable campaign of 'below the line' promotional activity to promulgate his name, and thus his product. He had Ricard pastis delivered to cafés in central Paris by camel train, himself at the head; he had himself featured in the press in the guise of horsebreeder, aesthete and paternalistic employer. On one occasion he took all 1500 of his workers to Rome to be blessed by the Pope. The Paul Ricard motor racing circuit is the venue of France's Formula One Grand Prix.

The company grew exponentially and began to take over others before merging with Pernod in 1975 to form what is now one of the largest drinks corporations worldwide. Paul Ricard died in 1997, aged eighty-eight, and his pastis still carries the slogan he coined when it made its legal début on the market in 1932: *Un peu de soleil en bouteille.* ❦

Riedenburger organic brewery in Bavaria, Germany, known for pale lager.

Riedersbückele vineyard at Lauffen in Württemberg region, Germany.

Riegelfeld vineyard at Bad Neuenahr-Ahrweiler in Ahr region, Germany.

Riegelnegg, Otto wine producer in Südsteiermark, Austria.

Rieschen vineyard at Meersburg in Baden region, Germany.

Rieslaner white grape variety of Franken region, Germany. Cross between Riesling and Silvaner.

Riesling noble white grape variety of Germany, often called Rhine Riesling. Also important in Alsace, France and, increasingly, in the New World. Other 'Riesling' varieties such as Weschriesling or Laski Rizling, are not comparable.

Riesling Italico synonym for Welschriesling, Italy.

Riesling Renano regional name for Riesling grape variety, Italy.

Riesling-Silvaner synonym for the Müller-Thurgau grape in New Zealand and Switzerland.

Rieussec, Château great wine estate of AC Sauternes, Bordeaux, France. Classified *1er Cru Classé*.

Rigal wine grower and *négociant-éleveur* of AC Cahors, SW France. Owner of Château St-Didier at Parnac.

Riggwelter Strong Yorkshire Ale (5.7% alc) by Black Sheep Brewery, Masham, North Yorkshire, England. 'Riggwelter: from the Old Norse *rygg* – back – and *velte* – to overturn. When a sheep is on its back and cannot get up without help, local dales dialect says it's *rigged* or *riggwelted*.'

Rignes beer brand of Rignes brewery, Norway. **Rignes Gold Extra Strong** (6.4% alc).

Rikki-Tikki-Tavi Cocktail. Into a champagne flute place 1 sugar lump soaked with Angostura bitters, 1 teaspoon curaçao, 1 teaspoon brandy. Top with chilled champagne.

Riley's Rye rye beer by Steelhead brewery, Eugene, Oregon, USA.

Rimski vodka brand of Hiram Walker & Sons, Canada.

rince cochon aperitif of Beaujolais region, France. Cassis liqueur and red beaujolais. Name means 'pig-swill'.

Ringnes brewery in Oslo, Norway.

Ringwood brewery in Ringwood, Hampshire, England. Fortyniner and Old Thumper ales.

Rioja DOCa (Denominación de Origen Calificada) wine region of northern Spain. Red wines renowned for rich, oaky flavours gained from cask ageing over varying periods, defined in ascending durations as *joven, sin crianza, con crianza, reserva* and *gran reserva*, plus bottle-ageing before release. Grape varieties chiefly Tempranillo (57% of the total), Garnacha, Graciano, Mazuelo. White wines

from Viura, Malvasia and Garnache Blanca grapes. The region has 17,000 individual growers and 398 registered wineries. Some producers label their wines only with the *cosecha* (vintage) and not with the classifications *crianza*, *reserva* etc, even though the wines would qualify.

Rioja Alavesa district of Rioja region, Spain. Reputed to produce the finest wines.

Rioja Alta district of Rioja region, Spain.

Rioja Alta, La Rioja *bodega* of Haro in Rioja Alta district, Spain. Noted wines include Viña Ardanza and '904' *reserva*.

Rioja Baja largest district forming SE section of Rioja region, Spain. Less-valued wines than those of Alavesa and Alta districts.

Riojanes, Bodegas wine producer of Rioja region, Spain. Known for Monte Real red and other brands.

Rio Negro wine-producing province of Argentina.

Ripaille wine *cru* of Savoie, France.

ripasso stage of winemaking process of Valpolicella, Veneto, Italy. In spring following vintage, new wine is pumped briefly on to lees of *recioto*, the specialised wine made from dried grapes, to give it the characteristic tang of Valpolicella.

Ripeau, Château wine estate of AC St-Emilion, Bordeaux, France. Classified *Grand Cru Classé*.

Riquewihr important wine town of Alsace, France. Great vineyards include Schoenenberg and Sporen, and several famous producers are headquartered in the town.

riserva in most regions of Italy, a wine aged longer in cask and/or bottle than is strictly required under DOC and DOCG rules.

riserva speciale occasional refinement of *riserva*, Italy. Implies period of ageing even longer than is customary for a region's *riserva* wines.

Rising Sun brew pub at Audley, Stoke-on-Trent, Staffordshire, England.

Ritsch vineyard at Thörnich in Mosel-Saar-Ruwer region, Germany.

Rittenhouse Cocktail. Over ice shake 2 parts bourbon, 1 crème de cacao, 1 fresh cream. Strain.

Ritterberg vineyard at Schornsheim in Rheinhessen region, Germany.

Ritter Bock seasonal (Lent) lager by Kaltenberg brewery, Bavaria, Germany.

Ritter Export lager by Dortmunder Union brewery, Dortmund, Germany.

Rittergarten vineyard at Bad Dürkheim in Rheinpfalz region, Germany.

Ritterhalde vineyard at Gailingen in Baden region, Germany.

Ritterhölle vineyard at Dalberg in Nahe region, Germany.

Ritterpfad vineyards at Kanzem and Wawern in Mosel-Saar-Ruwer region, Germany.

Rittersberg *Grosslage* incorporating vineyards in Baden region, Germany at, respectively: Dossenheim, Heidelberg, Hemsbach, Hirschberg (Grossachsen), Hirschberg Leutershausen), Laudenbach, Schriesheim, Weinheim, Weinheim (Hohensachsen), Weinheim (Lützelsachsen), Weinheim (Sulzbach).

Rittersberg vineyard at Ilbesheim in Rheinpfalz region, Germany.

Riunite major agglomeration of wine co-operatives of Emilia-Romagna region, Italy. Industrial quantities of Lambrusco for export.

Riva brewing company of Dentergem, Belgium. Owner of Liefmans brewery, Oudenaarde.

Riva, La sherry producer and shipper est 1776, Jerez de la Frontera, Spain. Owned by Domecq. Tres Palmas fino, Guadaloupe amontillado, Oloroso Riva (from solera est 1830).

Rivalerie, Château La wine estate of AC Premières Côtes de Blaye, Bordeaux, France.

Rivaner regional name for Müller-Thurgau grape variety, Luxembourg.

Rivanis Normandy pastis brand of Prodis Boissons, Bayeaux, France.

Riverhead brewery at Marsden, West Yorkshire, England.

Riverina preferred name for Murrumbidgee Irrigation Area, a wine district of New South Wales, Australia.

Riverland wine district of Murray Valley, South Australia.

Rivero, JM believed to be oldest sherry house, est 1653 or earlier, Jerez de la Frontera, Spain. Rivero 'CZ' brand is now shipped by Antonio Núñez.

Riverside brewery at Pallion, Sunderland, Tyne & Wear, England.

Riverside wine district south of Los Angeles, California, USA.

Rivesaltes AC for *vin doux naturel* of Pyrénées Orientales, SW France.

Riviera del Garda di Bresciano DOC for red wines from Groppello,

Sangiovese and Barbera grapes, Brescia region, Lombardy, Italy.

Rivière, Château de la leading wine estate of AC Fronsac, France.

Rizling Szilvani regional name for Müller-Thurgau grape variety, Hungary.

RM on champagne labels, indicates producer is a *récoltant-manipulant*, a grower who also makes the wine.

Road Runner Cocktail. Over ice shake 2 parts vodka, 1 amaretto, 1 coconut liqueur.

Roaix wine village of AC Côte du Rhône Villages, France.

robe in winetasting, the appearance and colour of the wine. French.

Robert Brown blended whisky brand of Kirin Breweries, Japan.

Robert Cain brewery at Stanhope Stret, Liverpool, Merseyside, England.

Robert Mondavi Winery leading wine producer of Napa Valley, California, USA. Many famed wines from Cabernet Sauvignon, Chardonnay, Pinot Noir and other grapes varities.

see label opposite ➡

Robertson important Wine of Origin area of Breede River Valley, South Africa.

Robertson Brothers port shipper est 1847 Vila Nova de Gaia, Portugal. Old tawnies, Game Bird brand, vintages: 1955, 60, 63, 66, 67, 70, 72, 75, 77, 80, 83, 85, 87.

Robertson Winery booming wine co-operative of Robertson region, South Africa. Cabernet Sauvignon, Chardonnay, Muscadel and other wines on a big scale.

Robin, Jules cognac house est 1782, Cognac, France. XXX, VSOP etc and a leading producer of Pineau des Charentes.

Robin Hood ale brand of Home Brewery, Nottingham, England. Ceased production 1996.

Robinson, Frederick brewery in Stockport, Cheshire, England.

Robinvale wine producer in Murray River district, Victoria, Australia. Biodynamic methods.

Robinwood brewery in Todmorden, Yorkshire, England. Reputed to produce Old Fart ale.

roble oak, Spanish.

Rob Roy blended scotch whisky by Morrison Bowmore, Glasgow, Scotland.

Rob Roy Cocktail. Over ice stir 2 parts scotch whisky, 1 sweet vermouth, 1 dash Angostura bitters. Strain.

Robson Cocktail. Over ice shake 4 parts rum, 2 grenadine, 1 lemon juice, 1 orange juice. Strain.

robust in winetasting, a flavour with assertiveness and body.

Roc-a-Coe Cocktail. Over ice stir 1 part dry gin, 1 dry sherry. Strain and add cocktail cherry to glass.

Rocca delle Macie wine producer of Chianti Classico, Tuscany, Italy.

Roche, Château La wine estate of AC Premières Côtes de Bordeaux, France.

Roche, Clos de La large (38 acres) *Grand Cru* vineyard in Morey-St-Denis, Burgundy, France.

Roch-aux-Moines, La AC of Savennières, Loire Valley, France. Noted white wines from producers including Château de Chamboureau.

Rochefort abbey brewery, since 1595, of Abbaye de Notre-Dame de Saint-Rémy, Rochefort, Belgium. Three famed abbey ales numbered as per now-defunct original-gravity scale: **Rochefort 6** (red crown cap, 7.5% alc), **Rochefort 8** (green, 9.2%), **Rochefort 10** (black, 11.3%).

Rochefort-sur-Loire wine village of Coteaux du Layon, Loire Valley, France.

Rochemorin, Château de wine estate of AC Pessac-Léognan, Bordeaux, France.

Rocher, Château du wine estate of AC St-Emilion, Bordeaux, France. Classified *Grand Cru*.

Rocher-Bellevue, Château wine estate of AC Côtes du Castillon, Bordeaux, France.

Rochette, Château La second wine of Château des Laurets, Bordeaux, France.

Rocheuses, Côtes wine brand of Union des Producteurs St-Emilion, Bordeaux, France.

Rochioli wine estate in Russian River Valley, Sonoma County, California, USA.

Rochusfels vineyards at Nittel and Nittel (Köllig) in Mosel-Saar-Ruwer region, Germany.

Rockford wine brand of Tanunda Vintners, Barossa Valley, South Australia. Outstanding Eden Valley Riesling and Shiraz wines.

Rockies Brewing Co producer of Boulder beers. Boulder, Colorado, USA.

Rockley former sugar estate and distillery of Barbados. The original pot still continues in production in the West Indian Rum Refinery at Blackrock.

Rocky Mountain Cocktail. Over ice shake 1 part amaretto, 1 Southern Comfort. Strain.

Rödchen vineyard at Eltville in Rheingau region, Germany.

Rodenbach brewery in Roeselare, West Flanders, Belgium. Famed for dark red, wine-like **Rodenbach**, **Rodenbach Grand Cru** and **Alexander Rodenbach** ales.

Rodet, Antonin wine grower and *négociant-éleveur* of Mercurey, Côte Chalonnaise, Burgundy, France. Vineyards include Château de Chamirey, Château de Rully.

Rodger's Old Scots Brand blended scotch whisky by Slater, Rodger & Co, Hurlford, Ayrshire, Scotland. Also, **Rodger's Special**.

Roederer, Louis *Grande Marque* champagne house, Reims, France. Famed for Cristal vintage champagne in clear bottle, first made for Czar of Russia, 1876.

Roederer Estate sparkling wine producer in Anderson Valley, Mendocino, California, USA. Owned by Louis Roederer of Champagne, France.

Roero DOC for red wines chiefly from Nebbiolo grapes, Cuneo, Piedmont, Italy.

Roffignac, Comte Ferdinand de cognac producer at Cognac, France.

Roggen rye beer, Germany.

Rogue shared brand since 1988 of breweries at Ashland and at Newport, Oregon, USA. Brews include Rogue American Amber (5.3% alc), Rogue Artisan Vienna Lager (5.2% alc), Rogue Hazelnut Brown Nectar Ale (6.2% alc), Rogue Honey Cream Ale (5.3% alc).

Rogue Valley wine district of Oregon, USA.

Roi, Clos du second wine of Château La Louvière, Bordeaux, France.

Roi des Rois cognac brand of Unicognac co-operative, Cognac, France.

Rol, Château de wine estate of AC St-Emilion, Bordeaux, France. Classified *Grand Cru*.

Roland Rivière cognac grower-producer, Jonzac, France.

Rolin, Nicolas benefactor of Hospices de Beaune, Burgundy, France, commemorated in name of three *cuvées* of wine auctioned annually in the Hôtel Dieu, which he endowed in 1443.

Rolland, Château de wine estate of AC Barsac, Bordeaux, France. Classified *Cru Bourgeois*.

Rolle white grape variety of AC Bellet, Provence, France.

Rolling Rock popular beer of Latrobe Brewery, Pennsylvania, USA.

Rolls-Royce Cocktail. Over ice shake 2 parts dry gin, 1 dry vermouth, 1 sweet vermouth, 1 dash Bénédictine. Strain. Alternatively, over ice shake 2 parts vermouth, 1 dry gin, 1 whisky, 1 dash orange bitters. Strain. (Attrib. HE Bates, *The Darling Buds of May*, 1958.)

Roma Cocktail. Over ice stir 2 parts dry vermouth, 2 sweet vermouth, 1 Campari, 1 dry gin, 1 dash Strega. Strain and add slice of lemon to glass.

Roman brewery in Mater, Oudenaarde, Belgium. Ales include Dobbleden Bruinen and Oudenaardes.

Romanée, La *Grand Cru* vineyard, Vosne-Romanée, Côte de Nuits, Burgundy, France.

Romanée-Conti tiny 4-acre *Grand Cru* vineyard of Vosne-Romanée, Côte de Nuits, Burgundy, France. Owned by Domaine de La Romanée-Conti, and producing the world's most expensive wine – red, from Pinot Noir grapes.

Romanée-Conti, Domaine de La producer of several of the greatest red wines of Burgundy with holdings in *Grand Cru* vineyards of Echézeaux, Grands-Echézeaux, Richebourg and Romanée St-Vivant as well as all of La Romanée-Conti and La Tâche. Also owns part of *Grand Cru* Le Montrachet, source of Burgundy's greatest white wine.

Romanée St-Vivant *Grand Cru* vineyard, Vosne-Romanée, Côte de Nuits, Burgundy, France.

Romania major wine-producing nation. Many indigenous grape varieties and increasing plantings of French.

Roman Road Cocktail. Over ice shake 1 part rum, 1 brandy, 1 lemon juice, 1 teaspoon raspberry syrup. Strain.

Romassan, Château wine property of Domaines Ott in AC Bandol, Provence, France.

Römer traditional wine glass of Germany.

Römerberg

Römerberg the name of 23 individual vineyards in Germany. Region by region, as follows: in Baden at Badenweiler, Müllheim; in Mittelrhein at Oberheimbach, Rheinbrohl; in Mosel-Saar-Ruwer at Burgen, Nehren, Oberbillig, Perl, Riol. Senheim; in Nahe at Bingen, Weiler, Gutenberg, Merxheim, Münster-Sarmsheim, Waldböckelheim, Windesheim; in Rheingau at Alsheim; in Rheinhessen at Alzey, Badenheim, Dorn-Dürkheim, Engelstadt, Essenheim, Gutenberg.

Römerbrunnen vineyard at Neustadt an der Weinstrasse in Rheinpfalz region, Germany.

Romer-du-Hayot, Château wine estate of AC Sauternes, Bordeaux, France. Classified *2ème Cru Classé*.

Römergarten vineyard at Briedern in Mosel-Saar-Ruwer region, Germany.

Römerhalde vineyard at Bad Kreuznach in Nahe region, Germany.

Römerhang vineyard at Kinheim in Mosel-Saar-Ruwer region, Germany.

Römerkrug vineyards at Oberwesel and Oberwesel (Delhofen) in Mittelrhein region, Germany.

Römerlay *Grosslage* incorporating vineyards in Mosel-Saar-Ruwer region, Germany at, respectively: Franzenheim, Hockweiler, Kasel, Mertesdorf, Mertesdorf (Lorenzhof), Mertesdorf (Maximin Grünhaus), Morscheid, Plowig, Riveris, Sommerau, Trier, Trier (Biewer), Trier (Eitelsbach), Trier (Filsch), Trier (Irsch), Trier (Kernscheid), Trier (Korlingen), Trier (Kürenz), Trier (Matthias), Trier (Olewig), Trier (Ruwer), Trier (Tarforst), Waldrach.

Römerpfad vineyards at Unkenbach and Zell in Mosel-Saar-Ruwer region, Germany.

Römerquelle vineyard at Zell in Mosel-Saar-Ruwer region, Germany.

Römerschanze vineyard at Eimsheim in Rheinhessen region, Germany.

Römersteg vineyard at Worms in Rheinhessen region, Germany.

Römerstrasse vineyard at Kircheim an der Weinstrasse in Rheinpfalz region, Germany.

Römerweg vineyard at Kirrweiler in Rheinpfalz region, Germany.

ron rum, Spanish.

Ron Anejo Cacique rum brand formerly of Seagram, Costa Rica.

Ron Cabana rum brand of Pernod-Ricard.

Ronceray, Château de la wine estate of AC St-Estèphe, Bordeaux, France. Classified *Cru Bourgeois*.

Rondinella red grape variety of Veneto region, Italy. Bardolino and Valpolicella wines.

Ron Llave white rum brand formerly of Seagram, Puerto Rico.

Ron Montilla rum brand formerly of Seagram, Argentina.

Ron Paraiso Cuban aged rum brand of McKinley Vintners, UK.

Ronrico white rum brand formerly of Seagram, Puerto Rico.

Roodeberg red wine from Pinotage, Shiraz and Tinta Barocca grapes by KWV, South Africa.

Roosje Zonder Doornen rose-essence liqueur by van Zuylekom distillery, Amsterdam, Netherlands. Name means 'roses without thorns'.

Roosters brewery at Harrogate, North Yorkshire, England.

rootstock in viticulture, the roots of American vine species such as *vitis labrusca* on to which cuttings of the wine-grape producing vine *vitis vinifera* are grafted. *Vitis labrusca* and its kin are resistant to the phylloxera grub; *vitis vinifera* is not.

Ropiteau Frères *négoçiants-éleveurs* in Meursault, Burgundy, France.

Roque-de-By, Château La wine estate of AC Médoc, Bordeaux, France.

Roques, Château de wine estate of AC Puisseguin-St-Emilion, Bordeaux, France.

Roquetaillade-le-Bernet, Château second wine of Château Roquetaillade-la-Grange, Bordeaux, France.

Roquetaillade-la-Grange, Château wine estate of AC Graves, Bordeaux, France.

rosado pink (wine). Spanish.

Rosatello *rosato* wine from Sangiovese grapes, Tuscany, Italy.

rosato pink (wine). Italian.

Rose, Château de la wine estate of AC Entre-Deux-Mers, Bordeaux, France.

rosé pink (wine). French and English.

Rosebank Lowland malt whisky distillery est 1840, Falkirk, Stirlingshire, Scotland. Single malts: 12-year-old, 17-year-old.

Rosechatel, Château wine brand of Schröder & Schÿler, Bordeaux, France.

Rose Cocktail. Over ice stir 2 parts dry gin, 1 cherry brandy, 1 dry vermouth, 2 dashes lemon juice. Strain.

Rose-Côte-de-Rol, Château La- wine estate of AC St-Emilion, Bordeaux, France. Classified *Grand Cru*.

Rosé d'Anjou pink wine from Groslot and numerous other grape varieties, Anjou, Loire Valley, France.

Rose de Chambertin Cocktail. Over ice shake 3 parts dry gin, 1 crème de cassis, 1 fresh lime juice, 1 teaspoon beaten egg white, 1 teaspoon gomme syrup. Strain.

Rosé de Gambrinus lambic fruit (raspberry-cherry) beer by Cantillon brewery, Brussels, Belgium.

Rosé de Loire AC for pink wines in drier style than those of Rosé d'Anjou, Loire Valley, France.

Rosé des Riceys AC for still rosé wine from Pinot Noir grapes, Champagne, France.

Roselyn Cocktail. Over ice shake 2 parts dry gin, 1 dry vermouth, 2 dashes grenadine. Strain and squeeze lemon peel over.

Rose-Maréchale, La

Rose-Maréchale, La second wine of Château Coufran, Bordeaux, France.

Rosemount major wine estate est 1975 Upper Hunter Valley, New South Wales, Australia. Famed Chardonnay wines, particularly Roxburgh, and many others. Amalgamated with rival Australian producer Southcorp in 2000.

Rosenberg the name of 48 individual vineyards in Germany. Region by region, as follows: in Ahr at Bad Neuenahr-Ahrweiler; in Baden at Dielheim, Ehrenkirchen, Mühlhausen, Müllheim (Britzingen), Müllheim (Dattingen), Müllheim (Zunzingen); in Franken at Bad Windsheim, Frankenwinheim, Sommerach, Volkach; in Mittelrhein at Leutesdorf, St Goar; in Mosel-Saar-Ruwer at Bernkastel-Kues (Kues), Bernkastel Kues (Wehlen), Bruttig-Frankel, Cochem, Kinheim, Klotten, Konz, Minheim, Moselkern, Neef, Oberfell, Osann-Monzel, Palzem, Pommern, Pünderich, Rivenich, Wiltingen, Wittlich; in Nahe at Bad Kreuznach, Mannweiler-Cölin, Monzingen, Niederhausen and der Nahe, Windesheim; in Rheingau at Lorch; in Rheinhessen at Biebelnheim, Nierstein; in Rheinpfalz at Billigheim-Ingenheim (Billigheim), Billigheim-Ingenheim (Mühlhofen), Steinweiler; in Württemberg at Hardthausen.

Rosenborn vineyard at Zell in Mosel-Saar-Ruwer region, Germany.

Rosenbühl *Grosslage* incorporating vineyards at Erpolzheim, Freinsheim, Lambsheim, Weisenheim am Sand in Rheinpfalz region, Germany.

Rosengärtchen vineyard at Neumagen-Dhron in Mosel-Saar-Ruwer region, Germany.

Rosengarten brewery in Einsiedeln, Switzerland, known for Maisgold maize beer.

Rosengarten *Grosslage* incorporating vineyards at Bockenau, Braunweiler, Burgsponheim, Hüffelsheim, Mandel, Roxheim, Rüdesheim, Sponheim, St Katharinen and Weinsheim in Nahe region, Germany.

Rosengarten the name of 12 individual vineyards in Germany. Region by region as follows: in Baden at Karlsruhe; in Mosel-Saar-Ruwer at Starkenburg; in Rheingau at Rüdesheim; in Rheinhessen at Bechtheim, Bingen, Gabsheim, Monsheim; in Rheinpfalz at Edesheim, Friedlesheim, Kapellen-Drusweiler, Obrigheim, Rhodt unter Rietburg.

Rosenhang *Grosslage* incorporating vineyards in Mosel-Saar-Ruwer region, Germany at, respectively: Beilstein, Bremm, Briedern, Bruttig-Fankel (Bruttig), Bruttig-Fankel (Fankel), Cochem, Ediger-Eller, Ellenz-Poltersdorf, Mesenich, Senheim, Treis-Karden, Valwig.

Rosenheck vineyards at Bad Kreuznach and Niederhausen an der Nahe in Nahe region, Germany.

Rosenhügel vineyard at Königswinter in Mittelrhein region, Germany.

Rosenkranz vineyards at Böchingen in Rheinpfalz region and Vogtsburg in Kaiserstuhl in Baden region, Germany.

Rosenkränzel vineyard at Roschbach in Rheinpfalz region, Germany.

Rosenkranzweg vineyard at Östringen in Baden region, Germany.

Rosenlay vineyard at Lieser in Mosel-Saar-Ruwer region, Germany.

Rosental vineyard at Perscheid in Mittelrhein region, Germany.

Rosenteich vineyard at Guldental in Nahe region, Germany.

Rosenthal vineyard at Bad Neu-enahr-Ahrweiler in Ahr region, Germany.

Rose Pauillac, La wine brand of Cave Co-opérative La Rose Pauillac, Bordeaux, France.

Rose-Peruchon, La second wine of Château du Lyonnat, Bordeaux, France.

Rose-Pourret, Château La wine estate of AC St-Emilion, Bordeaux, France. Classified *Grand Cru*.

Rose Street pub-brewery in Edinburgh, Scotland. Owned by Allied Breweries and named in honour of the humble alley giving rear access to the city's two lordly thoroughfares, George Street and Prince's Street and long notorious for the number of its public houses.

Roseworthy agricultural college and cradle of Australian oenology, South Australia.

Rosita Cocktail. Over ice stir 3 parts tequila, 2 Campari, 1 dry vermouth, 1 sweet vermouth. Strain.

Roslyn brewery in Washington state, USA.

Ross liqueur brand of Canadian Schenley Distilleries, Canada.

Rossberg vineyards at Essingen in Rheinpfalz region, Rossdorf in Hessiche Bergstrasse region and Winnenden in Württemberg region, Germany.

Rossel vineyard at Waldalgesheim in Nahe region, Germany.

Rossese di Dolceacqua DOC for red wines from Rossese grapes, Dolceacqua, Liguria, Italy.

rosso red (wine). Italian.

Rosso Barletta DOC for red wine from Uva di Troia grape, Barletta, Apulia, Italy.

Rosso Canosa DOC for red wine from Uva di Troia grapes, Canosa, Apulia, Italy.

Rosso Cònero DOC for red wine chiefly from Montepulciano grapes, Monte Conero hills, Ancona, Marches, Italy.

Rosso d'Arquata noted red wine from Barbera, Canaiolo and Merlot grapes by Adanti, Umbria, Italy.

Rosso delle Colline Lucchesi DOC for red wines chiefly from Sangiovese and Cannaiolo grapes, hills of Lucca, Tuscany, Italy.

Rosso di Cerignola DOC for red wine from Negroamaro and Uva di Troia grapes, Cerignola, Apulia, Italy.

Rosso di Montalcino DOC for red wines from Brunello grapes, Montalcino, Tuscany, Italy.

Rosso Piceno DOC for red wines from Sangiovese and Montepulciano grapes, Marches region, Italy.

Rossstein vineyard at Kaub in Mittelrhein region, Germany.

Rosstal *Grosslage* incorporating vineyards in Franken region, Germany at, respectively: Arnstein, Eussenheim, Gössenheim, Himmelstadt, Karlstadt, Karlstadt (Gambach), Karlstadt (Karlburg), Karlstadt (Stetten), Laudenbach, Mühlbach, Retzstadt.

Rotari sparkling wine brand of Gruppo MezzaCorona, Trentino, Italy.

Rotberger grape variety principally of Baden region, Germany. Cross between red Trollinger and white Riesling.

Rote Halde vineyard at Sasbach in Baden region, Germany.

Rotenberg vineyards at Altenbamberg and Oberhausen an der Nahe in Nahe region, Sugenheim in Franken region and Wachenheim in Rheinhessen region, Germany.

Rotenbusch vineyard at Pfinztal in Baden region, Germany.

Rotenfels vineyards at Alzey and Alzey (Heimersheim) in Rheinhessen region and Traisen in Nahe region, Germany.

Rotenfelser im Winkel vineyard at Bad Münster am Stein-Ebernburg in Nahe region, Germany.

Rotenpfad vineyard at Flonheim in Rheinhessen region, Germany.

Rotenstein vineyard at Westhofen in Rheinhessen region, Germany.

Roter Berg vineyards at Hochstadt in Rheinpfalz region, Ilsfeld in Württemberg region, Ipsheim in Franken region and Kenzigen in Baden region, Germany.

Roter Bur vineyard at Glottertal in Baden region, Germany.

Roterd vineyard at Neumagen-Dhron in Mosel-Saar-Ruwer region, Germany.

Rotes Kreuz vineyard at Ingelheim in Rheinhessen region, Germany.

Rotfeld vineyard at Nussbaum in Nahe region, Germany.

Rotgipfler white grape variety of Austria. Blended with other varieties for Gumpoldskirchner.

Rotgold pink wine from Ruländer and Spätburgunder grapes, Baden region, Germany.

Rotgrund vineyard at Breisach in Baden region, Germany.

Röth vineyard at Grünstadt in Rheinpfalz region, Germany.

Rothbury Estate leading wine producer of Hunter Valley, New South Wales, Australia. Famed Chardonnay wines as well as Semillon, Shiraz, Cabernet Sauvignon etc.

Röthen vineyards at Schliengen (Niedereggenen) and Schliegen (Obereggenen) in Baden region, Germany.

Rothenack vineyard at Bornich in Mittelrhein region, Germany.

Rothenberg vineyards at Duchroth, Langenlonsheim and Rümmelsheim mit Orsteil Burg Layen in Nahe region, Eltville and Geisenheim in Rheingau region and Gau-Algesheim and Nackenheim in Rheinhessen region, Germany.

Rother Valley brewery at Sedlescombe, East Sussex, England.

Rothschild banking dynasty of which two of original five branches are important wine-estate owners based in Bordeaux, France. Château Mouton-Rothschild of late Baron Philippe is the centre of a major wine business including other Bordeaux estates and famed brand Mouton Cadet. Château Lafite-Rothschild is owned by a separate family branch and is one of several Domaines Rothschild properties in France and abroad.

Rotlay vineyards at Platten, Sehlem and Trier in Mosel-Saar-Ruwer region, Germany.

Rotling cheap pink wine of Germany.

Rotsteig vineyard at Malsch in Baden region, Germany.

Rott *Grosslage* incorporating vineyards at Alsbach, Bensheim-Auerbach, Bensheim-Schönberg and Zwingenberg in Hessiche Bergstrasse region, Germany.

Rotterdam pub-brewery in Toronto, Ontario, Canada.

Roudier, Château wine estate of AC Montagne-St-Emilion, Bordeaux, France.

Rouet, Château wine estate of AC Fronsac, Bordeaux, France.

rouge red (wine). French.

Rouge du Manoir red wine of Chiddingstone Vineyard, Kent, England.

Rougemont Castle 'British wine' brand of Matthew Clark, Bristol, England.

Rouget, Château wine estate of AC Pomerol, Bordeaux, France.

Roughton-Mothschild wine brand of distinguished producer Sam Roughton formerly of Cambarn vineyard near Bath, England.

Rouillac, Château de wine estate of AC Pessac-Léognan, Bordeaux, France.

Roulette Cocktail. Over ice shake 2 parts apple brandy, 1 rum, 1 Swedish Punsch. Strain.

Roullet cognac house, Jarnac, France. Brands include Très Rare 57 and 60 year-old cognacs.

see label opposite ➡

Roumier, Georges important wine domaine of Chambolle-Musigny, Burgundy, France. Famed village wines of AC Chambolle-Musigny and *Premier Cru* les Amoureuses etc.

Roumieu, Château wine estate of AC Barsac, Bordeaux, France.

Roumieu-Goyaud, Château wine estate of AC Sauternes, Bordeaux, France. Classified *Cru Bourgeois*.

Roumieu-Lacoste, Château wine estate of AC Sauternes, Bordeaux, France. Classified *Cru Bourgeois*.

Roussanne white grape variety of northern Rhône Valley, France.

Rousse major winery of northern Bulgaria, est close to city of Rousse on Danube shore 1932. Privatised by Seaboard Corporation 1998.

Rousseau, Armand wine estate in Gevrey-Chambertin, Burgundy, France. Vineyard holdings in Clos de Bèze, Mazis-Chambertin etc.

Rousset, Château wine estate of AC Côtes de Bourg, Bordeaux, France.

Roussette de Bugey white wine chiefly from Chardonnay grapes (rather than Roussette of old) of Savoie, France.

Roussette de Savoie AC for white wine from Chardonnay and Roussette grapes, Savoie, France.

see label over ➡

Rouyer

Rouyer cognac brand of Rouyer Guillet est 1701, Cognac, France.

Roxton's sloe gin brand of Roxton Bailey Robinson, Wiltshire, England.

Royal Ambrosante old solera sherry entirely from Pedro Ximenez grapes by House of Sandeman, Jerez de la Frontera, Spain.

Royal Arrival Cocktail. Over ice shake 4 parts dry gin, 2 lemon juice, 1 crème de noyaux, 1 kümmel, 1 egg white, 1 dash blue food colouring. Strain.

Royal Brackla North Highland malt whisky distillery, Nairn, Scotland. Est 1812, closed 1993. Single malts: 10-year-old, 18-year-old.

Royal Blend blended scotch whisky by Wm Sanderson & Son, South Queensferry, Scotland.

Royal Canadian Canadian whisky brand of Jas Barclay & Co, Canada.

Royal Charter Canadian whisky brand of Hudson's Bay Company, Canada.

Royal Clover Club Cocktail. Over ice shake 1 egg yolk, 4 parts dry gin, 1 grenadine, 1 lemon juice. Strain.

Royal Cocktail. Over ice shake 1 part cherry brandy, 1 dry vermouth, 1 dry gin, 1 dash maraschino. Strain and add cocktail cherry to glass.

Royal Command Canadian whisky brand of Canadian Park & Tilford, Canada.

Royal Corregidor rare *oloroso* sherry by Sandeman Hermanos, Jerez de la Frontera, Spain.

Royal Court Brewery the Hofbräuhaus, Munich, Germany.

Royal Culross eight-year-old vatted malt scotch whisky by Glen Scotia Distillery, Campbeltown, Scotland.

Royal Edinburgh blended scotch whisky of Ainslie & Heilbron, Glasgow, Scotland.

Royal Escort twelve-year-old blended scotch whisky by Gibson International, London, England.

Royal Esmeralda 20-year-old Fine Dry Amontillado from an original solera est 1894 by House of Sandeman, Jerez de la Frontera, Spain.

Royal Findhorn five-year-old blended scotch whisky by Gordon & MacPhail, Elgin, Scotland.

Royal Game blended scotch whisky of Winerite Ltd, Lees, England.

Royal Household blended scotch whisky by James Buchanan, Glasgow, Scotland.

Royal Lochnagar East Highland malt whisky distillery est 1845, Crathie, Deeside, Aberdeenshire, Scotland. Overlooking Balmoral and visited by Queen Victoria in 1848. Single malt: 12-year-old.

Royal Oak brandy by Oude Meester distillers, South Africa.

Royal Oak pale ale by Eldridge Pope brewery, Dorchester, Dorset, England.

Royal Oporto Wine Co former state port-trade organisation est 1756 now trading as a private port shipper (the largest of any), Vila Nova de Gaia, Portugal. Many brands and 'vintage' ports from 1953, 54, 55, 58, 60, 61, 62, 63, 67, 70, 77, 78, 79, 80, 82, 83, 85, 87, 89, 91, 94, 97, 2000, 03.

Royal St-Emilion, wine brand of Union des Producteurs St-Emilion, Bordeaux, France.

Royal Salute twenty-one-year-old blended scotch whisky brand of Seagram, Montreal, Canada. Sold to Pernod-Ricard, 2001.

Royal Shakespeare Stout beer by Rogue brewery, Ashland, Oregon, USA.

Royal Smile Cocktail. Over ice shake 2 parts apple brandy, 1 dry gin, 1 grenadine. Strain.

Royal Somerset apple variety traditionally valued for cider-making. English.

Royal Stag whisky brand of Pernod-Ricard.

Royal Stag Autumn Ale season beer by Mansfield Brewery, Nottingham, England.

Royal Triple Sec white curaçao by Aktiebolaget Vin & Spritcentralem, Sweden.

Royal Wedding Cocktail. Over ice shake 2 parts orange juice, 1 kirsch, 1 peach brandy. Strain into flute glass and top with champagne. Stir occasionally to deter separation.

Royal Wilding apple variety traditionally valued for cider-making. English.

Roy Howard Cocktail. Over ice shake 2 parts Lillet, 1 brandy, 1 orange juice, 2 dashes grenadine. Strain.

Roy René cognac producer, Segonzac, France.

Rozenberg vineyard at Mundelsheim in Württemberg region, Germany.

Rozès French (Moët-Hennessy) owned port shipper, Vila Nova de Gaia, Portugal. Vintages: 1963, 67, 77, 78, 82, 83, 85, 87, 91.

Rozier, Château wine estate of AC St-Emilion, Bordeaux, France. Classified *Grand Cru*.

Rozova Dolina Controliran wine region of Bulgaria.

RTD UK drinks trade acronym for ready to drink – a class of individual-serving usually based on white spirit and fruit flavouring, more popularly known as alcopops.

Ruat second wine of Château Ruat-Petit-Poujeaux, Bordeaux, France.

Ruat-Petit-Poujeaux, Château wine estate of AC Moulis, Médoc, Bordeaux, France. Classified *Cru Bourgeois*.

Rüberberger Domherrenberg vineyards at Briedern, Ellenz-Polterberg and Senheim in Mosel-Saar-Ruwer region, Germany.

Rubesco red wine brand of Lungarotti, Torgiano, Italy.

Rubicon pub-brewery in Sacramento, California, USA.

Rubicon red wine from Bordeaux grape varieties of Meerlust Estate, Stellenbosch, South Africa.

Rubin black grape variety of Bulgaria. Crossing of Nebbiolo and Syrah.

Ruby Ale brand name of former Lett brewery, Co Wexford, Eire, now licensed to Pelforth brewery in France and Coors in USA.

Ruby Cabernet red grape variety of California, USA.

ruby port basic port aged in wood for minimum period, thus retaining its dense ruby colour. Portugal.

Ruby Ratchet's Porter seasonal (winter) ale (5.3% alc) by Hydes brewery, Manchester, England. 'An unusual porter, ruby claret in colour and exceptionally strong.'

Ruchottes-Chambertin *Grand Cru* vineyard of Gevrey-Chambertin, Burgundy, France.

Ruddles brewery at Oakham, Rutland, England, famed for **Ruddles' Best Bitter** and **Ruddles' County** ale.

Rüdesheim great wine village of Rheingau region, Germany. *Grosslage*: Burgweg. Individual vineyards include Bischofsberg, Klosterberg, Klosterlay, Roseneck, Rosengarten, Rottland, Schlossberg etc.

Rüdesheim minor wine village of Nahe region, Germany. *Grosslage*: Rosengarten.

Rudgate brewery at Tockwith, York, North Yorkshire, England.

Rueda DO wine region of Spain. White wines including traditional sherry-like style, from Palomino and Verdejo grapes.

Rue de la Paix Cocktail. Over ice stir 1 part brandy, 1 dry vermouth, 2 dashes orange bitters, 4 dashes each of curaçao, maraschino, pastis. Strain.

Ruedo white table wine of Montilla-Moriles region, Spain.

Ruffino wine grower and producer based at Pontassieve, Tuscany,

Italy. Chianti wines including famed Chianti Classico Riserva Ducale, and others.

Rufina zone of Chianti Putto, Tuscany, Italy. Chianti Rufina wines are of quality comparable to Chianti Classico.

Ruinart Père & Fils *Grande Marque* champagne house est 1727 Reims, France.

Rulandac Sivi regional name for Pinot Gris grape variety, Croatia.

Ruländer German synonym for Pinot Gris grape variety.

Rully village and AC for red and and white wines, Côte Chalonnaise, Burgundy, France. *Premier Cru* vineyards: la Bressande, Champ-Clou, Chapitre, Cloux, Ecloseaux, la Fosse, Gresigny, Margoté, Marisson, Meix-Caillet, Mont-Palais, Moulesne, les Pierres, Pillot, Préau, Rabourcé, Raclot, la Renarde, Vauvry. Producers include Bouton, Chandesais, Delorme.

rum spirit distilled from fermented molasses. See box.

Rumartini Cocktail. In a cocktail glass combine 1 part chilled rum, 1 dash chilled dry vermouth. Add an ice cube and squeeze lemon peel over.

Rum Cocktail. Over ice stir 3 parts rum, 1 sweet vermouth. Strain.

Rum Collins Cocktail. Over ice shake 2 parts white rum, 1 fresh lime juice, 1 teaspoon caster sugar. Strain into a tall, ice-filled glass and top with soda water.

Rum Daisy Cocktail. Over ice shake 2 parts rum, 2 lemon juice, 1 raspberry syrup. Strain.

Rum Fix Cocktail. Over ice shake 2 parts rum, 1 lemon juice, 1 teaspoon sugar, 1 dash grenadine. Strain into an ice-filled glass and add a lemon slice.

Rum Punch in punch bowl mix 1 litre brandy, 1 litre rum, juice of 12 lemons, 4 tablespoons sugar. Add fruit slices. If serving cold, add 1 litre soda water and ice. If hot, add 1 litre boiling water.

Rumpy Pumpy bottle-conditioned beer (3.9% alc) by Wessex Brewery, Forest of Dean, Gloucestershire, England.

Rum Runner Cocktail. Over ice shake 2 parts white rum, 1 fresh lime juice, 1 pineapple juice, 2 dashes orange bitters. Strain into an ice-filled glass and add an orange slice.

Rum Tee Tum Cocktail. Over ice shake 2 parts rum, 1 lemon juice, 1 teaspoon sugar, 1 dash grenadine. Strain into an ice-filled glass and add a lemon slice.

Rum

spirit from sugar cane

Rum may well be the most widely produced spirit in the world, because it is made from by-products of an abundant crop, sugar cane. There is distilling, licensed or otherwise, not just in famous Caribbean centres such as Demerara, Jamaica and Puerto Rico, but throughout Latin America, southern Africa, India, the Pacific islands and Australia.

The raw material for distillation is called molasses – the dark and sticky residue left after the base syrup has been centrifuged to extract the crystals of refined sugar. Water is added to the molasses and the mix fermented. In commercial production, special culture yeasts are usually introduced, but wild yeasts are still used – introduced by adding yeast-bearing *bagasse* (residual pulp) from the original sugar-cane pressings.

Light rums are fermented for 24 to 36 hours and darker ones for up to two weeks and the dead wash (distilling mash) is then distilled in patent (continuous) stills, which have largely replaced the pot stills used before the 20th century. Only a minority of rums are now made in the original pot stills.

Rum from a continuous still is colourless and typically emerges at 68% alcohol by volume. It is diluted, usually to the standard 40% alc, for bottling. Top-quality rums are aged in casks or vats for at least three years and the finest for ten or more years. In the best white rums, colour is extracted by charcoal filtering. In golden or dark rums, the colour may be natural from contact with wood, or (particularly in dark or 'Navy' rums) added as caramel colourant. Rums are commonly shipped in cask for ageing and bottling in their destination markets, especially Great Britain and France.

Rum Yellowbird Cocktail. Over ice shake 2 parts rum, 1 teaspoon Cointreau, 1 teaspoon Galliano, 2 dashes fresh lime juice. Strain into a glass filled with crushed ice and add a straw.

Ruppertsberg great wine village of Rheinpfalz region, Germany. *Grosslage*: Hofstück. Vineyards: Gaisböhl, Hoheburg, Nussbien etc.

Russell House Cocktail. Over ice shake 1 part rye whisky, 3 dashes blackberry brandy, 2 dashes orange bitters, 2 dashes sugar syrup. Strain.

Russe Riverside Controliran wine region of Bulgaria.

Russia vodka is the national drink, produced in all regions. Large-scale production of wine is concentrated around Rostov, and in the Black Sea region. Ordinary red and white wines from indigenous and French varieties, and oceans of *champanski*.

Russian Cocktail. Over ice shake 1 part crème de cacao, 1 dry gin, 1 vodka. Strain.

Russian River Valley AVA of Sonoma County, California, USA.

Rust Burgenland town of white wine of Austria.

Rustenberg leading wine estate of Stellenbosch, South Africa. French grape varieties.

Rusty Nail Cocktail. Over ice stir 1 part Drambuie, 1 scotch whisky. Strain.

Ruthe vineyards at Nordheim and Schwaigern in Württemberg region, Germany.

Rutherford & Miles leading Madeira shipper est 1814 now part of Madeira Wine Company. Island of Madeira, Portugal.

Rutherford Hill Winery wine producer in Napa Valley, California, USA. Chardonnay wines and noted Gewürztraminer among others.

Rutherglen wine district of NE Victoria, Australia.

Rutland bitter by Ruddles Brewery, Rutland, England.

Ruwer river tributary (of Mosel) and wine-producing subregion of Mosel-Saar-Ruwer region, Germany.

ruzica pink (wine). Serbo-Croat.

Ryburn brewery at Sowerby Bridge, West Yorkshire, England.

rye beer beer made with a proportion (usually under 50 per cent) of rye along with barley for the mash.

rye whisk(e)y whisky distilled from mash including a high proportion of rye grain. Mostly north America.

Rye Whisky Cocktail. Over ice stir 1 part rye whisky, 4 dashes sugar syrup, 1 dash Angostura bitters. Strain and add cocktail cherry to glass.

S

Saar river tributary (of Mosel) and wine-producing subregion of Mosel-Saar-Ruwer region, Germany.

Saarburg wine town of Mosel-Saar-Ruwer region, Germany. *Grosslage*: Scharzberg. Vineyards include Antoniusberg, Fuchs, Klosterburg etc.

Saarfeilser Marienberg vineyard at Schoden in Mosel-Saar-Ruwer region, Germany.

sablant lost term for a softly-sparkling style of champagne. French.

Sablet wine village of AC Côtes du Rhône Villages, France.

Sablière-Fongrave, Château de la wine estate of AC Entre-Deux-Mers, Bordeaux, France.

SABMiller leading brewery company, South Africa.

Sabra orange liqueur brand, Israel.

saccharomyces class of yeasts (the name means 'sugar-splitting') acting to form alcohol. Includes the natural yeast variety **saccharomyces ellipsoideus**.

sack archaic term for white wine of SW Europe, especially sherry. Possibly from 16th century English *wyne seck*, a rendering of French *vin sec*.

Sackträger vineyard at Oppenheim in Rheinhessen region, Germany.

Sacramento extensive wine district of Central Valley, California, USA.

Sacy white grape variety of northern Burgundy, France. Mostly for sparkling Crémant de Bourgogne.

Saddleworth brewery at Saddleworth, Greater Manchester, England.

Sagebrush Stout beer by Wynkoop brewery, Colorado, USA.

Sagrantino di Montefalco DOC for red wines from Sagrantino grapes of Montefalco, Umbria, Italy. Two styles: dry and rich, the latter from part-dried grapes giving minimum 14% alc.

sahti traditional beer of Finland and the Baltic states, made with rye or oats as well as barley and sometimes seasoned with juniper as an alternative to hops.

Sailer brewery in Marktoberdorf, Germany.

Sainsbury's well-known own-label brand of J Sainsbury (supermarkets), London, England. Included are many wines and spirits, plus beers and ciders.

St Agnes Château Tanunda brandy by Angoves, Barossa Valley, South Australia.

St-Agrèves, Château wine estate of AC Graves, Bordeaux, France.

St-Amand, Château wine estate of AC Sauternes, Bordeaux, France. Classified *Cru Bourgeois*.

Saint-Amour wine *cru* and AC of Beaujolais region, France. Name commemorates a Roman soldier called Amor who settled in the area after surviving a massacre in Switzerland in the 4th century. He converted to Christianity and was canonized after founding a local mission. A statue in his honour stands at the church in Saint Amour-Bellevue.

St-Ambroise ale by McAuslan brewery, St Henri, Montreal, Canada.

St-André-Corbin, Château wine estate of AC Montagne-St-Emilion, Bordeaux, France.

St Andrew's Cocktail. Over ice shake 1 part Drambuie, 1 scotch whisky, 1 orange juice. Strain.

St Arnould brewery in Lille, France. Ales include L'épi de Facon wheat beer and *bière de garde* Réserve du Brasseur. St Arno(u)ld is a patron saint of brewing in Belgium and France.

St-Aubin wine village and AC of Burgundy, France. Most of the red and white wines are sold as AC Côte de Beaune-Villages, apart from wines of *Premiers Crus*: Champlots, la Châtenière, les Combes, les Frionnes, sur Gamay, les Murgers-des-Dents de Chien, en Remilly, sur le Sentier du Clou. Producers include Clerget, Jadot, Lamy, Roux etc.

Saint-Aubin de Luigné wine village of Coteaux du Layon, Loire Valley, France.

St Austell brewery at St Austell, Cornwall, England. Brands include Tinner's, HSB.

St-Bonnet, Château wine estate of AC Médoc, Bordeaux, France. Classified *Cru Bourgeois*.

St Brendan's Irish Ale beer by Marin Brewing Co, San Francisco, California, USA.

St-Bris-Le-Vineux wine village near Chablis in northern Burgundy, France. Noted new AC for white wines from Sauvignon Blanc grapes sold as Sauvignon de St-Bris. Also white wines from Aligoté and Chardonnay grapes and reds from Gamay and Pinot Noir.

St-Chinian AC for chiefly red wines from Carignan, Cinsaut, Grenache, Mourvèdre and Syrah grapes of St-Chinian, Coteaux de Languedoc, France.

St Christoffel brewery est 1986 in Roermond, Netherlands. Christoffel pilsner beer.

St-Christoly, Château wine estate of AC Médoc, Bordeaux, France. Classified *Cru Bourgeois*.

St-Denis, Clos *Grand Cru* vineyard in Morey-St-Denis, Burgundy, France.

St-Drézery wine village of AC Coteaux du Languedoc, Midi, France.

Ste-Cathérine, Clos vineyard of Jean Baumard, AC Coteaux du Layon, Loire Valley, France.

Sainte Chapelle wine producer of Idaho state, USA.

Ste-Colombe, Château wine estate of AC Côtes de Castillon, Bordeaux, France.

Ste-Croix-du-Mont commune and AC of Bordeaux, France. Neighbouring Sauternes and known for sweet white wines.

Sainte Famille wine producer at Falmouth, Nova Scotia, Canada.

Sainte-Foy-Bordeaux AC for red and white wines, Bordeaux, France.

Ste-Hélène, Château second wine of Château de Malle, Bordeaux, France.

Ste Michelle, Château wine property of Washington State, USA.

St-Emilion grape variety of Charentes region, France. Synonymous with Ugni Blanc and Trebbiano.

St-Emilion historic ramparted town, AC and major wine-producing district of Libournais, Bordeaux, France. Second only to Médoc in importance among Bordeaux districts, but with estates first classified for quality only in 1954 (99 years after original Médoc classification). Two estates (Chx Ausone and Cheval Blanc) classified *Premier Grand Cru Classé 'A'* and nine or ten *Premier Grand Cru Classé 'B'*, around 70 *Grands Crus Classés* and more than 150 *Grands Crus*, the latter depending on annual reclassification. 'Satellite' St-Emilion ACs are those from outlying communes Lussac, Montagne, Parsac, Puisseguin, St-Georges, which append their name to that of St-Emilion itself. Red wines from, principally, Merlot and Cabernet Franc grapes.

St-Estèphe wine-producing commune and AC of Haut-Médoc, Bordeaux, France. Red wines from renowned estates including Chx Calon Ségur, Cos d'Estournel, Montrose, de Pez etc.

St-Estèphe, Château wine estate of AC St Estèphe, Médoc, Bordeaux, France. Classified *Cru Bourgeois*.

St Feuillien abbey beer by Roeulx brewery, Belgium.

Saint-Fiacre wine village of AC Muscadet de Sèvre et Maine, Loire Valley, France.

St Georgenbräu brewery in Buttenheim, Bamberg, Germany. Known for *Kellerbier*.

St-George's vineyard at Waldron, Heathfield, East Sussex, England.

St-Georges satellite AC of St-Emilion, Bordeaux, France. Wines are designated AC **St-Georges-St-Emilion**.

St-Georges, Château wine estate of AC St-Georges-St-Emilion, Bordeaux, France.

St-Georges-Côte-Pavie, Château wine estate of AC St-Emilion, Bordeaux, France. Classified *Grand Cru Classé*.

St-Georges d'Orques wine village of AC Coteaux du Languedoc, Midi, France.

St Germain Cocktail. Over ice shake 1 egg white, 2 parts green Chartreuse, 1 grapefruit juice, 1 lemon juice. Strain.

St Gervais wine village of AC Côtes du Rhône Villages, Rhône Valley, France.

St Guibert brewery at Mont-St-Guibert, Belgium. Vieux Temps ale.

St Honoré brandy by Landy Frères distillery, Rastignano, Italy.

St Hubertus Vineyard wine producer est 1948 at Kelowna, British Columbia, Canada.

St James's twelve-year-old blended scotch whisky by Berry Bros & Rudd, 3 St James's Street, London, England.

St-Jean, Cave Co-opérative largest wine coop of AC Médoc, Bordeaux, France.

St Jean, Château wine property in Sonoma Valley, California, USA.

St Josef's convent-brewery at Ursberg, Bavaria, Germany.

St-Joseph AC for red wine from Syrah grapes and white from Marsanne and Roussanne, northern Rhône Valley, France. Leading producers include Chave, Dard & Ribo, Grippat, Jaboulet.

St-Julien commune and AC of Médoc, Bordeaux, France. Famed red wines from *grand cru classé* estates including Ducru Beaucaillou, Léoville Barton, Léoville Lascases, Gruaud Larose, Talbot etc.

St-Lambert du Lattay wine village of AC Coteaux du Layon, Loire Valley, France.

St Laurent red grape variety principally of Austria.

St Laszlo Vineyards wine producer at Keremeos, British Columbia, Canada.

St Louis *gueuze* beer by Van Honsebrouck brewery, Ingelmunster, Belgium.

St Magalene Lowland malt whisky distillery, Linlithgow, West Lothian, Scotland. Est 1795, closed 1983.

Saint-Marceaux, De champagne house est 1837, Reims, France.

St Mark Cocktail. Over ice shake 2 parts dry gin, 2 dry vermouth, 1 cherry brandy, 1 redcurrant syrup. Strain.

St Martin fourth-century French prelate said to have discovered principles of vine-pruning and sometimes called the patron saint of drinkers.

St-Martin, Clos wine estate of AC St-Emilion, Bordeaux, France. Classified *Grand Cru Classé*.

St-Maurice-sur-Eygues wine village of AC Côtes du Rhône Villages, Rhône Valley, France.

St-Nicolas du Bourgueil village and AC for red wine from Cabernet Franc grapes, Loire Valley, France.

Saint Pantaleimon sweet white wine brand of Keo, island of Cyprus.

St-Pantaléon Les Vignes wine village of AC Côtes du Rhône Villages, Rhône Valley, France.

St-Paul, Château wine estate of AC Haut-Médoc, Bordeaux, France.

St Pauli brewery in Bremen, Germany, famed for **St Pauli Girl** beer.

Saint Péray village and AC for still and sparkling white wines mainly from Marsanne grapes at southern end of northern Rhône Valley, France. Method of producing *mousseux* wines is claimed locally to have been imparted to Champagne's Dom Pérignon in person.

St Peters brewery at South Elmham, Suffolk, England.

St-Pierre, Château wine estate of AC St Julien, Médoc, Bordeaux, France. Formerly Château St-Pierre-Sevaistre. Classified *4ème Grand Cru Classé*. *see label opposite* ➡

St-Pierre, Château de wine estate of AC Graves, Bordeaux, France.

St-Pierre, Château de wine estate of AC St-Emilion, Bordeaux, France. Classified *Grand Cru*.

St-Pierre de Mons wine commune of Graves district, Bordeaux, France.

St Piran's golden ale (4.5% alc) by Skinners Brewing, Truro, Cornwall, England.

Saint Pourçain-sur-Sioule VDQS for red, rosé and white wines, Loire Valley, France. Red and rosé wines largely from Gamay, plus Pinot Noir, grapes. White from Chardonnay, Tresallier and Sauvignon.

St Raphaël vermouth-style wine-based aperitif drink of France. Red and white versions.

Saint Reol Champagne brand of Sélection des Producteurs Associés, Ambonnay, Champagne, France.

St-Roch, Cave Co-operative wine coop of AC Médoc, Bordeaux, France.

St-Roch, Château second wine of Château Andron-Blanquet, Bordeaux, France.

Saint-Romain village and AC for red and, mainly, white wines, Côte de Beaune, Burgundy, France.

St-Saturnin, Château wine estate of AC Médoc, Bordeaux, France. Classified *Cru Bourgeois*.

St-Sauveur wine commune of Haut-Médoc, Bordeaux, France.

Saintsbury leading wine producer in Carneros, California, USA. Famed Pinot Noir red wines.

St-Seurnin de Cadourne wine commune of Haut-Médoc, Bordeaux, France.

St Severin's Kölsch beer by Boulder Creek Brewing Co, California, USA.

Saint Simon Champagne brand of Coopérative la Crayère, Bethon, Champagne, France.

St Sixtus abbey brewery and beer brand, Westvleteren, Belgium.

St Sylvestre brewery at St Sylvestre-Cappel, Steenvorde, France. Hoppeland Bier; 3 Monts strong (8.5% alc) *bière de garde*; Bière des Templiers abbey beer.

St Thomas Brau *Altbier* by Nussdorf brewery, Vienna, Austria.

Saint-Véran AC for white wine from Chardonnay grapes of villages of Chanes, Leynes, Pruzilly, St-Amour and St-Vérand, Côte de Maconnais, Burgundy, France.

Saint Vincent French patron saint of winemaking. Festival day is January 22nd.

St-Yzans-de-Médoc, Cave Co-opérative wine coop of commune of St-Yzans, AC Médoc, Bordeaux, France.

Sais wine appellation of Meknès Fez, Morocco.

saison dry beer style traditional in French-speaking Belgium, formerly made only during cold months for summer drinking.

Saison Régal popular brand of *saison* beer by Du Bocq brewery, Hainaut, Belgium.

Saison Silly widely exported *saison* beer, Hainaut, Belgium. Name is from the brewery, in the village of Silly.

Sakar Controliran wine region of southern Bulgaria. Known for quality red wines from Merlot grapes.

Sakar Liubimetz, Domaine winery est 1974 southern Bulgaria. Principally Merlot wines. Owned by Menada Stara Zagora.

sakazuki porcelain drinking cups for sake. Japan.

sake rice 'wine' (process is in fact more akin to brewing) of Japan. Typically around 17% alc. So-called after its reputed origin in Osaka, the drink is traditionally claimed to have been devised by a Japanese monarch in 712.

Sakini Cocktail. Over ice stir 3 parts dry gin, 1 sake. Strain.

Saku brewery at Tallinn, Estonia.

Sakura Masamune sake brand, Japan.

Sales, Château de wine estate of AC Pomerol, Bordeaux, France.

Salice Salentino DOC for red and rosato wines chiefly from Negro-amaro grapes from town of Salice Salentino, Puglia, Italy.

Salignac Courvoisier-owned cognac house, Cognac, France.

Salinas Valley wine district of California, USA.

Salins du Midi, Les major wine producer of Midi, France. Listel brand.

Salisbury Estate large-scale wine producer, Murray River, Victoria, Australia. Mostly bulk wine for blending but well-known Reserve Chardonnay.

Salitos lager brand incorporating Mexican Tequila de Jalisco. Germany.

Salle-de-Poujeaux, La second wine of Château Poujeaux, Bordeaux, France.

salmanazar large-format champagne bottle of 9 litres. Equals 12 standard bottles.

Salome Cocktail. Over ice shake 1 part dry gin, 1 dry vermouth, 1 Dubonnet. Strain.

Salomon, Fritz wine producer at Krems, Austria. Noted Riesling and other wines.

Salomon-Undhof wine producer based in Kremstal, Nieder-österreich, Austria.

Salon *Grande Marque* champagne house est 1914 by Eugène-Aimé Salon, le Mesnil-sur-Oger, Avize, France. The first *blanc de blancs* champagne, from Chardonnay grapes from le Mesnil-sur-Ogier vineyard.

Salonbier beer by Borbecker Dampf-bier brewery, Essen, Germany.

Salopian Brewing Company brewer in Shrewsbury, Shropshire, England. Brands include wheat beers Answer, Jigsaw and Puzzle, porter **Salopian Entire Butt** and traditional ale **Salopian Firefly**.

Saltram winery est 1859, Barossa Valley, South Australia.

Salty Dog Cocktail. Prepare a cocktail glass by dipping its rim first in grapefruit juice then in coarse salt to encrust. Shake 1 part dry gin, 2 grapefruit juice and strain into the prepared glass.

salud 'cheers' in Spanish.

salut 'cheers' in French.

Salutation Cocktail. Over ice stir 2 parts dry gin, 1 Bénédictine, 1 dash cherry brandy. Strain and add cocktail cherry to glass.

salute 'health'. Italian toast.

Salvagnin red wine from Gamay and Pinot Noir grapes, Vaud, Switzerland.

Salzberg *Grosslage* incorporating vineyards in Württemberg region, Germany at, respectively: Eberstadt, Ellhofen, Lehrensteinsfeld, Löwenstein, Löwenstein (Hösslinsülz), Obersulm (Affaltrach), Obersulm (Eichelberg), Obersulm (Eschenau), Obersulm (Sülzbach), Obersulm (Weiler), Obersulm (Willsbach), Weinsberg, Weinsberg (Grantschen), Weinsberg (Wimmental).

Samalens major armagnac producer, Laujuzan, Gascony, France.

Sambuca Italian sweet liqueur flavoured with aniseed, elder fruit and flower etc. Brands include Luxardo and Romana.

Sambuca Shooter Cocktail. Over ice shake 1 part Sambuca, 1 tablespoon vodka, 1 tablespoon cream. Strain into a shot glass.

Samichlaus Christmas beer (name means 'Santa Claus') by Hürlimann brewery, Zürich, Switzerland. Brewed each December 6th, the festival day of St Nicholas, for sale from the following December 6th.

At up to 14% alc, said to be the strongest of all bottom-fermented beers.

Samlesbury Silver premium lager (5.0% alc) made by Whitbread's Samlebury Brewery, Preston, Lancashire, England. First brewed 1997 to celebrate 25th anniversary of the brewery's opening. The brewery now produces 576 million pints per annum – 'a substantial proportion of the Whitbread Beer Company's production.'

samogon bootleg vodka, Russia.

Samos Aegean island known for dessert wine from Muscat grapes. Greece. Said to be the oldest of all the world's wines in continuous production.

Sam's cider brand of Winkleigh Cider Company, Winkleigh, Devon, England.

samshoo or **samshu** rice beer of China.

Samson beer brand of Budweiser Bürgerbräu, Budweis, Czech Republic.

Samson bitter ale by Vaux brewery, Sunderland, England.

Sam Trueman's brewery at Medmenham, Buckinghamshire, England.

Samuel Adams brand of Boston Brewing Co, Massachusetts, USA. Famed beers include **Samuel Adams Boston Lager** and **Samuel Adams Boston Stock Ale**.

Samuel Middleton's Pale Ale beer by Wild Goose brewery, Cambridge, Maryland, USA.

Samuel Smith renowned brewery in Tadcaster, Yorkshire, England. Beers include Museum Ale (exported as **Samuel Smith's Pale Ale**), Nourishing Strong Stout (exported as **Samuel Smith's Porter**) and Strong Brown Ale (exported as **Samuel Smith's Nut Brown**).

San Andreas brewery in Hollister, California, USA. Beers include Earthquake Pale Ale, Earthquake Porter, Survivor Stout.

Sanatogen tonic wine brand of Matthew Clark, Bristol, England.

San Benito vineyard district of Central Coast region, California, USA.

Sancerre town and AC of Loire Valley, France. Famed dry white wines from Sauvignon grapes and red/rosé wines from Pinot Noir. Producers include Bonnard, Cordier, Vatan.   *see label opposite* ➡

San Colombano al Lambro DOC for red wines from Barbera, Bonarda and French (Bordeaux) grape varieties. Also, white wine from Pinot Grigio, Riesling Tocai and Vedrea grapes.

Sand vineyard at Mainz in Rheinhessen region, Germany.

Sandalford wine producer of Margaret River, Western Australia.

Sandeman port and sherry shipper est 1790 by Scots-born George Sandeman (1765–1841) at Vila Nova de Gaia, Portugal, and Jerez de la Frontera, Spain. Ports include Apitiv, Founder's Reserve, Imperial Reserve Tawny, 20-year-old Tawny and vintages: 1950, 55, 58, 60, 63, 66, 67, 70, 75, 77, 80, 82, 85, 91, 94, 97, 99, 2000, 03. Sherries include Armada, Character, Dry Seco, Original Dry Don, Rare Fino, Rich Golden, Royal Ambrosante, Royal Corregidor, Royal Esmeralda. Family owned company until 1961 when shares were offered on the stock exchange and subsequently taken up by American drinks corporation Seagram which in 1999 disposed of its stock to French media group Vivendi, who sold Sandeman on to Portuguese wine company Sogrape in 2002.

Sandberg vineyard at Wiltingen in Mosel-Saar-Ruwer region, Germany.

Sanderberg vineyard at Obernau in Franken region, Germany.

Sanderson's Gold blended scotch whisky by Wm Sanderson, South Queensferry, Scotland.

Sandgrub vineyards at Eltville and Kiedrich in Rheingau region, Germany.

Sand Martin Cocktail. Over ice shake 2 parts dry gin, 2 sweet vermouth, 1 green Chartreuse. Strain.

Sandora cava sparkling wine brand of Penedes, Spain.

Sando Stout beer by McCallum brewery, Sri Lanka.

Sandrocken vineyard at Hirschberg in Baden region, Germany.

Sandy Macdonald blended scotch whisky by Macdonald Greenlees, Edinburgh, Scotland.

Sandy Macnab blended scotch whisky by Macnab Distilleries, Montrose, Scotland.

San Felice wine estate of Chianti Classico, Tuscany, Italy.

San Francisco brewery in Tucson, Arizona, USA. Home of Wildcat Ale.

San Francisco brewery in city of San Francisco, California, USA. Gold Rush Ale.

sangaree spiced wine-based mixed drink of Spain. Similar to sangria.

Sängerhalde vineyards at Markdorf, Meersburg and Stetten in Baden region, Germany.

San Giorgio renowned red wine by Lungarotti of Umbria, Italy. Torgiano and Cabernet Sauvignon grapes.

Sangiovese red grape variety chiefly of Tuscany, Italy. The major constituent of chianti.

Sangiovese d'Aprilia DOC for red and *rosato* wines from Sangiovese grapes grown near Rome, Italy.

Sangiovesi dei Colli Pesaresi DOC for red wines from Sangiovese grapes, Pesaro, Marches, Italy.

Sangiovese di Romagna DOC for red wine from Sangiovese grapes, Emilia-Romagna region, Italy.

Sangioveto regional name for Sangiovese grape variety, Tuscany, Italy.

San Giusto a Rentennano wine producer of Chianti Classico, Tuscany, Italy.

sangria red-wine based mixed drink of Spain commonly including citrus fruit, sugar, soda water and brandy. Named means 'bleeding'.

sangsom generic grain spirit of Thailand.

San Joaquin wine producing county of Central Valley, California, USA.

San Juan wine district of western Argentina.

Sankt Alban *Grosslage* incorporating vineyards at Bodenheim, Gau-Bischofsheim, Harxheim, Lörzweiler, Mainz (Ebersheim), Mainz (Hechtsheim) and Mainz (Laubenheim) in Rheinhessen, Germany.

Sankt Annaberg vineyards at Burrweiler in Rheinpfalz region and Worms in Rheinhessen region, Germany.

Sankt Anna Kapelle vineyard at Flörsheim in Rheingau region, Germany.

Sankt Antoniousweg vineyard at Langenlonsheim in Nahe region, Germany.

Sankt Castorhöhle vineyard at Müden in Mosel-Saar-Ruwer region, Germany.

Sankt Cyriakusstift vineyard at Worms in Rheinhessen, Germany.

Sankt Georgen vineyard at Partenheim in Rheinhessen region, Germany.

Sankt Georgenberg vineyards at Jugenheim and Worms in Rheinhessen region, Germany.

Sankt Georgshof vineyard at Temmels in Mosel-Saar-Ruwer region, Germany.

Sankt Jakobsberg vineyard at Ockenheim in Rheinhessen region, Germany.

Sankt Johännser vineyards at Markgröningen and Vaihingen in Württemberg region, Germany.

Sankt Jost vineyard at Bacharach in Mittelrhein region, Germany.

Sankt Julianenbrunnen vineyard at Guntersblum in Rheinhessen region, Germany.

Sankt Kathrin vineyard at Wolfsheim in Rheinhessen region, Germany.

Sankt Kiliansberg vineyard at Mainz in Rheingau region, Germany.

Sankt Klausen vineyard at Ramstahl in Franken region, Germany.

Sankt Laurenzikapelle vineyard at Gau-Algesheim in Rheinhessen region, Germany.

Sankt Martin vineyards at Bad Kreuznach and Guldental in Nahe region and Ensch in Mosel-Saar-Ruwer region, Germany.

Sankt Martiner Hofberg vineyards at Trier (Irsch) and Trier (Tarforst) in Mosel-Saar-Ruwer region, Germany.

Sankt Martiner Klosterberg vineyards at Trier (Irsch) and Trier (Tarforst) in Mosel-Saar-Ruwer region, Germany.

Sankt Martinsberg vineyard at Oberwesel in Mittelrhein region, Germany.

Sankt Martinskreuz vineyard at Mertesheim in Rheinpfalz region, Germany.

Sankt Matheiser vineyard at Trier in Mosel-Saar-Ruwer region, Germany.

Sankt Maximiner Kreuzberg vineyards at Trier and Trier (Kürenz) in Mosel-Saar-Ruwer region, Germany.

Sankt Michael *Grosslage* incorporating vineyards in Mosel-Saar-Ruwer region, Germany at, respectively: Bekond, Detzem, Ensch, Klüsserath, Köwerich, Leiwen, Longen, Mehring, Mehring (Lörsch), Pölich, Schleich, Thörnich.

Sankt Michaelsberg vineyard at Riegel in Baden region, Germany.

Sankt Nikolaus vineyard at Oestrich-Winkel in Rheingau region, Germany.

Sankt Oswald vineyard at Manubach in Mittelrhein region, Germany.

Sankt Petrusberg vineyard at Trier in Mosel-Saar-Ruwer region, Germany.

Sankt Quirinusberg vineyard at Perl in Mosel-Saar-Ruwer region, Germany.

Sankt Rochuskapelle *Grosslage* incorporating vineyards in Rheinhessen region, Germany at, respectively: Aspisheim, Badenheim, Biebelsheim, Bingen (Büdesheim), Bingen (Dietersheim), Bingen (Dromersheim), Bingen (Gaulsheim), Bingen (Kempten), Bingen (Sponsheim), Gensingen, Grolsheim, Horrweiler, Ockenheim, Praffen-Schwabenheim, Welgesheim, Zotzenheim.

Sankt Ruppertsberg vineyard at Gutenberg in Nahe region, Germany.

Sankt Remigiusberg vineyard at Laubenheim in Nahe region, Germany.

Sankt Stephan vineyard at Grünstadt in Rheinpfalz region, Germany.

Sankt Werner-Berg vineyard at Oberwesel in Mittelrhein region, Germany.

Sanlúcar de Barrameda seaside sherry-producing town of Andalucia, Spain. Known for manzanilla dry sherries.

San Luis Obispo wine district of Central Valley, California, USA.

San Michele tangerine-peel flavoured liqueur by Peter Heering, Denmark.

San Miguel worldwide pilsner beer brand of San Miguel breweries originally in Spain and Manila, Philippines.

San Pasqual AVA of San Diego County, California, USA.

San Patricio *fino* sherry brand of Garvey, Jerez de la Frontera, Spain. Spanish for St Patrick, patron saint of Ireland (birthplace of Garvey's founder).

Sanraku Ocean whiskey distiller, Japan. **Sanraku Ocean White Label**.

San Sebastian Cocktail. Over ice shake 3 parts dry gin, 1 white rum, 1 Cointreau, 1 grapefruit juice, 1 fresh lime juice. Strain.

San Severo DOC for red and *rosato* wines Montepulciano and Sangiovese grapes and white from Bombino and Trebbiano grapes, Apulia, Italy.

Sansonnet, Château wine estate of AC St-Emilion, Bordeaux, France. Classified *Grand Cru* (1996).

Sans Soucis beer brand of Italy.

Santa Barbara wine-producing county of Central Coast region, California, USA.

Santa Clara wine-producing county of Central Coast region, California, USA.

Santa Cruz brewery in Santa Cruz, California, USA. Beacon Barley Wine, Lighthouse Lager and other noted beers.

Santa Cruz wine-producing county of Central Coast region, California, USA.

Santa Fe Pale Ale popular bottle-conditioned beer by **Santa Fe Brewing Co**, Galisteo, New Mexico, USA.

Santa Julia wine brand of La Agricola, Mendoza, Argentina.

see label opposite ➡

Santa Maddelena red wine from Schiava grapes of village of Santa

Maddalena near Bolzano, Trentino-Alto Adige, Italy.

Santa Maria Valley AVA of Santa Barbara county, California, USA.

Sant'Anna di Isola Capo Rizzuto DOC for red wines chiefly from Gaglioppo grapes, Calabria, Italy.

Santa Ynez Valley AVA of Santa Barbara county, California, USA.

San Telmo wine brand of Diageo, Argentina.

Santenay village and AC of Côte de Beaune, Burgundy, France. Chiefly red wines. *Premier cru* vineyards: Beauregard, Beaurepaire, le Clos des Tavannes, la Comme, les Gravières, le Maladière, le Passe Temps.

Santiago Cocktail. Over ice shake 1 part Bacardi rum, 2 dashes grenadine, 2 dashes lemon juice. Strain.

Santorini Aegean (Cyclades) island known for strong white wines from Nycteri grapes. Greece.

Santos, AP port shipper late of Vila Nova de Gaia, Portugal. Vintages: 1963, 66, 75.

Sao Francisco leading *cachaca* brand of Brazil.

Saperavi red grape variety of Bulgaria and Russia.

Sapin, Paul leading producer and *négoçiant* of Beaujolais at Lancié, France.

sappy in winetasting, a concentrated character to the flavour of young wine, indicating good future development.

Sarah Hughes brewery at Sedgley, West Midlands, England.

Saran, Château de wine property of AC Coteaux Champenois, Champagne, France. Still white wines. Owned by Moët & Chandon.

Saransot-Dupré, Château wine estate of AC Listrac, Médoc, Bordeaux, France. Classified *Cru Bourgeois Supérieur*.

sarap 'wine'. Turkish.

Saratoga Cocktail. Over ice shake 1 part brandy, 2 dashes Angostura bitters, 2 dashes maraschino, 1 small slice pineapple. Strain and add a splash of soda water to glass.

Sardinia wine-producing Mediterranean island, Italy. DOCs for red and white wines chiefly from Cannonau, Torbato and Vermentino grapes. Also many *vino da tavola* wines and fortified wines.

Sarget du Gruaud-Larose second wine of Château Gruaud-Larose, Bordeaux, France.

Sarmento light red wine from Sangiovese and Canaiolo grapes.

Sarrau wine-producer and *négoçiant* based in Beaujolais, Burgundy, France.

Sartène wine district of island of Corsica, France.

Sartre, Château Le wine estate of AC Pessac-Léognan, Bordeaux, France.

Sassella DOC for red wine from Nebbiolo grapes, Valtellina, Lombardy, Italy.

Sassicaia famed red wine from Cabernet Sauvignon and Cabernet

Franc grapes, made by Marchese Incisa della Rochetta, near Bolghieri, Tuscany. A *vino da tavola* from first vintage in 1968 until 1994, when a new DOC – Bolghieri – was created exclusively for the estate's wine, Sassicaia now has an exclusive DOCG.

Satan's Whiskers Cocktail. Over ice shake 2 parts dry gin, 2 dry vermouth, 2 orange juice, 1 Grand Marnier, 1 dash orange bitters. Strain.

Sattler, Wilhelm Jr wine producer in Südsteiermark, Austria.

Sattler, Willi wine producer at Gamlitz, Austria.

Satzenberg vineyard at Wertheim in Baden region, Germany.

Sätzler vineyards at Baden-Baden and Sinzheim in Baden region, Germany.

Sauberg vineyard at Ötisheim in Württemberg region, Germany.

Saucy Sue Cocktail. Over ice stir 1 part apple brandy, 1 brandy, 1 dash apricot brandy, 1 dash pastis. Strain and squeeze orange peel over.

Saukopf vineyards at Gau-Bickelheim in Rheinhessen region and Windesheim in Nahe region, Germany.

Sauloch vineyard at Flörsheim-Dalsheim in Rheinhessen region, Germany.

Saul's farm and farmhouse cider, Wembworthy, Chumleigh, Devon, England.

Saumagen vineyard at Kallstadt in Rheinpfalz region, Germany.

Saumur town and AC of Loire Valley, France. Red wine chiefly from Cabernet Franc grapes, white from Chenin Blanc plus Chardonnay and Sauvignon. Sparkling wines, **Saumur Crémant** or **Saumur Mousseux** are red, rosé or white and from several grape varieties.

Saumur Champigny AC for superior red wines from Cabernet Franc grapes grown around villages of Saumur district, Loire Valley, France. Producers include Filliatreau and Coop of St Cyr en Bourg.

Sauschwänzel vineyard at Billigheim-Ingenheim in Rheinpfalz region, Germany.

Saussignac village and AC of Bergerac, SW France.

sautchoo grain spirit of China, similar to whisky. Arguably the oldest of all spirits, as Chinese archaeologists claim to have found evidence of distilling activity dating from more than 2,000 years ago.

Sauternes AC of Bordeaux, France, for sweet white wines from, typically, four parts Sémillon and one part Sauvignon grapes. Muscadelle grapes are sometimes included in fractional quantities. With neighbouring AC Barsac, the principal top-quality dessert wine producing district of the world. Estates classified in 1855 included 1 *premier grand cru classé*, Château d'Yquem, 11 *premiers crus classés*, 15 *deuxièmes crus* and a number of *crus bourgeois*.

Sauternes Punch in punch bowl mix 2 litres Sauternes, 1 measure each of curaçao, Grand Marnier, maraschino, 400 grams sugar. Add ice and fruit slices.

Sauvignon Blanc principal white grape variety of Loire Valley and (along with Sémillon grape) of

Bordeaux region, France. Sole constituent of AC wines of Pouilly-Fumé and Sancerre. Important in dry white wines of all Bordeaux ACs and in great sweet white wines of Barsac, Sauternes, etc. Widely planted in most wine-producing regions of the world, most successfully in Chile, New Zealand, United States.

Sauvignon de St Bris noted white wine from Sauvignon grapes of St-Bris-le-Vineux, Burgundy, France.

Sauvignon Vert regional name for Muscadelle grape variety, California, USA.

Sauvion & Fils wine producer in AC Muscadet, Loire Valley, France.

Sauza leading tequila distiller of Mexico, est 1873 by Don Cenobio Sauza at Jalisco and still a family concern (though owned by Allied Domecq, UK) under name of grandson of the founder, Francisco Javier Sauza Mora.

Sauza Hornitos tequila brand Don Cenobio Sauza.

Savagnin white grape variety of Jura region, France. Sole constituent of sherry-like wines Château Chalon and *vin jaune*.

Savatiano white grape variety of Greece. Retsina wine.

Savennières AC for white wine from Chenin Blanc grapes, Loire Valley, France.

Savès, Camille *récoltant manipulant* champagne producer, Bouzy, Champagne, France.

Savigny-lès-Beaune village and AC of Côte de Beaune, Burgundy, France. Chiefly red wines. *Premier Cru* vineyards: Basses-Vergelesses, Bataillière, les Charnières, aux Clous, la Dominode, aux Fourneaux, aux Grands Liards, aux Gravins, aux Guettes, Haut Marconnets, Haut Jarrons, les Jarrons, les Lavières, les Marconnets, les Narbantons, Petits Godeaux, aux Petits Liards, les Peuillets, Redrescuts, les Rouvrettes, aux Serpentières, les Talmettes, Vergelesses. Producers include Bize, Doudet Naudin, Leroy, Tollot-Beaut.

Savoie region and AC of eastern France. Red and rosé wines from Gamay, Mondeuse and Pinot Noir grapes. Whites (still and sparkling) chiefly from Chasselas, Jacquère and Roussette. Within Vin de Savoie AC, wines from individual sites (*crus*) may be labelled by name: Abymes, Apremont, Arbin, Ayze, Charpignat, Chignin, Chignin-Bergeron, Cruet, Jongieux, Marignan, Montmélian, Ripaille, St Jean de la Port, St Jeoire-Prieuré, Ste Marie d'Alloix.

Savoy Cocktail. Into a liqueur glass, pouring carefully to avoid mixing ingredients, put 1 part Bénédictine, 1 brandy, 1 crème de cacao.

Savoy Corpse Reviver Cocktail. Over ice shake 1 part brandy, 1 Fernet Branca, 1 white crème de menthe. Strain.

Savoy Sangaree

Savoy Sangaree Cocktail. Stir 1 part port or sherry, 1 teaspoon powdered sugar. Strain, add lemon or orange peel and pinch of ground nutmeg.

Savoy Special Cocktail. Over ice shake 2 parts dry gin, 1 dry vermouth, 2 dashes grenadine, 1 dash pastis. Strain and squeeze lemon peel over.

Savoy Tango Cocktail. Over ice shake 1 part apple brandy, 1 sloe gin. Strain.

Savuto DOC for red wines from Gaglioppo and Greco Nero grapes of Savuto valley, Calabria, Italy.

Saxon Cocktail. Over ice shake 2 parts rum, 1 fresh lime juice, 1 dash grenadine. Strain.

Sazerac Cocktail. Over ice stir 1 part rye whisky, 1 dash Angostura bitters, 1 sugar lump. Strain into chilled glass, add 1 dash pastis and squeeze lemon peel over.

Scanlon's Fine Ales brewery at Uxbridge, Middlesex, England.

Scapa Island malt whisky distillery est 1885, Kirkwall, Orkney, Scotland. Single malt: eight-year-old.

Scarlett O'Hara Cocktail. Over ice shake 2 parts Southern Comfort, 1 cranberry juice, 1 dash fresh lime juice. Strain.

Schaapskooi abbey brewery in Koningshoeven monastery, Tilburg, Netherlands. Ales marketed under Koningshoeven, La Trappe and Tilburg labels.

Schäf vineyards at Auggen and Neuenburg am Rhein in Baden region, Germany.

Schafberg vineyard at Grossniedesheim in Rheinpfalz region, Germany.

Schäfergarten vineyards at Insheim and Rohrbach in Rheinpfalz region, Germany.

Schäferlay vineyard at Briedel in Mosel-Saar-Ruwer region, Germany.

Schäfersberg vineyard at Schüneberg in Nahe region, Germany.

Schäffbräu brewery in Altmühltal Natural Park, Treuchtlingen, Germany.

Schafsteige vineyards at Niederstetten, Niederstetten (Oberstetten), Niederstetten (Vorbachzimmern), Niederstetten (Wermutshausen), Weikersheim (Laudenbach) and Weikersheim (Haagen) in Württemberg region, Germany.

Schalk vineyard at Elsenfeld in Franken region, Germany.

Schalkstein *Grosslage* incorporating vineyards in Württemberg region, Germany at, respectively: Affalterbach, Aspach (Allermsbach), Aspach (Kleinaspach), Aspach (Rietenau), Asperg, Benningen, Besigheim, Bietigheim-Bissingen (Bietigheim), Bietigheim-Bissingen (Bissingen), Erdmannshausen, Freiburg/Neckar (Beihingen), Gemmrigheim, Hessigheim, Ingersheim (Kleiningersheim), Ingersheim (Grossingersheim), Kirchberg/Murr, Löchgau, Ludwigsburg (Hoheneck), Ludwigsburg (Neckarweihingen), Ludwigsburg (Poppenweiler), Marbach/Neckar, Marbach/Neckar (Rielingshausen), Markgröningen, Mundelsheim, Murr, Steinheim, Steinheim (Höpfigheim), Vaihingen, Walheim.

Schandl, Peter wine producer in Neusiedlersee Hügelland, Burgenland, Austria.

Schanzreiter vineyards at Illingen and Vaihingen in Württemberg region, Germany.

Scharlachberg vineyards at Bingen in Rheinhessen region and Thüngersheim in Franken region, Germany.

Scharlachberg Meisterbrand *Weinbrand* distiller, Bingen am Rhein, Germany.

Scharrenberg vineyard at Stuttgart in Württemberg region, Germany.

Scharzberg *Grosslage* incorporating vineyards in Mosel-Saar-Ruwer region, Germany at, respectively: Ayl, Irsch, Kanzem, Kastel-Staadt, Konz, Konz (Falkenstein), Konz (Filzen), Konz (Hamm), Konz (Krettnach), Konz (Kommlingen), Konz (Könen), Konz (Niedermennig), Konz (Oberemmel), Konz (Obermenning), Ockfen, Pellingen, Saarburg, Saarburg (Krutweiler), Schoden, Serrig, Wawern, Wiltingen, Wiltingen (Scharzhofberg).

Scharzhofberg vineyard at Wiltingen in Mosel-Saar-Ruwer region, Germany.

Schatzgarten vineyard at Traben-Trarbach in Mosel-Saar-Ruwer region, Germany.

Schaumwein style of sparkling wine, Germany.

Schäwer vineyard at Burrweiler in Rheinpfalz region, Germany.

Scheibenbuck vineyard at Sasbach in Baden region, Germany.

Scheiblhofer, Johann, Harald & Erich wine producer in Neusiedlersee, Burgenland, Austria.

Scheidterberg vineyard at Ayl mit Ortsteil Biebelhausen in Mosel-Saar-Ruwer region, Germany.

Scheinberg vineyard at Euerdorf in Franken region, Germany.

Schellenbrunnen vineyard at Stringen in Baden region, Germany.

Schellmann, Gottfried wine producer in Thermenregion, Niederösterreich, Austria.

Schelm vineyard at Briedel in Mosel-Saar-Ruwer region, Germany.

Schelmen vineyard at Wahlheim in Rheinhessen region, Germany.

Schelmenklinge vineyard at Ilsfeld in Württemberg region, Germany.

Schelmenstück vineyards at Bingen (Bündesheim) and Bingen (Dietersheim) in Rheinhessen region, Germany.

schelvispekel style of herbal-flavoured (mainly cinnamon) *brandewijn*, Netherlands. Name means 'haddock pickler'.

Schemelsberg vineyard at Weinsberg in Württemberg region, Germany.

Schenk leading wine producer of Switzerland.

Schenkenberg vineyards at Esslingen and Esslingen (Mettingen) in Württemberg region, Germany.

Schenkenböhl collective vineyard (*Grosslage*) incorporating vineyards at Bad Dürkheim and Wachenheim in Rheinpfalz region, Germany.

Scheuerberg vineyard at Neckarsulm in Württemberg region, Germany.

Scheurebe white grape variety of Germany. Cross of Riesling and Silvaner.

Schiava red grape variety of Trentino-Alto Adige region, Italy.

Schieferlay vineyards at Bad Neuenahr-Ahrweiler, Dernau and Mayschoss in Ahr region, Germany.

Schierlinger Roggen rye beer by Schierling brewery, Germany.

Schiesslay vineyard at Thörnich in Mosel-Saar-Ruwer region, Germany.

Schickanenbuckel vineyard at Rehborn in Nahe region, Germany.

Schiedam once-common alternative name for Dutch gin or *genever*. From Dutch town of Schiedam where first distillery opened 1575.

Schilcher specialty wine of Styria, Austria. Blauer Wildbacher grapes.

Schild *Grosslage* incorporating vineyards at Abstwind, Castell, Castell (Greuth) and Prichsenstadt in Franken region, Germany.

Schildberg vineyard at Sulzheim in Rheinhessen region, Germany.

Schillerwein light red or rosé wine of Germany, especially Baden region.

Schilling, Herbert wine producer in Wien (Vienna), Austria.

Schindler, Franz wine producer in Neusiedlersee Hügelland, Burgenland, Austria.

Schioppettino red wine from Schioppettino (also called Ribolla Nera) grapes, Albano di Prepotto, Friuli-Venezia Giulia, Italy.

Schirf brewery in Park City, Utah, USA.

schist shaley granite soil of Douro Valley, Portugal, contributing much to the weight and ripeness of grapes cultivated there for port production.

Schladerer, Alfred renowned *eau de vie* distiller est 1844, Staufen im Breisgau in the Black Forest, Germany.

Schlangengraben vineyard at Wiltingen in Mosel-Saar-Ruwer region, Germany.

schlante 'cheers' in Scotland.

Schleidberg vineyard at Tawern in Mosel-Saar-Ruwer region, Germany.

Schlemmertröpfchen vineyard at Bremm in Mosel-Saar-Ruwer region, Germany.

Schlenkerla Rauchbier famed smoked beer of Schlenkerla inn, Bamberg, Germany. Produced by Heller brewery in Bamberg.

Schlichte, HW leading *Steinhäger* distiller, Steinhägen, Westphalia, Germany. Brands include Echt Schinkenhäger, Original Schlichte.

Schlierbach vineyard at Obersulm in Württemberg region, Germany.

Schlipf vineyard at Weil am Rhein in Baden region, Germany.

Schlittberg vineyard at Römerberg (bei Speyer) in Rheinpfalz region, Germany.

Schlitz major beer brand of USA. Originally brewed in Milwaukee, Wisconsin, and promoted as the beer 'that made Milwaukee famous'.

Schlorlemer, Hermann Freiherr von major wine producer in Mosel-Saar-Ruwer region, Germany.

Schloss 'castle' in German. In wine-estate names equivalent to but much rarer than, French *château*.

Schloss vineyards at Dienheim, Edesheim, Grünstadt, Obrigheim and Oppenheim in Rheinpfalz region, Schonungen in Franken region and Uelversheim in Rheinhessen region, Germany.

Schlossberg *Grosslagen* incorporating vineyards at Grosslangheim, Iphofen, Kitzingen, Kleinlangheim, Rödelsee and Wiesenbronn in Franken region and Heppenheim (einschliesslich Erbach und Hambach) in Hessiche Bergstrasse region, Germany.

Schlossberg *grand cru* vineyard at Kientzheim, Alsace, France.

Schlossberg the name of 90 individual vineyards in Germany. Region by region, as follows: in Baden at Appenweier, Baden-Baden, Freiburg, Hohberg, Ihringen, Kenzingen, Ortenberg, Rauenberg, Salem, Schriesheim, Staufen im Breisgay, Staufen im Briesgau (Grunern), Vogtsburg im Kaiserstuhl (Achkarren), Vogtsburg im Kaiserstuhl (Oberrotweil), Wertheim; in Franken at Alzenau, Castell, Elfershausen (Engenthal), Elfershausen (Trimberg), Hammelburg, Klingenberg am Main, Knetzgau, Volkach, Würzburg; in Mittelrhein at Bad Hönningen, Hammerstein, Nassau; in Mosel-Saar-Ruwer at Beilstein, Bekond, Bernkastel-Kues (Andel), Bernkastel-Kues (Bernkastel), Burg, Cochem, Kanzem, Kobern-Gondorf (Gondorf), Kobern-Gondorf (Kobern), Lieser, Perl, Saarburg, Sommerau, Traben-Trarbach, Wiltingen, Zeltingen-Rachtig; in Nahe at Altenbamberg, Bad Münster am Stein-Ebernburg, Braunweiler, Burgsponheim, Dalberg, Gutenberg, Mandel, Martinstein, Obermoschel, Raumbach/Glan, Rümmelsheim mit Ortsteil Burg Layen, Sponheim; in Rheingau at Eltville, Lorch, Oestrich-Winkel; in Rheinhessen at Gau-Heppenheim, Harxheim, Ingelheim, Mettenheim, Oppenheim, Saufheim, Schwabenheim; in Rheinpfalz at Battenberg, Bockenheim an der Weinstrasse, Bolanden, Neuleiningen, Neustadt an der Weinstrasse, Pleisweiler-Oberhofen, Rhodt unter Rietburg, Wachenheim, Weingarten; in Württemberg at Brackenheim, Brackenheim (Neipperg), Heilbronn, Ilsfeld (Auenstein), Islfeld (Helfenberg), Ingersheim (Grossingersheim), Ingersheim (Kleiningersheim), Stuttgart (Rotenberg), Stuttgart (Uhlbach), Stuttgart (Untertürkheim), Talheim, Winnenden.

Schlossberg Schwätzerchen vineyards at Bingen (Büdesheim) and Bingen (Kempten) in Rheinhessen region, Germany.

Schlossblick vineyard at Stuttgart (Hohenheim) in Württemberg region, Germany.

Schlossböckelheim wine village of Nahe region, Germany. *Grosslage*: Burgweg.

Schloss Bübinger *Grosslage* incorporating vineyards at Besch, Perl, Perl (Nennig), Perl (Sehndorf), Tettingen and Wochern in Mosel-Saar-Ruwer region, Germany.

Schlössel vineyard at Neustadt an der Weinstrasse in Rheinpfalz region, Germany.

Schloss Esterhazy wine producer in Neusiedlersee Hügelland, Burgenland, Austria.

Schlossgarten the name of 11 individual vineyards in Germany. Region by region, as follows: in Baden at Müllheim, Vogtsburg im Kaiserstuhl; in Nahe at Bretzenheim, Schweppenhausen; in Rheingau at Geisenheim, Hochheim; in Rheinhessen at Offstein; in Rheinpfalz at Burrweiler, Friedelsheim, Kirchheimbolanden, Kleinniedesheim.

Schloss Gobelsburg wine producer in Kamptal, Niederösterreich, Austria.

Schloss Grafenegg leading wine estate near Krems, Austria.

Schloss Groensteyn wine estate est 1400 in Kedrich, Rheingau region, Germany. Renowned Riesling wines.

Schloss Grohl vineyard at Durbach in Baden region, Germany.

Schloss Gutenburg vineyard at Gutenberg in Nahe region, Germany.

Schloss Hammerstein vineyards at Albig and Alzey in Rheinhessen region, Germany.

Schlosshölle vineyards at Gumbsheim and Wöllstein in Rheinhessen region, Germany.

Schloss Hohenrechen vineyard at Nierstein in Rheinhessen region, Germany.

Schloss Hohneck vineyard at Niederheimbach in Mittelrhein region, Germany.

Schloss Johannisberg great wine estate in Rheingau region, Germany. Traditional original site of the production of *edelfäule* wines (those affected by noble rot late in ripening season). Famed Riesling wines.

Schlosskapelle *Grosslage* incorporating vineyards in Nahe region, Germany at, respectively: Bingen, Dorsheim, Eckenroth, Guldental, Laubenheim, Münster-Sarmsheim, Rümmelsheim, Schweppenhausen, Waldalgesheim, Waldlaubersheim, Weiler, Windesheim.

Schlosskellerei Halbturn wine producer in Neusiedlersee, Burgenland, Austria.

Schlossleite vineyard at Eltmann in Franken region, Germany.

Schloss Ludwigshöhe *Grosslage* incorporating vineyards at Edenkoben and St Martin in Rheinpfalz region, Germany.

Schlosspark vineyard at Volkach in Franken region, Germany.

Schloss Randeck vineyard at Mannweiler-Cölln in Nahe region, Germany.

Schloss Reichenstein *Grosslage* incorporating villages at Niederheimbach, Oberheimbach, Oberheimbach (Schloss Fürstenberg) and Trechtingshausen in Mittelrhein region, Germany.

Schloss Reichhartshausen vineyard at Oestrich-Winkel in Rheingau region, Germany.

Schloss Rheinburg vineyard at Gailingen in Baden region, Germany.

Schloss Reinhartshausen leading wine estate of Rheingau region, Germany. Vineyards for noted Riesling wines at Erbach, Hattenheim, Kiedrich, Rüdesheim etc.

Schloss Rodeck *Grosslage* incorporating vineyards in Baden region, Germany at, respectively: Achern (Mösbach), Achern (Oberachern), Baden-Baden, Baden-Baden (Neuweier), Baden-Baden (Steinbach), Baden-Baden (Varnhalt), Bühl (Altschweier), Bühl (Eisental), Bühl (Neusatz), Bühlertal, Gernsbach (Obertsrot), Gernsbach (Staufenberg), Kappelrodeck, Kappelrodeck (Waldulm), Lauf, Ottersweier, Renchen, Sasbach, Sasbachwalden, Sinzheim, Weisenbach.

Schloss Saarfelser Schlossberg vineyard at Serrig in Mosel-Saar-Ruwer region, Germany.

Schloss Saarsteiner vineyard at Serrig in Mosel-Saar-Ruwer region, Germany.

Schloss Schönborn leading wine estate based at Hattenheim, Rheingau region, Germany. Est 1349 by, and still in ownership of, von Schönborn family. Vineyards at Erbach, Hattenheim, Hockheim, Oestrich, Rüdesheim etc.

Schloss Schönburg *Grosslage* incorporating vineyards at Damscheid, Niederburg, Oberwesel, Oberwesel (Dellhofen), Oberwesel (Engehöll), Oberwesel (Langscheid), Oberwesel (Urbar) and Perscheid in Mittelrhein region, Germany.

Schloss Schwabsburg vineyards at Nierstein and Nierstein (Schwabsburg) in Rheinhessen region, Germany.

Schloss Stahlberg vineyards at Bacharach (Breitscheid) and Bacharach (Steeg) in Mittelrhein region, Germany.

Schloss Stahlech *Grosslage* incorporating vineyards at Bacharach, Bacharach (Breitshcheid), Bacharach (Medenscheid und Neurath), Bacharach (Steeg), Manubach, Oberdiebach, Oberdiebach (Rhein-diebach) and Oberheimbach in Mittelrhein region, Germany.

Schlossteige vineyards at Beuren, Frickenhausen, Frickenhausen (Linsenhofen), Kohlberg, Metzingen, Neuffen, Neuffen (Kappishäusern) and Welheim in Württemberg region, Germany.

Schloss Stolzenberg vineyard at Bayerfeld-Steckweiler in Nahe region, Germany.

Schlossstück *Grosslage* incorporating vineyards in Franken region, Germany at, respectively: Bad Windsheim (Humprechtsau), Bad Windsheim (Ickelheim), Bad Windsheim (Külsheim), Bad Windsheim (Rüdisbronn), Dietersheim (Dottenheim), Dietersheim (Walddachsbach), Ergersheim, Ippesheim, Ippesheim (Bullenheim), Ipsheim, Ipsheim (Kaubenheim), Ipsheim (Weimersheim), Seinsheim, Sugenheim (Ingolstadt), Sugenheim (Krassolzheim), Weigenheim, Weigenheim (Reusch), Willanzheim, Windsheim.

Schloss Thorner Kupp vineyard at Palzem in Mosel-Saar-Ruwer region, Germany.

Schloss Vollrads great wine estate at Oestrich-Winkel in Rheingau, Germany. Proprietor Count Erwein Matuschka-Greiffenclau's ancestors were making wine here in 1211. Outstanding Riesling wines, with *halbtrocken* (semi-dry) styles a speciality. Wines are known for their distinguishing coloured capsules: green for *QbA*, blue for *kabinett*, pink for *spätlese*, white for *auslese*, gold for *trockenbeerenauslese*.

see label opposite ➡

Schlosswengert

Schlosswengert vineyard at Beilstein in Württemberg region, Germany.

Schlossweingut Hardegg wine producer in Weinviertel, Niederösterreich, Austria.

Schloss Westerhaus vineyards at Ingelheim and Ingelheim (Gross-Winternheim) in Rheinhessen region, Germany.

Schlück popular white wine brand of Lenz Moser, Austria. Grüner Veltliner grapes.

Schlumberger leading wine producer in Guebwiller, Alsace, France. Distinguished *grand cru* and *vendange tardive* wines.

Schlumberger wine producer in Thermenregion, Niederösterreich, Austria.

Schlüsselberg vineyard at Schöntal in Württemberg region, Germany.

Schmeker vineyard at Weikersheim in Württemberg region, Germany.

Schmelz, Johann wine producer in Wachau, Niederösterreich, Austria.

Schmelzer, Georg wine producer in Neusiedlersee, Burgenland, Austria.

Schmid, Josef wine producer in Kremstal, Niederösterreich, Austria.

Schmidl, Franz wine producer in Wachau, Niederösterreich, Austria.

Schmittskapellchen vineyard at Nackenheim in Rheinhessen region, Germany.

Schnapdragon mixed drink of schnapps and bitter lemon.

schnapps generic term for spirits, Germany. Also describes colourless potato spirit of Netherlands.

schnaps colourless spirit, Danish. See box.

Schneckenberg vineyard at Worms in Rheinhessen region, Germany.

Schneider Weisse wheat beer of George Schneider brewery, Kelheim, near Munich, Germany.

Schnekenhof vineyards at Bretzfeld (Adolzfurt), Bretzfeld (Geddelsbach), Bretzfeld (Unterheimbach) and Wüstenrot in Württemberg region, Germany.

Schnepfenflug an der Weinstrasse *Grosslage* incorporating vineyards at Deidesheim, Forst an der Weinstrasse, Friedelsheim and Wachenheim in Rheinpfalz region, Germany.

Schnepfenflug vom Zellertal *Grosslage* incorporating vineyards in Rheinpfalz region, Germany at, respectively: Albisheim, Bolanden, Bubenheim, Einselthum, Gauersheim, Immesheim, Kerzenheim, Kirchheimbolanden, Morschheim, Ottersheim/Zellertal, Rittersheim, Rüssingen, Stetten, Zellertal (Harxheim), Zellertal (Niefernheim), Zellertal (Zell).

Schnepp vineyard at Obersülzen in Rheinpfalz region, Germany.

Schnorbach Brückstück vineyard at Koblenz in Mittelrhein region, Germany.

Schoenenberg *Grand Cru* vineyard (since 1987) at Riquewihr, Alsace, France.

Schollerbuckel vineyard at Eberbach in Baden region, Germany.

Schnaps

spirit with a place at court

The spellings vary – schnaps in Denmark, schnapps in Germany and Holland, snaps in Sweden – but the meaning of the word is the same. It translates as a 'snatch', the tug in the throat that induces the gasp when taking a stiff swig of this ardent spirit.

Distilling schnaps dates back as far as 600 years in Denmark, where the name is more or less synonymous with aquavit for white spirits, variously flavoured, made from both grain and potatoes. Schnaps has also enjoyed a long synonymity with the Danish royal family, since King Kristian III became an enthusiastic distiller himself in 1555 after acquiring a working pot still from a Copenhagen pawnbroker. Strong spirits thus became *de rigueur* in the Danish Court.

Kristian's heir, Frederik II, who built the legendary Kronborg castle at Elsinore amidst a prosperous reign (1559–1588) is said to have drunk himself to death on schnaps. His son, Kristian IV, carried on the tradition and introduced the rowdy custom of accompanying the drinking of loyal toasts with drum rolls and trumpet blasts (and even the occasional round of cannon fire), just as portrayed in *Hamlet*.

Kristian IV's sister, Anne, married King James VI of Scotland (later also James I of England) in 1589 and as part of her dowry brought with her to Edinburgh a volume detailing 181 recipes for schnaps. Among her courtiers was a formidable Dane who was reputed to have triumphed in drinking contests in every court in Europe. He had not reckoned with the Scots. In a session that lasted three days and nights, the Viking challenger was comprehensively drunk under the table by a stalwart laird, Sir Robert Lawrie. The occasion is recorded, with gleeful embellishment, in Robert Burns's poem *The Whistle*.

Scholtz Hermanos leading producer of Málaga wines, Málaga, Spain. Brands include Lágrima Delicioso (10-year-old), Málaga Dulce Negro, Solera 1885.

Schön vineyards at Bad Friedrichshall (Duttenberg) and Bad Friedrichshall (Offenau) in Württemberg region, Germany.

Schönauer leading brand of *Korn* spirit by Schönau distillery, Friedrichsruh, Germany.

Schönberg vineyards at Bornheim and Lonsheim in Rheinhessen region, Germany.

Schönburger pink grape variety of Germany, and England. Crossing of Pinot Noir and Piovano 1.

Schönhell vineyard at Oestrich-Winkel in Rheingau region, Germany.

Schönhölle vineyard at Ockenheim in Rheinhessen region, Germany.

Schöntal vineyard at Alsbach in Hessische Bergstrasse region, Germany.

Schollerbuckel vineyard at Eberbach in Baden region, Germany.

schooner a drinking glass characterised by a tall, concave-formed bowl on a short stem. Once a popular vessel for sherry. Now rare. In some English-speaking countries notably Australia and the United States, a schooner is a tall beer glass.

schope traditional tankard for wine, Alsace, France.

Schoppenwein carafe wine of bars and cafés, Germany.

Schozachtal *Grosslage* incorporating vineyards at Abstatt, Ilsfeld, Ilsfeld (Auenstein), Insfeld (Helfenburg), Löwenstein and Untergruppen-bach (Unterheinreit) in Württemberg region, Germany.

Schramsberg renowned sparkling wine of Schramsberg Vineyard est 1862 by Jacob Schram, Napa Valley, California, USA. Featured in *Silverado Squatters* by Robert Louis Stevenson (1850–94) who visited the vineyard on his honeymoon.

Schröck, Heidi wine producer in Neusiedlersee Hügelland, Burgenland, Austria.

Schubert, C von leading wine estate at Maximin-Grünhaus, Mosel-Saar-Ruwer region, Germany. Est 966 and a von Schubert property since 1882. Famed *Einzellagen* of Abstberg, Bruderberg, Herrenberg.

Schubertslay vineyard at Piesport in Mosel-Saar-Ruwer region, Germany.

Schultheiss major brewery of Berlin, Germany, famed for **Schultheiss Berliner Weisse** wheat beer.

Schuster, Karl wine producer in Donauland, Niederösterreich, Austria.

Schuster, Rosi wine producer in Neusiedlersee Hügelland, Burgenland, Austria.

Schutterlindenberg *Grosslage* incorporating vineyards in Baden region, Germany at, respectively: Ettenheim (Münchweier), Ettenheim (Wallburg), Friesenheim, Friesenheim (Heiligenzell), Friesenheim (Oberschopfheim), Friesenheim (Oberweler), Kippenheim, Kippenheim (Mahlberg), Kippenheim (Schmieheim), Lahr, Lahr (Hugsweier), Lahr (Kippenheimweiler), Lahr (Mietersheim), Lahr (Sulz).

Schutzenberger brewery in Amos, Lorraine, France.

Schützenhaus vineyard at Eltville in Rheingau region, Germany.

Schützenhütte vineyards at Dolgesheim and Oppenheim in Rheinhessen region, Germany.

Schützenlay vineyard at Ediger-Eller in Mosel-Saar-Ruwer region, Germany.

Schwaben Bräu brewery in Vaihingen, Stuttgart, Germany. Meister Pils.

Schwalben vineyard at Wackernheim in Rheinhessen region, Germany.

Schwalbennest vineyard at Raumbach/Glan in Nahe region, Germany.

Schwanleite vineyard at Rödelsee in Franken region, Germany.

Schwartze Katz *Grosslage* incorporating vineyards at Zell, Zell (Kaimt) and Zell (Merl) in Mosel-Saar-Ruwer region, Germany.

Schwarz, Reinhold & Thomas wine producer in Neusiedlersee Hügelland, Burgenland, Austria.

Schwarzenberg vineyards at Bingen in Rheinhessen region and Walwig in Mosel-Saar-Ruwer region, Germany.

Schwarzenstein vineyard at Geisenheim in Rheingau region, Germany.

Schwarzerde *Grosslage* incorporating vineyards in Rheinpfalz region, Germany at, respectively: Bissersheim, Dirmstein, Gerolsheim, Grosskarlbach, Grossniedesheim, Grünstadt Land, Hessheim, Kirchheim an der Weinstrasse, Kleinniedesheim, Laumersheim, Obersülzen. *see label opposite* ➡

Schwarzer Letten vineyard at Edenkoben in Rheinpfalz region, Germany.

Schwarzes Kreuz vineyard at Friensheim in Rheinpfalz region, Germany.

Schwarzlay *Grosslage* incorporating vineyards in Mosel-Saar-Ruwer region, Germany at, respectively: Bausendorf, Bengel, Burg, Drels, Enkirch, Erden, Flussbach, Hupperath, Kinheim, Lösnich, Platten, Starkenburg, Traben-Trarbach (Traben, Trabenbach and Wolf), Ürzig, Wittlich.

Schwarzriesling regional name for Pinot Meunier grape variety, Germany.

Schwechat brewery in Vienna, Austria. Birthplace of Viennese lager in 1841 under the ownership of Anton Dreher. Current brands in production include Hopfenperle and Steffl.

Schwenker capacious drinking glass for brandy. German.

Schwobajörgle vineyards at Neuenstein (Eschelbach) and Neuenstein (Kesselfeld) in Württemberg region, Germany.

Sciacarello red grape variety of Corsica.

Scoff-Law Cocktail. Over ice shake 2 parts dry vermouth, 2 rye whisky, 1 grenadine, 1 lemon juice, 1 dash orange bitters. Strain.

Scolca, La leading producer of dry white Cortese di Gavi wine, Piedmont, northwest Italy.

1993
Kirchheimer Schwarzerde
Beerenauslese
Qualitätswein mit Prädikat

8.5%vol   PFALZ   37.5 d ℮

Scorpion Cocktail. Over ice shake 2 parts rum, 1 brandy, 1 lemon juice, 1 orange juice, 2 dashes curaçao. Strain.

Scorpion Lager strong (5.0% alc) lager brand of Vaux Breweries, Sunderland, England.

Scotch ale descriptive, if not defining, term for strong and malty dark ales brewed in Scotland.

Scotch Kilt Cocktail. Over ice stir 2 parts scotch whisky, 1 Drambuie, 2 dashes orange bitters, 1 strip orange peel. Strain.

Scotch Mist Cocktail. Over crushed ice shake 1 part scotch whisky and pour into flute glass. Add lemon peel twist and serve with straws.

Scotch Weekend Sour Cocktail. Over ice shake 3 parts scotch whisky, 2 cherry brandy, 1 sweet vermouth, 2 lemon juice, 1 egg white. Strain into ice-filled tumblers.

scotch whisky indigenous spirit of Scotland distilled from malted barley or other grain and sold mainly as a blend of both. All scotch must be produced in Scotland, but distilling ingredients may be – and are – imported from outside the country. To be sold as scotch, the spirit must have been aged at least three years in oak casks. See box.

Scotia Royale twelve-year-old blended scotch whisky by Glen Scotia Distillery, Campbeltown, Scotland.

Scotsmac ginger-wine-based 'whisky mac' premixed drink originally of J H Wham Co now of Matthew Clark, Bristol, England.

Scottish & Newcastle British brewing company formed by 1960 merger between McEwan's and Younger's breweries of Scotland and Newcastle's Tyne Brewery. Through further acquisitions, and disposal of pub interests, S&N became the largest brewing business in Britain. The company's Edinburgh site, the Fountain Bridge Brewery, closed 2004, and Tyne Brewery in Newcastle closed 2005. Brewing centres are now in Gateshead and Tadcaster.

Scottish Courage British brewing and drinks company incorporating Scottish & Newcastle breweries.

Scottish Leader blended scotch whisky by Burn Stewart Distillers, Glasgow, Scotland.

Scottish Oatmeal stout (4.2% alc) by Broughton Ales, Peeblesshire, Scotland.

Scotts brewery-hotel at Lowestoft, Suffolk, England.

Scott system micro-biologically controlled yeast-processing system in brewing industry.

Screwdriver Cocktail. Over ice shake 1 part vodka, 2 orange juice. Strain into ice-filled glass and add orange slice.

scrumpy unfiltered and unsweetened rustic cider, so-called after term scrump for a withered or windfall apple. English.

Scotch Whisky

five fiery centuries

History does not record when whisky distilling began in the Highlands of Scotland, but the process did not originate there. The necessary skills were imported with the Irish missionary monks who came to the region in the Middle Ages. Ireland is known to have discovered the art of distilling in the 12th century, if not earlier.

By the 1500s, Scotch whisky distilling was firmly established. The first stills were erected in the Irish-founded monasteries, but many farms and larger houses would have had their own apparatus by then. This dynamic industry inevitably attracted the attentions of regulators, and in 1505 the first quality-assurance scheme was set up in Edinburgh – under the aegis of the city's College of Surgeons. In the interest of the city's good health, it was ordained, producers must use only the purest ingredients. To ensure standards were met, the College secured the right to dispense whisky – a privilege shared with only one other exclusive professional group, the barbers.

Official interference has since done much to determine the history of Scotland's national liquor. The Scots Parliament, before its final dissolution in 1707, regularly attempted to restrict production, fearing that such a large proportion of the barley harvest was diverted to distillation in some years that the country might face famine from shortage of flour for breadmaking. And distillers were taxed. As early as 1664, a huge levy of two shillings and eight pence was imposed on every pint of whisky, to be paid by the distiller. Evasion was, naturally, widespread, and the excise men appointed to collect the despised tax had a hard time of it.

But the real blow fell in 1784. Parliament in London ruled that whisky distilling was illegal. Excise officers were diverted from the task of collecting duties to suppressing production altogether.

Among their number, appointed in 1789, was the poet Robert Burns. It was 40 years before the government in England relented, persuaded by the Scottish Duke of Gordon that the anarchy north of the border, where distilling had continued unabated, could only be controlled if the prohibition was lifted and a licensing system introduced.

Thus in 1823 the first of the countless acts governing Scotch whisky production was passed in Parliament. Successful applicants for the new licences would pay a £10 fee and two shillings excise duty on every gallon distilled. By the end of the 20th century, that levy had increased three-hundredfold to a swingeing £30. In the meantime, enthusiasm for the product has nevertheless spread south to England – and throughout the world.

Scrumpy Jack cider brand of Symonds Cider & English Wine Co, Hereford, England. Owned by HP Bulmer (Scottish Courage).

Sculler brewery in St Catherine's, Ontario, Canada. **Sculler Premium Lager**.

Scuppernong grape variety (of genus *vitis vulpina*) and wine of the valley of the River Scuppernong, North Carolina, USA.

Sea Breeze Cocktail. Over ice shake 1 part Absolut vodka, 2 cranberry juice, 2 grapefruit juice. Strain into ice-filled glass.

Sea Breeze Cooler Cocktail. Into tall glass with ice add 2 parts apricot brandy, 2 dry gin, 1 lemon juice, 2 dashes grenadine. Top with soda water and add mint sprig to glass.

Seabright pub-brewery in Santa Cruz, California, USA.

Seagram whisky distiller of Canada active since 1857. Incorporated 1883 at the Waterloo distillery, Ontario, Canada, by Joseph Seagram, it was to become among the largest liquor companies in the world. Following takeover of the company's drinks interests by Vivendi of France in 2000, Seagram's many brands of wines and spirits have been dispersed among several new owners – principally Diageo and

Pernod-Ricard – around the world.

Seagram's Extra Dry gin brand of Seagram, Canada, purchased by Pernod-Ricard, 2001.

Seagram's 5 Star Canadian whisky brand acquired by Diageo, 2001.

Seagram's VO and **Seagram's Seven Crowns** top-selling whiskies in both Canada and the USA, sold to Diageo, 2001.

Seagram Vodka brand sold to Pernod-Ricard, 2001.

Seaview sparkling wine brand of Southcorp, South Australia.

Sebastiani wine producer in Sonoma, California, USA.

Sebourg beer brand of Brasserie Duyck, Jenlain, France.

sec 'dry' (usually wine). French.

Séché part of *premier cru* vineyard of Vaillons in Chablis, France. Also spelt **Séchet**.

secco 'dry' (wine). Italian.

seco 'medium dry' (sparkling wine). Spanish.

secondary fermentation a carbon-dioxide-producing refermentation subsequent to the alcoholic fermentation (as in production of sparkling wines where new sugars and yeasts are introduced into bottle or tank which is then sealed). Also called malolactic fermentation.

Second Vin de Mouton-Rothschild, Le second wine of Château Mouton-Rothschild, Bordeaux, France.

second wine now-common term, originally from Bordeaux, France, for wine of a well-known estate made from vats of a quality not deemed suitable for the main product (*grand vin*). Second wines of some *châteaux*, eg Les Forts de Latour from Château Latour, fetch higher prices than *grands vins* of many *grand cru classé* estates.

Seder wine made (usually at home, from raisins) for the Jewish service of Seder.

Sedlescombe vineyard at Robertsbridge, Sussex, England. Organic methods.

Seehalde vineyard at Nonnenhorn in Württemberg region, Germany.

Seeweine former common name for wine of Lake Constance region, Germany.

Seewinkel wine-producing area of Neusiedlersee, Austria.

Segonnes, Château second wine of Château Lascombes, Bordeaux, France.

Segonzac, Château wine estate of AC Premières Côtes de Blaye, Bordeaux, France.

Séguinot, Pierre cognac producer, Segonzac, France.

Ségur, Château wine estate of AC Haut-Médoc, Bordeaux, France. Classified *Cru Grand Bourgeois*.

Segura Vidas wine producer at San Sadurniu da Noya, Penedès, Spain. *Cava* wines.

Ségur-d'Arsac, Château second wine of Château d'Arsac, Bordeaux, France.

Séguret wine village of AC Côtes du Rhône Villages, Rhône Valley, France.

Seidenberg vineyard at Mannweiler-Cölln in the Nahe region, Germany.

Seigneur de la Teste armagnac-producing co-operative, Condom, Gascony, France.

Seiler, Friedrich wine producer in Neusiedlersee Hügelland, Burgenland, Austria.

Seilgarten vineyard at Bermersheim in Rheinhessen region, Germany.

Sekt sparkling wine of Germany. Mostly Charmat or 'tank' method.

Selaks wine producer at Kumeu, New Zealand. Noted Sauvignon wines.

Selby brewery at Selby, North Yorkshire, England.

Sélection de Grains Nobles specialised wine from late-harvested grapes, Alsace, France. Rich and expensive wines from selected extra-ripe grapes (*grains nobles*) which must reach specified natural-sugar levels determined under AC rules.

Self-Starter Cocktail. Over ice shake 4 parts dry gin, 3 Lillet, 1 apricot brandy, 2 dashes pastis. Strain.

Seligmacher vineyards at Landau in der Pfalz and Ranschbach in Rheinpfalz region, Germany.

Sella & Mosca leading wine producer of island of Sardinia, Italy.

Selle, Château de wine property of Domaines Ott in AC Côtes de Provence, France.

Selosse, Jacques *récoltant manipulant* champagne producer, Avize, Champagne, France.

Selvapiana leading wine estate of Chianti Rufina, Tuscany, Italy.

Sémeillan Mazeau, Château wine estate of AC Listrac, Médoc, Bordeaux, France. Classified *Cru Bourgeois Supérieur*.

Sémillon white grape variety chiefly known as principal constituent of sweet wines of Barsac and Sauternes in Bordeaux, France. Also important in dry white wines of Bordeaux

and, increasingly, in New World, especially Australia.

semisecco medium sweet, Italian. Sparkling wines.

Sempé armagnac house est 1934 by Henri-Abel Sempé, Aignan, Gascony, France.

Seña premium wine brand of Viña Errazuriz, Chile, in co-operation with Robert Mondavi of California, USA.

Senailhac, Château wine estate of AC Entre-Deux-Mers, Bordeaux, France.

Sénéjac, Château wine estate of AC Haut-Médoc, Bordeaux, France. Classified *Cru Bourgeois Superieur*.

Senez, Christian *récoltant manipulant* champagne producer, Fontette, Champagne, France.

Senilhac, Château wine estate of AC Haut-Médoc, Bordeaux, France. Classified *Cru Bourgeois*.

Senn vineyard at Kleinkarlbach in Rheinpfalz region, Germany.

Señorio de Sarría wine producer at Pamplona, Navarra region, Spain.

Señor Lustau solera gran reserva brandy by Emilio Lustau, Jerez de la Frontera, Spain.

Sensation Cocktail. Over ice shake 3 parts dry gin, 1 lemon juice, 3 dashes maraschino, 3 sprigs fresh mint. Strain.

Seppelt wine producer est 1850 at Seppeltsfield, Barossa Valley, South Australia. Many renowned table wines from vineyards of several regions, plus Australia's most-prized (and expensive) 'ports'. Owned by Southcorp.

Seppelt Great Western leading sparkling wine producer of Australia. Part of Seppelt.

September Morn Cocktail. Over ice shake 1 egg white, 2 parts rum, 1 lime (or lemon) juice, 2 dashes grenadine. Strain.

Septimer grape variety chiefly of Rheinhessen region, Germany.

Serbia wine-producing state. Red and white wines from French and indigenous varieties.

Sercial grape variety for and style-name of dry madeira. Island of Madeira, Portugal.

Sergant, Château wine estate of AC Lalande-de-Pomerol, Bordeaux, France.

Serradayres wine brand of Carvalho, Ribeiro and Ferreira of Ribatejo, Portugal.

Serre, Château La wine estate of AC St-Emilion, Bordeaux, France. Classified *Grand Cru Classé*.

Serrig wine village of Mosel-Saar-Ruwer region, Germany. *Grosslage*: Scharzberg. Vineyards include Antoniusberg, Heiligenborn, Herrenberg, Kupp, Schlossberg, Schloss Saarsfelser, Vogelsang, Würzburg.

Servatiusberg vineyard at Briedern in Mosel-Saar-Ruwer region, Germany.

Sester *Kölschbier* brand, Cologne, Germany.

Sestignan, Château wine estate of AC Médoc, Bordeaux, France. Classified *Cru Bourgeois*.

Setinum red wine of ancient Rome, produced at Setia and reputed favourite of Caesar Augustus (63BC–AD14).

Settesoli major cooperative wine producer in Sicily, Italy.

Sétubal designated wine district south of Lisbon, Portugal. Best known for fortified wines from Moscatel grapes.

Setzer, Hans wine producer in Weinviertel, Niederösterreich, Austria.

Sève de Sapin pine-sap flavoured liqueur by Distilleries Associées Belge, Jumet, Belgium.

Seven Crowns American blended whisky brand originally of Seagram.

Sevenhill Cellars wine producer est 1851 Clare Valley, South Australia. Sacramental wines as well as popular commercial brands.

Seventh Heaven Cocktail. Over ice shake 1 part Caperitif, 1 dry gin, 2 dashes maraschino, 1 dash Angostura bitters. Strain and add cocktail cherry to glass. Squeeze orange peel over.

Séverin-Doublet *récoltant manipulant* champagne producer, Vertus, Champagne, France.

Sevilla Cocktail. Over ice shake 1 part rum, 1 sweet vermouth, 1 piece orange peel. Strain. Alternatively, over ice shake 1 egg, 1 part port, 1 rum, sprinkling sugar. Strain.

Sex on the Beach Cocktail. Over ice shake 2 parts vodka, 1 peach brandy, 2 cranberry juice, 1 equal mix lemon and orange juice. Strain into shot glasses and add a maraschino cherry to each.

Seyssel town and AC of Savoie region, France. Sparkling **Seyssel Mousseux** wine from Molette grapes and still Roussette de Seyssel from Roussette grape. Leading producer is Varichon & Clerc.

Seyval Blanc white grape variety of France. Also cultivated in England.

Sezoens summer-season beer by Martens brewery, Bocholt, Limburg, Belgium.

Sforzato alternative spelling of Sfursat.

Sfursat DOC for strong red wine from part-dried Nebbiolo grapes, Valtellina, Lombardy, Italy.

SG Cocktail. Over ice shake 1 part rye whisky, 1 lemon juice, 1 orange juice, 1 teaspoon grenadine. Strain.

Shady Grove Cocktail. Into tall glass with ice add 2 parts dry gin, 1 lemon juice, 1 teaspoon sugar. Top with chilled ginger beer.

Shady Lady Cocktail. Over ice shake 3 parts tequila, 1 apple brandy, 1 cranberry juice, 1 teaspoon fresh lime juice. Strain.

Shaftebury brewery in Vancouver, Canada. 'English-style' beers include **Shaftebury Bitter, Shaftebury ESB**.

Shakemantle bottle-conditioned ale (5.0% alc) by Freeminer Brewery, Forest of Dean, Gloucestershire, England. Brewed with real ginger and named after former iron mine, the deepest in the Forest of Dean.

Shamrock Cocktail. Over ice shake 1 part Irish whiskey, 1 dry vermouth, 3 dashes crème de menthe, 3 dashes green Chartreuse. Strain.

shandy mixed drink of beer with ginger beer or lemonade. In USA, **shandygaff**.

Shanghai Cocktail. Over ice shake 4 parts rum, 3 lemon juice, 1 Anisette, 2 dashes grenadine. Strain.

Shao-Hsing Shan Niang Chiew rice-based 'wine' brand of state trading monopoly, Shanghai, People's Republic of China.

shao shing Chinese rice beer or 'wine,' Possibly synoymous with shamshoo.

Shardlow brewery at Cavendish Bridge, Shardlow, Derbyshire, England.

Sharky Punch Cocktail. Over ice shake 3 parts apple brandy, 1 rye whisky. Strain into tumbler glass and top with soda water.

sharp in winetasting, a flavour with unpleasant acidity.

Sharp's brewery at Rock, Wadebridge, Cornwall, England. Ales include Cornish Coaster (3.6% alc), Eden (4.4% alc), Doom Bar Bitter (4.0% alc), **Sharp's Own** (4.4% alc), **Sharp's Special** (5.2% alc), Will's Resolve (4.6% alc),

Shawsgate vineyard at Framlingham, Suffolk, England.

Sheep Dip scotch whisky brand of Bailey Robinson, Bristol, England.

Sheep Stagger cider brand of Torre Farm, Washford, Somerset, England.

Sheffield Stout traditional shandy (beer-lemonade) drink of Yorkshire, England, made with Mather's (of Leeds, Yorkshire) Black Beer.

shekar an intoxicating drink, Hebrew. Also spelt *schechar*.

shemahrin wine of unquestioned authenticity and quality. Biblical.

Shenandoah Valley AVA of Amador County, California, USA.

Shepherd Neame brewery in Faversham, Kent, England. Established in 1698, it is said to be the country's oldest. Ales include Bishops Finger (5.0% alc), Masterbrew Bitter (3.7% alc), Spitfire (4.5% alc).

Sheppy's cider producer, Bradford-on-Tone, Somerset, England. Brands include Bullfinch, Goldfinch, Oakwood and a number of individual-variety bottled ciders including Dabinett, Kingston Black, Taylor's Gold and Tremlett's Bitter. And new certified-organic Sheppy's cider was launched in 2004.

Shere Beer lager (6% alc) brewed in UK under licence from Mysore Breweries, Bangalore, India.

Sheridan's 'Irish cream liqueur' brand of IDV, UK.

Sherlock's Home brewery in Minneapolis, Minnesota, USA. English style Bishop's Bitter, Scottish style Piper's Pride and Stag's Head Stout.

sherry the fortified wine of Jerez de la Frontera, Spain. Four styles are pale *fino*, tawny *amontillado*, the rare *palo cortado* and the dark *oloroso*. Wines are all naturally dry, but commonly sweetened, especially for export markets. Name is an English corruption of Jerez, originally Phoenician Xera and latterly Seris and Xeres of Moorish and Christian Spain respectively.

Sherry Cocktail. Over ice stir 1 part dry sherry, 2 dashes dry vermouth, 2 dashes orange bitters.

shicker a strong drink. Thus **shickered**, drunk. Yiddish.

Shields pub-brewery in Ventura, California, USA.

Shillelah Cocktail. Over ice shake 2 parts Irish whiskey, 1 sherry, 1 teaspoon rum, 1 teaspoon sloe gin, 1 teaspoon lemon juice, 1 pinch caster sugar. Strain.

Ship Cocktail. Over ice shake 2 parts sherry, 1 rum, 1 whisky, 1 prune syrup. Strain.

Shipstone brewery in Nottingham, East Midlands, England.

Ship Stout brand of Shipstone brewery, Nottingham, England.

Shiraz regional name for Syrah grape variety, Australia and South Africa. Said to be named after the ancient city, trading post and winemaking centre of Persia.

Shires Bitter ale by Wychwood Brewery, Witney, Oxfordshire, England. Also the name given to the house bitter of The Bull public house, Ambridge, Borsetshire, in BBC Radio's eternal soap-opera series *The Archers*.

shive stubby cork for closing wide-mouthed bottles or casks.

shochu type of white spirit distilled from rice beer. Japan.

Shock Cider strong (8.4% alc) cider in light-bulb-style bottle. German, but licensed for bottling abroad.

Shoes brew pub (Three Horseshoes Inn), Hereford, England.

Shoot Cocktail. Over ice shake 1 part scotch whisky, 1 dry sherry, 1 equal mix lemon and orange juice, 1 pinch sugar. Strain.

shooter style of cocktail in which small measures are shaken or stirred together then served in a 'shot' glass for drinking in one swallow.

short in winetasting, a flavour that lasts no time in the mouth. Indicates poor quality.

Shortridge Lawton madeira shipper. Island of Madeira, Portugal.

shot bottle product of antiquated custom of placing lead shot inside port bottles and shaking vigorously to etch the inner glass surface. The process was believed to improve adhesion of wine's sediment and facilitated decanting.

shot glass small tumbler-shaped glass for spirits.

Shriner Cocktail. Over ice shake 1 part sloe gin, 1 brandy, 1 dash Angostura bitters, 1 pinch sugar. Strain.

Shropshire Lad bottle-conditioned seasonal (Spring) bitter by Wood Brewery, Winstantow, Shropshire, England. Name commemorates immortal poem of 1896 by Worcestershire-born A E Housman (1859–1936).

shrub mixed drink of brandy or rum, fruit juices, spice and sugar. Also bottled commercially for adding to spirits, especially rum.

Shugborough Hall bottle-conditioned beer (4.5% alc) named after and brewed at ancestral home of the Earls of Lichfield, Shugborough, Staffordshire, England.

Shumen winery est 1962 in northeast Bulgaria. Taken over 1997 by Domaine Boyar. Well-known 'Premium' wines from French grape varieties.

Siaurac, Château wine estate of AC Lalande-de-Pomerol, Bordeaux, France.

Siberian Sunrise Cocktail. Into an ice-filled tall glass pour 1 part vodka, 1 orange juice, 1 pineapple juice, 2 dashes grenadine.

Sibirskaya Russian vodka brand from Siberian winter wheat.

Sichel, Peter (d. 1998) wine producer (Chx d'Angludet and Palmer) and *négoçiant*, as Maison Sichel, in Bordeaux, France.

Sichel Söhne US-based wine company and producer of Germany's most-famous Liebfraumilch brand, Blue Nun.

Sicily wine-producing island of Italy. Famed Marsala and other sweet and fortified wines plus table wines from DOC and countless unclassified origins.

Sidecar Cocktail. Over ice shake 2 parts brandy, 1 Cointreau, 1 lemon juice. Strain.

Sidi Rais rosé wine of Tunisia.

Sidi Salem red wine produced at Kanguet, Tunisia.

Sieben brewery in Chicago, Illinois, USA.

Sieben Jungfrauen vineyard at Oberwesel in Mittelrhein region, Germany.

Siegelsberg vineyard at Eltville in Rheingau region, Germany.

Siegerrebe white grape variety of Germany.

Sierra Nevada brewery in Chico, California, USA. Famed for Big Foot barley wine, **Sierra Nevada Draught Ale** and **Sierra Nevada Pale Ale** (5.5% alc).

sifone unfermented grape must added to marsala wines. Sicily.

Sigalas-Rabaud, Château wine estate of AC Sauternes, Bordeaux, France. Classified *1er Cru Classé*.

Signature cognac brand of Thomas Hine & Co, Jarnac, France.

Signature ruby port brand of Sandeman, Vila Nova de Gaia, Portugal.

Sigognac, Château wine estate of AC Médoc, Bordeaux, France. Classified *Cru Grand Bourgeois*.

Sigoulès village of cooperative wine producer in AC Bergerac, SW France.

Siklós wine-producing region of southern Hungary.

Silberberg the name of 11 individual vineyards in Germany. Region by region, as follows: in Ahr at Bad Neuenahr-Ahrweiler, Mayschoss; in Baden at Bahlingen, Kraichtal; in Mosel-Saar-Ruwer at Ellenz-Poltersdorf; in Nahe at Niedermoschel, Obermoschel; in Rheinhessen at Bodenheim, Mölsheim, Monsheim; in Rheinpfalz at Niederhorbach, Walsheim.

Silberberg college of oenology and wine producer in Südsteiermark, Austria.

Silbergrube vineyard at Mommenheim in Rheinhessen region, Germany.

Silberquell vineyard at Tauberbischofsheim in Baden region, Germany.

Siliusbrunnen vineyard at Dienheim in Rheinhessen region, Germany.

Silk Stocking Cocktail. Over ice shake 3 parts dry gin, 1 apple brandy, 2 orange juice. Strain.

Sillery village of Champagne region, France and, formerly, name given to red wine of the locality.

Silva, C Da port producer and shipper est 1862 Vila Nova de Gaia, Portugal. Aged tawny ports and vintages: 1963, 70, 77, 78, 82, 83, 85, 87, 91, 97, 2000, 03.

Silva & Cozens port shipper, Vila Nova de Gaia, Portugal. Vintages: 1955, 60, 63, 66, 70, 72, 75, 77, 80, 83, 85, 90, 91, 94, 97, 2000, 03.

Silvaner white grape variety chiefly of Germany, Switzerland and Alsace region of France. Also spelt Sylvaner (mainly France).

Silven Controliran wine region of Bulgaria. Red wines from French grape varieties.

Silverado Trail wine-producing district of Napa Valley, California, USA.

Silver Arrow Cocktail. Over ice shake 3 parts vodka, 1 crème de cassis, 1 fresh cream. Strain.

Silver Cocktail. Over ice shake 1 part dry gin, 1 dry vermouth, 2 dashes maraschino, 2 dashes orange bitters. Strain.

Silver Bells Cocktail. Over ice shake 1 part dry gin, 1 rum, 1 lemon juice, 2 dashes Crème de Noyau. Strain into glass with rim frosted by dipping first into fruit juice and then into sugar.

Silver Bullet Cocktail. Over ice shake 2 parts dry gin, 1 kümmel, 1 lemon juice. Strain.

Silver Jubilee Cocktail. Over ice shake 2 parts dry gin, 2 banana liqueur, 1 fresh cream. Strain.

Silver King Cocktail. Over ice shake 1 egg white, 2 parts dry gin, 1 lemon juice, 2 dashes orange bitters, 1 teaspoon sugar. Strain.

Silver Streak Cocktail. Over ice shake 1 part dry gin, 1 kümmel. Strain.

Simi wine producer at Healdsburg, California, USA. Noted Cabernet Sauvignon wine of Alexander Valley vineyards.

Simmern, Langwerth von leading wine producer at Eltville in Rheingau region, Germany. Famed Riesling wines from Marcobrunn and other vineyards.

Simmonet-Fèbvre wine producer and *négociant-éleveur* of Chablis, France.

Simon brewery in Wiltz, Luxembourg.

Simon, André champagne brand of Vintners International, UK. Named after famed British wine merchant André Simon (1877–1970), founder of the International Wine & Food Society.

Simon, Bert wine estate at Serrig in Mosel-Saar-Ruwer region, Germany.

Simon, Château wine estate of AC Sauternes, Bordeaux, France. Classified *Cru Bourgeois*.

Simone, Château sole wine property of AC Palette, Aix-en-Provence, France. Traditionally made red, white and rosé wines of renowned quality.

Simonsgarten vineyard at Roschbach in Rheinpfalz region, Germany.

Simonsig leading wine estate of Stellenbosch, South Africa. Tiara red wine from Cabernet Sauvignon grapes and many varietal brands.

Simonsvlei cooperative wine producer of Paarl, South Africa.

see label opposite ➧

sin crianza on labels of Spanish wine (usually Rioja), 'without nursing' – a wine not aged in cask, but bottled from the vat in the year following the harvest.

Singapore Sling Cocktail. Over ice shake 4 parts cherry brandy, 2 dry gin, 1 lemon juice. Strain into tumbler glasses and add ice. Top with soda water. Alternatively, over ice shake 2 parts dry gin, 1 cherry brandy, 1 lemon juice, teaspoon grenadine. Strain into ice-filled tall glasses and top with soda water.

Singha strong (6.0% alc) lager brand of Boon Rawd brewery, Bangkok, Thailand.

Singleton of Auchroisk, The Speyside single malt whisky of Auchroisk distillery est 1974, Mulben, Banffshire, Scotland. Single malt: 10-year-old and single vintages..

singlings first-distillation brandy, usually destined for re-distilling.

Sion inn-brewery in Unter Taschenmacher, Cologne, Germany.

Sion white wine of town of Sion in Valais, Switzerland. Fendant grapes.

Sioner Klosterberg vineyard at Mauchenheim in Rheinhessen region, Germany.

Sipon grape variety and wine of Drava, Slovenia. Synonymous with Furmint of Hungary.

Siran, Château wine estate of AC Margaux, Médoc, Bordeaux, France. Classified *Cru Bourgeois Supérieur*.

Sirius wine brand of Maison Sichel, Bordeaux, France.

Sir John large leather drinking pot of 17th century.

Sir Robert Burnett's White Satin gin brand formerly of Seagram, UK.

Sir Walter Cocktail. Over ice shake 4 parts brandy, 4 rum, 1 curaçao, 1 grenadine, 1 lemon juice. Strain.

Sissons restaurant-brewery in Baltimore, Maryland, USA.

Sitges Cocktail. Over ice shake 1 part Spanish brandy, 1 orange juice, 1 dash orange bitters. Strain into a wine glass and top with chilled cava.

Sitia sweet red wine of island of Crete. Greece.

Sittmann, Carl major wine producer of Rheinhessen region, Germany.

Six Bells brewery at Bishop's Castle, Shropshire, England.

6X bitter ale (4.3% alc) by Wadworth brewery, Northgate, Devizes, England.   *see label over* ➡

Sizzano DOC for red wine from Nebbiolo, Bonarda and Vespolina grapes of Sizzano, Novara hills, Piedmont, Italy.

skaal 'health'. Scandinavian toast.

Skalli wine producer of Languedoc, France. Popular Fortant de France brand.

Skane aquavit flavoured with aniseed, caraway and fennel. Sweden.

skhou spirit distilled from koumiss (*qv*). Central Asia.

Skinners brewery at Truro, Cornwall, England. Cornish Knocker (4.5% alc), Jingle Knocker (5.5% alc), St Piran's (4.5% alc), Who Put The Lights Out? (5.0% alc).

Skoff, Walter wine producer in Südsteiermark, Austria.

sköl 'cheers' in Norway and Sweden.

Skol international lager brand of Allied Breweries (UK). Originally Dutch.

Skringer, Johann Jr wine producer in Südsteiermark, Austria.

Skullsplitter strong (8.5% alc) ale by Orkney Brewery, Orkney, Scotland. Brewed 'in celebration of Thornfinn (Hausakluif) Skullsplitter, 7th Earl of Orkney.' *see label opposite* ➡

Skyrme's Kernel apple variety traditionally valued for cider-making. English.

SKYY American vodka brand of Skyy Spirits, San Francisco, California of American inventor Maurice Kanbar whose innovations have included Multiplex cinemas and the safety hypodermic needle.

Slack-my-Girdle apple variety traditionally valued for cider-making. English.

slainte mha 'good health'. Gaelic toast, Scotland and Ireland.

Slaintheva twelve-year-old blended scotch whisky by Alexander Dunn, Bracknell, Berkshire, England.

Slamnak medium sweet white wine of Ljutomer region, Slovenia. Rizling grapes.

Slaviantzi winery est 1935 in sub-Balkan Bulgaria. Principally white wines.

Slavonia wine-producing region of northern Croatia.

Sleeman's brewery in Guelph, Ontario, Canada.

Sleepy Head Cocktail. In a tumbler glass put 1 part brandy, 1 strip orange peel, 1 sprig fresh mint. Top with ginger ale.

sling spirit-based, sweetened mixed drink.

Slippery Nipple Cocktail. Pour 1 part chilled Baileys Irish Cream into a liqueur or shot glass and top with 1 teaspoon Sambuca.

slivovitz plum brandy made in various regions of eastern Europe. Originally Serbo-Croat (from *sljiva* for plum).

Sliwowica plum-flavoured potato vodka, Poland.

SLO acronymous brewery in San Luis Obispo, California, USA.

Sloeberry Cocktail. Over ice shake 1 part sloe gin, 1 dash Angostura bitters, 1 orange bitters. Strain.

sloe gin flavoured gin made by steeping sloe fruits (of blackthorn bush) in, or adding sloe juice to, gin.

Sloe Gin Cocktail. Over ice stir 2 parts sloe gin, 1 dry vermouth, 1 sweet vermouth. Strain.

Sloe Measure Cocktail. Over ice stir 1 part Lillet, 1 sloe gin, 2 dashes crème de noyaux, 2 dashes orange bitters. Strain.

Sloe Teq Cocktail. Over ice shake 2 parts tequila, 1 sloe gin, 1 fresh lime juice. Strain into ice-filled tumblers.

Sloe Vermouth Cocktail. Over ice shake 2 parts sloe gin, 2 dry vermouth, 1 lemon juice. Strain.

slop aside from any general deprecatory sense, the residue of distillation.

slug in US from 1756 any kind of strong drink. More recently, a serving of any strong drink.

sly grog alcohol made by an illicit producer. Also, a furtively consumed drink. Australian origin.

small beer archaic term for weak or poor-quality beer. Now with more-general pejorative applications.

Smaragd quality designation for wine in Wachau region, Austria. Minimum grape must weights and alcohol levels are stipulated. Name is that of a species of green salamander found in the region.

smash small mixed drink of the cobbler or julep type (*qv*).

Smederevka white grape variety of Serbia.

Smeets *jenever* and liqueur producer, Hasselt, Belgium.

Smile Cocktail. Over ice shake 1 part dry gin, 1 grenadine, 3 dashes lemon juice.

Smiler Cocktail. Over ice shake 2 parts dry gin, 1 dry vermouth, 1 sweet vermouth, 1 dash Angostura bitters, 1 dash orange bitters. Strain.

Smiles brewery at Colston Yard, Bristol, England. **Smiles Best** (4.1% alc) and **Smiles Heritage** (5.2%) bottled cask ales and draught ales.

Smirnoff world's leading vodka brand. Blue and Red Label styles are produced internationally and premium **Smirnoff Black Label** is triple distilled and bottled in

Moscow, Russia. Originally Polish, Smirnoff has been distilled in the United States since 1934 and the United Kingdom since 1952.

Smith & Reilly Honest Beer lager brand, Vancouver, Washington, USA.

Smith-Haut-Lafitte, Château wine estate of AC Pessac-Léognan, Bordeaux, France. Classified *Cru Classé.*

Smithwick's beer brand of Irish Ale Breweries, Kilkenny, Eire.

Smith Woodhouse port shipper, Vila Nova de Gaia, Portugal. Owned by Symingtons. His Majesty's Choice and Old Lodge Finest old tawnies, white port, and vintages: 1960, 63, 66, 70, 75, 77, 80, 83, 85, 91, 92, 94, 97, 2000, 03.

snakebite drink mixed from cider and ale or lager traditional in West of England.

Snake Dog Ale India pale ale (5.3% alc) by Broadway Brewing, Denver, Colorado, USA. Originally brewed exclusively for the Flying Dog Brewpub, Aspen, Colorado, but now exported in bottle.

Snake River brewery in Caldwell, Idaho, USA.

snaps colourless spirit, Swedish.

Sneaky Pete lost wine brand of California, USA, distinguished by an entry in early editions of the *Guinness Book of Records*. Listed as the world's 'least exclusive wine' it was described as a favourite with "Winos' (alcoholics with a penchant for fomented [*sic*] grape juice)'.

Sneck Lifter dark bitter ale by Jenning Brothers brewery, Cumbria, England. Name derives from northern English dialect term for a door latch – metaphor for drinker's solitary coin enabling entry to the pub and the purchase of one pint – in the hope that fellow drinkers would fund subsequent refreshment.

Snicker Cocktail. Over ice shake 1 egg white, 2 parts dry gin, 1 dry vermouth, 2 dashes maraschino, 1 dash orange bitters, 1 teaspoon sugar syrup. Strain.

Snowball 'light wine' brand of Matthew Clark, Bristol, England.

Snowball Cocktail. Over ice shake 4 parts dry gin, 1 Anisette, 1 Crème de Violette, 1 white crème de menthe, 1 sweetened cream. Strain. Alternatively, into an ice-filled glass pour 1 part Advocaat and top with lemonade. Add orange slice and cocktail cherry.

Snowflake Cocktail. Over ice shake 2 parts dry gin, 1 lemon juice, 1 fresh cream, 1 egg white, 1 teaspoon grenadine, 1 teaspoon sugar. Strain into tumblers and top with chilled soda water.

Snyder Cocktail. Over ice shake 4 parts dry gin, 2 dry vermouth, 1 curaçao. Strain and squeeze orange peel over.

Soave town and DOC for dry white wines from Garganega and Trebbiano grapes near Verona, Veneto region, Italy. Soave Classico wines are from vineyards closest to the town. Recioto di Soave is sweet wine from part-dried grapes. Noted producers include Bolla, Boscaini, Pieropan.

Soberano brandy by Gonzalez Byass, Jerez de la Frontera, Spain.

sochu spirit distilled from rice beer. China.

Sociando-Mallet, Château wine estate of AC Haut-Médoc, Bordeaux, France. Classified *Cru Grand Bourgeois*.

Sodap wine producer, island of Cyprus.

Sogrape wine producer of Vila Nova de Gaia, Portugal. Owners of Mateus Rosé brand, and purchaser in 2002 of Sandeman.

Soho Cocktail. Over ice shake 2 parts chianti wine, 1 sweet vermouth, 1 grapefruit juice. Strain.

Söhrenberg vineyard at Waiblingen in Württemberg region, Germany.

Solaia red wine from Cabernet Sauvignon and Sangiovese grapes by Marchesi Antinori, Tuscany, Italy.

Soleil, Château wine estate of AC Puisseguin-St-Emilion, Bordeaux, France.

solera system of ageing and blending sherry, Jerez de la Frontera, Spain. Series of 500-litre oak butts, stacked in up to four tiers and collectively called criaderas ('nurseries'), contain wines of successive vintages; as wine is drawn off for blending or bottling from the rank of butts with the oldest wine, it is topped up from the second oldest, and so on back to the newest butt. Finest sherries may come from one solera but most are blended from numerous different soleras. The word comes from Spanish *suelo*, meaning soil or ground, referring to the fact that the solera itself is, strictly speaking, the row of butts at ground level, from which the final wine is tapped off for fining and bottling.

Solera (Gran) Reserva quality designation for Spanish brandy. See Brandy de Jerez.

Solopaca DOC for red and white wines of Benevento, Campania, Italy.

Solva brewery at Solva, Haverfordwest, Dyfed, Wales.

S.O.M. Superior Old Marsala. Quality designation for wines of Marsala, Sicily.

Soma wine associated in ritual with warrior god Indra of India's Indus civilisation, said to date back to 3000 BC.

Sombrero Cocktail. Over ice shake 2 parts Tia Maria, 1 fresh cream. Strain.

Somerset Cider Brandy Company producer of UK's leading apple brandies. Brands are Somerset Royal Cider Brandy 3-year-old, 5-year-old, 10-year-old, apple *eau de vie* and Kingston Black aperitif.

Somerset Redstreak strong dry cider (7.4% alc) by Thatcher's Cider, Sandford, Somerset, England. From Somerset Redstreak apple variety.

Something Special blended scotch whisky brand previously of Seagram, UK. Bought by Pernod-Ricard, 2001.

Somló wine-producing district north of Lake Balaton, Hungary.

sommelier a wine waiter. French for butler, originally from Greek *sagma* (packhorse).

Sommer, Leopold wine producer in Neusiedlersee Hügelland, Burgenland, Austria.

Sommerberg vineyards at Abstatt, Löwenstein and Untergruppenbach in Württemberg region and Ebringen in Baden region, Germany.

Sommerhalde vineyards at Eberstadt, Korb and Reutlingen in Württemberg region and Kenzingen in Baden region, Germany.

Sommerheil vineyard at Hochheim in Rheingau region, Germany.

Sommerleite vineyard at Elfershausen in the Franken region, Germany.

Sommerstuhl vineyard at Güntersleben in Franken region, Germany.

Sommertal vineyard at Knetzgau in Franken region, Germany.

Sommerwende vineyard at Hangen-Weisheim in Rheinhessen region, Germany.

Sonnberg vineyard at Laudenbach in Baden region, Germany.

Sonne vineyard at Oberheimbach in Mittelrhein region, Germany.

Sonneberg vineyard at Sugenheim in Franken region, Germany.

Sonneck vineyards at Bullay and Zell in Mosel-Saar-Ruwer region, Germany.

Sonnema Dutch bitters distiller and brand, Netherlands.

Sonnenberg the name of 69 individual vineyards in Germany. Region by region, as follows: in Ahr at Bad-Neuenahr-Ahrweiler; in Baden at Angelbachtal (Eichtersheim), Angelbachtal (Michelfeld), Baden-Baden, Pfinztal, Reiburg, Sinsheim (Eschelbach), Sinsheim (Waldangelloch), Sinzheim, Wertheim (Dertingen), Wertheim (Kembach); in Franken at Markbreit, Marsteft; in Mittelrhein at Unkel; in Mosel-Saar-Ruwer at Cochem, Irsch, Kanzem, Konz, Schleich, Trier, Waldrach; in Nahe at Dalberg, Guldental, Hergenfeld, Norheim, Nussbaum, Roxheim, Schöneberg, Sommerloch; in Rheingau at Eltville; in Rheinhessen at Alsheim, Alzey, Aspisheim, Bechtolsheim, Gundheim,

Guntersblum, Hackenheim, Hohen-Sülzen, Ingelheim, Nieder-Olm, Pfaffen-Schwabenheim, Schwabenheim, Sprendlingen, Stein-Bockenheim, Udenheim, Vendersheim, Wonsheim; in Rheinpfalz at Bockenheim an der Weinstrasse, Ellerstadt, Essingen, Gönnheim, Ilbesheim, Leinsweiler, Neuleiningen, Oberotterbach, Schweigen-Rechtenbach, Schweighofen, Weisenheim am Berg; in Württemberg at Bönnigheim, Flein, Heilbronn, Korb, Remshalden, Schwaigern, Schwaigern (Stetten), Talheim, Weinstadt (Beutelsbach), Weinstadt (Schnait).

Sonnenborn collective vineyard (*Grosslage*) at Langenlonsheim in Nahe region, Germany.

Sonnenbrunnen vineyard at Lörrach in Baden region, Germany.

Sonnenbüchel vineyard at Nonnenhorn in Württemberg region, Germany.

Sonnenbühl *Grosslage* incorporating vineyards at Kernen (Rommelshausen), Kernen (Stetten), Weinstadt (Beutelsbach), Weinstadt (Endersbach), Weinstadt (Schnait) and Weinstadt (Strümpfelbach) in Württemberg region, Germany.

Sonnengold vineyard at Klotten in Mosel-Saar-Ruwer region, Germany.

Sonnenhain vineyard at Remlingen in Franken region, Germany.

Sonnenhalden vineyard at Tübingen in Württemberg region, Germany.

Sonnenhang vineyards at Eimsheim, Guntersblum, Ingelheim and Schornsheim in Rheinhessen region, Germany.

Sonnenhof vineyard at Gundelfingen in Baden region, Germany.

Sonnenköpfchen vineyard at Eckelsheim in Rheinhessen region, Germany.

Sonnenlauf vineyard at Gutenberg in Nahe region, Germany.

Sonnenlay vineyards at Ensch, Mülheim and Traben-Trarbach in Mosel-Saar-Ruwer region and Rhens in Mittelrhein region, Germany.

Sonnenleite vineyards at Dettelbach, Dettelbach (Brück), Dettelbach (Schnepfenbach) and Volkach in Franken region, Germany.

Sonnenmorgen vineyard at Windesheim in Nahe region, Germany.

Sonnenplätzchen vineyard at Obermoschel in Nahe region, Germany.

Sonnenring vineyards at Löf and Müden in Mosel-Saar-Ruwer region, Germany.

Sonnenschein vineyard at Bad Neuenahr-Ahrweiler in Ahr region, Germany.

Sonnenseite ob der Bruck vineyard at Heidelberg in Baden region, Germany.

Sonnenstock vineyard at Damscheid in Mittelrhein region, Germany.

Sonnenstück vineyards at Bad Bellingen, Neuenburg am Rhein, Schliengen, Schliengen (Liel), Schliengen (Mauchen) and Schliengen (Niedereggen) in Baden region and Immesheim in Rheinpfalz region, Germany.

Sonnenstuhl vineyard at Randersacker in Franken region, Germany.

Sonnenufer *Grosslage* incorporating vineyards in Baden region, Germany at, respectively: Bermatingen, Bodman, Hagnau, Hilzingen, Immenstaad, Immenstaad (Kippenhausen), Konstanz, Markdorf, Meersburg, Reichenau, Salem, Singen (Hohentwiel), Stetten, Überlingen, Uhldingen-Mühlhofen.

Sonnenuhr vineyards at Bernkastel-Kues, Maring-Noviand, Neumagen-Dhron, Pommern and Zeltingen-Rachtig in Mosel-Saar-Ruwer region, Germany.

Sonnenweg vineyards at Gimbsheim in Rheinhessen region and Wallhausen in Nahe region, Germany.

Sonnenwinkel vineyard at Michelau in Franken region, Germany.

Sonnhalde vineyards at Denzlingen, Heitersheim, Konstanz, Müllheim, Müllheim (Vögisheim) Sexau and Waldkirch in Baden region, Germany.

Sonnheil vineyard at Hillesheim in Rheinhessen region, Germany.

Sonnhohle vineyards at Bad Bellingen, Binzen, Efringer-Kirchen, Efringen-Kirchen (Egringen), Eimeldingen, Fischingen, Rümmingen, Schallbach and Weil am Rhein in Baden region, Germany.

Sonnhole vineyards at Müllheim (Britzingen) and Müllheim (Dattingen) in Baden region, Germany.

Sonnleite vineyard at Zellingen in Franken region, Germany.

Sonntagsberg vineyards at Heilbronn, Nordheim and Nordheim (Nordhausen) in Württemberg region, Germany.

Sonora Cocktail. Over ice shake 1 part apple brandy, 1 rum, 2 dashes apricot brandy, 1 dash lemon juice. Strain.

Sony & Cher Cocktail. Over ice shake 1 part Japanese rice wine, 1 crème de cassis. Strain into flute glass and top with champagne.

Sonza's Wilson Cocktail. Over ice shake 2 parts cherry brandy, 2 gin, 1 grenadine, 1 lemon juice. Strain.

Soonecker Schlossberg vineyard at Niederheimbach in Mittelrhein region, Germany.

sophistication a fading euphemism in brewing and distilling. Synonymous with adulteration.

Soplica brandy- and apple-spirit-flavoured vodka, Poland.

Sopron wine-producing district of western Hungary. Sweet white wines.

Sorentberg vineyard at Reil in Mosel-Saar-Ruwer region, Germany.

Sorrento Cocktail. Over ice shake 2 parts dry gin, 1 Galliano, 1 lemon juice, 1 dash amaretto. Strain.

So-So Cocktail. Over ice shake 2 parts dry gin, 2 sweet vermouth, 1 apple brandy, 1 grenadine. Strain.

sot drunkard. English from Old French.

Soudars, Château wine estate of AC Haut-Médoc, Bordeaux, France. Classified *Cru Bourgeois*.

Souley-Ste-Croix, Château Le wine estate of AC Haut-Médoc, Bordeaux, France. Classified *Cru Bourgeois*.

Soul Kiss Cocktail. Over ice shake 2 parts dry vermouth, 2 sweet vermouth, 1 Dubonnet, 1 orange juice. Strain. Alternatively, over ice shake 2 parts dry vermouth, 2 rye whisky, 1 Dubonnet, 1 orange juice, 1 slice orange. Strain.

sour a mixed drink from spirits, lemon juice and ice.

sour in winetasting, a flavour indicating excess acidity.

sour mash in American distilling, process of adding de-alcoholised mash from an earlier fermentation, plus fresh yeast, to new mash – starting fermentation, giving consistency of style and enhancing flavour and aroma. Mainly bourbon whiskies.

Soussans wine village of AC Margaux, Bordeaux, France.

Soutard, Château wine estate of AC St Emilion, Bordeaux, France. Classified *Grand Cru Classé*.

South Africa reinvigorated wine-producing nation with Cape vineyards divided into Wines of Origin regions including Constantia, Klein Karoo, Paarl, Robertson, Stellenbosch etc. Production is mainly by co-operatives but individual estates are burgeoning. French grape varieties increasingly dominate. Brandy and fortified wines in style of port and sherry are as important as table wines for the domestic market.

South Australia Brewing brewery in Adelaide, South Australia.

Southcorp leading wine producer of Australia. The company's domestic brands include Lindemans, Penfolds, Seaview, Seppelt, Tullochs and Wynns, and James Herrick in France. In 2000, Southcorp merged with rival Rosemount to form self-styled 'largest quality-wine company in the world'.

South Down Harvest ale (5.0% alc) by Harveys Brewery, Lewes, East Sussex, England.

Southern Bitter 'mellow session' ale brand (3.7% alc) of Cottage Brewing Co, Lovington, Somerset, England.

Southern Comfort see box.

Southern Gin Cocktail. Over ice shake 1 part dry gin, 1 dash curaçao, 1 dash orange bitters. Strain.

Southern Vales wine district bordering Adelaide, South Australia.

South Ken Cocktail. Over ice shake 1 part dry gin, 1 grapefruit juice, 1 pineapple juice, 1 dash Angostura bitters. Strain.

Southern Comfort

the Mississippi liqueur

The name of this American liqueur was coined by bartender M W Heron for a peach-flavoured whisky-based drink of his own invention. He served it as a consoling beverage to Confederate drinkers in his New Orleans hotel in the hard years after the Civil War of 1861–65.

The drink became a favourite with the crews of great paddle steamers such as the *Natchez* and *Robert E. Lee*. They carried enthusiastic reports of Southern Comfort hundreds of miles up and down the Mississippi.

A shrewd promoter, Heron began to offer the drink, ready-bottled, as the victor's prize in the hair-raising riverboat races that were at the time becoming a dangerous feature of Mississippi life. Prospering, Heron moved to the boom town of St Louis, where his new bar displayed the sign: 'St Louis Cocktail, made with Southern Comfort. Limit two to a customer. No gentleman would ask for more.'

Southern Comfort is the biggest-selling of all American-made liqueurs and Great Britain is second only to the United States itself in annual consumption. It is drunk neat, with or without ice and is an ingredient in numerous classic cocktails including the Alabama Slammer, the Helen Twelvetrees and the Long Slow Comfortable Screw.

South of the Border Cocktail. Over ice shake 2 parts tequila, 1 Tia Maria, 1 fresh lime juice. Strain.

South Quining apple variety valued for cider-making. English.

South Side Cocktail. Over ice shake 2 parts dry gin, 1 lemon juice, 1 teaspoon sugar, 1 mint sprig. Strain and add another mint sprig.

Southwark Premium beer by South Australia Brewing, Adelaide.

soutirage in winemaking, racking (drawing wine off the lees). French.

Souverin Cellars wine producer based in Sonoma, California, USA.

Sovereign bitter ale by Samuel Smith brewery, Yorkshire, England.

Sovereign 'British wine' brand of Halewood International, Huyton, Merseyside, England.

Sovereign Dry gin brand of Halewood International, Huyton, Merseyside, England.

Spain once known principally for sherry but now a major table-wine producer as well. Quality wine regions ranked *Denominación de Origen* (DO) increase in number continually (45 by 2000) and cover all regions of the country. Standards are controlled in each DO by a local Consejo Regulador. Major DOs include Rioja and Priorat (which have the higher *Denominación de Origen Calificada* classification), Navarra, Ribera del Duero, Somontano, Penedès, Valencia, Valdepeñas. Table wines in all styles plus *cava* sparkling wine and fortified wines of Malaga and Montilla in addition to Jerez.

Spanish clay mineral substance for fining wine and other drinks.

Spanish Main Cocktail. Over ice shake 3 parts rum, 1 curaçao, 3 dashes fresh lime juice. Strain.

Spanish Town Cocktail. Over ice stir 1 part rum, 2 dashes triple sec. Strain.

Spanna regional name for Nebbiolo grape variety, best known in wines bearing the name in DOCG Gattinara, Piedmont, Italy.

sparging in brewing, sprinkling heated water over the mash at the end of the process to improve sugar extraction. English.

sparkling wine generic term for effervescent wine of any type, from carbonated to champagne.

Spätburgunder red grape variety of Germany, principally in Baden and Württemberg regions, producing all the country's best red wines. Synonymous with Pinot Noir.

Spaten historic brewery of Munich, Bavaria, Germany, est 1397. Renowned for beers including Münchner Hell, Ur-Märzen, **Spatengold** and **Spaten Pils**.

spätlese 'late picked'. German wine-quality designation within the *Prädikat* range. The second level (after *kabinett*) of grape ripeness which must reach a minimum Oechsle (sugar density) level of between 76° and 95° according to region of production. Grapes may not be picked until at least a week after commencement of the main harvest.

Spätrot white grape variety for Gumpoldskirchen wine of Austria.

Special Brew famously alcoholic lager brand of Carlsberg, now widely imitated.

Special Rough Cocktail. Over ice stir 1 part apple brandy, 1 brandy, 1 dash pastis. Strain.

Special Vat cider brand of Matthew Clark, Bristol, England.

specific gravity measurement of sugar content in grape must, in-dicating potential alcohol.

Speculation bottle-conditioned ale (4.7% alc) by Freeminer Brewery, Forest of Dean, Gloucestershire, England. Named after former Speculation coal mine of Forest of Dean.

Spencer Cocktail. Over ice shake 2 parts dry gin, 1 apricot brandy, 1 dash Angostura bitters, 1 dash orange juice. Strain and add cocktail cherry to glass.

Spendrup brewing company of Sweden noted for **Spendrup's** lager and premium **Spendrup's Old Gold**.

spent liquor dealcoholised residue of distilling process.

Speyburn Speyside malt whisky distillery est 1897, Rothes, Moray-shire, Scotland. Single malt: 10-year-old.

Spey Cast twelve-year-old blended scotch whisky by Gordon & MacPhail, Elgin, Scotland. Fly-fishing connotations.

Speyside Rare blended scotch whisky brand by Speyside Distillery Co, Glasgow, Scotland. Also, eight, 12-, 15- 17- and 21-year-old blends.

Spezial brewery est 1536 in Bamberg, Germany. Known for *Rauchbier*. **Spezial Lager** and **Spezial Märzen**.

Sphinx Cocktail. Over ice stir 2 parts dry gin, 1 dry vermouth, 1 sweet vermouth. Strain.

Spice Route wine company and brand of Malmesbury, South Africa. A collaborative enterprise between winemakers Gyles Webb of Thelema, Charles Back of Fair-view and Jabulani Ntshangese with author John Platter to produce 'impeccable wines created by per-sonalities who aim to support their black employees to ensure that long-term prospects within South Africa's wine industry continue to improve.'

Spiegel vineyard at Neustadt an der Weinstrasse in Rheinpfalz region, Germany.

Spiegelberg *Grosslage* incorporating vineyards at Nackenheim, Nierstein and Nierstein (Schwabsburg) in Rheinhessen region, Germany.

Spiegelberg vineyards at Eppingen, Kraichtal and Östringen in Baden region, Germany.

Spielberg vineyards at Bad Dürk-heim and Meckenheim in Rhein-pfalz region, Germany.

Spiess vineyard at Ruppertsberg in Rheinpfalz region, Germany.

spigot peg for sealing vent holes in casks. Also used in the opening of a faucet to regulate flow.

Spikes brewery at Southsea, Hamp-shire, England.

spile peg for stopping up vent holes in casks. Similar to spigot (*qv*).

Spinnaker Ale brand of Spinnakers brewery, Canada.

Spion Kop Cocktail. Over ice stir 1 part Caperitif, 1 dry vermouth. Strain.

spirit distilled alcohol as defined by medieval alchemists. The term has been in use for distilled liquor only since 1610.

Spirytus Rektyfikowany pure rectified spirit for vodka production, Poland.

Spitalberg vineyard at Sobernheim in Nahe region, Germany.

Spitalhalde vineyards at Lindau and Wasserburg in Württemberg region, Germany.

Spitfire beer brand (4.5% alc) of Shepherd Neame brewery, Kent, England.

Spitzberg vineyard at Stadecken-Elsheim in Rheinhessen region, Germany.

Spitzenberg vineyard at Wiesloch in Baden region, Germany.

Spitzenwein generic term for wine of highest quality, Austria.

Splügen Fumée 'red ale' brand by Poretti brewery, Italy.

Spodka vodka brand of Polmos Distillers, Poland.

Spokane Cocktail. Over ice shake 1 egg white, 2 parts dry gin, 1 lemon juice, 2 dashes sugar syrup. Strain.

Sporen *grand cru* vineyard at Riquewihr, Alsace, France.

Spreading Redstreak apple variety traditionally valued for cider-making. English.

Sprecher brewery in Milwaukee, Wisconsin, USA.

Springbank Campbeltown malt whisky distillery, Campbeltown, Argyll, Scotland. Est 1828 in place of an illicit distillery of farmer Archibald Mitchell, Springbank remains a Mitchell-family business. Single malts: 10-, 15-, 21-, 25- and 30-year-old.

Springbock 'Bavarian style' wheat beer (5.2% alc) by Pilgrim Brewery, Reigate, Surrey, England.

Springbok Cocktail. Over ice stir 1 part Lillet, 1 dry sherry, 1 Van der Hum, 2 dashes orange bitters. Strain.

Spring Cocktail. Over ice shake 3 parts dry gin, 1 Bénédictine, 1 quinquina, 1 dash Angostura bitters. Strain.

Springeton wine district of Barossa Valley, South Australia.

Spring Feeling Cocktail. Over ice shake 2 parts dry gin, 1 green Chartreuse, 1 lemon juice. Strain.

Springhead Fine Ales brewery at Sutton on Trent, Newark, Nottinghamshire, England.

Spring Mountain Vineyards wine producer in Napa Valley, California, USA. Noted Cabernet Sauvignon and Chardonnay wines. 'Falcon Crest' wine brand reminds consumers that Spring Mountain was the property used as the setting for the television drama series of that name.

spritzer a mixed drink of wine and soda or sparkling water.

spritzig 'slightly sparkling' (wine) of Germany. Equates to French *pétillant*.

spruce beer drink from fermented molasses flavoured with cones and twigs of spruce trees.

SP Sporting Ales brewery at Leominster, Herefordshire, England.

spumante sparkling wine, Italy.

Squinzano DOC for red and *rosato* wines from Negroamaro grapes of Squinzano, Apulia, Italy.

Squires dry gin brand of Squires Gin Ltd, London, England. Named after Squire Thomas Pope of Dorset, and owned by his descendants, the Dorchester brewing family of Pope.

SS Politician scotch whisky blended with fractional quantity of 1938-distilled Martin's whisky salvaged 1989 from the wreck of the steamship *SS Politician*, which sank off the Outer Hebrides in 1941. By Douglas Laing of Glasgow, Scotland, for SS Politician plc.

Staatlicher Hofkeller state wine domain of Bavaria, Germany. Cellars at Würzburg, vineyards in Franken region.

Staatlicher Weinbaudomänen state wine domain of Germany. Main vineyards are at Kloster Eberbach in Rheingau region, Schlossböckelheim in Nahe region, Trier in Mosel-Saar-Ruwer region.

Stad Krems wine producer in Kremstal, Niederösterreich, Austria.

Stadlmann wine producer in Thermenregion, Niederösterreich, Austria.

Stag bitter ale (4.1% alc) by Tomintoul Brewery, Ballindalloch, Banffshire, Scotland.

Stag's Breath Liqueur scotch whisky and heather-honey liqueur by Meikle's, Newtonmore, Baddenoch, Scotland. 'Husbanded to mellow maturity in the cool aisles of glenside bonds.'

Stag's Leap district and AVA of Napa Valley, California, USA. Site of two separate wine producers, **Stag's Leap Wine Cellars**, famed for its Cabernet Sauvignon wines, and **Stag's Leap Winery**.

Stahlberg vineyard at Kühlsheim in Baden region, Germany.

Stahlbühl vineyard at Heilbronn in Württemberg region, Germany.

Staig vineyard at Brackenheim in Württemberg region, Germany.

Stambolovo Controliran wine region of Bulgaria.

Stancombe Cyder cider by Stancombe farm, Sherford, Devon, England.

Stanislaus altbier brewery in Modesto, California, USA.

Stanley Cocktail. Over ice shake 2 parts dry gin, 2 rum, 1 grenadine, 1 lemon juice. Strain.

Stanley Wine Company wine producer in Clare-Watervale, South Australia. Leasingham brand of wines.

Stanway brewery at Cheltenham, Gloucestershire, England.

Staple St James vineyard at Canterbury, Kent, England.

Starboard 'port-style' fortified wine brand of Andrew Quady, California, USA.

Starboard Light Cocktail. Over ice shake 2 parts dry gin, 1 crème de menthe, 1 lemon juice. Strain.

Star Cocktail. Over ice shake 1 part apple brandy, 1 dry gin, 4 dashes grapefruit juice, 1 dash dry vermouth, 1 dash sweet vermouth. Strain. Alternatively, over ice shake 1 part apple brandy, 1 sweet vermouth. Strain.

Star Daisy Cocktail. Over ice shake 2 parts dry gin, 2 apple brandy, 1 crème de framboise, 1 lemon juice. Strain.

Starka apple and pear-leaf flavoured vodka, Russia. Also, a dark vodka from rye flavoured with malaga wine and aged in casks for minimum ten years, by Polmos distillers, Poland.

Staropramen brewery est 1869 and renowned Pilsner beer (5.0% alc) of Prague, Czech Republic.

see label opposite ➡

Stars and Stripes brand of Pernod-Ricard.

Stars and Stripes Cocktail. Into a liqueur glass, pouring carefully to avoid mixing ingredients, put 1 part crème de cassis, 1 green Chartreuse, 1 maraschino.

Star Tipsy Toad brewery at St Peters, Jersey, Channel Islands (UK). Proprietor is Mr S. Beer.

Station Porter bottle-conditioned beer (6.1% alc) by Wickwar Brewing, Gloucestershire, England.

Staudenberg vineyards at Hirschberg and Schriesheim in Baden region, Germany.

Stauder renowned brewery in Essen, Germany. Pilsener beers.

Staufenberg *Grosslage* incorporating vineyards in Württemberg region, Germany at, respectively: Bad Friedrichshall (Duttenberg), Bad Friedrichsall (Offenau), Eberstadt, Ellhofen, Erlenbach-Binswangen (Binswangen), Erlenbach-Binswangen (Erlenbach), Gundelsheim, Heilbronn, Langenbrettach, Neckarsulm, Neckarsulm (Untereisesheim), Oedheim, Talheim, Weinsberg, Weinsberg (Gellmersbach).

Stay the Night Cocktail. In a shaker, muddle small section fresh ginger root with 1 part gomme syrup then add 3 parts Sauza Hornitos (or other) tequila, 2 lemon juice, 1 cassis. Shake and strain into a tumbler filled with crushed ice. Garnish with lemon twist and drink through straws.

Steam Packet brewery at Knottingley, North Yorkshire, England.

steely in winetasting, the flavour of a dry white wine with marked, but correct, acidity. Often applies to Chablis.

Steen white grape variety of South Africa. Similar (perhaps identical) to Chenin Blanc.

Steenberg distinguished wine producer of Constantia, South Africa.

steeneeyasas 'cheers' in Greek.

Steiermark wine-producing region of southern Austria.

Steigerwald *Bereich* of Franken region, Germany.

Steinwein former name for wines of Franken region, Germany. Since wine-law reform of 1971, confined to wines of Stein estate, Würzburg.

Steiner, Julius wine producer in Neusiedlersee, Burgenland, Austria.

Steinschaden Weinschlössl wine producer in Kamptal, Niederösterreich, Austria.

Stefansberg vineyard at Zell in Mosel-Saar-Ruwer region, Germany.

Stefanslay vineyard at Wintrich in Mosel-Sarr-Ruwer region, Germany.

Steffensberg vineyards at Enkirch and Kröv in Mosel-Saar-Ruwer region, Germany.   *see label over* ➡

Stehlerberg vineyard at Kasbach-Ohlenberg in Mittelrhein region, Germany.

Steig vineyards at Bissersheim in Rheinpfalz region, Eisingen in Baden region, Flörsheim-Dalsheim (Dalsheim) and Flörsheim-Dalsheim (Niederflörsheim) in Rheinhessen and Mainz in Rheingau region, Germany.

Steige vineyard at Fürfeld in Rheinhessen region, Germany.

Steigerberg vineyard at Wendelsheim in Rheinhessen region, Germany.

Steigerdell vineyard at Bad Münster am Stein-Ebernburg in Nahe region, Germany.

Steig-Terrassen vineyard at Guntersblum in Rheinhessen region, Germany.

Steil *Grosslage* incorporating vineyards at Rüdesheim (Assmannshausen) and Rüdesheim (Aulhausen) in Rheingau region, Germany.

Stein vineyards at Bechteim in Rheinhessen region, Flörsheim and Hochheim in Rheingau region and Karlstadt and Würzburg in Franken region, Germany.

Steinacker vineyards at Ellhofen, Lehrensteinsfeld and Weinsberg in Württemberg region, Heidesheim, Ingelheim and Nieder-Hilbersheim in Rheinpfalz region, Kallstadt and Kirchheim an der Wein-

strasse in Rheinpfalz region and Rheinfelden in Baden region, Germany.

Steinbach vineyards at Sommerhausen and Eiberstadt in Franken region, Germany.

Steinbachhof vineyard at Vaihingen in Württemberg region, Germany.

Steinberg the name of 13 individual vineyards in Germany. Region by region, as follows: in Baden at Bollschweil, Durbach; in Franken at Alzenau; in Nahe at Bad Kreuznach, Niederhausen an der Nahe; in Rheingau at Eltville (Hattenheim); in Rheinhessen at Dalheim, Guntersblum, Partenheim, Sankt Johann, Wackernheim; in Rheinpfalz at Bad Dürkheim; in Württemberg at Beilstein.

Steinberger vineyard at Konz in Mosel-Saar-Ruwer region, Germany.

Steinbier see stone beer.

Steinbiss vineyard at Billigheim-Ingenheim in Rheinpfalz region, Germany.

Steinbuck vineyard at Vogtsburg im Kaiserstuhl in Baden region, Germany.

Steinchen vineyards at Löf in Mosel-Saar-Ruwer region and Langenlonsheim in Nahe region, Germany.

Steinert vineyard at Gau-Algesheim in Rheinhessen region, Germany.

Steinfelsen vineyards at Ihringen and Vogtsburg im Kaiserstuhl in Baden region, Germany.

Steingässle vineyards at Efringen-Kirche, Efringen-Kirchen (Welmlingen), Efringen-Kirchen (Wintersweiler), Kandern (Feuerbach), Kandern (Holzen), Kandern (Riedlingen), Kandern (Tannenkirch)

and Kandern (Wollbach) in Baden region, Germany.

Steingebiss vineyard at Billigheim-Ingenheim in Rheinpfalz region, Germany.

Steingeröll vineyard at Zwingenberg in Hessische Bergstrasse region, Germany.

Steingerück vineyard at Gross Umstadt in Hessische Bergstrasse region, Germany.

Steingrube vineyards at Brackenheim and Stuttgart (Uhlbach) in Württemberg region, Edingen, March, Sasbach and Teningen in Baden region and Westhofen in Rheinhessen region, Germany.

Steingrüble vineyards at Bad Krozingen, Bad Krozingen (Schlatt) and Endingen in Baden region and Korb, Korb (Kleinheppach) and Weinstadt in Württemberg region, Germany.

Steingrübler vineyards at Baden-Baden in Baden region and Miltenberg in Franken region, Germany.

Steinhäger colourless juniper-flavoured spirit of Steinhägen, Westphalia, Germany. Rated as the finest version of *Wacholder*.

Steinhalde vineyards at Edingen in Baden region and Stuttgart (Bad Cannstatt), Stuttgart (Mühlhausen) and Stuttgart (Münster) in Württemberg region, Germany.

Stein/Harfe vineyard at Würzburg in Franken region, Germany.

Steinhöhl vineyard at Monzemheim in Rheinhessen region, Germany.

Steinkaul vineyard at Bad Neuenahr-Ahrweiler in Ahr region, Germany.

Steinkaut vineyard at Weinsheim in Nahe region, Germany.

Steinklinge vineyard at Lauda-Königshofen in Baden region, Germany.

Steinkopf vineyards at Grünstadt Land in Rheinpfalz region, Heppenheim and Heppenheim (Hambach) in Hessische Bergstrasse region and Münster-Sarmsheim in Nahe region, Germany.

Steinköpfchen vineyard at Rümmelsheim mit Ortsteil Burg Layen in Nahe region, Germany.

Steinkreuz vineyard at Sankt Katherinen in Nahe region, Germany.

Steinler vineyards at Freiburg and Lottstetten in Baden region, Germany.

Steinmächer *Grosslage* incorporating vineyards at Eltville, Eltville (Martinsthal), Eltville (Rauenthal), Walluf (Nieferwalluf), Walluf (Oberwalluf), Wiesbaden (Dotzheim), Wiesbaden (Frauenstein) and Wiesbaden (Schierstein).

Steinmauer vineyard at Freiburg in Baden region, Germany.

Steinmorgen vineyards at Eltville and Eltville (Erbach) in Rheingau region, Germany.

Steinrossel vineyard at Sommerloch in Nahe region, Germany.

Steinsberg vineyards at Sinsheim (Steinsfurt) and Sinsheim (Weiler) in Baden region, Germany.

Steinschmetzer vineyard at Tauberbischofsheim In Baden region, Germany.

Steinwengert vineyard at Pfinztal in Baden region, Germany.

Steinwingert vineyard at Niederhausen an der Nahe in Nahe region, Germany.

Stella Artois pilsner lager of Artois brewery, Leuven, Belgium. The brewery, said to have been founded in 1366, introduced Stella in 1926 as a seasonal beer for Christmas (the name Stella referring to the Star of Bethlehem). Owned by Interbrew.

Stellenbosch town and important wine region of South Africa, east of Cape Town.

Stellenbosch Farmers Winery largest wine producer of Stellenbosch region, South Africa.

Stellenryck Collection prestige wine brand of Bergkelder, Stellenbosch, South Africa.

Stellenvale wine brand of Beram's winery, Devon Valley, Stellenbosch, South Africa.

Stelvin leading brand of screwcap wine closure, similar to Stelcap for spirits. Alcan company, USA.

Stemmier vineyards at Heppenheim and Heppenheim (Hambach) in Hessische Bergstrasse region, Germany.

stengah drink of whisky and soda in equal measure. English from Malay *sa tengah* (one half).

Stephansberg vineyards Bad Münster am Stein-Ebernburg in Nahe region, and Weinheim (Hohensachsen) and Weinheim (Lützelsachsen) in Baden region, Germany.

Stephanus-Rosengärtchen vineyard at Bernkastel-Kues in Mosel-Saar-Ruwer region, Germany.

stepony extinct seventeenth-century English drink of lemons and raisins steeped in spirit.

Sterling brewery in Evansville, Indiana, USA.

Sterling Vineyards wine producer in Napa Valley, California, USA. Noted Cabernet Sauvignon and other wines. Acquired by Diageo, 2001.

Sternberg vineyard at Pleitersheim in Rheinhessen region, Germany.

Sternenberg vineyards at Bühl (Altschweier) and Bühl (Neusatz) in Baden region, Germany.

Stewart's Cream of the Barley blended scotch whisky by Alexander Stewart, Dundee, Scotland.

Steyer vineyard at Hüffelsheim in Nahe region, Germany.

Steyerberg vineyard at Schweeppenhausen in Nahe region, Germany.

Stich den Buben vineyard at Baden-Baden in Baden region, Germany.

Sticky Nuts Cocktail. Over ice stir 2 parts Dooley's Vodka Toffee, 1 amaretto. Strain.

Stiefel vineyard at Seinsheim in Franken region, Germany.

Stiege vineyards at Weil am Rhein, Weil am Rhein (Haltingen) and Weil am Rhein (Ötlingen) in Baden region, Germany.

Stielweg vineyard at Hochheim in Rheingau region, Germany.

Stift vineyard at Bad Neuenahr-Ahrweiler in Aher region, Germany.

Stiftsberg *Grosslage* incorporating vineyards in the Baden region, Germany at, respectively: Angelbachtal (Eichtersheim), Angelbachtal (Michelfeld), Bad Rappenau, Binau, Bretten, Eberbach, Eppingen, Eppingen (Elsenz), Eppingen (Mühlbach), Eppingen (Rohrbach a G), Gemmingen, Hassmersheim, Hassmersheim (Neckarmühlbach), Kirchardt, Kraichtal (Bahnbrücken Gochsheim und Oberacker), Kraichtal (Landshausen und Menzingen), Kraichtal (Menzingen, Münzesheim und Neuenbürg), Kürnbach, Mosbach, Neckarzimmern, Neudenau, Neudenau (Herbolzheim), Oberderdingen, Östringen (Eichelberg), Östringen (Odenheim), Östringen (Tiefenbach), Sinsheim (Eschelbach), Sinsheim (Hilsbach), Sinsheim (Steinsfurt), Sinsheim (Waldangelloch), Sinsheim (Weiler), Sulzfeld, Zaisenhausen.

Stiftsberg vineyards at Bad Neuenahr-Ahrweiler in Ahr region and at Heilbronn, Heilbronn (Horkheim) and Talheim in Württemberg region, Germany.

Stiftsweingut Heiligenkreuz wine producer in Thermenregion, Niederösterreich, Austria.

still apparatus for distilling spirits. Two principal types are patent (devised and patented by Aeneas Coffey) for continuous distillation and rigorous purity, and pot still for a less-refined process.

still wine wine free of carbon dioxide and thus without effervescence.

Stillman's Dram brand name for long-matured whiskies of Invergordon Distillers, Leith, Edinburgh, Scotland. Used for Highland single grain by The Invergordon distillery, Highland single malt by Tullibardine distillery, Island single malt by Isle of Jura distillery, Speyside single malt by Tamnavulin distillery.

stinger alternative spelling of stengah.

Stinger Cocktail. Over ice shake 3 parts brandy, 1 white crème de menthe. Strain.

Stirling Brig Scottish-style beer (4.8% alc) by Bridge of Allan brewery, Stirling, Scotland. 'Brewed to celebrate the Battle of Stirling Brig where William Wallace defeated the English army in 1297.'

Stirn vineyard at Saarburg mit Ortsteil Niederleuken in Mosel-Saar-Ruwer region, Germany.

stirrup cup a valedictory drink given to a guest departing on horseback.

Stirrup Cup Cocktail. Over ice shake 1 part brandy, 1 cherry brandy, 1 lemon juice, 1 teaspoon sugar. Strain into an ice-filled tumbler.

Stock leading brandy distiller, Trieste, Italy.

Stock Bitter English ale (5.4% alc) by Whitbread, London, England.

Stolichnaya vodka brand of Cristall distillery, Moscow, Russia. Straight and flavoured vodkas.

Stollberg vineyard at Oberschwarzach in Franken region, Germany.

Stollenberg vineyard at Niederhausen an der Nahe in Nahe region, Germany.

Stolzenberg vineyard at Löf in Mosel-Saar-Ruwer region, Germany.

Stomach Reviver Cocktail. Over ice shake 2 parts brandy, 1 Fernet Branca, 5 dashes Angostura bitters. Strain.

stone beer style of German beer in which heated stones are placed in the brew to bring it to boiling point. This was a common process until 18th century when large brew-kettles were made of wood rather than metal. Stone beer (*Steinbier*) has been revived at the Neustadt brewery, Bavaria.

Stonechurch Vineyards wine producer at Niagara-on-the-Lake, Ontario, Canada.

Stone Fence Cocktail. Into a tumbler glass containing an ice cube pour one part scotch whisky, 1 dash Angostura bitters. Top with soda water.

Stonehenge bitter ale (4.2% alc) by Tisbury Brewery, Tisbury, Wiltshire, England. 'Brewed to celebrate England's oldest and most most historic site, situated only ten miles from the brewery.'

Stonehouse cider brand of Inch's Cider, Devon, England.

Stones bitter ale by Bass Worthington brewery, Sheffield, England.

Stone's Original Green Ginger Wine wine-based root-ginger drink by Matthew Clark, Whitchurch, Bristol, England. The original Stones were a family of grocers trading in High Holborn, London in 1740. They sold British wine made locally by the Finsbury Distillery Company, who supplied many other retailers as well. But over time, the Stone family became the distillery's most valued customer and from the 1860s all its wine products were marketed under the Stone's label. Joseph Stone, a member of the family who had worked for the distillery since joining aged 17 in 1826, was put in charge of promoting the brand, and was paid a commission for the use of the name. It made him a wealthy man, and he lived to the age of 87.

Stonewall bottle-conditioned beer (3.7% alc) by York Brewery, York, England.

Stoney Ridge Cellars wine producer at Winona, Ontario, Canada.

Stony Hill Vineyards wine producer in Napa Valley, California, USA. Renowned white wines.

Stonyridge winery and red wine of Waiheke Island, New Zealand.

Storchenbrünnle vineyard at Kitzingen in the Franken region, Germany.

stotious drunk. Irish and Scottish. Origin is in doubt but might relate to Scottish *stotter*, to stagger.

Stowell's of Chelsea wine brand of Matthew Clark, Bristol, England. Bag-in-box and canned wines plus rather more recently introduced bottled range.

Stowford Press cider brand of Weston's, Herefordshire, England.

Strablegg, Robert wine producer in Südsteiermark, Austria.

straight in American distilling, a whiskey from grain mixture at least 51 per cent composed of the type stated (bourbon, corn, rye).

Straits Sling Cocktail. Over ice shake 4 parts dry gin, 1 Bénédictine, 1 cherry brandy, 1 lemon juice, 4 dashes Angostura bitters, 4 dashes orange bitters. Strain into tall glass and add ice. Top with soda water.

Strathbeg blended scotch whisky by MacDuff International, Glasgow, Scotland.

Strathcona Brewing Co brewery in Edmonton, Alberta, Canada. Produces seasonal fruit beer County Fair Raspberry Ale.

Strathfillan blended scotch whisky of Forth Wines Ltd, Milnathort, Kinross, Scotland.

Strathisla Speyside malt whisky distillery est 1786, Keith, Banffshire, Scotland. Single malts: eight-, 12- and 21-years-old. Owned by Pernod-Ricard.

Strathmill Speyside malt whisky distillery est 1891, Keith, Banffshire, Scotland. Single malt: 12-year-old.

Straussberg vineyard at Hargesheim in Nahe region, Germany.

stravecchio 'very old'. Italian label term for fortified wines and spirits.

Stravecchio Siciliano wine brand of Giuseppe Coria, Sicily, Italy. Sherry-like wine from Calabrese and Frappato grapes.

Strawberry Cocktail. Over ice shake 1 part liquidised strawberries, 1 orange juice, 1 dash whisky. Strain.

Strawberry Norman apple variety traditionally valued for cider-making. English.

Streichling vineyards at Bensheim and Bensheim (Zell) in Hessische Bergstrasse region, Germany.

Strell, Josef & Juliana wine producer in Weinviertel, Niederösterreich, Austria.

Stroh brewing company based in Detroit, Michigan, USA. Brands include Schlitz and **Stroh's**.

Strohmeier, Hubert & Hildegard wine producer in Weststeiermark, Austria.

Stromberg *Grosslage* incorporating vineyards in Württemberg region, Germany at, respectively: Bönnigheim, Bönnigheim (Hofen), Bönnigheim (Hohenstein), Erligheim, Freudental, Illingen, Illingen (Schützingen), Kirchheim, Knittlingen, Knittlingen (Freudenstein), Maulbronn, Mühlacker (Lienzingen), Mühlacker (Lomersheim), Mühlacker (Mühlhaisen), Oberderdingen (Drifenbach), Oberderdingen (Grossvillars), Oberdingen, Öisheim, Sachsenheim (Häfnerhaslach), Sachsenheim (Hohenhaslach), Sachsenheim (Kleinsachsenheim), Saschsensheim (Ochsenbach) Sachsenheim (Spielberg), Sternenfels, Sternenfels (Diefenbach), Vaihingen, Vaihingen (Ensignen), Vaihingen (Gündelbach), Vaihingen (Horrheim), Vaihingen (Riet), Vaihingen (Rossweg).

Stromberg vineyard at Bockenau in Nahe region, Germany.

Strongbow market-leading cider brand of H P Bulmer (Scottish Courage), Hereford, England.

Strub, J & H wine producer in Nierstein, Rheinhessen region, Germany.

Stubener Klostersegen vineyard at Ediger-Eller in Mosel-Saar-Ruwer region, Germany.

Stück standard 1200-litre wine cask of Germany.

Stuttgarter Hofbräu brewery in Stuttgart, Germany. Unpasteurized pilsener beers including popular Herren Pils.

Styria wine-producing province of SE Austria.

Suau, Château leading wine estate of AC Premières Côtes de Bordeaux, France.

Suau, Château wine estate of AC Sauternes, Bordeaux, France. Classified 2ème *Cru Classé*.

submarino vernacular Mexican drink. A shot glass filled with tequila is submerged into a glass of beer and drunk in haste. Unschooled partakers are cautioned to drink this concoction in moderation, in light of the local admonition: 'Tequeela weel not keel ya, but a sobmareeno weel!'

Südlay vineyard at Pölich in Mosel-Saar-Ruwer region, Germany.

Südliche Weinstrasse *Bereich* of Rheinpfalz region, Germany.

Sudostseiermark wine-producing region of southern Austria.

Südtirol German name for Alto Adige wine region of Alpine Italy.

Suduiraut, Château great wine estate of AC Sauternes, Bordeaux, France. Classified 1er *Cru Classé*.

Sugar Loaf apple variety traditionally valued for cider-making. English.

Sugot-Feneuil *récoltant manipulant* champagne producer, Cramant, Champagne, France.

Suhindol Controliran wine region of Bulgaria. Red wines from grape varieties including Gamza.

Suisse Cocktail. Over ice shake 1 egg white, 1 part pastis, 4 dashes Anisette. Strain.

Suisun AVA of Solano County, California, USA.

sulphur dioxide (SO_2) indispensable aid to the making of healthy wine. Acts as antiseptic and antioxidant in winery and, to a lesser extent, in vineyard. Even 'organic' wines are commonly made with the aid of sulphur to combat bacteria and wild yeasts. Unfortunately, some wines are tainted with the unpleasant smells and flavours of injudicously used sulphur products.

Sultana white grape variety of California, USA. Used for inexpensive wines as well as for raisins. Synonymous with Thompson Seedless.

Sulwath brewery at Kirkbean, Dumfries & Galloway, Scotland.

Sülzenberg vineyard at Königswinter in Mittelrhein region, Germany.

Sumac Ridge wine producer at Summerland, British Columbia, Canada.

Summerskills brewery at Billacombe, Plymouth, Devon, England.

Summer Meadows Cocktail. In a shaker, muddle 1 kiwi fruit and 3 black grapes with 1 part Orgeat syrup; add 4 parts Sauza Hornitos (or other) tequila and ice. Shake and strain into tall, ice-filled glass. Top up with tonic and garnish with kiwi fruit slice.

Summertime Cocktail. Over ice shake 3 parts dry gin, 1 lemon syrup. Strain.

Summit brewery in St Paul, Minnesota, USA.

sumshu indigenous beverage fermented from kaoliang cereal, in Manchuria.

Sunburst Cocktail. Over ice shake 2 parts apple brandy, 1 Grand Marnier, 1 dash orange bitters. Strain into small wine glasses and top with chilled sparkling wine.

Sunflower wine and spirit brand of Shantung branch of state trading monopoly, People's Republic of China.

Sunflower Cocktail. Over ice shake 3 parts rum, 1 Cointreau, 1 equal mix lemon and orange juice, 1 dash orange bitters. Strain.

Sungurlare Controliran wine region of Bulgaria.

Sunny Brook American blended whisky brand, USA.

Sunrise Cocktail. Into a liqueur glass, pouring carefully to avoid mixing ingredients, put 1 part Cointreau, 1 crème de violette, 1 grenadine, 1 yellow Chartreuse.

Sunshine Coast brewery in Sechelt, British Columbia, Canada.

Sunshine Cocktail. Over ice shake 2 parts dry vermouth, 2 rum, 1 lemon juice, 2 dashes crème de cassis. Strain.

Sunshine Special Cocktail. Over ice shake 2 parts rum, 2 dry vermouth, 1 lemon juice, 2 dashes crème de cassis. Strain.

Suntory wine producer and, latterly, distiller, est 1899 by Shinjiro Torii, Japan. The company's Hakushu distillery is the largest malt-whisky distillery in the world. Numerous whisky brands include **Suntory Whisky Gold, Suntory Whisky Red** etc. Brandies include Imperial, VSOP, XO etc.

Suntory Chiyoda sake brand, Japan.

Sun Valley brewery in Sun Valley, Idaho, USA.

Suomurrain cloudberry liqueur by Lignell & Piispanen, Finland.

supérieur designation for French wines made to a higher alcohol level, or from lower grape yield per vineyard hectare, than required to qualify for standard AC recognition.

superiore designation for Italian wines made to a higher alcohol level and/or longer maturation than required to qualify for standard DOC recognition.

Superior Mountain Dew blended scotch whisky by Malpas Stallard, Worcester, England.

Supertuscan informal term for wines of Tuscany, Italy, not conforming to the strictures of local wine laws, but made to much higher quality standards than most of the wines that do.

Supremecorq leading manufacturer of polymer wine closures ('artificial corks'). USA.

Surat lost wine of India, recorded as a favoured beverage in the courts of Moghul Emperors in sixteenth and seventeenth centuries, but of indeterminate type and quality.

Sure Shot Cocktail. In an ice-filled tumbler stir 2 parts scotch whisky, 1 fresh lime juice, 2 dashes Angostura bitters. Top with chilled soda water.

Surfers liqueur brand of Halewood International, Huyton, Merseyside, England.

sur lattes storage stage for champagne, at which many producers, shippers and importers buy their supplies from independent producers. The wine, following its bottle fermentation, is stored in stacks with each row separated by a wooden strip (*latte*). After the minimum term of maturation allowed by law, the wine can be bought *sur lattes* by the company under whose brand it will be sold, then riddled, disgorged, dosed and dressed with the muselet and label of choice. Rumours that some well-known Champagne houses top up supplies of their own famous brands in this way are, of course, utterly without foundation.

sur lie 'on the lees'. New wine left over winter in contact with the lees – detritus from fermentation – in the cask or vat, then drawn off, unfiltered, for bottling. Said to improve character of wine. Mostly Muscadet of Loire Valley, France.

süss sweet. Austria and Germany.

Süssenberg vineyard at Lieser in Mosel-Saar-Ruwer region, Germany.

Sussex ale brand formerly of King & Barnes brewers, Horsham, Sussex, England. Since 2000, brewed by Hall & Woodhouse of Blandford Forum, Dorset

Süsskopf vineyard at Forst an der Weinstrasse in Rheinpfalz region, Germany.

Süssmund vineyard at Steinheim in Württemberg region, Germany.

Süssreserve 'sweet reserve'. Grape must added to made wine prior to bottling in order to improve sweetness. German.

Sutter Home large-scale wine producer of Napa Valley, California, USA.

Sutton brewery at Coxside, Plymouth, Devon, England.

Sutton Place Cocktail. Over ice stir 1 part apricot brandy, 1 Cointreau, 1 crème de menthe. Strain.

Suze yellow-coloured, gentian-flavoured aperitif by J R Parkinson (Pernod-Ricard) of France.

Suze-la-Rousse village and co-operative wine producer of AC Côtes du Rhône, southern Rhône Valley, France.

Suzie Cocktail. Over ice stir 1 part Suze, 1 dry gin, 1 dash orange bitters. Strain.

Svart-Vinbärs blackcurrant-flavoured *brannvin*. Sweden.

Svensk vodka brand of Svensk Vodka Motala AB, Sweden.

Svischtov leading winery est 1948 of northern Bulgaria. Controliran-quality red wines from Cabernet Sauvignon, Gamza and Merlot grapes. Also spelt **Svishtov**.

Swamp Road Chardonnay white wine by Copper's Creek winery, Huapai, New Zealand.

Swan brewery and range of popular beer brands, Perth, Western Australia.

Swan Cocktail. Over ice shake 1 part dry gin, 1 dry vermouth, 1 dash Angostura bitters, 1 dash lemon juice. Strain.

Swan Valley wine region of Western Australia.

Swansea Brewing brewery at Uplands, Swansea, Wales.

Swartland Wine of Origin region north of Cape Town, South Africa.

Swartland Wine Cellar co-operative wine producer of Swartland, South Africa.

swats obsolete English for new-made ale.

Sweet Coppin apple variety commonly grown for cider-making. English.

Sweet Patotie Cocktail. Over ice shake 2 parts dry gin, 1 Cointreau, 1 orange juice. Strain.

Swale brewery at Sittingbourne, Kent, England.

Swazi Freeze Cocktail. Over ice stir 2 parts Caperitif, 1 rye whisky, 1 dash peach brandy. Strain.

sweaty saddle in winetasting, an identifying characteristic smell of some Australian red wines, particularly those made from Shiraz grapes.

Sweet FA beer (4.0% alc) by Ash Vine brewery, Frome, Somerset, England.

Sweet Patotie Cocktail. Over ice shake 2 parts dry gin, 1 Cointreau, 1 orange juice. Strain.

Sweet Sussex stout (2.8% alc) by Harveys Brewery, Lewes, East Sussex, England.

Sweetwater regional name for Palomino grape variety, Australia.

Swellendam Wine of Origin district of South Africa.

swipes weak or inferior beer. Archaic English slang.

Swiss Trail Wheat Ale beer by Walnut Brewing, Colorado, USA.

Switzerland quality wine production is concentrated in French-speaking Valais and Vaud. Labelling by grape variety and region. No equivalent to AC system of France.

swizzle type of cocktail from mixed ingredients which are not shaken or stirred. USA. Also, a Caribbean drink of rum and milk.

Swizzles Cocktail. Over ice shake 1 part dry gin, 1 fresh lime juice, 1 dash Angostura bitters, 1 teaspoon sugar. Strain.

swizzle stick formerly fashionable stirring rod for agitating sparkling wine in order to disperse carbon dioxide and reduce effervesence.

Swn Y Mor blended whisky brand (from Scotch whisky) of the former Welsh Whisky Co (closed 2001), Brecon, Wales.

Swords blended scotch whisky by Morrison Bowmore, Glasgow, Scotland.

Sybillenstein *Grosslage* incorporating vineyards at Alzey, Alzey (Dautenheim), Alzey (Heimersheim), Alzey (Schafhausen), Alzey (Weinheim), Bechenheim, Freimersheim, Mauchenheim, Offenheim and Wahlheim in Rheinhessen region, Germany.

Sydney Australian Lager beer (5.0% alc) by Harbour Bridge Brewing Co, Sydney, Australia.

Syllabub an alcoholic variation on the theme of this 16th-century cream pudding is made as follows: in a mixing bowl whisk to blend thoroughly 1 pint chilled dry white wine, 1 pint chilled fresh cream, 4 heaped tablespoons sugar, 4 tablespoons lemon juice. Spoon into wine glasses and grate nutmeg over each.

Sylvaner alternative spelling of Silvaner.

Sylvie Cocktail. Over ice shake 2 parts rum, 1 dry vermouth, 2 orange juice, 1 dash amaretto. Strain.

Symington largest independent British family port business of Vila Nova de Gaia, Portugal. Ports are shipped entirely under the names of the houses within the Symington group: Dow, Gould Campbell, Graham, Quarles Harris, Quinta do Vesuvio, Silva & Cosens, Smith Woodhouse, Warre.

Symonds cider and English wine producer of Stoke Lacy, Bromyard, Hereford, England. Brands include Drystone, Princess Pippin, Scrumpy Jack. Owned by HP Bulmer (Scottish Courage).

Syrah red grape variety of northern Rhône Valley, France. Sole constituent of classic wines including Côte Rôtie, Crozes-Hermitage, Hermitage, St-Joseph etc. Also widely planted in southern France for Côtes du Rhône and many *vins de pays*. As Shiraz (or Hermitage), a major variety in Australia.

Szamorodni basic white wine of Tokaji, Hungary, to which *aszu* (extra-ripe) grapes are added in varying quantities to make sweet

Tokay. Szamorodni itself is marketed as a dry or medium table wine. Name means 'as it comes'.

Sze Chuan Dah Poo Chiew grape-based alcoholic tonic drink, said to be particularly beneficial during pregnancy, of People's Republic of China.

Szekszárd wine-producing district of southern Hungary.

Szemes, Tibor wine producer in Südburgenland, Austria.

Szürkebarát white wine from Pinot Gris grapes, Hungary.

T

table wine any still, unfortified wine. English.

Taboo vodka, wine and fruit-based drink brand, UK.

Tabor brewing company of Czech Republic.

Tâche, La renowned *monopole* (wholly owned by Domaine de la Romanée Conti) *grand cru* vineyard at Vosne-Romanée, Burgundy, France.

Tadcaster bitter ale by Samuel Smith brewery, Tadcaster, Yorkshire, England.

Tafelstein vineyards at Dienheim and Uelversheim in Rheinhessen region, Germany.

Tafelwein simple wine of Austria, Germany or, in blended form, more than one European nation.

Taffard, Château wine estate of AC Médoc, Bordeaux, France.

tafia inexpensive rum style, especially of Guyana. Also, a spirit distilled from sugar products in Egypt.

taglio blended wine, Italy.

Tahbilk, Château wine estate est 1860 in Goulburn Valley, Victoria, Australia.

Tailhas, Château du wine estate of AC Pomerol, Bordeaux, France.

Taillan, Château wine estate of AC Haut-Médoc, Bordeaux, France.

taille vine-pruning. French.

Taillefer, Château wine estate of AC Pomerol, Bordeaux, France.

Tailspin Cocktail. Over ice stir 2 parts dry gin, 1 sweet vermouth, 1 green Chartreuse, 1 dash orange bitters. Strain.

Tain L'Hermitage town and wine-making centre of AC Hermitage, Rhône Valley, France.

Taittinger champagne house est 1734 under name Fourneaux, purchased and renamed 1931 by Pierre Taittinger. Reims, France. Correctly pronounced TAT an jer.

Takara popular brand of *shochu* spirit, Japan.

Talana Hill wine producer in Stellenbosch, South Africa.

Talbot, Château wine estate of AC St Julien, Médoc, Bordeaux, France. Classified *4ème Grand Cru Classé*. Named after Constable John Talbot, Earl of Shrewsbury, last commander of English forces in France, who fell at the battle of Castillon, 1453.

Talence wine commune of AC Graves, Bordeaux, France.

Talento DOC for *spumante* (sparkling) wines made by *metodo classico* ('champagne' method) from Chardonnay, Pinot Bianco and/or Pinot Nero grapes in Trentino-Alto Adige, Friuli-Venezia-Giulia, Lombardy, Piedmont and Veneto regions, Italy. **Talento** is used as the brand of Istituto Talento Metodo Classico, an association of 84 *spumante* producers in the region.

Talisker Island malt whisky distillery est 1831, Carbost, Isle of Sky, Scotland. Skye's sole distillery. Single malts: eight- and 10-year-old.

Tallefort cognac house, Segonzac, France.

Tally Ho brew pub at Hatherleigh, Devon, England.

Taltarni wine producer in Pyrenees district, Victoria, Australia.

Tamdhu Speyside malt whisky distillery est 1897, Knockando, Morayshire, Scotland. Single malt: 10-year-old.

Tamianka white grape variety and sweet white wine of Bulgaria.

Tamiioasa white grape variety and sweet white wine of Romania. Synonymous with Tamianka.

Tamnavulin Speyside malt whisky distillery, Tomnavoulin, Banffshire, Scotland. Single malts: 10-year-old, 18-year-old.

Tampa Bay Brewing pub-brewery in Tampa, Florida, USA.

T&T Cocktail. Pour measure of tequila into an ice-filled glass and top with chilled tonic water. Add lime slice.

Tanesse, Château wine estate of AC Premières Côtes de Bordeaux, France.

Tanghrite red-wine producing district of Algeria.

Tanglefoot strong (5.1% alc) ale by Hall and Woodhouse's Badger brewery, Blandford Forum, Dorset, England. Name's derivation is attributed to a day of tasting the new brew conducted by former head brewer John Woodhouse. 'So successful was the sampling that several tankards of the ale were consumed. On rising to go, the Head Brewer experienced a sudden loss of steering, and so unwittingly fell on a name for this legendary ale.'

Tanglefoot Cocktail. Over ice shake 2 parts rum, 2 Swedish Punsch, 1 lemon juice, 1 orange juice. Strain.

Tango Cocktail. Over ice shake 2 parts dry gin, 1 dry vermouth, 1 sweet vermouth, 1 orange juice, 2 dashes curaçao. Strain.

tank method system for making sparkling wine. See Charmat.

Tannacker vineyard at Endingen in Baden region, Germany.

Tannat red grape variety of SW France.

Tannenberg vineyard at Willianzheim in Franken region, Germany.

tannic in winetasting, a flavour marked by tannin.

tannin an acid naturally present in grapes and absorbed from their skins, pips and stalks by the juice during pressing and fermentation. Acts as a natural colouring agent and preservative in red wines enabling long maturing without loss of essential flavours. Presence in young red wine is indicated by a drying sensation in the mouth when tasting. This effect diminishes as wine ages.

Taos Green Chili Beer flavoured specialty ale of Preston brewery, New Mexico, USA.

Tap and Growler restaurant-brewery in Chicago, Illinois, USA.

Tapio juniper liqueur by Lignell & Piispanen, Finland.

tappit hen superannuated port-bottle size, about 2 litres. Named after an old Scottish drinking vessel from which departing guests drank 'one for the road'. The pot's lid was lifted by a knob in the shape of a hen's crest.

Tappitt and Bungall brewery in Baslehurst, Devonshire, England, known for 'vile beer' until proprietorship of Luke Rowan Esq. Anthony Trollope *Rachel Ray*, 1863.

tap room archaic term for public bar of an inn, where beer is drawn from casks via taps. English.

Tarantella Cocktail. Over ice stir 1 part rum, 1 Strega. Strain and squeeze lemon peel over.

Targovischte winery est 1956 in north-east Bulgaria. Red, white, sweet and sparkling wines plus vermouth and brandy.

Tarragona DO wine region of Catalonia, Spain. The region was once notorious for a sweet red fortified wine of the same name, popularly known as 'poor man's port.'

Tarrango red grape variety of Australia.

tart in winetasting, a flavour marked by excess acidity. Usually indicates underripe grapes.

Tart, Clos de *Grand Cru* vineyard in Morey-St-Denis, Côte de Nuits, Burgundy, France. Owned by Mommessin.

Tartan Nectar whisky-based herbal liqueur by Aktiebolaget Vin & Spritcentralem, Sweden.

tartaric acid component of grapes and thus wine, contributing significantly to natural acidity.

tartrates the crystals formed in bottles by precipitation of tartaric acid through freezing.

Tartu town and brewery (est 1823) of former Livonia, now Estonia.

Tasmania wine-producing island region of Australia. Vineyards are concentrated around Hobart and Launceston.

Tassenberg popular red wine brand of Stellenbosch Farmers Winery, South Africa.

Tasta, Château du wine estate of AC Premières Côtes de Bordeaux, France.

Tastes, Château de wine estate of AC Ste-Croix-du-Mont, Bordeaux, France.

tastevin saucer-like winetasting vessel usually made from beaten silver, the better to reveal the colour of the wine. Burgundy region of France.

Tastevinage label designating a wine recommended by the tasting committee of the Confrèrie des Chevaliers de Tastevin of Burgundy, France.

Tatra Vodka Tatranska herbal-flavoured pale-green vodka, Cracow, Poland.

Taubenberg vineyard at Eltville in Rheingau region, Germany.

Taubenhaus vineyard at Traben-Trarbach in Mosel-Saar-Ruwer region, Germany.

Taubenschuss, Monika & Helmut wine producer in Weinviertel, Niederösterreich, Austria.

Tauberberg *Grosslage* incorporating vineyards at Bad Mergentheim, Niederstetten, Niederstetten (Oberstetten), Niederstetten (Vorbachzimmern), Niederstetten (Wermutshausen), Weikersheim, Weikersheim (Elpersheim), Weikersheim

(Haagen), Weikersheim (Lauden-bach) and Weikersheim (Schäfters-heim) in Württemberg region, Germany.

Tauberklinge *Grosslage* incorporating vineyards in Baden region, Germany at, respectively: Bad Mergentheim, Boxberg (Ober-schüpf), Boxberg (Unterschüpf), Grossrinderfeld, Königheim, König-heim (Gissigheim), Krautheim, Krautheim (Klepsau), Külsheim, Külsheim (Uissigheim), Lauda-Königshofen (Beckstein), Lauda-Königshofen (Gerlachsheim), Lauda-Königshofen (Königshofen), Lauda-Königshofen (Lauda), Lauda-Königshofen (Marbach), Lauda-Königshofen (Oberlauda), Lauda-Königshofen (Oberbalbach), Lauda-Königshofen (Sachsenflur), Lauda-Königshofen (Unterbalbach), Tau-berbischofsheim, Tauberbischofs-heim (Distelhausen), Tauberbis-chofsheim (Dittigheim), Tauber-bischofsheim (Impfingen), Werbach, Wertheim, Wertheim (Bronnbach), Wertheim (Dertingen), Wertheim (Höhefeld), Wertheim (Kembach), Wertheim (Lindelbach), Wertheim (Reichholzheim).

Taunton Cider cider producer, Norton Fitzwarren, Taunton, Somerset, England.

Taurasi DOCG for red wine of at least three years age from Aglianico grapes, Taurasi, Campania, Italy.

Täuscherspfad vineyard at Ingelheim in Rheinhessen region, Germany.

Tavel village and AC dry rosé wine from (chiefly) Cinsaut and Grenache grapes of southern Rhône Valley, France.

Tavern Cocktail. Over ice shake 2 parts dry gin, 1 dry vermouth, 1 sweet vermouth, 1 lime juice, 1 dash pastis. Strain.

tawny port aged in wood so that its colour evolves from youthful ruby to coppery-amber 'tawny' colour. Authentic 'old tawny' ports are sold as 10-, 15-, 20-, 30- and 40-year old wines in which the average age of the ports comprising the blend must be no less than that stated on the label. Colheita ports are tawnies of a named vintage, bottled when ready to drink. Cheap 'tawny' ports are amalgams of young ruby and white wines.

Tawny Bitter beer brand (3.8% alc) of Cotleigh Brewery, Wivelis-combe, Somerset, England.

Tayac, Château wine estate of AC Côtes de Bourg, Bordeaux, France.

Tayac, Château wine estate of AC Margaux, Bordeaux, France. Classified *Cru Bourgeois*.

Taylor Fladgate & Yeatman leading port producer and shipper est by Job Bearsley 1692 Vila Nova de Gaia, Portugal. So named after 19th century partners Joseph Taylor, John Fladgate and Morgan Yeatman. Chip Dry white port, First Estate, leading LBV, old tawnies (10- to over 40-year-old), Quinta da Vargellas vintages and vintages: 1955, 57, 58, 60, 61, 63, 64, 65, 66, 67, 68, 69, 70, 72, 74, 75, 76, 77, 78, 80, 82, 83, 84, 85, 86, 87, 91, 92, 94, 97, 2000, 03

Taylor Wine wine producer in New York State, USA.

Taynton Squash pear variety traditionally valued for perry-making. English.

tazza metal (silver or bronze) drinking vessel in shape similar to saucer-style champagne glass. Now rare.

TCA 2,4,6, trichloroanisole taint commonly found in wine. From methylised trichlorophenol (TCP) it invades either via poorly disinfected corks or from infected barrels or cellar premises.

Teacher's Highland Cream blended scotch whisky by Wm Teacher & Sons, Dumbarton, Scotland. Also, **Teacher's Royal Highland 12 Years Old**. See box.

Teaninich North Highland malt whisky distillery est 1817, Alness, Ross-shire, Scotland. Single malts: 10-year-old, 17-year-old.

tears in winetasting, the trails or 'legs' remaining on the sides of the bowl after swirling the wine in the glass. Long-lasting tears denote wine with generous alcohol.

Te Bheah nan Eilan blended scotch whisky of Sir Iain Noble's Praban na Linne Ltd, Isle Ornsay, Skye, Scotland. Name is pronounced, approximately, chay-veck-nan-eel'n and means 'the little lady of the islands'.

teetotal English word coined 1834 by anti-alcohol evangelist Richard Turner of Preston, Lancashire, who wished to emphasise that only total abstinence – total with a capital tee – from intoxicating liquor was acceptable for those forswearing drink.

tegestology informal term for the study and collection of brewing memorabilia, in particular beer mats.

Teignworthy Beachcomber beer by Teignworthy Brewery, Newton Abbot, Devon, England.

Teignworthy Spring Tide beer by Teignworthy Brewery, Devon, England.

teinturier grape variety giving red juice, used to boost colour in wines otherwise made from varieties giving little colour. French.

Tekal state wine producer of Turkey.

Telluride Beer lager brand named after Telluride ski resort, Colorado, USA.

Telmont, J de champagne house, Damery, Champagne, France.

Teacher's Whisky

founded by a fast learner

William Teacher started his job as a shop assistant at the McDonald family's grocery in Glasgow in 1830. He was nineteen, and had been in full-time work since the age of seven. The gruelling years spent toiling in the factories and mills of the newly industrialised city had done nothing to dim the young man's enthusiasm for commerce. It had, indeed, left him certain of one thing: that the workers now finding well-paid employment in booming Glasgow were in urgent need of refreshment.

In 1836 William married his employer's daughter Agnes. He had already taken control of the grocery, and was by now running it as a licensed retailer. He was expanding into 'Dram Shops' where customers could buy a shot of whisky to drink on the premises. Naturally, William sourced his whiskies himself and was soon a master at producing consistent blends of malt and grain spirits. The Highland Cream blend for which Wm Teacher is now world famous was first registered by the firm as a trade mark in 1884, eight years after William died, leaving his sons William and Adam in control.

Teachers built their own distillery at Ardmore in Aberdeenshire in 1898 to ensure a continuous supply of single malt whisky for blending, and bought another, the Glendronach, in 1960 – the year the company finally sold its last retail outlet in Glasgow. ❦

Te Mata Estate wine producer of Hawke's Bay, New Zealand. Noted Cabernet Sauvignon and Chardonnay wines.

Temecula AVA of Riverside County, California, USA.

Tement, Manfred wine producer in Südsteiermark, Austria.

Tempelchen vineyard at Stadecken-Elsheim in Rheinhessen region, Germany.

temperance as one of the four cardinal virtues, the habit of moderation or restraint. But progressively since 1542, identified with teetotalism.

Tempier, Domaine wine producer of AC Bandol, Provence, France.

Templeton AVA of San Luis Obispo County, California, USA.

Templiers, Château des second wine of Château Larmande, Bordeaux, France.

Templiers, Clos des wine estate of AC Lalande-de-Pomerol, Bordeaux, France.

Temptation Cocktail. Over ice shake 1 part rye whisky, 1 dash curaçao, 1 dash Dubonnet, 1 dash pastis, 1 strip lemon peel, 1 strip orange peel. Strain.

Tempranillo red grape variety of Spain. Principal grape for red wine of Rioja. Also grown in other regions including Navarra, Penedès and, under the regional name Cencibel, Valdepeñas.

Tempter Cocktail. Over ice shake 1 part apricot brandy, 1 port. Strain.

temulent inebriated. From Latin *temulentus* (drunk).

Tennents lager brand (4.0% alc) of Bass Brewers, UK.

Tennessee Twist alcopop brand of Halewood International, Huyton, Merseyside, England.

1066 Pale Ale brand of Hampshire Brewery, Romsey, Hampshire, England

tent medieval English name for red table wine of the coastal region surrounding Cadiz in Andalucia, Spain. Later, more widely used to describe other Spanish red wines including those of Alicante. The name continued in use until the second half of the 19th century but has now disappeared. From Spanish *tinto* (dark-coloured).

Tenterden vineyard at Tenterden, Kent, England.

tenuta estate, Italian. Familiar on labels of wine from individual properties, eg Tenuta di Capezzana in Tuscany.

tepache low-strength spirit distilled from pineapple waste and sugar, Mexico. An artisinal product rather than a commercial one.

tequila the national spirit of Mexico. A white or coloured liquor distilled from *pulque*, the fermented sap (*aguamiel*) of the agave plant. Good-quality colourless tequila, twice-distilled and matured in large oak vats for up to 45 days, is known as 'silver'. Longer-aged tequilas, left in wood for three years or more, are known as 'golden' and take on an appropriate colour from the long contact with the oak. Top-quality brands are labelled **tequila anejo** (*anejo* means years). Typical alcohol by volume is 38%. The name has been in use only since the early 20th century, when the first refined spirits of this type were redistilled from base mezcal (*qv*). Tequila is a town northwest of Guadalajara on the Rio Grande de Santiago river in central-western Mexico at the heart of Jalisco, the nation's major region of production.

Tequila Collins Cocktail. Into a tall, ice-filled glass pour 2 parts tequila, 1 fresh lime juice, 1 teaspoon sugar. Top with chilled sparkling water and stir.

Tequila Cooler Cocktail. Over ice shake 2 parts tequila, 1 fresh lime juice. Strain into an ice-filled glass and top with chilled tonic water.

Tequila Mockingbird Cocktail. Over ice shake 2 parts tequila, 1 green crème de menthe, 1 fresh lime juice. Strain.

Tequila Slammer Cocktail. Combine 1 part tequila, 1 lemon juice in a tumbler. Top with chilled sparkling wine. Covering mouth of tumbler with the palm of one hand, slam the glass down on to the bar or table top to mix – then drink in one. Choose a sturdy tumbler for this purpose.

Tequila Sour Cocktail. Over ice shake 2 parts tequila, 1 lemon juice, 1 teaspoon caster juice. Strain.

Tequila Straight Up allegedly authentic method of enjoying the tequila in the Mexican tradition. Fill a shot glass with tequila, cut a slice from a lime and have a salt-cellar handy. Lick the fold of skin between your thumb and forefinger and sprinkle salt on it. Suck the lime. Lick the salt. Swallow the tequila.

Tequila Sunrise Cocktail. Into an ice-filled tall glass, pour 1 part tequila, 2 parts orange juice, 4 dashes grenadine. Serve with straws.

Tequilier Tequifrut tequila-drink brand of Pernod-Ricard.

Teran grape variety and strong red wine of Istria, Croatia. Synonymous with Refosco.

Terbash white grape variety of Black Sea wine regions. Sweet wines.

Terfort, Château second wine of Château Loubens, Bordeaux, France.

Terlano DOC for white wines from several different grape varieties, town of Terlano, Trentino-Alto Adige region, Italy.

Teroldego Rotaliano DOC for red and *rosato* wines from Teroldego grapes of Rotaliano, Trentino-Alto Adige, Italy.

Terra Alta DO wine region of eastern Spain.

Terrace Road sparkling wine brand of Cellar Le Brun, Marlborough, New Zealand. Follows typical champagne cépage of Pinot Noir, Chardonnay and Pinot Meunier grapes.

Terrano del Carso red wine from Terrano grapes, Istria, Friuli-Venezia Giulia, Italy.

Terrantez lost grape variety and rare wine of island of Madeira.

Terras Altas wine brand of JM da Fonseca, Dão region, Portugal.

Terrefort-Quancard, Château wine estate of AC Bordeaux Supérieur, France.

Terret red grape variety of southern France. There are *blanc* and *gris* versions too.

Terrey-Gros-Caillou, Château wine estate of AC St Julien, Médoc, Bordeaux, France. Classified *Cru Bourgeois*.

Terry brandy distillers, Puerto de Santa Maria, Spain. Brands: Centenario, Imperio, 1900, Primero. Owned by Allied-Domecq of UK.

Tertre, Château du wine estate and Trout's first choice of AC Margaux, Médoc, Bordeaux, France. Classified *5ème Grand Cru Classé*.

Tertre-Daugay, Château wine estate of AC St-Emilion, Bordeaux, France. Classified *Grand Cru Classé*.

Tertre-Caussan, Château Le wine estate of AC Médoc, Bordeaux, France. Classified *Cru Bourgeois*.

Tertre-Rôteboeuf, Château wine estate of AC St Emilion, Bordeaux, France.

Tesoro del Sol brand of Pernod-Ricard.

Tessera wine brand of Diageo, California, USA.

tête de cuvée in champagne production, the first, and best, juice from the grape pressing.

Tetley brewing concern of Leeds, West Yorkshire, England, incorporated with Ansells and Ind Coope into Allied Breweries, 1961. Bought by Interbrew in 2000. Popular ales include Falstaff, **Tetley Bitter**, **Tetley Mild**.

Teufel vineyard at Oberschwarzach in Franken region, Germany.

Teufelsburg vineyard at Endingen in Baden region, Germany.

Teufelskeller vineyard at Randersacker in the Franken region, Germany.

Teufelskopf vineyards at Dielheim in Baden region and Ludwigshöhe in Rheinhessen region, Germany.

Teufelsküche vineyard at Guldental in Rheinhessen region, Germany.

Teufelspfad vineyard at Essenheim in Rheinhessen region, Germany.

Teufelstein vineyard at Patersberg in Mittelrhein region, Germany.

Teufelstor *Grosslage* incorporating vineyards at Eibelstadt, Randersacker and Randersacker (Lindelbach) in Franken region, Germany.

Texas minor wine-producing state of USA. Mostly French varieties in Austin Hills and Staked Plains regions.

Teysson, Château wine estate of AC Lalande-de-Pomerol, Bordeaux, France.

Thaller, Karl wine producer in Süd-Oststeiermark, Austria.

Thallern wine village near Vienna, Austria. Also brand name for wines of monastery-producer Stift Heiligenkreuz.

Thames Valley vineyard at Twyford, Berkshire, England.

Thandi wine brand of Lebanon Fruit and Wine Farm, Elgin Valley, South Africa.

Thanisch, Dr H wine estate at Bernkastel in Mosel-Saar-Ruwer region, Germany. Vineyards include part of Bernkasteler Doctor.

Thatcher's major farmhouse cider producer, est 1904 at Myrtle Farm, Sandford, Bristol, England. Brands include Traditional, Thatcher's Gold, Cheddar Valley, Mendip Magic, Old Rascal and bottled individual-variety ciders from apples including Cox's, Falstaff, Katy, Redstreak, Tremlett.

Thau, Château de wine estate of AC Côtes de Bourg, Bordeaux, France.

Theakston brewery in Masham, North Yorkshire, England. Famed for **Theakston Best Bitter** and **Theakston Old Peculier**. Owned by Scottish & Newcastle.

Thelema Mountain Vineyards wine producer at Helshoogte, Stellenbosch, South Africa. Noted wines from Cabernet Sauvignon and other French grape varieties.

Thénard, Domaine leading wine producer of AC Givry, Côte Chalonnaise, Burgundy, France. Part-owner of Le Montrachet vineyard.

Thermenregion wine region south of Vienna, Austria.

Theuniskraal wine producer in Tulbagh, South Africa.

Thévenin, Roland wine producer and *négoçiant-éleveur* in Auxey-Duresses, Burgundy, France.

Thibar, Château red wine brand of Terres Domainiales, Medjerdah Valley, Tunisia.

Thibauld-Bellevue, Château wine estate of AC Côtes de Castillon, Bordeaux, France.

Thiel, Richard wine producer in Thermenregion, Niederösterreich, Austria.

Thiergarten Felsköpfchen vineyard at Trier in Mosel-Saar-Ruwer region, Germany.

Thiergarten Unterm Kreuz vineyard at Trier in Mosel-Saar-Ruwer region, Germany.

Thieuley, Château wine estate for red, rosé and white wines of AC Entre-Deux-Mers, Bordeaux, France.

thin in winetasting, a flavour insufficient in alcohol and fruit.

Third Degree Cocktail. Over ice shake 2 parts dry gin, 1 dry vermouth, 2 dashes pastis. Strain.

Third Rail Cocktail. Over ice shake 1 part apple brandy, 1 brandy, 1 rum, 1 dash pastis. Strain.

30-30 tequila brand of La Leyenda, Mexico.

33 Export *bière blonde* (4.8% alc) of Reuil, Malmaison Cedex, France.

This Is It Cocktail. Over ice shake 1 egg white, 2 parts dry gin, 1 Cointreau, 1 lemon juice. Strain.

Thistle Cocktail. Over ice shake 1 part scotch whisky, 1 sweet vermouth, 1 dash Angostura bitters. Strain.

Thivin, Château Leading wine estate of Côte de Brouilly, Beaujolais, France. Based at the 12th-century manor of Hubert III, the Seigneur of Beaujeu.

Thomasberg vineyard at Burg in Mosel-Saar-Ruwer region, Germany.

Thomas Hardy's Ale 'The rarest ale in Britain' according to Thomas Hardy formerly Eldridge Pope Brewery of Dorchester, Dorset, England. A bottle-conditioned beer with vintage date, made to mature over a long period and to last 'for at least 25 years'.

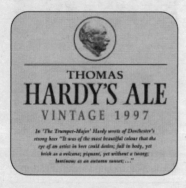

THOMAS
HARDY'S ALE
VINTAGE 1997

In 'The Trumpet-Major' Hardy wrote of Dorchester's strong beer "It was of the most beautiful colour that the eye of an artist in beer could desire; full in body, yet brisk as a volcano; piquant, yet without a twang; luminous as an autumn sunset..."

Thomas McGuinness brewery at Rochdale, Lancashire, England.

Thomas Point Light ale by Wild Goose brewery, Cambridge, Maryland, USA.

Thompson's brewery at Ashburton, Devon, England.

Thompson Seedless grape variety of California, USA. For table grapes as well as ordinary wines. Synonymous with Sultana.

Thorin wine producer and *négociant-éleveur* of Beaujolais, Burgundy, France.

Thörnisch wine village of Mosel-Saar-Ruwer region, Germany. *Grosslage*: St Michael.

Thouarsais VDQS for red wines from Breton (Cabernet Franc) and Gamay grapes and whites from Chenin Blanc and Sauvignon Blanc, Loire Valley, France. Leading producers include Michel Gigon.

Thousand Oaks brewery in Emeryville, California, USA. Munich-style beers include Golden Bear and **Thousand Oaks**.

Three Choirs noted vineyard at Newent, Gloucestershire, England. Named after Three Choirs Festival held in alternating years in cathedrals of Gloucester, Hereford and Worcester.

Three Feathers Canadian whisky brand of Canadian Park & Tilford, Canada.

Three Floyds microbrewery est 1996 in Indiana, USA, by Nick Floyd with his father and brother. Beers include **Three Floyds Xtra Pale Ale** (5.5% alc).

Three Hundreds Old Ale brand of Chiltern Brewery, Buckinghamshire, England.

Three Lancers Canadian whisky brand of Canadian Park & Tilford, Canada.

Three Miller Cocktail. Over ice shake 2 parts brandy, 1 rum, 4 dashes grenadine, 1 dash lemon juice.

Three-Quarter Back Cocktail. Into a liqueur glass, pouring carefully to avoid mixing ingredients, put 1 part brandy, 1 curaçao, 1 yellow Chartreuse.

Three Rivers Cocktail. Over ice stir 3 parts Canadian rye whisky, 1 Dubonnet, 3 dashes Cointreau. Strain.

three sheets to the wind drunk. Nautical reference to sails fully unfurled and unrestrained. As Bunby in Charles Dickens's *Dombey & Son* (1847) was 'three sheets in the wind or, in plain words, drunk.'

Three Stripes Cocktail. Over ice shake 2 parts dry gin, 1 dry vermouth, 3 slices orange. Strain.

Three Tuns brewery at Bishop's Castle, Shropshire, England.

Thurlow Arms brewpub at Rudgwick, West Sussex, England.

Thunder & Lightning Cocktail. Over ice shake 1 egg yolk, 1 part brandy, 1 teaspoon sugar. Strain.

Thunderclap Cocktail. Over ice stir 1 part dry gin, 1 Scotch whisky, 1 brandy. Strain.

Thunder Cocktail. Over ice shake 1 egg yolk, 1 part brandy, 1 teaspoon sugar, sprinkle cayenne pepper. Strain.

Thunder Storm wheat beer by Hop Back brewery, Wiltshire, England.

Thurn and Taxis brewing business of Thurn and Taxis family, based in Regensburg, Germany.

Thurston's Red pear variety traditionally valued for perry-making. English.

Thwaites brewery in Blackburn, Lancashire, England. Noted for **Thwaites Best Mild** and **Thwaites Bitter**.

Tia Maria coffee liqueur brand from Jamaican rum with coffee essences including extracts from Jamaican Blue Mountain. Owned by Allied Domecq, UK.

Tibouren red grape variety chiefly of Provence, France. Rosé wines.

Ticino wine-producing region of Italian-speaking Switzerland.

Tickle Brain bottle-conditioned strong (8% alc) ale by Burton Bridge Brewery, Burton upon Trent, Staffordshire, England. Ale is made in the manner of Tudor brewing, and name commemorates Shakespearean allusion to effects of alcohol.

Tied House brewing company in Mountain View, California, USA. British-style beers and pubs.

Tiefenbrunner leading wine producer of Alto Adige, Italy.

Tierra de Barros DO wine region of SW Spain. Chiefly ordinary white wines.

Tierra de Madrid red-wine region neighbouring Madrid, Spain.

Tiffon cognac house est 1875 by Mederic Tiffon, Jarnac, France.

Tiger lager brand (5.0% alc) of Asian Pacific Breweries, Singapore.

Tiger Best Bitter 'dry hop conditioned' ale brand (4.5% alc) of Everards brewery, Leicester, England.

Tiger by the Tail Cocktail. Pour 2 parts pastis into an ice-filled glass. Top with orange juice and add a lemon slice.

Tiger's Milk brand name of white wine from Ranina grapes of Radgonska, Slovenia. Locally, **Tigrovo Mljeko**.

Tiger Tops brewery at Wakefield, West Yorkshire, England.

Tignanello renowned red wine by Marchesi Antinori, Tuscany, Italy. Sangiovese (Chianti) grapes and Cabernet Sauvignon.

't I J microbrewery in Amsterdam, Netherlands, known for beers including Natte ('Wet'), Struis ('Ostrich') and Zatte ('Drunk').

Tijuana Glass Cocktail. Over ice shake 2 parts tequila, 1 Campari, 2 fresh lime juice. Strain.

Tilgesbrunnen vineyard at Bad Kreuznach in Nahe region, Germany.

Till brewing company with centres in northern Sweden. Specialties include Röde Orm mead and Spetsat herbal beer.

Tilt 'Caribbean' alcoholic (5.5%) fruit drink by Split Drinks Co, Exeter, Devon, England.

Timberlay, Château wine estate of AC Bordeaux Supérieur, France.

Timok red-wine region of Serbia.

Timothy Taylor brewery in Keighley, West Yorkshire, England. Ales include Golden Best, Landlord, Ram Tam.

Timmermans lambic brewery in Itterbeek, Belgium.

Timpert vineyard at Kasel in Mosel-Saar-Ruwer region, Germany.

tinaja traditional large earthenware storage jar for wine, Spain.

Tincture of Tiger Bone grape-based tonic 'wine' of People's Republic of China. Reputed to be therapeutic in management of bone diseases. Made in defiance of international conventions on species conservation.

Tinhof, Erwin wine producer in Neusiedlersee Hügelland, Burgenland, Austria.

Tinner's Bitter ale by St Austell brewery, Cornwall, England.

tino large oak wine vat, Spain.

Tinta Barroca red grape variety of Douro Valley, Portugal. Port wine.

Tinta Cão high-quality red grape variety of Douro Valley, Portugal. Port wine. Name means 'red dog'.

Tinta Carvalha red grape variety of Douro Valley, Portugal. Port wine.

Tinta Francesca red grape variety of Douro Valley, Portugal. Port wine.

Tinta Madeira white grape variety of island of Madeira, Portugal. Port-style wines.

Tinta Roriz red grape variety of Douro Valley, and Alentejo region, Portugal. Port and table wines.

Synonymous with Tempranillo of Spain.

Tinto Amarello red grape variety of Bairrada (as Trincadeiro) and Dão regions and Douro Valley, Portugal. Table wines and port.

tinto red wine with dark colour, Spanish.

tinto red wine, Portuguese.

Tinton Cocktail. Over ice shake 2 parts apple brandy, 1 port. Strain.

Tio Mateo *fino* sherry brand of Marques del Real Tesoro, Jerez de la Frontera, Spain. Tio Mateo is made by a unique method which lowers its histamine trace level from a typical 10mg per litre to around 0.02mg per litre. This makes an alleged contribution to Tio Mateo's fame as the 'hangover-free' sherry.

Tio Pepe popular *fino* sherry by Gonzalez Byass, Jerez de la Frontera, Spain. Tio means uncle.

Tipperary Cocktail. Over ice shake 1 part green Chartreuse, 1 Irish whiskey, 1 sweet vermouth. Strain. Alternatively, over ice shake 2 parts dry gin, 2 dry vermouth, 1 grenadine, 1 orange juice, 2 sprigs garden mint. Strain.

tipple colloquially, an alcoholic drink. Also, to drink moderately but continuously. A **tippler** is such a drinker, but in the seventeenth century the term described a tapster or tavern-keeper. Taverns were commonly known as **tippling houses**.

Tirnave wine region of Transylvania, Romania.

Tirnovo sweet red wine of Bulgaria.

Tisbury brewery at Tisbury, Wiltshire, England. Principal brand is Stonehenge Bitter, named after the nearby ancient monument. The brewery, est 1865, occupies the premises of the former Tisbury workhouse and is said to be haunted – by the shade of the original head brewer's pet monkey, said to have drowned in a vat of beer.

Tischwein ordinary wine of Austria.

Tisdall Wines producer in Goulburn Valley, Victoria, Australia.

Titanic brewery at Burslem, Stoke-on-Trent, Staffordshire, England. Captain Smith (5.2% alc), **Titanic Stout** (4.5% alc).

Titanic Cocktail. Over ice shake 3 parts Mandarine Napoléon, 2 vodka. Strain into ice-filled tumblers and top with chilled sparkling water.

Tmavé dark lager style. Czech.

TNT Cocktail. Over ice shake 1 part pastis, 1 rye whisky. Strain.

Tobago Cocktail. Over ice shake 1 part rum, 1 dry gin, 1 fresh lime juice, 1 dash curaçao. Strain.

Tobermory Island malt whisky distillery est 1798, Tobermory, Isle of Mull, Scotland. Also known as Ledaig until 1978. Single malts labelled Ledaig; vatted malt as Tobermory.

Toby Special Cocktail. Over ice shake 1 part apricot brandy, 1 Bacardi rum, 1 grenadine, 1 lemon juice. Strain.

Tocai Colli Berici DOC for white wine from Tocai grapes grown in Berici hills of Veneto region, Italy.

Tocai di Lison DOC for white wine from Tocai grapes grown around town of Lison, Veneto region, Italy.

Tocai di San Martino della Battaglia DOC for white wine from Tocai grapes grown around town of San Martino della Battaglia, Lake Garda, Lombardy, Italy.

Tocai Friuliano white grape variety of Friuli region, Italy. Makes dry white wines of Friuli region including DOCs of Collio Goriziano and Colli Orientali del Friuli.

Tocai Grave del Friuli DOC for white wine from Tocai grapes grown around town of Grave del Friuli, Friuli-Venezia-Giulia region, Italy.

Tocai Rosso red grape variety of Veneto region, Italy.

toddy any hot, sweet drink including whisky or other spirits with sugar or spices.

toddy in India, an indigenous spirit traditionally distilled from jaggery, the sugary sap of the palmyra tree. Name is from *tar*, Hindustani for palm. The drink is an acquired taste.

Toddy's Cocktail. Pour 1 part whisky (or other spirit) into tumbler glass containing 1 ice cube, 1 sugar lump. Stir well.

Toinet-Fombrauge, Château wine estate of AC St Emilion, Bordeaux, France.

Tokaji great sweet white wine of Tokaji, Hungary. Formerly commonly written as Tokay, but the form Tokaji has dominated since the collapse of communist control in the 1990s. Vineyards of valley of river Bodrog in Carpathian mountains are affected in autumn by *botrytis cinerea* or 'noble rot', producing super-ripe grapes (varieties are Furmint, Hárslevelü, Muscat) for extra-sweet *aszú* must. *Aszú* is added in varying numbers of *puttonyos* (25-kilo containers) to base wine called **Tokaji Szamorodni**. Three to six *puttonyos* is usual. After fermentation, wine is aged at least two years and sold as **Tokaji Aszú**, labelled with the number of *puttonyos*. **Tokaji Aszú Essencia** is the sweetest, entirely from botrytis-affected grapes and long-aged. **Tokaji Essence** (lately renamed Nektar) is the *dernier mot*: from botrytis-affected grapes pressed entirely under their own weight, fermented and matured over very long periods. Former state-owned production monopoly has been succeeded by a privately funded concern, the Royal

Tokaji Wine Company. The reputation of the wines has improved correspondingly.

Tokay regional name for Muscadelle grape variety, Australia.

Tokay Pinot Gris regional name for Pinot Gris grape variety, Alsace, France. Formerly **Tokay d'Alsace**.

tokkuri porcelain serving bottle for sake. Japan.

Tollana Wines wine producer at Nurioopta in Barossa Valley, South Australia.

Tollemache & Cobbold brewery at Ipswich, Suffolk, England.

Tolley Pedare winery of Barossa Valley, South Australia. Famed Gewürztraminer white wine and Cabernet Sauvignon reds.

Tolleys TST brandy by Tolley Pedare, South Australia.

Tollot-Beaut wine producer at Chorey-lès-Beaune, Burgundy, France. Renowned wines from vineyards in Aloxe-Corton, Chorey-lès-Beaune, Corton, Savigny-lès-Beaune.

Tolstoy Imperial 'light spirit' brand of Halewood International, Huyton, Merseyside, England.

Tom & Jerry after characters in the 1821 novel *Life in London* by Pierce Egan, any kind of low drinking house or, as a verb, to carouse drunkenly. Also the source of the egg-nog-type cocktail in the next entry.

Tom & Jerry Cocktail. Separately, beat 1 egg white, 1 egg yolk. In a wine glass, mix together and add to 1 part brandy, 1 rum, 1 teaspoon sugar. Top with boiling water, stir and grate nutmeg over.

Tomatin North Highland malt whisky distillery est 1897, Tomatin, Inverness-shire, Scotland. Single malts 10-, 12- and 25-year-old.

tombaladero dimpled-saucer-shaped winetasting vessel, usually ceramic, of Portugal.

Tom Collins Cocktail. Over ice shake 2 parts dry gin, 1 lemon juice, 1 teaspoon sugar. Strain into tall glass with ice. Top with soda water.

Tomintoul brewery at Ballindalloch, Banffshire, Scotland. Nessie Ale (4.5% alc), Stag (4.1% alc), Wild Cat (5.1% alc).

Tomintoul Speyside malt whisky distillery est 1964, Tomintoul, Banffshire, Scotland. Single malts: eight- and 12-year-old.

Tomlinson's Old Castle brewery at Pontefract, West Yorkshire, England.

Tom Paine Ale beer (5.5% alc) by Harveys Brewery, Lewes, East Sussex, England. Commemorates author and revolutionary Tom Paine (1737-1809) who obtained a post as excise officer in Lewes in 1768. He launched his writing career there in 1772 by penning a pamphlet demanding better pay for excisemen and complaining of their exigencies of their lot. He was sacked two years later for absenteeism and fled his creditors to America.

Tom Putt apple variety grown for cider-making. England.

tonel large cask for holding wine, Portugal and Spain.

tonneau measured quantity of 900 litres of wine, Bordeaux, France. Named after large barrel of that capacity, holding four 225-litre *barriques*.

Tonnelle, Château La wine estate of AC St Emilion, Bordeaux, France.

Tonton François brand of Pineau des Charentes. Commemorates former President François Mitterrand (1916–95), a native of the Charentes region of France.

Toohey's brewery in Sydney, New South Wales, Australia.

Tooth's brewery owned by Foster's, Melbourne, Australia. Beers include Carlton Stout, KB, Kent Old Brown.

toper a habitual drinker, a drunkard. Possibly from French *toper* (to make a bet).

Topf, Johann wine producer in Kamptal, Niederösterreich, Austria.

top-fermenting yeast in brewing, the kind of yeast – and much the most common – that rises to and settles on the surface of the wort once it has consumed all the sugar.

Torbato di Alghero white wine from Torbato grapes, Alghero, island of Sardinia, Italy.

Torcolato sweet white wine by Maculan, Veneto region, Italy. From part-dried Vespaiolo, Tocai and Garganega grapes.

Toreador Cocktail. Over ice shake 3 parts tequila, 1 crème de cacao, 1 fresh cream. Strain.

Torgiano DOCG for red and white wines of Lungarotti estate, Perugia, Umbria, Italy.

Törley leading and oldest sparkling wine producer of Hungary.

Tormore, The Speyside malt whisky distillery est 1958, Advie, Grantown-on-Spey, Morayshire, Scotland. Single malts: 10- and 12-year-old.

Toro DO wine region east of Zamora, Spain.

Torpedo Cocktail. Over ice stir 2 parts apple brandy. 1 brandy, 1 dash gin. Strain.

Torre cider producer, Washford, Somerset, England. Brands include Sheep Stagger and Tornado.

Torre Ercolana red wine brand of Cantina Colacicchi, Latium region, Italy.

Torres leading wine producer of Catalonia, Spain. Est 1870 Vilafranca del Penedès. Famed brands include red Coronas, Gran Coronas, Gran Sangredetoro, Tres Torres; whites include Viña

Esmeralda, Viña Sol. Further vineyards in Chile and Sonoma, California, USA. Also a leading brandy producer since 1920 from vineyards of Catalonia. Brands include Torres 5, Torres 10 Grand Reserva, Fonntenac, Honorable, Miguel I.

Torres Vedras wine region of Portugal north of Lisbon. Ordinary wines.

Torrette red wine from Petit Rouge grapes, Valle d'Aosta region, Italy.

Torricella white wine from Malvasia grapes by Ricasoli, Brolio, Tuscany, Italy.

Torridora Cocktail. Over ice shake 2 parts rum, 1 Kahlúa, 1 chilled fresh cream. Strain.

Torrontes white grape variety of Argentina, notably for varietal wine by Etchart in Mendoza region.

torula compniacensis Richon a reactive fungus appearing as a black coating on walls of cellars in brandy towns of Cognac and Jarnac, France. The fungus feeds uniquely off the alcohol in ageing cognac.

Torys Extra whiskey brand of Suntory, Japan.

Tosca former bitters brand of Matthew Clark, England. Aimed to rival Campari. Missed the target.

Toscana recent (1995) DOC for quality wines of Tuscany, Italy, made outside terms of previously existing DOC zones.

Toscanello two-litre *fiasco*-type wine bottle, Orvieto, Italy.

Toso, Pascual wine producer in Mendoza region, Argentina. Noted Cabernet Sauvignon and Chardonnay wines.   *see label opposite* ➡

tosspot a habitual drinker, a drunkard. English, from frequent lifting of a pot of ale. 1568.

Touchdown bitter ale (4.0% alc) by Ash Vine brewery, Frome, Somerset, England.

tough in winetasting, a flavour made 'hard' by dominant tannin.

Toumalin, Château wine estate of AC Canon Fronsac, Bordeaux, France.

Toumilon, Château wine estate of AC Graves, Bordeaux, France.

Touraine province and wine region of Loire Valley, France. ACs include Bourgueil and Chinon for red wines, Montlouis and Vouvray for still and sparkling whites.

Touraine Amboise AC for red and rosé wines from grape varieties including Cabernet Franc, Cabernet Sauvignon, Gamay and Malbec and white wine from Chenin Blanc. Province of Touraine, Loire Valley, France.

Touraine Azay-le-Rideau AC for rosé and white wine of village of Azay-le-

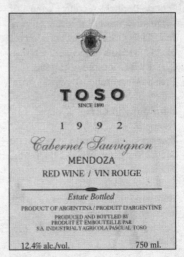

Rideau, Touraine, Loire Valley, France. Rosé chiefly from Groslot grapes; white from Chenin Blanc.

Touraine Mesland AC for red wines mainly from Gamay grapes and whites from Chenin Blanc, village of Mesland, Touraine, Loire Valley, France.

Tour-Bicheau, Château La wine estate of AC Graves, Bordeaux, France.

Tour Blanche, Château La wine estate of AC Médoc, Bordeaux, France. Classified *Cru Bourgeois*.

Tour-Blanche, Château La wine estate of AC Sauternes, Bordeaux, France. Classified *1er Cru Classé*.

Tour-Carnet, Château La wine estate of AC Haut-Médoc, Bordeaux, France. Classified *4ème Grand Cru Classé*.

Tour d'Aspic, Château La second wine of Château Haut-Batailley, Bordeaux, France.

Tour-de-Bessan, Château wine estate of AC Margaux, Bordeaux, France.

Tour-de-Bonnet second wine of Château Bonnet, Bordeaux, France.

Tour-de-By, Château La wine estate of AC Médoc, Bordeaux, France. Classified *Cru Grand Bourgeois*.

Tour-de-Marbuzet, Château wine estate of AC St-Estèphe, Médoc, Bordeaux, France. Classified *Cru Bourgeois*.

Tour-de-Mons, Château wine estate of AC Margaux, Médoc, Bordeaux, France. Classified *Cru Bourgeois Supérieur*.

Tour-des-Termes, Château wine estate of AC St-Estèphe, Médoc, Bordeaux, France. Classified *Cru Bourgeois*.

Tour-de-Tourteau, Château wine estate of AC Côtes de Bourg, Bordeaux, France.

Tour-du-Haut-Moulin, Château wine estate of AC Haut-Médoc, Bordeaux, France. Classified *Cru Grand Bourgeois*.

Tour-du-Mirail, Château wine estate of AC Haut-Médoc, Bordeaux, France. Classified *Cru Bourgeois*.

Tour-du-Pas-St-Georges, Château wine estate of AC St-Emilion, Bordeaux, France.

Tour-du-Pin-Figeac, Château wine estate of AC St-Emilion, Bordeaux, France. Classified *Grand Cru Classé*.

Tour-du-Pin-Figeac (Giraud Belivier), Château wine estate of AC St Emilion, Bordeaux, France. Classified *Grand Cru Classé*.

Tour-du-Roc, Château wine estate of AC Haut-Médoc, Bordeaux, France. Classified *Cru Bourgeois*.

Tour-Figeac, Château La wine estate of AC St Emilion, Bordeaux, France. Classified *Grand Cru Classé*.

Tour-Haut-Brion, Château La wine estate of AC Pessac-Léognan, Bordeaux, France. Classified *Cru Classé*.

Tour-Haut-Causson, Château La wine estate of AC Médoc, Bordeaux, France. Classified *Cru Grand Bourgeois*.

Touriga Francesca red grape variety of Douro Valley, Portugal. Port wines.

Touriga Nacional the most-valued red grape variety for port, Douro Valley, Portugal. Other sites include Dão region of Portugal.

Tour-Léognan, Château wine estate of AC Graves, Bordeaux, France.

Tour-Martillac, Château La wine estate of AC Pessac-Léognan, Bordeaux, France.

Tour Mont d'Or, Château La wine estate of AC Montagne-St-Emilion, Bordeaux, France.

Tour-Musset, Château wine estate of AC St Emilion, Bordeaux, France.

Tournefeuille, Château wine estate of AC Lalande-de-Pomerol, Bordeaux, France.

Tour-Pibran, Château La wine estate of AC Pauillac, Médoc, Bordeaux, France. Classified *Cru Bourgeois*.

Tour-Prignac, Château La wine estate of AC Médoc, Bordeaux, France. Classified *Cru Bourgeois*.

Tour-Puymirand, Château La wine estate of AC Entre-Deux-Mers, Bordeaux, France.

Tours, Château des wine estate of AC Montagne-St-Emilion, Bordeaux, France.

Tour-St-Bonnet, Château La wine estate of AC Médoc, Bordeaux, France. Classified *Cru Bourgeois*.

Tour St-Joseph, Château La wine estate of AC Haut-Médoc, Bordeaux, France. Classified *Cru Bourgeois*.

Tour-St-Pierre, Château wine estate of AC St-Emilion, Bordeaux, France. Classified *Grand Cru*.

Tour-Seran, Château La wine estate of AC Médoc, Bordeaux, France. Classified *Cru Bourgeois*.

Tourteau-Chollet, Château wine estate of AC Graves, Bordeaux, France.

Tourteran, Château alternative name for wine of Château Ramage-la-Bâtisse, Bordeaux, France.

Tour-Védrines, Château La second wine of Château Doisy-Védrines, Bordeaux, France.

Toussaint 'dry' coffee liqueur originally of Haiti, West Indies. Name commemorates black independence fighter General Toussaint L'Ouverture, born in the French colony of Sainte Domingue 1743, whose struggle against French colonists won him first the governorship of the island then traducement by Napoleon Bonaparte. He died in a French jail in 1803, the year before the independent republic of Haiti was established in one half of Sainte Domingue.

Toutigeac, Château de wine estate of AC Entre-Deux-Mers, Bordeaux, France.

Tovaric Cocktail. Over ice shake 3 parts vodka, 2 kümmel, 1 fresh lime juice. Strain.

Townes brewery at Chesterfield, Derbyshire, England.

Traben-Trarbach wine village on both sides of Mosel river, Mosel-Saar-Ruwer region, Germany. *Grosslage*: Schwarzlay.

Tracy, Château de long-established (1396) wine estate of AC Pouilly Fumé, Loire Valley, France.

Trade Winds Cocktail. Over ice shake 1 part rum, 1 teaspoon sloe gin, 1 teaspoon fresh lime juice, 1 pinch sugar. Strain.

Traditional fortified wine brand of Matthew Clark, Bristol, England.

Trafalgar bottle-conditioned India Pale Ale (6.0% alc) by Freeminer Brewery, Forest of Dean, Gloucestershire, England. Name after a local coal mine – named after the naval battle of 1805.

Traisen wine village of Nahe region, Germany. *Grosslage*: Burgweg.

Traiskirchen wine village south of Vienna, Austria.

Trakya wine region west of Bosphorus, Turkey.

Traminac white wine from Traminer grapes, Serbia and Slovenia.

Traminer white grape variety originally of village of Tramin (also called Termeno) in Alto Adige, Italy. Now synonymous with Gewürztraminer.

Traminer Aromatico DOC for white wines from Gewürztraminer grapes, Trentino-Alto Adige region, Italy.

Traminer Musqué synonym for Gewürztraminer.

Transvaal Cocktail. Over ice stir 1 part Caperitif, 1 dry gin, 2 dashes orange bitters. Strain.

Trappenberg *Grosslage* incorporating vineyards in Rheinpfalz region, Germany at, respectively: Altdorf, Bellheim, Böbingen, Bornheim, Essingen, Freimersheim, Gross- und Kleinfischlingen, Hochstadt, Knittelsheim, Lustadt, Ottersheim, Römerberg (bei Speyer) (Berghausen), Römerberg (bei Speyer) (Mechtersheim), Römerberg (bei Speyer) (Heiligenstein), Schwegenheim, Venningen, Weingarten, Zeiskam).

Trappist beer strictly speaking, the beers of six distinct Trappist monastery-breweries in Belgium and Holland. All, including the renowned Chimay, Orval and Rochefort, are bottle-conditioned ales.

Traquair House castle-brewery of Traquair, Peeblesshire, Scotland. Bear Ale (5.0% alc), Jacobite, **Traquair House Ale** (7.2% alc).

Trautberg vineyard at Castell in Franken region, Germany.

Trautlestal vineyard at Hammelburg in Franken region, Germany.

Travellers Inn brew pub at Caerwys, Mold, Wales.

treating in Britain in the First World War (1914-18) this social habit, of buying drinks for companions in a public house, was outlawed. The penalty for an infringement was a fine of £100 – equivalent to an unskilled labourer's earnings for up to a year. The government of the day was of the view that alcohol consumption reduced the productivity of workers in munitions factories. 'Britain faces three enemies,' said Prime Minister David Lloyd George in 1915. 'Germany, Austria, and drink.'

Trebbiano white grape variety widely planted in Italy under differing regional names; a constituent of many famous white wines including Frascati, Galestro, Orvieto, Soave, Verdicchio etc and even of (red) Chianti. New World plantings are mainly for distilling. Synonymous with Ugni Blanc of Charente and Gascony, France (grown for table wines and for distilling into cognac and armagnac).

Trebbiano di Abruzzo DOC for white wine from Trebbiano grapes, Abruzzi, Italy.

Trebbiano di Romagna DOC for white wine from Trebbiano grapes, Emilia-Romagna region, Italy.

Treble Chance Cocktail. Over ice stir 1 part Cointreau, 1 dry vermouth, 1 scotch whisky. Strain.

Trefethen wine producer in Napa Valley, California, USA. Noted wines from Cabernet Sauvignon, Chardonnay, Pinot Noir etc. Eschol wine brand recalls former (to 1973) name of estate.

Treille-des-Girondiers, Château wine estate of Côtes de Castillon, Bordeaux, France.

Tremletts Bitter dry cider (7.4% alc) by Thatcher's Cider, Sandford, Somerset, England. From Tremletts Bitter apple variety.

Trentino Italian section of wine-producing Italo-Germanic **Trentino-Alto Adige** region of northern Italy.

Treppchen vineyards at Erden, Piesport, Piesport (Niederemmel) and Treis-Karden in Mosel-Saar-Ruwer region, Germany.

Tres Magueyes tequila brand of Pernod-Ricard, Mexico.

Treuenfels vineyard at Altenbamberg in Nahe region, Germany.

Treuil Nailhac, Château wine estate of AC Monbazillac, SW France.

Trévallon, Domaine de great wine estate of Coteaux des Baux, Provence, France. Renowned red wines from six parts Cabernet Sauvignon to four Syrah do not conform to *cépage* of local AC rules, so are designated *vin de pays*. New white wine (from 1995 vintage) is from Marsanne and Rousanne grapes.

triage selective picking of *botrytis*-affected grapes for sweet-wine production. Collecting the harvest can call for many passes (*tries*) through the vineyard over a period of weeks. French.

Tribute five- and 15-year-old blended scotch whiskies by William Lundie & Co, Glasgow, Scotland.

Tricolor Cocktail. Into a shot glass, adding each ingredient with a steady hand to form separate layers, pour 1 part chilled green crème de menthe, 1 chilled Baileys Irish Cream, 1 chilled Grand Marnier.

Triebaumer, Ernst wine producer in Neusiedlersee Hügelland, Burgenland, Austria.

Triebaumer, Paul wine producer in Neusiedlersee Hügelland, Burgenland, Austria.

Trier wine city of Mosel-Saar-Ruwer region, Germany. *Grosslage*: Römerlay.

Triguedina, Clos wine estate of AC Cahors, SW France.

Trilby Cocktail. Over ice shake 1 part Parfait Amour liqueur, 1 scotch whisky, 1 sweet vermouth, 2 dashes orange bitters, 2 dashes pastis. Strain.

Trimbach, FE leading wine producer at Ribeauvillé, Alsace, France.

Trimoulet, Château wine estate of AC St-Emilion, Bordeaux, France. Classified *Grand Cru* (1996).

Tring brewery at Tring, Hertfordshire, England.

Trinity white wine brand formerly of Wootton Vineyard, Shepton Mallet, Somerset, England, closed 1999).

Trinity Cocktail. Over ice stir 1 part dry gin, 1 dry vermouth, 1 sweet vermouth. Strain.

Tripel traditional strong beer style of Trappist breweries of Belgium and the Netherlands. The term is now used for many strong beers of the region.

triple sec dry, strong, colourless style of curaçao made in France and the Netherlands. Leading brand labelled as triple sec is by Bardinet of Bordeaux, France. Cointreau is the leading brand name.

Triple Rock brewery in Berkeley, California, USA. Black Rock Porter, Pinnacle Pale Ale, Red Rock Ale.

Trittenheim wine village of Mosel-Saar-Ruwer region, Germany. *Grosslage*: Michelsberg.

Trocadero Cocktail. Over ice shake 1 part dry vermouth, 1 sweet vermouth, 1 dash grenadine, 1 dash orange bitters. Add cocktail cherry to glass.

trocken dry (wine). Germany.

Trockenbeerenauslese 'selected dried berries'. Wine-quality designation at the top of the *Prädikat* range. Grape ripeness must reach 150° Oechsle (sugar density) level and the resulting wine is very sweet indeed with great ageing potential. Rare and very expensive. Austria and Germany.

Troischardons, Château des wine estate of AC Margaux, Médoc, Bordeaux, France.

Trois Moulins, Château wine estate of AC St-Emilion, Bordeaux, France. Classified *Grand Cru Classé*.

Trollberg vineyards at Dorsheim and Münster-Sarmsheim in Nahe region, Germany.

Trollinger regional name for Schiava grape, Württemberg region, Germany.

Tronçais oak valued for barrel making. From forests neighbouring Nevers, France, producing timber with similar qualities.

Tronquoy-Lalande, Château wine estate of AC St-Estèphe, Médoc, Bordeaux, France. Classified *Cru Grand Bourgeois*.

Tropica Cocktail. Over ice shake 1 part rum, 3 pineapple juice, 1 dash grenadine. Strain into an ice-filled tumbler.

Tropical Cocktail. Over ice shake 1 part crème de cacao, 1 dry vermouth, 1 maraschino, 1 dash Angostura bitters, 1 dash orange bitters. Strain.

Tropicana white rum brand originally of Seagram, UK.

Troplong-Mondot, Château wine estate of AC St-Emilion, Bordeaux, France. Classified *Grand Cru Classé*.

Trotanoy, Château great wine estate of AC Pomerol, Bordeaux, France.

Trotsky mourned former cherry brandy, curaçao and kümmel brand by Davis & Co. Axed in the 1980s.

Trottevieille, Château wine estate of AC St-Emilion, Bordeaux, France. Classified *1er Grand Cru Classé*.

Trotzenberg vineyard at Bad Neuenahr-Ahrweiler in Ahr region, Germany.

Trousseau synonym for Bastardo grape variety. French.

Truck Act famed item of British parliamentary legislation. From the 18th century it became customary for agricultural employers to pay labourers' wages at least partially in truck (farm produce). A considerable proportion of this bounty might be alcoholic beverages, ale or cider. It was found that many farmers were paying such a great part of workers' wages in drink that men and women were becoming addicted, and their children malnourished. In England, it was quite usual for labourers to receive four pints of cider per day and twice that quantity during harvest and haymaking. The Truck Act of 1887 prohibited payment of wages in this manner. The practice nevertheless continued, as a mutually beneficial one, between farm workers and employers well into the 20th century.

try-box in distilling, a device for checking progress.

Tscheppe, Roland wine producer in Weststeiermark, Austria.

Tschida, Johann wine producer in Neusiedlersee, Burgenland, Austria.

Tsen Gon rice-based 'wine' of state trading monopoly, Fukien, People's Republic of China.

Tsingtao wine-producing district of Shantung, People's Republic of China.

Tsingtao Beer lager brand of Tsingtao Brewery, Tsingtao, People's Republic of China. *see label opposite* ➡

tsuica spirit drink of Romania.

Tuaca Italian liqueur from 'fine aged brandy and Tuscan fruit essences'.

Tualatin wine producer in Oregon, USA.

Tuborg brewery in Copenhagen, Denmark, co-owned with Carlsberg and known for international brands **Tuborg Gold** and **Tuborg Pilsener**.

Tucher major brewery of Nürnberg, Franconia, Germany.

Tudor Rose fortified wine brand of Matthew Clark, Bristol, England.

Tuilerie, Château de second wine of Château Moulin-de-Launay, Bordeaux, France.

Tuilerie, Château de la leading wine estate in AC Costières de Nîmes, France.

Tuilerie, Château La wine estate of AC Graves, Bordeaux, France.

Tuileries, Château Les wine estate of AC Premières Côtes de Blaye, Bordeaux, France.

Tulbagh town and Wine of Origin district of South Africa.

Tulip Cocktail. Over ice shake 2 parts apple brandy, 2 sweet vermouth, 1 apricot brandy, 1 lemon juice. Strain.

Tullamore Dew Irish whiskey liqueur brand of Irish Distillers, Midleton, Dublin.

Tullibardine Highland malt whisky distillery est 1949, Blackford, Perthshire, Scotland. Single malt: 10-year-old.

Tulloch wine producer est 1893 Hunter Valley, New South Wales, Australia. Owned by Penfolds.

tumbler a glass or other drinking vessel without a handle or stem. Originally a vessel with a rounded bottom which had to be emptied before it could be set down, lest it tumble over.

Tumbleweed Cocktail. In a jug, stir together 1 part vodka, 1 Kahlúa, 1 scoop chocolate ice cream. Pour into a wine glass.

tumultuous fermentation first and most yeast-active stage of alcoholic fermentation.

tun a large cask or vat. As a specific measure of wine or other liquids, equivalent to 2 pipes or 4 hogsheads – formerly 252 wine-gallons or 210 imperial gallons. Name is believed to reflect calculation that the weight of wine in one such tun is one imperial ton.

Tunisia North African nation of diminishing importance as a wine producer. Quality is nominally determined under an *appellation d'origine contrôlée* system inspired by that of France.

Tunny Cocktail. Over ice stir 2 parts apple brandy, 1 dry gin, 2 dashes pastis, 1 dash sugar syrup. Strain.

Tuppers' brewery at Ashburn, Virginia, USA. Brands include **Tuppers' Hop Pocket Pils** (5.0% alc). Owner Bob Tupper gives one half of all profits to charitable causes.

Tuquet, Château Le wine estate of AC Graves, Bordeaux, France.

Turckheim, Cave Vinicole de leading co-operative wine producer of Alsace, France.

Turf Cocktail. Over ice shake 1 part dry vermouth, 1 dry gin, 1 dash maraschino, 1 dash orange bitters, 1 pastis. Strain.

Türk wine producer in Kremstal, Niederösterreich, Austria.

Turkey traditionally the cradle of postdiluvian winemaking, since Noah's planting of a vineyard on Ararat from cuttings thoughtfully stowed aboard the Ark, but now a minor source of alcoholic beverages for export and tourist consumption. Wine principally from state producer, Tekal.

Turmberg vineyards at Karlsruhe (Durlach), Karlsruhe (Grötzingen) and Landau-Königshofen in Baden region, Germany.

Tursan VDQS for, chiefly, red wines from Cabernet Franc and Tannat grapes. Landes region, SW France.

Tuscany province of Italy known principally for DOCGs Chianti and Chianti Classico, plus Brunello di Montalcino and Vino Nobile di Montepulciano. The region has a new (1995) DOC covering quality red and white wines not covered by previously existing DOCs.

Tusker premium lager (5.0% alc) by Kenya Breweries, Nairobi, Kenya. 'Brewed from Bima Equatorial Barley and the pure waters of Mzima Springs.'

Tustal, Château wine estate of AC Entre-Deux-Mers, Bordeaux, France.

Tuxedo Cocktail. Over ice shake 1 part dry gin, 1 dry vermouth, 2 dashes orange bitters, 1 dash maraschino, 1 dash pastis.

twankay archaic English slang for gin.

Twee Jonge Gezellen Estate wine producer est 1710 Tulbagh, South Africa. Dry and sweet, sparkling and still white wines.

Twelve Miles Out Cocktail. Over ice shake 1 part apple brandy, 1 rum, 1 Swedish Punsch. Strain and squeeze orange peel over.

Twin Peaks Cocktail. Over ice shake 2 parts bourbon, 1 Bénédictine, 1 fresh lime juice, 2 dashes Cointreau. Strain and add lime slices.

Twin Six Cocktail. Over ice shake 1 egg white, 3 parts dry gin, 1 sweet vermouth, 4 dashes orange juice, 1 dash grenadine. Strain.

Twin Towers beer by Willys Brewery, Cleethorpes, England.

Twister Cocktail. Over ice shake 2 parts vodka, 1 fresh lime juice. Strain into an ice-filled tumbler and top with chilled tonic water.

Two Dogs Australian 'alcoholic lemon brew' (4.0% alc) brand made under licence by Merrydown Co, Horsham, East Sussex, England.

Twyford's beer brand of Irish Ale Breweries, Eire.

tyg extinct two-handled drinking vessel of seventeenth century, used as a ceremonial loving cup. English. Also spelt tig.

Tynllidiart Arms brewpub at Capel Bangor, Aberystwyth, Wales.

Typhoon Cocktail. Over ice shake 2 parts dry gin, 1 Anisette, 2 fresh lime juice. Strain into tall ice-filled glasses and top with chilled sparkling wine.

typicity in winetasting, a character in the wine immediately associable with that of the constituent grape variety.

Tyrconnell single malt Irish whiskey by Cooley Distillery, Riverstown, Dundalk, County Louth, Republic of Ireland.

Tyrni liqueur brand of Oy Suomen Marjat Ab, Finland.

Tyrrells leading and long-established (1853) wine producer of Hunter Valley, New South Wales, Australia. Renowned varietal wines and popular brands Long Flat Red and Long Flat White.

U

Übereltzer vineyard at Moselkern in Mosel-Saar-Ruwer region, Germany.

Übigberg vineyards at Altenahr, Altenahr (Kreuzberg) and Altenahr (Pützfeld) in Ahr region, Germany.

Ueli brewery at Fischerstube tavern in Basel, Switzerland.

U Fleku brewery of U Fleku tavern (est 1499) in Prague, Czech Republic. Known for dark lagers.

Ugni Blanc white grape variety of SW France. Principally grown for distilling into spirits of Armagnac and Cognac. Synonymous with Trebbiano of Italy.

Uhlen vineyards at Kobern-Gondorf and Winningen in Mosel-Saar-Ruwer region, Germany.

Uiterwyk wine producer in Stellenbosch, South Africa.

Uitkyk Estate vineyard est 1788 in Stellenbosch, South Africa. Wines are made by Bergkelder.

Ukiah Valley wine district of Mendocino County, California, USA.

Ukraine CIS state with wine-producing regions in Carpathian hills and Black Sea coast.

UKVA United Kingdom Vineyards Association. Formerly English Vineyards Association est 1967. Federation of vineyard owners and wine producers of England and Wales. In the absence, to date, of an Appellation Contrôlée-type quality-guarantee system, the UKVA has its own set of standards.

Ulanda Cocktail. Over ice shake 2 parts dry gin, 1 Cointreau, 1 dash pastis. Strain.

Uley brewery ay Uley, Gloucestershire, England.

ullage in an upright beer or wine bottle, the space between the top of the liquid and the bottom of the cap or cork. Over long periods, stored beverages become the more 'ullaged' the larger this space is. Also a term both for the first beer drawn from a cask and poured away and for the last, sediment-bearing quantity.

Ull de Llebre regional name for Tempranillo grape variety, Spain.

Ulrichsberg vineyard at Östringen in Baden region, Germany.

Ultimate Beefeater Martini Cocktail. Over ice stir 1 part Beefeater gin, 1 dash dry vermouth. Strain and add a sliver of uncooked fillet steak.

Ultraa vodka brand, Russia

Ultra Brut extra dry champagne brand of Laurent Perrier, Tours-sur-Marne, France.

Umani Ronchi wine producer in Marches region, Italy. Verdicchio etc.

Umathum wine producer in Neusiedlersee, Burgenland, Austria.

Umbria wine region of central Italy. DOCs include Colli del Trasimeno, Colli Perugini, Colli Montefalco, Orvieto, Torgiano.

Umpqua Valley wine district of Oregon, USA.

Underberg herbal digestive bitters sold in 'one-shot' bottles, Rheinberg, Germany. First produced 1846. Reputed hangover remedy.

Undurraga leading wine producer of Maipo Valley, Chile. Noted Cabernet Sauvignon, Chardonnay and Pinot Noir wines.

Une Idée Cocktail. Over ice shake 1 part dry gin, 1 cognac, 1 sweet vermouth, 1 teaspoon apricot brandy. Strain.

Un Emile 68 absinthe blanche (68% alc) by Pontalier, France.

Un Hombre Legendario spirit brand of Pernod-Ricard, France.

Ungeheuer vineyard at Forst an der Weinstrasse in Rheinpfalz region, Germany.

Ungsberg vineyard at Traben-Trarbach in Mosel-Saar-Ruwer region, Germany.

Unger, Alexander wine producer in Neusiedlersee Hügelland, Burgenland, Austria.

Unger, Wolfgang wine producer in Kremstal, Niederösterreich, Austria.

Ungstein wine village of Mittelhaardt district in Rheinpfalz region, Germany. *Grosslagen*: Hochmess and Honigsäckel.

Uniacke Estate wine producer in British Columbia, Canada.

Unicognac growers' and distillers' co-operative of Cognac, France. Brands include Ansac, Jules Gautret, Roi des Rois.

Unicum herbal liqueur (42% alc) of Zwack Unicum Company, est 1790, Hungary.

Union brewery at Jumet, Charleroi, Belgium.

Union Brewery restoration of 1864 brewery in Virginia City, Nevada, USA. Has the distinction of being the only brewery in the state. **Union Beer**.

Union des Producteurs de St-Emilion wine coop of AC St-Emilion, Bordeaux, France.

Union Jack Cocktail. Over ice stir 3 parts dry gin, 1 Crème Yvette. Strain. Alternatively, over ice stir 2 parts dry gin, 1 sloe gin, 3 dashes grenadine. Strain. As a further alternative, into a liqueur glass, pouring carefully to avoid mixing ingredients, put 1 part grenadine, 1 maraschino, 1 blue curaçao.

United Breweries major brewer in Bangalore, India. Known for Jubilee and Kingfisher lagers.

Unterberg vineyard at Konz in Mosel-Saar-Ruwer region, Germany.

Unzip A Banana Cocktail. Over ice stir 1 part Baileys Irish Cream, 1 banana liqueur. Strain.

Upper Canada brewery in Toronto, Canada. **Upper Canada Dark Ale**, **Upper Canada Wheat** and other ales.

Upright Redstreak apple variety traditionally valued for cider-making. English.

Upstairs Cocktail. Into an ice-filled tumbler glass pour 2 parts Dubonnet, 1 lemon juice. Top with soda water.

Up-to-Date Cocktail. Over ice shake 1 part rye whisky, 1 dry sherry, 1 dash Angostura bitters, 1 dash Grand Marnier. Strain.

Ur- prefixing beer names, 'original' in German.

Urbelt vineyard at Konz in Mosel-Saar-Ruwer region, Germany.

Urgüp white wine from Emir grapes, Anatolia, Turkey.

Ursulinengarten vineyard at Bad Neuenahr-Ahrweiler in Ahr region, Germany.

Ursus UK vodka brand 'distilled to a unique Icelandic recipe.' Straight and flavoured (blackcurrant, lemon, sloeberry) styles.

Urtyp beer by Bavaria-St Pauli brewery, Hamburg, Germany.

Ushers brewery formerly at Trowbridge, Wiltshire, England. Closed 2000. Brands include cask-conditioned Founder's Ale, canned Ploughman's Ale. Owned by Diageo.

Usher's Green Stripe blended scotch whisky by Andrew Usher, Edinburgh, Scotland.

Usquaebach whisky brand of Twelve Stone Flagons distillers, Pittsburgh, Pennsylvania, USA.

usquebaugh whisky. The modern word whisky is corrupted from Gaelic and Irish *uisge* (water) and *beatha* (life).

Usquebaugh brand of coriander-flavoured liqueur whiskey, Eire.

Utena town and brewery of Lithuania.

Utiel Requena DO wine region of NE Spain.

Utility Cocktail. Over ice stir 2 parts dry sherry, 1 dry vermouth, 1 sweet vermouth. Strain.

Utkins UK5 organic vodka by Thames Distillers, Bramley, England. 'The UK's first organic vodka.'

Uto Mij leading distiller of *genever* and other spirits, Netherlands.

uva grape. Italian, Portuguese, Spanish.

Uza, Clos d' second wine of Château de St-Pierre, Bordeaux, France.

V

Vaakuna lager brand of Olvi brewery, Iisalmi, Finland.

Vaccarese red grape variety of AC Châteauneuf du Pape, Rhône Valley, France.

Vacheron wine producer of AC Sancerre, Loire Valley, France.

Vacqueyras AC and village of Côte du Rhône, France. Rich red wines.

CUVÉE SPÉCIALE

VACQUEYRAS

Appellation Vacqueyras Contrôlée

VINIFIÉ ET MIS EN BOUTEILLE
12% vol   À VACQUEYRAS   750 ml

PASCAL, NÉGOCIANT-VINIFICATEUR À VACQUEYRAS (VAUCLUSE) FRANCE
PRODUCE OF FRANCE

Vaduzer red wine from Blauburgunder grapes, Liechtenstein.

Vail Ale local brew of Vail Ale, Colorado, USA. Produced by Kentucky brewer Oldenberg.

Vaillante, Château La second wine of Château Launay, Bordeaux, France.

Vaillons *Premier Cru* vineyard of Chablis, Burgundy, France. The name incorporates vineyards of Beugnon, Châtains, Les Lys and Séchet as well as Vaillons itself.

Val, Clos du wine estate in Napa Valley, California, USA.

Valade, Château La wine estate of AC Fronsac, Bordeaux, France.

Valais major wine-producing canton of French-speaking Switzerland.

Valandraud, Château wine producer of St Emilion, Bordeaux, France. Est 1991 but already commanding among the highest prices in Bordeaux.

Valbuena name given to young (three- and five-year-old) wines of Bodegas Vega Sicilia, Ribera del Duero, Spain.

Valcalepio DOC for red wine from Merlot and Cabernet Sauvignon grapes and white from Pinot Bianco and Pinot Grigio, Lake Iseo, Lombardy, Italy.

Valdadige all-embracing DOC for red, *rosato* and white wines of Trentino-Alto Adige region, Italy.

Val d'Arbia DOC for dry white wine and *vin santo*, Tuscany, Italy.

Valdeorras DO wine region of Galicia, Spain.

Valdepeñas DO wine region within DO of La Mancha, central Spain. Noted red wines from Cencibel (Tempranillo) and Garnacha grapes.

Val de Salnés wine district of Galicia, Spain. White wines from Albariño grapes.

Valdespino, AR leading sherry producer, Jerez de la Frontera, Spain.   *see label over* ➡

Valdiguié red grape variety of SW France.

Valdivieso leading wine producer of Chile.

Vale brewery at Haddenham, Buckinghamshire, England.

Valençay VDQS chiefly for red and rosé wines from Cabernet Franc, Cabernet Sauvignon, Gamay, Malbec and Pinot Noir grapes, Touraine, Loire Valley, France.

Valencia city and DO wine region of Levante, Spain. Ordinary wines.

Valencia Cocktail. Over ice shake 1 part apricot brandy, 1 orange juice, 2 dashes orange bitters. Strain. Alternatively, over ice shake 1 part apricot brandy, 1 orange juice, 2 dashes orange bitters. Strain into flute glass and top with Spanish sparkling wine.

Valentino district of DO Valencia, Spain. Sweet white wines from Moscatel grapes.

Valgella DOC for red wine from Nebbiolo grapes, Valtellina, Lombardy, Italy.

Valière, Château La wine estate of AC Médoc, Bordeaux, France. Classified *Cru Bourgeois.*

Valckenberg, PJ wine producer and merchant at Worms in Rhein-hessen region, Germany. Brands include Madonna Liebfraumilch.

Valle d'Aosta wine region and expansive DOC of Alpine Italy.

Valle Isarco DOC for white wines from Müller Thurgau, Pinot Grigio, Silvaner, Traminer Aromatico and Veltliner grapes, Isarco Valley, Trentino-Alto Adige region, Italy.

Vallée de la Marne vineyard district of AC Champagne, France.

Vallet wine village of AC Muscadet de Sèvre et Maine, Loire Valley, France.

Vallformosa wine brand of Bodegas Masia Vallformosa, Penedés, Spain.

Valmur *Grand Cru* vineyard of Chablis, Burgundy, France.

Valpolicella DOC for red wine from Corvina Veronese, Rondinella and Molinara grapes grown around Veronese town of Valpolicella and surrounding districts of Veneto region, Italy. *Classico* wines are from an inner zone of vineyards and *superiore* wines have 12% alc plus one year's ageing. See also Recioto. Reputable producers include Allegrini, Masi, Quintarelli, Tedeschi.

Valpolicella Valpantena DOC for Valpolicella wine from Valpantena district, Veneto, Italy.

Valréas wine village of AC Côtes du Rhône Villages, southern Rhône Valley, France.

Valrone, Château wine estate of AC Premières Côtes de Blaye, Bordeaux, France.

Valtellina DOC for red wines chiefly from Nebbiolo (local name Chiavennasca) grapes of Sondrio, Lombardy, Italy. *Superiore* wines made within the DOC are labelled respectively Grumello, Inferno, Sassella, Valgella.

Valvanera liqueur by Abadia de Valvanera, La Rioja, Spain. Bears a passing similarity to Bénédictine and claims connection with Benedictine monastery of Valvanera.

Van Zuylekom major liqueur distillery est 1684, Amsterdam, Netherlands.

Varichon et Clerc leading sparkling wine producer of AC Seyssel, Savoie, France.

Vancouver Island brewery at Victoria, Vancouver Island, Canada.

Van Damme *jenever* distillery, Balagem, Belgium.

Vanderbilt Cocktail. Over ice shake 3 parts brandy, 1 cherry brandy, 2 dashes sugar syrup, 1 dash Angostura bitters. Strain.

Vanderlinden brewery at Halle, Payottenland, Belgium. Lambic beers.

Vandermint mint-flavoured liqueur by Bols, Netherlands.

Vandervelden brewery in Beersel, Belgium. Lambic beers under Oud Beersel label.

Van Dusen Cocktail. Over ice shake 2 parts dry gin, 1 dry vermouth, 1 dash Grand Marnier. Strain.

vanilla in winetasting, a smell indicating a wine aged in oak barrels.

Van Loveren wine producer in Robertson district, South Africa.

Van Zellers port shipper, Vila Nova de Gaia, Portugal. Vintages: 1991, 94, 97, 2000, 03.

varietal a wine labelled with the name of its constituent grape variety. Originally, Americanese for variety.

Varna Controliran wine region of Bulgaria. Chardonnay wines.

Varoilles, Domaine de wine estate of Gevrey-Chambertin, Côte de Beaune, Burgundy. Noted wines from vineyards including wholly-owned Clos des Varoilles, Clos du Couvent, Clos du Meix des Ouches, la Romanée.

Vasse Felix wine producer of Margaret River region, Western Australia.

Vassilinsky's Black Russian Beer bottle-conditioned stout brand by McMullen brewery, Hertford, England.

vat container for fermentation and storage of wine. Originally wood (chestnut, oak etc) but now mostly concrete, glass-fibre or steel lined with enamel, glass or resin. Stainless steel vats are commonly used for high-value wines. Formerly, vat was a specific measurement of liquid, eg 100 litres in the Low Countries.

VAT 69 blended scotch whisky by Wm Sanderson & Son, South Queensferry, Scotland. The vat was number 69 among 100 from which samples were assembled by blender Wm Sanderson (b 1839) for tasting by friends and colleagues in 1882. It was the unanimous preference.

vatted malt whisky blended from two or more malt whiskies from different distilleries. Retailer own-brands are commonly vatted.

Vaucoupin *Premier Cru* vineyard of Chablis, Burgundy, France.

Vaud wine-producing canton of Switzerland.

Vaudésir *Grand Cru* vineyard of Chablis, Burgundy, France.

Vaudevey *Premier Cru* vineyard of Chablis, Burgundy, France.

Vaux brewery in Sunderland, Tyne & Wear, England. Double Maxim brown ale, Samson bitter, Weizenbier wheat beer.

Vazart-Cocquart *récoltant manipulant* champagne producer, Couilly, Champagne, France.

VDN common abbreviation of *Vin Doux Naturel*.

vdp informal abbreviation of *vin de pays*. France.

VdP Verband Deutscher Prädikats und Qualitätsweingüter. Federation of leading wine producers of Germany.

vdt informal abbreviation of *vino da tavola*. Italy.

VDQS abbreviation of Vin Délimité de Qualité Supérieur.

V.E.B. Getrankekombinat brewery in Berlin, Germany, known for Berliner Weisse beer.

vecchio old, Italian.

Vecchio Samperi renowned long-aged style of marsala from, chiefly, Grillo grapes; dry and unfortified. Made by De Bartoli, Sicily, Italy.

Vedrenne leading producer of cassis (blackcurrant) liqueurs, France.

Vega de la Reina, Bodegas wine producer in Rueda, Castillo-León, Spain. Oak-aged red wines.

Vega Sicilia, Bodegas distinguished wine producer at Valbuena de Duero, DO Ribera del Duero, Castillo-León, Spain. Renowned red wines from Bordeaux (Cabernet Sauvignon, Merlot, Malbec) and indigenous (Tinto Aragonés, Garnacha, Albillo) grape varieties. Premium wines are aged in oak ten or more years.

Velich, Roland & Heinz wine producer in Neusiedlersee, Burgenland, Austria.

Velika Morava wine-producing district of Serbia. Laski Rizling white wine.

Velletri DOC for red and *rosato* wines from Cesanese, Montepulciano and Sangiovese grapes and white from Malvasia and Trebbiano, Latium region, Italy.

vellinch a pipette for drawing samples from casks.

Velocity Cocktail. Over ice shake 2 parts sweet vermouth, 1 dry gin, 1 slice orange. Strain.

Veltins brewery in Sauerlands, Germany, known for Veltins Pilsener.

Veltliner grape variety of DOC Valle Isarco, Alto Adige, Italy. Also known as Frühroter Veltliner, in Austria. Related to but distinct from Grüner Veltliner.

velvety in winetasting, a flavour of exceptional smoothness, denoting balance and maturity.

vendange grape harvest, French.

vendange tardive 'late harvest'. In Alsace region of France, a style of wine from extra-ripe grapes picked after the main harvest. Under AC rules instituted 1984, restricted to Gewürztraminer, Muscat, Pinot Gris or Riesling grapes, which must reach minimum natural sugar level. Vintage must be declared.

vendangeur grape picker, French.

vendemmia year or vintage, Italian.

venencia cylindrical silver cup attached to long handle for drawing samples from sherry butts, Jerez de la Frontera, Spain. In the expert hands of a **venenciador**, the cup is used to pour sherry into narrow-mouthed *copita* tasting glasses, held at arm's length, without spilling a drop of the wine. A ritual that has to be seen to be believed.

vendimia year or vintage, Spanish.

vendita diretta 'direct sale'. Indicates wines on sale at point of production. Italian.

Veneto major wine region of NW Italy. Many DOCs include Soave and Valpolicella.

Venegazzù noted red wine from Bordeaux grape varieties, Treviso, Veneto, Italy. Also **Venegazzù Bianco** from Pinot Bianco grapes, and *spumante* wine.

vente directe 'direct sale'. Indicates wines on sale at point of production. French.

Ventnor brewery at Ventnor, Isle of Wight, England.

Venusbuckel vineyard at Billigheim-Ingenheim in Rheinpfalz region, Germany.

véraison grape ripening stage at which skins begin to take on mature colour. French.

Verbesco white, slightly sparkling (*frizzante*) wine chiefly from Barbera grapes, Piedmont, Italy.

Verdejo white grape variety of Rueda, Spain.

Verdelho medium-dry style of madeira wine from Verdelho grapes, island of Madeira, Portugal.

Verdelho white grape variety principally of Portugal and Spain.

Verdenz wine village of Mosel-Saar-Ruwer region, Germany.

Verdicchio white grape variety of central Italy.

Verdicchio dei Castelli di Jesi DOC for white wine from (chiefly) Verdicchio grapes of the hills of the town of Jesi, Marches region, Italy. Traditional bottling in amphora-shaped bottles commemorates Etruscan (pre-200 BC) origins of this wine. Producers include Brunori, Garofoli, Umani Ronchi. Also *spumante* wine.

Verdicchio di Matelica DOC for white wine from (chiefly) Verdicchio grapes, Matelica, Marches region, Italy.

Verdicchio di Montanello white wine from (chiefly) Verdicchio grapes, Montanello, Marches region, Italy.

Verdignan, Château wine estate of AC Haut-Médoc, Bordeaux, France. Classified *Cru Grand Bourgeois*.

Verdigny wine village of AC Sancerre, Loire Valley, France.

Verdiso white grape variety of northern Italy.

Verduzan armagnac brand of Morel, Ténarèze, Gascony, France.

Verduzzo Colli Orientali del Friuli DOC for white wines from Verduzzo grapes, Friuli-Venezia-Giulia region, Italy. Noted dry and sweet styles.

Verduzzo del Piave DOC for white wine from Verduzzo grapes, Piave, Veneto, Italy.

Verduzzo Friuliano white grape variety of NW Italy.

Vereinigten Hospitien hospice and charitably endowed wine estate at Trier in Mosel-Saar-Ruwer region, Germany. Vineyards include Schloss Saarsfelser, Serriger Schlossberg, Wiltinger Hölle etc.

Vergelegen wine producer in Somerset West, South Africa.

vergine dry and most-valued style of marsala wine, Sicily, Italy. From free-run grape juice, unfortified but at least 18% alc and cask aged five years. **Vergine stravecchio** is aged 10 years.

Verhoeven *genever* distiller, Netherlands.

Verín town known for strong red wines, Galicia, Spain.

Vermentino white grape variety principally of coastal Liguria and islands of Corsica and Sardinia, Italy.

Vermentino di Gallura DOCG (1997) for white wine from 95% Vermentino grapes of Nuori and Sassari provinces, Sardinia, Italy.

Vermentino Riviera Ligure di Ponente DOC for white wine from Vermentino grapes, Pietra Ligure and San Remo, Liguria, Italy.

Vermont Pub & Brewery restaurant-brewery in Burlington, Vermont, USA. Known for high-quality German-style beers.

vermouth see box.

Vermouth Cocktail. Over ice stir 1 part dry or sweet vermouth, 1 dash Angostura bitters. Strain.

Vermouth & Cassis Cocktail. Into an ice-filled tumbler glass pour 2 parts dry vermouth, 1 crème de cassis. Top with soda water.

Vermouth & Curaçao Cocktail. Into an ice-filled tumbler glass pour 4 parts dry vermouth, 1 curaçao. Top with soda water.

Vernaccia white grape variety of Italy. Variety includes two white forms, **Vernaccia di Oristano** (*qv*) for sherry-style wine, **Vernaccia di San Gimignano** (*qv*) for dry white wine, and one red, **Vernaccia di Serrapetrona** (*qv*).

Vermouth

from medicinal potion to fashionable mixer

Just as liqueurs are made by steeping wild herbs in spirits, vermouths are made by flavouring wines in the same way. Wine has been used as a preservative for thousands of years. Doctors in the ancient world discovered that alcohol extended the life of plucked plants, allowing for year-round supplies of the most-valued herbs. And they found, too, that alcohol absorbed the essential oils of the preserved herbs, and became medicines in their own right.

Thus, as with so many alcoholic drinks, vermouth owes its origins to the pursuit of a cure. By the Middle Ages, herbal medicines had become relatively sophisticated. Monasteries, traditional centres both of herb-growing and winemaking, were the main source, particularly in France and Italy.

As a drink for 'recreational' purposes, vermouth has a short history. The word, derived from German *wermut* for wormwood (a group of plants long valued in medicine) entered the English language as recently as 1806. Today, wormwood is just one among 50 or more herbal and other flavourings employed in making vermouths. Others are chamomile, cloves, coriander, elderflower, forget-me-not, horehound, gentian, ginger, juniper, quinine and rose petals.

Ingredients, including fruits as well as herbs and spices, are macerated in wine (always white) and fortified with a grape juice (or sugar) and brandy mix. Red vermouths take their colour from oxidation of the wine or from cochineal dye. Commercial production dates from late 18th century Italy, where Antonio Carpano of Turin has been credited with the first brand.

Vernaccia di Oristano

Vernaccia di Oristano DOC for fortified (up to 18% alc) and unfortified (15-16%) sherry-style white wines from extra-ripe Vernaccia grapes, island of Sardinia, Italy. *Superiore* wines are barrel-aged three years and *riserva* wines barrel-aged four years. Dry and sweet styles.

Vernaccia di San Gimignano DOC for white wine from Vernaccia and (up to 10%) Chardonnay grapes grown around historic hilltown of San Gimignano, Tuscany, Italy. Said to have been a favourite of Michelangelo (1475–1564), it was the first wine to be nominated DOC, in 1966, and promoted to DOCG with the 1993 vintage. Producers include Falchini, San Quirico, Terruzi & Puthod.

Vernaccia di Serrapetrona DOC for red *spumante* wine from Vernaccia Nera grapes grown around town of Serrapetrona, Marches region, Italy.

Vernay, Georges leading wine producer of AC Condrieu, Rhône Valley, France. Famed single-site wines Chaillées de l'Enfer and Coteau de Vernon plus Cépage Viognier.

Vernous, Château wine estate of AC Médoc, Bordeaux, France. Classified *Cru Bourgeois*.

véronique *flûte*-shaped wine bottle decorated with neck rings. French.

Verrenberg vineyard at Öheringen in Württemberg region, Germany.

Versailles former sugar estate and distillery of Demerara, Guyana giving its name to a still producing renowned golden rums for long ageing. Locals are insistent the Versailles Still is pronounced 'ver sales'.

Verschnitt style of blended spirit, Germany.

Versinthe La Blanche wormwood absinthe by Liqueurs de Provence, France.

Vertheuil wine commune of AC Haut-Médoc, Bordeaux, France.

Vertzami red grape variety of Ionian islands, Greece.

Verwaltung on German wine labels, administration of a wine estate.

Verwaltung der Staatsweingüter Eltville major wine estate, owned by state of Hessen, at Kloster Eberbach in Rheingau region, Germany. Vineyards include Erbacher Marcobrunn, Hochheimer Kirchenstück, Rauenthaler Baiken, Steinberg.

Verwaltung der Staatlichen Weinbaudomänen state-owned (Rheinland-Pfalz) wine estate est 1896 in Mosel-Saar-Ruwer region, Germany. Vineyards include Avelsbacher Hammerstein, Ockfener Bockstein, Serriger Vogelsang.

Verwaltung der Staatlichen Weinbaudomänen Niederhausen-Schlossböckelheim state (Rheinland-Pfalz) wine domain of Nahe region, Germany. Vineyards include Schlossböckelheim, Niederhausen Hermannsberg, Traisen *usw*.

Veryan Vineyard cider and English wine producer, Tregenna, Truro, Cornwall, England.

Verzenay wine village of Montagne de Reims, Champagne, France.

vesou juice of sugar cane distilled for agricultural rums of Martinique.

Vespa Cocktail. Over ice shake 1 part dry gin, 4 dashes vodka, 2 dashes dry vermouth. Strain.

Vespaiolo white grape variety of Veneto region, Italy.

Vespetro caraway-flavoured liqueur of Italy.

Vesselle, Jean *récoltant manipulant* champagne producer, Bouzy, Champagne, France.

Vesselle, Maurice *récoltant manipulant* champagne producer, Bouzy, Champagne, France.

Vesuvinum the name engraved into wine jars excavated at Pompeii, Italy, destroyed by the eruption of Vesuvius, 79AD. Vesuvinum is credited as the oldest trademark in history.

Vesuvio modern dry white wine of Naples, Italy.

Veterano three-year-old brandy by Osborne, Puerto de Santa Maria, Spain.

Veuve Clicquot Ponsardin *Grand Marque* champagne house made famous by Nicole-Barbe Clicquot (née Ponsardin), widow of François Clicquot (d 1805). Reims, France.

Veuve du Vernay sparkling wine by Charmat method, Bordeaux, France.

Vézelay village and AC of northern Burgundy, France. Distinguished Chardonnay wines comparable with better-known Chablis. Leading producers include Elise Villiers.

see label opposite ➡

Via Veneto Cocktail. Over ice shake 3 parts brandy, 1 Sambuca, 1 lemon juice, 1 teaspoon sugar, 1 egg white. Strain.

Vickers spirit (especially gin) brand of United Distillers, Australia.

Vickery's cider producer, Hisbeer's Farm, Buckland St Mary, Somerset, England.

Vicomtesse, Château La second wine of Château Laffitte-Carcasset, Bordeaux, France.

Victoria wine-producing state of Australia. Includes well-known regions such as Great Western, Milawa, Murray River, Rutherglen, Yarra Valley.

Victor's Special Cocktail. Over ice shake 1 egg white, 2 parts dry gin, 1 Cointreau, 1 lemon juice. Strain.

Victory Cocktail. Over ice shake 1 part pastis, 1 grenadine. Strain into wine glass and top with soda water.

Vidal wine producer in Hawke's Bay, New Zealand. Red and white wines.

Vidal Fleury, J wine producer and *négociant* of Rhône Valley, France. Wines of ACs Côte Rôtie, Hermitage, Muscat de Beaumes de Venise etc.

VIDE Vitivinicoltori Italiani di Eccellenza. Association of diverse wine producers (Associazione Viti-

vinicoltori Italiani) in several regions of Italy working to high standards. Initials VIDE are displayed on neck labels of bottles.

~~Videau, Château~~ wine estate of AC Premières Côtes de Bordeaux, France.

Vie en Rose Cocktail. Over ice stir 2 parts dry gin, 2 kirsch, 1 lemon juice, 1 grenadine. Strain.

Vieille Cure, Château La wine estate of AC Fronsac, Bordeaux, France.

Vieille France, Château La wine estate of AC Graves, Bordeaux, France.

vieilles vignes 'old vines'. On bottle labels signifies wine from vines older than average from a given property. Sometimes refers to an individual enclosed vineyard (*clos*) of ungrafted vines, eg the highly valued champagne Bollinger Vieilles Vignes, from vines predating and unaffected by the phylloxera outbreak of the 19th century.

Vieira de Sousa port shipper, Vila Nova de Gaia, Portugal. Vintages: 1965, 70, 74, 75, 77, 78, 79, 80, 82, 83, 85, 87, 89, 91, 94, 97, 2000, 03.

Vienna Austrian capital embraces large areas of vineyard within its purlieus, supplying the city's famous cafés and *Heurigen*.

Vienna bier loosely, a beer style between those of Pilsner and Munich.

Viénot, Charles wine producer and *négoçiant-éleveur*, Nuits-St-Georges, Burgundy, France. Wines from *grand cru* vineyards including Bonnes Mares, Charmes-Chambertin, Corton, Musigny and *premiers crus* including Les Damodes, Gevrey-Chambertin, Nuits-St-Georges.

Vie Rose Cocktail. Over ice shake 2 parts dry gin, 2 Kirsch, 1 grenadine, 1 lemon juice. Strain.

Vietti wine producer of Piedmont, Italy. Renowned Barbaresco and Barolo wines.

vieux 'old' in French, but in Netherlands, domestic grape brandy.

Vieux Château Certan great wine estate of AC Pomerol, Bordeaux, France.

Vieux Château Landon wine estate of AC Médoc, Bordeaux, France. Classified *Cru Bourgeois*.

Vieux Château Mazerat wine estate of AC St-Emilion, Bordeaux, France.

Vieux-Clocher, Cave Co-opérative de wine coop of AC Médoc, Bordeaux, France.

Vieux Donjon, Le wine estate of Louis Michel in AC Châteauneuf-du-Pape, Vaucluse, France.

Vieux Foudre brand name for famed lambic beers of Vanderlinden brewery, Halle, Belgium.

Vieux-Moulin, Château du wine estate of AC Loupiac, Bordeaux, France.

Vieux-Robin, Château wine estate of AC Médoc, Bordeaux, France. Classified *Cru Bourgeois*.

Vieux Sarpe, Château wine estate of AC St-Emilion, Bordeaux, France. Classified *Grand Cru*.

Vieux Télégraphe, Domaine du leading wine estate of AC Châteauneuf-du-Pape, Rhône Valley, France. Named after the erection on the site in 1793 of a mast by Claude Chappe (1763–1805) as a stage in his visual telegraph system, precursor of the electric telegraph.

Vigerie, Château La second wine of Château Moulin-de-Launay, Bordeaux, France.

vigna vineyard, Italian.

vignaiolo grape grower, Italian.

vigne vine, French.

Vignelaure, Château leading wine estate of AC Coteaux d'Aix-en-Provence, France.

vigneron vine-grower and wine-maker, French.

vignes mères hybrid rootstock vines for grafting to produce phylloxera-resisting plants. French.

vigneto vineyard, Italian.

vignoble vineyard, French.

Vigouroux, Georges wine producer in AC Cahors, SW France.

Viking Premium Lager beer by Vancouver Island brewery, Canada.

Vila Nova de Gaia borough of Oporto, Portugal, and centre of port trade. Location for port shippers' lodges and thus of maturing wines.

Vilafranca del Penedés winemaking centre of Penedés, Catalonia, Spain.

Vila Santa wine brand of João Portugal Ramos, Alentejo, Portugal.

Villa Antinori renowned Chianti Classico brand of Marchesi Antinori, Florence, Italy.

Villa Lobos absinthe brand of Mexico.

Villa Maria wine producer in South Auckland, New Zealand. Red wines from Cabernet Sauvignon and Merlot grapes and whites from Riesling, Sauvignon and other varieties.

Villány wine-producing centre of southern Hungary. Red wines from Cabernet Sauvignon, Pinot Noir and indigenous grape varieties.

Villa Pancho Cocktail. Over ice shake 2 parts tequila, 1 fresh lime juice, 1 teaspoon sugar. Strain.

Villard white grape variety of southern France. Ordinary wines. Also, **Villard Noir**.

Villars, Château wine estate of AC Fronsac, Bordeaux, France.

Villa Sachsen wine producer at Bingen in Rheinhessen region, Germany.

Villegeorge, Château wine estate of AC Haut-Médoc, Bordeaux, France. Classified *Cru Bourgeois Supérieur Exceptionnel*.

Villenave-d'Ornon wine-producing commune of AC Graves, Bordeaux, France.

Villenkeller vineyard at Klein-Winternheim in Rheinhessen region, Germany.

Villiera Estate wine producer in Paarl, South Africa. Well-known Bordeaux-style wines and sparkling wines.

Villiers, Elise leading wine producer of AC Bourgogne Vézelay, Burgundy, France.

vin wine, French.

viña vineyard, Spanish.

Viña Anita wine estate of Cachapoal Valley region, Chile.

Viña Sol well-known dry white wine brand of Bodegas Torres, Penedés, Spain.

Viña Toña white wine from Xarello grapes by Celler R Balada, Catalonia, Spain.

vin bourru new-harvest wine, still fermenting (and thus slightly sparkling), traditionally sold direct from the cask in cafés during the vintage. Now rare. French.

Vincent, Château wine estate of AC Margaux. Médoc, Bordeaux, France. Classified *Cru Bourgeois*.

Vincor leading wine-producing company, Canada.

vin cotto 'cooked wine'. Speciality of Abruzzi region, Italy, from grape must heated before fermentation.

vin cuit heated grape must used for sweetening wine. French.

vindaloo the notoriously incendiary Indian culinary sauce is popularly believed to take its name from the inclusion of vinegar as an ingredient. In fact, the word is a recent rendering of Portuguese *vin d'alho*, from *vinho* (wine) and *alho* (garlic), a sauce exported by colonists to Goa, a coastal territory of India in Portuguese possession from 1505 to 1962.

Vin de Corse AC for red and white wines of Corsica, France.

vin de cuvée in Champagne, France, the most-valued must from first pressing of grapes, set aside to make superior wine.

vin de garde 'wine to keep'. Wine made not for immediate consumption but for 'laying down' in bottle for years (or even decades) before reaching its ideal state. Applies to all the leading estates of Bordeaux and many Burgundy and northern Rhône wines. French.

vin de goutte new free-run wine from fermented grapes prior to pressing. French.

Vin Délimité de Qualité Supérieur under French wine law, a zone in which qualifying wine must be made from specified grape varieties grown within a defined area. The designation will ultimately disappear as wine laws evolve, with existing VDQS zones being either uprated to the higher AC ranking or demoted to *vin de pays* status.

vin de liqueur heavy sweet wine. French.

vin de paille 'straw wine'. Sweet specialty wine from grapes dried out (traditionally on beds of straw) to concentrate juice before pressing and slow-fermenting then long-ageing in oak casks. Mostly Jura region, France.

vin de pays 'country wine' of France. To qualify, the wine must be from a designated *vin de pays* zone (there are more than 100 varying in size from entire regions and *départements* to individual communes) but can be made from numerous permitted grape varieties.

vin de pays départementaux wine-producing zones of France defined by *département*. Wines produced under these designations are supposed to be of better quality than mere *vin de table*. Synonymous zones include Ain, Alpes du Haute Provence, Alpes Maritime, Ardèche, Aude, Bouches du Rhône, Deux Sèvres, Dordogne, Drôme, Gard, Gironde, Haute Garonne, Hérault, Indre et Loire, Loir-et-Cher, Loire Atlantique, Loiret, Maine et Loire, Meuse, Nièvre, Puy de Dôme, Pyrenées Atlantiques, Pyrenées Orientales, Sarthe, Tarn et Garonne, Var, Vaucluse, Vendée, Vienne.

Vin de Pays de Zone country wine zone of France. The most regulated of the *vin de pays* designations, with stricter quality requirements than those demanded of wines from *vins de pays départementaux* or *régionaux*. Zones are numerous and continually added to or altered. Notable are the following (with *département*/region in brackets): Allobrogie (Savoie), Ardailhou (Hérault), Argens (Var), Balmes Dauphinoises (Isère), Bénovie (Hérault), Bérange (Hérault), Bessan (Hérault), Bigorre (AC Madiran), Bourbonnais (Allier), Cassan (Hérault), Catalan (Pyrenées Orientales), Caux (Hérault), Cessenon (Hérault), Charentais (Charente/Charente Maritime), Collines de la Moure (Hérault), Comté de Grignan (Drôme), Condomois (Gers), Coteaux de l'Ardèche (Ardèche), Coteaux des Baronnies (Drôme), Coteaux de Bessilles (Hérault), Coteaux de la Cabrerisse (Aude), Coteaux Cevenols (Gard), Coteaux de Cèze, Coteaux Charitois (Nièvre), Coteaux du Cher et de l'Arnon (Loire), Coteaux de la Cité de Carcassonne (Aude), Coteaux d'Enserune (Hérault), Coteaux des Fenouillèdes (Pyrenées Orientales), Coteaux Flaviens (Gard), Coteaux de Fontcaude (Hérault), Coteaux de Glanes (Lot), Coteaux du Gresivaudan (Isère and Savoie), Coteaux de Laurens (Hérault), Coteaux du Lézignanais, Coteaux du Libron (Hérault), Coteaux du Littoral Audois (Aude), Coteaux de Miramont (Aude), Coteaux de Murviel (Hérault), Coteaux de Narbonne (Aude), Coteaux de Peyriac (Aude), Coteaux du Pont du Gard (Gard), Coteaux du Quercy (Lot), Coteaux du Salagou (Hérault), Coteaux du Salavès (Gard), Coteaux du Termenès (Aude), Coteaux et Terrasses de Montauban (Tarn et Garonne), Coteaux Vidourle (Gard), Côtes du Brian (Hérault), Côtes Catalanes (Pyrenées Atlantiques), Côtes du Céréssou (Hérault), Côtes de Gascogne (Gers), Côtes de Lastours (Aude), Côtes de Montestruc (Gers), Côtes de Pérignan (Aude), Côtes de Prouille (Aude), Côtes de Tarn (Tarn et Garonne), Côtes de Thau (Hérault), Côtes de Thongue (Hérault), Cucugnan (Aude), Gorges et Côtes de Millau (Tarn), Gorges de l'Hérault (Hérault), Hauts de Badens (Aude), Haute Vallée de l'Aude (Aude), Haute Vallée de l'Orb (Hérault), Hauterive en Pays d'Aude (Aude), Ile de Beauté (Corsica), Littoral Orb-Hérault (Hérault), Marches de Bretagne (Loire Atlantique), Maures (Var), Mont Baudile (Hérault), Mont Bouquet (Gard), Mont Caume (Var), Monts de la Grage (Hérault), Petite Crau (Bouches du Rhône), Pézanas (Hérault), Principauté de l'Orange (Vaucluse), Sables du Golfe du Lion (Bouches du Rhône, Grad, Hérault), Saint-Sadros (Tarn et Garonne, Haute Garonne), Serre du Coiran (Gard), Thézard-Perricard (Lot et Garonne), Torgan (Aude), Urfé (Loire), Uzège (Gard), Vals d'Agly (Pyrenées Atlantiques), Val de Cesse (Aude), Val de Dagne (Aude), Val de Montferrand (Hérault), Val d'Orbieu (Aude), Vallée du Paradis (Aude), Vaunage (Gard), Vicomté d'Aumerlas (Hérault), Vistrenque (Gard).

Vin de Pays d'Oc one of four *vin de pays régionaux* zones of France, covering the Midi and Provence, and the most productive of all defined *vin de pays* designations.

Vin de Pays du Comté Rhodaniens one of four *vin de pays régionaux* zones of France covering upper Rhône Valley and Savoie.

Vin de Pays du Comté Tolosan one of four *vin de pays régionaux* zones of France, covering SW France from south of Bordeaux to the Pyrenees.

Vin de Pays du Jardin de La France one of four *vin de pays régionaux* zones of France, covering Loire Valley and much of the area to the south-west.

vin de presse wine pressed from grapes, as distinct from free-run *vin de goutte* (*qv*).

vin de table humblest wine of France, ungoverned as to grape variety, region, country or vintage. Examples from outside France (usually Italian) are commonly labelled *Mélange de vins de differents pays de la Communauté Européenne*.

vin de taille in Champagne region, France, the second batch of juice from the grape pressing, following the *vin du cuvée*.

vin de tête regional term for wine from first (and most valued) pressing of grapes, Barsac and Sauternes, Bordeaux, France.

vin doux naturel 'naturally sweet wine'. A sweet style of wine defined in southern France under AC rules as one made through interrupted fermentation of high-sugar grapes. Grape alcohol is added to stop the fermentation and prevent all the sugar turning into alcohol. Examples are Banyuls, Muscat de Beaumes de Venise, Muscat de Rivesaltes.

vin d'une nuit informal French term for a rosé with an ephemeral hue gleaned from the briefest (one night) contact with the red skins of the grapes.

vine woody, climbing, grape-bearing plant. Species *vitis vinifera* is cultivated for wine production.

vineyard plantation of vines, usually for wine production.

vin gris 'grey wine'. A type of pale rosé from juice of red grapes run off the skins before fermentation begins. Usually Mediterranean France.

vinho wine, Portuguese.

vinho de mesa table (ordinary) wine of Portugal.

Vinho de Qualidade Produzido em Região Demarcada designation for quality wine, Portugal.

vinho verde the red and white wine of Minho region, northern Portugal. Red wines are chiefly from Vinhão grapes and whites from Alvarinho, Loureiro and Trajadura. Many top-quality whites are entirely or largely from Alvarinho. Name *vinho verde* means 'green' wine, referring to wine's suitability for drinking while young and fresh.

Vinícola de Castilla major wine producer in La Mancha region, Spain. Known for Castillo de Alhambra brand.

Vinícola Navarra, Bodegas wine producer in DO Navarra, Spain.

Vinifera Wine Cellars wine producer in New York State, USA.

vinification the process of turning grapes into wine.

Vini Sliven winery est 1920, Stara Planina, in sub-Balkan Bulgaria. Wines from French grape varieties.

vinititulist a collector of paper wine labels.

vin jaune 'yellow wine'. Regional speciality of Jura region, France. From Savagnin grapes and matured for six or more years in oak casks prior to bottling in distinctive *clavelin* bottles. Similar to *fino* sherry in that it acquires its yellow colour through oxidation in cask but forms a yeast-detritus crust akin to *flor*, preserving its freshness.

Vinmonopolet the alcohol-retailing state-controlled monopoly of Norway. Similar monopoly in Sweden was dismantled under free-market condition of membership of the European Union.

vin noir mythical 'black wine' of Cahors, SW France. Mostly a colouring and strengthening wine for blending with light Bordeaux reds in unregulated era of 19th century.

vino wine, Italian and Spanish.

vino da arrosto informal term for a wine of maturity and status worthy of serving with a meal of *arrosto* (roast meat). Italian.

vino da pasto informal term for everyday wine suitable for drinking with food. Italy.

vino da tavola 'table wine' of Italy. Mostly ordinary wine, but in some cases the description of a highly valued wine made by methods or from grape varieties that do not conform with the requirements of local DOC conventions and thus disallowed the designation.

see label opposite ➡

vino de color in sherry-making, the dark grape must or *arrope* added to the main fermentation to produce brown wine. Jerez de la Frontera, Spain.

vino de la tierra 'country wine' of guaranteed quality from a defined region, Spain.

vino de mesa table (ordinary) wine, Spain.

Vino Nobile di Montepulciano DOCG for red wines from Sangiovese, Canaiolo, Trebbiano and Malvasia grapes from slopes of hilltown of Montepulciano, Tuscany, Italy.

vino novello wine made for immediate drinking within weeks of the grape harvest, Italy.

VINO DA TAVOLA!

vino santo aperitif or dessert wine (dry to sweet styles) usually from Nosiola grapes, Trentino region, Italy. Bunches are part-dried, traditionally in lofts, before pressing. The must is long-fermented and aged in closed barrels.

Vinòt red *vino novello* from Nebbiolo grapes by Angelo Gaja, Barbaresco, Piedmont, Italy.

vino tipico 'country wine' from a defined region and thus with geographical typicity, Italy.

vinous in winetasting, a pleasing smell indicating a wine of authenticity.

Vinprom former state-owned wine monopoly of Bulgaria.

vin santo aperitif or dessert wine (dry to sweet styles) usually from Malvasia and Trebbiano grapes, Tuscany region, Italy. Bunches are part-dried, traditionally in lofts, before pressing. Fermentation is protracted and the wine is aged over long periods in closed barrels.

Vinsobres wine village of AC Côtes du Rhône Villages, Rhône Valley, France.

vintage grape harvest. The vintage on a wine label is the year in which the constituent grapes for the wine were picked. All, or in some nations (eg Australia) most, of the wine in the bottle must come from one year's harvest if a vintage is to be stated.

vintage character a style of port blended from wines of several vintages but claimed to resemble wine from one good vintage year. Portugal.

vintage charts comparative evaluations of series of vintages in a given country or region. Much used to price wines of Bordeaux etc but at best a very general guide to relative quality and value for money.

vintage champagne champagne made entirely from the fruit of one year's harvest, especially in years when grapes reach optimum ripeness. Needs longer ageing in bottle than non-vintage (blend of different years' harvests). Champagne, France.

vintage port port wine made entirely from grapes harvested in the year stated. Treacherous weather conditions of the vineyards, in the Douro Valley of northern Portugal, mean that ideal vintages are comparatively rare so vintage ports are in short supply, and expensive. Port houses 'declare' a vintage about 18-20 months after the harvest. Recent generally declared years (in which top-quality wines were made by most producers) are 2003, 2000, 1997, 1994, 1991, 1985, 1983, 1977, 1970, 1966, 1963.

vintner wine merchant.

vin vert light, sharp-tasting young white wine traditional in Midi, France.

Viognier white grape variety originally of northern Rhône Valley, France. Brought to the region by immigrant Phocaean immigrants around 1st century BC and the sole constituent of AC Condrieu wine. Plantings have lately spread elsewhere in southern France and to the Americas.

Viole, Le grappa brand of Cantina Sociale Copertino, Mombercelli, Italy.

Violette, Château La wine estate of AC Pomerol, Bordeaux, France.

Vipava white wine from Laski Rizling grapes, Slovenia.

Viré village of Mâconnais region, Burgundy, France. White wines labelled Mâcon-Viré (until 1999 vintage) from producers include Château de Viré, Clos du Chapitre.

Viré-Clessé new (1998) appellation contrôlée for the white wines of chardonnay grapes grown in the villages of Viré and Clessé in Mâconnais, Burgundy, France. Replaces the appellations Mâcon-Viré and Mâcon-Clessé.

Virgin Cocktail. Over ice shake 1 part dry gin, 1 Forbidden Fruit Liqueur, 1 white crème de menthe. Strain.

Virginia Brewing Co brewery at Virginia Beach, Norfolk, Virginia, USA.

Virgin's Kiss Cocktail. Over ice shake 3 parts peach brandy, 1 amaretto, 1 fresh cream, 2 dashes orange bitters. Strain.

Virgin Vodka British triple-distilled vodka brand of Virgin Trading.

Virou, Château wine estate of AC Premières Côtes de Blaye, Bordeaux, France.

Viru Valge vodka brand of Liviko, Tallinn, Estonia.

Visan wine village of AC Côtes du Rhône Villages, France.

viscous in winetasting, a wine of exceptional richness leaving long-lasting 'legs'.

Vitacée, La wine estate at Sainte-Barbe, Quebec, Canada.

viticoltore wine-grower, Italian.

viticulteur wine-grower, French.

viticulture the science and practice of growing grapes for wine production.

vitigno vine or grape variety, Italian.

Vitis Labrusca vine species widely planted in USA. Concord is best-known variety.

Vitis Riparia vine species of North America. Grown for provision of phylloxera-resistant rootstocks.

Vitis Vinifera vine species cultivated worldwide for wine grapes.

Vitivino, Bodegas wine producer in DO Jumilla, Levante, Spain. Altos de Pío brand.

Vitusberg vineyard at Walluf in Rheingau region, Germany.

Viura regional named for Maccabeo grape, Rioja, Spain.

vivace lively, as in lightly bubbly wine. Italian.

Vladimir dark lager (5.0% alc) by Irkutsk brewery, Siberia, Russia. Said to be Siberia's biggest-selling beer.

Vladimir I the first Christian sovereign of Russia (956–1015). Since canonised as St Vladimir the Great, he considered Islam as a possible state religion before imposing the Christian faith. While still undecided, he summoned Mohammedan representatives to explain their beliefs, but soon discovered there would be a problem. 'Drink is the joy of the Russians,' he felt compelled to tell the mullahs. 'We cannot live without it.'

Vladivar vodka brand of Whyte & Mackay, Warrington, Cheshire, England. Named after a British racehorse.

VO a short form of VSOP.

Vodga Cocktail. Over ice shake 3 parts vodka, 2 Strega, 1 orange juice. Strain.

vodka see box.

Vodka-Cranberry Punch to make this delicious concoction prepare an ice block by freezing water in a plastic container such as an old ice cream carton. In a punch bowl combine the ice block with 1 bottle vodka, 2 pints cranberry juice, half pint dry red wine, 1 sliced orange, 6 medium strawberries.

Vodka Martini Cocktail. Over ice shake 1 part vodka, 1 teaspoon dry vermouth. Strain. Recipe is said to be the device of novelist Ian Fleming (1908–64).

Vodka Poolside Cocktail. Over ice shake 3 parts vodka, 1 lemon juice, 1 dash grenadine, 1 pinch sugar. Strain into an ice-filled glass and top with chilled sparkling water. Add orange slice.

Vodkatini Cocktail. Over ice stir 1 part vodka, 1 dash dry vermouth. Strain and add lemon peel twist.

Vögelein vineyard at Nordheim in Franken region, Germany.

Vogelsang the name of 19 individual vineyards in Germany. Region by region, as follows: in Baden at Gemmingen, Kirchardt; in Franken at Iphofen, Markt Einersheim; in Mosel-Saar-Ruwer at Serrig; in Nahe at Bretzenheim, Merxheim; in Rheingau at Geisenheim (Johannisberg); in Rheinhessen at Erbes-Bündesheim, Gau-Odernheim, Wallertheim, Zornheim; in Rheinpfalz at Bockenheim an der Weinstrasse, Kindenheim, Weisenheim am Berg; in Württemberg at Brackenheim, Untereisesheim.

Vogelsberg vineyard at Lauda-Königshofen in Baden region, Germany.

Vogelschlag vineyard at Duchroth in Nahe region, Germany.

Vogelsgärten *Grosslage* incorporating vineyards at Guntersblum and Ludwigshöhle in Rheinhessen region, Germany.

Vodka

purity as a selling point

The clear, neutral spirit of Poland and Russia has its origins in the eleventh century AD, when low-strength vodka then known as *gorzalka* in Poland was made for medicinal purposes by monks and lay apothecaries. The drink first became popular as an alcoholic beverage in the 1400s. It was by then commonly distilled from grain mash. In the centuries since, successive governments in Poland and Russia have struggled vainly to restrict, regulate and tax both the production and consumption of a spirit to which large sections of their respective populations have been firmly addicted.

Modern vodka, especially the brands made for export or produced in western countries, is distilled from grain mash (usually rye) in pot stills and unaged. Vodkas distilled from other grains (maize, barley and, rarely, wheat), potatoes and sugar beet molasses are now largely confined to regions of Russia where these crops are abundant, and rye unavailable.

The renowned purity and neutrality of vodka is largely attributable to the filtering of the spirit through charcoal, especially from silver birch wood. In the regions which are its home, vodka is less refined, with residual colour and a greater weight than western versions. Some vodka produced in the Baltic regions for export has glycerine added to give extra body.

Flavoured vodkas proliferate in Poland and Russia. Popular flavourings include bison grass, pepper and other herbs and spices, fruits such as cherry, lemon, plum and rowanberry, and materials as diverse as ginseng, honey and walnuts.

The name vodka means 'little water', a diminutive of Polish *woda* or Russian *voda*.

Vogelsprung vineyard at Flemlingen in Rheinpfalz region, Germany.

Vogteiberg vineyard at Senheim in Mosel-Saar-Ruwer region, Germany.

Vogtei Rötien *Grosslage* incorporating vineyards in Baden region, Germany at, respectively: Bad Bellingen (Bamberg), Bad Bellingen (Hertingen), Bad Bellingen (Rheinweiler), Binzen, Efringen-Kirchen, Efringen-Kirchen (Blansignen), Efringen-Kirchen (Egringen), Efringen-Kirchen (Huttingen), Efringen-Kirchen (Istein), Efringen-Kirchen (Kleinkems), Efringen-Kirchen (Welmlingen), Efringen-Kirchen (Wintersweiler), Eimeldingen, Fischingen, Grezach-Whylen, Kandern (Feuerbach), Kandern (Holzen), Kandern (Riedlingen), Kandern (Tannenkirch), Kandern (Wollbach), Lörrach, Rheinfelden, Rümmingen, Schallbach, Weil am Rhein, Weil am Rhein (Haltingen), Weil am Rhein (Ötlingen).

Vogüé, Comte Georges de leading wine domaine of Chambolle-Musigny, Burgundy, France. Vineyards include parts of *Grands Crus* Bonnes-Mares and Le Musigny.

Vojvodina wine-producing province of Serbia. French and indigenous grape varieties.

VOK leading liqueur producer, Australia.

volatile acidity in winetasting, a noticeable vinegary character associated with acetic acid. Usually due to bacterial infection.

Vollburg vineyard at Michelau in Franken region, Germany.

Volnay great wine village and AC of Côte de Beaune, Burgundy, France. Renowned red wines from the AC and from *Premier Cru* vineyards les Angles, les Aussy, la Barre, Bousse d'Or, les Broouillards, en Cailleret, Cailleret Dessus, Carelle Dessous, Carelle sous La Chapelle, Champans, Chanlin, Clos des Chênes, en Chevret, Clos des Ducs, Fremiet, les Lurets, les Mitans, en l'Ormeau, les Petures, Pitures Dessus, Pointes d'Angles, Robardelle, Ronceret, les Santenots, Taille-Pieds, en Verseuil, Village de Volnay. Leading producers include Marquis D'Angerville, Clerget, Lafarge, Pousse d'Or.

Vom heissen Stein *Grosslage* incorporating vineyards at Briedel, Pünderich and Peil in Mosel-Saar-Ruwer region, Germany.

von Buhl, Weingut Reichsrat leading wine estate of Rheinpfalz region, Germany. Renowned Riesling wines from vineyards of Deidesheim, Forst, Ruppertsberg.

von Kesselstadt see Kesselstadt.

von Schubert see Schubert.

voorburg citrus-flavoured *brandewijn*, Netherlands.

Vorderberg vineyard at Kleinniedesheim in Rheinpfalz region, Germany.

Vor der Hölle vineyard at Hesloch in Nahe region, Germany.

voros red (wine), Hungary.

Vosgros *Premier Cru* vineyard of Chablis, Burgundy, France.

Vöslau wine town south of Vienna, Austria. Noted red wines.

Vosne-Romanée village and AC of Côte de Nuits, Burgundy, France. Site of famed *Grand Cru* vineyards

Richebourg, Romanée, Romanée-Conti, Romanée-St-Vivant, la Tâche. Also *Premier Cru* vineyards: les Beaumonts, aux Brulées, les Chaumes, les Gaudichots, la Grande Rue, aux Malconsorts, le Clos de Réats, les Peitis Monts, les Reignots, les Suchots. Leading producers include Jean Grivot, Henri Jayer, Leroy, Méo-Camuzet, Domaine de La Romanée-Conti etc.

Votrix mourned former 'British vermouth' brand of Vine Products Co, late of Kingston-upon-Thames, Surrey, England.

Vougeot village and AC of Côte de Nuits, Burgundy, France.

Vougeot, Clos (de) largest (124 acres) *Grand Cru* vineyard of Côte de Nuits, Burgundy, France. Divided up among some 80 owners and producing red wine of quality varying from the execrable to the divine. **Vougeot AC** and **Vougeot Premier Cru** red and white wines are those from within the appellation, but without the Clos.

Vouvray village and AC of Loire Valley, France. Noted still and sparkling white wines from Chenin Blanc grapes. Softly sweet still wines from extra-ripe grapes are labelled *moelleux*. **Vouvray Mousseux** (sparkling) is made by *méthode traditionelle* (champagne method in all but name). Leading producers include Marc Brédif, Daniel Jarry.

VP 'British wine' brand of Matthew Clark, Bristol, England. Initials stand for Vine Products, name of the product's original perpetrator.

VQA Vintners Quality Alliance. Wine producers' association of Ontario, Canada est 1988. Standards of VQA members approximate to those of France's *Appellation Contrôlée* and qualifying wines bear the VQA symbol.

VQPRD Vinho de Qualidade Produzido em Região Demarcada (*qv*).

vrac 'bulk' (wine), French. **Vin en vrac** is bought in cask, drum or tanker for bottling by purchaser.

Vrai-Canon-Bouché, Château wine estate of AC Canon-Fronsac, Bordeaux, France.

Vranac red grape and wine of Balkan province of Montenegro.

Vranje wine region of Serbia. Red wines from French grape varieties.

Vranken Monopole wine brand and corporate producer of Champagne, France.

Vray-Canon-Boyer, Château wine estate of AC Canon-Fronsac, Bordeaux, France.

Vraye-Croix-de-Gay, Château wine estate of AC Pomerol, Bordeaux, France.

Vredendal co-operative wine producer of Olifants River, South Africa.

Vreez liqueur producer, Mexico.

Vriesenhof wine producer in Stellenbosch, South Africa. Kallista red from Cabernet Sauvignon and Merlot grapes, and other brands.

VSOP Very Superior Old Pale. An age designation for the brandy of Cognac, France. No brandy in the blend may have been distilled less than 4 years and six months prior to blending and bottling.

Vugava white grape variety and wine of Dalmatian island of Vis, Croatia.

Vulkanfelsen *Grosslage* incorporating villages in Baden region, Germany at, respectively: Bahlingen, Bötzingen, Breisach, Eichstetten, Endingen, Endingen (Amoltern), Endingen (Kiechlinsbergen), Endingen (Königschaffhausen), Ihringen, Ihringen (Blankenhornberg), Ihringen (Wasenweiler), March, Riegel, Sasbach, Sasbach (Jechtingen), Sasbach (Leiselheim), Teningen, Vogtsburg im Kaiserstuhl (Achkarren), Vogtsburg im Kaiserstuhl (Bischofflingen), Vogtsburg im Kaiserstuhl (Burkheim), Vogtsburg im Kaiserstuhl (Oberbergen), Vogtsburg im Kaiserstuhl (Oberrotweil) Vogtsburg im Kaiserstuhl (Schelingen).

Vve Champion producer of famed Noyau liqueur. Bordeaux, France.

W

Wachau wine region along Danube river, southern Austria. Highly valued white wines from Grüner Veltliner and Riesling grapes.

Wachenheim important wine village of Rheinpfalz region, Germany. Famed vineyards include Böhlig, Fuchsmantel, Gerümpel, Mandelgarten, Rechbächel. *Grosslagen*: Mariengarten, Schenkenböhl, Schnepfenflug. Principal producer Dr Bürklin Wolf.

Wachhügel vineyard at Wiesenbronn in the Franken region, Germany.

Wacholder clear spirit flavoured with juniper – Germany's answer to gin. Qualities range from simple flavoured neutral spirit **Wacholderkornbrannt** to finest crock-bottled *Steinhäger*.

Wachter, Franz wine producer in Südburgenland, Austria.

Wachtkopf vineyard at Vaihingen in Württemberg region, Germany.

Wadworth & Co brewery est 1885 in Devizes, Wiltshire, England. Famed for ales including Farmer's Glory, Henry Wadworth IPA, 6X.

Waggledance gold-coloured, sweet honey beer (5.0% alc) first made 1995 by Vaux brewery, Sunderland, England.

Wagner, Günther wine producer in Südsteiermark, Austria.

Wahrheit vineyard at Oberheimbach in Mittelrhein region, Germany.

Wahrsager vineyard at Senheim in Mosel-Saar-Ruwer region, Germany.

waiter's friend a style of corkscrew incorporating a lever to facilitate withdrawal of the cork. Based on an original prototype by German engineer Karl Wienke, 1883.

Wakka Saké vodka-saké brand of Extreme Drinks, UK.

Waldorf Cocktail. Over ice shake 2 parts Swedish Punsch, 1 dry gin, 1 lemon juice. Strain.

Waldrach wine village of Mosel-Saar-Ruwer region, Germany. *Grosslage*: Römerlay. Producers include Bischofliche Weinguter.

Waldschütz, Reinhard wine producer in Kamptal, Niederösterreich, Austria.

Walfart, Armand Belgian-born inventor of the current process of freezing the neck of champagne bottles in advance of releasing the cap and disgorging the wine of its detritus in a plug of ice. The method, dating from 1884, involves dipping the bottles in low-temperature brine. First adopted by Moët & Chandon in 1891.

Walkenberg vineyard at Walluf in Rheingau region, Germany.

Walker, John see Johnnie Walker.

Wallaby Cocktail. Over ice shake 1 part peach brandy, 1 Dubonnet, 4 dashes lime juice, 1 dash grenadine. Strain.

Wallace single malt whisky liqueur brand of Burn Stewart Distillers, Scotland.

Wallis Cocktail. Prepare cocktail glass by dipping rim in fruit juice then in sugar to encrust. Over ice shake 1 part dry gin, 1 blue curaçao, 1 fresh lime juice. Strain.

Wallmauer vineyard at Neckarzimmern in Baden region, Germany.

wallop informal name for beer, probably from 16th century verb meaning to boil rapidly (as in fermentation).

Wall Street Cocktail. Over ice shake 2 parts dry gin, 1 lemon juice, 1 teaspoon white crème de menthe. Strain into a champagne glass and top with chilled champagne or other sparkling wine.

Walluf wine village of Rheingau region, Germany. *Grosslage*: Steinmächer.

Walnut Brewing brewery in Boulder, Colorado, USA.

Walporzheim Ahrtal *Bereich* encompassing entire Ahr wine region, Germany.

Walthari-Hof wine producer at Edenkoben, Rheinpfalz region, Germany.

Walterstal vineyards at Lauda-Königshofen (Königshofen) and Lauda-Königshofen (Sachsenflur) in Baden region, Germany.

Walzer, Ewald wine producer in Kremstal, Niederösterreich, Austria.

Wanne vineyard at Weinstadt in Württemberg region, Germany.

Warday's Cocktail. Over ice shake 1 part apple brandy, 1 dry gin, 1 sweet vermouth, 2 dashes Chartreuse. Strain.

Ward Eight Cocktail. Over ice shake 2 parts rye whisky, 1 lemon juice, 1 orange juice, 1 teaspoon grenadine. Strain.

Warden brewery at Chipping Warden, Banbury, Oxfordshire, England.

Ward's Cocktail. In cocktail glass place ring of lemon peel and crushed ice. Pour in, first, 1 part Chartreuse then, gently to avoid mixing, 1 part brandy.

Ward Ten Cocktail. Over ice shake 2 parts rye whisky, 1 lemon juice, 4 dashes grenadine, 1 teaspoon sugar. Strain.

Ward's brewery at Sheffield, Yorkshire, England.

Warre & Ca oldest British port shipper est 1670 Vila Nova de Gaia, Portugal. Owned by Symington. Late-bottled vintage, Nimrod tawny, Quinta da Cavadinha single-estate vintage, **Warre's Warrior** 'vintage character' and vintages: 1955, 58, 60, 63, 66, 70, 75, 77, 80, 83, 85, 91, 92, 94, 97, 2000, 03.

Warsteiner brewery in Sauerland, Germany, known for for **Warsteiner Pilsener**.

Wartberg vineyards at Alzey in Rheinhessen region and Beilstein in Württemberg region, Germany.

Wartbühl *Grosslage* incorporating vineyards in Württemberg region, Germany at, respectively: Aichwald, Kernen (Rommelshausen), Kernen (Stetten), Korb, Korb (Kleinheppach), Remshalden (Geradstetten), Remshalden (Grunbach), Remshalden (Hebsack), Weinstadt (Beutelsbach), Weinstadt (Endersbach), Weinstadt (Grossheppach), Weinstadt (Schnait), Weinstadt

(Strümpelbach), Winnenden, Winnenden (Baach), Winnenden (Breuningsweiler), Winnenden (Hahnweiler), Winnenden (Hertmannsweiler).

Warteck brewery in Basel, Switzerland.

Warwick Estate wine producer in Stellenbosch, South Africa. Trilogy red from Cabernet Franc, Cabernet Sauvignon and Merlot grapes, and varietal wines.

Warwickshire brewery at Kenilworth, Warwickshire, England.

wash in distilling, the fermented liquid – wine or beer-type products from grain, fruit or sugar – which is heated in a closed container to create alcohol-bearing vapour.

Washington Cocktail. Over ice shake 2 parts dry vermouth, 1 brandy, 2 dashes Angostura bitters, 2 dashes sugar syrup. Strain.

wassail a toast (from Old Norse *ves heill* 'be in health') and the drink involved, usually of ale with apples, sugar, nutmeg and bread.

Wasseros vineyard at Kiedrich in Rheingau region, Germany.

Waterbury Cocktail. Over ice shake 1 egg white, 2 parts brandy, 1 lemon juice, sprinkle sugar. Strain.

Waterfall Cocktail. Over ice shake 1 part vodka, 1 puréed fresh watermelon. Strain into a tumbler filled with crushed ice.

Waterloo bottle-conditioned bitter ale (4.0% alc) by Freeminer Brewery, Forest of Dean, Gloucestershire, England. Named after a former local coal mine – named after the decisive battle of the Napoleonic Wars, 1815.

Water Street pub-brewery in Milwaukee, Wisconsin, USA.

Watney formerly famed London brewery (Watney Combe Reid) and brand diminishingly admired since takeover by Grand Metropolitan company in 1972. Watney's 'Red Revolution' campaign of replacing cask-conditioned ales with 'keg' beer – most notoriously **Watney's Red Barrel** – has been credited with giving crucial impetus to the Campaign for Real Ale in the UK.

Wawern wine village of Mosel-Saar-Ruwer region, Germany. *Grosslage*: Scharzberg.

Wax Cocktail. Over ice shake 1 part dry gin, 2 dashes orange bitters. Strain.

Webster Cocktail. Over ice shake 4 parts dry gin, 2 dry vermouth, 1 apricot brandy, 1 fresh lime juice. Strain.

Webster's brewery est 1838 by Samuel Webster in Halifax, West Yorkshire, England. Closed 1996 following takeover by Scottish & Newcastle breweries. Webster's brands since produced at John Smith brewery, Tadcaster, Yorkshire.

Wedding Belle Cocktail. Over ice shake 2 parts dry gin, 2 Dubonnet, 1 cherry brandy, 1 orange juice.

Wedding Bells Cocktail. Over ice stir 3 parts rye whisky, 2 orange curaçao, 1 Lillet, 1 dash orange bitters. Alternatively, over ice stir 2 parts rye whisky, 2 Lillet, 1 curaçao, 1 dash orange bitters.

Weedkiller ale by Wiltshire brewery, Tisbury, England.

weeper bottle leaking from cork.

Weeping Radish brewing company in Roanoke Island, North Carolina, USA. Bavarian-style beers.

Weesuer Special Cocktail. Over ice shake 1 part dry gin, 1 dry vermouth, 1 orange curaçao, 1 sweet vermouth, 4 dashes pastis. Strain.

Weetwood Ales brewery at Tarporley, Cheshire, England.

Wegeler-Deinhard famed wine estate of Rheingau region, Germany. See Deinhard.

Wehlen wine village of Mittelmosel, Mosel-Saar-Ruwer region, Germany. Site of renowned Sonnenuhr vineyard. Producers include Dr Loosen, J J Prum, Wegeler-Deinhard. *Grosslage*: Münzlay.

Weil, Dr wine estate at Kiedrich, Rheingau region, Germany.

Weilberg vineyard at Bad Dürkheim in Rheinpfalz region, Germany.

Wein wine, German.

Weinbaugebiet wine-producing region as defined for production of *Tafelwein*. Germany.

Weinberge vineyard at Viereth in Franken region, Germany.

weinbrand 'burnt wine'. Style of grape brandy devised by Hugo Asbach, Rudesheim, Germany.

Weingarten vineyard at Fischingen in Baden region, Germany.

Weingrube vineyard at Boppard in Mittelrhein region, Germany.

Weingut wine estate (wine producer), Germany.

Weinhaus Kaisergarten wine producer in Neusiedlersee, Burgenland, Austria.

Weinhecke vineyards at Bruchsal and Ubstadt-Weiher in Baden region, Germany.

Weinhex *Grosslage* incorporating vineyards in Mosel-Saar-Ruwer region, Germany at, respectively: Alken, Brodenbach, Burgen, Dieblich, Kobern-Gondorf (Gondorf), Kobern-Gondorf (Kobern), Koblenz (Güls und Metternich), Koblenz (Lay), Koblenz (Moselweiss), Lehmen, Löf, Löf (Hatzenort), Löf (Kattenes), Moselsürsch, Niederfell, Oberfell, Winningen.

Weinkammer vineyard at Enkirch in Mosel-Saar-Ruwer region, Germany.

Weinkeller brewer and major retailer (500 beer brands) in Berwyn, Chicago, Illinois, USA.

Weinkeller vineyard at Mainz in Rheinhessen region, Germany.

Weinkellerei place for making and/or storing wine, Germany.

Weinrieder wine producer in Weinviertel, Niederösterreich, Austria.

Weinsack vineyard at Odernheim am Glan in Nahe region, Germany.

Weinsteig vineyards at Erlabrunn and Leinach in Franken region, Germany.

Weinsteige *Grosslage* incorporating vineyards in Württemberg region, Germany at, respectively: Esslingen, Fellbach, Gerlingen, Stuttgart, Stuttgart (Bad Cannstatt), Stuttgart (Degerloch), Stuttgart (Feuerbach), Stuttgart (Gaisburg), Stuttgart (Hedelfingen), Stuttgart (Hofen), Stuttgart (Hohenheim), Stuttgart (Mühlhausen), Stuttgart (Münster), Stuttgart (Obertürkheim), Stuttgart (Rohracker), Stuttgart (Rotenberg), Stuttgart (Uhlbach), Stuttgart (Untertürkheim), Stuttgart (Wangen), Stuttgart (Zuffenhausen).

Weinstrasse wine route. A road through vineyards. Germany.

Weischler GmbH brandy and fruit-spirit distiller, Austria.

Weisenstein vineyard at Benkastel-Kues in Mosel-Saar-Ruwer region, Germany.

Weissbier 'white beer'. In German, a pale beer made with wheat.

Weissburgunder white grape variety of Austria. Synonymous with Pinot Blanc.

Weisse synonym for *Weissbier*.

Weissenberg vineyard at Kobern-Gondorf in Mosel-Saar-Ruwer region, Germany.

Weissenstein vineyards at Mann-weiler-Cölln and Oberndorf in Nahe region, Germany.

Weisserberg vineyard at Briedel in Mosel-Saar-Ruwer region, Germany.

Weiss Erd vineyard at Mainz in Rheingau region, Germany.

Weisses Kreuz vineyard at Leubsdorf in Mittelrhein, Germany.

Weissherbst style of pale pink wine of Germany.

Weizenbier 'wheat beer'. German. Commonly shortened to **Weizen**.

Welcome Stranger Cocktail. Over ice shake 1 part brandy, 1 dry gin, 1 grenadine, 1 lemon juice, 1 orange juice, 1 Swedish Punsch. Strain.

Welgemeend wine producer in Paarl, South Africa. Bordeaux-style red wines.

Wellanschitz, Stefan wine producer in Mittelburgenland, Austria.

Wellings brand of Dutch bitters, Netherlands.

Wellington County brewery in Guelph, Ontario, Canada. Beers include Iron Duke, **Wellington Premium Lager**, **Wellington Special Pale Ale**.

Wells, Charles brewery in Bedford, Bedfordshire, England. Beers include Bombardier, Charles Wells, Noggin.

Welschriesling white grape variety of Austria and eastern Europe. Widely planted under names such as Laski Rizling (former Yugoslav states) and Olaszrizling (Hungary). Not comparable with Rhine Riesling.

Welsh Whisky extinct since 1906 when Wales's last whisky distillery, Frongoch at Bala, North Wales, closed, but revived 1995 by **Welsh Whisky Company**, Brecon. This enterprise in turn ceased after a short period of marketing scotch whisky as Welsh and was superseded by new owners in 1998 who had a still built to their own design and proceeded to make 'Penderyn' Welsh whisky from raw materials supplied by Cardiff brewers Brains.

Weltons North Downs brewery at Dorking, Surrey, England.

Wembley Cocktail. Over ice shake 2 parts dry gin, 2 dry vermouth, 2 dashes apple brandy, 1 dash apricot brandy. Strain. Alternatively, over ice shake 1 part dry vermouth, 1 Scotch whisky, 1 pineapple juice. Strain.

Wendelstück vineyard at Burg in Mosel-Saar-Ruwer region, Germany.

Weninger, Franz wine producer in Mittelburgenland, Austria.

Wente Brothers wine producer of Livermore, California, USA.

Wenzel, Michael wine producer in Neusiedlersee Hügelland, Burgenland, Austria.

Werner, Domdechant wine producer at Hochheim in Rheingau region, Germany.

Werner Klein, Mosbacher Hof wine producer in Rheinpfalz region, Germany.

Wernleite vineyard at Gemünden in Franken region, Germany.

Wertek, Franz wine producer in Thermenregion, Niederösterreich, Austria.

Wessex Brewery brewery and bottler at Mitcheldean, Forest of Dean, Gloucestershire, England. Rumpy-Pumpy bottle-conditioned beer.

Wessex Sup ale brand (4.3% alc) of Cottage Brewing Co, Lovington, Somerset, England.

Westbrook Cocktail. Over ice shake 7 parts dry gin, 3 sweet vermouth, 1 whisky, sprinkle of sugar. Strain.

Westbury vineyard at Reading, Berkshire, England.

West Coast brewery of King's Arms pub, Chorlton-on-Medlock, Manchester, England.

West Country Liqueurs flavoured liqueur brand of Friary Vintners, Witham Friary, Somerset, England.

see label opposite ➡

West Croft cider producer, Brent Knoll, Highbridge, Somerset, England. Brands include Janet's Jungle Juice.

West End Draught beer by South Australia Brewing, Adelaide.

Western Rose Cocktail. Over ice shake 2 parts dry gin, 1 apricot brandy, 1 dry vermouth, 1 dash lemon juice. Strain.

West Indian Cocktail. In a tumbler glass with one ice cube stir 1 part dry gin, 1 teaspoon lemon juice, 1 teaspoon sugar, 4 dashes Angostura bitters. Strain.

Westmalle Trappist monastery brewery at Westmalle, Antwerp, Belgium. Westmalle Trappist Lager (7.0% alc).

West Monckton cider producer, Overton, West Monckton, Somerset, England.

Westons cider producer est 1880 Much Marcle, Herefordshire, England. Present master cider maker Henry Weston is great-grandson of founder. Brands include Stowford Press draught cider and bottled Henry (8.5% alc) plus Organic Strong (6.5% alc), Stowford Press

LA (low alcohol, 1%) and Stowford Press LC (low calorie/carbohydrate 5% alc).

Westrum vineyard at Bodenheim in Rheinhessen region, Germany.

Weststeiermark wine region of Austria.

Westvleteren brewery of Trappist monastery of St Sixtus est 1830 at Westvleteren, Belgium. The monastery's Abbot beer is among Belgium's strongest at 10.6% alc.

Wetterkreuz vineyard at Braunweiler in Nahe region, Germany.

Wetzstein vineyards at Fellbach, Stuttgart and Weinstadt in Württemberg region, Germany.

Whatley Vineyard wine and spirit producer at Whatley, Somerset, England. Still and sparkling wines and Whatley St George Somerset Brandy.

What the Dickens Cocktail. Stir 1 part gin, 1 teaspoon icing sugar in a sturdy glass. Top with warm water and stir. A favourite, furtive beverage of Mr and Mrs Bumble in Dickens's *Oliver Twist*. Their habit was to pour the gin from a milk jug and the water from a teapot.

What the Hell Cocktail. Over ice stir 1 part dry gin, 1 apricot brandy, 1 dry vermouth, 1 dash lemon juice.

Wheel Tapper's ale brand (4% alc) of Cottage Brewing Co, Lovington, Somerset, England.

Which Way Cocktail. Over ice shake 1 part Anisette, 1 brandy, 1 pastis. Strain.

Whim Ales brewery at Hartington, Buxton, Derbyshire, England.

Whin Hill cider producer, Wells next the Sea, Norfolk, England.

Whip Cocktail. Over ice shake 2 parts brandy, 1 dry vermouth, 1 sweet vermouth, 3 dashes curaçao, 1 dash pastis. Strain.

whiskey alternative spelling of whisky, eg in Ireland and USA.

Whiskey Cobbler Cocktail. Over ice shake 3 parts bourbon, 1 orange juice, 1 teaspoon sugar. Strain into ice-filled glasses and top with chilled sparkling water.

Whiskey Flip Cocktail. Over ice shake 3 parts bourbon, 1 teaspoon sugar, 1 egg. Strain.

whisky spirit distilled from malted cereal grains. Formerly, spirit distilled from any starch-bearing source. Name is a contraction of Gaelic *uisgebeatha*, water of life. There are four pricipal national producers, giving their names to distinctive styles: Scotch, Irish, Canadian and American. Whisky is also widely distilled in Asia, with Japan the largest producer.

Whisky Cocktail. Over ice stir 1 part rye whisky, 2 dashes sugar syrup, 1 dash Angostura bitters. Strain and add cocktail cherry to glass.

Whisky Collins Cocktail. Over ice shake 3 parts whisky, 1 lemon juice, 1 teaspoon sugar syrup. Strain into tall glass and add ice. Top with soda water.

Whisky Insurrection name given to a revolt in the American state of Pennsylvania in 1794. Thousands of Scottish and Irish Pennsylvanians operated whisky stills and made loud protests when, in 1791, the Federal Government introduced an excise duty on domestic spirits. Federal excise officers attempting to enforce the law in Western Pennsylvania (also in Virginia and North Carolina) were violently repelled, and in some cases tarred and feathered. Protests whipped up by the notorious agitator David Bradford turned into widespread lawlessness by 1794, and President Washington despatched an armed force to the state in September. The insurgency was put down without bloodshed and the ringleaders (excepting Bradford, who escaped to Louisiana) were tried and convicted for treason – but immediately pardoned. The Insurrection has an important place in American history because its suppression was the first occasion on which the Federal Government employed the powers bestowed upon it by Congress (in May, 1792) to enforce federal laws within the 13 states. Some historians maintain that the excise law of 1791 was enacted not to collect whisky duties but to provoke just such a rebellion – in order to afford the executive an opportunity to exercise its new powers and demonstrate its willingness to exert them.

Whisky Mac Cocktail. Over ice stir 2 parts scotch whisky, 1 ginger wine. Strain.

Whisky Sour Cocktail. Over ice shake 2 parts scotch whisky, 1 lemon juice, 1 teaspoon sugar. Strain.

Whisky Special Cocktail. Over ice shake 6 parts whisky, 4 dry vermouth, 1 orange juice, pinch nutmeg. Strain and add olive to glass.

Whisper Cocktail. Over ice shake 1 part dry vermouth, 1 sweet vermouth, 1 whisky. Strain.

Whist Cocktail. Over ice stir 2 parts apple brandy, 1 rum, 1 sweet vermouth. Strain.

Whistler Brewing resort brewery at Whistler, Vancouver, Canada.

Whitbread major UK brewer styled Whitbread Beer Company with holdings in many well-known smaller breweries and producing well-known foreign brands (eg Heineken, Murphys) under licence. The company's brewing operations were sold to Belgium's Interbrew in 2000. Brands include Tankard, Trophy draught ales, Gold Label, Mackeson Stout, Pale Ale. Founded by Samuel Whitbread (1720–1796) in London in 1742 with partners Godfrey and Thomas Sewell, the company came into Whitbread's sole ownership in 1761. The brewery established by the partners in Chiswell Street, London EC, in 1750 remained in continuous production for 226 years until its closure in 1976.

White Cocktail. Over ice stir 4 parts dry gin, 1 Anisette, 2 dashes orange bitters. Strain and squeeze lemon peel over.

White & Gold blended scotch whisky by Alistair Graham, Leith, Scotland.

White Baby Cocktail. Over ice shake 2 parts dry gin, 1 Cointreau, 1 lemon syrup. Strain.

White Bache apple variety traditionally valued for cider-making. Synonymous with Norman. Anglo-French.

White Cargo Cocktail. Shake 1 part dry gin, 1 vanilla ice cream. Dilute with iced water to thin as necessary.

White Cloud Cocktail. Into a glass with ice pour 2 parts Sambuca, 1 teaspoon lemon juice. Top with chilled sparkling water and stir.

White Cloud Ale beer by Sun Valley brewery, Idaho, USA.

White Horse blended scotch whisky by White Horse Distillers, Edinburgh, Scotland. Blend created by J L Mackie of Lagavulin distillery, 1883, and named after the White Horse pub in Edinburgh, a *de facto* officer's mess during the Rebellion of 1745.

White Knight Cocktail. Over ice stir 2 parts dry gin, 4 dashes Anisette, 1 dash orange bitters. Strain and squeeze lemon peel over.

White Label low alcohol (1%) bitter ale by Whitbread, London, England.

see label opposite ➡

White Lady Cocktail. Over ice shake 2 parts dry gin, 1 Cointreau, 1 lemon juice. Strain.

White Lightning cider brand of Inch's Cider, Devon, England.

White Lily Cocktail. Over ice shake 1 part Cointreau, 1 dry gin, 1 rum, 1 dash pastis. Strain.

White Overproof Rum spirit brand of Wray & Nephew, Jamaica.

White Plush Cocktail. Over ice shake 8 parts milk, 1 dry gin, 4 dashes maraschino. Strain.

white port port from white grapes (principally Malvasia) formerly made traditionally to be a sweet after-dinner drink. Now commonly made as an aperitif from fermented-out wine plus brandy, to make it drier-tasting.

White Rose Cocktail. Over ice shake 6 parts dry gin, 2 maraschino, 2 orange juice, 1 lemon (or lime) juice. Strain.

White Russian Cocktail. Over ice stir 2 parts vodka, 1 white crème de menthe. Strain.

White Slave Cocktail. Over ice shake 1 egg white, 1 part champagne, 1 dry gin, 1 dry sherry. Strain.

White Spider Cocktail. Over ice shake 1 part crème de menthe, 1 vodka. Strain.

White Swan gin brand of Hiram Walker & Sons, Canada.

White Velvet Cocktail. Over ice shake 3 parts vodka, 2 white crème de menthe, 1 fresh cream, 1 dash orange bitters. Strain.

White Way Cocktail. Over ice stir 2 parts dry gin, 1 white crème de menthe. Strain.

Whitewater brewery at Kilkeel Newry, County Down, Northern Ireland.

White Wings Cocktail. Over ice shake 2 parts dry gin, 1 white crème de menthe, 1 teaspoon Cointreau. Strain.

Whizz-Bang Cocktail. Over ice shake 2 parts scotch whisky, 1 dry vermouth, 2 dashes grenadine, 2 dashes orange bitters, 2 dashes pastis. Strain.

Whoopee Cocktail. Over ice stir 1 part apple brandy, 1 brandy, 1 pastis. Strain.

Who Put the Lights Out? golden ale (5.0% alc) by Skinners Brewing, Truro, Cornwall, England. Specially made to mark the total eclipse of the sun seen (momentarily if at all through the dense cloud) over the county on 11 August 1999.

Why Not Cocktail. Over ice shake 2 parts dry gin, 1 apricot brandy, 1 dry vermouth, 2 dashes lemon juice. Strain.

Whyte & Mackay blended scotch whiskies of Whyte & Mackay, Glasgow, Scotland. **Whyte & Mackay Special Reserve, Whyte & Mackay 12 Years Old, Whyte & Mackay 21 Years Old.**

Whyte Avenue Amber bitter ale by Strathcona brewery, Edmonton, Canada.

Wickham vineyard at Shedfield, Hampshire, England.

Wicküler brewery in Wuppertal, Germany, known for **Wicküler Pilsener**.

Wickwar brewery est 1800 at Wickwar, Gloucestershire, England.

Widmer brewery in Portland, Oregon, USA.

Widmers Wine Cellars wine producer in New York State, USA.

Widow's Dream Cocktail. Over ice shake 1 egg, 1 part Bénédictine. Strain into tumbler glass and top with cream.

Widow's Kiss Cocktail. Over ice shake 2 parts apple brandy, 1 Bénédictine, 1 Chartreuse. Strain.

Widow's Wish Cocktail. Over ice shake 2 parts Bénédictine, 1 egg. Strain into a tumbler and top with chilled fresh cream.

Wieder, Juliana wine producer in Mittelburgenland, Austria.

Wieninger, Fritz wine producer in Wien (Vienna), Austria.

Wiesbaden spa, wine town and capital of Hessen State in Rheingau region, Germany. *Grosslage*: Steinmächer.

Wiesberg vineyard at Rüdesheim in Nahe region, Germany.

Wiese Krohn Sucrs port shipper est 1865 by Norwegians Theodor Wise and Dankert Krohn, Vila Nova de Gaia, Portugal. Single-estate and vintage tawnies and vintages: 1957, 58, 60, 61, 63, 65, 67, 70, 75, 78, 82, 85, 87, 91.

Wiesen beer brewed for festival occasions. German.

Wiibroe Carlsberg-owned brewery, Elsinore, Denmark.

Willamette Valley wine district south of Portland, Oregon, USA.

Wild Boar Special Amber beer brand of Wild Boar company, Atlanta, Georgia, USA.

Wild Cat beer (5.1% alc) by Tomintoul Brewery, Ballindalloch, Banffshire, Scotland.

Wildenberg vineyards at Elhofen and Weinsberg in Württemberg region, Germany.

Wilderness Wheat ale by Wynkoop brewery, Denver, Colorado, USA.

Wild Goose brewery in Cambridge, Maryland, USA. **Wild Goose Amber Beer**.

Wild Goose Vineyards wine producer at Okanagan Falls, British Columbia, Canada.

Wildgrafenberg vineyard at Kirschroth in Nahe region, Germany.

Wild Irish Rose Cocktail. Over ice shake 3 parts Irish whiskey, 1 fresh lime juice, 1 grenadine. Strain into ice-filled glasses and top with chilled soda or sparkling water.

Wild Night Out Cocktail. Over ice shake 3 parts tequila, 2 cranberry juice, 1 fresh lime juice. Strain into ice-filled glasses and add a squirt of soda water.

Wildsau vineyard at Eltville in Rheingau region, Germany.

Wild Turkey Kentucky Straight Bourbon Whiskey by Austin Nichols Distilling Co, Laurenceburg, Kentucky, USA.

Wilhelmsberg vineyards at Kitzingen in Franken region and Nussloch in Baden region, Germany.

Wilkins Farmhouse cider producer est 1917, Mudgeley, Wedmore, Somerset, England. Present cidermaker is Roger Wilkins.

William & Mary five-year-old blended whisky by Edwin Cheshire Ltd, Stansted, Essex, England. Launched 1988, tercentenary of the Glorious Revolution.

William Grant's blended scotch whisky brand of William Grant & Sons, Glasgow, Scotland. Whiskies include William Grant's Classic (18-year-old), Family Reserve, Royal (de luxe 12-year-old), Superior Strength ('100° Proof'), 21 Years Old.

William Lawson's blended scotch whisky by William Lawson, Coatbridge, Lanarkshire, Scotland.

William Low's Finest blended scotch whisky by Peter Russell & Co for William Low (supermarkets), Dundee, Scotland.

Williams & Humbert sherry *bodega*, Jerez de la Frontera, Spain. Owned by Barbadillo. Many brands including Pando Fino, Dry Sack, Walnut Brown.

Willie Smith Cocktail. Over ice shake 2 parts brandy, 1 maraschino, 1 dash lemon juice. Strain.

Willm, AN wine producer in Barr, Alsace, France.   *see label opposite* ➡

Will Rogers Cocktail. Over ice shake 2 parts dry gin, 1 dry vermouth, 1 orange juice, 4 dashes curaçao. Strain.

Will's Resolve ale (4.6% alc) by Sharp's Brewery, Rock, Cornwall, England.

Willys pub-brewery at Cleethorpes, Lincolnshire, England.

Wilsons whisky brand of Wilson Distilleries, Dunedin, New Zealand.

Wiltingen principal wine town of Saar, Mosel-Saar-Ruwer region, Germany. *Grosslage*: Scharzberg. Producers include Egon Müller, von Kesselstadt.

Wiltshire brewery in Tisbury, Wiltshire, England.

Wimmer-Czerny leading wine producer in Donauland, Niederösterreich, Austria.

Windy Corner Cocktail. Over ice shake 1 part blackberry brandy. Strain and add pinch of nutmeg to glass.

Windsor Premier Scotch whisky brand of Diageo, bottled in Korea.

Windsor Rose Cocktail. Over ice stir 3 parts dry gin, 2 Dubonnet, 1 Campari, 1 dash crème de noyaux. Strain.

wine the fermented juice of grapes, from Greek *oinos*. See box.

Wineapple Cooler Cocktail. In a large wine glass combine 1 part chilled dry white wine, 1 chilled apple juice, 1 chilled sparkling water, half teaspoon caster sugar. Stir, add ice and top with extra sparkling water to taste.

Wine Cobbler Cocktail. In a wine glass mix 1 part sparkling water, 1 teaspoon sugar. Add 2 parts dry red wine, ice, 1 orange slice and stir.

Wine of Origin designated wine-producing region, South Africa. Instituted 1973 under a system intended to resemble European appellation regimes.

winery wine-producing establishment. Originally American.

Wingertsberg vineyards at Dietzenbach in Hessische Bergstrasse region and Nieder-Wiesen in Rheinhessen region, Germany.

Wingertstor vineyard at Bechtolsheim in Rheinhessen region, Germany.

Winkel wine village of Rheingau region, Germany. *Grosslagen*: Erntebringer, Honigberg. Producers include Prinz von Hessen, Schloss Schönborn, Schloss Vollrads.

Winkleigh Cider Company new cider producer at Winkleigh, Devon, England, est 1998 in premises of former Inch's Cider Co. Brands include Sam's Dry, Sam's Medium, Sam's Sweet ciders (all 6% alc), named after founder Samuel Inch and Autumn Scrumpy (7.6% alc).

Winklerberg vineyard at Ihringen in Baden region, Germany.

Winkler-Hermaden, Georg wine producer in Süd-Oststeiermark, Austria.

Wine

one version of its beginnings

There is a romantic story about the origin of wine. It concerns a concubine in the harem of an Arabian prince long before history began. The young woman, Ayshia, had for days been plagued with a headache so persistent and severe that she could be of no service to her master. She resolved to take her own life to escape the pain, and had already determined the means.

In the palace at this season of the year, mid-winter, were to be found great clay jars of grapes, in store for banquets. Ayshia knew the fruit was forbidden to all but the Prince and his guests. But she knew, too, that the valuable contents of the jars sometimes spoiled – the grapes would mysteriously grow warm, burst their skins and issue forth a sweet-smelling liquor. All in the palace believed the liquor to be a lethal poison, and affected jars were always disposed of immediately. But Ayshia was aware of a jar, forgotten in a remote part of the harem, which had been oozing for weeks. She took a cup and filled it to the brim. She drank, and soon fell into a deep sleep.

When Ayshia awoke, she believed she must be in heaven. She felt refreshed, free of pain. And the Prince, she saw, was standing over her. He enquired, tenderly, after her condition. She could only confirm she felt not just alive, but well. Now she feared the Prince's wrath, knowing the grape jars were forbidden.

But the Prince, hearing the girl had taken the liquor, had hurried to her bedside in fear for her life – for she was, unknown to Ayshia herself, the favourite among all his concubines. So he was twice blessed. He made Ayshia his first consort and, after tasting the wine that had brought him enlightenment, ordered one tenth of his realm planted with vineyards. ❦

Winningen wine village of Mosel-Saar-Ruwer region, Germany. *Grosslage*: Weinhex.

Wintrich wine village of Mittelmosel, Mosel-Saar-Ruwer region, Germany. *Grosslage*: Kurfürstlay.

Winzergenossenschaft wine co-operative. German.

Winzerhaus NÖ wine co-operative in Wien (Vienna), Austria.

Winzerkeller Neckenmarkt wine producer in the Mittelburgenland, Austria.

Winzer Krems wine producer in Kremstal, Niederösterreich, Austria.

Winzerverein wine co-operative. German.

Wirra Wirra wine producer in Langhorne Creek, South Australia. Well-known red wines.

Wirsching, Hans wine producer at Iphofen in Franken region, Germany.

Wisdom & Warter sherry *bodega* est 1854 Jerez de la Frontera, Spain.

Wisdom Solera brandy by Wisdom & Warter, Jerez de la Frontera, Spain.

Wisniowka cherry-flavoured vodka, Poland.

Wissberg vineyards at Gau-Weinheim and Sprendlingen in Rheinhessen region, Germany.

Wisselbrunnen vineyard at Eltville in Rheingau region, Germany.

wit style of 'white' wheat beer, Belgium.

Wit beer brand of Spring Street Brewing Co, St Paul, Maine, USA.

witbier 'white' wheat beer of Belgium.

Withy Cutter bitter ale (3.8% alc) by Moor Beer Co, Ashcott, Somerset, England. Name celebrates harvesting of withies (willows) for basket-making on surrounding moors.

WKD Alcoholic fruit-flavoured 'ready-to-drink' brand, UK. Initials suggest an abbreviation of 'wicked'.

Wöber, Anton wine producer in Weinviertel, Niederösterreich, Austria.

wodka vodka, Poland. From 18th century *woda*, 'little water'.

Wohlfahrtsberg vineyard at Löwenstein in Württemberg region, Germany.

Wohlmuth, Gerhard wine producer in Südsteiermark, Austria.

Wolf brewery at Attleborough, Norfolk, England.

Wolfer vineyards at Efringen-Kirchen (Blansignen) and Efringen-Kirchen (Kleinkems) in Baden region, Germany.

Wolfhag vineyards at Bühl and Ottersweier in Baden region, Germany.

Wölflein vineyard at Veitshöchheim in Franken region, Germany.

Wolfsaugen vineyard at Brackenheim in Württemberg region, Germany.

Wolfsberg vineyard at Schweighofen in Rheinpfalz region, Germany.

Wolfshöhle vineyard at Bacharach in Mittelrhein region, Germany.

Wolfsmagen collective vineyard (*Grosslage*) at Bensheim einschliesslich Zell und Gronau in Hessiche Bergstrasse region, Germany.

Wolfsnach vineyard at Dörscheid in Mittelrhein region, Germany.

Wolverhampton & Dudley brewery at Wolverhampton, West Midlands, England.

Wonne vineyard at Neundorf in Franken region, Germany.

Wonneberg vineyards at Bad Bergzabern and Dörrenbach in Rheinpfalz region, Germany.

Wonnegau *Bereich* covering southern wine districts of Rheinhessen region, Germany.

Wood brewery at Wistanstow, Craven Arms, Shropshire, England.

Woodbine 1 apple variety traditionally valued for cider-making. Synonymous with Slack-ma-Girdle. English.

Woodbridge winery of Robert Mondavi, California, USA.

Woodchuck cider brand of Green Mountain Cidery, Vermont, USA. Owned by HP Bulmer, UK.

Wooden Hand brewery and ale brand (4% alc) of Cornwall, England.

Woodford bourbon brand of Labrot and Graham distillery, Woodford County, Kentucky, USA.

Woodforde's Norfolk Ales brewery at Woodbastwicke, Norwich, Norfolk, England. Great Eastern Golden Ale (4.3% alc), Head Cracker Pale Norfolk Ale (7% alc), Nelson's Revenge Premium Ale (4.5% alc), Norfolk Nog Old Dark Ale (4.6% alc), Norfolk Wherry Best Bitter (3.8% alc), Norkie Beer (5.0% alc).

Woodhampton Brewing Co brewery at Leominster, Herefordshire, England.

Woodhouse marsala brand of Florio, Sicily, Italy. Commemorates John Woodhouse, founder of Marsala trade in 1773 and whose company, Woodhouse & Ingham, was bought by Florio in 1929.

Woodpecker cider brand of Bulmer, Hereford, England, owned by Scottish Courage.

wood port informal term for port aged in cask and bottled only when ready for drinking. Does not improve in bottle. Old tawny ports are most noted examples.

Wood's Old Navy dark rum brand originally of Seagram, UK.

Woodstock wine producer in McLaren Vale, South Australia.

Woodstock Cocktail. Over ice stir 2 parts apple brandy, 1 dry vermouth. Strain.

Woodward Cocktail. Over ice shake 2 parts scotch whisky, 1 dry vermouth, 3 dashes grapefruit juice. Strain.

woody in winetasting, a dull flavour more of wood than of wine; a fault of wines kept too long in cask before bottling.

Woody Woodward's pub-brewery at Stottesdon, Kidderminster, Shropshire, England.

Woogberg vineyard at Ellenz-Poltersdorf in Mosel-Saar-Ruwer region, Germany.

Woolworths Wines famed range of South African wines made for the retailer FW Woolworth.

Wootton vineyard formerly at North Wootton, Wells, Somerset, England. Noted wines from Auxerrois, Seyval Blanc, Schönburger and other varieties and *eau de vie*. Vineyard closed 1999.

Woo Woo Cocktail. Over ice shake 1 part peach schnapps, 1 vodka, 2 cranberry juice. Strain.

Worcester Wine of Origin district east of Paarl, South Africa.

Worldham brewery at East Worldham, Alton, Hampshire, England.

Worms wine city of Rheinhessen region, Germany. *Grosslage*: Liebfrauenmorgen.

wort infusion from mashing process in brewing. In whisky production, the name given to the malt before and during fermentation. Old English *wyrt* (root).

Worth brewery at Keighley, West Yorkshire, England.

Wray & Nephew, J rum distillers, Jamaica. Brands include Appleton.

Wülfel brewery in Hanover, Germany.

Wülfen vineyard at Eltville in Rheingau region, Germany.

Wunnenstein *Grosslage* incorporating vineyards in Württemberg region, Germany at, respectively: Beilstein, Beilstein (Hohenbeilstein), Grossbottwar, Grossbottwar (Hof und Lembach), Grossbottwar (Winzerhausen), Ilsfeld, Ludwigsburg, Oberstenfeld, Oberstenfeld (Gronau), Steinheim, Steinheim (Kleinbottwar).

Wurmberg vineyards at Besigheim, Bitigheim-Bissingen, Gemmrigheim, Hessigheim and Walheim in Württemberg region and Neubrunn in Franken region, Germany.

Württemberg wine region of southern Germany. Vineyards are concentrated in valley of river Neckar. Quality white wines from Riesling grapes plus better-known reds from Spätburgunder, Trollinger and other varieties.

Württembergisch Unterland *Bereich* of Württemberg region, Germany.

Württembergische Hofkammer Kellerei wine estate based in Stuttgart, Württemberg region, Germany.

Würtzberg vineyard at Serrig in Mosel-Saar-Ruwer region, Germany.

Würzburg principal wine city of Franken region, Germany.

Würzburger Hofbräu royal brewery est 17th century in Wurzburg, Germany.

Würzburg Staatlicher Hofkeller the leading wine estate of Franken region, Germany.

Würzgarten vineyards at Detzem, Traben-Trarbach and Ürzig in Mosel-Saar-Ruwer region and Oestrich-Winkel (Hallgarten) in Rheingau region, Germany.

Würzhölle vineyard at Unkenbach in Nahe region, Germany.

Würzlay vineyard at Lehmen in Mosel-Saar-Ruwer region, Germany.

Wüstberg vineyard at Weinheim in Baden region, Germany.

Wutschenberg vineyard at Klein-langheim in Franken region, Germany.

Wyborowa vodka brand of Polmos Poznan, Warsaw, Poland. Wyborowa Blue Label, Wyborowa Red Label. Flavoured versions include spice-and-honey **Wyborowa Krupnik**. Producer was acquired by Pernod-Ricard, 2001.

Wychwood brewery at Witney, Oxfordshire, England.

Wye Valley brewery at Stoke Lacy, Herefordshire, England. Beers include Butty Bach, Dorothy Goodbody Wholesome Stout, Hereford Pale Ale, Trekkers Ale.

Wyken Vineyards wine producer in Stanton, Suffolk, England. Red and white wines.   *see label opposite* ➡

Wynand Fockink liqueur distillery est 1679, Amsterdam, Netherlands. Owned by Bols.

Wyndham Estate wine producer in Hunter Valley, New South Wales, Australia. Many well-known varietal wines.

Wynkoop brewery in Denver, Colorado, USA.

Wynns large-scale wine producer est 1891 Coonawarra, South Australia. Many brands including prestige John Riddoch Cabernet Sauvignon.

Wyoming Swing Cocktail. Over ice shake 2 parts dry vermouth, 2 sweet vermouth, 1 orange juice, sprinkle of sugar. Strain into tumbler glass and top with soda water.

Wyre Piddle brewery at Fladbury, Evesham, Hereford & Worcester, England.

X, Y, Z

X the custom of chalking or branding barrels with one or more X may derive from a medieval monastic practice, indicating that the contents (usually beer) have been inspected and found to be of acceptable quality and/or have been blessed. But the origin may be earlier. Ancient Roman brewers were known to distinguish between small (weak) and stronger beers by marking the respective container X for *birra simplex* (single beer) and XX for *birra duplex* (double beer).

Xamprada sparkling wine from Chardonnay, Godello and Doña Blanca grapes by Bodegas Prada a Tope, Cacabelos, El Bierzo, Spain.

Xanath vanilla liqueur by Montini, Mexico.

Xanthia Cocktail. Over ice shake 1 part cherry brandy, 1 dry gin, 1 yellow Chartreuse. Strain.

Xanthos white wine by Hatzimichalis, Atalanti, Greece.

Xarel-lo white grape variety of Penedés, Catalonia, Spain. Chiefly for blending with Maccabeo and Parellada grapes for *cava* sparkling wine.

Xenius *cava* brand of Cooperativa Vinicola del Penedes/Covides, Spain.

Xenoloo red wine by Ampelona Gavala, Santorini, Greece.

Xeres Cocktail. Over ice stir 1 part dry sherry, 1 dash orange bitters, 1 dash peach bitters. Strain.

Xerolithia white wine by Creta Olympias, Heraklion, Crete, Greece.

Xerxes Cocktail. Over ice shake 1 part white port, 2 tomato juice, 2 dashes Worcestershire sauce. Strain.

Xerxes II Cocktail. In a wine glass combine 2 parts red wine, 1 brandy, 1 port.

Xibeca beer brand of Damm brewery, Barcelona, Spain.

Xingu beer brand of Brazil.

Xinomavro black wine grape of northern Greece.

Xipella wine brand of Concavins, Conca de Barbera, Spain.

XM distillery and rum brand of Guyana. Classic, 5-year-old and 10-year-old rums and **XM Cream Liqueur**.

XO an age designation for brandies of Cognac and Armagnac, France. Introduced by Hennessy and since adopted by other producers for spirits of great quality and age. Also imitated by distillers of other nations. Hennessy XO includes brandies aged from ten to 70 years and other houses' versions are commonly of average 20 years' ageing. The term is governed by convention rather than law, since no legal definition for brandies over six years of age has been laid down.

X-Ray Cocktail. Over ice shake 1 part blue curaçao, 1 green crème de menthe, 1 double cream. Strain.

XV du Président wine estate in Languedoc-Roussillon, France.

XX beer brand favoured by British brewers. Greene King, Shepherd Neame etc.

XXX beer brand favoured by British brewers. Brakspear, Ridley etc.

XXXB beer brand of Bateman's brewery, Lincolnshire, England.

XXXD and **XXXL** beer brands of George Gale brewery, Hampshire, England.

XXXX beer brand favoured by British brewers including Bass, Harvey etc, but now most famously by Australian brewer Castlemaine of Brisbane, Queensland.

XXXXX seasonal (winter) ale brand of George Gale brewery, Hampshire, England.

Xynisteri white grape variety, island of Cyprus. Makes (along with Mavro grapes) the famed wine Commandaria.

Xynomavro red grape variety of northern Greece. Wines include Amindeo, Naoussa, Rapsani.

XYZ Cocktail. Over ice shake 2 parts rum, 1 Cointreau, 1 lemon juice. Strain.

'Y' (Ygrec) dry white wine of Château d'Yquem, Sauternes, Bordeaux, France.

Yacht Club Cocktail. Over ice shake 2 parts rum, 1 lemon juice, 2 dashes pastis, 2 dashes grenadine. Strain into an ice-filled glass and top with soda water.

Yakima Valley wine district of Washington State, USA.

Yale Cocktail. Over ice shake 1 part dry gin, 3 dashes orange bitters, 1 dash Angostura bitters. Strain, add a little soda water and squeeze lemon peel over.

Yalumba wine producer est 1863 Angaston, Barossa Valley, South Australia. Famous brands include Angas Brut sparkling, Heggies, Hill Smith Estate, Oxford Landing etc. Owned by Hill Smith family.

Yamagata vineyard region of Honshu, Japan.

Yamanashi the major vineyard region of Honshu, Japan.

Yamazaki whisky brand of Suntory, Japan.

Yanjing Brewery major brewing concern of China, based in Beijing. Said to be nation's third-largest brewer.

Yankee Prince Cocktail. Over ice shake 3 parts dry gin, 1 Grand Marnier, 1 orange juice. Strain.

Yankee Punch to make this traditional American punch first prepare a large block of ice for the punch bowl by freezing water in a plastic container such as an old ice-cream carton. Into the punch bowl add 3 bottles rye whisky, 1 bottle rum, 8 pints chilled water, 8 heaped table-spoons sugar. Float orange slices on top.

Yantra Valley Controliran wine region of Bulgaria. Cabernet Sauvignon wines.

Yarlington Cocktail. Over ice shake 1 part dry gin, 1 Cointreau, 1 pine-apple juice. Strain.

Yarlington Mill apple variety com-monly cultivated for cider-making. English.

Yarra Ridge wine producer in Yarra Glen, Victoria, Australia.

Yarra Valley small wine region near Melbourne, Victoria, Australia. Expanding since first new winery, Yarra Yering, was est 1969.

Yarra Yering wine producer est 1969 Coldstream, Victoria, Australia. Well-known Dry White No 1 etc.

Yates brewery at Westnewton, Aspatria, Cumbria, England.

Yates famed chain of 'wine lodges'. UK.

Yattarna premium white wine of Penfold's, Australia. Chardonnay grapes. First vintage 1995.

yayin wine, Biblical Hebrew.

Yburgberg vineyard at Baden-Baden in Baden region, Germany.

Ycoden-Daute-Isora DO wine region of island of Tenerife, Spain.

yeast natural or cultured fungal matter producing zymase and thus prompting alcoholic fermentation of carbohydrates. Wild yeasts cause spontaneous fermentation, but in modern processes of alcoholic-drinks manfacture the organisms used are almost invariably cultured.

The function of yeast was not fully understood until the discoveries made by French scientist Louis Pasteur in the 1860s.

yeasty in winetasting, a smell redolent of fermentation. A fault that probably indicates, in a bottled wine, that a second fermentation is under way. Champagnes described as yeasty, on the other hand, are usually being praised.

Yebisu pilsener beer by Sapporo brewery, Japan.

Yecla DO wine region of Levante, Spain.

Yellow Daisy Cocktail. Over ice shake 2 parts dry gin, 2 dry ver-mouth, 1 Grand Marnier, 1 dash pastis. Strain.

Yellowglen major sparkling-wine producer in Ballarat, South Australia. Also some still wines.

Yellow Label blended scotch whisky by John Robertson & Son, Leith, Scotland.

Yellow Label informal name for Veuve Clicquot Brut non-vintage champagne, which bears, curiously, an orange label.

Yellow Label renowned wine brand of Wolf Blass, Barossa Valley, Australia.

Yellow Mongrel wheat beer by Geebung Polo Club brewery, Melbourne, Australia.

Yellow Parrot Cocktail. Over ice shake 1 part apricot brandy, 1 pastis, 1 yellow Chartreuse. Strain.

Yellow Rattler Cocktail. Over ice shake 1 part dry gin, 1 dry ver-mouth, 1 sweet vermouth, 1 orange juice. Strain and add cocktail onion to glass.

Yellow Redstreak apple variety traditionally valued for cider-making. English.

Yellow Torrish whisky brand of Merchant International, UK.

Yeltsin Cocktail. Over ice stir 3 parts vodka, 1 dry vermouth, 1 medium sherry. Strain and squeeze lemon peel over.

Yeni raki brand of Tekel distillers, Turkey and Cyprus.

Ye Olde Bishopsgate London dry gin brand of Merchant International, UK.

Yerassa wine village of island of Cyprus. Commandaria wine.

Yeringberg wine producer est 1862 Coldstream in Yarra Valley, Victoria, Australia.

yeso gypsum (calcium sulphate) dusted over grapes to improve acidity in wine. A process traditional in fortified-wine production, notably of sherry. Spanish.

Ye Whisky of Ye Monks blended scotch whisky of Donald Fisher & Co, Edinburgh, Scotland.

Ygay brand name of Bodegas Marqués de Murrieta, Rioja, Spain.

Yianakohori red wine brand of Kyr-yanni, Naoussa, Greece.

yield in viticulture, the quantity of grapes (and thus of wine) obtained per acre or hectare of vineyard. As a rule, lower yields mean better wine. Appellation controls in some countries, especially France, restrict yields to ensure quality.

Yikes Cocktail. Over ice shake 1 part amaretto, 1 peach schnapps. Strain into a shot glass.

Yllera non-DO red wine of Rueda, Spain, by Bodegas SAT Les Curros, est 1973 by Jesus Gonzalez Yllera.

Yodel Cocktail. In tumbler glass with ice stir 1 part Fernet Branca, 1 orange juice. Top with soda water.

Yon-Figeac, Château wine estate of AC St-Emilion, Bordeaux, France. Classified *Grand Cru Classé*.

York brewery in Brampton, Ontario, Canada. **York Pilsner Lager**.

York brewery est 1996 in Micklegate, York, North Yorkshire, England. Brideshead Bitter, Stonewall Ale.

York Mountain AVA of San Luis Obispo County, California, USA.

Yorkshire Bitter beer brand successively of Webster, Samuel Smith and Scottish & Newcastle brewers. UK.

Yorkshire Grey Brewery brew pub in London WC1, England.

Yorkshire Square Ale strong (5.0% alc) ale by Black Sheep Brewery, Masham, North Yorkshire, England. 'Yorkshire Squares – a particular fermentation system originated by Timothy Bentley over two hundred years ago in the West Riding of Yorkshire. The system utilises double decked vessels, which were originally made of stone or slate. Black Sheep beers are all brewed using this original system. Some of our Yorkshire Squares are actually 100 year old slate vessels – surely the ultimate in traditional ale brewing.'

York Special Cocktail. Over ice shake 3 parts dry vermouth, 1 maraschino, 2 dashes orange bitters. Strain.

York Tavern brew pub at Norwich, Norfolk, England.

Young & Co famed independent brewery in Wandsworth, London,

England. Ales include **Young's Bitter**, **Young's Export Special London Ale**, **Young's Special**.

Younger, Wm beer brand of Scottish & Newcastle, UK.

Young Man Cocktail. Over ice shake 3 parts brandy, 1 sweet vermouth, 2 dashes curaçao, 1 dash Angostura bitters. Strain.

Yquem, Château great wine estate of AC Sauternes, Bordeaux, France. Producer of the world's foremost sweet white wine, Château D'Yquem. Classified *1er Grand Cru Classé*.

Yucatan brewery owned by Mexican brewing giant Modelo.

Yuengling brewery est 1829 at Pottsville, Pennsylvania, and the longest-established in the USA. Renowned for Celebrated Pottsville Porter.

Yukon Gold beer brand of Old Fort brewery, British Columbia, Canada.

Yukon Jack strong (50% alc) spirit 'cordial' of Canada.

yum sing 'cheers' in Cantonese.

Yuntero brand for red, white and *rosado* wines of Cooperativa Nuestro Padre Jesus del Perdon, Manzanares, La Mancha, Spain.

Yvon Mau leading *négociant* of Bordeaux, France.

zabaione famed marsala-based dessert of Sicily. Official recipe from Consorzio Volontario del Vino Marsala is: 6 large egg yolks; 120g sugar; 1 wine glass sweet marsala. Beat the egg yolks in a Pyrex bowl and heat over a bain-marie. Add the sugar, stirring continuously. If the mixture appears to be too thick add a little water. Mix well then add the sweet marsala little by little. Whisk until smooth. Place in small glass bowls and refrigerate. Remove immediately prior to serving. Alternative, anglicised spelling is *zabaglione*.

Zaca Mesa wine producer in Santa Barbara County, California, USA.

Zagarolo DOC for dry-to-sweet white wines from Malvasia and Trebbiano grapes, Zagarolo town, outh of Rome, Latium region, Italy.

Zala Gyöngye white grape variety principally of Hungary. Used diminishingly for wine production.

Zalema disappearing white grape variety of southern Spain, mostly Condado de Huelva region.

Zamba Cocktail. Over ice shake 3 parts rum, 1 lemon juice, 2 dashes sweet vermouth, 1 dash Angostura bitters. Strain.

Zamek beer brand of Budweiser Bürgerbräu, Budweis, Czech Republic.

Zamoyski vodka brand of Bass (Channel Islands).

Zanatta, Vigneti wine producer est 1986 at Glenora, Duncan, British Columbia.

Zandvliet wine producer in Robertson district, South Africa. Renowned Shiraz and other wines.

Zandwijk Wine Farm wine producer in Paarl, South Africa. Kosher wines.

Zanna Montepulciano wine brand of Illuminati, Abruzzi, Italy.

Zanzibar Cocktail. Over ice shake 3 parts dry vermouth, 1 dry gin, 1 lemon juice, tablespoon sugar syrup. Strain and add lemon peel twist to glass.

zapenka flavoured vodka-based liquor of Ukraine.

Zaragozana brewery in Aragon, Spain, known for Ambar de Zaragozana beer.

Zatte beer by 't I J microbrewery, Amsterdam, Netherlands. Name means 'Drunk'.

Zaza Cocktail. Over ice stir 2 parts Dubonnet, 1 dry gin, 1 dash orange bitters. Strain.

ZD wine producer, California, USA.

Z de Zédé second wine of Château Labégorce Zédé, Bordeaux, France.

Zebulon's smoked beer by Phantom Canyon brewery, Colorado Springs, USA.

Zechberg vineyard at Framersheim in Rheinhessen region, Germany.

Zechpeter vineyard at Flemlingen in Rheinpfalz region, Germany.

Zedda Piras producer of sweet liqueur Alchernes, Italy.

Zee Rons Cocktail. Over ice shake 1 part white rum, 1 dark rum, 1 fresh lime juice, 1 dash Cointreau. Strain.

Zefir white grape variety of Hungary, derived from Harslevelu and Leanyka varieties.

Zefyros Breeze rosé wine of Metaxa, Cephalonia, Greece.

Zehmorgen vineyard at Nierstein in Rheinhessen region, Germany.

Zehntgraf vineyard at Wipfeld in Franken region, Germany.

Zeilberg vineyards at Löwenstein, Obersulm (Affaltrach) and Obersulm (Willsbach) in Württemberg region, Germany.

Zeisel vineyard at Pommern in Mosel-Saar-Ruwer region, Germany.

Zele brewery at Dubuque, Iowa, USA. Produces **Zele** fruit beers.

Zell *Bereich* covering lower Mosel region of Germany from village of Zell to Koblenz.

Zell wine village of Mosel-Saar-Ruwer region, Germany. *Grosslage*: Schwartze Katz.

Zellerberg vineyards at Longen, Mehring and Mehring (Lörsch) in Mosel-Saar-Ruwer region, Germany.

Zellerweg am schwarzen Herrgott vineyard at Mölsheim in Rheinhessen region, Germany.

Zeltingen wine village of Mittelmosel, Mosel-Saar-Ruwer region, Germany. *Grosslage*: Münzlay.

Zema wine estate in Coonawarra, South Australia.

Zenit white grape variety of Hungary.

Zens, Josef wine producer in Weinviertel, Niederösterreich, Austria.

Zentralkellerei Badischer Winzergenossenschaft better known, mercifully, as ZBW. Co-operative wine-producing establishment at Breisach in Baden region, Germany. Vinifies wines from more than 100 co-operatives of Baden and produces nine-tenths of the entire region's wine under 500 different descriptions.

Zeppwingert vineyard at Enkirch in Mosel-Saar-Ruwer region, Germany.

Zerkhoun wine appellation of Meknès Fez region, Morocco.

Zero Mist Cocktail. In a shaker combine 2 parts green crème de menthe, 1 water. Place in a freezer for one to two hours. When the mix is slushy, pour into a cocktail glass.

Zest flavoured-cider brand of Matthew Clark, Shepton Mallet, Somerset, England.

Zhirinovsky vodka brand inaugurated 1994 by Russian nationalist politician Vladimir Zhirinovsky.

Zibibbo regional name for Muscat d'Alexandrie grape variety, Italy.

Zickelgarten vineyard at Ockfen in Mosel-Saar-Ruwer region, Germany.

Zierer, Harald wine producer in Thermenregion, Niederösterreich, Austria.

Zierfandler white grape variety principally of Thermenregion, Austria, where it goes into famed Gumpoldskirchen wine, along with the Rotgipfler grape.

Zig-Zag stout by Milk Street Brewery, Frome, Somerset, England.

Zilavka white grape variety and wine of Mostar, Herzegovina.

Zimbabwe wine is produced on a small scale.

Zimmermann, Alois wine producer in Kremstal, Niederösterreich, Austria.

Zinck, Paul wine producer at Eguisheim, Alsace, France.

Zind-Humbrecht leading wine producer est 1658 Wintzenheim, Alsace, France. Famed wines from *Grand Cru monopole* vineyards of Clos Hauserer, Clos St Urbain, Herrenweg plus those of Brand, Hengst and Rangen. Still family run.

see label opposite ➡

Zinfandel black grape variety of California, USA. Makes many styles of wine from off-white 'blush' to long-lived rich reds. Said to be synonymous with Primitivo of Italy, but there is room for doubt.

Ziolowy herb-flavoured vodka-based liqueur by Polmos distillers, Poland.

Zip City pub-brewery in Manhattan, New York City, USA.

Zitadelle vineyard at Sankt Martin in Rheinpfalz region, Germany.

Zitsa sparkling white wine from Debina grapes, Epirus, Greece.

zivania colourless grape spirit similar to *marc* and commonly illicit, island of Cyprus.

zivio 'cheers' in Serbo-Croat.

ZO *zeer oude* (very old). A common designation for aged *genever*. Netherlands.

Zobelsberg vineyard at Segnitz in Franken region, Germany.

Zöhrer, Anton wine producer in Kremstal, Niederösterreich, Austria.

Zöldszilváni regional name for Silvaner grape variety, Hungary.

Zollturm vineyard at Traben-Trarbach in Mosel-Saar-Ruwer region, Germany.

Zolo Pacchharan liqueur brand, Spain.

Zombie Cocktail. Over ice shake 3 parts rum, 1 apricot brandy, 1 fresh lime juice, 1 pineapple juice, 1 teaspoon sugar. Strain and add orange slice and maraschino cherry to each glass.

Zona di Crianza under Spanish wine law, the defined region within which a wine qualifying for DO status can be stored for maturation before sale.

Zonchera Barolo wine by Ceretto, Piedmont, Italy.

Zonin leading wine producer est 1821, Gambellara, Italy.

Zonnebloem wine range of Stellenbosch Farmers Winery, South Africa.

Zoopiyi wine village of island of Cyprus. Commandaria wine.

Zorzal Viña Nava wine producer in DO Navarra, Spain.

Zoumiatiko white grape variety of Macedonia and Thrace, Greece.

Zuber, Ernst distillery at Arisdorf, Switzerland. Kirsch and other liqueurs.

zubrowka traditional bison-herb-flavoured vodka of Poland and Russia.

zucco Sicilian sweet wine eclipsed by marsala.

Zuckerberg vineyard at Oppenheim in Rheinhessen region, Germany.

Zuckerkulor liqueur description, Germany. Spirit has been coloured and sweetened with a sugar preparation.

Zuckerle vineyards at Stuttgart (Bad Cannstatt), Stuttgart (Mühlhausen) and Stuttgart (Münster) in Württemberg region, Germany.

ALSACE
APPELLATION ALSACE CONTROLEE

DEPUIS

DOMAINE
MISE

Domaine
Zind Humbrecht
PINOT D'ALSACE

700 ml

LEONARD HUMBRECHT PROPR. VITIC. A WINTZENHEIM (HAUT-RHIN) FRANCE

Zügernberg vineyard at Weinstadt in Württemberg region, Germany.

Zull, Werner wine producer in Weinviertel, Niederösterreich, Austria.

Zum Schlüssel restaurant-brewery in Düsseldorf, Germany.

Zum Uerige renowned Altbier of equally renowned **Zum Uerige** inn-brewery on Berger Strasse, Düsseldorf, Germany.

Zunft *Kölschbier* brand, Cologne, Germany.

Zupa wine-producing district of Serbia. Red wines named **Zupsko** from Plovdina and Prokupac grapes.

Zürich wine-producing canton of Switzerland.

zurra mixed drink of wine, brandy and fruit similar to sangria, but made with white wine. Also known as **zurracapote**. Spain.

Zwack, L liqueur distillery est 1840 Vienna, Austria.

Zwack Unicum distiller est 1790, Budapest, Hungary, of Unicum herbal liqueur.

Zwarte Kip Black Hen. Advocaat brand of van Olffen company, Netherlands.

Zweifelberg vineyard at Brackenheim in Württemberg region, Germany.

Zweigelt most prolific black grape variety of Austria, contrived by Dr Zweigelt from a crossing of Blaufränkisch and St Laurent vines in 1922. Zweigelt was exiled from Austria in recognition of his collaboration with the Nazis during the *Anschluss* of 1938.

zwetgenwasser *eau de vie* distilled from quetsch plums, Switzerland.

zwetschenwasser *eau de vie* distilled from mirabelle plums, Switzerland.

Zwetschken plum brandy, mostly farm-distilled. Germany.

Zweytick, Alois wine producer in Südsteiermark, Austria.

Zwickelbier unfiltered beer, Germany.

zwicker wine made from a blend of grape varieties. Alsace, France.

Zwierlein, Freiherr von wine producer at Geisenheim in Rheingau region, Germany. Renowned Riesling wines from vineyards including Kläuserberg and Rothenberg.

zymase enzyme present in yeast cells prompting alcoholic fermentation.

zymology scientific study of fermentation.

zymurgy in applied chemistry, the science of fermentation in brewing and winemaking.

zythum beer of ancient Egypt recorded (and recommended) by Greek historian Diodorus Siculus, 1st century BC.

Zytnia vodka flavoured with fruit brandies. Polmos distillers, Poland.

Zywiec brewery and renowned 'Premium Quality Beer' brand of Poland.

Acknowledgements

The author is grateful to a great many people who have helped me write, check and provide illustrations for this book. These are the names, individual and corporate, to whom special thanks are owed – with apologies for all the unwitting omissions:

Geoff Adams; Adnams & Co; Will Ainley; Allied Domecq; Peter Amor; Stig Anderson; Archers Ales; Mimi Avery; Bacardi-Martini; Fiona Bacon; Tom Baring; Anthony Barne MW; Nick Barnwell; John Barrett; Stephen Barrett; Chris Bongo Beckwith; Simon Billinghurst; Black Sheep Brewery; Peter Booth; Georgina Borrows; Philippe Boucheron; Julian Brind MW; Bristol Spirits Co; Jim Budd; HP Bulmer; Jonathan Butt; Campaign for Real Ale; Andrew Campbell; Fiona Campbell; David Capps-Tunwell; Graeme Carmichael; Marcus Clapham; Coates & Co; Peter & Suzie Coe; Liz Copas; Cotleigh Brewery; Cottage Brewing; Kim Crawford; Ben Crichton; Alan Darby; Paul Davey; Nick Davies; HL Delaney; Diageo; Tim Doubleday; Ivor Dunkerton; Nick Dymoke-Marr; Eldridge Pope; Michael Eavis; Everards Brewery; Exe Valley Brewery; Lucy Faulkner; Richard Fergé; First Quench; Marcus FitzGibbon; Ken Fletcher; Fourcroy; Percy Fox & Co; Arthur Frampton; Fuller, Smith & Turner; German Wine Information Service; Sue Glasgow; William Glasson; Gonzalez Byass; Peter Goodden; Greene King; Hall & Woodhouse; Lydia and Max Halley; Colin Hamilton; Roger Harris Wines; Laelia Hartnoll; John Harvey & Son; Heck's Cider; Bernard Hine; Hoegaarden; Mike Holt; Tim Holt; Niki Hunter; Hydes Anvil Brewery; Tom Innes of Irma Fingal-Rock; International Brewers Guild; Chris Jelley; Hugh Johnson; Donald Kenwrick-Cox; Bodo Klingenberg; Christopher Lee; Simon Loftus; Ernest Loosen; Majestic Wine; Matthew McCulloch; Mentzendorff & Co; Carole Minto;

Jonathan Montagu-Pollock; Montana Wines; Quita Morgan; Victoria Morral; Morris & Verdin; Angela Mount; Greig Nicholls; Noilly Prat; Oddbins; Su-Lin Ong; Orkney Brewery; Patricia Parnell; Pernod-Ricard; Marguerite Perry; Phillips & Co; Rupert Ponsonby; Port Wine Institute; Mario and Claudia Priester-Reading; Richard Purdey; Matthew Quirk; Clive Reynard; Ringwood Brewery; Liz Robertson MW; Charles Rolls of Plymouth Gin; Hugo Rose MW; Royal Tokaji Wine Co; Sam Roughton; Simon Russell; Piers Russell-Cobb; Safeway; George Sandeman; Keith Sayers; Jules Schad; Anne Scott; Jan Scott; Seagram; David Sheppy; Christian Siegl; Smiles Brewery; Sopexa; Southcorp; Jenny Stewart; J Straker Chadwick; Ian Sumner; Jay Swaff; Taylor, Fladgate & Yeatman; Julian Temperley; Tesco Stores; Martin Thatcher; Thierrys; George Thomas; John Thorne; John Townend; Neil Tully MW; Bettina von Bülow; Welsh Whisky Co; Whitbread; Nick & Barbie White; Simon Whitmore; Vaughan Williams; Willys Brewery; Wine Bank; Karen Wise; Michael Witt; Woodforde's Brewery; Mike Wren; Wye Valley Brewery; Jason Yapp; Robin Yapp.